Collins

SOCIOLOGY AS
FOR AQA

Stephen Moore

Steve Chapman

INTRODUCTION

Features of the textbook

The book is divided into chapters that match the AQA AS-level topics (see p. 282 for more information). Each chapter contains a number of features designed to help you with learning, revision and exam-preparation.

Getting you thinking

The opening activity draws on your existing knowledge and experiences to lead in to some of the main issues of the topic. The questions are usually open and, although suitable for individual work, may be more effectively used in discussion in pairs or small groups, where experiences and ideas can be shared.

Getting you thinking

<<A visit to Isabella Mackay's home is like a walk through the pages of *Little Women*. She opens the door wearing a pretty pink blouse, children hiding in her flowing skirt. Isabella has some interesting ideas about motherhood. She says 'I could no more go out to work, abandon my children or disobey my husband than I could grow an extra head. I don't have any of the modern woman's confusion about her role in life. From the day I was born I knew I was destined to be a wife and mother. By the age of 16, I knew that all I really wanted from life was to get married, have children and make a lovely home. That was my ambition.'

She not only believes that a mother's place is in the home, but that the feminist movement is a 'dangerous cancer and perversion'. The world, she says, would be a better place if the Equal Opportunities Commission was shut down and workplace crèches were scrapped. The rape-within-marriage law should be abolished too. She says 'in the rare event of a wife refusing sex with her husband he has every right, perhaps even a duty, to take her as gently as possible. Once a woman is married she loses the right to say no to her husband's advances. The female role is a submissive one. The male role is assertive and aggressive.' >>

1 List the stereotypical and non-stereotypical masculine and feminine characteristics that come to mind on first seeing the images above.

2 What aspects of Isabella Mackay's view of femininity do you agree or disagree with?

AQA specification table

At the start of each chapter, a clearly laid out table shows how the topics in that chapter cover the AQA AS-level specification.

AQA Specification	Topics	Pages
Candidates should examine:		
Different definitions and ways of measuring poverty, wealth and income.	Definitions of income and wealth are covered in Topic 1, poverty in Topic 2.	124–35
The distribution of poverty, wealth and income between different social groups.	Explanations of the distribution of income and wealth are covered in Topic 1. Topic 2 discusses the distribution of poverty.	124–35
The existence and persistence of poverty in contemporary society.	Topic 3 investigates the groups most at risk of poverty. Topic 4 covers sociological explanations of poverty.	136–41 142–47
Different responses to poverty, with particular reference to the role of social policy since the 1940s.	Topic 5 looks at possible solutions to poverty.	148–53
The nature and role of public, private, voluntary and informal welfare provision in contemporary society.	Topic 6 focuses on welfare provision.	154–59

Key terms

These are simple definitions of important terms and concepts used in each topic, linked to the context in which the word or phrase occurs. Most key terms are sociological, but some of the more difficult but essential vocabulary is also included. Each key term is printed **in bold type** the first time it appears in the main text.

Key terms

11+ IQ test taken at the age of 11 to determine what sort of school you would attend under the tripartite system.

IQ tests supposedly objective tests that establish a person's 'intelligence quotient' (how clever they are).

Marketization the move towards educational provision being determined by market forces.

National Curriculum what every pupil in every state school must learn, decided by the government.

New vocationalism a series of measures in the 1980s that re-emphasized the importance of work-related education.

Parity of esteem equal status, equally valued.

Public schools the top private fee-paying schools, e.g. Eton, Harrow, Roedean.

Secondary education education between ages 11 and 16.

Social democratic perspective supports the view that a democratically elected government can work to reduce the perceived injustices of the capitalist market system.

Social exclusion the situation where people are unable to achieve a quality of life that would be regarded as acceptable by most people.

Specialist schools schools which have a particular focus within their curriculum and links to specialist areas of work, e.g. arts and media, business, languages, healthcare and medicine. They can select 10 per cent of their intake on the basis of ability.

Vocational work-related.

Activities

At the end of each topic, there are two types of activity that will help you take your learning further:

- Research ideas – Suggestions for small-scale research which could be used for class or homework activities.

- Web tasks – Activities using the worldwide web to develop your understanding and analysis skills. This feature also serves to identify some of the key websites for each topic.

Activities

Research ideas

1 If you know people from ethnic or religious backgrounds different from your own, ask if you can interview them about their experience of family life. Make sure your questionnaire is sensitive to their background and avoids offending them.

2 Design a research tool that allows you to gather quantitative and qualitative information about your classmates' relationships with their elderly relatives. Does this confirm or challenge previous sociological research?

Web.task

Visit the following sites which focus on recent research into family life. What changes have they documented in family life since the turn of the century?

- The Institute for Social and Economic Research: www.iser.essex.ac.uk
- Centre for Family Research: www.sps.cam.ac.uk/CFR/
- Joseph Rowntree Foundation: www.jrf.org.uk
- Centre for Research in Family, Kinship and Childhood: www.leeds.ac.uk/family

Chapter summary

Each chapter ends with a summary in the form of a 'mind map' that provides an attractive visual overview of the whole chapter using key headings. This clearly shows how the topics fit together and is useful for revision.

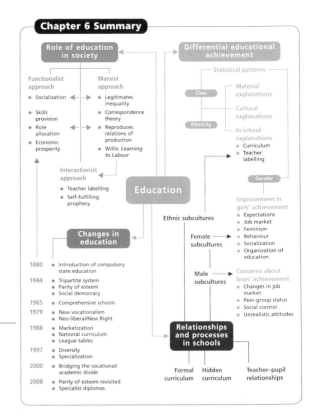

Chapter 6 Summary

Role of education in society

Functionalist approach
- Socialization
- Skills provision
- Role allocation
- Economic prosperity

Marxist approach
- Legitimates inequality
- Correspondence theory
- Reproduces relations of production
- Willis: *Learning to Labour*

Interactionist approach
- Teacher labelling
- Self-fulfilling prophecy

Changes in education

- 1880 — Introduction of compulsory state education
- 1944 — Tripartite system; Parity of esteem; Social democracy
- 1965 — Comprehensive schools
- 1979 — New vocationalism; Neo-liberal/New Right
- 1988 — Marketization; National curriculum; League tables
- 1997 — Diversity; Specialization
- 2000 — Bridging the vocational/academic divide
- 2008 — Parity of esteem revisited; Specialist diplomas

Education

Differential educational achievement

Statistical patterns
- Class
- Ethnicity

- Material explanations
- Cultural explanations

In-school explanations
- Curriculum
- Teacher labelling

Gender

Improvement in girls' achievement
- Expectations
- Job market
- Feminism
- Behaviour
- Socialization
- Organization of education

Ethnic subcultures

Female subcultures

Male subcultures

Concerns about boys' achievement
- Changes in job market
- Peer-group status
- Social control
- Unrealistic attitudes

Relationships and processes in schools

- Formal curriculum
- Hidden curriculum
- Teacher–pupil relationships

Focus on research activities

These appear in Chapters 1 to 4: a recent piece of interesting and relevant research is summarized, followed by questions that encourage you to evaluate the methods used as well as the conclusions drawn.

Research methods activities

These appear in Chapters 5 to 7: they are similar to the Focus on research activities in Chapters 1 to 4, but concentrate on the research methods used in the piece of research described. Questions are asked that reflect the types of questions that appear in the AQA AS Unit 2 exam paper.

Research methods

George Davey Smith et al. (2003)
The health of ethnic minorities: a meta-study

George Davey Smith and his colleagues were concerned that there was relatively little information on the health of ethnic minorities in Great Britain. They therefore conducted a **meta-study** to try to provide an overall picture of health care. They looked at data from a range of surveys including official publications, small-scale surveys and earlier sociological studies. Putting all of this together, they provided a picture of standards of health for different ethnic groups in Britain, taking into account the impact of social class. In order to do this, they also had to review a wide range of theoretical and methodological books and articles. The study therefore includes secondary research based upon both theoretical and statistical studies, from government as well as academic sources.

They found that, overall, the health standards of ethnic minorities in Britain were worse than those of the general population, and that these differences were most apparent in childhood and old age. They found that most previous studies tended to explain any differences in health between ethnic minorities and the majority population in terms of cultural, dietary or genetic differences. However, they concluded that ethnicity by itself does not explain these differences. They suggest instead that differences in health are closely linked to social class and income.

Davey Smith, G., Chaturvedi, N., Harding, S., Nazroo, J. and Williams, R. (2003) Health Inequalities. Lifecourse approaches, Bristol: Policy Press

1 Why did the researchers use a meta-study?
2 How did the use of secondary sources allow them to reach different conclusions from earlier research?

Focus on research

Charlotte Cooper (1998)
Fatness as disability

Sociologists have been critical of official definitions and measurements of disability because they are frequently based upon medical discourse, which views the impaired as inadequate, dependent and problematic. In contrast, sociologists suggest that disabled people are 'disabled by society', i.e. by the stereotypes of disability held by the able bodied. Charlotte Cooper takes this

Challenging stereotypes: pop star Beth Ditto

analysis a stage further when she claims that fat people are disabled because both the disabled and fat people are made invisible by the media and a fat-hating culture dominated by 'able-bodied, slender white bodies'. Fat people are seen as unworthy, pitiful and ugly because they are seen to have brought their condition upon themselves.

Cooper, C. (1998) Fat and Proud: The politics of size, London: Women's Press

1 How would you define 'disability'?
2 Identify two reasons why you might agree or disagree with Charlotte Cooper's analysis.

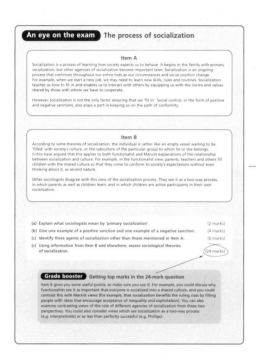

An eye on the exam The process of socialization

Item A

Socialization is a process of learning how society expects us to behave. It begins in the family with primary socialization, but other agencies of socialization become important later. Socialization is an ongoing process that continues throughout our entire lives as our circumstances and social position change. For example, when we start a new job, we may need to learn new skills, rules and routines. Socialization teaches us how to fit in and enables us to interact with others by equipping us with the norms and values shared by those with whom we have to cooperate.

However, socialization is not the only factor ensuring that we 'fit in'. Social control, in the form of positive and negative sanctions, also plays a part in keeping us on the path of conformity.

Item B

According to some theories of socialization, the individual is rather like an empty vessel waiting to be 'filled' with society's culture, or the subculture of the particular group to which he or she belongs. Critics have argued that this applies to both functionalist and Marxist explanations of the relationship between socialization and culture. For example, in the functionalist view, parents, teachers and others fill children with the shared culture so that they come to conform to society's expectations without even thinking about it, as second nature.

Other sociologists disagree with this view of the socialization process. They see it as a two-way process, in which parents as well as children learn, and in which children are active participants in their own socialization.

(a) Explain what sociologists mean by 'primary socialization'. (2 marks)
(b) Give one example of a positive sanction and one example of a negative sanction. (4 marks)
(c) Identify three agents of socialization other than those mentioned in Item A. (6 marks)
(c) Using information from Item B and elsewhere, assess sociological theories of socialization. (24 marks)

Grade booster Getting top marks in the 24-mark question

Item B gives you some useful points, so make sure you use it. For example, you could discuss why functionalists see it as important that everyone is socialized into a shared culture, and you could contrast this with Marxist views (for example, that socialization benefits the ruling class by filling people with ideas that encourage acceptance of inequality and exploitation). You can also examine contrasting views of the role of different agencies of socialization from these two perspectives. You could also consider views which see socialization as a two-way process (e.g. interpretivists) or as less than perfectly successful (e.g. Phillips).

An eye on the exam

Data-response activities – one at the end of each topic – which reflect the AQA AS-level exam questions. Use these to assess your progress, as well as providing regular exam practice.

Check your understanding

These comprise a set of basic comprehension questions – all answers can be found in the preceding text.

Check your understanding

1 Using examples, define what is meant by the terms 'values' and 'norms'.
2 Give an example of an ascribed status in Britain.
3 Why do sociologists believe that human behaviour is not biologically determined?
4 What is the difference between primary and secondary socialization?
5 What role does culture play in the construction of identity?

Exam practice

At the end of each chapter is a complete exam-style question of the type you will find in the relevant AQA AS-level exam paper. A candidate's 'answer' is provided, together with comments and a mark from a real AQA examiner. The comments point out where the answer scores good marks and when it fails to score.

Finally, an essay-style question is provided, together with some hints from the examiner about the best way to tackle it. Free answers are available online at

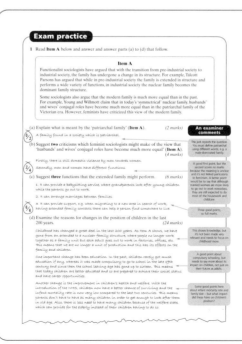

Exam practice

1 Read **Item A** below and answer and answer parts (a) to (d) that follow.

Item A

Functionalist sociologists have argued that with the transition from pre-industrial society to industrial society, the family has undergone a change in its structure. For example, Talcott Parsons has argued that in pre-industrial society the family is organized in structure and performs a wide variety of functions, in industrial society the nuclear family becomes the dominant family structure.

Some sociologists also argue that the modern family is much more equal than in the past. For example, Young and Willmott claim that in today's 'symmetrical' nuclear family, husbands' and wives' conjugal roles have become much more equal than in the patriarchal family of the Victorian era. However, feminists have criticized this view of the modern family.

(a) Explain what is meant by the 'patriarchal family' (**Item A**). (2 marks)

(b) Suggest **two** criticisms which feminist sociologists might make of the view that 'husbands' and wives' conjugal roles have become much more equal' (**Item A**). (4 marks)

(c) Suggest **three** functions that the extended family might perform. (6 marks)

(d) Examine the reasons for changes in the position of children in the last 200 years. (24 marks)

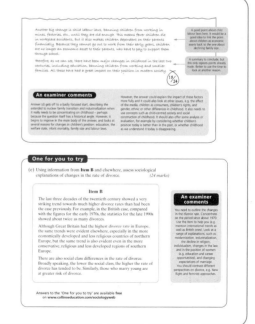

(e) Using information from **Item B** and elsewhere, assess sociological explanations of changes in the rate of divorce. (24 marks)

Item B

The last three decades of the twentieth century showed a very striking trend towards much higher divorce rates than had been the case previously. For example, in the British case, compared with the figures for the early 1970s, the statistics for the late 1990s showed about twice as many divorces.

Although Great Britain had the highest divorce rate in Europe, the same trends were evident elsewhere, especially in the more economically developed and less religious countries of northern Europe, but the same trend is also evident even in the more conservative, religious and less developed regions of southern Europe.

There are also social class differences in the rate of divorce. Broadly speaking, the lower the social class, the higher the rate of divorce has tended to be. Similarly, those who marry young are at greater risk of divorce.

Answers to the 'One for you to try' are available free on www.collinseducation.com/sociologyweb

www.collinseducation.com/sociologyweb

CONTENTS

Sociology AS for AQA

Introduction to Sociology: key themes and perspectives

Socialization, culture and identity

Getting you thinking

Feral children

Feral or 'wild' children are those who, for whatever reason, are not brought up by humans. One famous example of feral children is that of two infant girls, Kamala and Amala, who were lost in the jungle in India in about 1918. The girls had been found living with wolves, in a cave-like den. The older girl was 6 or 7 years old and the other, who died a year later, perhaps a year younger.

When captured, the girls were like animals. They were naked and ran in a sort of stooped crouch. They were afraid of artificial light. They were afraid of

Kamala, one of the 'wolf children', being taught to accept food and drink by hand

humans and kept a good distance. They did not display any characteristically human qualities. For example, they did not use tools of any kind, not even a stick. They did not know how to make a shelter. They did not walk upright. They did not laugh. They did not sing. They did not show any affection or attraction or curiosity towards humans. But what is especially striking is that the girls used no language. They used no noises or gestures to communicate. They didn't point at things or directions, or nod their head in agreement or disagreement. They preferred to eat with the dogs in the compound, who seemed to accept them. They ate by pushing their faces into the food, the way dogs do, and they drank by lapping from a bowl.

Adapted from Singh, J.A. and Zingg, R.N. (1942) *Wolf Children and the Feral Man*, New York: Harper

Shirbit culture

The Shirbit culture believes that the human body is ugly and that its natural tendency is to feebleness and disease. The Shirbit therefore indulge in rituals and ceremonies designed to avoid this, and consequently every household has a shrine devoted to the body. The rituals associated with the shrine are private and secret. Adults never discuss the rituals and children are told only enough for them to be successfully initiated. The focal point of the shrine is a box built into the wall in which are kept charms and magical potions for the face and body. These are obtained from the medicine men who write down the ingredients in an ancient and secret language which is only understood by the herbalist who prepares the potion. These potions are kept in the charm-box for many years. Beneath the charm-box is a small font. Every day, twice a day, every member of the family enters the shrine room in succession and bows his or her head before the charm-box, mingles different sorts of holy water in the font and proceeds with a brief rite of ablution.

The Shirbit have an almost pathological horror of and fascination with the mouth, the condition of which is believed to have a supernatural influence on all social relationships. Were it not for the rituals of the mouth, they believe their teeth would fall out, their friends would desert them and their lovers would reject them. Finally, men and women indulge in barbaric acts of self-mutilation. Men engage in a daily body ritual of scraping and lacerating their faces with a sharp instrument, while women bake their heads in a small oven once a month.

Based on Levine, R. (1956) 'Body language of the Nacirema', *American Anthropologist*, 58

1 Make a list of the things that the feral girls could not do and compare them with what you were capable of at the age of 6 or 7 years.

2 In your opinion, what skills were the feral girls likely to have that you lack?

3 What does the first extract tell us about the behaviour of human beings?

4 What aspects of Shirbit cultural behaviour seem alien to you?

5 In what ways might Shirbit behaviour be thought to resemble British culture?

Defining culture

What would you be like if all human influences were removed from your life? Tragic stories of **feral children**, such as that described on the left, show us very clearly that being human is about contact with other people. Without that contact we are reduced to basic and **instinctive** behaviour. But when humans work together – as they usually do – they create **cultures** that are complex, fascinating and utterly different. Our own culture always appears to be the most 'normal', while other cultures may seem strange, different and even inferior in some cases (a view known as **ethnocentrism**). Did you notice that the odd culture of the 'Shirbit' (described on the left) was actually a description of 'British' behaviour, especially our obsession with cleanliness, as it might appear to someone from a very different culture? ('Shirbit' is an anagram of 'British'.)

The idea of 'culture' is very important for sociologists. Culture is commonly defined as the way of life of a social group. More specifically, the term refers to 'patterns of belief, **values**, attitudes, expectations, ways of thinking, feeling and so on' which people use to make sense of their social worlds (Billington *et al.* 1998).

Some sociologists argue that culture also consists of **customs** and rituals, **norms** of behaviour, **statuses** and **roles**, language, symbols, art and material goods – the entire way in which a **society** expresses itself. Culture brings people together because it is shared and taken for granted. The idea of culture helps us to understand how individuals come together in groups and identify themselves as similar to or different from others.

When societies become larger and more complex, different cultures may emerge in the same society. Think of Britain today, where there are cultures based on different ages, genders, classes, ethnic groups, regions and so on – a situation known as **cultural diversity**. Sociologists refer to these 'cultures within cultures' as **subcultures**. They share some aspects of what we think of as 'British culture' – maybe eating with a knife and fork and speaking English – but they also possess distinctive cultural features that are all their own, for example, ways of dressing, accents and attitudes to the family.

The formation of culture

Culture is made up of several different elements, including values, norms, customs, statuses and roles.

Values

Values are widely accepted beliefs that something is worthwhile and desirable. For example, most societies place a high value on human life – although during wartime this value may be suspended. Other examples of British values include fair play, democracy, free speech, achievement, tolerance, wealth, property, romantic love, marriage and family life.

Norms

Norms are values put into practice. They are specific rules of behaviour that relate to specific social situations, and they govern all aspects of human behaviour. For example, norms govern the way we prepare and eat food, our toilet behaviour and so on. Norms also govern how we are supposed to behave according to our gender – that is, there are rules governing what counts as masculine or feminine behaviour. These norms have changed in recent years – for example, only 40 years ago, women with young babies going out to work or wearing trousers to work would have met with social disapproval.

Customs

Customs are traditional and regular norms of behaviour associated with specific social situations, events and anniversaries which are often accompanied by rituals and ceremonies. For example, in Britain many people practise the custom of celebrating Bonfire Night on November 5th, and this usually involves the ritual of burning a Guy Fawkes effigy and setting off fireworks.

It is also the social custom to mourn for the dead at funerals, and this usually involves an elaborate set of ritualistic norms and a ceremony. For example, it is generally expected that people wear black at funerals in Britain. Turning up in a pink tuxedo would be regarded as **deviant**, or norm-breaking, behaviour.

Statuses

All members of society are given a social position or status by their culture. Sociologists distinguish between 'ascribed' statuses and 'achieved' statuses. Ascribed statuses are fixed at birth, usually by inheritance or biology. For example, gender and race are fixed characteristics (which may result in women and ethnic minorities occupying low-status roles in some societies). Achieved statuses are those over which individuals have control. In Western societies, such status is normally attained through education, jobs and sometimes marriage.

Roles

Society expects those of a certain status to behave in a particular way. A set of norms is imposed on the status. These are collectively known as a role. For example, the role of 'doctor' is accompanied by cultural expectations about patient confidentiality and professional behaviour.

Culture and biology

Some people, known as **sociobiologists**, believe that human behaviour is largely the product of nature, so we can learn much about humans by studying animals. Most sociologists reject this view. If human behaviour were biologically determined, they argue, we could expect to see little variation in how people behave, whereas human behaviour is actually richly diverse. For example, if we look at other societies, we can see very different values and norms relating to gender roles, marriage, family and bringing up children. If human behaviour is influenced by biology at all, it is only at the level of physiological need – for example, we all need to sleep, eat and go to the toilet. However, when you look more closely, you find that even these biological influences are shaped by culture. Cultural values and norms determine what we eat. For example, insects are not popular as a food in Britain, and cannibalism would be regarded with horror. Cultural norms also determine *how* we eat. For example, eating behaviour is accompanied by a set of cultural norms called 'table manners', while the binge eating associated with bulimia is normally conducted in secret because of cultural disapproval.

Socialization and the transmission of culture

At birth, we are faced with a social world that already exists. Joining this world involves rapidly learning 'how things are done' in it. Only by learning the cultural rules of a society can a human interact with other humans. Culture needs to be passed on from generation to generation in order to ensure that it is shared. Shared culture allows society's members to communicate and cooperate. The process of learning culture is known as **socialization**. This involves learning the norms and values of a culture so that ways of thinking, behaving and seeing things are taken for granted or **internalized**.

Primary socialization

The family, and specifically parents, are central to **primary socialization**, the first stage in a lifelong process. Children learn language and basic norms and values. These can be taught formally, but they are more likely to be picked up informally by children imitating their parents. Parents may use **sanctions** to reinforce approved behaviour and punish behaviour defined as unacceptable. Such processes develop children's roles within the family and society so that children learn how they are expected to behave in a range and variety of social situations.

Feral children

We can illustrate the importance of primary socialization and contact with culture by examining feral children (children brought up in the wild by animals) to see what cultural characteristics they lack. If we consider the case of Kamala and Amala (see p. 2), we can see that they lacked toilet training, table manners and any sense of decorum. They had no sense of humour and consequently did not know how to laugh. They had no sense of music and could not sing. They did not know how to show affection. All of these things are cultural products that we pick up within the family.

Secondary socialization

Other institutions and groups also participate in the socialization of children. These are often referred to as agents of **secondary socialization**. Schools, religion, the mass media and the peer group all play a role in teaching society's members how to behave in particular situations and how to interact with people of a different status.

Socialization in all its varied forms involves children interacting with others and becoming aware of themselves as individuals. It is the process through which children acquire both a personal and a social **identity**.

Culture, socialization and history

Norbert Elias (1978) argues that the process of socialization has grown more influential throughout history, so that culture exerts a greater civilizing influence over our behaviour now than in any other historical age. He points out that in the

Key terms

Cultural diversity describes a society in which many different cultures exist.

Culture the way of life of a particular society or social group.

Customs traditional forms of behaviour associated with particular social occasions.

Deviance rule-breaking behaviour.

Ethnocentrism the belief that one culture is 'normal' and others inferior.

Feral children children brought up with limited contact with humans.

Identity the sense of who we are.

Instinct a genetic or biological code in animals that largely determines their behaviour.

Internalize accept something so that it becomes 'taken for granted'.

Norms rules of behaviour in social situations.

Primary socialization socialization in the very early years of life, normally through parents.

Roles positions in society such as 'mother' or 'police officer'. Roles are made up of norms.

Sanctions actions that encourage or discourage particular behaviour, such as smiling or frowning at a young child.

Secondary socialization socialization that continues throughout life. Education, the media and religion are all important influences.

Socialization the process by which we learn acceptable cultural beliefs and behaviour.

Society a social system made up of social institutions such as the family, education, law, politics, the media, religion, peer groups, and so on.

Sociobiology the study of similarities between the natural and social worlds.

Status social position.

Subculture a group within a larger culture that shares aspects of that culture but also has some of its own values, customs and so on.

Values widely accepted beliefs that some things are worthwhile.

Middle Ages, there were fewer cultural constraints on individual behaviour. People ate with their fingers, urinated and defecated in public, and engaged in explicit sexual behaviour that today would be defined as indecent and obscene. Moreover, burping, breaking wind, spitting and picking one's nose in public were regarded as perfectly normal forms of behaviour.

Culture and society

The concept of 'culture' is often used interchangeably with the concept of 'society', but it is important to understand that they do not mean exactly the same thing. Culture forms the connection between the individual and society – it tells the individual how to operate effectively within social institutions such as the family, marriage, education and so on. Zygmunt Bauman (1990) notes that socialization into culture is about introducing and maintaining social order in society. Individual behaviour that lies outside the cultural norm is perceived as dangerous and worth opposing because it threatens to destabilize society. Consequently, societies develop cultural mechanisms to control and repress such behaviour.

Culture and identity

Culture plays an important role in the construction of our identity. Identity is made up of two components – how we see ourselves and how others see us. It involves some choice on our part – that is, we often actively identify with aspects of our culture with regard to particular groups or activities, e.g. a football team, a friendship network, a fashion or trend. However, our identity is partly imposed on us by our culture. We are born into particular cultural positions or statuses – we do not choose our social class, gender, ethnic group, age, religion and nationality. Social forces like these shape our identity.

Check your understanding

1   Using examples, define what is meant by the terms 'values' and 'norms'.

2   Give an example of an ascribed status in Britain.

3   Why do sociologists believe that human behaviour is not biologically determined?

4   What is the difference between primary and secondary socialization?

5   What role does culture play in the construction of identity?

Activities

Exploring socialization

Socialization is the process whereby the helpless infant gradually becomes a self-aware, knowledgeable person, skilled in the ways of the culture into which she or he is born. Children obviously learn a great deal from their parents but they also learn basic values, norms and language, from a range of people, including grandparents (especially grandmothers), childminders and baby-sitters, siblings and neighbours who act as 'aunts', etc. There are other secondary influences, such as playgroups and nurseries, as well as television, video and computer games and traditional media such as comics or storybooks. Children do not passively absorb these influences. They are from the very beginning active beings. They 'make sense' of their experience and decide for themselves how to react.

Adapted from Giddens, A. (2006) *Sociology* (5th edn), Cambridge: Polity Press, p.26

1   Explain what is meant by 'culture'.
    (2 marks)

2   Identify two social institutions that are responsible for the transmission of culture.
    (4 marks)

3   Identify three norms that are important in British culture today.   (6 marks)

4   Identify and briefly illustrate two cultural influences on our sense of identity.
    (8 marks)

Research idea

Draw up a questionnaire to give to other students which aims to find out the extent to which culture is shared. You might ask about aspects of culture such as mealtimes and food customs, leisure activities, values and beliefs, and taste in music. Carry out the survey and analyse your results.

Web.task

Visit www.feralchildren.com

Choose a child and write a report on them detailing how the child differs from children who have experienced normal socialization.

TOPIC 2

Social differentiation, power and stratification

Getting you thinking

Where you rate in the new social order

1 Higher managerial & professional occupations

1.1 Employers & managers in large organizations – Company directors, corporate managers, police inspectors, bank managers, senior civil servants, military officers

1.2 Higher professionals – Doctors, barristers and solicitors, clergy, librarians, social workers, teachers

2 Lower managerial & professional occupations – Nurses and midwives, journalists, actors and musicians, prison officers, police, soldiers (NCO and below)

3 Intermediate occupations – Clerks, secretaries, driving instructors, computer operators, telephone fitters

4 Small employers & own account workers – Publicans, playgroup leaders, farmers, taxi drivers, window cleaners, painters and decorators

5 Lower supervisory, craft & related occupations – Printers, plumbers, butchers, bus inspectors, TV engineers, train drivers

6 Semi-routine occupations – Shop assistants, traffic wardens, cooks, bus drivers, hairdressers, postal workers

7 Routine occupations
Waiters, road sweepers, cleaners, couriers, building labourers, refuse collectors

8 Never worked/long-term unemployed

Source: *The Guardian*, 15 January 1999

1 The *Guardian* cartoon above shows the government's new social classification of the population, which is based on eight job categories. Examine it carefully and try and work out what has been used to distinguish the categories.

2 Where would the Royal Family fit into this classification?

3 Using the occupational examples listed in each category, allocate David and Victoria Beckham, and Richard Branson (owner of Virgin) to a social class.

4 What problems have you identified with this classification system?

Despite being a wealthy country that can offer its citizens a very good standard of living, the UK is still characterized by great inequalities in wealth and income that affect people's **life chances**, such as their level of educational qualification and life expectancy. A great number of people in the UK are **socially excluded** from taking part in activities which the rest of society takes for granted. For instance, in 2005/6 it was estimated by the charity Barnardos that 3.8 million children were living in poverty. What these inequalities tell us is that the UK is a society characterized by social class **stratification** – people are ranked hierarchically according to social and economic factors such as wealth, income, qualifications, skills and so on.

One way in which the government attempts to keep tabs on the extent of these inequalities is through the use of the occupational classification, illustrated in the cartoon on the left, known as the National Statistics Socio-Economic Classification (NS-SEC). This system, introduced in 2000, is based on a rather complex collection of criteria related to the jobs people do, e.g. levels of skill, authority over others, salary, promotion prospects, control over the work process and hours worked, and so on. However, many sociologists are unhappy with this system for reasons which you may have spotted when you attempted to allocate the Royal Family to it. The system fails to account for those wealthy enough not to have to work – in other words, a significant proportion of the rich who live off inherited wealth, share dividends, rents and so on are not covered by it. Moreover, you will have seen that it was also difficult to allocate our 'celebrities' to these occupational categories. By rights, Victoria Beckham (as 'Posh Spice') should have been allocated to social class 2, while David Beckham doesn't fit in any of the categories. Moreover, their extreme wealth makes a mockery of this system.

Other sociologists point out that social class, i.e. our socio-economic position in society, is only one form of inequality and stratification that exists in UK society. It is argued by feminists that gender is an important source of inequality, while other sociologists point out that the UK is a **multicultural** society in which racism and, consequently, inequalities experienced by ethnic minorities are a daily fact of life. More recently, sociological research has suggested that disability, age and sexuality are producing newer forms of inequality and stratification.

Whatever forms of stratification exist, we can see that those at the top of the system experience many more benefits in terms of life chances and standard of living than those beneath them. We have already identified inequalities in education and health, but there are also differences in political **power**. Those at the top of the stratification system are often in a position to maintain inequality against the will of others and to generate further economic and social advantages for themselves.

Differentiation and stratification

Social differences exist in every society. Social **differentiation** takes the form of variations in aspects of culture such as dress, language and customs as well as in the degree of power, wealth and **status** accorded to individuals and groups. Stratification refers to the process by which groups of people

are ranked hierarchically into strata or layers. These strata often share specific characteristics, such as being wealthy or poor, powerful or powerless and so on, as well as cultural characteristics such as sharing similar values, norms and lifestyles.

There are a number of different types of stratification. The oldest form is probably **slavery**. Many ancient societies practised this and, as recently as the early 19th century, the slave trade – the transportation to the New World of millions of Africans – was dominated by the British. Slave labour still continues in varied forms around the world today. Some sociologists see it as the basis of inequalities that exist around race and ethnicity in contemporary Britain.

Another type of stratification is **feudalism**. This medieval system was based on a hierarchical system of land ownership, with the king at the top lending land in return for services and loyalty from his nobles. At the bottom of this system was the peasant who had few rights – for example, they often could not marry without permission of the local lord of the manor.

Caste is a stratification system found in India and amongst ethnic-minority groups that migrated to Britain from South Asia. It is usually associated with Hinduism (although Sikhs and some Muslims also practise forms of caste). In the Hindu version, people are born into closed groups called *varna,* which are ranked on the basis of religious purity achieved in a previous life. If you were especially bad in a previous life, you might be born into the non-caste group called 'untouchables', who have the least status in Hindu society.

Some sociologists point out that many societies often stratify on the basis of belonging to particular tribes or clans, as was the case in Scotland until the late 18th century. Others stratify along racial or ethnic lines. The system of segregation found in the Southern states of the USA until the 1960s, and the South African system of apartheid, which was only dismantled in the late 1980s, are good examples of stratification based on notions of racial superiority.

Social class

In the UK, social class is regarded as the main form of stratification. Class societies such as the UK are regarded as 'open' societies because it is possible to achieve **upward mobility** through educational qualifications, hard work, and even marriage. In contrast, societies in which we find slavery, feudalism, caste and racial and ethnic apartheid are 'closed' societies because mobility is restricted by the more powerful groups. Class societies are also regarded as achievement-orientated or **meritocratic** systems (although some sociologists disagree and point out that some people, especially those from upper-class backgrounds educated in the public schools such as Eton and at Oxbridge have more opportunities to succeed than the majority of the population). Tony Blair, Prime Minister of the UK between 1997 and 2007, believed the UK to be an open society – in 1999, he said 'I believe we will have an expanded middle class, with ladders of opportunity for those of all backgrounds'. However, Marxist sociologists are sceptical of this claim, as you will see in Topic 4.

The class structure

It is generally agreed that four broad social classes exist in the UK.

The upper class

The upper class is thought to be made up of three categories of rich people in Britain:

1 *Landowners* – people whose wealth in the form of land and property has been largely inherited
2 *The entrepreneurial rich* – those who wealth is wrapped up in stocks and shares. Some, such as the Sainsbury family, have inherited their wealth, whereas others, like Sir Richard Branson (shown on p. 6) and Sir Alan Sugar, are self-made millionaires
3 *The jet-set rich* – including film stars, rock stars and sports professionals.

The middle classes

This term refers to a number of **non-manual** social groups. The term implies that they have a great deal in common, whereas there are often distinct differences between them:

● *Professionals* – Doctors, solicitors, teachers, lecturers, etc. This group is characterized by high levels of education which equips them with **cultural capital**, i.e. the knowledge, attitudes and skills required so that their children can also take advantage of further and higher education.
● *Managers* – This group tends to have worked its way up from the shop or office floor and tends to have skills specific to particular organizations. The job security of this group is constantly under threat from economic recession.
● *White-collar workers* – Clerks, secretaries, etc., carrying out routine tasks and employed by organizations such as banks, building societies and insurance firms. Some sociologists argue that the pay and working conditions of this group have deteriorated so much that they have more in common with the working classes than the middle class.
● *The petit bourgeoisie* – The self-employed, such as farmers and hauliers. There are signs that this group is increasingly adopting radical methods to protect their interests, which they see as under threat.

The working classes

This concept refers to skilled, semi-skilled and unskilled **manual workers** who only make up about 28 per cent of the workforce in 2007. They generally enjoy fewer privileges than middle-class workers in terms of holidays, sick pay, opportunities for promotion, pensions, etc., and their jobs are generally less secure. There are also major differences in educational qualifications, life expectancy, infant mortality, housing type and leisure pursuits between the working class and other social classes.

The underclass

New Right sociologists have claimed that an **underclass** has appeared at the bottom end of the working class in recent years. This group is allegedly workshy, happy to live off state benefits, involved in criminal activities and promiscuous. However, critics suggest that the New Right use the label of 'underclass' to stereotype the poor as 'undeserving'. It has been pointed out that the majority of the poor are in poverty through no fault of their own – because of economic recession, cuts in welfare spending and so on.

Social status

Some sociologists argue that social differences are just as important as class differences in the UK. It is argued that social status does not always derive from economic factors such as wealth and income. It can also derive from education, occupation, speech, dress, age, gender and race. For example, people do not look up to doctors and follow their orders unquestioningly because doctors are wealthy or earn more than they do. Rather, we respect doctors because they have spent years in training, learning what the rest of us see as very difficult skills. This issue of status has led sociologists to explore a range of social differences which they suggest are just as important as social-class differences.

Gender

Feminists see British society as **patriarchal** (male dominated). They claim that men have used their economic and cultural power to define women and women's interests as subordinate to men and men's interests. They claim that in every sphere of social life, patterned gender inequalities can be seen. These ideas are explored in further detail in Topic 4.

Race and ethnicity

It can be argued that inequalities are also stratified across ethnic lines in the UK. If we examine the evidence, we can see that White children generally do better in education than children from minority ethnic groups (with the exception of Indian and Chinese children, who do slightly better on average than Whites). With regard to indicators such as unemployment, low-skilled and low-paid jobs, life expectancy, infant mortality rates and housing, people from African-Caribbean, Pakistani and Bangladeshi backgrounds do substantially worse than White people. Moreover, there is evidence of racism in the way the police and courts treat members of ethnic-minority groups.

These inequalities and the lack of power that results from them have led some sociologists to conclude that institutional racism exists across a range of British institutions, including the police, the judicial system, the prison service and the NHS. It is suggested that such institutions discriminate against ethnic minorities because they are organized around a set of often unconscious stereotypes and discriminatory practices that are taken for granted, habitual and often not recognized as racism.

Disability

In recent years, we have increasingly recognized that disability is not only a medical condition, but also a social condition, in that the way that society reacts to the disabled can have a negative effect on them. In other words, they have been 'disabled by society'. It is argued that disabled people have been socially marginalized and discriminated against by social attitudes. This has led to exclusion from mainstream employment, education, housing, and leisure opportunities. A growing number of disabled people have challenged negative stereotypes and discriminatory social policies by organizing pressure groups to develop positive identities among the disabled and to petition for fairer treatment.

Ageism

Age is another source of status inequality. The young and elderly both lack status in modern British society. In many societies around the world, the elderly acquire status as they get older. They are revered as wise and society feels a strong duty to care for them. This is not the case in the UK, where the elderly often experience **ageism** – prejudicial attitudes and discriminatory practices which dismiss them as a problem or burden. In 2006, age discrimination laws came into force. These make it illegal for employers to make workers retire at the age of 65. It is also now illegal for companies to advertise for 'young' or 'mature' candidates for jobs.

Focus on research

Charlotte Cooper (1998) Fatness as disability

Sociologists have been critical of official definitions and measurements of disability because they are frequently based upon medical discourse, which views the impaired as inadequate, dependent and problematic. In contrast, sociologists suggest that disabled people are 'disabled by society', i.e. by the stereotypes of disability held by the able bodied. Charlotte Cooper takes this analysis a stage further when she claims that fat people are disabled because both the disabled and fat people are made invisible by the media and a fat-hating culture dominated by 'able-bodied, slender white bodies'. Fat people are seen as unworthy, pitiful and ugly because they are seen to have brought their condition upon themselves.

Challenging stereotypes: pop star Beth Ditto

Cooper, C. (1998) *Fat and Proud: The politics of size*, London: Women's Press)

1 **How would you define 'disability'?**

2 **Identify two reasons why you might agree or disagree with Charlotte Cooper's analysis.**

Key terms

Ageism discrimination based upon negative stereotypes, usually focusing on the elderly.

Cultural capital cultural skills, such as knowing how to behave, speak and learn, passed on by middle-class parents to their children.

Differentiation ways of distinguishing between social groups through variations in aspects of culture, language, customs, power, wealth and status.

Feudalism medieval system of stratification based on the ownership of land.

Homophobia prejudice and discrimination against gay people.

Life chances opportunities or lack of them to acquire material, social and cultural rewards, such as jobs, qualifications or good health.

Manual work physical labour.

Meritocratic where rewards are given on the basis of achievement, i.e. effort, ability and intelligence.

Multicultural characterized by a variety of ethnic groups.

Non-manual work work that mainly involves mental labour.

Patriarchal male dominated.

Power the ability to maintain inequality against the will of others.

Social exclusion missing out on opportunities and activities that most other people take for granted because of poverty or other factors beyond your control.

Status prestige.

Slavery form of stratification where people are either owned by others or are forced to work for no or very little pay.

Stratification hierarchical ranking based on social status, resulting in patterns of inequality.

Underclass a social group in poverty which (depending on your perspective) is a product of workshy attitudes and an overgenerous benefit system or a product of economic recession.

Upward social mobility the ability to move upwards through the class system, e.g. from working class to middle class.

Focus on research

Babb *et al.* (2006)
Social Trends

Poverty

- In 2003/4, 17 per cent of the UK population were estimated to be living in poverty, i.e. these individuals were receiving less than 60 per cent of the average wage. Some 21 per cent of children (2.6 million) were living in poverty-stricken households in 2003/4.

Inequality

- Although the gender pay gap has narrowed, only very slow progress has been made. In 1986, women in full-time work earned on average 74 per cent of what men earned. By 2004, this had only increased to 82 per cent.
- Wealth distribution has continued to widen in the last decade. Between 1991 and 2003, the percentage of wealth held by the wealthiest 1 per cent of the population increased from 17 per cent to 21 per cent. In 2003, half the population owned only 7 per cent of total wealth.
- People from ethnic-minority groups were more likely to be unemployed compared with White people in 2004. 15 per cent of males from African-Caribbean backgrounds were unemployed compared with 5 per cent of White males. 20 per cent of Pakistani women were unemployed compared with 4 per cent of White females.

Education

- The socio-economic status of parents can have a significant impact on the GCSE attainment of their children. In England and Wales, 76 per cent of pupils whose parents were in higher professional occupations achieved five or more GCSEs at grades A* to C in 2004 compared with 33 per cent of those whose parents were in lower social classes.
- There was also variation by social class in the qualifications that 16 year olds in full-time education studied. 74 per cent of 16 year olds whose parents were in higher professional occupations were studying for GCE A-level or its equivalent compared with 31 per cent of working-class 16 year olds.
- Entry to higher education increased from 19 per cent in 1990 to 31 per cent in 2000, but it has benefited the well-off more than the poor. In 2004, while 44 per cent of teenagers from higher professional backgrounds were in higher education, the figure for those from the lowest social class was just 13 per cent.
- In 2003/4, around 25 in every 10 000 pupils of mixed ethnic origin were permanently excluded from schools in England, compared with 41 in every 10 000 of African-Caribbean pupils, 14 White pupils in every 10 000 and 6 Asian pupils in every 10 000.

Health

- In 1901, males born in the UK could expect to live to around 45 years and females to 49 years. By 2004, life expectancy at birth had risen to almost 77 years for males and just over 81 years for females. However, males living in the most economically and socially deprived areas of the UK had a life expectancy at birth of only 71 years.
- Middle-class men are less likely than working-class men to die from the major causes of death in the UK such as cardiovascular disease (angina, heart attacks and strokes) and cancer. Cardiovascular disease seems linked to income. About 14 per cent of men in the top 20 per cent of income earners died from cardiovascular conditions compared with 22 per cent of men in the lowest 20 per cent of earners.
- Household income may influence whether people have access to a healthy diet and the recommended five daily portions of fruit and vegetables. In 2003, 40 per cent of women and 27 per cent of men in the highest 20 per cent of income group ate five or more portions compared with 17 per cent of women and 14 per cent of men in the lowest 20 per cent of income group.
- There was a clear relationship between social class and participation rates in sports, games and physical activities. 59 per cent of professionals took part in regular physical exercise compared with 30 per cent of manual workers. Walking was the most popular activity among all socio-economic classifications but professionals were almost twice as likely to engage in this activity compared with those in working-class occupations.

Quality of life

- Perceptions of crime vary by demographic and socio-economic characteristics. In 2002/3, unskilled workers were more than twice as likely as professionals to think there was a lot more crime than two years previously.
- The risk of being a victim of crime is also linked to social class. Single-parent families are at a higher risk of burglary than other family types, as are households with a low income compared with households with higher incomes. Households in council estates and in rented accommodation were at a higher risk of burglary than homeowners.

Adapted from Babb, P., Butcher, H., Church, J. and Zealey, L. (eds) (2006) *Social Trends 36*, Office for National Statistics/Palgrave MacMillan

Choose any two of the points outlined above.

1 **How might the data have been collected? How accurate do you think it is? Explain your answer.**

2 **Suggest ways in which any two of these inequalities might be reduced.**

Sexuality

Finally, sexuality may be another source of inequality. It is certainly the case that gay men and lesbians do not enjoy equal status with heterosexual people, despite nearly 40 years of legalization. There is still a strong tendency in society that defines these types of sexuality as deviant and unnatural. Moreover, this **homophobia** (dislike of homosexuality) has extended to erroneous media coverage of Aids as a 'gay plague', despite Aids being overwhelmingly a heterosexual problem worldwide. It has also led to discrimination in the form of physical attacks on – and the murder of – people solely because they are homosexual.

Check your understanding

1   What is the NS-SEC used for?

2   Explain why the caste system is 'closed' and class systems are 'open'.

3   What groups make up the upper class and the middle class?

4   What is meant by 'social status'?

5   Identify five sources of social status that exist in modern Britain, apart from social class.

Activities

Exploring social class

Sociologists typically approach the unequal distribution of scarce resources as a study of stratification. The term 'stratification' refers to the fact that there is inequality of resources between groups of people, and that these form a structured, or systematic, hierarchy. As a matter of fact, on average, men have more resources than women; property owners more than employees; professional workers more than unskilled manual workers; White people more than Black; older people more than younger ones, and so on.

Class divisions remain the most important of inequalities in British society. Class continues to exert a great influence on our lives, and inequalities between the poor and wealthy have increased in the last 20 years. Gender and ethnicity are increasingly important but it is important to acknowledge that middle-class women enjoy more opportunities than working-class men and women, whilst the middle-class members of minority ethnic groups are advantaged compared to working-class people of any ethnicity.

1   Explain what is meant by 'stratification'.
(2 marks)

2   Identify two advantages in terms of life chances that the middle class enjoy over the working class.
(4 marks)

3   Identify three sources of inequality associated with age.
(6 marks)

4   Identify and briefly describe two ways in which disabled people might be disabled by society.
(8 marks)

Research idea

Conduct a survey to find out the extent of class identity among a sample of young people.

- What classes do they think exist?
- Do they believe that class is still important?
- Do they feel that they belong to any particular class?
- Do they feel that their gender, ethnicity, age or sexuality is more important?

Web.task

Visit the following websites and document the different types of inequalities experienced by a variety of status groups:

- The Disability Archive of the Centre for Disability Studies at Leeds University includes a range of resources written by disabled sociologists, including Colin Barnes and Tom Shakespeare www.leeds.ac.uk/disability-studies

- Age Concern – www.ageconcern.org.uk – this site contains details of the different forms that ageism takes today

- Outrage is an organization which fights discrimination against gay people – www.outrage.org.uk

- The Commission for Racial Equality documents inequality relating to ethnic minorities in the UK – www.cre.gov.uk/ – as does The Runnymede Trust – www.runnymedetrust.org/

- The Equal Opportunities Commission documents inequalities experienced by women – www.eoc.org.uk

Consensus, culture and identity

Getting you thinking

Examining the homes in a typical English suburb, Nigel Barley noticed how similar they were in their organization. Most had front gardens kept in good order with flowerbeds and so on. However, he observed that people very rarely sat in these or used them for family activities such as barbecues. This was the function of back gardens, although people maintained their privacy through the use of hedges and fences. Rooms on the ground floor were generally regarded as public rooms – some had best front rooms used only for entertaining at the weekend. Kitchens were used to prepare and eat meals. Most had a sitting room in which the television was kept and this was the focus of most family activity, especially entertaining guests. The most private rooms were the toilets. Visitors would seek permission to use these. Upstairs bedrooms, too, were generally regarded as private because these were associated with intimate activities. Consequently, family members knocked on doors before entering. Bedrooms were also individually furnished and decorated so that it was not difficult to identify which family members occupied them.

Adapted from Billington, R. *et al.* (1998) *Exploring Self and Society*, Basingstoke: Macmillan, pp. 38–9

1 Can Barley's description of the typical suburban home be applied to your general experience of home?

2 Do you think this description is typical of most homes in the UK?

3 Barley is describing a very ordered and structured world. What do you think is the reason for all this order and predictability? Where does it come from?

We learn from an early age to see our status as wrapped up with our home, and to see a happy family and home as important goals. In other words, there exists a great deal of agreement in society about how we ought to organize our daily lives. Sociologists refer to this agreement among members of society as **consensus**. This consensus means that we have a good idea of how we should behave in most situations. It also means that we can anticipate pretty accurately how other people are going to behave, just as we can guess the layout of their house or flat. Some sociologists see this order and predictability as the key to understanding society. If this order did not exist – if we were always confused and uncertain about our own and others' values and behaviour – then, they believe, chaos and anarchy would be the result. This theory of society is known as **functionalism** or consensus theory.

Functionalism

Functionalism is a **structuralist theory**. This means that it sees the individual as less important than the **social structure** or organization of society. It is a 'top-down' theory that looks at society rather than the individuals within it. Society is more important because the individual is produced by society. People are the product of all the social influences on them: their family, friends, educational and religious background, their experiences at work, in leisure, and their exposure to the media. All of these influences make them what they are. They are born into society, play their role in it and then die. But their deaths do not mean the end of society. Society continues long after they are gone.

Social order

Functionalists study the role of different parts of society – social institutions – in bringing about the patterns of shared and stable behaviour that they refer to as **social order**. They might study, for example, how families teach children the difference between right and wrong, or how education provides people with the skills and qualifications needed in the world of work. For functionalists, society is a complex system made up of parts that all work together to keep the whole system going. The economic system (work), the political system, family and kinship, and the cultural system (education, mass media, religion and youth culture) all have their part to play in maintaining a stable society from generation to generation.

A major function of social institutions is to socialize every individual into a system of norms and values that will guide their future behaviour and thinking. People need to be taught the core values of their society and to internalize them, so that they become shared and 'taken for granted'. The end result of this process is **value consensus** – members of society agree on what counts as important values and standards of behaviour. Such consensus produces a sense of **social solidarity**, i.e. we feel part of a community that has something in common. We feel a sense of common **identity**.

Another important foundation stone of social order in modern societies is the specialized division of labour. This refers to the organization of jobs and skills in a society. All members of society are dependent upon this division of labour, which supplies a vast and invisible army of workers to maintain the standard of living we take for granted. For example, hundreds of unskilled and skilled manual workers, professionals and managers are involved in supplying us with essential services such as electricity, gas, water, sewage systems, transport, food in supermarkets, and so on. The fact that you are able to sit in a classroom and read this book is also the product of hundreds of workers you will never see or meet. For example, someone has decided that your area needs a school or college, somebody has hired a caretaker to open and maintain the building, cleaners to clean, secretaries to run the office, teachers to teach and managers to decide to put on AS Sociology. The presence of this book in front of you required an author, editors, proofreaders, graphic designers, picture researchers, illustrators, a publisher, printers, people involved in the production of paper and ink, lorry drivers to transport the finished product to warehouses and bookshops, and someone behind the counter or a computer to sell it on to schools, teachers and students. Note, too, that you are already part of this division of labour. Without students, educational institutions would be pointless. The list of people we are dependent upon is endless. Think about how your life would change if all electricity workers were abducted by aliens overnight!

The specialized division of labour, therefore, is crucial because without it, society would soon descend into chaos. Consequently, another function of **social institutions** is to prepare young people to take their place in the division of labour by transmitting the idea that education, qualifications, working hard and a career are all worthwhile things. This ensures that young people will eventually come to replace workers who have retired or died, and so social order is maintained.

Figure 1.1 Understanding functionalism

Functionalism looks at society as though it were a living thing like a human being.

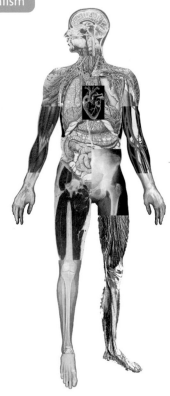

How is society like a human body?

The body

Every part of the body has a function which helps to keep it alive and healthy.

- The human body grows and develops.
- All of the parts of the body link together into one big system.
- The body fights disease.

Society

Every part of society helps to keep society going – for example, the family helps by bringing up the next generation.

- Societies gradually develop and change.
- All of the parts of society work together and depend on each other – they are interdependent.
- Society has mechanisms to deal with problems when they occur, such as the police and the legal system.

Talcott Parsons

Talcott Parsons (1902–79) was a key functionalist thinker. He argued that socialization is the key to understanding human behaviour patterns. The role of social institutions, such as the family, education, religion and the media, is to ensure the passing on, or reproduction, of socially acceptable patterns of behaviour. Social institutions do this in a number of ways:

● They socialize people into key values of society, such as the importance of nuclear family life, achievement, respect for authority and hierarchy, and so on. The result is that most members of our society share common values and norms of behaviour (value consensus), and so we can predict how people are going to behave in the vast majority of social situations. The family, education and the mass media are primarily responsible for this function.

● Social institutions give some values and norms a sacred quality, so that they become powerful formal and informal moral codes governing social behaviour. These moral codes underpin our definitions of criminal, deviant and immoral behaviour. An example of a formal moral code is 'do not steal', because it is embodied in the law, while examples of more informal moral codes are 'do not lie' or 'do not commit adultery'. The social institutions of religion and the law are primarily responsible for the transmission of these codes, although media reporting of crime and deviance also contributes by reminding members of society about what counts as normality and deviance, and publicizing the punishments handed out to those who indulge in behaviour that lies outside the consensus.

● They encourage social solidarity (a sense of community) and **social integration** (a sense of belonging). For example, the teaching of history is an important means of achieving this goal, because it reminds members of society about their shared culture.

So, our behaviour is controlled by the rules of the society into which we are born. The result is that we don't have to be told that what we are doing is socially unacceptable. We will probably feel inhibited from indulging in deviant behaviour in the first place because we are so successfully immersed in the common values of society by our experience of socialization.

Identity

Identity is the way we feel about ourselves, which is partly shaped by how others view us. People's identity as fathers, mothers and children, for example, is controlled by a value consensus. This defines and therefore largely determines what roles each status has to adopt if it is to fit successfully into society. In other words, there is a clear set of expectations about what makes a 'good' mother or father, son or daughter. For example, people defined as 'normal' parents will engage in socially approved behaviour – they will protect their children from harm rather than neglect them or inflict excessive physical punishment on them; they will give them unconditional love; they will support them economically, and so on. Note that

these expectations may change according to gender – hence the commonly held belief that working mothers, rather than working fathers, may be a cause of psychological damage in children. Functionalists point out that our experience of socialization and social control ensures that most of us will attempt to live up to these social and cultural expectations without question.

Criticisms of functionalism

Functionalism is far less popular in sociology today than it was in the 1950s. Part of its decline in popularity is probably linked to the problems it had attempting to explain all the diversity and conflict that existed in society from the 1960s onwards. Criticism of its core ideas has therefore been widespread:

● Functionalism has been criticized for overemphasizing consensus and order, and failing to explain the social conflicts that characterize the modern world. We see clear differences in behaviour all around us every day, and there may be clear cultural differences present in the same society. For example, behaviours on which most of society might have been agreed 50 years ago, such as women with young children going out to work, cohabitation, abortion or homosexuality (which were all regarded as wrong), now attract a range of differing opinions. Some functionalists have attempted to explain this by reference to subculture. This can be defined as a way of life subscribed to by a significant minority who may share some general values and norms with the larger culture, but who may be in opposition to others. For example, in a multicultural society like the UK, some minority ethnic groups may retain very traditional ideas about women's roles, marriage, homosexuality, etc.

Key terms

Consensus a general agreement.

Functionalism a sociological perspective that focuses on understanding how the different parts of society work together to keep it running smoothly.

Identity the way we feel about ourselves.

Social institution a part of society, such as education or the family.

Social integration a sense of belonging to society.

Social order patterns of shared and predictable behaviour.

Social solidarity a sense of community.

Social structure an alternative term for the social organization of society.

Structuralist theory a theory that believes that human behaviour is influenced by the organization of society.

Value, or moral, consensus an agreement among a majority of members of society that something is good and worthwhile.

- Functionalism has also been accused of ignoring the freedom of choice enjoyed by individuals. People choose what to do – they do what makes sense to them. Their behaviour and ideas are not imposed on them by structural factors beyond their control. In this sense, functionalism may present 'an oversocialized' picture of human beings.
- There may also be problems in the way functionalists view socialization as a positive process that never fails. If this were the case, then delinquency, child abuse and illegal drug-taking would not be the social problems they are.
- Finally, functionalism has been accused by Marxists of ignoring the fact that power is not equally distributed in society. Some groups have more wealth and power than others and may be able to impose their norms and values on less powerful groups. The next few topics focus on this process.

Check your understanding

1 Using your own words, explain what is meant by 'value consensus'.

2 What are the key values of society according to Parsons, and what agencies are mainly responsible for their transmission?

3 What agencies are responsible for turning key values into powerful moral codes that guide our most basic behaviour?

4 Why do social agencies such as the law and the media need to regulate our behaviour?

5 How might the teaching of British history encourage a sense of community and integration in British schools?

Activities

Exploring social institutions

Read the following text and then answer the questions on the right.

Durkheim believed that the function of social institutions was to promote and maintain social order and social solidarity. He regarded the family as the most important institution because it links the individual to society. Romantic love and marriage provide society with an orderly means of reproduction, while the family unit provides physical and economic support for children during the early years of dependence. Most importantly, the family is the primary agent of socialization – children learn society's essential ideas and values, the accepted ways of behaving and the social roles (such as feminine and masculine roles) required for adult life. Education, too, develops both the values and skills required for children to take their place eventually as working adults in the specialized division of labour. The discipline structure and secondary socialization that occurs in schools also function to maintain consensus, as most people accept that a future of work and a career are the norm. Finally, religious beliefs provide people with moral guidelines and practices which socially integrate people into a common identity and community.

1 Explain what is meant by 'the specialized division of labour'. (2 marks)

2 Identify two functions of religion. (4 marks)

3 Identify three examples which suggest that socialization is not as successful as functionalists claim. (6 marks)

4 Identify and briefly explain two reasons why functionalists might be criticized for overemphasizing consensus and order. (8 marks)

Research idea

Interview a sample of males and females of different ages about what they see as important. You could ask them about issues such as love, marriage, how family life should be organized, how children should be brought up, what they regard as deviant, their religious beliefs and so on. However, remember to explain the aims of this research to your participants and gain their informed consent.

Web.task

Search for the website 'Dead Sociologists' Society'. Use it to find out about the ideas of the founding father of functionalism, Emile Durkheim.

TOPIC 4

Conflict, culture and identity

Getting you thinking

Imagine that everybody in the British economy was to march past you in an hour-long parade, and that the marchers are organised by income, with the poor at the front and the rich at the back. Now imagine that the height of the people marching by is proportional to their income, so a person with average income will be average height, a person earning half the average income will be half the average height, and so on.

What would this parade look like? Most of us would picture a parade where people slowly but steadily got taller. We'd be wrong. As the parade begins, the first marchers are really tiny. For five minutes or so, you are peering down at people just inches high – single mothers, the disabled, the elderly and the unemployed. Ten minutes in, the full-time labour force has arrived: to begin with, mainly unskilled manual and clerical workers, standing about waist-high to the observers. At this point things start to get dull, because there are an incredible number of these very small people. The minutes pass, and pass, and they just keep on coming. It is only in the last 20 minutes of the parade that you are able to look anyone in the eye – and then, only for a fleeting moment because,

suddenly, heights begin to surge upward at a madly accelerating rate. Doctors, lawyers, and senior civil servants 20 feet tall speed by. Moments later, bankers and stockbrokers peer down from 50 feet, 100 feet, 500 feet. And then in the last seconds you see the unimaginably huge giants: the great untaxed. The very soles of their shoes are hundreds of feet thick. Most of them are businessmen, owners of companies, film stars, and a few members of the Royal Family. Robbie Williams and Prince Charles are over a mile high. Britain's richest man is the last in the parade – he measures over four miles high.

Adapted from Johann Hari, *The Independent*, 25 June 2007

1 **What does this parade tell us about the way income is divided in the UK?**

2 **Give examples of how long it took for people on different incomes to appear in the parade.**

3 **Does the parade surprise you in any way? Is Britain more, or less, unequal than you thought?**

Lots of students have part-time jobs. Perhaps you have. If so, you sell your time and your ability to work to an employer who, in return, gives you money. But is this a fair exchange? Think about why they employ you. It's not to do you a favour, but because they benefit: the work you do is worth more to them

than the amount they pay you. They would benefit even more if they paid you less for the same work or got you to do more work for the same pay. Of course, it would be better for you if you were paid more for the same work or worked less for the same pay. To put it another way, what is good for your boss is bad for you, and vice versa. There's a very basic conflict of interest between you and your employer. This conflict occurs not because you are unreasonable or your boss is money-grabbing. It occurs simply because the system works that way.

Marxism

This is the starting point for **Marxism**, a sociological perspective based on the ideas of Karl Marx (1818–83). For Marxists, the system we live in (which he called **capitalism**) divides everyone up into two basic classes: bosses and workers. Marx called the bosses the **bourgeoisie** or ruling class (because they controlled society), and the workers he called the **proletariat** or working class. The ruling class benefit in every way from how society operates, while the workers get far less than they deserve.

Like functionalism, Marxism is a structuralist theory – that is, it sees the individual as less important than the social structure of society. In particular, Marxism sees the economic organization of societies as responsible for the behaviour of individuals. This is because Marxism claims that individuals are the products of the class relationships that characterize economic life.

Society is based on an exploitative and unequal relationship between two economic classes. The bourgeoisie are the economically dominant class (the ruling class) who own the **means of production** (machinery, factories, land, etc.). The working class, on the other hand, own only their ability to work. They sell this to the bourgeoisie in return for a wage. However, the relationship between these two classes is unequal and based on conflict because the bourgeoisie aim to extract the maximum labour from workers at the lowest possible cost.

According to Marxists, the result is that the bourgeoisie exploit the labour of the working class. The difference between the value of the goods and services produced by the worker and the wages paid is pocketed by the capitalist class and lies at the heart of the vast profits made by many employers. These profits fuel the great inequalities in wealth and income between the ruling class and the working class. For example, according to HM Revenue and Customs, in 2003, 71 per cent of all financial wealth in the UK was owned by just 10 per cent of the population. Even if we add property ownership to financial wealth, the least wealthy 50 per cent of the population only own about 7 per cent of all wealth in the UK in 2003. These figures are also likely to be underestimates, because people generally do not declare the full sum of their wealth to the tax authorities – for instance, they may keep wealth abroad.

If society is so unfair, why do the working class go along with it? Why aren't there riots, strikes and political rebellion? Why does society actually appear quite stable, with most people seemingly content with their position?

Ideology

Marxists argue that the working class rarely challenge capitalism because those who control the economy also control the family, education, media, religion – in fact, all the cultural institutions

that are responsible for socializing individuals. Louis Althusser (1971) argued that the function of these cultural institutions is to maintain and **legitimate** class inequality. The family, education, the mass media and religion pass off ruling-class norms and values as 'normal' and 'natural'. Marxists refer to these ruling-class ideas as **ideology**.

Marxists argue that socialization is an ideological process in that its main aim is to transmit the ruling-class idea that capitalist society is **meritocratic** – that is, if you work hard enough, you can get on – despite the fact that the evidence rarely supports this view. This ideological device is so successful that the majority of the working class are convinced that their position in society is deserved. In other words, they are persuaded to accept their lot and may even be convinced that capitalism has provided them with a decent standard of living.

Marxists argue that capitalist ideology shapes the way of life of a society – its culture. A good example of this, say Marxists, is the way that the mass media convince us through advertising and popular culture – television, cinema, pop music, tabloid newspapers, etc. – that our priority should be to buy more and more material goods (see Figure 1.2 below). We want to be rich so that we can buy more consumer goods, and, somehow, this will make us happy. What is more, while we are all watching soap operas and reading the latest celebrity gossip, we fail to notice the inequalities and exploitation which are the norm in the capitalist system.

This means that most of us are unaware of our 'real' identity as exploited and oppressed workers. We experience what Marxists describe as **false class consciousness**. Eventually though, Marxists believe, we will learn the real truth of our situation and rebel against the capitalist system.

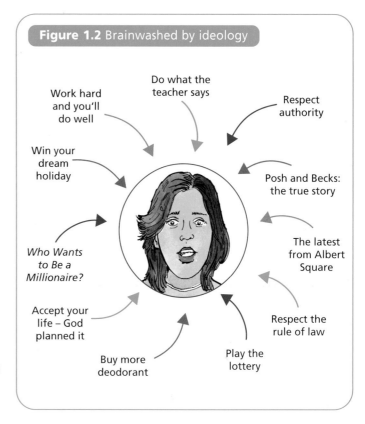

Figure 1.2 Brainwashed by ideology

Work hard and you'll do well

Do what the teacher says

Respect authority

Win your dream holiday

Posh and Becks: the true story

Who Wants to Be a Millionaire?

The latest from Albert Square

Accept your life – God planned it

Respect the rule of law

Buy more deodorant

Play the lottery

Criticisms of Marxism

- The notion of 'false class consciousness' has been undermined by surveys such as those conducted by Marshall *et al.* (1988), and the government in the form of the British Social Attitudes survey (Jowell *et al.* 1995). The British Social Attitudes survey found that 69 per cent of people thought their opportunities were influenced by their social class 'a great deal' or 'quite a lot'. Marshall argued that over 70 per cent of his survey sample believed that social class was an inevitable feature of British society and over 50 per cent felt that class conflict existed in the UK between a ruling class that monopolized economic and political power and a lower class that could do little to change its position. Marshall noted that most people were aware of social injustices, especially relating to inequalities in the distribution of wealth and income, but felt there was little they could do practically to bring about more equality. However, in support of the concept of ideology, Charlesworth's (2000) study of working-class people in Rotherham blames the educational system for this indifference and cynicism. He argues that the working-class experience of education results in them devaluing themselves and restricting their ambitions to 'being disappointed' in life.
- Like functionalism, Marxism has been accused of ignoring the freedom of choice enjoyed by individuals. People choose what to do and think – they are not 'brainwashed' by ideology. In this sense, Marxism too may present an 'oversocialized' picture of human beings.
- This criticism is not true of all Marxists. Some have argued that **oppositional subcultures** can exist within the capitalist system. For example, Hall and Jefferson (1993) argued that youth subcultures are often a means by which young people can express dissatisfaction with the capitalist system. They argued that the value systems, dress codes and behaviour of groups such as mods, skinheads and punks are a form of symbolic and temporary resistance to society. Their resistance is symbolic in that their behaviour often shocks society, but temporary in that they eventually become passive adults.
- Marxism may put too much emphasis on conflict. After all, despite all its inequalities, capitalism has managed to improve most people's standard of living. Marxism also neglects the common interests that employers and workers may have. If workers work well, then the business does well and employers can afford to increase wages.
- Marxism, in general, has been criticized for claiming that all cultural activity is geared to class or economic interests. Consequently, Marxists neglect the fact that culture may reflect religious, **patriarchal**, nationalistic and ethnic interests.

The work of Max Weber

Another sociologist who took a conflict perspective was Max Weber (1864–1920). He agreed with Marx that social class was an important source of inequality but argued that

inequality could also be rooted in influences that have nothing to do with economics. Weber claimed that 'status differences' were at the heart of inequality – class was only one form of status. For example, Weber pointed out that in many societies, power is acquired from being born into a particular tribe or ethnic group. Inequality between Blacks and Whites in apartheid South Africa in the period 1950 to 1990 stemmed from status rather than social class, in that even the poorest White was regarded as having more status and power than educated and economically successful Black people.

In Hindu India, the caste system (even though illegal) still exerts a strong influence on inequality. In this system, every person is born into one of four closed status groups or, situated below these, the non-caste group known as 'untouchables'. This system of status differences is based upon religious purity – the better the life you lead, the more likely you will be reborn (reincarnated) as a member of a higher caste. Meanwhile, you cannot work your way out of your caste, your job is determined by it and you must marry within it.

Feminism

Feminists argue that another important status difference and source of inequality and conflict is gender. They point out that the UK is a patriarchal society – that is, men generally have more power and prestige than women across a range of social institutions. Women generally have less economic power than men. In 2006, women working full time earned on average 17 per cent less than men working full time and they were more likely to be in poverty. Natasha Walter, in *The New Feminism*

Key terms

Bourgeoisie (or **capitalists**) the owners of businesses, and the dominant class in capitalist societies.

Capitalism an economic system associated with modern societies, based on private ownership of businesses.

False class consciousness the state of not being aware of our true identity as exploited workers.

Feminism a set of ideas that suggest that women are oppressed and exploited by men.

Ideology the norms and values that justify the capitalist system.

Legitimate make something appear fair and reasonable.

Marxism a sociological perspective based on the writings of Karl Marx. It believes that societies are unequal and unfair.

Means of production the land, factories, machines, science and technology, and labour power required to produce goods.

Meritocratic based on ability and effort.

Oppositional subcultures social groups whose value systems and behaviour challenge the dominant capitalist value system.

Patriarchal dominated by males.

Proletariat the working class in capitalist societies.

(1999), claimed that women do not enjoy equality of access to jobs, especially the top jobs in the city. Males still monopolize professional and managerial positions – for example, in 2006, only 17 per cent of directors and chief executives of major organisations, 8 per cent of top judges and 7 per cent of surgeons were women. Moreover, women are still expected to be predominantly responsible for the upkeep of the home and childrearing – surveys continue to indicate that family life is not yet characterized by equality between the sexes in terms of household labour.

Feminists believe that sexual discrimination is still a problem today and Walter argues that women still need to achieve financial, educational, domestic and legal equality with men. Liberal feminists are optimistic that this will eventually happen. They believe that there has been a steady improvement in the position of women, as old-fashioned attitudes break down, more girls do well in education and more women have successful careers.

Other types of feminists are not so hopeful. Marxist-feminists argue that patriarchy suits the capitalist system as well as men, because women are unpaid domestic labourers who service the male labour force, making them fit and healthy for work, and who produce and rear the future workforce. True equality between the sexes can only occur when the capitalist system is dismantled.

Radical feminists believe that the patriarchal oppression and exploitation of women is built into every aspect of the way society is organized. In particular, the family is identified as the social institution in which patriarchy is rooted. Radical feminists argue that, through gender-role socialization, women are socialized into accepting female subordination and into seeing motherhood as their main goal in life. Moreover, radical feminists argue that men aggressively exercise their physical, economic and cultural power to dominate women in all areas of social life, and particularly in personal relationships, such as marriage, domestic labour, childcare and sex. All men benefit from this inequality – there are no good guys!

Check your understanding

1 What is the relationship between the bourgeoisie and the proletariat?

2 What is the function of ideology?

3 Describe two important criticisms of Marxism.

4 What is the purpose of socialization according to Marxists?

5 How do youth subcultures challenge capitalism?

6 What other sources of inequality exist, apart from social class, according to Weber and feminist sociologists?

Activities

Exploring capitalist values

Marxists believe that social institutions such as the education system, the media, the legal system and religion are agents of capitalism that transmit ruling-class ideology. For example, the education system socializes the working class into believing that their educational failure is due to lack of ability and effort, when, in reality, the capitalist system deliberately fails them so that they will continue to be factory workers. Television socializes the working class into believing that consensus is the norm and that serious protest about the way society is organized is 'extremist'. The law socializes the working class into believing that the law is on their side when, in reality, it mainly supports and enforces the values and institutions of the capitalist ruling class. Finally, Marxists argue that religions are also ideological because they convince some working-class people that their poverty is the product of sin and moral weakness, and that they should seek solutions in the form of salvation and spirituality.

1 Explain what is meant by the term 'ideology'. (2 marks)

2 Identify the two basic classes that characterize capitalist societies. (4 marks)

3 Identify three ways in which the working class are socialized into accepting inequality. (6 marks)

4 Identify and briefly describe two trends or patterns that suggest that the UK is a society characterized by economic inequality. (8 marks)

Research idea

Conduct a small survey to see how aware people are of (a) their social class and (b) inequalities in income and wealth in the UK.

Web.tasks

1 Using the website of the Office for National Statistics at www.statistics.gov.uk, try to find statistics that give an indication of the extent of inequality in Britain. You might look for figures on income, wealth, education and health.

2 Search for the website 'Dead Sociologists' Society'. Use it to find out about the ideas of Karl Marx.

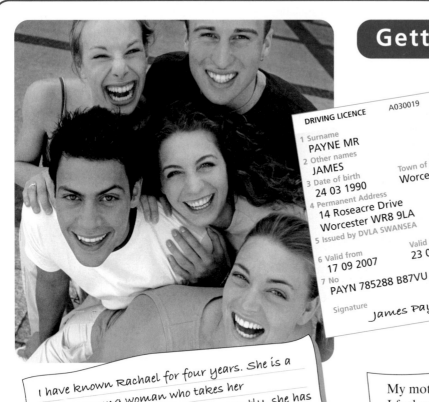

Getting you thinking

DRIVING LICENCE   A030019

1 Surname
PAYNE MR
2 Other names
JAMES   Town of birth
3 Date of birth   Worcester
24 03 1990
4 Permanent Address
14 Roseacre Drive
Worcester WR8 9LA
5 Issued by DVLA SWANSEA
6 Valid from   Valid until
17 09 2007   23 03 2060
7 No
PAYN 785288 B87VU

Signature
James Payne

EUROPEAN UNION

UNITED KINGDOM OF
GREAT BRITAIN
AND NORTHERN IRELAND

PASSPORT

I have known Rachael for four years. She is a mature young woman who takes her responsibilities seriously. Consequently, she has a conscientious and industrious approach to her academic studies and can be trusted to work independently and with initiative. She also works well as a member of a team and is well liked and respected by both her peers and teachers. I have no doubt that you will find Rachael to be a thoroughly honest and reliable person. I was always impressed by her enthusiasm, persistence, motivation and ability to work under pressure. I have no hesitation in recommending her to your institution.

My mother loves me.
I feel good.
I feel good because she loves me.

I am good because I feel good
I feel good because I am good
My mother loves me because I am good.

My mother does not love me.
I feel bad.
I feel bad because she does not love me
I am bad because I feel bad
I feel bad because I am bad
I am bad because she does not love me
She does not love me because I am bad.

R.D. Laing (1970) *Knots*,
Harmondsworth: Penguin

1 What do these documents tell us about a person? What do they not tell us?

2 What does the reference tell us about Rachael's identity? What doesn't it tell us?

3 What does the poem tell us about this person's identity?

4 How does the self-identity apparent in the poem contrast with the picture of the individual in the reference?

Official documents tell us about the identity we present to the world – our date and place of birth, age, nationality, address, marital status and so on. References, like the example on the left, give us some insight into **social identity** – how well we perform our social roles, such as our jobs. However, poems, like the one on the left, can tell us about the way we see ourselves – our **self-identity** – and how this is often the result of how we interpret other people's reactions to us.

Think about a small child. Children try out different sorts of behaviour and then watch how the people important to them (significant others) react. By doing this, they learn what is acceptable and unacceptable behaviour. This assists the development of their conscience, which modifies and regulates future behaviour – children remember whether they were rewarded or punished for particular types of behaviour and usually choose to avoid those activities that previously resulted in disapproval. Parents further contribute to this interactive process by encouraging children to imitate socially approved adult behaviour, such as good manners, gendered dress codes and so on.

Social action theory

What has just been described is the view of **social action** or **interactionist** sociologists. They reject the structuralist assumption that social behaviour is determined, constrained and even made predictable by the organization of society. They see people as having a much more positive and active role in shaping social life. If structuralist theory is a 'top-down' theory, then social action theory is 'bottom-up', as it starts with people rather than society.

Social action theorists reject the view that people's behaviour is the product of external forces over which they have little control. Most people do not feel themselves to be puppets of society. Rather, as Chris Brown (1979) notes:

>> *they feel they are living their own lives, making their own decisions and engaging, for the most part, in voluntary behaviour. There may be things they have to do which they resent, but resentment is, of course, tangible evidence of an independent self, forced to comply, but unwillingly and under protest.*>>

However, although we operate as individuals, we are aware of other people around us. Social action theorists argue that the attitudes and actions of those other people influence the way we think and behave – that society is the product of people coming together in social groups and trying to make sense of their own and each other's behaviour.

People are able to work out what is happening in any given situation because they bring a set of **interpretations** to every interaction and use them to make sense of social behaviour. In particular, we apply meanings to symbolic behaviour. For example, gestures are symbols – putting up two fingers in a V-sign may be interpreted as insulting, because it has an obscene meaning. When we are interacting with others, we are constantly on the lookout for symbols, because these give us clues as to how the other person is interpreting our behaviour –

for instance, if they are smiling, we might interpret this as social approval, and if they maintain prolonged, intense eye contact, we might interpret this as a 'come-on'.

Our experience of this 'symbolic interaction' means we acquire a stock of knowledge about what is appropriate behaviour in particular situations. We learn that particular contexts demand particular social responses. For example, I might interpret drinking and dancing at a party as appropriate, yet the same behaviour at a funeral as inappropriate. It is likely that other people will share my interpretations and so it is unlikely that the behaviour described would occur at the funeral.

Socialization and identity

Socialization involves learning a stock of shared interpretations and meanings for most given social interactions. Families, for example, teach us how to interact with and interpret the actions of others; education brings us into contact with a greater range of social groups and teaches us how to interpret social action in a broader range of social contexts. The result of such socialization is that children acquire an identity.

Social action theorists suggest that identity has three components:

1 Personal identity refers to aspects of individuality that identify people as unique and distinct from others. These include personal name, nickname, signature, photograph, address, National Insurance number, etc.

2 Social identity refers to the personality characteristics and qualities that particular cultures associate with certain social roles or groups. For example, in our culture, mothers are supposed to be loving, nurturing and selfless; therefore, women who are mothers will attempt to live up to this description and hence acquire that social identity. As children grow up, they too will acquire a range of social identities, such as brother, sister, best friend, student. Socialization and interaction with others will make it clear to them what our culture expects of these roles in terms of obligations, duties and behaviour.

3 The individual has a **subjective** (internal) sense of their own uniqueness and identity. Sociologists call this the 'self'. It is partly the product of what others think is expected of a person's social identity. For example, a mother may see herself as a good mother because she achieves society's standards in that respect. However, 'self' is also the product of how the individual interprets their experience and life history. For example, some women may have, in their own mind, serious misgivings about their role as mother. The self, then, is the link between what society expects from a particular role and the individual's interpretation of whether they are living up to that role successfully.

The concept of self has been explored extensively by social action sociologists. Some have suggested that the self has two components – the 'I' and the 'me'. The 'I' is the private inner self, whereas the 'me' is the social self that participates in everyday interaction. When a person plays a social role as a teacher or student, it is the 'me' that is in action. The 'me' is shaped by the reactions of others – that is, we act in ways that we think are socially desirable. However, the 'I' supplies the confidence or self-esteem to play the role successfully.

Goffman (1959) argues that interaction is essentially about successful role-playing. He suggests that we are all social actors engaged in the drama of everyday life. Stage directions are symbolized by the social and cultural context in which the action takes place. For example, the classroom as a stage symbolizes particular rules that must be followed if the interaction is to be successful, e.g. students sit at desks while teachers can move around the room freely. Sometimes the script is already in place, so for instance, we adhere to cultural rules about greeting people – 'Good morning, how are you?' – although often the script has to be improvised. Goffman argues that the public or social identity we present to the world is often simply a performance designed to create a particular impression. This makes sense if we think about how we behave in particular contexts or company. For example, your behaviour in front of your grandparents is likely to be very different compared with your behaviour in front of friends. Therefore, you have a catalogue of different identities you can adopt.

Goffman invents a number of concepts that he claims people as social actors use in everyday action to assist in the management of other people's impression of them. Some people will use 'front' to manage an interaction. This refers to items of physical or body equipment that a social actor uses to enhance their performance – for example, teachers who want to convey authority may wear formal clothing to distance themselves from students. Another concept is 'region' – the classroom is the front region where the teacher 'performs',

while the staffroom is where they relax and become another person, such as the colleague or friend.

Labelling theory

Labelling theory is closely linked to the social action approach and helps us to understand how some parts of society may be responsible for socializing some people into identities that may have negative consequences. Take education as an example. Interactionists believe that the social identity of pupils may be dependent on how they interact with teachers. If teachers act in such a way that pupils feel negatively labelled – as 'lazy' or 'thick', for example – then this will seriously affect their behaviour and progress.

Howard Becker (1963) pointed out that labels often have the power of a **master status**. For example, the master status of 'criminal' can override all other statuses, such as father, son or husband. In other words, deviant labels can radically alter a person's social identity. For example, someone labelled as 'criminal' may be discriminated against and find it difficult to get employment, make new friends and be accepted into their community. They may end up seeking others with similar identities and values, and form deviant subcultures. A **self-fulfilling prophecy** is the result, as the reaction to the label makes it come true.

Think about how the experience of streaming or setting may affect the self-esteem of a pupil. How do pupils who are placed in low streams or sets feel? They may well accept a view of themselves as 'failures' and stop trying – after all, what's the point if you're 'thick'? Or what if a pupil feels labelled as a 'troublemaker' because they are Black? The negative label may be internalized (accepted) and a self-fulfilling prophecy may

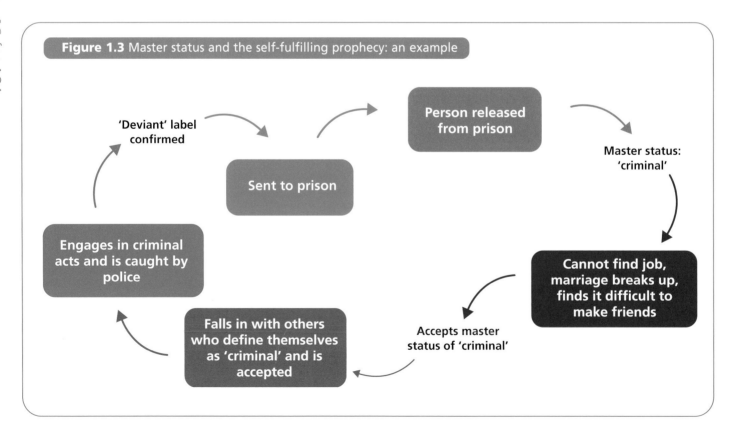

Figure 1.3 Master status and the self-fulfilling prophecy: an example

occur. The self sees itself as a 'failure' or as 'deviant' and reacts accordingly. The label becomes true (see Figure 1.3).

Goffman (1961) illustrated the power of such labelling in his ethnographic study of inmates in a mental hospital in the USA. Goffman refers to such hospitals as 'total institutions' because they attempt to shape all aspects of their inmates lives, e.g. by organizing their routine. Goffman argues that total institutions deliberately break down a person's sense of self through a process he calls 'mortification' – they are stripped, given a common uniform to wear and referred to by a serial number. In other words, the institution sets about destroying individuality. The institution then attempts to rebuild the self in its own collective image. However, Goffman notes that the inmates he studied reacted in various ways to this process. Some conformed to the institution's demands; some even became institutionalized – they became so completely dependent on the institution that they could no longer survive in the outside world. Some, however, hung on to their individuality by giving the impression that they were conforming, while others openly opposed the system. What Goffman's work indicates is that the self and self-esteem can be very resilient and that labelling does not always have to be such a destructive process. Those who have been labelled can actually resist the definitions of the powerful.

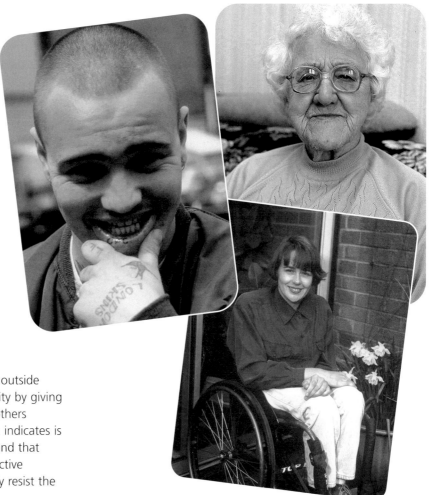

Body image

Recent studies in a social action context have focused on how we interpret our bodies. It is argued that the way people view themselves and others is shaped by the dominant cultural ideas and images about ageing, body shape, weight and beauty that we see in media products such as magazines, advertisements, television and films. It is argued by feminist commentators that British culture sees the slim or thin female form as the ideal, with the result that young girls are socialized into seeing the slim figure as a source of status and success, while 'too much' weight is unattractive and socially inadequate. It is suggested that eating disorders, such as anorexia and bulimia, may be the outcome of these dominant cultural ideas, as female identity is often bound up with how women perceive their bodies. Research on female eating disorders suggests that those with the disorders often have low self-esteem and often subscribe to distorted images about their weight and attractiveness. A survey of 25 000 women aged 17 to 34 conducted by Radio 1's *NewsBeat* in 2006 found that 51 per cent would have surgery to improve their looks and a third of size 12 women thought they were overweight. Furthermore, almost half the sample said they had skipped a meal to lose weight, while 8 per cent had made themselves sick. More than half of girls aged 12 to 16 felt that their body image either stopped them from getting a boyfriend or from relaxing in a relationship.

Suggest how labelling might affect the lives and the identities of the people in these photographs.

Disability

Social action studies of disability by sociologists such as Colin Barnes and Tom Shakespeare are very critical of official and medical definitions of disability. As Shakespeare and Watson (1997) note, disabled people are defined by society and social institutions such as the mass media as 'that group of people whose bodies do not work; or who look or act differently; or who cannot do productive work'. In other words, the disabled are defined as abnormal or deviant by society, and disability is something to be avoided at all costs. Furthermore, Shakespeare and Watson argue that medical approaches to disability consider any negative self-identity held by disabled people to be exclusively the product of their physical impairment and 'focus on the need for adjustment, mourning, and coming to terms with loss'.

In contrast, social action theory advocates a social model of disability which suggests that disabled people are actually 'disabled by society' – by social attitudes based on prejudicial stereotypes and by social policy which assumes that physical impairment results in dependency. Social action theory argues that we learn our social identity through the process of socialization and this forms the basis of how we see ourselves and, most importantly, how we think we are seen by others.

It is argued that if disabled people are constantly subjected to the view that they are dependent, weak, abnormal and have little status, the disabled individual may actually take on a 'disabled identity' in order to interact successfully with doctors, social workers, the general public and so on. The prophecy of dependency and weakness is fulfilled as the disabled person lives up to social expectations and is not encouraged to be an independent person. Social policy also contributes to this process by failing to provide the disabled with practical facilities, such as wheelchair access to buildings and public transport, that would enable them to lead a normal life.

Focus on research

Anne Becker (2003)
Eating disorders in Fiji

Anne Becker (2003) carried out a study to evaluate the impact of the introduction of Western television in the 1990s on Fijian adolescent girls. Traditionally, Fijian society favoured robust appetites and plump body shapes among women, and eating disorders were rare. However, the study found that subjects living in a house with a TV set were three times more likely to show symptoms of eating disorders. Dieting, too, became common among the study population, with 74 per cent reporting that they felt 'too big or fat'. Analysis of interview data found that 77 per cent of girls strongly admired TV characters, and wanted to copy them by changing behaviour, clothing or hairstyle, or through reshaping their body.

Adapted from Becker, A. *et al.* (2003) 'Binge eating and binge eating disorder in a small-scale, indigenous society: the view from Fiji', published online in Wiley InterScience (www.interscience.wiley.com)

1 **What was the main cause of the appearance of eating disorders in Fiji in your view?**

2 **How did Fijians view the female body before the introduction of television?**

3 **Identify three ways in which Fijian girls' identity has been negatively influenced by Western media imagery.**

Shyness

A recent symbolic interactionist study focused on shyness. Scott (2003) carried out in-depth interviews with 16 'shy' individuals in the South Wales area who volunteered after responding to an advertisement. She also set up a website about 'shyness and society' that included an email distribution list. Over a period of nine months, a virtual community composed of 42 individuals was created which exchanged ideas and discussed online the social aspects of shyness.

Scott found evidence of the notion of an 'I' and a 'me', in that shyness was often experienced as a conflict between a desire to be part of a social scene and the fear of being negatively judged or criticized. The shy 'I' was often beset by feelings of 'anxiety, uncertainty and inhibition', while the shy 'me' was concerned about how other people would view them – that is, they were afraid of making a fool of themselves or not fitting in. Many participants felt plagued by 'what if' feelings, such as 'what if they don't like me?'. Scott's sample often felt shy in particular social contexts in which the reactions of others were perceived as important. Scott notes that shyness is often seen as a 'deviant' activity, although society is likely to interpret it as 'normal' in particular social groups, e.g. among girls. She argues that there is a lot of moral pressure put on shy people to overcome their 'problem' through the use self-help books, miracle drugs and shyness clinics.

Criticisms of social action theory

Social action theories have been criticized because they tend to be very vague in explaining who is responsible for defining acceptable norms of behaviour. They do not explain who is responsible for making the rules that so-called deviant groups break. In this sense, they fail to explore the origin of power and neglect potential sources, such as social class, gender and ethnicity. For example, Marxists argue that the capitalist ruling class define how social institutions such as education and the law operate. In other words, social action theories tend to be descriptive rather than explanatory.

Check your understanding

1 **How is society formed, according to social action theorists?**

2 **From an interactionist perspective, what is the function of socialization?**

3 **What is meant by 'social identity'?**

4 **Explain the meaning of 'self'.**

5 **What causes a 'self-fulfilling prophecy'?**

6 **What is the result of deviant labels becoming master statuses?**

Key terms

Interpretations the meanings that we attach to particular objects or situations, e.g. we usually interpret classrooms as learning environments and act accordingly.

Labelling theory the idea that categorizing or stereotyping individuals or groups can seriously affect their behaviour. Used especially in the fields of education and deviance.

Master status a label or status that can override all others (e.g. criminal, child abuser).

Self-identity refers to how we see ourselves, usually in reaction to how we think others see us.

Self-fulfilling prophecy a prediction that makes itself become true.

Social action theory or **interactionism** a sociological perspective that focuses on the ways in which people give meaning to their own and others' actions.

Social identity refers to how society sees us, in terms of whether we live up to the cultural expectations attached to the social roles we play.

Subjective personal, based on your own view.

Activities

Exploring social institutions

Individuals, like actors, are performing for an audience. Speech, acts and gestures all require someone else to be watching or listening. Our identities, therefore, are the product of how we present ourselves and how others perceive us. For example, you have to persuade your tutor that you have seriously adopted the identity and role of student. Your tutor may respond by according you an 'ideal' student label or identity. If you fail to convince, you may be labelled as a 'deviant' student, i.e. as idle or troublesome. This 'deviant' label is a 'master status' which overshadows other aspects of identity. Often, people who are considered deviant in one respect are assumed to be deviant in other respects. For example, other teachers may judge you negatively in staffroom discussions.

Those labelled as 'deviants' often experience stigma – people behaving differently towards them. In reaction, those labelled may pursue a deviant career by adopting a lifestyle which confirms their deviant status. In other words, a self-fulfilling prophecy results.

Adapted from Woodward, K. (ed.) (2000) *Questioning Identity: Gender, Class, Nation,* London: Routledge, pp. 14–15

1 **Explain what is meant by the term 'self-fulfilling prophecy'.** (2 marks)

2 **Identify two aspects of your own identity.** (4 marks)

3 **Identify three possible consequences of being labelled by an institution, such as a school, the police or a mental hospital.** (6 marks)

4 **Identify and briefly describe two criticisms of the concept of 'labelling'.** (8 marks)

Research ideas

1 Observe an everyday situation involving interaction between people. It could be in a library, at a bus stop, in a common room or a pub.

   – What is going on?
   – Does everyone share the same interpretation of the situation?
   – How do people try to manage the impression they give of themselves?

2 Find two groups of students: one group who have experience of being placed in a high stream, and one group who have experience of being placed in a low stream. Give a questionnaire to, or interview, each group in order to find out how streaming affected their self-image, motivation and progress. Compare the responses of the two samples.

Web.task

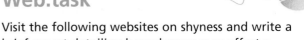

Visit the following websites on shyness and write a brief report detailing how shyness may affect a person's self-esteem and identity:

● Susie Scott's 'Shyness and Society' website at **www.sussex.ac.uk/Users/ss216/**

● The Shyness Institute, a major shyness research centre at **www.shyness.com/shyness-institute.html**

● The Shyness Home Page detailing the work of the American sociologists, L. Henderson and P.G. Zimbardo, at **www.shyness.com**

Postmodernism

Getting you thinking

Try to imagine the life ahead for the woman from the 1930s in the photograph above.

1 What sort of family life do you think she would have had?

2 Might she have had paid employment? What problems might she have faced in pursuing a career?

3 What about the roles played by her and her husband?

Now think about the future for the young woman of today.

4 What sort of family life do you think she is likely to have?

5 Is she likely to have paid employment?

6 What about her relationship with her husband?

You may well have found it fairly straightforward to plot out the future for the young woman of 70 years ago. Attempting the same task for a woman today is much more difficult. Maybe she will choose not to marry or live in a family. Maybe she won't have children. Alternatively, she could devote her life to a family, but then again she might decide to focus on following a career – or she could do both. The choices appear endless. Being a woman today seems much more flexible and uncertain – and less predictable – than in the past.

Sociologists have watched recent social changes with great interest. Some have reached the conclusion that society has experienced such major upheavals that the old ways of explaining it just won't work any more. They believe that we are entering a new sort of society, which they refer to as the postmodern world or **postmodernity**. But before we can consider this, we need to head back to the beginnings of sociology.

Have you ever wondered why sociology came about? History tells us that sociology developed in order to explain the rapid social changes associated with **industrialization** and **urbanization** during the 19th century. Lives changed so drastically during this period that, not surprisingly, people began to look for theories and explanations that would help make sense of the bewildering changes taking place. Families left the rural communities where they had lived for centuries, to find work in the new cities. They had to adjust to a different lifestyle, different work, different bosses and different kinds of relationships with family and community.

On the whole, early sociologists approved of these changes and the kind of society they created – now commonly referred to as **modernity** or the modern world. They set out to document the key features of what they saw as an exciting new order.

The nature of the modern world

Sociologists have identified four major characteristics of the modern world:

1 *Industrialization* – Production is industrial and economic relationships are capitalist. Factories produce goods, bosses own factories, and workers sell their labour to bosses. Social class is therefore the basic source of difference and identity in modern societies.
2 *Urbanization* – Early modernity was associated with great population movement to the cities, known as urbanization. Twentieth-century theories of modernity tended to celebrate the bright lights and innovation of the city while ridiculing rural culture as living in the past.
3 *Centralized government* – Government is characterized by a **bureaucratic** state that takes a great deal of responsibility both for the economy and for the welfare of its citizens.
4 *Rational, scientific thinking* – What really made modern society stand apart from premodern societies was the revolution in the way people thought about the world. Before industrialization, tradition, religion and superstition had provided the basis for views of the world. The modern world adopted a new way of thinking, shaped by science and reason.

New ideas and theories (referred to by postmodernists as '**big stories**' or **meta-narratives**) competed with each other to explain this constantly changing modern world and these theories frequently called for more social progress. Some of these theories were political (e.g. socialism), while others were cultural (e.g. the ideas of feminism). To paraphrase Marx, one of the leading modernist thinkers, their job was not just to explain the world – the point was to change it.

Sociology and the modern world

Sociologists were caught up in this excitement about modernity, and attempted to create scientific theories that would explain the transition from the traditional to the modern. One of the founding fathers of sociology, Auguste Comte, believed that sociology was the science of society. This **positivist** view argued that sociological research based upon scientific **rationality** could rid the world of social problems such as crime.

Marx, too, celebrated modernity, despite his criticism of its economic relationships, because he believed that science had given people the power to change the world. Sociological theories such as functionalism and Marxism, therefore, also developed into meta-narratives as they attempted to provide us with knowledge or 'truth' about the nature of modernity.

The postmodern world

In the past 20 years or so, some sociologists have identified trends and developments which, they claim, show that modernity is fragmenting or dissolving. They argue that it is being replaced by a postmodern world in which many sociological ideas and concepts are becoming irrelevant.

Characteristics of postmodernity have been identified in aspects of work, culture, identity, globalization and knowledge.

Work

The nature of work and economic life has changed. Work is no longer dominated by mass factory production in which thousands of people work alongside each other. Work today is mainly located within the **service sector**, and is dominated either by jobs that mainly involve the processing of information (e.g. the financial sector), or by jobs that involve the servicing of **consumption** (e.g. working in a shop).

Our ideas about work have also changed. People today are less likely to expect a job for life, and are more willing to accept a range of flexible working practices, such as part-time work, working from home and job-sharing.

Culture

As our society has grown wealthier, so the media and other cultural industries – such as fashion, film, advertising and music – have become increasingly central to how we organize our lives. It is suggested that we are a 'media-saturated' society in which media advice is available on how we can 'make over' our homes, gardens, partners and even ourselves. Look, for example, at the lifestyle magazines ranged on the shelves of bookshops and newsagents, advising you on skin care, body size and shape, hair colour and type, fitness, cosmetic surgery and so on. What these trends tell us is that consumption is now a central defining feature in our lives.

Postmodern culture is also about mixing and matching seemingly contradictory styles. For example, think about the way in which different music from different times and different styles is 'sampled', with musical phrases from one recording being used in another recording.

Identity

Our identities are now likely to be influenced by mainstream popular culture which celebrates **diversity**, consumerism and choice. In other words, the old 'me' was about where I came from in terms of my family and class background, the area I lived in and so on. The new postmodern 'me', however, is about designer labels, being seen in the right places, the car I drive, listening to the right music and buying the right clothes. Style has become more important than substance. As Steve Taylor (1999) argues, society has been transformed into:

« *something resembling an endless shopping mall where people now have much greater choice about how they look, what they consume and what they believe in.*»

Globalization

The global expansion of **transnational companies** – such as McDonald's, Sony, Coca-Cola and Nike – and the global marketing of cultural forms – such as cinema, music and computer games – have contributed to this emphasis on consumption. Such globalization has resulted in symbols that are recognized and consumed across the world. Images of Britney Spears and Michael Jackson are as likely to be found adorning the walls of a village hut in the interior of New Guinea as they are a bedroom wall in Croydon. Brands like Nike and Coca-Cola use global events like the World Cup and the Olympic Games to beam themselves into millions of homes across the world.

It is therefore no wonder that this global culture is seen to be challenging the importance of national and local cultures, and challenging **nationalism** as a source of identity. Information technology and electronic communication, such as email and the internet, have also been seen as part of this process.

Knowledge

In the postmodern world, people no longer have any faith in great truths. In particular, people have become sceptical, even cynical, about the power of science to change the world, because many of the world's problems have been brought about by technology. In the political world, ideologies such as **socialism** – which claimed they were the best way of transforming the world – have been discredited in many people's eyes, with the collapse of communism in Eastern Europe. Postmodernists insist that truth is both unattainable and irrelevant in the postmodern world. Instead, they stress the **relativity** of knowledge, ideas and lifestyles, such that many different yet equally authentic values are possible.

Postmodernism and sociology

Steve Taylor argues that these developments have three main consequences for sociology:

1 Most sociology is concerned with explaining the nature and organization of modern societies and social institutions. However, the key relationships that underpin such societies – class, family, gender – are no longer relevant.

2 Sociologists can no longer claim to produce expert knowledge about society, because in postmodern societies, relativity and uncertainty have replaced absolute judgements about what is or should be. As Swingewood (2000) argues, in postmodern societies 'knowledge is always incomplete, there are no universal standards, only differences and **ambiguity**'. The big sociological stories, such as functionalism and Marxism, have become redundant, because 'knowledge' is now judged in terms of its usefulness rather than its claim to be a universal 'truth'.

3 Sociologists can no longer make judgements or claim that they know what is best for societies. Sociology is only one set of ideas competing with others. All have something relevant to offer. If people want to listen to sociologists and act upon their findings, it is up to them. It is equally relevant not to do so.

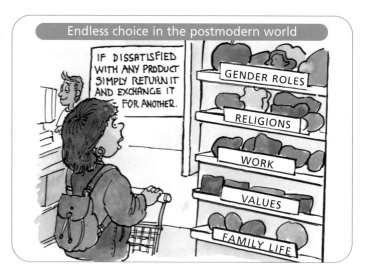

Endless choice in the postmodern world

Criticisms of postmodernism

Critics of postmodernism suggest that it is guilty of making too much of recent social changes. Evidence suggests that aspects of the postmodernist argument – especially the decline of social class, ethnicity and nationalism as sources of identity – are exaggerated. For example, surveys indicate that people still see social class as a strong influence in their lives, and use aspects of it to judge their success and status and that of others. There is no doubting that consumption has increased in importance, especially among young people, but it is pointed out that consumption does not exist in a vacuum. The nature of your consumption – what and how much you consume – still very much depends upon your income, which is generally determined by your occupation and social class. Similarly, our ability to make choices is still also constrained by our gender and ethnicity, because of the influence of patriarchy and institutional racism.

Check your understanding

1 What term is used by postmodernists to describe theories of society?

2 What was the role of sociology, according to Auguste Comte?

3 Identify two social changes that have led some sociologists to argue that we are entering a postmodern world.

4 How do the media contribute to our sense of identity?

5 What is the relationship between globalization and postmodernism?

6 How did the collapse of communism in Eastern Europe contribute to people's cynicism about meta-narratives?

7 What is the role of the internet in postmodern society?

Key terms

Ambiguity the state of being open to a range of interpretations – the meaning is not clear.

Bureaucratic based on rules and procedures.

Consumption the use of goods and services, especially as part of forming an identity.

Diversity variety.

Industrialization the transformation of societies from being agricultural to industrial, that took place in the 18th and 19th centuries.

Meta-narratives or **'big stories'** the postmodernist term for theories like Marxism and functionalism, which aim to explain how societies work.

Modernity period of time starting with the industrial revolution, associated with industrial production, urban living, rational thinking and strong central government.

Nationalism belief system or political view that stresses shared geographical location, history and culture.

Positivism the view that sociological research based upon scientific principles could rid the world of social problems such as crime.

Postmodernity term used by postmodernists to describe the contemporary period, which is characterized by uncertainty, media-saturation and globalization.

Rationality actions decided by logical thought.

Relativity the idea that no one example of something (e.g. political view, sociological

theory, lifestyle, moral) is better than any other.

Service sector a group of economic activities loosely organized around finance, retail and personal care.

Socialism a political belief system based on the idea of collective ownership and equal rights for all.

Transnational companies companies that produce and market goods on a global scale.

Urbanization the trend towards living in towns and cities rather than in rural areas.

Activities

Exploring postmodernism

Although there are many strands to 'postmodernism', the basic idea is that individual freedom has combined with increased geographical mobility, better communication and a media-saturated society to create a world in which 'consumers' select elements of culture from a global cafeteria. Economies based on the production and distribution of things have been superseded by economies based on the production and distribution of ideas and images. We are now bombarded with a mass of different media images, which has led to greater individual choice in terms of personal style, tastes and beliefs so that it makes little sense to talk of a mass of people being shaped by influences such as social class.

An obvious illustration can be found in the matter of accents. Before the 1970s, there was a clear link in British society between certain accents and social status. British broadcasters, particularly on the BBC, spoke in the accents of the upper classes. It used to be possible to guess the political party of a politician by accent. Conservative party politicians spoke like members of the Royal Family, whereas Labour politicians spoke in the regional accent of the working class. Such typing is now vastly more difficult. Well-educated, middle-class children listen to 'gangsta rap' and other musical styles associated with the Black poor of the inner cities and borrow not only vocabulary and accent, but also dress and posture styles.

In politics, it is no longer possible to 'read off' people's preferences from their social class. Instead, we find a variety of consciously created interest groups:

radical student movements, environment movements, animal rights campaigns, gay rights groups and women's groups.

Adapted from Bruce, S. (1999) *Sociology: A Very Short Introduction*, Oxford University Press

1. Explain what is meant by a 'media-saturated society'. (2 marks)

2. Identify two sources of identity in modern societies. (4 marks)

3. Identify three characteristics of postmodern society. (6 marks)

4. Identify and briefly describe two ways in which postmodernism may challenge sociological thought. (8 marks)

Research idea

Interview a sample of 16 to 19 year olds about their expectations of the future (jobs, relationships, family, etc.). To what extent are they uncertain or clear about their future?

Web.task

Use the world wide web to search for information on:

- postmodernism – find out about its influence on art, architecture and literature
- Jean Baudrillard, a key postmodern thinker.

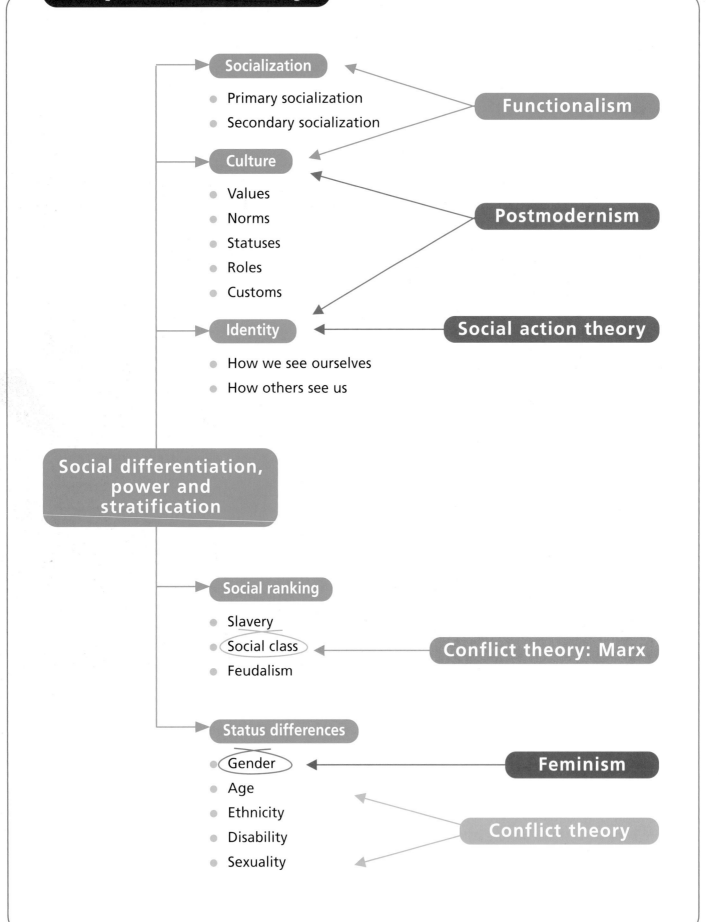

Socialization
- Primary socialization
- Secondary socialization

Functionalism

Culture
- Values
- Norms
- Statuses
- Roles
- Customs

Postmodernism

Identity
- How we see ourselves
- How others see us

Social action theory

Social differentiation, power and stratification

Social ranking
- Slavery
- Social class
- Feudalism

Conflict theory: Marx

Status differences
- Gender
- Age
- Ethnicity
- Disability
- Sexuality

Feminism

Conflict theory

Culture and identity

TOPIC 1

Culture

Getting you thinking

1 Examine the images above and rank them into hierarchical order with the ones which you think are the most valued by society at the top and those least valued at the bottom.

2 What criteria did you use to judge 'value'?

3 Did your judgements coincide with those of your teacher? If not, why not?

The aim of this exercise is to get you to think about what our culture values in terms of the creative arts. You probably found it difficult to divorce your feelings about Shakespeare (who you have probably been forced to study over the years) and actor Hugh Grant from an objective assessment of their respective value to society. However, have you ever wondered why Shakespeare, rather than, say, J.K. Rowling, is considered worthy of your study of English Literature, or why classical composers such as Beethoven, rather than singer Amy Winehouse, dominate our study of music in schools?

The simple answer is that those with power are able to define some creative activities as more important than others.

As we shall see in this topic, the same may also be true of other important aspects of our culture.

Defining culture

The concept of '**culture**' has been interpreted and used in a number of ways by sociologists. For this reason, defining precisely what is meant by culture is not a straightforward process. However, most sociologists would agree that culture can generally be defined as the shared beliefs, **values**, **norms**, **customs**, **rituals**, language, symbols, history and knowledge that make up the way of life of a social group or society. Kidd (2002) argues that all these features influence the way members of a society live their lives. For example, culture is partly composed of symbols that people use to convey meaning. As Abbott (1998) notes, language is the most obvious set of symbols through which members of society share meanings – think about how powerful the verbal and non-verbal symbols of swearing are in terms of their ability to shock others.

Culture as all that is learned

Another way of defining culture is to see it as being made up of all the non-biological aspects of human societies. Marshall (1998) suggests 'culture is all that in human society which is socially rather than biologically transmitted'. Culture, therefore, refers to all that is learned from others in society. When people are born, they join a social world with a culture already in existence. Children learn how things are done, i.e. they learn the cultural rules in order to take their place successfully in society. This teaching and learning process is known as **socialization** and will be explored in greater depth in Topic 2.

Culture and society

At this stage, it is useful to stress that culture is not the same as **society**. As Giddens (1997) notes: 'no cultures could exist without societies. But equally, no societies could exist without culture. Without culture no one can be "human" at all.'

Society is made up of all the formal and informal social institutions that people create by coming together and interacting with each other. These include marriage and the family, the **peer group**, education, government (sometimes referred to as the **State**), mass media, religions and the workplace. Culture dictates how those institutions work by setting behavioural rules (norms) and by shaping expectations about the **social roles** people should play in those institutions. For example, culture is responsible for shaping how we should behave as mothers, fathers, sons, daughters, teachers, students, police officers, doctors, etc.

Culture and identity

Identity, like culture, is also not a straightforward concept. It generally refers to our 'sense of self', which means our subjective feelings, how we see ourselves and, very importantly, how we think other people see and judge us. Kidd (2002) suggests that identity is being able to figure out who we are as people, and how we are similar to or differ from others. The notion of self, identity and difference is explored in depth in Chapter 1, pp. 20–5.

Most sociologists suggest that culture and identity are closely related. Culture is what links the individual and their sense of self to society because, as Kidd argues, who we think we are is related to what society – in the shape of cultural values and norms – says we should do and be.

High culture

It is important to acknowledge alternative and narrower ways in which the concept of culture has been used by sociologists. Kidd, for example, identifies 'the highest intellectual achievements of a group in the fields of science, art, literature,

theatre, music, etc.' as a vital component of culture. Kidd is referring here to '**high culture**' – this controversial and sometimes **elitist** concept suggests that some cultural creations should have the greatest status because they represent the highest levels of human creativity and are **aesthetically** superior to other cultural products and leisure activities. These cultural products are usually established historically and include classical music, opera, ballet, art (in the form of traditional paintings and sculpture), Shakespeare, great literature and poetry, and so on. As we shall see in Topic 3, high culture is an important part of the identity of the economic and political elite in the UK – that is, the upper class.

Folk culture

Folk culture refers to traditional cultural products and activities that originate with ordinary people and are rooted in pre-industrial societies. They have been passed down, usually by word of mouth, over the generations, e.g. Morris dancing, folk singing and traditional storytelling. These activities do not claim to be art or high culture – rather they claim to tell **authentic** stories about real lives and experiences.

Mass popular culture

Mass or popular culture refers to the products of the mass media in modern capitalist societies, such as television programmes, films, popular fiction, magazines and comics, and popular music. Some sociologists have argued that this type of culture is manufactured for mass consumption rather than created for its own sake and, consequently, has little or no artistic merit compared with the products of high culture. Moreover, it is suggested that popular culture is harmful because it discourages critical thought. Others suggest that it is a corrupting influence on young people, e.g. a recent debate in 2007 has focused on the alleged negative influence of hip hop or rap music.

Theoretical perspectives on culture

Kidd notes that theories have developed which aim to answer three main questions about culture:

- How is culture patterned?
- How is culture maintained?
- Why is culture as it is?

Sociobiology

Sociobiologists generally believe that culture is the product of biology or nature. This contrasts with the sociological point of view that culture is the product of social learning or **nurture**. For example, Morris (1968) argued that biology shapes culture, because sharing culture is based on the in-built or genetic need to continue the life of the social group over time, i.e. to survive.

On the other hand, sociologists argue that if human behaviour is influenced by biology at all, it is only at a reflex or physical level, e.g. we feel hungry. They argue that culture determines *what* is eaten – for example, in the UK, we culturally disapprove of cannibalism and eating certain creatures such as dogs, horses and insects. We also express some cultural anxieties about overeating (obesity) and not eating enough (dieting and eating disorders). Even *when* and *how* we eat are shaped by cultural rules – think, for example, about what time you have 'dinner'.

Culture as a system – functionalism

The founder of functionalism, Emile Durkheim (1858–1917) believed that society and culture were more important than the individual. This belief was based on a simple observation: society exists before the individual is born into it and continues relatively undisturbed after the death of the individual.

Durkheim (1893) noted that modern industrial societies are characterized by social order rather than chaos or anarchy. People's behaviour is generally patterned and predictable. Durkheim argued that this was because society's members were united by a **value consensus**, meaning that they shared the same cultural values, goals and norms. As Kidd notes, functionalists see culture as the cement that bonds individuals together in the form of society and allows people to interact successfully with each other.

Culture in pre-industrial societies

Durkheim argued that the function of the social institutions that make up society – the family, religion, education, etc. – was to socialize individuals into the value consensus. He noted that in traditional pre-industrial societies, socialization agencies such as religion were extremely powerful cultural influences over individual behaviour. Consequently, in these societies, individual identity was secondary to cultural conformity. In other words, people went along with what society demanded; they rarely spoke out or complained. These societies, therefore, demonstrated high levels of solidarity or social belonging because people felt very similar to each other. Social order was a natural outcome of these processes.

Culture in modern societies

Durkheim notes, however, that industrial societies are much more complex. The social changes that occurred during the 18th and 19th centuries, such as industrialization and urbanization, have the potential to undermine value consensus and cultural conformity because we experience a great deal more choice in our beliefs and actions; we have more opportunity to be individuals. As a result, we become less like each other. This is potentially disruptive, because people may become confused about what values, beliefs, rules, etc., they should live by and come into conflict with each other. Durkheim called this '**anomie**'.

Despite this, Durkheim believed that social order would still be generally maintained (although in a weaker form than

previously), because social institutions continue to socialize people into a shared culture – in particular, the cultural goals that achievement, competition and hard work are all important, and that people should be prepared to take their place in the **specialized division of labour**, i.e. the way the economy organizes work. This specialized division of labour reinforces social order because it results in people being dependent upon each other for society's survival and continuation. Jobs do not exist in isolation from each other – teachers need supermarket workers, sewage workers, plumbers, bus drivers, and vice versa.

Criticizing Durkheim

Durkheim has been criticized for exaggerating cultural consensus and hence social order. Social conflict between groups within the same society is generally neglected. Interpetivist sociologists (see Chapter 5, p. 171) are critical of Durkheim because he sees people as less important than society and culture, i.e. as if their actions and choices are shaped solely by social and cultural forces, and socialization. There is little acknowledgement that people play an active role in shaping culture. However, on the positive side, Durkheim is probably correct to suggest that there is a core culture that is widely shared by a majority of people in a society. The fact that you are sitting reading this text now in pursuit of an A-level in Sociology supports this observation.

Culture as a system – Marxism

Marxism focuses on the economic organization of modern societies, particularly the fact that societies like the UK are **capitalist** societies characterized by class inequalities in wealth, income and power. **Social class** refers to the amount of economic power, i.e. wealth, that social groups have or do not have. Karl Marx (1818–83) saw capitalist societies as characterized by class inequality and conflict. One group – the bourgeoisie – owned and controlled the means of production – the factories, raw materials, investment capital – and exploited the labour power of another group – the proletariat or working class – in order to make even greater wealth.

Culture as ideology

Marx noted that the bourgeoisie, in order to protect their interests, used their wealth to acquire political and cultural power. As Marx and Engels (1974) stated: 'the ideas of the ruling class are in every epoch the ruling ideas, i.e. the class which is the ruling material force of society, is at the same time its ruling intellectual force.' In other words, cultural ideas and values are dominated by ruling-class ideas and values. Marx called this ruling-class culture '**ideology**'. He argued that social institutions such as religion, education, the mass media and even the family, functioned to socialize society's members – especially its working-class members – to accept ruling-class culture and, consequently, to see their own low status and lack of opportunity as 'normal', 'natural' and a product of their own shortcomings. How these agencies do this in practice will be explored further in Topic 2.

Criticizing Marx

Marx's theory may be guilty of overemphasizing social class as the main source of conflict in modern societies. There is evidence that gender, religion, **ethnicity** and **nationalism** may be just as important as causes of inequality. Marxism also assumes that the working class are the passive victims, or puppets, of ruling-class culture and ideology. However, surveys suggest that the working class are aware of inequality and exploitation, but may choose to live with it because of the benefits that capitalism brings in the form of living standards and materialism.

Cultural diversity and subcultures

Functionalist and Marxist accounts of culture are probably correct in their assumption that culture is generally shared. On the whole, people get married, live in families, see education as a good thing, vote in elections, follow the Highway Code and respect the law. Shared culture also helps us to make sense of the world. However, both theories are probably guilty of overstating this sharing of culture and, as a result, fail to note that modern societies are characterized by **cultural diversity**.

Although the cultures of modern societies may seem to be dominated by cultural agreement, in reality, cultures are fragmented into competing **subcultures**. These are social groups based on social class, age, religion and ethnicity that subscribe to the values and norms of mainstream society in most respects, but also subscribe to cultural values, norms, customs, etc., that are unique to them. Some of these subcultures may even be regarded as deviant by wider society or by those who wield power. These groups will be explored further in Topics 3 to 6.

Global culture

Cultural diversity has also been influenced by **globalization**. Only 30 or so years ago, our culture was local and familiar. Travelling abroad was not a common activity; most of the products we consumed were produced in the UK and, although we watched Hollywood films and listened to American singers, there was also a reasonably healthy British entertainment industry focused on pop music and television. Today, however, it can be argued globalization is now a profound influence on how we live our cultural lives. As Marsh and Keating (2006) note:

<< *The British are increasingly a globalized people. We appear willing to travel far and wide. We increasingly eat and drink the foods and beverages that our European or even North American neighbours consume. We drive similar, if not identical cars, albeit on the other side of the road. Moreover, our consumption patterns are increasingly influenced and shaped by the growth of global media and advertising. I can now sit in my hotel room in the USA or Egypt, and watch my favourite Premier League side lose yet again. Our world, that is to say the affluent Western world, is the world of Levi's, a world of Gap, a world of Coca-Cola, McDonald's, H&M, a world of Oil of Ulay.* >> (p. 431)

Some sociologists, especially postmodernists, argue that globalization is good for us because it offers us more choice in terms of constructing our identities and lifestyles. Consequently, postmodernists argue that our personal identities as well as our cultural identity are now influenced in a positive way by a range of cultures from around the world. See Chapter 1, pp. 26–9, for further discussion of these trends.

Focus on research

Kate Fox (2004) Watching the English queuing

The English expect each other to observe the rules of queuing and feel highly offended when these rules are violated. However, they lack the confidence or social skills to express their annoyance in a straightforward manner. In England, queue-jumping is regarded as deeply immoral, but the queue-jumper is likely to get away with the offence. Usually, nobody would even think of simply barging to the front of a queue. This is so unthinkable that when it does happen, people assume either that it is a genuine dire emergency or that the person is a foreigner who is unaware of the 'rules'. If you jump a queue in England, you will be subjected to frowns, glares, raised eyebrows and contemptuous looks – accompanied by heavy sighs,

pointed coughs, tutting and muttering. However, few English people want to 'cause a scene' or 'make a fuss', and usually direct their comments to each other rather than directly to the offender. They prefer to shame the offender into retreating to the back of the queue.

Adapted from Fox, K. (2004) *Watching the English: The Hidden Rules of English Behaviour*, London: Hodder & Stoughton

1 **What sort of research method do you think would produce the most valid data on queuing, and why?**

2 **What does queuing tell us about how the English interpret conformity and deviance?**

Conclusions

The debate about culture is generally focused on three major questions:

1 Is nature responsible for culture, or is culture the product of learning? This will be further explored in Topic 2.

2 Are society and culture integrated into a unified shared whole, or is society characterized by subcultural diversity and possible conflict? This will be explored in greater detail when we examine subcultures based on social class, ethnicity, sexuality and age (Topics 3 to 6).

3 Are human beings cultural robots passively reacting to the demands of cultural and social forces beyond their control, or are they the masters/mistresses of their own destinies?

Interpretivists are critical of both functionalism and Marxism for ignoring the role of human agency in the construction of culture and identity. They argue that culture is actively created by people via social interaction. They would argue that culture is not static – rather it is constantly evolving, as people interpret the actions of others around them and make their own choices about their behaviour.

Key terms

Aesthetic pleasing, appreciating beauty.

Anomie moral confusion and uncertainty.

Authenticity reflecting reality.

Capitalist economic system based on competition to produce manufactured goods.

Cultural diversity differences between groups with regard to beliefs, values, norms, etc.

Culture a way of life of a society.

Customs traditional ways of doing things.

Elitist belief in the superiority of a powerful group.

Ethnicity characteristics associated with particular ethnic group based on factors such as shared race, religion, history and language.

Globalization the influence on British culture of cultural products and activities produced outside the UK.

High culture cultural products and activities that are defined as superior in their creativity to those that make up mass or popular culture.

Identity how the individual sees themselves – influenced, too, by how others see the person.

Ideology a set of ideas that originate with powerful people and function to justify some type of inequality.

Mass culture cultural products that are consumed by large numbers of people.

Nationalism strong belief and devotion to the concept of a nation, e.g. strong pride in being English.

Norms ways of behaving.

Nurture bringing up or teaching (usually children).

Peer group friendship networks.

Popular culture cultural products such as films, television, pop music, etc., enjoyed by large numbers of people.

Rituals traditional ceremonies, e.g. the State opening of Parliament.

Social class socio-economic status, usually based on job and income.

Socialization the process of teaching and learning culture.

Social roles the norms attached to particular statuses.

Society community bound together by social institutions, culture, etc.

Specialized division of labour the organization of work and jobs in society.

State the government and all its supporting apparatuses, e.g. the armed services.

Subcultures groups that exist within and alongside the wider majority culture.

Value consensus shared agreement on important beliefs/actions.

Values important general beliefs.

Check your understanding

1 Identify six key components of culture.

2 Identify four key values in British culture relating to family life.

3 What is the difference between culture and society?

4 What are the supposed differences between folk culture, high culture and popular culture?

5 How do functionalists and Marxists differ in their view of culture?

6 Why are interpretivists critical of both the functionalist and Marxist accounts of culture?

Activities

Research idea

Obtain the Review pages from a Sunday broadsheet newspaper such as *The Sunday Times*, *The Sunday Telegraph* or *The Observer*. Work out how many column inches or pages are dedicated to specific cultural activities such as literature (book reviews), films, popular and classical music. Does this evidence suggest that these newspapers distinguish between high culture and popular culture?

Web.tasks

1 Visit the web sites www.morrisdancing.org and www.efdss.org

   What cultural traditions are these two organizations attempting to preserve?

2 Visit www.sociology.org.uk and click on the on-line resource bank, the 'video vault' and access the films on culture and identity, particularly the HSBC adverts. What do these tell us about culture?

Culture

Item A

Culture is not an easy term to define. However, it is not too difficult to identify some of the elements that go to making a culture. These include language, norms, values and beliefs.

Nor is there complete agreement on what the role or purpose of culture is. However, sociologists are united in the view that culture is something which is learned from other members of a group or community, rather than being transmitted biologically or genetically. Culture is also something which is shared by members of a society. For example, it would be hard to imagine a language spoken by only one person – unless of course he or she was the last surviving member of a group that spoke the language.

However, especially in large complex societies, not every individual shares exactly the same culture, and different 'kinds' of culture may exist alongside one another within the same society, such as high culture and folk culture, for example.

Item B

According to functionalist sociologists, everything in society performs a function. This is also the case for culture. In the view of functionalists such as Emile Durkheim, the key feature of society is that it is orderly and harmonious – despite the fact that different individuals may have competing or conflicting interests, they are still able to live together and cooperate with one another.

Durkheim argues that this is because of the existence of a shared culture or value consensus. This shared culture binds individuals together by giving them a sense of belonging and a set of common goals which they can achieve through cooperation. This helps to safeguard individuals and society from anomie.

(a) Explain what is meant by 'anomie' (Item B). (2 marks)

(b) Identify two types of culture other than those mentioned in Item A. (4 marks)

(c) Suggest three other elements of culture other than those mentioned in Items A and B. (6 marks)

(d) Using information from item B and elsewhere, assess the functionalist theory of culture. (24 marks)

Grade booster   Getting top marks in the 24-mark question

Make sure you use Item B to help you to give an account of the functionalist view of culture, but you should also include ideas about culture in both pre-industrial and industrial societies (for example, on solidarity, anomie, the division of labour, etc.). Once you have described the functionalist view, you need to evaluate it. You can do this by considering criticisms that others have made of it, e.g. its over-emphasis on value consensus and harmony, and its view that individuals' beliefs, values, choices, etc., are entirely shaped by society. You can use other perspectives on culture, such as Marxism or postmodernism, to contrast with the functionalist view.

TOPIC 2

The process of socialization

Ofcom's 2006 survey of young people aged 8 to 15 years and new media in Britain found that:

- 63% of girls and 54% of boys use the internet
- 49% of girls and 36% of boys read newspapers or magazines
- two thirds of the whole sample thought that most or all of what was on the internet was 'true'
- one third thought that 'reality TV' was 'true' most of the time.

Source: Ofcom 2006, quoted in R. Boyle (2007) 'The "now" media generation', *Sociology Review*, 17(1), September 2007

It's a dilemma of modern working parents: finding enough time for their children. Now a major study reveals that parents who fail to do so put their teenagers at risk of problems including drug use and teenage pregnancies. Teenagers who felt emotionally 'connected' to at least one parent were up to a third less likely to show some type of problem behaviour. Professor Blum, the author of the report, said that parents should supervise free time and make themselves available at four key times of the day: early mornings, immediately after school, suppertime and bedtime.

Adapted from G. Hinsliff, 'Peril of the parents who have no time', *The Observer*, 14 April 2002.

1 How might the effectiveness of socialization in the family be undermined by the processes described above?

2 What evidence is there that the mass media may be replacing the family as the main agency of socialization?

The process by which human babies, infants, adolescents and even adults learn behaviour is known as 'socialization'. The primary agency of socialization has always been the family, but – as we can see above – pressures on parenting may be reducing the effectiveness of this particular child-rearing institution. Secondary agencies of socialization, such as the mass media, may be increasing in importance. Some commentators, notably Postman (1982) and Palmer (2007), have expressed anxiety at the quality of the socialization experienced by children viewing television, reading teenage magazines and surfing the internet.

Socialization, culture and subculture

Although the first few years of a person's life are crucial to learning how to behave, it is important to understand that socialization is a life-long process. This is because humans are social animals who live in complex and sophisticated societies based on detailed rules and traditions. For this reason, we have a great deal more to learn than other animals over the course of our lifetime. This learning process is, therefore, a continuous process, which really only ends at death.

For socialization to be effective, it should not be experienced as forced or as an imposition. The individual should not feel that they are being subjected to a form of brainwashing. Such feelings run the risk of rejection, dissent and rebellion. Instead, as Paul Taylor (1997) notes, socialization should be organized in such a way 'that the ways of thinking, behaving and perceiving things that are accepted by culture come to appear normal, natural and inevitable'. As Marsh and Keating (2006) argue, effective socialization should happen to children without them even noticing it.

Stages of socialization – primary socialization

The main agent of primary socialization is the family. The first few years of socialization in the family are crucial to a person's development, having a profound effect upon all later social learning. Close social relationships with other people are essential in order for children to learn to interact and to communicate. These processes allow children to become aware of themselves as 'social beings'. They recognize that they occupy particular social roles, such as son, daughter, brother, sister, etc., and that they are capable of social action that has consequences for others.

As this process develops, they acquire uniquely human skills; they learn that love, sadness and humour are appropriate emotional responses in certain situations, and they acquire the ability to smile, to laugh, to cry, etc. In other words, the socialization process results in children acquiring most of the skills necessary to **empathize** with others. Consequently, the helpless infant becomes a self-aware, competent, skilled and knowledgeable member of society. Children learn to function as good and useful citizens in their community.

Feral children

Feral children are a good example of what happens when a child is denied human contact, interaction and communication. These children have usually grown up with minimal human contact because they have been confined and isolated and, in some cases, been raised by animals. As a result, they have tended to behave like their animal foster parents – walking on all fours, making animal noises, being unable to talk, smile or laugh, biting and being aggressive, eating raw meat, urinating and defecating in public.

Socialization and identity

Baumeister (1986) notes that family socialization provides children with an identity. A very young child has no life apart from its role in the family, and so a child will believe that the family will love and care for it so long as it does what it is supposed to do. Many children successfully learn what they are supposed to do through **imitative play**. Social roles, particularly the significant roles played by parents, provide children with blueprints for action – examples and illustrations

of how to behave that they can then copy. Play activities may involve imitating parents by playing 'house' or 'mummies and daddies' – this too encourages empathy, as they gradually learn what it might feel like to be a father or mother.

Socialization and social control

Morgan (1996) suggests that a great deal of socialization is concerned with social control and encouraging **conformity**. This can be illustrated in a number of ways:

- Parents often use **sanctions** to reinforce and reward socially approved behaviour, and to discipline and punish 'naughty', i.e. deviant, behaviour. Positive sanctions might include praise, sweets, and the promise of extra television-viewing or new toys, while negative sanctions include smacking, 'grounding' and especially the threat to withdraw love.
- Sanctions encourage the development of a conscience in the child. It is culturally expected that a child will eventually know the difference between 'good' and 'bad' behaviour, and that guilt will act as a deterrent, preventing deviant behaviour. Socialization is seen to be successful when the child realizes that the costs in terms of parental punishment outweigh the benefits of deviant actions, and so exercises self-control. This is the first step to independent action, i.e. actions not shaped solely by parents.
- Morgan suggests that the function of toilet training is to instil in the child some sense of control over their bodily functions so that the child is accepted into wider society as a 'civilized' being. Similarly, children will be taught 'civilized' norms such as politeness and table manners. At the same time, they will learn to avoid uncivilized behaviours, such as swearing, and vulgar behaviours, such as burping, picking their nose and breaking wind in public.
- Socialization also involves becoming aware of what being a boy or a girl entails. Children internalize cultural expectations with regard to femininity and masculinity, and generally conform to traditional gender roles. Durkin (1995) notes that most children can categorize themselves correctly and consistently as a boy or a girl between the ages of 2 and 3 years of age. The reasons for this will be explored more fully in Topic 4.

Functionalists and primary socialization

Functionalists such as Parsons see the family as a 'personality factory' – the child is seen as a 'blank slate' at birth and the function of parents, especially the nurturing mother, is to train and mould the passive child in the image of society. The child is to be filled up with the shared cultural values and norms, so that it assumes that cultural values are somehow naturally its own values. This ensures that the child subscribes to value consensus and so feels a strong sense of belonging to society.

Marxism and primary socialization

Marxists are critical of the functionalist view that children are socialized into shared cultural values and norms. Zaretsky (1976),

Julia Brannen and Ellen Heptinstall (2003)

Children's view of family life

This study of nearly one thousand London 10 to 12 year olds focused on how children view care, parental responsibility and family life. A questionnaire survey was conducted with the children, as well as 63 in-depth interview-based case studies from four different types of family: two-parent, lone-mother, stepfather and foster-care.

The researchers found that children saw the process of family life, especially parental unconditional love and care, as far more important than family structure. Furthermore, the children emerged as active contributors to family life. They showed considerable ability to understand other people's feelings and circumstances. Some expressed a strong appreciation of what their parents had done for them and wanted to reciprocate by being caring, as well as offering practical help. One girl wrote on her questionnaire: 'It gives me a chance to do something for my parents instead of them doing things for me.'

The research suggests that children are active co-participants in care and co-constructors in family life. They make a contribution to family life while also trying to fulfil their increasingly onerous responsibilities at school. In this context, it is not surprising that children also think adults should listen to them more than they do at present.

Brannen, J. and Heptinstall, E. (2003) 'Family Life – what the children think', *Young Minds Magazine*, 54, www.youngminds.org.uk

1 How might the research methods that were used have increased the validity of the findings?

2 How do the findings support the view that socialization is a two-way rather than a one-way process?

for example, argues that the family is used by the capitalist class to instil values, such as obedience and respect for authority, that are useful to the capitalist ruling class. Such values ensure that individuals can be exploited later in life by the ruling class, because ordinary people will have learnt that power, authority and inequality should be viewed as normal and natural.

Secondary agents of socialization

Sociologists note that, in addition to the family, a range of other social institutions are involved in socialization. These are called the secondary agents of socialization and function to build on what has been learned during primary socialization in order to help the child to take their place in wider society.

The functionalist theory of education as an agent of secondary socialization

Functionalists see education systems as essential in that they transmit shared cultural values, thus producing conformity and **consensus**. Durkheim believed that subjects such as history, language and religious education link the individual to society, past and present, by encouraging a sense of pride in the historical and religious achievements of their nation; this reinforces their sense of belonging to society.

Parsons argued that the main function of education was to act as a social bridge between the family unit and wider society.

Education socializes children into important values such as achievement, competition and **individualism** – functionalists see the transmission of these values as essential in preparing young people for the world of work.

The Marxist theory of education as an agent of secondary socialization

In contrast to functionalist theorists, Marxists, such as Althusser (1971), argue that education as an agency of socialization is dominated by a **hidden curriculum** – a ruling-class ideology that encourages conformity and an unquestioning acceptance of the organization of the capitalism.

Althusser claimed that few students are allowed to access educational knowledge that challenges the existence of capitalism. It is claimed that when the national curriculum was introduced in 1988, critical subjects such as Sociology, Economics and Politics were deliberately excluded from mainstream education because the ruling class believed that socialization into ideas commonly taught by these subjects might lead to students becoming too critical of capitalist inequality.

Marxists also claim that schools socialize pupils into uncritical acceptance of hierarchy, obedience and failure. In particular, working-class pupils are socialized to see their failure as their own fault and as deserved rather than being caused by capitalism's need for a relatively uneducated manual labour force.

The functionalist theory of religion as an agent of secondary socialization

According to Durkheim (1912), the major function of religion is to socialize society's members into value consensus by investing certain values with a sacred quality, i.e. by infusing them with religious symbolism and special significance. These values consequently become 'moral codes' – beliefs that society agrees to revere and socialize children into. Such codes regulate our social behaviour with regard to crime, sexual behaviour and obligation to others. The Ten Commandments are a good example of a set of moral codes that have influenced both formal controls, such as the law (e.g. 'thou shalt not kill', 'thou shalt not steal'), as well as informal controls such as moral disapproval (e.g. 'thou shalt not commit adultery').

The Marxist theory of religion as an agent of secondary socialization

Marxists, on the other hand, describe religion as an ideological apparatus that serves to reflect ruling-class ideas and interests. According to Marxists, religion socializes the working class into three sets of false ideas:

- It promotes the idea that material success is a sign of God's favour, whereas poverty is interpreted as caused by wickedness, sin and immorality.
- Religious teachings and the emphasis on blind faith serve to distract the poor and powerless from the true extent of their exploitation by the ruling class.
- Religion makes exploitation, poverty and inequality bearable by promising a reward in the afterlife for those who accept without question their suffering or poverty here and now.

The mass media as an agent of secondary socialization

Many sociologists argue that the mass media – newspapers, magazines, television, films, pop music, computer games, the internet, etc. – comprise the most significant socialization agency today, as far as influence over values and norms (and especially those of young people) are concerned. Many people use the mass media to make sense of the world around them. The media offer a window onto the wider world and provide much of the information required to make sense of events that have a bearing on our everyday lives. The media may also provide us with role models and designs for living, i.e. images and ideas that we use to fashion our identities. It is, therefore, important that all points of view are presented to us in an objective and neutral fashion, because the media may have the power to structure how and what we think.

The Marxist critique of the mass media as an agent of secondary socialization

Marxist sociologists are also critical of the mass media because they argue that it is mainly responsible for mass culture. Sociologists such as Marcuse suggested that popular culture, especially television and advertising, has had a negative effect on culture because, as Marsh and Keating (2006) note, 'popular culture is a false culture devised and packaged by capitalism to keep the masses content' – its function is to encourage 'false needs' (e.g. the acquisition of non-essential consumer goods) and to discourage any serious or critical thought, especially that relating to the inequalities caused by the organization of capitalism.

This theme has been taken up by modern commentators such as Steve Barnett, who argues that media output in the UK that once encouraged a critical outlook, such as quality drama, documentaries and serious news coverage, have gone into decline and are being increasingly replaced with dumbed-down light entertainment – reality shows, soap operas and the like, which focus on transmitting superficial, mindless entertainment (Barnett and Curry 1994). Such critics argue that we are being socialized into not being able to think for ourselves.

In defence of the media, research does indicate that different people interpret media messages in different ways. There is no evidence that audiences passively accept what is being fed to them. Audiences are selective and, at times, critical. The idea that the audience can be manipulated does not recognize the ways in which they actively and critically use the media to enhance their lives and identities.

The peer group

The peer group refers to people of similar status who come into regular contact with each other, either on a social or work-related basis. Peer groups, therefore, include friendship networks, school subcultures and occupational subcultures, i.e. workmates.

Peer groups have a particularly strong influence over adolescent behaviour and attitudes. Teenagers may feel a tension between parental controls and their desire for more responsibility and independence, and so come into conflict with parents. A common site for this conflict may be the teenager's choice of friendships – and especially the choice of boyfriend or girlfriend.

Peer pressure

Adolescents may feel a great deal of peer pressure to fit in with their friends, and this may lead to radical changes in their identity during their teenage years in terms of image and behaviour. Some teenagers may feel that they have to engage in 'deviant' behaviour, such as drug-taking, delinquency and sex, in order to be accepted by their peers. Friendship networks may put considerable pressure on teenagers to conform; they may use negative sanctions such as gossip and bullying to control the behaviour of their fellow adolescents.

Peer group and young adulthood

Some sociologists, most notably Sue Heath (2004), have suggested that friendship networks are becoming increasingly important as agents of socialization in the period known as 'young adulthood'. This period is characterized by movement in and out of a variety of independent living arrangements – for example, a student may move between living in a hall of residence, flatsharing and going home to stay with parents. It is also marked out as the period when a person is likely to be single. Cote (2000) suggests that in young adulthood, peer-group or friendship networks eventually become more important than relationships with parents as a source of knowledge about how to live one's life.

Occupational peer groups

The workplace is another important source of peer-group relationships. Our experience at work teaches us not only skills and work discipline, but also the informal rules that underpin work, i.e. the tricks of the trade. We may also be influenced by our membership of more formal work-based organizations to behave in particular ways. For example, membership of a trade union may produce a **collectivist** outlook, in which the person puts the interest of the group before their individual interests, whereas membership of a professional organization, such as the Law Society or the British Medical Association, will make clear how a professional person should behave in practice.

Criticisms of the concept of socialization

Many accounts of socialization discuss this process as if it is a relatively straightforward, positive and, hence, unproblematical process. However, not all adults acquire the skills that are required to nurture children towards adulthood; as a result, such poor parenting may, unfortunately, result in neglect or child abuse.

Other commentators suggest that childhood socialization is not as effective today as it was in the past. Postman (1982) suggests that childhood is a much shorter period today compared with 50 years ago and bemoans children's loss of innocence, which he sees as the result of overexposure to sex and violence in the media. Palmer (2007) also notes the negative influence of television and computer games, and argues that parents all too often use these as a substitute for spending quality time interacting with children. Consequently, children today are less likely to be socialized into important

moral codes of behaviour. Phillips (1997) argues that children have too many rights today and claims that they have used these to resist parental power, so undermining socialization. She suggests that the antisocial behaviour associated with young people today is a direct result of parents being too content not to take responsibility for their children's upbringing. These themes are explored further in Chapter 3, pp. 116–17.

Finally, many accounts of socialization portray it as a one-way process – the child being a vessel waiting to be filled up with the wisdom of its parents. However, interpretivist sociologists point out that socialization is a two-way process, and that parenting itself is a learning process.

Check your understanding

1 Identify six skills that children acquire during primary socialization.

2 How do children learn to differentiate between right and wrong during primary socialization?

3 What does Parsons mean when he describes the family as a 'personality factory'?

4 Why do functionalists and Marxists disagree on the role of education as an agency of secondary socialization?

5 Why is the peer group such an important agency of socialization?

6 Identify three ways in which socialization might have negative consequences for some children.

Activities

Research idea

Using the contents of this chapter, design a questionnaire that focuses on:

● what parents think are important in bringing about effective primary socialization
● whether parents share the concerns of commentators such as Postman, Palmer and Phillips.

Web.task

Access the Open University website **www.open2.net/childofourtime/2007/index.html** and explore the 'Child of Our Time' pages. View the videos on the site on parenting. What do these experts tell us about the nature of family socialization?

Key terms

Collectivist putting the group interest before your own.

Conformity obeying the rules without question.

Consensus agreement.

Empathy being able to imagine how others feel about something.

Hidden curriculum the invisible ways in which schools encourage conformity.

Imitative play games that involve children copying adults, e.g. playing 'mummies and daddies' or 'doctors and nurses'.

Individualism putting one's own needs and wishes before those of the group or society.

Sanctions punishments and rewards.

Item A

Socialization is a process of learning how society expects us to behave. It begins in the family with primary socialization, but other agencies of socialization become important later. Socialization is an ongoing process that continues throughout our entire lives as our circumstances and social position change. For example, when we start a new job, we may need to learn new skills, rules and routines. Socialization teaches us how to fit in and enables us to interact with others by equipping us with the norms and values shared by those with whom we have to cooperate.

However, socialization is not the only factor ensuring that we 'fit in'. Social control, in the form of positive and negative sanctions, also plays a part in keeping us on the path of conformity.

Item B

According to some theories of socialization, the individual is rather like an empty vessel waiting to be 'filled' with society's culture, or the subculture of the particular group to which he or she belongs. Critics have argued that this applies to both functionalist and Marxist explanations of the relationship between socialization and culture. For example, in the functionalist view, parents, teachers and others fill children with the shared culture so that they come to conform to society's expectations without even thinking about it, as second nature.

Other sociologists disagree with this view of the socialization process. They see it as a two-way process, in which parents as well as children learn, and in which children are active participants in their own socialization.

(a) Explain what sociologists mean by 'primary socialization' (Item A). (2 marks)

(b) Give one example of a positive sanction and one example of a negative sanction (Item A). (4 marks)

(c) Identify three agents of socialization other than those mentioned in Item A. (6 marks)

(d) Using information from Item B and elsewhere, assess sociological theories of socialization. (24 marks)

Grade booster Getting top marks in the 24-mark question

Item B gives you some useful points, so make sure you use it. For example, you could discuss why functionalists see it as important that everyone is socialized into a shared culture, and you could contrast this with Marxist views (for example, that socialization benefits the ruling class by filling people with ideas that encourage acceptance of inequality and exploitation). You can also examine contrasting views of the role of different agencies of socialization from these two perspectives. You could also consider views which see socialization as a two-way process (e.g. interpretivists) or as less than perfectly successful (e.g. Phillips).

Identity and social class

1 **Does this survey suggest that class identity is still important?**

2 **Why might sociologists be cautious about the findings of surveys like this?**

3 **How would you define 'working class'?**

Class rules

A Guardian/ICM poll published in October 2007 shows that Britain remains a nation dominated by class division, with a huge majority certain that their social standing determines the way they are judged. Of those questioned, 89 per cent said they think people are still judged by their class – with almost half saying that it still counts for 'a lot'. Only 8 per cent think that class does not matter at all in shaping the way people are seen.

Despite the collapse of industrial employment, 53 per cent of people consider themselves 'working-class'. Despite huge economic change and the government's efforts to build what it calls an opportunity society, people who think of themselves as 'middle-class' are still in a minority. In 1998, 41 per cent of people thought of themselves as middle-class – exactly the same proportion as today. Only 2 per cent of those who took part in the poll claimed to be 'upper-class'.

Adapted from Glover, J. (2007) 'Class rules', *The Guardian*, 20 October 2007

Defining social class

As we can see from the above exercise, social class can be a difficult concept to define. This is because a person's subjective sense of identity, i.e. what they think they are, may differ from objective attempts to measure the importance of social class.

Objectively, social class refers to the socio-economic status and identity that are attached to a person because of their job. The government categorizes people into one of eight social classes using an occupational scale known as the National Statistics Socio-Economic Classification (NS-SEC) – see Chapter 1, pp. 6–7. The NS-SEC differentiates between different jobs on the basis of **employment relations** (whether people are employers, self-employed, employees and how much authority they exercise over others) and **market conditions** (how much they earn, their promotion opportunities, job security, etc.). Sociologists have observed that groups of people who share similar socio-economic status also share similar educational backgrounds and experiences, lifestyles and outlooks. There is also evidence that there exist distinct inequalities between social classes in terms of **infant mortality**, life expectancy, the educational achievement of their children and the distribution of wealth and poverty.

It is generally agreed that there are three broad social class identities that exist in the UK today: the upper class, the middle classes and the working class.

Upper-class identity

The upper class is made up of a fairly small number of wealthy **extended families** who are often interconnected by marriage. They tend to share a common background in terms of an elite education at expensive **public schools**, such as Eton College or Harrow, and Oxford and Cambridge universities. Scott (1991) argues that the main purpose of these schools is to mould the ideas and outlooks of their pupils so that they quickly realize their common upper-class interests. In particular, he notes that such schools socialize upper-class pupils into a common culture that promotes the values of conservatism and especially respect for tradition, nationalism, superior breeding and upbringing as well as hostility towards socialist ideals. Moreover, these schools produce **'old-boy'** or **'old school-tie'** networks made up of people who share the same cultural values and assets, and who use these contacts to further each other's adult careers and influence.

There is some evidence that the value system of the upper class differs from that of other social classes. Scott notes that the **conservative** values of tradition and the acceptance of privilege, hierarchy and authority are regarded as particularly important aspects of upper-class identity. Upper-class tastes and activities generally focus on higher cultural pursuits such as classical music, theatre, opera and ballet. Other leisure activities revolve around exclusive social events that provide a distinctive upper-class lifestyle, such as debutantes' balls, hunting, shooting and sports such as polo and rowing.

The upper class, therefore, is a self-selecting and exclusive elite which is closed to outsiders, i.e. this is known as '**social closure**'. This is reinforced by parents encouraging their children to choose partners from other upper-class families and by the practice of sending children away to boarding schools.

The middle classes

The term 'middle classes' is used in a broad way to describe **non-manual** workers. Savage's research (1995) describes four distinct types of middle-class groups and, therefore, identities:

- *Professionals such as doctors and lawyers* – Savage claims that these subscribe to an intellectual identity gained from a long and successful education. He claims that they value **cultural** assets or **capital** such as knowledge, qualifications, achievement, experience of higher education and **altruism** (i.e. they often see themselves as serving a higher purpose – namely, society).
- *Managers* are generally less qualified than professionals and are more likely to have worked their way up in a company, i.e. from the shop or office floor. Savage suggests that this group generally defines its status and identity in terms of its standard of living and leisure pursuits. Managerial middle-class identity is less secure today compared with the past because of factors such as globalization, economic recession, mergers and takeovers.
- Roberts (2001) notes that the *self-employed owners of small businesses* have traditionally been very individualistic. Surveys suggest that they believe that people should be independent and stand on their own two feet rather than rely on the welfare state. They also have great faith in hard work and discipline – believing firmly that success in life is a result of effort and application rather than luck.
- *White-collar or clerical workers* – Clerks and secretaries, for example, have traditionally been seen as having a middle-class identity, despite often being the children of manual workers, because their pay and working conditions were superior to manual workers. However, the introduction of technology such as computers has led to their pay and status going into decline, and it is suggested that they now have more in common with the working class. However, surveys of clerical workers indicate that they still see themselves as middle-class. They rarely mix with manual workers, and spend their leisure time and money in quite different ways.

Despite these differences in material circumstances, sociologists such as Ken Roberts argue that these different groups do share some values. A general middle-class identity, therefore, can be seen to exist which is mainly focused on the home. The middle classes value home ownership – they are more likely than other social groups to have mortgages and to own their own home. They are more likely to live in the suburbs – they are generally a commuting class.

Members of the middle classes generally encourage their children to do well in education. They are keen on private education, although their children also do exceptionally well within the state sector. Middle-class parents often move home to get their children into the catchment area for the best state primary and secondary schools. Their children dominate the top streams of state schools, get the best GCSE results, are more likely to stay on and do A-levels and dominate the university sector (80 per cent of students are from middle-class backgrounds).

The middle classes generally believe in the concept of **meritocracy** – that high position and status can be achieved by ability or effort. It is said that the middle classes are more willing than other social groups to '**defer gratification**' (e.g. financial rewards, pleasure) in the pursuit of education. In other words, they are more willing to make sacrifices whilst qualifications are achieved.

The working classes

The traditional working class

Sociological evidence suggests that those engaged in traditional manual work, especially in industries such as mining and factory work – i.e. the working class – had a very strong sense of their economic or social-class position. This traditional working-class identity was dominant for most of the 20th century and is still very influential in some parts of the UK even today.

Manual workers, probably more than any other group of workers, identified very strongly with each other. This was partly due to the dangerous nature of some manual jobs (such as mining) but was also due to the collective nature of their jobs; for example, factories were often made up of thousands of workers controlled by a minority of supervisors, managers and employers. This led to a strong sense that the world was divided into 'them', i.e. the bosses (capital), who were only interested in exploiting the workers and making profits, and 'us', i.e. the worker on the shop-floor (labour). Consequently, relations between management and labour until the 1980s were often characterized by mistrust and hostility. Many workers belonged to trade unions, which represented workers' interests and engaged in industrial action when it was thought that such interests were being threatened by management.

There is evidence that the traditional working class had a strong political identity and saw the Labour party as representing its natural interests against those of the employers. At general elections until the 1970s, the Labour Party could, therefore, count on the loyal support of about 80 per cent of the working-class electorate. Trade-union support for Labour reinforced this political allegiance.

Such workers also had a strong sense of their class identity because they often lived in close-knit communities made up of extended **kinship** networks. Adult children often lived close to their parents and saw them on a regular basis. **Mutual support** was offered by a range of relatives especially in terms of childcare, financial help and finding work.

The decline of traditional working-class identity

However, more recently, some researchers have claimed that traditional working-class identity is less important today because of the decline in manual work over the last 30 years. The numbers employed in traditional heavy industries such as mining and shipbuilding have fallen rapidly since the 1970s and

1980s. Consequently, manual workers now make up well under half of the total workforce and so the economic basis for class identity and solidarity has weakened.

The new working class

Research has also identified a new sort of working-class identity, mainly found in the South East, which sees work as a means to an end, i.e. a wage, rather than as a source of community, status and identity. This working-class identity tends to be found in the newer types of high-tech manufacturing industries.

This new working class has no heightened sense of class injustice or political loyalty. They believe in individualism (i.e. putting themselves and their immediate families first), rather than collective or community action. They define themselves through their families, their lifestyle and their standard of living, rather than through their work. They vote for whichever political party furthers their individual financial interests.

The underclass

Another type of working-class identity may be held by those who exist at the margins of society. In recent years, a number of commentators, most notably Murray (1994) and Mount (2004), have identified a supposed 'new' form of working-class identity organized around dependency upon state benefits – this is the so-called **urban underclass** allegedly found on run-down council estates and in the depressed inner cities. This group allegedly consists of individuals who are long-term unemployed and single parents, as well as drug addicts, criminals, etc. Murray suggests that the culture and identity of this underclass revolve around being work-shy, feckless, anti-authority, anti-education, immoral and welfare-dependent. It is suggested, too, that the children of the underclass are being socialized by their inadequate parents into a culture of idleness, failure and criminality.

Unemployment, poverty and identity

Not everyone agrees that this so-called deviant underclass exists. Studies of the poor and long-term unemployed carried out by Jordan (1992) suggest that those living in poverty share the same ideas about work and family as everyone else. Surveys also show that the unemployed want to work in order to gain the respect of their loved ones and to regain their dignity. Surveys indicate that unemployment often brings with it negative self-image or identity, shame, guilt, low self-esteem, insecurity and poor mental and physical health. These are not feelings or effects that people choose to have. Surveys clearly show that the long-term unemployed want to work in order to gain the respect of their loved ones. Furthermore, most unemployed people do not enjoy a high standard of living. They often lack basics, are in debt and feel guilty because their children go without at crucial times such as birthdays and Christmas.

Jordan also notes that most people do not choose to be unemployed or poor, or to be dependent on welfare benefits. Rather, it is often the fault of global recession, government

Focus on research

Simon Charlesworth (2000) Deadman's Town

Charlesworth takes a phenomenological approach to working-class experience on an extremely deprived council estate in Rotherham. 'Phenomenological' means looking at a social phenomenon from the perspective of those experiencing it, usually in their own words. Charlesworth's account of the experience of long-term unemployment in one of Britain's poorest and bleakest towns (known by locals as 'Deadman's Town') puts working-class people's interpretations at the heart of the study.

Charlesworth found that working-class identity was still a very strong feeling among the poor in Rotherham, although it had been adapted to cope with the conditions of exclusion, hardship and humiliation that are a normal part of everyday life. From the outside, and particularly from a middle-class perspective, the everyday culture of working-class people on this estate might seem narrow and irresponsible. Charlesworth notes that people on the estate do not seem proud of their heritage nor are they positive about their futures. Instead, they indulge in behaviour – heavy drinking, drug use, stealing, etc. – that brings them criticism as 'chavs' or as a deadbeat idle underclass. However, the reality, says Charlesworth, is that their response is a rational one to the economic decay of their area.

Charlesworth, S. (2000) *A Phenomenology of Working Class Experience*, Cambridge: Cambridge University Press

1 How do you think Charlesworth gathered the information for this study?

2 How was working-class identity interpreted and expressed by people living on this council estate in Rotherham?

policies and the fact that capitalist companies find it more profitable to close down factories in the UK and instead exploit workers in the developing world. The unemployed and poor are therefore excluded by society.

Simon Charlesworth's (2000) study of working-class people in Rotherham (see above) suggests that those at the bottom end of the working class are often misunderstood by other social classes because they experience negative self-identity and low self-esteem. He argues that their negative experience of education results in them devaluing themselves, restricting their ambitions to 'being disappointed' in life and hence turning to drink, drugs or antisocial behaviour as a form of compensation.

The decline of social class as a source of identity?

In recent years, some sociologists have argued that class has ceased to be the main factor in creating identity. Postmodernists argue that class identity has fragmented into numerous separate identities – young people, in particular, have more choice today as to how they construct their identity. For example, a young male might experiment with identity by taking ideas from femininity (e.g. make-up, accessories), global culture (e.g. a t-shirt celebrating an American band), a media role model (e.g. copying their hero's hairstyle or attitude) and consumption (e.g. wearing designer shades or labelled clothing). It is argued, therefore, that social class as a source of identity is no longer recognized by the young, and **hybrid** identities are increasingly the norm.

However, there is some evidence that postmodern ideas may be exaggerated. Marshall's survey research into how people viewed themselves suggests that the majority of people in the UK still think that social class is still a significant source of identity. Members of a range of classes are aware of class differences and are happy to identify themselves using class categories. Furthermore, a Guardian/ICM poll conducted in October 2007 showed that 89 per cent of the sample, including the majority of 18 to 24 year olds who took part believed that social class was still a significant influence on their lives.

Postmodernists also ignore the fact that, for many, consumption – i.e. the ability to buy designer labels and so on – depends on having a job and an income. Poverty is going to limit any desire to pursue a postmodern lifestyle. In other words, consumption – what we buy – depends ultimately on social class.

Key terms

Altruism putting the interests of society and others before self-interest.

Conservative belief in traditional ways of doing things.

Cultural capital positive attitudes towards education, work, etc., based on personal experience; seen to be a middle-class characteristic.

Deferred gratification putting off rewards or pleasure in pursuit of education or training.

Employment relations how much independence and authority a person has in their job.

Extended family family units that include parents and children, as well as relatives such as grandparents, aunts, uncles and so on.

Hybrid a mix of different components.

Infant mortality the number of child deaths at birth and in the first year of life for every 1000 children born.

Kinship relatives.

Market conditions the value of your job in terms of pay, pension, fringe benefits, promotion opportunities, etc.

Meritocracy the idea that achievement is solely the result of intelligence, talent, skill and hard work, rather than inheritance or luck.

Mutual support a system of social, economic and emotional supports, commonly found in traditional working-class communities.

Non-manual jobs that require mental rather than manual labour.

Old-boy network a system of economic and social supports maintained by ex-public-school boys in adulthood.

Old school-tie network see old-boy network above.

Public schools exclusive, elite and expensive private schools, such as Eton College.

Social closure the process by which the upper class maintain wealth and privilege, e.g. by keeping marriage within the class, by sending children to expensive schools.

Underclass a class subculture generally made up of the poor.

Urban living in the city (as opposed to the countryside).

Check your understanding

1 What is 'social closure' and how does the upper class ensure it?

2 Identify four groups that make up the middle classes. How do they differ from one another?

3 What are the main components of traditional working-class identity?

4 What economic and social factors have led to a dramatic fall in the number of traditional manual workers?

5 How do the new working class differ from the traditional working class?

6 Identify the main arguments for and against the idea that a deviant underclass exists in the UK's inner cities.

Activities

Research idea

Watch the DVDs of *Brassed Off* and *The Full Monty*. How are the working classes portrayed in these films? How are social and economic changes affecting working-class values and behaviour, according to these films?

Web.task

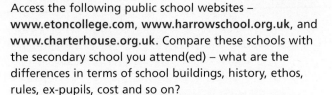

Access the following public school websites – www.etoncollege.com, www.harrowschool.org.uk, and www.charterhouse.org.uk. Compare these schools with the secondary school you attend(ed) – what are the differences in terms of school buildings, history, ethos, rules, ex-pupils, cost and so on?

Item A

Sociological definitions of social class are usually based on the idea that they are large groups of people who share significant things in common. For example, the manual working class has, on average, poorer health chances than the middle class.

Members of a class also tend to share a common culture and identity with others of their class. For example, members of the middle class not only have more wealth than the working class, but they also are said to possess more cultural capital.

Members of a social class maintain a shared identity by following a similar lifestyle and holding similar values to one another.

Item B

Some sociologists have argued that social class is becoming less and less relevant as a source of identity for people in today's society. For example, it has been argued that traditional working-class identity is disappearing. This identity was based on what Goldthorpe and Lockwood described as the 'solidaristic collectivism' of manual workers in manufacturing, mining, engineering, shipbuilding and other heavy industries.

These workers regarded individual advancement as impossible and instead sought to improve their position by collective action in trade unions and by voting Labour, which they saw as the party of the working class. They identified strongly with other manual workers and had a two-class, 'them-and-us' view of society, seeing themselves as a distinct class with separate interests opposed to those of the employers or capitalist class.

Some sociologists argue that this traditional working-class identity is being replaced by a new working-class identity based on individualism rather than collectivism.

(a) Explain what sociologists mean by 'cultural capital' (Item A). (2 marks)

(b) Suggest two characteristics of a social class other than those mentioned in Item A. (4 marks)

(c) Identify three aspects of lifestyle or values that help to maintain the identity of the upper class (Item A). (6 marks)

(d) Using information from item B and elsewhere, assess the view that traditional class identities are no longer important. (24 marks)

Grade booster   Getting top marks in the 24-mark question

You could begin by making use of Item B to outline the idea of traditional working-class identity. Discuss the possible reasons for its decline, such as the decline of manufacturing industry, as well as the characteristics of the 'new' working class, such as their voting patterns. You can evaluate in various ways, e.g. by linking your answer to different perspectives (e.g. Marxism, postmodernism) or using evidence that shows most people still think of themselves as belonging to a class and see society in terms of classes. Note that the question refers to 'identities' plural, so don't just focus on working-class identity – look at other class identities too (e.g. upper- and middle-class and underclass identities). Is it true that these are in decline?

TOPIC 4

Gender and sexuality

Getting you thinking

<< A visit to Isabella Mackay's home is like a walk through the pages of *Little Women*. She opens the door wearing a pretty pink blouse, children hiding in her flowing skirt. Isabella has some interesting ideas about motherhood. She says 'I could no more go out to work, abandon my children or disobey my husband than I could grow an extra head. I don't have any of the modern woman's confusion about her role in life. From the day I was born, I knew I was destined to be a wife and mother. By the age of 16, 1 knew that all I really wanted from life was to get married, have children and make a lovely home. That was my ambition.'

She not only believes that a mother's place is in the home, but that the feminist movement is a 'dangerous cancer and perversion'. The world, she says, would be a better place if the Equal Opportunities Commission was shut down and workplace crèches were scrapped. The rape-within-marriage law should be abolished too. She says 'in the rare event of a wife refusing sex with her husband, he has every right, perhaps even a duty, to take her as gently as possible. Once a woman is married she loses the right to say no to her husband's advances. The female role is a submissive one. The male role is assertive and aggressive.' >>

1 List the stereotypical and non-stereotypical masculine and feminine characteristics that come to mind on first seeing the images above.

2 What aspects of Isabella Mackay's view of femininity do you agree or disagree with?

Gender-role socialization

When examining the source of our identities as males and females, sociologists distinguish between the concepts of '**sex**' and '**gender**'. The term 'sex' refers to the biological differences between males and females, e.g. chromosomes, hormones, menstruation and genitalia. The concept of gender, however, refers to the cultural expectations that society associates with 'masculinity' and 'femininity'. Men and women are expected to conform to expectations about 'masculine' and 'feminine' behaviour. Such expectations are not fixed – they change over time and are often different in other cultures.

Gender expectations are transmitted to the next generation through **gender-role socialization**. Sociologists believe that gender differences between males and females are largely the result of society's expectations. Sociologists therefore argue that masculinity and femininity are **socially constructed** rather than being the product of biology.

Hegemonic definitions of masculinity and femininity

A very traditional set of ideas about how men and women are supposed to behave in the UK has dominated our culture until fairly recently. Connell (2002) refers to these ideas as **hegemonic** masculinity and femininity. This set of ideas has allocated very distinct family roles to men and women. Women were expected to occupy the maternal role and to take on much of the responsibility for housework, whereas men were expected to be the head of the household and the economic breadwinner. A range of characteristics were associated with males and females that were seen to shape their behaviour. For example, females were expected to show emotion and affection openly – it was regarded as perfectly acceptable for females to cry or to kiss, hug and hold hands with each other in public. Men and boys, in contrast, were not expected to show their emotions – rather aggression, rationality and toughness were seen as positive characteristics for males to have.

The family and gender-role socialization

Sociologists note that from an early age, infants and children are trained to conform to social expectations about their gender. Much of this training goes on in the family during primary socialization. Oakley (1982) identifies four processes central to the construction of gender identity:

- **Manipulation** refers to the way in which parents encourage and reward or discourage behaviour on the basis of whether it is appropriate for the child's sex. For example, a mother may encourage her daughter to see her appearance as all important, while a father may encourage a son to take part in sports or discourage him from crying.
- **Canalization** refers to the way in which parents direct children's interests into toys and play activities that are seen as normal for that sex.
- Domestic activities – Daughters may have cultural expectations about their future responsibilities reinforced by mothers insisting they help with housework.
- Verbal appellations – Parents may reinforce cultural expectations by referring to daughters and sons using stereotypical feminine and masculine descriptions such as 'pretty' and 'handsome'.

Gender codes

Gender-role socialization, therefore, involves the learning of gender codes, which generally result in social conformity to expectations about appropriate gender behaviour. These include:

- colour codes – e.g. our parents dress boys in blue and girls in pink
- appearance codes – e.g. we learn what dress, hairstyles, cosmetics and jewellery are appropriate for males and females
- toy codes – e.g. gender-specific toys give us clues about our expected future gender roles, i.e. girls get dolls for mothering whilst boys may receive aggressive or creative toys
- play codes – e.g. boys may be expected to play boisterously whereas girls may be expected to play in more docile or decorous ways
- control codes – e.g. boys and girls are subjected to different types of social control especially when they get to their teenage years, with girls often being interrogated more closely about their social lives, boyfriends, etc., than boys.

Statham (1986) found that by the age of 5, most children have acquired a clear gender identity. They know what gender they belong to and they have a clear idea of what constitutes appropriate behaviour for that gender.

The education system and traditional gender-role socialization

A number of feminist studies of education in the 1970s suggested that females were underachieving because their education was regarded by teachers as less important than that of boys. Females consequently saw the educational aspect of their identity as unimportant and often left school at 16. For example, Sue Sharpe's survey of working-class girls in the early 1970s found that such experiences meant that female identity revolved around 'love, marriage, husbands, children, jobs and careers, more or less in that order' (Sharpe 1994).

The mass media and traditional gender-role socialization

Billington et al. (1998) argue that the mass media has traditionally portrayed masculinity as dominant and femininity as subordinate, so that women were generally represented on television in a narrow range of social roles, whereas men were shown performing the full range of social and occupational roles. Women were rarely shown in high-status occupational roles; rather they tended to be overrepresented in domestic settings – as busy housewives, contented mothers, eager consumers and so on. Women were often presented as sexual objects to be enjoyed by men. The most extreme media version of this is pornography and 'Page 3 girls' in newspapers.

Criticizing gender-role socialization

The idea of gender-role socialization has been criticized on two main counts:

- The experiences of men and women vary greatly. There are huge differences in the experience of socialization because of factors such ethnicity, social class and age. Most accounts of gender socialization ignore these differences. For example, there is evidence that socialization into gender roles in Asian families may be more traditional and hegemonic than that found in other ethnic groups. See Topic 5 for further evidence of these processes.
- It is assumed that women passively accept the traditional gender identity imposed on them. It neglects the choices that people have in developing an identity and the fact that many women and men resist attempts to make them conform to hegemonic gender stereotypes. This can be illustrated with reference to recent social changes.

Social change and masculine identity in the 21st century

Bob Connell argues that masculinity today is experiencing change. There now exist, in addition to the hegemonic type of masculinity, other alternative types of masculinity:

- Some sociologists suggest that a '**new man**' has emerged in the last ten years who is more in touch with his feminine and emotional feelings and who shares childcare and housework with his female partner. However, others have suggested that this is merely a creation of the advertising industry and that surveys show that although men have increased their share of domestic and childcare tasks, true equality within the home is still a long way off.

- Mort (1996) has highlighted the emergence of **metrosexual** men – these are heterosexual males who are concerned with image and consequently invest in personal grooming products such as designer label fashion, hair conditioners and skin care products. David Beckham is often cited as a prime example of metrosexual man.

Focus on research

Linda McDowell (2001)
Young men leaving school: White working-class masculinity

Drawing on interviews with 23 young men in Cambridge and Sheffield in the year following the end of their compulsory schooling, this in-depth study explores young White working-class men and the ways in which they talk about their masculinity.

All the men had been classified as low achievers by their schools and, without exception, they were dismissive of their school experiences and anxious to leave. In both cities, the participants stressed being able to stick up for themselves if need be and to sort out any challenges. In their conversations they were casually sexist, often dismissive or at best tolerant of their female peers.

In their leisure time these young men moved between typical 'laddish' behaviour and more responsible behaviour. Many had a clearly gender-divided social life, going out with their girlfriend on Friday or Saturday but definitely not both.
One evening was strictly reserved for going out 'with me mates', usually to play pool or snooker in pubs, or sometimes to go clubbing. Although a small number  admitted to drinking too much and to occasional fighting, more commonly they stressed that they were not trouble-makers.

McDowell, L. (2001) *Young Men Leaving School: White working-class masculinity*, York: Joseph Rowntree Foundation

1 How did the men in this study express their masculinity?

2 In what ways might these men be experiencing a crisis of masculinity?

3 How would you criticize this research?

- Homosexuality was **decriminalized** in the 1960s and is becoming part of the mainstream. However, despite greater cultural tolerance, it still generally devalued as a masculine form and is often the subject of negative stereotyping.

Mac an Ghaill (1996) claims that hegemonic masculinity may be experiencing a '**crisis of masculinity**' because of the decline of traditional industries and the resulting unemployment. Work is central to the identity of traditional men, and unemployment can therefore lead to a loss of self-esteem and status as well as a loss of identification with others. Younger males may see their futures as bleak and so view schooling and qualifications as irrelevant to their needs. This may reinforce educational failure as they seek alternative sources of status in activities in which they can stress their masculinity, such as delinquency and gang violence.

However, although masculinity has undergone some change, it would be a mistake to exaggerate these trends. Collier (2002), for example, notes that lads' magazines still objectify women in an explicitly sexual fashion. Some of these magazines, most notably, *Loaded*, *Zoo* and *Nuts*, actively assert traditional notions of masculinity by celebrating 'birds, booze and football'. There is a whole media industry devoted to encouraging women to perfect their figure, make-up and sexual desirability for the benefit of men. The male equivalent of such media does not really exist.

Social change and feminine identity

Today, female achievement at all levels of the examination system outstrips that of males (although a significant number of working-class females continue to underachieve). This success is partly the result of educational initiatives such as Girls Into Science and Technology (GIST), coursework and a national curriculum that aimed to prevent the gender-stereotyping of subject choice. However, the main cause is probably the profound changes that the economy has experienced in the last 25 years. Changes in demand for British goods and the **globalization of the economy** have led to changes in the labour market, particularly a decline in traditional industries such as mining, iron and steel, heavy engineering, etc. (which mainly employed men). Whilst demand for men's jobs fell, there was a corresponding expansion in the **service sector** of the economy, i.e. white-collar and professional jobs in financial and government services, managers of retail outlets in new shopping centres, and so on. Most of these new jobs were aimed at employing women.

Genderquake and feminine identity

It is argued by sociologists such as Wilkinson (1994) and Sharpe (1994) that the increasing participation and success of women in the world of paid work mean that traditional notions of female identity are being abandoned. Helen Wilkinson (1994) argues that there has been a fundamental shift in values and attitudes amongst women aged under 35. She argues that this shift is so dramatic that it amounts to a '**genderquake**' and has led to a profound change in the distribution of power between men and women.

Wilkinson argues that the **feminization of the economy and the workplace** has led to a revolution in women's ambitions. Family commitments no longer have priority in women's lives; careers and economic independence are now the defining feature of young women's identity and self-esteem. Younger women and girls are encouraged to think along these lines because they are likely to experience the positive role model of a mother who enjoys a career rather than just a part-time job. Some young women may even choose voluntary childlessness and a career as an alternative to getting married and having children.

Sharpe's study (1994) suggests that young females are becoming more assertive about their rights and are now more likely to rank education and career above marriage and family as priorities in their lives. Moreover, there are signs that women are now more willing to use divorce to escape husbands who insist on their wives playing a subordinate domestic role. Consequently, hegemonic versions of femininity, i.e. being a good mother and housewife – the traditional domestic role – may be becoming less significant in terms of female identity.

Consumption, leisure and feminine identity

Increasing economic independence means that women are now viewed as significant consumers. There are signs that mass-media products are increasingly being targeted at single women. This means that young women today are also likely to see consumption and leisure as key factors in their identity. Such processes have supposedly led to the emergence of 'girl power' and '**ladettes**', who are increasingly adopting male forms of behaviour, such as drinking and smoking heavily, and being sexually aggressive.

Identity and sexuality

Homosexuality and identity

In the UK, heterosexuality has been traditionally defined as the dominant and ideal form of sexuality because of its links to reproduction. In contrast, homosexuality was seen in the early part of the 20th century as a form of deviant or abnormal sexuality. Some saw it as a type of mental illness brought about by factors such as too much mothering and the lack of a strong father figure. In the UK, homosexual activity between men was made illegal in the 19th century and was punishable by prison. Many homosexual men were subjected to electric shock treatment in the 1950s and 1960s in an attempt to 'cure' them of their condition.

These **repressive** attempts to control homosexuality made it exceptionally difficult for gay men to 'come out' and publicly declare their homosexuality. However, in the 1950s, cultural attitudes towards homosexuality began to shift, and homosexual acts between consenting adults over the age of 21 years were decriminalized in the 1960s. By the 1970s, homosexuality was no longer defined as a psychiatric condition by doctors. These social changes support Weeks' (2003) view that sexuality is the product of culture rather than biology.

As Taylor (1997) notes, female homosexuals, i.e. lesbians, have always had a much lower social profile than gay men. As we have seen, the law generally criminalized gay men until the 1960s, but this was rarely the case with gay women. Changes in the law, changing cultural attitudes towards homosexuality and the feminization of education and the economy benefited lesbian women; many sought to bring about greater social change for women in general by becoming involved in the **radical-feminist** movement, which sees political and sexual separateness from men as a necessity if patriarchy is to be overcome.

Gay subculture

By the 1970s, a distinct gay subculture could be seen to have emerged in British culture. Rich (1984) suggests that the eventual emergence of gay and lesbian subcultures is remarkable considering that Western societies tend to be characterized by a fierce '**compulsory heterosexuality**'. Hegemonic masculinity states that 'real men' are not homosexuals. The mass media constantly subject people to heterosexual images through films, television programmes and advertising. Religious organizations criticize homosexuality as sinful, wicked and immoral. Homosexuality is rarely portrayed as a normal or ideal condition.

Homosexuality, leisure and consumption

Much of the gay subculture that emerged from the 1970s focused on leisure and consumption – the 'pink pound' or spending power of gay professionals was targeted by gay bars, clubs and restaurants. At the same time, gay culture became politicized as gays sought to assert their identity. Organizations such as Stonewall actively sought changes in the law so that homosexuals enjoyed the same rights as heterosexuals whilst the Terrence Higgins Trust sought to educate the general public about AIDS and particularly aimed to counter the myth perpetrated by a homophobic tabloid media in the UK that homosexuals were mainly susceptible to, and hence responsible for, the HIV virus. Furthermore, in cities such as London, Brighton and Manchester, Gay Pride marches sought to increase the visibility and social acceptability of gay people. These strategies, aided by the increasing number of celebrities coming out as gay, have undoubtedly made it easier for gay people to lead a normal life today, although it should also be acknowledged that **prejudice** and **discrimination** have not totally disappeared. Unfortunately, homophobic attacks on gay people are still relatively common and suggest that this type of sexuality is not totally accepted by all sections of the community.

Heterosexuality and identity

Heterosexuality too is the product of culture rather than biology and this can be illustrated by examining the way that definitions of sexual attractiveness have changed over the course of the last 100 years in Western societies. Studies of 18th- and 19th-century paintings suggest that the ideal of feminine beauty in this period stressed plump women, whilst even in the 1950s, female sexual icons such as Marilyn Monroe were much bigger women than the waif-like supermodels and celebrities favoured by the fashion industry and championed by the media today.

Some feminist sociologists have suggested that these types of media representations of femininity may be responsible for eating disorders in modern societies. Hunt (2001) argues that 'the media recognize society's obsession with looking slim and perpetuate the idea that slimness equals success, health, happiness and popularity' (p.5). Although images of an ideal male body are increasingly being portrayed in the media, there is little sign that this is having the equivalent effect upon males.

Another clue that suggests that heterosexuality is socially constructed rather than being the product of biology is the double standard that exists with regard to comparable male and female sexual behaviour. There exists an assumption that males and females have different sexual identities. Males are supposed to be promiscuous predators (they supposedly want to have sex with as many women as possible), whereas females are supposed to be passive and more interested in love than sex. Because of this, women's sexual identity carries risks. Lees (1986) found that they may be subjected to being labelled a 'slag' or a 'slapper' by both men and other women if they appear to behave in similar ways to men.

Key terms

Canalization parental attempts to make sure children play with gender-appropriate toys, etc.

Compulsory heterosexuality the idea that culture automatically socializes its members into heterosexual roles.

Crisis of masculinity the idea that men who have been brought up in traditional ways might feel confused or anxious about the loss of their role as breadwinners, etc.

Decriminalization legalization, no longer criminal.

Discrimination treating someone unfairly because of their sexuality, race, age, etc.

Feminization of the economy/workplace the fact that most available new jobs are for women rather than men.

Gender the behaviour that culture associates with femininity and masculinity.

Genderquake the radical change in attitudes, especially towards education and work, experienced by younger women compared with women of previous generations.

Gender-role socialization the process by which people learn how to act in feminine or masculine ways.

Globalization of the economy the trend towards manufacturing goods more cheaply abroad, e.g. in China, which has contributed to the decline in British industry.

Hegemonic cultural dominance.

Ladettes girls who behave like boys.

Manipulation parental encouragement of gender-appropriate behaviour and disapproval of gender-inappropriate behaviour.

Metrosexual males who spend a lot of time and money on personal grooming.

New Man a caring, sharing male in touch with his own and his female partner's emotions.

Prejudice a preformed opinion, usually an unfavourable one, based on insufficient knowledge, irrational feelings or inaccurate stereotypes.

Radical feminism a set of sociological ideas that essentially sees men as repressing and exploiting women.

Repressive oppressive and exploitative.

Service sector that sector of the economy that provides services, e.g. financial or retail services, rather than manufactures goods.

Sex the biological differences between men and women.

Socially constructed produced by society, i.e. manufactured by culture rather than biologically inherited.

Check your understanding

1 Identify three differences between 'sex' and 'gender'.

2 Explain, using examples, what is meant by 'hegemonic' masculinity and femininity.

3 Explain why the family is the most important agency of gender-role socialization.

4 How do mass media representations of masculinity and femininity reinforce traditional stereotypes about men and women?

5 How have economic and social changes contributed to the emergence of new types of femininity and masculinity?

6 How have sexual identities evolved over the last 50 years?

Activities

Research idea

Get hold of at least two toy catalogues or catalogues that include toys. Analyse any links between gender and the presentation of the catalogues. Are girls or boys pictured playing with toys? Do the pictures reflect or challenge typical gender roles? Are some toys targeted more at girls and others more at boys? Which are targeted at which? How can you tell?

Web.tasks

1 Visit the web-site **www.theory.org.uk** and click on the link 'Media, Gender and Identity' – this will take you through to a range of resources on femininity and masculinity produced by David Gauntlett and his students, as well as internet links to various sites celebrating masculinity and femininity.

2 Find the website **www.feminist.com**. Access their 'Resources' page and pick an article that relates to some aspect of femininity. What social changes or issues are important to women today according to this website?

Item A

Sexuality or sexual orientation refers to a person's sexual preference – for example, heterosexual, homosexual (gay or lesbian) or bisexual. How far sexuality is biologically rather than socially constructed has been greatly debated, but there is some evidence for the latter view. For example, in Victorian England, the ideal of feminine beauty and sexual attractiveness – the characteristics that heterosexual men find desirable – differed from today's ideal: Victorian men found plump women attractive, whereas today the ideal seems to be much thinner.

There have also been changes in the social construction of homosexuality. The dominant 'hegemonic masculinity' in British society has traditionally defined gay men as effeminate (and lesbian women as 'butch' or masculine). However, recently this definition has been challenged, particularly since the 1970s, with the emergence of a distinctive gay and lesbian subculture.

Item B

Unlike sex, which refers to biological differences between males and females, gender is seen as a socially constructed difference. It refers to the cultural expectations concerning how males and females should act. In other words, gender is a set of norms regulating the behaviour of men and women.

Evidence that gender is a social construct comes from the fact that what is perceived as normal or even required behaviour for men or women in one group or society and at one point in time, may be seen as abnormal or even intolerable at another.

There is evidence that gender expectations and gender identity have been undergoing considerable change in Britain and other industrialized countries in the last 40 years or so. For example, many women no longer see marriage and the family – and especially the housewife role within it – as the main source of their gender identity. Sociologists see these shifts in gender identity as the product of a number of social, economic, political and cultural factors.

(a) Explain what sociologists mean by the idea that sexuality is 'socially constructed' (Item A). (2 marks)

(b) Identify two features of hegemonic masculinity (Item A). (4 marks)

(c) Suggest three reasons for the emergence of a gay and lesbian subculture since the 1960s (Item A). (6 marks)

(d) Using information from Item B and elsewhere, assess the view that there have been major changes in gender identity in the last 40 years. (24 marks)

Grade booster Getting top marks in the 24-mark question

You need to look at both male and female gender identities and how far each of these has changed, and at reasons for such changes. Make use of information from the Item. This includes the notion of social construction of gender identity, and the idea that the changes are the result of social and economic factors. You should go on to identify and discuss some of these – for example, changes in women's position as a result of changes in education, career opportunities, consumption patterns and the role of the mass media. You should contrast this with the ideas about women's identity put forward by traditional hegemonic femininity. Changes in men's gender identity can be considered in terms of similar factors.

Ethnicity and nationality

Getting you thinking

Rachel Billington: <<When I go away for holidays to Europe, I am conscious of 'being abroad', of being a foreigner. My passport bears the legend 'European Community' and states that I am a 'British Citizen'. While abroad, despite being dressed in what appears to be the inconspicuous clothes of a middle-aged, middle-class woman, I notice that people frequently address me in English, even before I have spoken. During a stay in the USA which, despite the dominance of the English language, felt 'foreign' to me, I was approached in shops and other places by people who noted my English accent, welcomed me to America, told me about their trips to England and, sometimes, their English ancestors. A sizeable audience for a university lecture I gave was explained to me in terms of the novelty of hearing a 'real English accent'! Formally asked my nationality, I usually reply 'British'. Asked to describe myself to people of other nationalities I say I am English. If asked to write an autobiographical piece, I probably would not include either of these two identities.>>

Source: Billington R. *et al* (1998) *Exploring Self and Society*, Basingstoke: MacMillan

Colin Wong: <<My parents arrived in England in the early 1960s from Hong Kong. They settled in rented accommodation in Liverpool working long hours in various poorly paid jobs in local Chinese restaurants and shops. Growing up in a large family was bliss. Being bilingual was the norm; we spoke Cantonese with our parents and English with others. I had a Scouse accent. It was only at secondary school that I began to consider my ethnic identity. Almost overnight, the duality of my life became evident. I attended Anglican schools, yet my home life reflected Buddhism. I celebrated Easter and Christmas yet my family also celebrated Chinese New Year. During my teenage years, it was difficult to decide on my true identity. I felt English, but my adversaries would remind me of my differences to them. I felt Chinese, but I had never been beyond the UK. However, on my first visit to Hong Kong, I felt instantly comfortable with the people, the place, the language and the culture. So who am I? When I complete Ethnic Monitoring Forms, I tick the Chinese box. When I clear Customs at the airport, I walk through the European channel. When I look in the mirror, I do not see a Chinese face or an English face … I just see plain Me.>>

Source: Marsh, I. and Keating, M. (2006) *Sociology: Making Sense of Society*, Harlow: Pearson Education, p. 313

1 **What factors make up the identity of Colin Wong?**

2 **Identify five factors that make up Rachel Billington's national identity.**

Ethnicity as cultural distinctiveness

If we examine the case study above of Colin Wong, we can see that he has the specific ethnic characteristic of speaking Cantonese. He also shares racial characteristics with Chinese people, i.e. he comes from a Chinese background. Note, though, that this does not mean he subscribes to an exclusively Chinese identity. His ethnic identity is more complex than that. Rather his ethnic identity overlaps with his national identities, as well as his regional identity.

Despite these difficulties, sociologists note that significant numbers of people in the UK share an ethnic identity, i.e. they recognize that they share cultural characteristics, and that their **ethnicity** is distinctive compared to the majority White and **Anglo-Saxon** culture. These characteristics include:

- *Common descent* – This may be represented by colour or other racial characteristics, e.g. Modood's (1997) research suggests that being Black is an important source of identity for young African-Caribbeans.
- *Geographical origins* – Links with a country of origin are important, and ethnic identity may involve seeing oneself as 'Pakistani' or 'Indian' or 'Irish' first and foremost.
- *History* – Members of minority ethnic cultures may share a sense of struggle and oppression, which originates in particular historical contexts, such as slavery, colonialism or persecution. For example, Jewish identity may be partially shaped by events like the Holocaust during the Second World War, while some African-Caribbeans may feel that the fact that they are descendants of slaves is central to their identity.
- *Language* – Members of particular groups may speak the language(s) of their country of origin at home, e.g. older-generation Chinese people may speak in Cantonese, while

young British-Pakistani Muslims may talk to each other in a combination of Urdu and English.

- *Religion* – This is the most important influence for some ethnic-minority groups, e.g. some Pakistanis will see themselves first and foremost as Muslim.
- *Traditions and rituals* – These may be religious or cultural, e.g. the Notting Hill Carnival, which is held annually in the UK to celebrate African-Caribbean culture.
- *Racism* – Prejudice and discrimination may be experienced and may take several forms, e.g. name-calling, police harassment, violence, and so on.

Ethnic minorities

In Britain, ethnicity is mainly associated with minority groups from the former British colonies on the Indian subcontinent, in the Caribbean and in Africa. However, this kind of categorization can be a problem because it emphasizes skin colour rather than common cultural characteristics. In doing so, it ignores significant White minority ethnic groups resident in the UK, such as Jews, gypsies and Irish people.

Ethnic identity and primary socialization

Singh Ghumann (1999) suggests that the first generation of Asian parents to arrive in the UK in the 1950s and 1960s were concerned to transmit the following key values to their children during primary socialization in the family:

- Children should be obedient, loyal to and respectful of their elders and community around them. Social conformity was demanded.
- Parents were considered to know best the interests of their children regardless of the child's age.
- The choice of marriage partner was thought to be best left to parents.
- Religious training was considered very important because it reinforced respect for family and stressed humility rather than self-pride and assertiveness.
- The role of the mother tongue was seen as crucial in maintaining links between generations. Children therefore tended to be bilingual, and were often able to use both the mother language, e.g. Urdu, Punjabi, Gujerati or Hindi, and English interchangeably.

Many of these family socialization practices are still the norm today. For example, Singh Ghumann (1999) found that Asian families – whether Hindu, Muslim or Sikh – socialize children into a pattern of duty, obligation and loyalty to the extended family community, as well as religious commitment, which, in most cases, they accept. The concept of corporate or family honour (*izzat*) is particularly important in Muslim kinship relations. Consequently, even when they leave home, children will often continue to live near their parents and visit them regularly.

Ethnic identity and arranged marriage

Evidence suggests continuing strong support for arranged marriages across all Asian groups, even among the young.

Hennink *et al.* (1999) found that 75 per cent of Sikh and 85 per cent of Muslim teenage girls expected an arranged marriage. Singh Ghumann (1999) notes that this is the product of successful socialization into a **collectivist** family culture that stresses obedience, loyalty to and respect for elders. Brah (1993) notes that the majority of Asian adolescents felt confident that they would not be forced into a marriage they did not want. Arranged marriage, then, was regarded as a joint undertaking with scope for negotiation.

Ethnic identity and potential family conflict

Anwar (1981) suggests that the family can be a site of conflict between grandparents, parents and children. The younger generation is seen by the older generation to have mixed with people, i.e. Westerners, who have very different values and attitudes, and this has supposedly resulted in the younger generation believing in values and ideas which their parents regard as alien. This may particularly be the case with regard to young females who wish to continue into further and higher education and pursue professional careers. The older generation might believe these wishes are too ambitious and attempt to restrict females to a more traditional domestic role.

Ethnic identity and religion

Religion has a profound influence as an agency of socialization in shaping the ethnic identity of young Asians. Modood (1997) questioned two generations of Asians, African-Caribbeans and Whites about the statement: 'Religion is very important to how I live my life'. He found that those most in favour of religion were the Pakistani and Bangladeshi samples: 82 per cent of the age 50+ sample and 67 per cent of the 16 to 34 year age group valued the importance of Islam in their lives. About one third of young Indians saw their religion as important. The lowest figure was for young Whites – only 5 per cent saw religion as important compared with 18 per cent of young African-Caribbeans.

Modood notes that the centrality of religion in Asian communities – and therefore in shaping their ethnic identity – can be illustrated in the fact that very few Asians marry across religious or **caste** lines, and that most of their children will be socialized into a religious value system. Singh Ghumann notes that the mosque is the centre for the religious, educational and political activities of Muslim communities and these religious institutions often exert a strong influence on the way parents rear and educate their children.

African-Caribbean identity

Modood (1997) found that skin colour is an important source of identity to many young African-Caribbeans. Some African-Caribbean youth stress their Black identity because of their experience of racial prejudice and discrimination from White society. Black pride and power may be celebrated, especially if Black youth perceives itself to be deliberately excluded from jobs or stereotyped by White people – in particular, by symbols of White authority such as teachers and the police.

African–Caribbean identity and peer group pressure

The African-Caribbean sociologist, Tony Sewell (1996) argues that peer-group pressure is extremely influential in shaping ethnic identity among disaffected African-Caribbean youth in British inner cities and that this is probably partly responsible for educational underachievement and the high levels of unemployment found in this group.

He argues that African-Caribbean male identity is focused on being a **hyper-male** and 'gangsta' in the eyes of their peers. This, he claims, often compensates for the lack of a father figure in the lives of many of these teenagers, i.e. many live in one-parent families headed by their mothers. Furthermore, Sewell notes that this street identity is partly shaped by media agencies such as advertising and MTV, which encourage young African-Caribbean males to subscribe to a consumer culture that views material things such as clothing, trainers, jewellery (i.e. 'bling') as more important than education.

Mixed-race identity

Recently, sociologists have observed that intermarriage, especially between Whites and African-Caribbeans, has risen considerably. As a result, more mixed-race children are being born. Tizard and Phoenix (1993) found that 60 per cent of the mixed-race children in their sample were proud of their mixed parentage, but they noted that 'it is still not an easy ride to be of mixed Black and White parentage in our society because of racism from both White and Black populations'.

Hybrid or dual identities

There is some evidence that ethnic identities are evolving and modern hybrid forms are now developing among Britain's younger ethnic-minority citizens. Johal (1998) focused on second- and third-generation British-Asians. He found that they have a **dual identity** in that they inherit an Asian identity and adopt a British one. This results in Asian youth adopting a 'White mask' in order to interact with White peers at school or college, but emphasizing their cultural difference whenever they feel it is necessary. He notes that many British-Asians adopt 'hybrid identities'. They select aspects of British, Asian and global culture relating to fashion, music and food in order to construct their identity. For example, many young British-Asians like Bhangra music – a mixture of Punjabi music married to Western rhythms.

National identity

National identity can be defined as 'the feeling of being part of a larger community in the form of a nation, which gives a sense of purpose and meaning to people's lives as well as a sense of belonging'.

National identity is not necessarily the same thing as **nationality**. The latter concept is a formal, legal category that derives from belonging to a 'nation-state', i.e. a country recognized by other countries as exercising authority and power over a geographical territory. Nationality is symbolized by legal rights, such as being able to carry a passport, being able to marry legally or vote at a particular age. It also involves certain duties, such as obeying the law of the land. The crime of 'treason', i.e. betraying one's country, is seen as one of the most heinous crimes one can commit.

It is important to recognize that the legal status of being British, i.e. formal nationality, does not necessarily mean that people will subscribe to a British identity. Many citizens of the United Kingdom, defined as British in the law, identify with 'nations within the nation', i.e. they see themselves primarily as English, Scottish, Welsh or Irish. Moreover, many British subjects may see their national identity as primarily tied up with their country or region of origin, and so see themselves as African-Caribbean, Punjabi, Bengali, Pakistani, etc. Others may subscribe first and foremost to identities deriving from their religious affiliations, such as Muslim or Jewish.

British national identity

The British are essentially a 'mongrel nation', i.e. a mix of social and immigrant groups that have settled in Britain since Roman times. As Guibernau and Goldblatt (2000) note, no case can be made for a single, original, authentic group of Britons. They note that until the 1707 Act of Union that linked Scotland to England and Wales there was no such thing as a British national identity. People identified more with the regions in which they lived than with a loyalty to the British nation-state.

However, Guibernau and Goldblatt argue that a sense of British identity was gradually created around five key themes:

- *Geography* – the fact that Britain is an island gave it a clear sense of boundaries that made it distinct from Europe. A result of this is that very few British people have identified themselves as European.
- *Religion* – Protestantism is the dominant religious identity of Great Britain. People who do not attend church on a regular basis still identify themselves as Church of England. In times of national celebration, such as royal weddings or disaster and remembrance of the war-dead, religion plays a central role in the proceedings. In the courts, people still swear to tell the truth using the Bible and the National Anthem asks God to look after the Queen, the ultimate symbol of the British nation.
- *War* – Wars have reinforced the sense of 'them' versus 'us' and especially the uniquely British themes of self-sacrifice, perseverance, fair play, heroism and putting up with exceptional hardship. Think, for example, about the sense of Britishness associated with historical events such as the London Blitz and Dunkirk. Public ceremonies and celebrations marking events such as the end of the Second World War symbolize both individual sacrifice for the nation and the preservation of the British way of life.
- *The British Empire* – Britain's success as an **imperial** power in the 18th and 19th centuries brought economic success and a sense of pride and achievement in what was perceived as British superiority over other cultures and races.
- *Monarchy* – The cultural symbols of British nationality, in particular, the anthem *God Save the Queen* and the Union Jack were invented in order to place the monarchy at the

heart of British identity. The outpouring of grief after the death of Diana, Princess of Wales, in 1997 illustrated very clearly how deeply the British feel about such symbols.

National identity and socialization

Schudsen (1994) points out that the British people are socialized into a British identity in several ways:

- *A common language* – English is seen as central to our cultural identity.
- *Education* – The teaching of history, English literature and religion in British schools tends to promote national identity. For example, Shakespeare is often proudly described as the world's greatest playwright, while traditional history teaching often focuses on Britain's positive achievements at the expense of such negative British activities as slavery, massacres and exploitation. The Education Reform Act (1988) stresses Christian worship in schools, despite the fact that the UK is a **multicultural** society.
- *National rituals* – Royal and state occasions are used to reinforce the British way of life, and the public are invited to take part, usually via television, e.g. the Cenotaph ceremony on Remembrance Sunday. Rituals unite us in Britishness. Think about how other uniquely British rituals, e.g. the changing of the guard, the State opening of Parliament, royal weddings and funerals, the Queen's televised Christmas speech and even Bonfire Night, do this.
- *Symbols* – These include styles of dress, uniforms, passports, styles of music, national anthems, and particularly, flags. The Union Jack is symbolic of Britishness, especially of the British Empire, the Queen and Parliament. It often indicates tradition and **patriotism**, especially during wartime or at sporting events.
- *The mass media* – Television, magazines and newspapers encourage people to identify with national symbols such as the Royal Family by taking a keen interest in their activities. Members of the Royal Family are treated as celebrities and their lives are closely scrutinized. The media also play a key role in reinforcing our sense of national identity by talking up British achievement. In times of war, the media focus on 'our boys', while sporting events such as the Olympic Games are reported almost as quasi-wars against other nations.
- *The mass production of fashion and taste* – Britishness can also be embodied in particular foods, e.g. fish and chips, and consumer goods such as the Rolls-Royce car and retail outlets such as Marks and Spencer.

Focus on research

Mark Urban (1999) English Identity

Urban's research confirms that people's sense of English identity differs according to factors such as region, ethnicity and age. He showed two videos of national images to focus groups around the country. Both concentrated on British themes: one on the traditional defiance of outsiders, the other on love of personal freedom. The 'traditional' video contained shots of war, the monarchy and emphasized teamwork. This video drew a very positive response from older audiences, especially those outside London. The 'liberal' tape featured images of innovation, freedom and tolerance, along with pictures of Shakespeare, the Notting Hill Carnival, great British inventions and Lenny Henry. Many people in London identified with these images, but people in the provinces were less convinced that these images represented Englishness and were less likely to identify with the images of race and multiculturalism.

Urban, M. (1999) 'Which is the true face of England?', *The Guardian*, 5 May 1999

1 **How did the contents of the two videos represent Britishness?**

2 **What factors influenced people's choice of images to represent Britishness?**

The decline of British identity

Waters (1995) suggests that British identity may be under threat in the 21st century for four reasons, outlined below.

Celtic identity

Celtic identity, especially Welsh and Scottish identity, has always been a powerful source of identity in those countries, and has recently been given political and legal legitimacy in the form of a Scottish Parliament and Welsh Assembly, which have the power to introduce legislation on a wide range of issues.

There is evidence that people in Wales are more likely to stress Welsh identity at the expense of Britishness, which historically has always been associated with Englishness. For example, a Labour Force Survey in 2001 found that 87 per cent of people born in Wales saw themselves as Welsh only.

Globalization

Globalization is becoming more significant as **transnational** companies and international financial markets increasingly dominate world trade. British identity may be diluted, as some British companies and products are taken over by foreign companies, while others close down their factories in the UK and move production to the cheaper developing countries. There are also concerns that American culture is taking over the British high street, as companies such as McDonald's, Starbucks and Borders expand their British operations. Moreover, television programmes, films and music are increasingly being produced for the international market. There are fears that these largely American products may erode Britishness and create a single commercialized culture offering superficial mass entertainment.

Multiculturalism

The multicultural nature of British society seems to be having an effect on our sense of British or national identity. The survey by Modood (1997) of ethnic-minority groups found that most of his second-generation sample thought of themselves as mostly – but not entirely – culturally and socially British. A survey conducted in March 2005 by ICM found that only 39 per cent of minorities saw themselves as 'fully British'. Modood (2005) found that Asians and African-Caribbeans did not feel comfortable with a 'British' identity because they felt that the majority of White people did not accept them as British because of their colour and cultural background.

English identity

Concerns have also been expressed about English identity. Research by Curtice and Heath (2000) suggests that the group who identify themselves as 'English' rather than 'British' has increased from 7 per cent of the population in 1996 to 17 per cent in 1999 (i.e. more than 6 million adults). This group are known as 'Little Englanders', with 37 per cent of this total openly admitting to being racially prejudiced.

A new form of Britishness?

Despite these negative trends, there are positive signs that a new sense of 'Britishness' is slowly emerging in the field of popular culture, especially in the worlds of food, fashion and music. It is best illustrated with the news that chicken tikka masala, a hybrid of Indian spices and English gravy, has now replaced fish and chips as the UK's most popular food. In other words, a new form of Britishness may be emerging, shaped both by 'traditional' British values and institutions, and by values and institutions that originate in the increasingly multicultural and globalized nature of UK society.

Key terms

Anglo-Saxon a White speaker of English as a first language.

Caste the Hindu system of organizing society into hereditary classes based on religious purity.

Celtic relating to Wales, Scotland and Ireland.

Collectivist group-orientated.

Dual identity hybrid identity, e.g. combination of British and Asian identity.

Ethnicity ethnic distinctiveness.

Hyper-male exaggerating masculine characteristics.

Imperial empire-building.

Multicultural lots of different cultures living side by side.

Nationality the status of belonging to a particular nation.

Patriotism proudly supporting or defending one's country and its way of life.

Transnational company one that operates across a number of countries.

Check your understanding

1   What seven factors contribute to a person's ethnic identity?

2   What sorts of values and norms are transmitted from generation to generation in the Asian family?

3   How important is religion in acquiring an ethnic identity?

4   What is 'dual' or 'hybrid' identity with regard to both ethnic and national identity?

5   Why has British identity developed in the way that it has?

6   How are people socialized into British identity?

7   How has British identity been challenged in recent years?

8   Why is English identity not as distinctive as Scottish or Welsh identity?

Activities

Research ideas

1   List 10 characteristics, images or symbols that constitute English, Welsh, Scottish and Irish identities. Visit the tourist board websites of these countries or look at holiday brochures for clues.

2   Put together two collections of photographs that constitute a 'traditional' and 'liberal' view of Britishness, just as Urban did. Show them to various samples within your college or community to see whether the views of what constitutes Britishness in your area have changed.

Web.task

Find the following websites to get to know more about ethnicity and racism in Britain:

●   Play Britkids – it's aimed at students a little younger than you but it's still worth a visit. Find it at: **www.britkid.org**

●   Test your knowledge by trying the quiz at the Institute of Race Relations site: **www.irr.org.uk/quiz/index.htm**

●   The Institute also has excellent pages about current issues. Head for **www.irr.org.uk/resources/index.htm**

Item A

Ethnicity refers to a sense of identity shared by the members of a group. That is, it involves a subjective recognition by group members that they have something important in common with one another – and something that makes them different from others. This 'something' can be a shared characteristic, such as skin colour, as in the case of 'racial' groups such as Whites or Blacks. However, while this is often an important source of ethnic identity, it is far from being the only one. For example, religion can be a source of ethnic identity, as in the case of Protestants and Catholics in Northern Ireland, or Catholics, Orthodox Christians and Muslims in the former Yugoslavia – all of whom are White. However, ethnic identities are not always clear cut, and some individuals may have 'hybrid' identities.

Item B

National identity involves, first, a belief in the existence of a social group called a 'nation' and, second, the feeling of being part of this nation. 'Nations' might seem easy to define, and nationalists tend to see them as fixed, permanent and real, but in fact they are social constructs. Definitions of what a particular nation is or should be, and what its 'national character' is – for example, what a 'true Brit' or a 'real Aussie' is – are often contested and sometimes even fought over.

Similarly, national identity may change over time. For example, in the 17th century, most of the people living in those territories that we now call Britain would not have recognized either themselves or each other as 'British'. Some would argue that the heyday of 'British' as a national identity coincides with the period of Britain's imperial power – roughly, from the late 18th to mid-20th centuries. Since then, it is suggested, British identity has been undermined by major economic, political and cultural changes.

(a) Explain what is meant by 'hybrid identities' (Item A). (2 marks)

(b) Explain the difference between nationality and national identity. (4 marks)

(c) Suggest three sources of ethnic identity apart from those referred to in Item A. (6 marks)

(d) Using information from Item B and elsewhere, examine the social factors that influence the construction of national identity. (24 marks)

Grade booster — Getting top marks in the 24-mark question

The notion that national identity is socially constructed or defined is a key sociological idea, so use examples to illustrate some of the processes involved. You could use the construction of British identity as an example. Examine factors such as language and geography, historical events such as wars, national rituals and symbols (Remembrance Sunday, the flag), agencies of socialization such as education, the media and so on. The Item suggests that national identity is contested, so you could look at how different people define Englishness (e.g. does it necessarily mean being White?). What factors today might be reshaping national identity (e.g. globalization, the EU)?

TOPIC 6

Age and disability

Getting you thinking

1 Examine the photographs of the three different age groups. List all the positive and negative characteristics that you associate with the identities of people in those age ranges.

2 What sorts of stereotypical assumptions does society make about people in wheelchairs and people with Down's syndrome? How do those assumptions affect how non-disabled people interact with disabled people?

3 What disability is associated with Heather Mills McCartney? How and why does her treatment as a disabled person differ from people confined to wheelchairs or people with Down's syndrome?

Age and identity

We have seen in previous topics that personal and social identity are shaped by social factors such as social class, gender, ethnicity and globalization. However, it is also a fact that the UK segregates its members by age, so that how young or how old people are has a significant influence on their identity. Marsh and Keating (2006, p. 358) note that age both enables us and constrains us.

<< Our age may influence where we shop, what we buy and even how we pay for our goods. Our age may affect the types of books we read, the music we listen to, the television programmes we watch, the leisure activities we engage in. Our everyday lives are shaped by the way our age is understood and expressed in the society we live in. >>

Biology and age

Biology obviously has some influence on the way that society divides people by age. Babies, infants and children are not physically or psychologically developed enough to perform adult tasks, whilst the ageing process may mean that the elderly may not be as physically or as mentally effective as they were when younger. However, sociologists point out that there are enough cultural differences across different societies and even across subcultural groups within the UK to suggest that age differences – and therefore, identities – are **socially or culturally constructed** rather than just the result of biological differences.

The social and cultural construction of age

This can be illustrated by comparing traditional pre-industrial societies with modern industrial societies such as the UK. In many traditional societies, people often do not have a precise age because births are not registered. People may not even know their birth date and so may not celebrate birthdays. In these traditional societies, people's identities in terms of their age generally go through three major stages:

● *Children* – This age group is regarded as dependent upon older groups for protection and survival.
● *Adults* – Children, usually at puberty, go through a rite of passage or initiation ceremony, in which they are instructed in adult ways. Boys may learn how to be warriors or hunters and have to go through several tests of skill and/or strength. They may also be subjected to physical change and pain, e.g. **circumcision** is common, as is the cutting of the face so that it leaves scars symbolizing manhood. Girls, too, are instructed on sexual matters so that they can become wives and mothers. Some may even undergo female circumcision. Girls can, therefore, be married and be having children shortly after puberty. An important difference between traditional and modern societies is that adolescence – the teenage years – is often not recognized as a distinct period by the former.
● *Elders* – As people get older in tribal societies, they often acquire greater status and power because they are regarded as having greater experience and wisdom than those who are younger. It is often taken for granted that a young man should defer to his elders.

Age and modern industrial societies

In contrast, in modern Western societies such as the UK, the state insist that all births are registered. It is taken for granted that people know their birth dates and that they celebrate birthdays. Bradley (1996) identifies five generational major stages in age identity in the UK. **Generations** are age groups that live through the same historical and social events, and whose common identity and attitudes are cemented by similar experiences of consuming cultural goods such as fashion, music, films, television programmes, etc.

1 Childhood

This is regarded as a special innocent time in which children are supposed to be cosseted and protected by their parents. They are supported in this enterprise by the state, which has introduced laws, e.g. various Children Acts, in order to regulate the quality of parenting. The state has also introduced legislation in order to draw up guidelines for what is acceptable behaviour for children; for example, the state has decided that schooling should be compulsory between the ages of 5 years and 16 years, and that 10 years should be the lowest age that a child can be held responsible for a criminal offence.

The experience of childhood is central to understanding age as a social construct. Some childhood experts, notably Aries (1962), argue that the experience of childhood identity has changed considerably over the last 500 years. Other commentators, such as Postman (see p. 116), argue that the nature of childhood continues to change even today. These themes of childhood identity are explored further in Topic 7 of Chapter 3.

2 Adolescence or youth

This is the period between puberty and the achievement of full adult status, i.e. the teenage years. Until the late 1960s, adulthood in the UK was usually celebrated at 21 years, but since the last part of the 20th century, 18 years has become more common – this is the age at which the state confers legal adulthood via being able to vote, to marry or leave home without parental consent, and to sit on a jury.

In the 1950s, **adolescence** or youth was recognized as a unique age group for the first time. Before this period, adolescence was generally regarded as part of adulthood because the majority of youth prior to the Second World War left school in their early teens and started work. They were not recognized as a separate social category because they were generally indistinguishable from their parents in terms of their values, tastes, behaviour, dress, etc. No specific teenage market existed for fashion, cosmetics and mass media such as films and popular music.

The postwar period saw the emergence of a **youth culture** based on specific teenage fashions, hairstyles and tastes in music, such as rock and roll, which the older generation found both shocking and threatening. This culture was the product of an increase in young people's spending power brought about by full employment in the 1950s. **Capitalist entrepreneurs** reacted to this lucrative new market by developing products specifically for youth, such as comics and magazines for teenagers, pop music, radio stations, transistor radios, fashion and cosmetics.

Studies of the mass media have focused on how youth is **demonized** by the mass media. Cohen (1980) was the first sociologist to observe how newspapers tend to sensationalize and exaggerate the behaviour of groups of young people in order to create **newsworthiness** and to sell papers. His study described how fights between two sets of youths in 1964 – labelled 'mods' and 'rockers' – produced a '**moral panic**',

Teenage rockers in the early 1960s

i.e. social anxiety about young people in general, and **'folk devils'**, with young people being blamed for the moral decline of the nation. According to Cohen, this generally illustrates how young people are seen as a 'social problem' by the older generation. Contemporary studies of the mass media's portrayal of teenagers, particularly Thornton (1995) and Savage (2007), suggest that teenagers are more frequently condemned than praised by the mass media.

However, studies of young people suggest that the **generation gap** implied by moral panics is exaggerated. There is little evidence that youth identity is significantly different in terms of what young people value compared with their parents. Very few young people have got involved with those youth subcultures defined as deviant by the mass media, such as teddy-boys (1950s), mods and rockers (1960s), skinheads (early 1970s), punks (late 1970s) or ecstasy-using ravers (1980s/1990s). Most young people are generally conformist – they get on well with their parents and place a high value on traditional goals such as getting married, having children and buying a house.

3 Young adulthood

This type of age identity is focused on the period between leaving the parental home and middle age. Pilcher (1996) points out that this age group has rarely been researched and so we have little information about this significant group of people. Jones and Wallace (1992) suggests that modern societies like the UK have private and public 'markers' that signify the beginning of adult status. For example, private markers might include a first sexual encounter or first cigarette, whilst public markers include the right to vote or the granting of a bank loan. Pilcher concludes that adult identity revolves around living with a sexual partner, having children, having a job and maintaining a home. Hockey and James (1993) see it as bound up with having freedom and independence from parents, having control over material resources and having responsibilities.

4 Mid-life

There is some disagreement as to when middle age begins. Brookes-Gunn and Kirsch (1984) set it as low as 35 years, whereas others have suggested it might be as high as 50 years. There are physical indicators of middle age, e.g. greying hair, the appearance of the 'middle-aged spread' and the menopause in women, as well as social indicators, e.g. children leaving home to go to university or having more money for leisure pursuits. There may even be emotional or psychological indicators, i.e. the mid-life crisis.

5 Old age

This period officially and legally begins at 65 years in the UK, when people are expected to retire from paid work and state pensions are paid. Pilcher argues that because of increasing life expectancy and differences in generational attitudes, tastes and behaviour that we should differentiate between the 'young old' (aged 65 to 74), the 'middle-aged old' (aged between 75 and 84 years) and the 'old old' (aged 85+). However, in contrast to traditional societies, the elderly in the UK are not accorded a

great deal of respect or status, because work is the major source of status in industrial societies. Loss of work due to retirement can result in a significant decline in self-esteem, social contacts with others and income, as well as a consequent rise in loneliness, poverty, depression and poor health in general.

Age and discrimination

The low status associated with elderly identity in UK society is not helped by the fact that people are often stereotyped and discriminated against because of their age. This is known as **ageism**. Johnson and Bytheway (1993) define it as the 'offensive exercise of power through reference to age' and suggest that it has three integral elements:

● Ageism is often institutionalized in that it is embedded in organizational and legal practices, e.g. people aged over 70 years are excluded from jury service.
● Ageism is often expressed through the stereotypical prejudices that underpin everyday interaction, in that people often assume without question that a person's competency is limited by their age, i.e. they are too old to carry out a particular task.
● Ageism can involve the well-meaning assumption that the very old are vulnerable and depend on younger and fitter adults for care and protection.

There is evidence, therefore, that old age as a stage in the life course is largely negatively perceived. This is reflected in everyday descriptions of elderly people as being 'past it' or 'over the hill' or having 'one foot in the grave'. Pilcher notes that old people are often described in derogatory or condescending ways such as 'old fogey', 'old biddy', 'old bat' or 'sweet little old lady/man'. Pilcher points out that such stereotypes tend to marginalize old people and to label them as inferior.

Arber and Ginn (1993) suggest that ageism is reinforced and perpetuated by institutional practices. It is often the case that workers who are made redundant in their mid-40s experience age barriers in finding new jobs. Bradley (1996) notes that old people may be seen as less suitable for employment because they are assumed to be 'physically slow, lacking in dynamism and not very adaptable to change'. However, the Employment Equality (Age) Regulations Act came into force in late 2006, providing protection against age discrimination in employment and education.

Ginn and Arber note too that the increasing number of the elderly – in 2002, for the first time people aged 60 years and over formed a larger part of the population than children aged under 16 years – has led to rising fears about the costs to society of the elderly. For example, the rising costs of pensions and of the increased use of health and welfare services have led to media reports portraying the elderly as a 'burden' on taxpayers.

Ageism and the mass media

Ageism is often reflected through mass media representations of youth and old age. Advertising reinforces the view that the appearance of youth is central to looking good and that ageing should be resisted at all costs. As a result, adverts for anti-ageing creams, hair dyes to conceal greyness and cosmetic surgery are common on television and particularly in women's magazines. Ageism may also be reflected through the underrepresentation of middle-aged and elderly women as news presenters and hosts of light-entertainment shows. Sontag (1978) suggests that there is double standard of ageing especially in television, whereby women are required to be youthful throughout their media careers but men are not. The newscaster, Moira Stuart claimed to be a victim of this type of ageism at the BBC in 2007 when she was 'retired' by the corporation at the age of 58, whilst male counterparts such as David Dimbleby (69 in 2007) and Peter Sissons (65 in 2007) were allowed to carry on beyond retirement age.

Age and identity – conclusions

Sociologists argue that age and generation are products of the culture of the society to which we belong. As Marsh and Keating (2006) observe, different cultures attach different cultural meanings and values to different age groups. These shape our behaviour in terms of how we respond to others of the same generation and how we treat people in other age groups. It is also important to note that how particular age groups or generations are treated will often be shaped by influences such as gender, social class and ethnicity. For example, the experience of being an elderly African-Caribbean woman may be quite different to that of a White middle-class elderly man. Evidence for this observation can be found in Topics 3, 4 and 5.

Disability and identity

The medical model of disability

Best (2005) notes that, traditionally, disability was seen:

>> *in terms of a person's inability to fully participate in various activities that the rest of us take for granted, such as washing yourself, cleaning the floor, walking and driving, shopping ... and generally looking after oneself.* >>

This definition reflected the **medical model of disability**, which assumed that disability is a personal tragedy and that the disabled deserve our pity. In terms of the disabled identity, it was also assumed that the disabled are dependent on the able-bodied and are unable to function effectively without constant help. In other words, disabled people were labelled by the medical model as inferior because it was assumed that to be disabled was to be abnormal, and that normalization could only occur with a medical cure or round-the-clock care.

The social model of disability

This interpretation of the disabled identity began to change in the 1980s with the appearance of the **social model of disability**. This view was developed by disabled people themselves, who argued that biological disability was less important than social disability – as Oliver (1996) argues 'it is society which disables physically impaired people' because the disabled are excluded from full participation in society by stereotypical attitudes held by able-bodied people. As Best notes:

>> *Society generates forms of discrimination and exclusion that disabled people have to cope with. The problem is to be found in the social constructions of prejudice that surround disability and not in the bodies of disabled people.* >>

Disability as a social construct

Disability activists and sociologists have suggested that most of the UK population are impaired in some way but are rarely classified as 'disabled'. They argue that there are degrees of difference in disability or impairment; for example, the author of this chapter is impaired in that his eyesight is extremely poor without glasses or contact lenses. However, he is not socially labelled as 'disabled' because society does not define short-sightedness as a problem and so does not produce a social environment in which people who wear glasses or contact lenses are handicapped. However, people who have to use wheelchairs *are* handicapped by society's failure to provide a social environment in which they can be as mobile as able-bodied people.

The disabled identity and independence

The disabled movement is also very critical of the concept of 'independence' as an aspect of normality. The negative social reaction to disability is often based on the view that the disabled are dependent and constantly in need of help. Marsh and Keating (2006) point out that very few of us are really independent.

>> *In modern societies, we are, of course, interdependent: we cannot manage to feed and clothe ourselves without relying on a vast network of other people and organizations. Similarly, we are all dependent on many aids for mobility and communication. Few of us could function without telephones, transport, ladders, tools and so on, and many of us cannot function at all without glasses, or medication, or other aids.* >>

Marsh and Keating go on to ask – why do some mobility aids like wheelchairs or white sticks attract such a negative social reaction in comparison?

The disabled identity and capitalism

Marxists, such as Finkelstein (1980), have suggested that our negative cultural attitudes towards the disabled may be the product of capitalism's emphasis on work as a source of identity, status and power. He suggests that in pre-industrial societies, the idea that disabled people should be segregated and treated differently simply did not exist. However, industrialization was responsible for a dramatic shift in cultural attitudes because capitalist society required a healthy and fit workforce to generate profits for the capitalist class; in this context, the disabled become an economic burden for society and are defined as abnormal and as a social problem.

Learned helplessness

Watson (1998) argues that the perception of disabled people is based upon stereotypical ideas about dependency and helplessness, and these can have a negative effect on how disabled people perceive themselves and their abilities. In other words, disabled people may respond to the constant assumption that they are helpless and dependent by developing low social esteem and worth. A classic study which illustrates this **self-fulfilling prophecy** very well is Scott's (1969) study of blind people. After observing the interaction between medical professionals and blind people in the USA, Scott argued that the blind developed a 'blind personality' because they internalized the experts' view that they should be experiencing psychological problems in adjusting to their loss of sight. Part of this process also involved '**learned helplessness**', i.e. that they should rely on sighted people for help. In other words, they became dependent because this is what the experts expected them to do.

Mass media representations of the disabled

A number of studies indicate that disability is represented in a negative fashion by the mass media. Longmore (1987) suggests that disabled people tend to be represented on television as evil, as monsters, as inhuman, as dependent on others, as maladjusted, as the objects of pity or charity, and as dangerous and deviant. If the disabled are portrayed as courageous, this is often contrasted with the tragedy of their situation. These stereotypes reinforce cultural stereotypes, and consequently prejudice and discrimination. As Cumberbatch and Negrine (1992) argue, media representations of the disabled rarely present them as 'a person, an individual, who happens also to have a disability'.

Prejudice and discrimination

Stereotypes and prejudices about the disabled affect their quality of life in several ways:

- The disabled may find themselves segregated from able-bodied society, e.g. in special schools, which consequently makes it more difficult for them to be 'normal' and for them to integrate into society.
- Prejudice may be translated into discrimination in the field of employment, as employers may be reluctant to take them on. The disabled therefore may be more likely to be on welfare benefits and to experience poverty.
- Brown (1994) argues that people with disabilities may be seen as either 'innocents or perverts'. Anderson and Kitchin (2000) found that a number of myths about disability and sex existed among professionals who worked in family planning clinics in Northern Ireland, e.g. it was believed that the disabled should be discouraged from having sex because they were not responsible enough to cope with sexual relationships (see Focus on research).
- Kallianes and Rubenfeld (1997) argue that women with disabilities are often discriminated against compared with other women. It is assumed by professionals that such

Focus on research

Anderson and Kitchin (2000)
Stereotyping, sexuality and disability

Anderson and Kitchin studied the attitudes of health professionals working in family planning clinics in Northern Ireland and found that many of them subscribed to cultural myths about the sexual behaviour of disabled people. For example, professionals tended to believe that:

- disabled people were unable to take part in sexual activities
- disabled people were sexually irresponsible and therefore needed to have their sexual appetite and behaviour controlled by professionals
- some disabled people were unable to sustain long-term relationships
- some disabled people lacked a sex drive.

Source: Best, S. (2005) *Understanding Social Divisions*, London: Sage, p. 112

1 **Do the beliefs held by health professionals in Northern Ireland support the medical or social model of disability?**

2 **How might these beliefs undermine integration and encourage learned helplessness among the disabled?**

women should not be having sex and that they are likely to make unsuitable mothers. There have been a number of cases in which disabled women have been forcibly sterilized or have had their children forcibly taken into care.

The disabled identity and resistance

The social model of disability argues that more positive disabled identities should be promoted stressing independence, choice and autonomy for disabled people. They believe that the state should invest in a disabled-friendly social environment and should address prejudice and discrimination against the disabled.

Recent sociological studies suggest that the disabled identity may now be underpinned by the social model of disability, and that disabled people are more likely to resist those definitions of disability that stress dependence and helplessness. Antle (2000) found that children with disabilities do not qualitatively differ in how they see themselves compared with children without disabilities. Olney and Kim (2001) argue that the disabled people in their study felt positive about their disability despite their awareness that people without disabilities negatively evaluated them. They rejected the medical labels and had a very positive self-image.

The disabled identity – recent developments

Critiques of the social model of disability have recently appeared. These acknowledge that prejudice and discrimination need to be addressed and that the social environment in which we live is not always conducive to the disabled. However, they argue that we cannot ignore the fact that physical and biological factors such as pain, mental impairment, and so on, *do* negatively impact on how disabled people experience social life and can make it unpleasant and difficult. The disabled identity is therefore probably made up of coping both with the limitations caused by the physical impairment of the body and mind, and the limitations of the social environment shaped by negative and stereotypical attitudes towards disability.

Activities

Research ideas

1 How do young people see the elderly? Design a questionnaire which explores the extent and social character of ageism. Use the ageism survey 'How ageist is Britain?', which can be found on **www.ageconcern.org.uk**, as the basis for your questionnaire.

2 Carry out three or four unstructured interviews with elderly people who fall into the categories of young elderly, middle-aged elderly and old elderly. How are their experiences of being elderly similar or different? How do they interpret their situation? Have they experienced ageism? In what shape or form?

3 Talk to people in your class about what constitutes 'disability'. Place these categories on a continuum with 'independence' at one end and 'dependence' at the other. How does their position on the continuum affect your interpretation of their condition and identity?

Web.tasks

1 Visit the sites **www.ace.org.uk** and **www.cpa.org.uk** How do these sites promote positive images of the elderly?

   Visit the web-site **www.campaignforrealbeauty.co.uk** How does this site challenge ageist stereotypes?

2 Visit the following disability websites:

   www.disabilitynow.org.uk
   www.bbc.co.uk/ouch/
   www.radar.org.uk

   How do these sites view the disabled identity? Do these sites support the medical or social model of disability?

   How does the site **www.disabilityfilms.co.uk** support points made by the social model of disability?

Key terms

Adolescence period from puberty to adulthood, i.e. teenage years.

Ageism discrimination and prejudice on the basis of age.

Capitalist entrepreneurs businessmen and -women.

Circumcision practice of removing foreskin from penis.

Culturally constructed product of culture or society, rather than biology.

Folk devils groups stereotyped by the media as deviants.

Demonized the process of being negatively labelled or stereotyped.

Generation a group of people born within the same historical period who share similar cultural experiences.

Generation gap the notion that teenagers and their parents are in conflict because they hold different sets of values.

Learned helplessness learning how to be dependent.

Medical model of disability the view that the disabled are handicapped by their physical or mental disabilities and need to be assisted in their everyday activities by the able-bodied.

Moral panics anxiety felt by members of society about the behaviour of social groups, caused by media sensationalism and exaggeration.

Newsworthiness the process by which a story becomes interesting and sells papers.

Self-fulfilling prophecy predictions about the behaviour of social groups that come true as a result of positive or negative labelling.

Social model of disability the view, held by disabled campaigners, that disabled people are disabled by prejudicial stereotypes and discrimination that assumes that they should be dependent on the able-bodied.

Socially constructed product of society or culture, rather than biology.

Youth culture set of values and norms of behaviour relating to fashion, dress, hairstyle, lifestyle, etc., subscribed to by some young people that may be seen as deviant by mainstream culture.

Check your understanding

1 How does age identity differ in traditional societies compared with modern industrial societies?

2 How does pre-Second World War youth identity in the UK compare with youth identity in the 1950s?

3 What is 'ageism' and how does it affect the social identity of the elderly?

4 What sort of disabled identity is encouraged by the medical model of disability?

5 What is 'learned helplessness' and how does it affect the identity of disabled people?

6 What are the consequences of being 'disabled by society'?

Item A

All societies make some kind of distinction between different age groups. However, the number of age groups that different societies identify and the status that they give to these groups both vary greatly. Nonetheless, in general, we can identify a broad pattern of differences between the way in which age is regarded in pre-industrial societies and they way it is seen in modern industrial societies. Such variations in how age is seen in different cultures and societies illustrate the view of sociologists that age is a social construct.

Despite the variations, however, there may be some common elements across different societies. For example, in all societies, adults have a higher status than children. This reflects the key features of adult identity.

Item B

In their study of the ways in which the mass media represent disability and the disabled, Cumberbatch and Negrine (1992) found that, in television drama, disabled people were usually portrayed as the objects of condescension and pity. In other studies, such as Longmore (1987), the disabled were frequently found to be presented by the media negatively, for example as monsters, as lacking humanity, as a sexual menace or as totally dependent on others.

On another level, the medical model of disability also defines the disabled as dependent on the able-bodied. It sees disability as a shortcoming within the individual that renders them abnormal and less than fully competent, whether mentally, physically or both. One danger is, of course, that people with disabilities will internalize such ideas and this will become a self-fulfilling prophecy in which they take on a 'disabled identity'.

(a) Explain what sociologists mean by the phrase 'age is a social construct' (Item A). (2 marks)

(b) Suggest two differences between the way in which age is regarded in pre-industrial and in industrial societies (Item A). (4 marks)

(c) Suggest three characteristics of adult identity (Item A). (6 marks)

(d) Using information from Item B and elsewhere, examine the factors affecting the identity of people with disabilities. (24 marks)

Grade booster Getting top marks in the 24-mark question

You can make use of the Item to develop an account of the medical model of disability. You should then go on to consider a range of different factors that influence the identity of those with disabilities. These can include media representations (e.g. using the studies in the Item), linking to the idea of stereotyping or labelling and the self-fulfilling prophecy (e.g. Scott's study of blindness). You can also consider the role of capitalism and the work ethic, as well as the attitudes of the caring professions, in shaping the identities of disabled people. You should also examine how far people can resist negative labelling, for example through disability rights campaigns, which you could relate to the social model of disability. Consider also whether different kinds of disability, e.g. physical or mental, might make a difference to identity.

Exam Practice

1 Read **Item A** below and answer the question that follows.

Item A

The socialization process involves instilling society's shared culture of norms, values, beliefs, traditions and so on, into its individual members. We can distinguish between primary and secondary socialization. Primary socialization takes place largely in the family and consists of the acquisition of basic social and communication skills such as language and how to cooperate with others, learning to feed oneself, knowledge of right and wrong, and so on. Some sociologists have argued that in today's society, the family may find it more difficult to carry out the primary socialization of children as effectively as in the past.

Although socialization involves instilling society's shared culture, there may be aspects of culture not shared by everyone in the same society. For example, many societies contain a high culture or a folk culture which are not shared by all their members.

An examiner comments

(a) Explain the difference between norms and values (**Item A**). *(4 marks)*

2/4 Norms are specific rules of conduct or behaviour, whereas values are more general.

> Correct as far as it goes, but this answer doesn't give us much idea of what values really are – more general what? It needs to say 'general guidelines' for behaviour. The definition of norms is fine.

(b) Explain the difference between high culture and folk culture (**Item A**). *(4 marks)*

2/4 High culture is the culture of the upper classes and includes things like opera, classical music and Shakespeare. Folk culture is more like the popular culture of the masses, e.g. soap operas and pop music.

> A correct account of high culture but not of folk culture. The answer needs to say that folk culture is authentic, created by the people and typical of pre-industrial societies.

(c) Suggest **two** reasons why the primary socialization of children in today's society may not be as effective as in the past (**Item A**). *(4 marks)*

4/4 First, many children today are brought up in single-parent families, so there may not be a male role model around, which could be a particular problem in socializing boys effectively.

Second, there is the influence of the mass media, which may give out messages that contradict the values that parents are putting forward and undermine their authority.

> Two good points, so full marks here.

(d) Examine the process of gender-role socialization. *(24 marks)*

From an early age, boys and girls begin to be socialized into seeing themselves as different from the opposite sex, and by the age of about two or three years old, they can identify themselves (and usually other people, too) correctly as male or female. Parents begin this process by things like the names they use to talk to their children, such as 'pretty girl' but not 'pretty boy'. This can reinforce the idea that girls are expected to think about how they look, whereas boys are not. By the age of five, most children have a clear idea of what the expectations are for girls' and boys' behaviour.

Once children start school, they are likely to be stereotyped by teachers and treated differently depending on their gender. Teachers may expect girls to be neat and tidy, quiet, etc., and to be good at subjects such as English. On the other hand, they expect boys to be more rowdy and naughty, and to like physical activities and to be good at subjects such as maths and sciences.

> A reasonable start, although it would be good to define key terms such as socialization, gender and gender role. It could also introduce the idea of 'verbal appellations'.

> Some potentially relevant ideas here, but a bit descriptive. It would benefit from concepts such as the self-fulfilling prophecy to explain the effect that teachers' expectations can have on gender identity.

68

Sociology AS for AQA

Another important part of the process of gender-role socialization is played by the mass media. Again, stereotyping is common, with males shown as dominant and females as subordinate or submissive, as Billington found. Other research shows females portrayed in a narrower range of roles than males, reinforcing their identity as housewives or low-paid workers in the service sector.

> Some relevant research findings used here to show the effect on gender identity.

However, these views ignore the impact of changes in gender identity. For example, recent years have seen the emergence of the 'new man' who takes on a more nurturing identity, e.g. involving childcare duties traditionally part of the female role. Some sociologists see this as a challenge to 'hegemonic masculinity'. This challenge may be part of the 'crisis of masculinity' that Mac an Ghaill describes, as traditional men's jobs decline and leave men in limbo.

> This brings in some useful evaluation, but 'hegemonic masculinity' needs defining and its relevance explaining.

Women's identities are also changing. Sue Sharpe found that, unlike in the 1970s, girls today no longer see themselves and their future in terms of love, marriage, motherhood and the housewife role. Instead, they are more focused on getting a good career and financial independence – very few want to be economically dependent on a man. This is a major reason why they are now doing better than boys in education, since this is the key to career success.

> Good points about changes in female identity and its consequences (e.g. girls wanting to succeed educationally), although it should also look at why this has happened.

An examiner comments

This is quite a good answer in several ways. First, it looks at a range of sources of gender role socialization, such as parents/the family, education and the media. Second, it deals with both males and females throughout. Third, it looks at changes in gender identity.

There are several ways in which the answer could be improved:

- It should use more concepts, such as canalization, gender codes, and the distinction between primary and secondary socialization.
- It should also define and explain the concepts it does use, such as hegemonic masculinity, crisis of masculinity, etc.
- It could bring in the idea of resistance to stereotyping – not everyone simply absorbs the gender 'messages'.
- It begins to lose sight of the issue of socialization and focuses more on identity. These are linked ideas but not the same thing.
- Lastly, it needs a brief conclusion.

One for you to try

Read **Item B** and answer the question that follows.

Item B

According to Marxist sociologists, culture can only be understood and explained in terms of its role in capitalist society. Marxists argue that capitalism is based on the division of society into two classes: the bourgeoisie (capitalists), who own the means of production, and the proletariat (the working class), who are forced to work for the capitalists to survive).

For Marxists, culture plays an important role in preventing the proletariat from overthrowing the capitalists. They ague that culture is really ruling-class culture, and this acts as an ideology to persuade the working class to accept their subordinate position.

An examiner comments

Use the Item to explain the Marxist theory of culture. You should develop some of its points, e.g. about ideology. For example, you could look at the role of education, the mass media or religion in producing ideas to support class inequality and capitalism. You need to evaluate the theory too, for instance by criticizing it from a functionalist standpoint. Equally, you could criticize its focus on class by noting that ideas about ethnic and gender inequality are also important elements of culture that need explaining.

(e) Using information from **Item B** and elsewhere, assess the Marxist theory of culture. *(24 marks)*

Answers to the 'One for you to try' are available **free** on **www.collinseducation.com/sociologyweb**

Chapter 2 Summary

High culture
- Aesthetically superior
- Elitist

Functionalism
- Culture is product of value consensus
- Core culture promotes social order

Mass culture
- Popular culture
- Manufactured by media

Marxism
- Culture shaped by capitalism
- Culture as ideology

Primary socialization
- Family and parenting
- Social control

Functionalism
- Family as personality factory
- Socialization into value consensus

Secondary socialization
- Education
- Mass media
- Religion
- Peer group

Marxism
- Socialization into ruling-class values
- False needs

Defining culture

Socialization

Ethnicity and nationality

Asian identity
- Family socialization
- Religious influences

African-Caribbean identity
- Peer-group pressure
- Mixed-race identity

National identity
- Britishness
- Celtic identity
- Multiculturalism
- Globalization

Culture and identity

Social class and identity

Upper-class identity
- Social closure
- Conservative value system

Middle-class identity
- Fragmentation
- Suburban and meritocratic

Working-class identity
- Traditional – work as source of identity
- New individualistic working class
- Underclass

Decline of class identity
- Hybrid identity
- Persistence of class inequality

Age and disability

Social construction of age
- Childhood
- Adolescence and youth subcultures
- Old age and ageism

Disability
- Medical model vs social model

Gender and sexuality

Hegemonic masculinity and femininity
- Gender-role socialization
- Traditional gender roles

Changing femininities and masculinities
- Genderquake
- Feminization of the workplace

Homosexuality
- Decriminalization
- Gay culture

Families and households

AQA Specification	Topics	Pages
Candidates should examine:		
The relationship of the family to the social structure and social change, with particular reference to the economy and to state policies.	Covered in Topics 1, 2 and 3.	72–91
Changing patterns of marriage, cohabitation, separation, divorce, child-bearing and the lifecourse, and the diversity of contemporary family and household structures.	Covered in Topics 4 and 5.	92–107
The nature and extent of changes within the family, with reference to gender roles, domestic labour and power relationships.	Covered in Topic 6	108–13
The nature of childhood, and changes in the status of children in the family and society.	Covered in Topic 7.	114–19
Demographic trends in the UK since 1900; reasons for changes in birth rates, death rates and family size.	Covered in Topic 4.	92–99

The family, social structure and social change

Getting you thinking

Above an Ik village clings to the hillside
Right: an Ik child called Lokiira

1 **How do the Ik define the family?**

2 **Given your own experience of family life, think of three features of the family that you would expect to find in all families, wherever they are. How do these three features differ from the Ik?**

3 **In what ways might some British families share some of the characteristics of the Ik?**

The family does not feature heavily in the culture of the Ik of Northern Uganda. In fact, as far as the Ik are concerned, the family means very little. This is because the Ik face a daily struggle to survive in the face of drought, famine and starvation. Anyone who cannot take care of him- or herself is regarded as a useless burden by the Ik and a hazard to the survival of the others. Families mean dependants such as children who need to be fed and protected. So close to the verge of starvation, family, sentiment and love are regarded as luxuries that can mean death. Children are regarded as useless appendages, like old people, because they use up precious resources. So the old are abandoned to die. Sick and disabled children too are abandoned. The Ik attitude is that, as long as you keep the breeding group alive, you can always get more children.

Ik mothers throw their children out of the village compound when they are 3 years old, to fend for themselves. I imagine children must be rather relieved to be thrown out, for in the process of being cared for he or she is grudgingly carried about in a hide sling wherever the mother goes. Whenever the mother is in her field, she loosens the sling and lets the baby to the ground none too slowly, and laughs if it is hurt. Then she goes about her business, leaving the child there, almost hoping that some predator will come along and carry it off. This sometimes happens. Such behaviour does not endear children to their parents or parents to their children.

Adapted from Turnbull, C. (1994) *The Mountain People*, London: Pimlico

You probably reacted to the description of the Ik with horror. It is tempting to conclude that these people are primitive, savage and inhuman, and that their concept of the 'family' is deeply wrong. However, sociologists argue that it is wrong simply to judge such societies and their family arrangements as unnatural and deviant. We need to understand that such arrangements may have positive functions. In the case of the Ik, with the exceptional circumstances they find themselves in – drought and famine – their family arrangements help ensure the survival of the tribe. Moreover, you may have concluded that family life in the UK and for the Ik have some things in common. British

family life is not universally experienced as positive for all family members. For some members – young and old alike – family life may be characterized by violence, abuse and isolation.

The problem with studying the family is that we all think we are experts – not surprisingly, given that most of us are born into families and socialized into family roles and responsibilities. For many of us, the family is the cornerstone of our social world, a place to which we can retreat and where we can take refuge from the stresses of the outside world. It is the place in which we are loved for who we are, rather than what we are. Family living and family events are probably the most important aspects of our lives. It is no wonder then that we tend to hold very fierce, emotional, and perhaps irrational, views about family life and how it ought to be organized. Such 'taken-for-granted' views make it very difficult for us to examine objectively family arrangements that deviate from our own experience – such as those of the Ik – without making critical judgements.

Defining 'the family'

The experiences of the Ik suggest that family life across the world is characterized by tremendous variation and diversity. However, the concepts of variation and diversity have created problems for those sociologists concerned with defining what counts as a family. The functionalist sociologist, George Peter Murdock (1949), for example, defined the family as: 'a social group characterized by common residence, economic co-operation and reproduction. It includes adults of both sexes, at least two of whom maintain a socially approved sexual relationship, and one or more children, own or adopted, of the sexually cohabiting adults'.

Murdock's definition, therefore, is focused on the **'nuclear family'** – a stereotypical two-generation family made up of a heterosexual couple with dependent offspring. This definition of the family has proved very popular with politicians and **right-wing** sociologists who suggest that this is the ideal type of family to which people should aspire. It was generally accepted that this family, which was the statistical norm until the 1980s should have the following characteristics:

- It should be small and compact in structure, composed of a mother, father and usually two or three children who are biologically related (see Figure 3.1).
- They should live together, i.e. share a common residence. Nuclear families are a type of **household**.
- The relationship between the adults should be **heterosexual** and based on romantic love. Children are seen as the outcome of that love and as symbolic of the couple's commitment to each other.
- The relationship between the adults should be reinforced by marriage, which, it is assumed, encourages **fidelity** (faithfulness) and therefore family stability.
- Marriage should be companionate, i.e. based on husband and wives being partners. There is an overlap between male and female responsibilities as men get more involved in childcare and housework. However, some 'natural' differences persist in the form of a gendered or **sexual division of labour** with regard to **domestic labour**. It is taken for granted that women want to have children and that they

should be primarily responsible for **nurturing** and childcare. The male role is usually defined as the main economic breadwinner and head of the household.

- The immediate family comes first and all other obligations and relationships come second. **Kinship**, therefore, is all important.
- It is assumed, almost without question, that the family is a positive and beneficial institution in which family members receive nurturing, unconditional love and care.

The influence of the traditional view of the family

The influence of these traditional beliefs about family life has been immense. It can be argued that they constitute a powerful **conservative 'ideology'** about what families should look like and how family members should behave. For example, the beliefs that the main responsibility for parenting lies with mothers, that lone parents are not as effective as two parents, and that homosexuals should not have the same fertility or parenting rights as heterosexuals, are still very influential today in the UK. We can even see such views reflected in our everyday behaviour and attitudes, as Jon Bernardes observes (1997, p.31):

<<It is not just that many people think of women as the most appropriate carers of children but rather that we all act on this belief in our daily lives. Men may hesitate or not know how to engage in certain tasks or, in public, men may be discouraged from comforting a lost child whilst a woman may 'naturally' take up this role. Examples of family ideology can be found in a wide range of everyday practices, from images on supermarket products to who picks up dirty laundry (or who drops it in the first place).>>

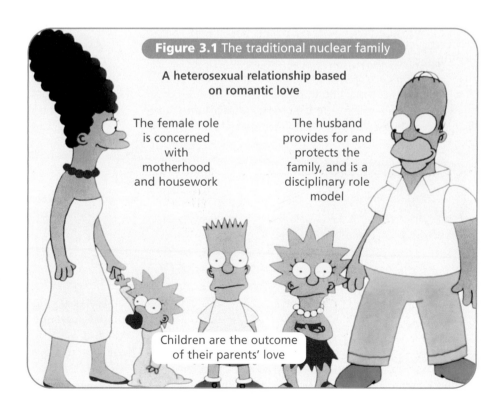

Figure 3.1 The traditional nuclear family

A heterosexual relationship based on romantic love

The female role is concerned with motherhood and housework

The husband provides for and protects the family, and is a disciplinary role model

Children are the outcome of their parents' love

Functionalism, the social structure and the family

Many of our traditional beliefs about the nuclear family are influenced by the theory of functionalism, which dominated thinking in the sociology of the family for many years. Functionalism is a structural theory in that it believes that the social structure of society (which is made up of social institutions such as the economy, education, media, law, religion and family) is responsible for shaping us as individuals and determining our experiences and life chances. Consequently, functionalists are interested in how the family functions for the greater good of society and, in particular, how it contributes to the maintenance of social order. They are also interested in how the family as an institution operates in conjunction with other institutions, particularly the economy, and how these interrelationships also contribute to **social solidarity**. Moreover, functionalists are interested in how the family, as part of the social structure, shapes and benefits its individual members.

Functionalism and the evolution of the family

Functionalist sociologists, such as Talcott Parsons (1965), have attempted to trace the historical development of the family in order to explain why the nuclear family form has been so dominant. Parsons' theory of the family focused on examining the influence of industrialization and the economy on family structures and relationships.

Parsons argued that the economic systems of **pre-industrial** societies were largely based on **extended kinship networks**. Land and other resources were commonly owned or rented by a range of relatives extending well beyond the nuclear family unit. For example, it was not uncommon to live with and work alongside cousins. This extended family was responsible for the production of food, shelter and clothing, and would trade with other family groups for those things they couldn't produce themselves. Very few people left home to go to work. Home and workplace were one and the same thing.

Roles in these families were the product of **ascription** rather than **achievement**. This means that both family status and job

were the product of being born into a particular extended family known for a particular trade or skill. For example, if the family were pig farmers, then there was a strong likelihood that all members of the family – men and women, old and young alike – would be involved in some aspect of pig farming. Moreover, these roles would be passed down from generation to generation. Few family members would reject the roles, because duty and obligation to the family and community were key values of pre-industrial society.

In return for this commitment, the extended family network generally performed other functions for its members:

- The family equipped its members with the skills and education they needed to take their place in the family division of labour, although this socialization rarely extended to literacy and numeracy.
- The family functioned to maintain the health of its members, in the absence of a system of universal health care. However, the high infant mortality rates and low life expectancy of the pre-industrial period tell us that this was probably a constant struggle.
- The family also provided welfare for its members. For example, those family members who did make it into old age would be cared for, in exchange for services such as looking after very young children.
- The extended family was expected to pursue justice on behalf of any wronged family member.

The effects of industrialization

Parsons argued that the industrial revolution brought about four fundamental changes to the family (see Fig 3.2):

1 **Industrialization** meant that the economy demanded a more **geographically mobile** workforce. At the same time, achievement became more important than ascription as mass education was introduced. People were, therefore, less likely to defer to their elders or feel a strong sense of obligation to remain near to kin. Parsons argued that nuclear families were formed as people moved away from their extended kin in the countryside in order to take advantage of the job opportunities brought about by industrialization in the towns.

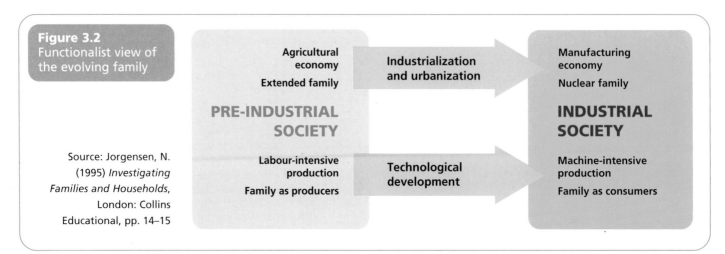

Figure 3.2
Functionalist view of the evolving family

Source: Jorgensen, N. (1995) *Investigating Families and Households*, London: Collins Educational, pp. 14–15

Agricultural economy
Extended family

PRE-INDUSTRIAL SOCIETY

Labour-intensive production
Family as producers

Industrialization and urbanization

Technological development

Manufacturing economy
Nuclear family

INDUSTRIAL SOCIETY

Machine-intensive production
Family as consumers

Figure 3.3 Structural differentiation

Multifunctional pre-industrial family

Structural differentiation

Nuclear family with specialized functions

2 Geographical mobility led to people becoming 'isolated' from their relatives and less reliant on kin for economic and social supports. Parsons claims that nuclear family members became more dependent and focused on each other, more home-centred and less prone to pressures from their extended kin and community.

3 Specialized agencies developed which gradually took over many of the functions of the family. Parsons referred to this economic process as 'structural differentiation' (see Fig. 3.3 above). For example, after the industrial revolution, families could buy food and clothing mass produced in factories. Companies developed that specialized in the mass production of homes. The result of these processes was that the family became less important as an agency of production. The home and the workplace became separated as people become wage earners in the factory system.

The state also eventually took over the functions of education, health and welfare. This left the nuclear family to specialize in two essential functions – the primary socialization of children and the stabilization of adult personalities. Parsons claimed that structural differentiation resulted in the family becoming a more streamlined and effective unit in terms of its contribution to the economy.

4 Parsons claimed that the new nuclear unit provided the husband and wife with very clear social roles. The male is the '**instrumental leader**', responsible for the economic welfare of the family group and protection of family members; he goes out to work and earns money. The female is the '**expressive leader**', primarily responsible for the socialization of children and the emotional care and support of family members. It is clearly implied that this sexual division of labour is 'natural' because it is based on biological differences. For example, women's **maternal instincts** made them best suited to be the emotional caretakers of both children and their spouses. Parsons saw relationships between husbands and wives as complementary, with each contributing to the maintenance of the family in a qualitatively different way.

Parsons concluded that only the nuclear unit could effectively provide the achievement-orientated and geographically mobile workforce required by modern industrial economies.

Focus on research

Elizabeth Roberts (1996)
Oral history of working-class women

Elizabeth Roberts interviewed 160 mothers and grandmothers in Lancashire and detailed the everyday lives of ordinary working-class women between 1890 and 1940. She resists the feminist analysis that working-class families were patriarchal institutions that benefited men. Instead, she notes that women blamed poverty, not men, for their plight, and women had power – of a sort – in household and family. The mother/daughter bond was the foundation stone of the family, and women gained much satisfaction from their family achievements such as the management of the family budget, the education and socialization of large families, and the upholding of the family and neighbourhood traditions.

Roberts, E. (1996) *A Woman's Place – an Oral History of Working Class Women, 1890–1940*, Oxford: Blackwell

1 **What are the strengths and weaknesses of oral histories?**

2 **How does Roberts' work challenge critical views of the family?**

Historical criticisms of Parsons' view

Historians suggest that Parsons was far too simplistic in his interpretation of the history of the family. They point out that the evidence suggests that industrialization may follow different patterns in different industrial societies. The Japanese experience of industrialization, for example, stressed the importance of a job for life with the same company. Employees were encouraged to view their workmates as part of a larger extended family and consequently duty and obligation were encouraged as important cultural values. The result of this was that extended kinship networks continued to exert a profound influence on their members and the isolated nuclear family failed to gain a significant toehold in Japanese culture.

Laslett's (1972) study of English parish records suggests that only 10 per cent of households in the pre-industrial period contained extended kin. In other words, most pre-industrial families may have been nuclear, and not extended as Parsons claimed. Such small families were probably due to late marriage, early death and the practice of sending children away to become servants or apprentices. It may also be the case that industrialization took off so quickly because nuclear families already existed – and so people could move quickly to those parts of the country where their skills were in demand. However, Laslett's data has been criticized as unreliable because statistics do not give us any real insight into the quality of family life, i.e. how people actually experienced the family or the meaning they attached to family life. For example, people may have lived in nuclear units but may have seen and spent quality time with other relatives on a daily basis.

Michael Anderson's historical study (1971) of the industrial town of Preston, using census records from 1851, also contradicts Parsons' view that, after industrialization, the extended unit was replaced by the nuclear family. Anderson found a large number of households shared by extended kin. These probably functioned as a **mutual economic support system** in a town in which unemployment and poverty were common. In other words, people probably pooled their low wages in order to share the cost of high rents and to help out those who were sick, disabled and elderly.

The evolution of the British family

The British sociologists Young and Willmott (1957) take issue with Parsons over the speed of change. They suggest that the movement towards the nuclear unit was not as sudden as Parsons suggests, but rather that it was more gradual in nature. Their empirical research, conducted in the 1950s in the East End of London (Bethnal Green), showed that extended families existed in large numbers even at this advanced stage of industrialization. This extended kinship network was based upon emotional attachment and obligation. It was also a mutual support network, offering its members assistance with money, jobs, childcare and advice.

Young and Willmott (1973) argue that the extended family unit went into decline in the 1960s, when working-class communities were rehoused in new towns and on council estates after extensive slum clearance. Moreover, the welfare state and full employment in the 1950s undermined the need for a mutual economic support system. Bright working-class young men made the most of the opportunities and qualifications made available by the 1944 Education Act and were less likely to follow their fathers into manual work. Their social mobility into white-collar and professional jobs often meant geographical mobility, i.e. moving away from traditional working-class areas, and less frequent contact with kin. Young and Willmott therefore concluded that the nuclear or **symmetrical family** only became the universal norm in Britain in the late 20th century.

Marxist views

Marxists are critical of the functionalist view that the modern nuclear family has evolved in order to benefit wider society. Instead, Marxists generally see the nuclear family as serving the interests of the ruling class because it mainly promotes capitalist values and so discourages dissent and criticism of inequality and the way capitalism is organized.

In particular, the nuclear family unit is seen as an **ideological apparatus** that promotes values and ways of thinking essential to the reproduction and maintenance of capitalism. It helps to ensure that the working class remain ignorant of the fact that they are being exploited by the capitalist system (see Chapter 1, p. 17). For example, nuclear families encourage their members to pursue the capitalist-friendly goals of materialism, consumerism and 'keeping up with the Joneses'. Marcuse (1964) claimed that working-class families are encouraged to pursue 'false needs' in the form of the latest consumer goods and to judge themselves and others on the basis of their acquisitions. He noted that this served the interests of capitalism rather than consumers, because it both stimulated the economy and distracted workers from the need to seek equality and justice.

Marxists argue that the working-class extended family has been deliberately discouraged by the capitalist ruling class, because its emphasis on a mutual support system and collective shared action encourages its members to be aware of their social-class position and hence inequality. Such class consciousness is regarded as threatening, because it may eventually challenge the wealth and power of the capitalist class.

Marxist-feminist views

Marxist-feminists are sceptical about Parsons' claim that the nuclear family meets the needs of industrial society. They, too, suggest that the nuclear family benefits capitalist society and therefore the bourgeoisie at the expense of the working class. Marxist-feminists have focused on the contribution of domestic labour, i.e. housework and childcare, to capitalist economies. They point out that such work is unpaid but has great value for capitalist economies. In other words, capitalism exploits women. Moreover, men benefit from this exploitation.

Margaret Benston (1972) suggested that the nuclear family is important to capitalism because it rears the future workforce at little cost to the capitalist state. Women's domestic labour and sexual services also help to maintain the present workforce's physical and emotional fitness. Mothers and housewives are also a useful reserve army of labour that can be hired cheaply as part-time workers in times of economic expansion and let go first in times of recession. Finally, it can be argued that the capitalist class directly exploit women's domestic labour by hiring women as cleaners, nannies and cooks. This enables the wealthy of both sexes to pursue careers outside the home.

Some feminists suggest that the nuclear family may also be useful to capitalism and men because it provides an emotionally supportive retreat for male workers who may be frustrated at their treatment in the workplace. The focus on a comfortable home and attaining a good standard of living may distract workers from their workplace problems and reduce the possibility of industrial unrest. However, some men may attempt to make up for their lack of power and control in the workplace by exerting control within the family. This may have negative consequences for some females, in the form of domestic violence (see Topic 6, p. 110).

Check your understanding

1 Identify four features of the traditional family.

2 What has been the impact of the traditional model of the family on popular thinking?

3 In Parsons' view:
   (a) What functions did the pre-industrial family perform?
   (b) What happened to the functions of the family after industrialization?

4 In what ways do historians challenge Parsons' ideas about family change?

5 From a Marxist perspective, whom does the nuclear family benefit? How?

6 Whom does the nuclear family benefit according to feminist thinkers? How?

Activities

Research idea

Visit your local reference library and ask to see a copy of the 1851 census for your area. Randomly choose a couple of streets and work out how households were organized. Does this evidence support Parsons or Anderson?

Web.task

Use an internet search engine such as www.google.co.uk and sites such as www.en.wikipedia.org to find out more about the work of G.P. Murdock, Talcott Parsons, Ronald Fletcher, and particularly Peter Wilmott and Michael Young's research on Bethnal Green in London. However, be cautious in your use of material from the net. Always attempt to check any information against textbook-based data.

Radical feminist views

Radical feminists argue that the main effect of industrialization was that women were generally excluded from paid work (and therefore, an independent income); they were redefined as mothers and housewives dependent upon the family wage earned by the male breadwinner. Men came to dominate paid work and, consequently, political and cultural power, whereas women were confined to the family in which they were generally exploited and oppressed by men. Radical feminists, therefore, argue that the emergence of the modern nuclear family meets the needs of men rather than the needs of all members of society.

Key terms

Achievement the allocation of roles and status on the basis of individual merit, e.g. through the acquisition of qualifications.

Ascription the allocation of roles and status on the basis of fixed characteristics, e.g. on the basis of gender or what family you are born into.

Conservative a belief in traditional ideas and institutions; suspicious of radical change.

Domestic labour housework and childcare.

Expressive leader Parsons' term for the female function of mother/housewife.

Extended kinship networks relationships between family members beyond the nuclear family, e.g. grandparents, cousins.

Fidelity being faithful to one's partner.

Geographical mobility the ability to move quickly around the country.

Heterosexual attracted to the opposite sex.

Household a social group sharing common residence.

Ideological apparatus according to Marxists, any institution that is involved in the transmitting of ruling-class ideas, e.g. education, mass media.

Ideology set of powerful ideas.

Industrialization the process (occurring during the 18th and 19th centuries in Britain) whereby societies moved from agricultural production to industrial manufacturing. It had a huge impact, creating cities (urbanization), changing the sort of work people did, and fundamentally altering their social experiences and relationships.

Instrumental leader Parsons' term for the male breadwinner.

Kinship related to each other by blood, marriage, etc.

Maternal instinct a 'natural' instinct to desire motherhood and want to care for children.

Mutual economic support system a system in which family members work to support each other.

Nuclear family family group consisting of two generations, i.e. parents and children, living in the same household.

Nurturing caring for and looking after others.

Pre-industrial before the industrial revolution.

Right-wing political ideas that are supportive of tradition.

Sexual division of labour the division of both paid work and domestic labour into men's jobs and women's jobs.

Social solidarity the feeling of belonging.

Symmetrical family a nuclear family in which both spouses perform equally important roles.

The family, social structure and social change

Item A

There are five traditional assumptions made about the nuclear family. First, marriage is regarded as the climax of romantic love, and children are seen as symbolic of the couple's commitment to each other. Second, it is assumed that the ultimate goal of women is to have children, stay at home and gain satisfaction through the socialization of their children. Women who choose not to have children may be viewed as 'unnatural'. Third, it is assumed that the family is a positive and beneficial institution in which family members receive nurturing, care and love. Fourth, the male is expected to be head of the household and to provide for the family. Finally, it is assumed that the immediate family comes first and all other obligations and relationships come second.

Adapted from Chapman, S. and Aiken, D. (2000) 'Towards a new sociology of families', *Sociology Review*, 9(3)

Item B

According to functionalists, industrialization led to greater geographical mobility and loss of regular contact with extended kin. The wider family network was no longer required, as emotional and personal needs were met by the nuclear unit. However, a number of sociological studies of the 1950s and 1960s suggested that the isolation of the nuclear family from the wider family had been exaggerated. The study of Bethnal Green in London by Young and Willmott (1957) found extended families with frequent and strong contact between kin. By the late 1960s, studies of new council estates and factory workers with high incomes were suggesting that contact with kin, although not totally severed, was in decline. Research indicated that people were mainly living in nuclear families which were more inward-looking, home-centred and less inclined to be sociable outside the home with kin and friends.

Adapted from Abercrombie, N. and Warde, A. (2000) *Contemporary British Society* (3rd edn), Cambridge: Polity Press, pp. 302–9

(a) **Explain what is meant by 'structural differentiation'.** (2 marks)

(b) **Explain the difference between 'instrumental' and 'expressive' leaders in the family.** (4 marks)

(c) **Identify three 'traditional assumptions made about the nuclear family' (Item A).** (6 marks)

(d) **Using information from Item B and elsewhere, assess the view that industrialization led to the decline of the extended family and the rise of the nuclear family.** (24 marks)

Grade booster Getting top marks in the 24-mark question

You need to identify the view in the question as a functionalist one and explain it in detail – in particular, how the extended family fits the needs of pre-industrial society, while the nuclear family fits those of industrial society. Include ideas such as structural differentiation and social and geographical mobility. To evaluate this view, you should use Laslett on the pre-industrial family, Anderson and Young and Willmott on the early industrial working-class family, and studies of the continued existence of the extended family in modern industrial society.

TOPIC 2

The functions of the family

Getting you thinking

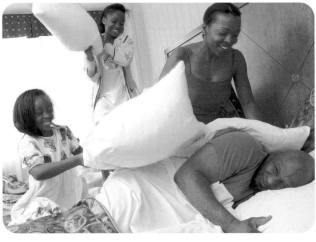
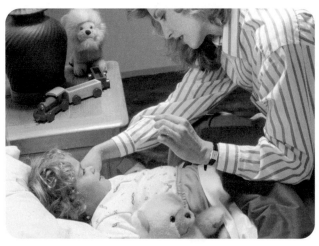

1 **Examine the photographs carefully. What functions are family members performing?**

2 **How do you think your family functions to benefit you?**

3 **In your opinion, can family functions be performed just as effectively by other agencies?**

It is likely that you have identified several family functions after examining the photographs and discussing your own families. You have probably concluded too that very few social institutions can perform these functions as well as the family. You will no doubt be pleased to see that your conclusions parallel those of many sociologists. However, it is important to understand that the experience of family functions is not the same for all of us. There may be very different experiences shaped by social class, ethnicity, age, gender and religion. Furthermore, some of these experiences may be damaging rather than beneficial.

The functionalist theory of the family

For many years, the sociology of the family was dominated by the theory of functionalism. Functionalists assume that society has certain basic needs or **functional prerequisites** that need to be met if it is to continue successfully into the future. For example, a successful society is underpinned by social order and economic stability, so the role of the social institutions that make up society is to make sure this continues by:

- transmitting values, norms, etc., to the next generation in order to reproduce **consensus** and therefore the culture of a society
- teaching particular skills in order that the economy – the engine of society – operates effectively
- allocating people to family and occupational roles which make best use of their talents and abilities.

Functionalists see the family as playing a major role in achieving these social goals. They view the family as the cornerstone of society because it plays the dominant role amongst all social institutions in making individuals feel part of wider society. Furthermore, the family is seen as meeting the needs of individuals for emotional satisfaction, social support, identity and security. Overall, then, functionalists see the family as extremely **functional**, i.e. its existence is both beneficial and necessary for the smooth running of society and the personal development of individuals.

The work of G.P. Murdock

Murdock (1949) compared over 250 societies and claimed that the nuclear family was universal, i.e. that some form of it existed in every known society, and that it always performed four functions essential to the continued existence of those societies:

- *Reproductive* – Society requires new members to ensure its survival – **procreation** generally occurs within a marital and family context.
- *Sexual* – This function serves both society and the individual. Unregulated sexual behaviour has the potential to be socially disruptive. However, marital sex creates a powerful emotional bond between a couple, encourages fidelity and therefore commits the individual to family life. Sex within marriage contributes to social order and stability because marital fidelity sets the moral rules for general sexual behaviour.
- *Educational* – Culture needs to be transmitted to the next generation, so children need to be effectively socialized into the dominant values, norms, customs, rituals, etc., of a society.
- *Economic* – Adult family members show their commitment to the care, protection and maintenance of their dependents by becoming productive workers and bringing home an income. This underpins the family standard of living with regard to shelter or housing, food, quality of care, etc. It also benefits society because it is assumed without question that family members should take their place in the economy and the **division of labour** as specialized wage-earners, thereby contributing to the smooth running of the economy and society.

Evaluation of Murdock

Interpretivist sociologists (see Chpater 5, p. 171) argue that Murdock fails to acknowledge that families are the product of culture rather than biology, and that, consequently, family relationships and roles will take different forms even within the same society. For example, a range of different attitudes towards bringing up children can be seen in the UK which have their roots in different religious beliefs, access to economic opportunity, belief in particular child psychology approaches, etc. Think about how the educational function may differ in an upper-class White family compared with a Muslim family or a White family living on a deprived inner-city estate.

Murdock's definition of the family and its functions is also quite conservative in that it deprives certain members of society of family status; it implies that certain types of parenting – single, foster, homosexual and surrogate – are not quite as beneficial as the classic two heterosexual parents' model. In this sense, Murdock's model is political because it is clearly saying there are 'right' and 'wrong' ways to organize family life.

Family functions

Despite these doubts about the universality of the nuclear unit, functionalist sociologists have focused their attention on the functions of the family in order to assess its benefits for both the social structure and its members. Several functions have been identified that allegedly contribute to the wellbeing of society as well as parents and children.

Primary socialization of children

As we saw in Topic 1, Parsons (1955) saw the pre-industrial extended family as evolving into the modern nuclear family which specialized in the primary socialization of children. Parsons believed that personalities are 'made not born' – for Parsons, a child could only become a social adult by internalizing the shared norms and values of the society to which they belonged. He therefore saw nuclear families as 'personality factories', churning out young citizens committed to the rules, patterns of behaviour and belief systems which make involvement in social life possible. In this sense, the family acts as a bridge between children and their involvement in wider society.

As Cheal (2002) puts it, more simply: 'Parents today are encouraged to believe they have a special responsibility to ensure every child grows up happy, strong, confident, articulate, literate and skilled in every possible respect.'

Other sociologists point out that the family is important in terms of both political and religious socialization. Many of our beliefs, prejudices and anxieties may be rooted in the strong emotional bonds we forge with our parents during childhood.

Parsons saw mothers as playing the major role in the process of nurturing and socialization in families. Mothers, he claimed, were the 'expressive leaders' of the family who were biologically suited to looking after the emotional and cultural development of children. Such ideas reflect the dominant domestic arrangements in the UK where women have long held primary responsibility for looking after children and housework. These arrangements will be further explored in Topic 6.

Although the family is viewed as the main agent of socialization, it is important to remember that socialization is a life-long process. It does not end with the onset of adulthood or when a child leaves home. We acquire experience and knowledge throughout our lives from a range of different sources. It is therefore important to acknowledge the existence of secondary agents of socialization, such as the educational system, religion, the mass media and the workplace. Such agencies also strongly support what goes on in families. Fletcher (1988), for example, argued that childrearing in families is made more effective by the support offered by state institutions in the form of antenatal and postnatal care, health clinics, doctors, health visitors, social workers, teachers and housing officers.

Stabilization of adult personality

Parsons argued that the second major specialized function of the family is to relieve the stresses of modern-day living for its adult members. This theory, often called the 'warm bath' theory, claims that family life 'stabilizes' adult personalities. Steel and Kidd note the family does this by providing 'in the home a warm, loving, stable environment where the individual adults can be themselves and even "let themselves go" in a childish and undignified way. At the same time, the supervision and socialization of children gives parents a sense of stability and responsibility' (Steel and Kidd 2001, p.42). This emotional support and security, and the opportunity to engage in play

Figure 3.4 The 'warm bath' theory

Commuting   Deadlines   Competition

Budgets   Pace of life

Money

Productivity   Stress

Overtime

Hard work

Promotion   Hiring and firing

Job insecurity

Home and family

with children, acts as a safety valve in that it prevents stress from overwhelming adult family members and, as a result, it strengthens social stability. In this sense, Parsons viewed the family as a positive and beneficial place for all its members – a 'home sweet home', a 'haven in a heartless world' and a place in which people can be their natural selves (see Fig. 3.4).

Gender-role socialization

A further important aspect of socialization is that children learn the cultural patterns of behaviour expected of their gender, i.e. what is regarded as appropriate masculine or feminine behaviour. From an early age, people are trained by their parents' childrearing practices to conform to social expectations of how males and females should behave.

Chapman (2004, p.200) notes that traditionally:

>> *girls, through play, through the chores they did and through formal schooling would learn the right kind of attitudes and skills to perform their adult role of homemaker and mother. Boys, by the same token, were aimed squarely at the role of breadwinner by toning down their emotionality so that they would have what were presumed to be the right kinds of skill for work.* >>

In this sense, then, gender differences are not biological or natural but are socially constructed by society. These differences too are further reinforced by secondary agents of socialization, such as education and the mass media.

Social control

The family serves as an important agent of **social control** and, alongside secondary agencies such as religion, the criminal justice system and the mass media, polices the behaviour of society's members in order to maintain value consensus and social order. As Murdock pointed out, the family is generally regarded as the moral centre of society and sets the rules with regard to how people should behave, particularly with regard to sex and sexuality, e.g. it is generally regarded as deviant to engage in adulterous behaviour.

Setting the boundaries of deviant behaviour is an important consequence of primary socialization. Effective childrearing involves the development of a moral conscience that trains children to know the difference between 'right' and 'wrong'. This is backed up through parental use of positive sanctions (e.g. rewards) and negative sanctions (e.g. punishments). In this sense, the family contributes to the maintenance of other social institutions by ensuring the moral education of children who usually grow up to become decent, law-abiding citizens and workers.

Social status

Being born into a family results in the acquisition of a number of **ascribed statuses** – i.e. status allocated by age, gender, birth order, ethnicity, religion and social class. There is some evidence that the socio-economic status of our family provides us with a sense of family identity. It also has a profound influence over the quality of opportunities that we experience as we grow up. For example, the social and cultural supports we receive from parents with regard to education, e.g. nursery education, private tuition, attendance at private schools, access to computers and so on, are often dependent upon the economic supports our parents can offer us. Some families are able to offer their children considerable economic support, not only during their early years of dependence, but often well after they have flown the family nest, e.g. to go on to university or to set up homes of their own. Bernardes argues that such inequalities in economic maintenance result in helpless newborn infants being channelled into becoming a wide range of very unequal mature adults.

Economic consumption

In Topic 1, we saw that the pre-industrial family was responsible for the production of goods. Industrialization, however, led to factories taking over this function. Family companies, farms and shops continue to exist in the 21st century, but it can be argued that the family's economic function today is as a unit of **consumption** – goods and services provided by the economy are mainly consumed by the family unit. As Day Sclater notes:

>> *from ready-made meals, through washing machines and cars, to telecommunication services, the advertisers on our TV sets and in magazines clearly regard families as providing the main market for the goods and services they promote. Family income is expended largely on things for the family.*>> (Sclater 2000, p.24)

Recreation and leisure

During the 20th century, the family became an important centre for recreation and leisure. This was especially true for children in the 1990s, when parents started to interpret the world as a much riskier place for children and children began to spend more time in the home. Evans and Chandler (2006) note how homes, and specifically children's bedrooms, are often now furnished with media and technological entertainment, such as televisions, DVD players and computer games.

Protective and welfare function

Unlike many newly-born animals, the human baby is generally helpless and requires adult physical support and protection for a prolonged period of time. However, the welfare support that a child receives from its parents, e.g. shelter, diet and education, very much depends on the family's socio-economic status. This, in turn, is dependent on the occupation and income of the major wage-earners.

The welfare function also takes the form of family members being cared for and supported by other family members if they are ill, disabled, elderly or in poverty. The family, therefore, makes an important contribution to the health and welfare of the more vulnerable members of society, and works alongside social institutions such as the National Health Service.

Focus on research

Morrow (1998) Children's views of the family

A qualitative study of 183 children aged between 8 and 14, carried out by Morrow in 1998, found that children's views of the functions of the family do not necessarily conform to stereotypical images of the nuclear family. The research asked pupils to draw and write about 'who is important to me?', and to complete a sentence on 'what is a family?' and 'what are families for?' They were also given a short questionnaire asking whether or not five one-sentence descriptions of family type counted as family. Group discussions also took place which explored their responses to the questionnaire. The children were found to have a pragmatic view of family life – love, care and mutual respect were regarded by them as the essential functions of family life. They also had a very inclusive view of who was family – absent relatives and pets were regarded as family members. This research can be downloaded from www.jrf.org.uk.

1 **In what ways did the children's views agree with sociological views about the functions of the family?**

Functionalists, therefore, see the family as a crucial social institution functioning positively to bring about healthy societies and individuals.

Criticisms of functionalist views of the family

Functionalists tend to view the family as very harmonious but as we shall see in Topic 6, this view has been challenged by accounts of child abuse, domestic violence and the fall-out from divorce. As Cheal notes, functional relationships can easily slip into **dysfunctional** relationships, and love can often turn into hate in moments of intense emotion. He notes that 'we have to face the paradox that families are contexts of love and nurturance, but they are also contexts of violence and murder' (Cheal 2002, p.8).

Functionalist analyses of the nuclear family tend to be based on middle-class and American versions of family life, and they consequently neglect other influences, such as ethnicity, social class or religion. For example, Parsons does not consider the fact that wealth or poverty may determine whether women stay at home to look after children or not. Since Parsons wrote in the 1950s, many Western societies, including the UK, have become **multicultural**. Religious and ethnic **subcultural** differences may mean that Parsons' version of the family is no longer relevant in contemporary society.

Social and cultural changes may mean that some of the functions of the family have been modified or even abandoned altogether as demonstrated in Table 3.1.

The Marxist critique

Marxists are very critical of the process of primary socialization in the nuclear family because they argue that it reproduces and maintains class inequality. They argue that the main function of the nuclear family is to distract the working class from the fact they are exploited by capitalism. This is done in two ways:

- The hierarchical way in which nuclear families are traditionally organized (e.g. the male as the head of the household) discourages workers from questioning the hierarchical nature of capitalism and the inequalities in wealth and power that result from it.
- Parents are encouraged to teach their children that the main route to happiness and status lies in consumerism and the acquisition of material possessions. Consequently, the organization of capitalism (and its inequalities) often goes unchallenged by a generation fixated on the acquisition of the latest designer labels and trendy gadgets.

From a Marxist perspective, then, the functions of the nuclear family benefit those who run the capitalist system rather than the whole of society, as functionalists suggest.

The Marxist-feminist critique

Marxist feminists argue that the nuclear family functions to benefit capitalism and, therefore, the wealthy rather than the whole of society. Men too benefit from family life at the expense of women. Marxist-feminists argue that the focus on women as mothers puts considerable cultural pressure on women to have children and to take time out of the labour market to bring them up. These children become the workforce of the future at little or no expense to the capitalist class. This also benefits men, because it means that women cannot compete on a level playing field for jobs or promotion opportunities if their first priority is looking after children.

Furthermore, it is argued that socialization of children ensures that the pattern of male dominance and female subordination (symbolized by men's traditional role as main economic earner and head of household, and the idea that women should primarily be responsible for children) is reproduced generation after generation.

The radical-feminist critique

Radical feminists argue that the nuclear family mainly functions to benefit men because gender-role socialization results in

Table 3.1 Changes in the functions of the family

Family function	Recent social trends – have these undermined or supported family functions?
Procreation	The size of families has declined as people choose lifestyle over the expense of having children. Many women prefer to pursue careers and are making the decision not to have children. The UK birth rate has consequently fallen.
Regulating sex	Sex outside marriage is now the norm. Alternative sexualities, e.g. homosexuality, are becoming more socially acceptable.
Stabilizing personalities	A high percentage of marriages end in divorce. However, some argue that divorce and remarriage rates are high because people continue to search for emotional security.
Economic	Although welfare benefits are seen by some as undermining family economic responsibilities, the family is still a crucial agency of economic support, especially as the housing market becomes more expensive for first-time buyers, and young people spend longer periods in education with the prospect of debt through student loans.
Welfare	A decline in state funding of welfare in the 1980s led to the encouragement of 'community care', in which the family – and especially women – became responsible for the care of the elderly, the long-term sick and the disabled.
Socialization	This is still rooted in the family, although there are concerns that the mass media and the peer group have become more influential, with the result that children are growing up faster.
Social control	Power has shifted between parents and children as children acquire more rights. This trend, alongside attempts to ban smacking in England and Wales, is thought by some sociologists to undermine parental discipline. Some sociologists argue that families need fathers and see the absence of fathers in one-parent families as a major cause of **delinquency**.

males and females subscribing to a set of ideas that largely confirm male power and superiority. They argue that the nuclear family is the main arena in which **patriarchal ideology** is transmitted to children. This ideology encourages the notion that the **sexual division of labour** is 'natural' and unchangeable. It also results in the exploitation of women because patriarchal ideology mainly views women as sexual objects when single, and mothers/housewives when married.

Evaluating Marxism and feminist theories of the family

Feminist theories of the family have dated fairly badly, because they fail to account for recent economic and social changes, such as the **feminization of the economy**, the educational success of young females, women's use of divorce, and many women's rejection of domestic labour as their unique responsibility.

Feminist theories portray women as passively accepting their lot – the reality, however, is that women can adopt a range of active social identities today, many of which do not involve playing a secondary role to men. In other words, many young women are resisting traditional male definitions of what their role should be.

There is an implicit assumption in feminist theories that all male–female relationships involve male exploitation of women. However, the bulk of male–female relationships are probably based on mutual love and respect rather than exploitation, domination and subordination.

Both Marxism and feminism have a good deal in common with functionalism despite their ideological differences. All three theories see the functions of the family as determined by the needs of society and the economy. All three theories are guilty of overemphasizing the nuclear family and

neglecting the rich diversity of family types in modern society. (This diversity will be explored further in Topic 5.)

From an interpretivist point of view, functionalism, feminism and Marxism tend to neglect the meanings families have for individuals and how family members interpret family relationships. Both feminism and Marxism, for example, can be accused of deliberately ignoring those accounts of family life in which some females suggest motherhood is a fulfilling and rewarding experience.

Marxism and feminism are also very critical of the nuclear family but fail to offer any practical alternatives to it.

Check your understanding

1   What are the four universal functions of the family according to Murdock?

2   What did Parsons mean when he described the nuclear family as a personality factory?

3   What is the 'warm bath' theory?

4   In what ways might recent social trends challenge the idea that the nuclear family functions to relieve the stresses of modern living for adults?

5   How are functionalist, feminist and Marxists alike in their analyses of the functions of the nuclear family?

Key terms

Ascribed status inherited status.

Consensus common agreement on shared values.

Consumption the ways in which individuals use goods and services.

Delinquency youth crime.

Dysfunctional having negative consequences.

Feminization of the economy an economic trend that began in the 1990s whereby the majority of newly available jobs were aimed at women.

Functional beneficial, fulfilling a purpose.

Functional prerequisites the basic needs of society, such as the need for social order.

Multicultural having more than one culture.

Patriarchal ideology male-dominated ideas.

Procreation having children.

Sexual division of labour the distribution of childcare and housework tasks according to gender.

Social control process of persuading, encouraging and enforcing conformity.

Subcultural subscribing to cultural values and norms that may be different from the mainstream.

Activities

Research idea

Using this chapter, make a list of the functions that the family performs. Find five people of different ages and ask them to rate on a scale of 1 to 5 how important these functions are to them (where 1 is 'very important' and 5 'not important'). Also ask two open questions 'what is a family?' and 'what are families for?'

Web.task

Visit websites dedicated to the family, such as: www.familyeducation.com and www.familiesonline.co.uk

Look at the content of these sites in terms of advice, news and letters from parents. What functions should families be performing according to these sites? Do such functions support the functionalist theory of the family?

The functions of the family

Item A

Ronald Fletcher distinguishes between 'essential' and 'non-essential' functions of the family. He argues that, while other agencies have become responsible for six 'non-essential' functions, the family still performs three 'essential' functions that only it can perform. These are the stable satisfaction of sexual needs, the production and rearing of children, and the provision of a home. Fletcher argues that the state actually supports the family in fulfilling these essential functions through the provision of health care, child benefit, council housing, etc. Fletcher argues that the family is no longer primarily responsible for production of housing, clothing and food for its own needs, education, recreation, religion, health and welfare, although he stresses that the family still continues to play an important role in most of these areas of social life.

Adapted from Steel, E. and Kidd, W. (2001) *The Family*, Basingstoke: Palgrave

Item B

During the 1970s and 1980s, feminist perspectives dominated most debates and research on the family. Many feminist writers questioned the functionalist vision that the family is a cooperative unit based on common interests and mutual support. They have sought to show that the presence of unequal power relationships within the family means that men benefit more than women from family life. They have emphasized two main themes. First, they argue that there exists a domestic division of labour in which women are exploited by men. Some feminists see this as a product of capitalism, while others claim that families were characterized by patriarchy well before industrialization came along. Second, feminists have drawn attention to the unequal power relationships that exist in many families that they see as responsible for domestic violence.

Adapted from Giddens, A. (2001) *Sociology* (4th edn), Cambridge: Polity Press, pp. 175–7

Item C

The existence of 'the family' has been taken for granted by many sociologists. For functionalists, in particular, any query over the use of 'the family' appears trivial and tends to be dismissed. The failure by functionalists to question the idea of 'the family' has allowed all sorts of mistaken ideas to persist, such as the naturalness of monogamy (whereas many societies permit more than one marriage), the inevitability of female inferiority (which many feminists dispute), the right of men to control and abuse women (which many women dispute), and the right of parents to smack children (which is banned in some European countries, including Scotland).

Adapted from Bernardes, J. (1997) *Family Studies: An Introduction*, London: Routledge, pp. 4–5

(a) **Explain what is meant by 'patriarchy' (Item B).** (2 marks)

(b) **Explain the difference between the Marxist feminist and radical-feminist views of the family.** (4 marks)

(c) **Suggest three functions that the family may perform for its members (Item A).** (6 marks)

(d) **Using information from Items A, B and C and elsewhere, assess the view that the nuclear family functions to benefit all its members and society as a whole.** (24 marks)

Grade booster Getting top marks in the 24-mark question

You should identify the view in the question as one put forward by functionalists and explain how it fits with their consensus view of society. You need to describe the kinds of functions they see the family as performing and explain how these benefit both individual members and wider society. You must evaluate the functionalist view, and you can do so by using different feminist and/or Marxist views of the role of the family in benefiting the men or the ruling class. Use concepts such as patriarchy, capitalism and reproduction of labour.

The family, morality and state policy

SUPER DADS OF FATHERS 4 JUSTICE

Getting you thinking

Valerie Riches, the founder president of a body called Family and Youth Concern, is a woman of conviction. She is convinced, for instance, that sex education harms the young and undermines the family. She is clear that sending childless housewives out to work means that men's 'masculine role as the provider and father' is being obliterated. She has also criticized the decision of a gay couple to have a child by a surrogate mother. 'It's against the natural order of things', she says. Interestingly, although Ms Riches is second to none in her opposition to single-parent families, she is none the less firmly opposed to the introduction of emergency contraception – the morning-after pill – which might reduce the creation of more such faulty units. 'Taking a morning-after pill will encourage girls to be easy and carefree', she says.

Adapted from Bennett, C. (2000) 'Valerie's moral lead', *The Guardian*, 14 December

1   Look carefully at the images above. How might some people see them as threatening the traditional family?

2   In the article, five things are identified that Valerie Riches thinks are undermining the family. What are they? Do you agree that these things are harming the family unit?

3   Think of any ways in which the government influences your family life. In your opinion, should it play a greater or a lesser role? What role, if any, should it play?

In the UK over the last 50 years, public debate about the family has focused on the changing nature of family life and its impact on society. This debate has often been dominated by those who, like Valerie Riches, take the view that the traditional nuclear family and the moral character of the young are under attack from a number of 'threats', including sex education, contraception, working mothers, homosexuality, divorce and single-parent families. Moreover, the state is accused of not doing enough to protect the traditional family. In fact, some commentators have suggested that liberal state policies, especially those introduced in the 1960s, are responsible for starting the perceived decline in traditional family values.

The golden age of family life

Those who claim that the family is in decline can be grouped under the label '**New Right**', in that they are usually conservative thinkers and politicians who believe very strongly in tradition. These commentators often assume that there was once a 'golden age' of the family, in which husbands and wives were strongly committed to each other for life, and children were brought up to respect their parents and social institutions such as the law.

Many New Right thinkers see the 1960s and early 1970s as the beginning of a sustained attack on traditional family values, particularly by the state. They point to social policies, such as the legalization of abortion in the 1960s and the NHS making the contraceptive pill available on prescription, as marking the beginning of family decline. The sexual freedom that women experienced as a result of these changes supposedly lessened their commitment to the family. At the same time, equal opportunities and equal pay legislation distracted women from their 'natural' careers as mothers. The 1969 Divorce Reform Act was seen as undermining commitment to marriage. The decriminalization of homosexuality and the lowering of the homosexual age of consent have been interpreted as particularly important symbols of moral decline, because the New Right see homosexuality as 'unnatural' and deviant.

Familial ideology

New Right views on the family reflect a **familial ideology** – a set of ideas about what constitutes an 'ideal' family. Their preferred model is the traditional nuclear family with a clear sexual division of labour, as described in Topic 1 (see p. 73). This ideology is transmitted by sections of the media and advertising, politicians, religious leaders, and pressure groups such as 'Family and Youth Concern'.

Family decline and the 'New Right'

This familial ideology also makes a number of assumptions about how not to organize family life. In particular, it sees the declining popularity of marriage, the increase in cohabitation, the number of births outside marriage, and teenage pregnancy as symptoms of the decline in family morality. Homosexuality,

single parenthood, liberal sex education, abortion and working mothers are all seen as threats, both to family stability and to the wellbeing of society itself.

A good example of the New Right approach to the family can be seen in the view that there exists an underclass of criminals, unmarried mothers and idle young men who are responsible for rising crime. It is argued that this underclass is welfare-dependent, and that teenage girls are deliberately getting pregnant in order to obtain council housing or state benefits. To make things worse, this underclass is socializing its children into a culture revolving around crime and delinquency, and anti-authority, anti-work and anti-family values.

State policy and the family

Three broad trends can be seen in state policy which suggest that the ideology of the traditional nuclear family has had, despite New Right misgivings, some positive influence on government thinking:

1   Tax and welfare policies have generally favoured and encouraged the heterosexual married couple rather than cohabiting couples, single parents and same-sex couples. Graham Allan (1985) goes as far as to suggest that these policies have actively discouraged cohabitation and one-parent families.
2   Policies such as the payment of child benefit to the mother, and the government's reluctance to fund free universal nursery provision, have reinforced the idea that women should take prime responsibility for children.
3   The fact that a coordinated set of family policies was not introduced until 1999 may reflect the state's traditional tendency to see the family as a **private institution** and its reluctance to interfere in the family's internal organization.

Nevertheless, New Right thinkers still believe that grave damage has been inflicted on the nuclear family ideal by misguided government policy. For example, they claim that governments have encouraged mothers to return to work and, consequently, generations of children have been 'damaged' by **maternal deprivation**. There have been few tax or benefit policies aimed at encouraging mothers to stay at home with their children. The New Right argue that commitment to marriage has been weakened by governments making divorce too easy to obtain. Morgan (2000) even suggests that the government is 'antimarriage'. The New Right also claim that 'deviant' family types, such as single-parent families, have been encouraged by welfare policies.

Criticisms of the New Right

State policy until 1997 was generally aimed at ensuring the family unit did not overwhelm the rights of the individuals within it. Therefore, legislation focused on improving the social and economic position of women. For example, the Conservative government made marital rape illegal in 1991. The rights of children have also been enhanced through successive Children's Acts, e.g. 1989. There is no doubt that such legislation has undermined traditional male dominance in families, but many people believe that improved rights for women and children strengthen the family rather than weaken it.

Post-1997 family policy

As Lewis (2007) notes, UK governments, unlike their European counterparts, did not 'do' explicit family policy. However, Labour appointed a Minister for Children in 2003, and in 2007, formed the new Department for Children, Schools and Families.

Lewis argues that Labour have particularly taken the idea of 'social investment in children' seriously and have increasingly recognized that family forms are changing. Lone mothers have ceased to be condemned as a moral problem and threat. Rather, Labour has introduced policies such as the New Deal of 1998, aimed at helping lone mothers back into paid work.

Labour has also recognized that there are few families in the 21st century which have exclusively a male breadwinner. Most families rely on two incomes and most women work (albeit often part time). Lewis notes that Labour has:

- invested in subsidies for nursery childcare
- lengthened maternity care from 14 weeks to nine months
- almost doubled maternity pay
- introduced the right for parents of young children to ask for flexible working patterns from their employers.

However, this explicit family policy has attracted criticism that it is undermining family privacy and that Labour has constructed a 'nanny state' which overinterferes in personal living arrangements. Furthermore, despite these innovations, the government is still accused of conforming to familial ideology in that the policy emphasis is still overwhelmingly on motherhood rather than on parenting in general or fatherhood, as seen in the limited rights of fathers to take paid paternity leave. Moreover, some cabinet ministers have regularly stated that married parents create the best environment for bringing up children. Critics suggest that, on the whole, state policy continues to reinforce familial ideology, as can be seen in Table 3.2.

Evaluating familial ideology

Feminists have claimed that familial ideology is merely patriarchal ideology – a set of ideas deliberately encouraged by men that ensure male dominance in the workplace. For example, Oakley points out that if society subscribes to the view that women have a maternal instinct, it follows on that society will believe that women who elect not to have children are somehow deviant, that 'real' women are committed to giving up jobs to bring up children, and that working mothers are somehow 'damaging' their children. Oakley argues that this aspect of familial ideology benefits men because it results in women withdrawing from the labour market – they do not compete with men for jobs which results in men enjoying advantages in promotion and pay. This ideology ties women to men, marriage, the home, children and, for a while, promotes economic dependence. Moreover, such family ideology permeates gender-role socialization – girls are taught from infancy that motherhood is their ultimate goal.

Other sociologists have argued that familial ideology has led to the nuclear family being over**idealized**. It fails to acknowledge that divorce and one-parent families might be

	State policy	Familial ideology
Care in the community	The state has encouraged families to take responsibility for the elderly and long-term sick and disabled. Female members of the family often carry the burden of this care, which means they are less likely to work full time and are more likely to be economically dependent upon a male.	The traditional sexual division of labour is reinforced: women as emotional and physical caretakers, and men as breadwinners.
Housing policy	Fox Harding (1996) argues that the best council housing is often allocated to married couples with children and the worst housing on problem estates is allocated to one-parent families. Housing in the UK is overwhelmingly designed for the nuclear family.	The traditional nuclear family is clearly the dominant family type. Other types of family are 'punished' or discouraged.
Parenting	Fathers can take either one or two weeks paid leave from work on the birth of a child, compared with up to 39 weeks for women. The Child Support Agency (CSA) was set up to pursue absent fathers in order that they take financial responsibility for their children. Mothers are often awarded custody of children after divorce and fathers are often denied access to children by the law. Unmarried fathers have few legal rights over their children compared with married men.	It is assumed that women's primary role is motherhood and childcare rather than paid work. It is implied that men have no childcare skills. The function of the CSA is to ensure women's continuing economic dependence on men. Marriage is seen as superior to cohabitation.

Table 3.2 State policy and familial ideology

'lesser evils' than domestic violence and emotional unhappiness. The ideology also neglects key cultural changes, such as the changing roles of men and women and, especially, cultural and ethnic diversity, as well as social and economic problems such as poverty, homelessness and racism.

The view that the family is a private institution has led to the general neglect of severe social problems, such as child abuse and domestic violence. Until the late 1980s, for example, only as a very last resort would social workers break up families in which they suspected abuse. It took a series of abuse-related child deaths to change this policy.

A similar theme suggests that the ideology results in the worsening of family problems, such as domestic violence, because women believe that their husbands 'punish' them for being 'bad' wives and mothers. They therefore see themselves as deserving of punishment and believe that they should stick by their man through thick and thin. This theme is explored further in Topic 6.

Barrett and McIntosh (1982) argue that familial ideology is antisocial because it dismisses alternative family types as irrelevant, inferior and deviant. For example, as a result of the emphasis on the nuclear family ideal and the view that families need fathers, one-parent families are seen as the cause of social problems, such as rising crime rates and disrespect for authority. This theme will be further explored in Topic 5.

The family: in decline or just changing?

New Right politicians strongly believe that the family – and therefore family ideology – is in decline, and that this is the source of all our social problems. However, it may simply be that family ideology is evolving rather than deteriorating, as we realize that the traditional family denies women and children the same rights as men. People today may be less willing to tolerate these forms of inequality and the violence and abuse that often accompany them. Increasing acceptance and tolerance of a range of family types may be healthy for society, rather than a symptom of moral decay.

Focus on research

Reynolds *et al.* (2003)
Caring and counting

The researchers interviewed 37 mothers and 30 fathers in couples who had at least one pre-school child (Reynolds *et al.* 2003). The mothers were working in a hospital or in an accountancy firm. All the mothers in the study had strong, traditional views about what being a 'good mother' and a 'good partner' was about. Employment did not necessarily lead to more egalitarian relationships with their partners.

In fact, most of the mothers and fathers interviewed subscribed to highly traditional and stereotypical views about the gendered division of labour within the home. The mothers had primary responsibility for the home and the conduct of family life. Mothers who worked full time were just as concerned as those working part time to 'be there' for their children and to meet the needs of their children and their family.

The researchers found no evidence of mothers becoming more 'work centred' at the expense of family life.

Apart from increasing the family income, mothers also felt their employment was helping them to meet their children's emotional and social development. Separate interviews with the women's partners revealed widespread agreement that the mother's work was

having a positive impact on family relationships. Most fathers felt their children had benefited from their mothers' work, which provided a positive role model for their children.

Some mothers, nevertheless, expressed concern that their job had a negative impact on the family, particularly when they were overstretched at work, felt tired or had trouble 'switching off' from a bad day at work. A number of fathers also felt uneasy about the demands placed on their partners at work and the effect that work-related stress could have on their children and their relationship with each other.

Reynolds, T., Callender, C. and Edwards, R. (2003) *Caring and Counting: The impact of mothers' employment on family relationships*, York: Joseph Rowntree Foundation (www.jrf.org.uk)

1 **Comment on the sample used in the study.**

2 **How did parents feel that mothers' employment was having a positive effect on their families?**

3 **What concerns were expressed about mothers' employment?**

Focus on research

Jonathan Gershuny (2000)
Standards of parenting

A major theme of those who believe that the family is in decline is working parents and particularly working mothers. However, research illustrates the complexity of the debate about whether standards of parenting have fallen. In 2000, Jonathan Gershuny, using data from the diaries of 3000 parents, suggested that the quality of parenting had significantly improved compared with the past. He noted that the time British parents spent playing with and reading to their children had increased fourfold and this was the case for both working and non-working parents.

1 How could the use of diaries in Gershuny's research be criticized?

Check your understanding

1 What legislation introduced in the 1960s and 1970s is seen as damaging to the family, according to New Right commentators?

2 What is the attitude of the Labour government towards the family?

3 What are the main symptoms of the decline in family morality, according to the New Right?

4 In what ways has familial ideology had an impact on state policy?

5 In what ways has state policy been good for family members?

Key terms

Familial ideology the view that a particular type of family (e.g. the nuclear family) and particular living arrangements (e.g. marriage, men as breadwinners, women as mothers and housewives) are the ideals that people should aspire to.

Idealized presented as an ideal, i.e. something perfect.

Maternal deprivation the view that if a child is deprived of maternal love for any significant period of time, it will grow up to be psychologically damaged.

New Right a group of thinkers and commentators who believe very strongly in tradition. They tend to be against change and to support the Conservative Party.

Private institution something that occurs 'behind closed doors', with few links with the wider community.

Activities

Research ideas

1 Conduct a mini-survey of teenagers and old-age pensioners to see whether there is any major difference in how they perceive family life and so-called 'threats' to it, such as homosexuality, cohabitation and illegitimacy.

2 Observe the media and other institutions for signs of familial ideology. You could, for example:

- study television commercials at different times of the day
- examine the content of specific types of programmes, such as soap operas or situation comedies
- analyse the content of women's magazines
- stroll through family-orientated stores, such as Mothercare, Boots and BHS, to see whether familial ideology is apparent in their organization, packaging, marketing, etc.

Web.tasks

1 Visit the websites of organizations dedicated to protecting family life, such as the Family Matters Institute at www.familymatters.org.uk and Family and Youth Concern at www.famyouth.org.uk and make a list of the family issues they consider to be important. In what ways do these issues support familial ideology?

2 Visit the website of the Department for Children, Schools and Families at www.dfes.org.uk as well as the websites of the major political parties. What specific statements do these sites make about the family?

The family, morality and state policy

Item A

Conservative thinkers have tended to define what the traditional family should be in terms of a heterosexual unit based on marriage and co-residence. A clear segregation of tasks based on sexual differences is seen as the 'traditional', 'natural' and 'God-given' way of ordering our lives. It is assumed that the man is the 'natural' head of the family. The family's key tasks are the reproduction of the next generation, the protection of dependent children and the inculcation of proper moral values in children. The family also disciplines men and women in economic and sexual terms: it keeps us in our proper place. Order, hierarchy and stability are seen as the key features of the 'healthy' family and the 'healthy' society. However, conservative commentators see this traditional family as under threat and in decline. This is seen as one of the main causes of the claimed wider moral decay in society.

Adapted from Sherratt, N. and Hughes, G. (2000) 'Family: from tradition to diversity?' in G. Hughes and R. Fergusson (eds) *Ordering Lives: Family, Work and Welfare*, London: Routledge

Item B

<<The state has intervened significantly in families for a considerable length of time, whether by providing support (such as family income credits for those earning low wages and with dependent children) or in overseeing the bringing up of children (if social workers think this is not being done properly, then children may be put temporarily or more permanently into the care of the local authority). This interference has not lessened – indeed, as politicians and the media have come together to discuss what they see as the decline of the family, so the extent of that interference has increased. However, conservative thinkers tend to believe that there has not been enough state input into protecting the traditional family, or that state interference has actually contributed to its decline by encouraging the development of 'deviant' living arrangements.>>

Source: Abercrombie, N. & Warde, A. (2000) *Contemporary British Society* (3rd edn), Cambridge: Polity Press

Item C

The House of Lords has ruled that a homosexual couple in a stable relationship can be defined as a family. One of the law lords, Lord Nicholls, defined a family as follows: 'The concept underlying membership of a family is the sharing of lives together in a single family unit living in one house. It seems to me that the bond must be one of love and affection, not of a casual nature, but in a relationship which is permanent, or at least intended to be so. As a result of that permanent attachment, other characteristics will follow, such as a readiness to support each other emotionally and financially, to care for and look after each other in times of need, and to provide a companionship in which mutual interests and activities can be shared'. Dr Adrian Rogers of the pressure group, Family Focus, deplored the ruling and said 'homosexual couples cannot be defined as families – the basis of true love is the ability to procreate and have children'.

Adapted from *The Guardian*, 29 October 1999

(a) **Explain what is meant by 'familial ideology'.** (2 marks)

(b) **Identify two ways in which the state may intervene in family life (Item B).** (4 marks)

(c) **Suggest three factors which conservative or New Right thinkers might see as undermining the traditional family (Item A).** (6 marks)

(d) **Using information from Items B and C and elsewhere, examine the ways in which state policy may affect families and households.** (24 marks)

Grade booster   Getting top marks in the 24-mark question

You need to identify a range of different state policies and explain how they affect families and households. Make sure you use the Items – for example, Item B includes reference to family income credits and the role of local authorities and social workers in child protection. Consider other policies too, such as maternity and paternity leave, tax and benefits, council housing, policies on homosexuality, abortion and contraception, equal pay, and so on – how are these likely to affect families and households? You should also link your answer to theories such as New Right and feminism.

Demographic trends and family life

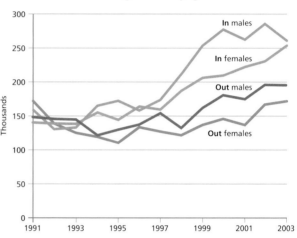

Getting you thinking

Births[1,2] and deaths[1,2] (UK)

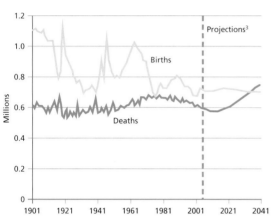

1 Data for 1901 to 1921 exclude Ireland which was constitutionally a part of the United Kingdom during this period.
2 Data from 1981 exclude the non-residents of Northern Ireland.
3 2004-based projections for 2005 to 2041.

International migration into and out of the United Kingdom: by gender

Source (both graphs): Babb, P. et al. (2006) Social Trends 36, Basingstoke: Palgrave Macmillan

© Posy Simmonds (from The Observer, 25 October 1998)

Single Parent Family · Advertising Family · Lesbian Family · Child-free Family · Gay Family · Step Family · Divorced Family · Socially Excluded · Nuclear Family · Long term Family

1 Examine the graphs above – what trends can be observed?

2 How do you think that the trends relating to births, deaths and migration will influence the nature of family life in the UK?

3 How do the family setups portrayed in the cartoon challenge the traditional view of the family?

The study of **demography** is focused on how the number of births and deaths, and the number of people entering and leaving the country (migration) all affect the size, sex and age structure of the population. As we shall see, demographic changes over the past 100 years have had a major influence on British family life. The nuclear family is no longer the main way in which living arrangements are organized in the UK. Consequently, some sociologists, notably Rapoport et al. (1982), have been very critical of the functionalist and New Right view

that the typical family is nuclear. They point out that even back in 1978, only 20 per cent of families fitted the traditionalist idea of a married couple household, i.e. a father who went out to work and a mother who stayed at home to look after the two children. Rapoport and colleagues argue that family life in Britain today is actually characterized by **diversity**. A range of family types exists with diverse internal setups reflecting the changing demography of British society.

The population of the UK

The population of the United Kingdom grew steadily between 1971 and 2003 to reach 59.8 million people in 2004. Population projections suggest that it will reach 65 million in 2023 and 67 million by 2031. The rate of population change over time depends upon four demographic factors:

- the **birth rate** – refers to the number of live births per 1000 of the population over a year
- the **fertility rate** – refers to the number of live births per 1000 women aged 15 to 44 over one year
- the **death rate** – refers to the number of deaths per 1000 of the population over the course of a year
- **migration** – refers to the number of people entering the UK (i.e. **immigration**) and the number of people leaving the UK (i.e. **emigration**).

Reasons for population growth

Up to the 1950s and 1960s, natural change (i.e. more births than deaths) was the main reason for population growth in the UK, although from the 1980s onwards, net migration (i.e. immigration exceeding emigration) has been the main factor. For example, in the 1950s, natural change accounted for 98 per cent of population change and net migration for only 2 per cent. Between 2001 and 2004, net migration accounted for two thirds of the increase in the UK population.

Changes in the birth rate

Only 716 000 children were born in 2004. This is 34 per cent fewer births than in 1901 and 21 per cent fewer than 1971. However, if we examine the birth rate over the course of the century, it has not been a straightforward history of decline. It is actually a history of fluctuations. There was a fall in births during the First World War, followed by a postwar 'baby boom', with births peaking at 1.1 million in 1920. The number of births then fell and remained low during the interwar period. Births increased again after the Second World War with another 'baby-boom'. There was also an increase in births in the late 1980s and early 1990s. This was the result of the larger cohort of women born in the 1960s entering their childbearing years. Since 2001, the birth rate has steadily risen. In 2007, the ONS announced that the 2006 birth rate was the highest for 26 years.

There are a number of reasons why the number of births in the 21st century is lower than the number of births in 1901:

- A major decline in the infant mortality rate, (i.e. the number of children dying at birth or in their first year of life per 1000 births) occurred. This began in the 19th century because of improvements in sanitation, water supplies and nutrition, and continued into the 20th century. Contrary to popular belief, medicine was not mainly responsible for children surviving into adulthood. Mass vaccination was not introduced until after the Second World War, although it obviously contributed to the better health enjoyed by

children. The decline in child mortality rates meant that parents did not need to have lots of children to ensure that a few survived.

- As standards of living increased and childhood came to be seen as a special period in our lives (see Topic 7), having children became an expensive business and, consequently, parents chose to limit the size of their families.
- Attitudes towards women's roles dramatically changed during the course of the 20th century and this had a profound effect upon women's attitudes towards family life, having children, education and careers. In particular, it resulted in a decline in fertility as women chose to have fewer children and some chose not to have children at all.

Changes in the fertility rate

The fertility rate generally refers to the number of children that women of childbearing age have in any one year. Fertility rates have generally declined over the past 100 years. For example, in 1900 there were 115 live births per 1000 women aged 15 to 44, compared with only 57 in 1999 and 54.5 in 2001.

Another way of looking at fertility is to examine the Total Fertility Rate (TFR) – the number of children that are born to an average woman during her childbearing life. In 2004, the UK had a TFR of 1.77 children per woman but recent ONS data suggests that the first baby boom of the 21st century may be on its way because the fertility rate rose to 1.8 babies per woman in 2005 and again to 1.87 in 2006. This was the fifth annual rise in a row and resulted in the most babies being born in a single year since 1993.

Fertility and age

There is evidence that women are delaying having families. Changes in fertility rates suggest that women are having children at an older age than they were 30 years ago. In general, fertility rates for women aged 30 and above have increased, while those for women aged below 30 have declined. The average age of married women giving birth has increased by six years since 1971 to 30 in 2003. The highest rate of fertility is found in the age group 30 to 34 whilst 2005 ONS figures showed a seven per cent increase in births among women aged between 35 and 39. Moreover, the number of children born to women aged 40 and over has doubled in the last 20 years.

Explanations for changes in fertility rate

There are three main reasons why fertility rates fell towards the end of the 20th century:

- Reliable birth control, particularly the contraceptive pill, gave women far greater power over reproduction.
- Educational opportunities expanded for females, particularly entry into university. This coincided with an increase in job opportunities for females as the service sector of the economy expanded. There is some evidence that the recent rise in the fertility rate of women aged 35 and above is due to high earners who took up their university places in the 1980s.

- Attitudes towards family life underwent a profound cultural change as a result of economic change. Women could see that there were other lifestyle choices in addition to getting married and having children.

The recent rise in fertility has been credited to the increase in the number of immigrants to the UK who tend to have larger families. For example, in 2005, 146 944 children were born to mothers who did not come from Britain. In 1998 the total was 86 345. Babies born to mothers from overseas accounted for 21.9 per cent of all births in 2005, up from 20.8 per cent in 2004.

Dual-earner families

There is some evidence that declining fertility rates have encouraged the decline of the full-time mother and encouraged the growth of dual-career families in which couples combine paid work with family life and childcare. Over 60% of couples with children now combine jobs and family life. There are generally two types of dual-earner families. Some professional couples are extremely committed to their careers but make the decision to have a child once these careers are established. These couples are probably partly responsible for the doubling in the number of women aged 40 or over having babies in the last 20 years. These couples can probably also afford professional childcare services such as nannies, au-pairs and private nurseries.

The other more common type of dual-earner family is composed of the husband who earns the major share of the family income and the female who works part-time. In this situation, it is likely that it is she who takes the major responsibility for childcare and the upkeep of the home.

Births outside marriage

New Right commentators have been especially disturbed by the fact that one in three babies is now born outside marriage. In particular, media **moral panics** have focused on the fact that the UK has the highest rate of teenage pregnancy in Europe. For example, in England and Wales in 2003, there were 34 138 pregnancies in the 16 to 17 age group, 7690 pregnancies in the 15 to 16 age group and 334 pregnancies in the 14 and under age group. Only 54 per cent of these conceptions resulted in a birth.

However, according to the National Council for One Parent Families, the under-16 conception rate has fallen considerably, compared with the 1960s, and it has fallen slightly over the last ten years to approximately 8 per 1000 girls. Only 3 per cent of unmarried mothers are teenagers, and most of them live at home with their parents. Experts are generally sceptical that such teenagers are deliberately getting pregnant in order to claim state housing and benefits. Moreover, four out of five births outside marriage are registered to both parents, and three-quarters of these are living at the same address. Most births outside marriage, therefore, are to cohabiting couples. It should also be pointed out that a significant number of marriages break up in the first year after having a child, which suggests that marriage is not always the stable institution for procreation that the New Right claim it is.

Childlessness

Some sociologists argue that we should be more concerned about the trend towards childlessness that has appeared in recent years. The Family Policy Studies Centre estimates that one woman in five will choose to remain childless, and this figure is expected to double in the next 20 years (McAllister 1998). In 2000, one in five women aged 40 had not had children compared with one in ten in 1980, and this figure is expected to rise to one in four by 2018.

The death rate

The annual number of deaths has remained relatively steady since 1901. There were peaks in the number of deaths during both the First and Second World Wars. The peak of 690 000 in 1918 represented the highest annual number of deaths ever recorded; these were due both to losses during the First World War and the influenza epidemic which followed it. However, as the population has increased, life expectancy has increased and death rates have fallen; between 1971 and 2004 the death rate for all males fell by 21 per cent, while the death rate for all females fell by 9 per cent.

Life expectancy

In 1851, life expectancy at birth in England and Wales was 40 years for males and 44 years for females. Just 150 years later, in modern-day industrialized UK, life expectancy has nearly doubled from Victorian levels: children born in 2004 will, on average, live for 78 years. This increase in life expectancy is the result of improved public health (sanitation and hygiene), medical technology and practice (drugs such as vaccines and antibiotics), rising living standards (which have improved nutritional intake and housing quality) and better care and welfare facilities (which have been mainly provided by the State).

However, life expectancy is not uniform across the country. There is some evidence that life expectancy differs according to region, e.g. male life expectancy in 2002 was 76.2 years in England, but 73.5 in Scotland. There is also evidence that life expectancy also depends on social class and ethnicity – those in middle-class jobs tend to live longer than those in manual jobs and the unemployed, whilst some ethnic minorities have lower life expectancy than White people.

The ageing population

The decline in the death rate, especially the infant mortality rate, and the increase in life expectancy has led to an ageing of the UK population. There are increasing numbers of people aged 65 and over and decreasing numbers of children under 16. In 1821, there were very large numbers of young people but very few of them were surviving into old age. Today, there are fewer young people – only 12 per cent of the population is aged under 10 years compared with 27 per cent in 1821, whilst the numbers of those aged over 80 years have increased from 1 per cent in 1821 to 4 per cent in 2004. However, the UK also saw an acceleration in this process in the late 20th century – the number of people aged under 16 declined by 18 per cent between 1971 and 2004 whilst the number of people aged over 65 increased by 29 per cent in the same period. It is predicted that people aged over 65 years will outnumber people aged under 16 for the first time in 2014 and that the gap will widen thereafter.

Elderly one-person households

The ageing of the population has led to an increase in the number of one-person households over state pension age as a proportion of all households. In 2005, 14 per cent of all households were of this type. Women aged 65 and over were more likely to live alone than men because of their superior life expectancy and because they tend to marry men older than themselves. In 2005, 59 per cent of women aged 75 and over were living alone.

Kinship diversity

Although older people are increasingly living alone, this does not mean that they are isolated. Evidence suggests that many of them have regular contact with extended kin. There is evidence that working-class families, in particular, still see great virtue in maintaining **extended families**. The study *Villains* by Janet Foster (1990) – of an East End London community – found that adults chose to live only a few streets away from their parents and other close relatives such as grandparents, aunts, uncles and cousins, and visited them regularly. Ties

between mothers and children were particularly strong. Emotional and material support was frequently offered to family members.

Other research by Phillipson and Downs (1999), and O'Brien and Jones (1996) found that children and grandchildren saw their elderly relatives on a frequent basis, whereas ONS survey data collected in 2003 found that 61 per cent of grandparents saw their grandchildren once a week. Many elderly relatives were using new technology such as e-mail to keep in contact with their extended kin.

Ross *et al.* (2006) found in their study that grandparents spoke positively about becoming and being a grandparent (see Focus on research below). When grandchildren were younger, time was spent together on outings and playing together, or with the grandparents teaching skills and providing childcare. As grandchildren grew older, the relationships were more likely to revolve around talking, giving advice and support.

Beanpole families

Brannen (2003) notes that the ageing of the population, the increasing tendency of women to pursue both higher education and a career, the consequent decline in fertility and the availability of divorce has led to the recent emergence of four-generation families – families that include great-grandparents and great-grandchildren. She notes that families today are less likely to experience horizontal intragenerational ties, i.e. we have fewer aunts, uncles and cousins. Brannen argues that we are now more likely to experience vertical intergenerational ties, i.e. closer ties

Focus on research

Ross *et al.* (2006)
Exploring intergenerational relationships

Interviews and group discussions were held with 73 grandparents aged between 55 and 88 and 75 grandchildren aged between 10 and 19 to explore in depth the meaning and significance of grandparent–grandchild relations.

Grandparents generally spoke positively about becoming and being a grandparent. When grandchildren were younger, time was spent together on outings and playing together, or with the grandparents teaching skills and providing childcare. Grandparents often referred to providing financial support to assist their grandchildren, ranging from pocket money to school fees. As grandchildren grew older, the relationships were more likely to revolve around talking, giving advice and support. Both generations described how grandparents usually played a key role in 'listening' to grandchildren. Many young people said they could

share problems and concerns with their grandparents and referred to the way grandparents would sometimes act as go-betweens in the family, particularly when there were disagreements between themselves and their parents.

Grandparents also provided a bridge to the past by acting as sources of family history, heritage and traditions: storytellers who kept grandchildren aware of their own family experiences and their culture. They were also active in keeping wider sets of relatives connected.

Ross, N., Hill, M., Sweeting, H. and Cunningham-Burley, S. (2006) *Grandparents and Teen Grandchildren: Exploring Intergenerational Relationships*, Edinburgh: Centre for Research on Families and Relationships

1 **Why might the research methods used by the researchers have increased the validity of the findings?**

2 **How did grandparents and grandchildren interpret each other's family role?**

with grandparents and great-grandparents (see Focus on research on p. 95). Brannen calls such family setups 'beanpole families'. She argues that the 'pivot generation', i.e. that sandwiched between older and younger family generations is increasingly in demand to provide for the needs of both elderly parents and grandchildren. For example, 20 per cent of people in their fifties and sixties currently care for an elderly person, while 10 per cent care for both an elderly person and a grandchild. Such services are based on the assumption of 'reciprocity', i.e. the provision of babysitting services is repaid by the assumption that daughters will assist mothers in their old age.

Migration

Historically, the population of Great Britain was made up of people from a White British ethnic background. The pattern of migration since the 1950s has produced a number of distinct, minority ethnic groups within the general population. In 2001, the majority of the population in Great Britain were White British (88 per cent). The remaining 6.7 million people (11.8 per cent of the population) belonged to other ethnic groups – White Other was the largest group (2.5 per cent), followed by Indians (1.8 per cent), Pakistanis (1.3 per cent), White Irish (1.2 per cent), those of mixed ethnic backgrounds (1.2 per cent), Black Caribbeans (1.0 per cent), Black Africans (0.8 per cent) and Bangladeshis (0.5 per cent).

Migration during the latter part of the 20th century also led to religious diversity in Great Britain. Christianity was the main religion in Great Britain; 41 million people identified themselves as Christians in 2001, making up 72 per cent of the population. Muslims formed the largest non-Christian religious group, comprising 3 per cent of the total population. Hindus were the next largest group (1 per cent), followed by Sikhs (0.6 per cent), Jews (0.5 per cent) and Buddhists (0.3 per cent).

Cultural diversity

Immigration has led to cultural and religious diversity in family life. Research carried out at Essex University in 2000 indicates that only 39 per cent of British-born African-Caribbean adults under the age of 60 are in a formal marriage, compared with 60 per cent of White adults (Berthoud 2000). Moreover, this

group is more likely than any other group to intermarry. The number of mixed-race partnerships means that very few African-Caribbean men and women are married to fellow African-Caribbeans and only one-quarter of African-Caribbean children live with two Black parents. Ali (2002) notes that such marriages result in interethnic families and mixed-race (sometimes called 'dual heritage') children. Some sociologists have suggested that these types of families have their own unique problems, such as facing prejudice and discrimination from both White and Black communities.

African-Caribbean families

There is evidence that African-Caribbean families have a different structure to White families. African-Caribbean communities have a higher proportion of one-parent families compared with White communities – over 50 per cent of African-Caribbean families with children are one-parent families. Rates of divorce are higher but there is also an increasing tradition in the African-Caribbean community of mothers choosing to live independently from their children's father. Berthoud notes two important and increasing trends:

● 66 per cent of 20-year-old African-Caribbean mothers remain single compared with 11 per cent of their White peers, while at 25 years, these figures are 48 per cent and 7 per cent respectively.
● At the age of 30, 60 per cent of African-Caribbean men are unattached, compared with 45 per cent of their White peers.

These trends indicate that African-Caribbean women are avoiding settling down with the African-Caribbean fathers of their children. Berthoud (2003) suggests that the attitudes of young African-Caribbean women are characterized by 'modern individualism' – they are choosing to bring up children alone for two reasons:

● African-Caribbean women are more likely to be employed than African-Caribbean men. Such women rationally weigh up the costs and benefits of living with the fathers of their children and conclude that African-Caribbean men are unreliable as a source of family income and are potentially a financial burden. Surveys indicate that such women prefer to be economically independent.
● Chamberlain and Goulborne (1999) note that African-Caribbean single mothers are more likely to be supported by an extended kinship network in their upbringing of children – interestingly, African-Caribbean definitions of kinship often extends to including family friends and neighbours as 'aunts' and 'uncles'.

Asian family life

The Essex study also found that the Pakistani and Bangladeshi communities are most likely to live in old-fashioned nuclear families, although about 33 per cent of Asian families – mainly Sikhs and East African Asians – live in extended families. East African Asian extended families are likely to contain more than

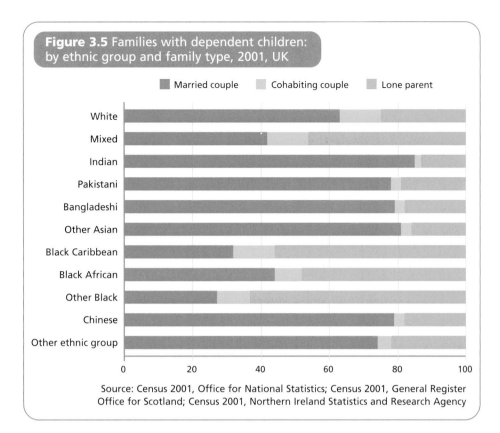

Figure 3.5 Families with dependent children: by ethnic group and family type, 2001, UK

Legend: ■ Married couple ■ Cohabiting couple ■ Lone parent

White
Mixed
Indian
Pakistani
Bangladeshi
Other Asian
Black Caribbean
Black African
Other Black
Chinese
Other ethnic group

0   20   40   60   80   100

Source: Census 2001, Office for National Statistics; Census 2001, General Register Office for Scotland; Census 2001, Northern Ireland Statistics and Research Agency

cultural advantages in terms of attitudes, values and practices (i.e. cultural capital – see Chapter 1, p.8) which assist their children through the educational system. However, critical sociologists argue that working-class parents are just as child-centred, but that material deprivation limits how much help they can give their children. Therefore, the working-class child's experience is likely to be less satisfactory because of family poverty, poor schools, lack of material support, greater risks of accidents both in the home and in the street, and so on.

There is also evidence that extended kinship ties are important to the upper class, in their attempt to maintain wealth and privilege. The economic and political **elite** may use marriage and family connections to ensure 'social closure' – that is, to keep those who do not share their culture from becoming part of the elite.

one generation, while Sikh extended units are organized around brothers and their wives and children.

Berthoud argues that South Asians tend to be more traditional in their family values than Whites. Marriage is highly valued and there is little divorce (although this may indicate empty-shell marriages). Marriage in Asian families – whether Muslim, Hindu or Sikh – is mainly arranged and there is little intermarriage with other religions or cultures. There is also evidence that Bangladeshi and Pakistani women have more children than Indian and White women, and at younger ages. Relationships between Asian parents and their children are also very different from those that characterize White families. Children tend to respect religious and cultural traditions, and they feel a strong sense of duty to their families, and especially to their elders. South Asian families, particularly, feel a strong sense of duty and obligation to assist extended kin in economic and social ways. This is important because Bangladeshi and Pakistani families in the UK are more likely to be in poverty compared with Indian and White families. Such obligations often extend to sending money to relatives abroad on a regular basis and travelling half way around the world to nurse sick or dying relatives.

Class diversity

Rapoport *et al.* (1982) suggest that there may be differences between middle-class and working-class families in terms of the relationship between husband and wife and the way in which children are socialized and disciplined. Some sociologists argue that middle-class parents are more child-centred (see Topic 7) than working-class parents. They supposedly take a greater interest in their children's education, and consequently pass on

Sexual diversity

The New Right have expressed concern at the increasing number of same-sex couples who are cohabiting – and particularly the trend of such couples to have families through adoption, artificial insemination and surrogacy. In 1999, the law lords ruled that a homosexual couple can be legally defined as a family, and the Government is now looking to introduce legislation which will mean that long-term same-sex partners will have similar rights to heterosexual married couples with regard to inheritance (of property and pensions, for example) and next-of-kin status. New Right commentators have suggested that such family setups are 'unnatural' and that children will either be under pressure to experiment with the lifestyles of their parents or will be bullied at school because of the sexuality of their parents. In the courts, such fears have meant that in the past mothers who have come out as lesbians have lost custody of their children.

There have been a number of sociological studies of homosexual couples and children. Studies of couples suggest that relationships between partners are qualitatively different from heterosexual partners in terms of both domestic and emotional labour because they are not subject to gendered assumptions about which sex should be responsible for these tasks. There may, therefore, be more equality between partners.

Studies of children brought up in single-sex families show no significant effects in terms of gender identification or sexual orientation. For example, Gottman (1990) found that adult daughters of lesbian mothers were just as likely to be of a heterosexual inclination as the daughters of heterosexual mothers. Dunne (1997) argues that children brought up by homosexuals are more likely to be tolerant and see sharing and equality as important features of their relationships with others.

Postmodernism and family diversity

Postmodernists argue that postmodern family life is characterized by diversity, variation and instability. For example, women no longer aspire exclusively to romantic love, marriage and children. Premarital sex, serial monogamy, cohabitation, economic independence, single-sex relationships and childlessness are now acceptable alternative lifestyles. Men's roles too are no longer clear cut in postmodern society, and the resulting 'crisis of masculinity' (see p. 111) has led to men redefining both their sexuality and family commitments. Beck and Beck-Gernsheim (1995) argue that such choice and diversity have led to the renegotiation of family relationships as people attempt to find a middle ground between individualization and commitment to another person and/or children.

Demography and diversity – some conclusions

As we can see, demographic changes in the number of births and deaths, the fertility rate and migration have had a fairly profound effect on the structure and internal organization of families in the modern UK. In particular, these demographic changes have undermined the traditionalist New Right view that the nuclear family is the most common type of family in the UK. In 2005, only 37 per cent of family households were made up of couples with dependent children. However, demographic changes also tell us that family life is not static – rather it is constantly in a state of change and flux. For example, 25 per cent of family households are made up of couples with no children. These and single-person households may have evolved out of nuclear families or may be about to evolve into them. It is important, therefore, not to dismiss the nuclear family as redundant, although we should be constantly aware that over 40 per cent of children live in a non-traditional family today. As we shall see in the next topic, demographic change in terms of marriage and divorce rates also exert influence over the form the family will take in the future.

(see p. 111)

Check your understanding

1 How have changes in the fertility rate affected the relationship between women and family life?

2 What have been the main causes of the ageing of the UK population?

3 What effects might the ageing of the population have on family life in the UK?

4 What differences might exist between working-class and middle-class families in the UK?

5 Identify three main differences in family life in multicultural Britain?

Activities

Research ideas

1 If you know people from ethnic or religious backgrounds different from your own, ask if you can interview them about their experience of family life. Make sure your questionnaire is sensitive to their background and avoids offending them.

2 Design a research tool that allows you to gather quantitative and qualitative information about your classmates' relationships with their elderly relatives. Does this confirm or challenge previous sociological research?

Web.task

Visit the following sites which focus on recent research into family life. What changes have they documented in family life since the turn of the century?

● The Institute for Social and Economic Research: **www.iser.essex.ac.uk**

● Centre for Family Research: **www.sps.cam.ac.uk/CFR/**

● Joseph Rowntree Foundation: **www.jrf.org.uk**

● Centre for Research in Family, Kinship and Childhood: **www.leeds.ac.uk/family**

Key terms

Birth rate number of live births per 1000 of the population.

Death rate number of deaths per 1000 population.

Demography the study of population change.

Diversity difference, variation.

Elite the most powerful, rich or gifted members of a group.

Emigration people moving abroad.

Extended family a family in which sons and daughters live in the same neighbourhood as their parents, see each other on a regular basis and offer each other various kinds of support.

Fertility rate number of children born per 1000 women aged 15 to 44.

Immigration people settling in the country to live or work.

Migration the number of people entering and leaving the country.

Moral panic public concern over some aspect of behaviour, created and reinforced in large part by sensational media coverage.

Item A

The fertility rate and the birth rate of the population of the United Kingdom have fallen in recent years, but the overall size of the population has nonetheless increased. One reason for this is that more people are immigrating than emigrating. From the 1940s, significant numbers of people arrived in the UK from the countries of the New Commonwealth, such as the Caribbean, Africa and South Asia, as well as from the Republic of Ireland.

More recently, the pattern of immigration has changed significantly, with most of the new arrivals into the UK coming from the new accession states of the European Union, such as Poland, Lithuania and the Czech Republic.

Item B

The twentieth century witnessed a significant decline in the numbers of children being born in the United Kingdom. At the same time, a greater proportion of these children survived childhood and adulthood to reach old age. This has produced a rapidly ageing population in which there will soon be more people aged over 65 than aged under 16 in the UK for the first time ever.

One result of these developments is that the UK is witnessing a steady rise in the number of one-person households over state retirement pension age. The great majority of the people living in these households are female.

(a) Explain what sociologists mean by the 'fertility rate'. (2 marks)

(b) Suggest two reasons for the increase in life expectancy. (4 marks)

(c) Suggest three reasons for the fall in the birth rate. (6 marks)

(d) Using information from Items A and B and elsewhere, assess the causes and consequences of changes in the UK population. (24 marks)

Grade booster Getting top marks in the 24-mark question

For this question, you need to consider the major changes in the population. This involves looking at both births and deaths, and at immigration and emigration, as well as aspects such as life expectancy, overall size and so on. You should consider the different factors at work in each case – for example, how changes in women's position might affect birth rates, or reasons why people choose to (or have to) migrate. You can show evaluation by considering the relative importance of different factors in producing these changes. You must also look at consequences, such as poverty among female pensioners or the implications for government spending on welfare and education.

Marriage, divorce and family diversity

Getting you thinking

Households by type, 1971–2026, England

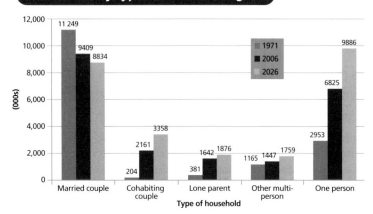

Source: Murphy, M. (2006) *Household and Family – Past, present & future*, ESRC Public Policy Seminar

Marriages and Divorces (UK)

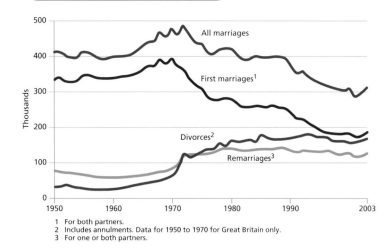

1 For both partners.
2 Includes annulments. Data for 1950 to 1970 for Great Britain only.
3 For one or both partners.

Source: Babb, P. *et al.* (2006) *Social Trends 36*, Basingstoke: Palgrave Macmillan

Above: Marriage in the 21st century? A couple on the escalator on their way to tying the knot in the clothing department at the supermarket where they work.

1 **What have been the general trends in divorce and marriage between 1950 and 2003?**

2 **How have households evolved since 1971? What will be the dominant types of household in 2026?**

3 **Suggest possible explanations for the trends illustrated in the graphs.**

4 **Why might the image above and the statistical trends be alarming for supporters of the traditional family?**

It is not difficult to see why supporters of the traditional family, such as the New Right, are so alarmed by figures and images such as those above. They believe these indicate a crisis in the family, which will inevitably result in increasing antisocial behaviour and moral breakdown.

Many postmodernists and feminists look at the figures and images in a very different way – they see them as indicators of greater personal choice in our private lives, and as evidence of a rejection of patriarchal family arrangements. So who is right?

Marriage

In 1972, the highest ever number of couples (480 000) since the Second World War got married. According to the Office for National Statistics (ONS), this was due to the baby boom generation of the 1950s reaching marriageable age and these people choosing to marry at a younger age compared with previous generations. However, the annual number of marriages in England and Wales then went into decline and, despite a slight revival in marriage in 2004 when 273 000 couples got married, reached an all-time low in 2005 when only 244 710 couples tied the knot.

This decline in the total number of marriages has been paralleled by a decline in marriage rates (i.e. the number of people marrying per 1000 of the population aged 16 and over). In 1994, the marriage rate was 11.4 but this had declined to 10.3 by 2004. The male rate declined from 36.3 in 1994 to 27.8 in 2004 whilst the female rate declined from 30.6 to 24.6. Furthermore, only 32 per cent of marriages in 2004 involved a religious ceremony, compared with 51 per cent in 1991.

We can also see some ethnic variations in marriage. Research by Berthoud (2000) suggests that three quarters of Pakistani and Bangladeshi women are married by the age of 25, compared with just over half of White women. Moreover, British African-Caribbeans are the group least likely to get married – only 39 per cent of Caribbean adults under the age of 60 are in a formal marriage, compared with 60 per cent of White adults.

These figures have recently provoked a keen debate between New Right commentators and feminists. New Right commentators express concerns about the decline in marriage. Patricia Morgan (2000) argues that marriage involves unique 'attachments and obligations' that regulate people's behaviour. For example, she claims that married men are more likely to be employed than unmarried or cohabiting men, and earn more (i.e. 10 to 20 per cent more in 2001) because they work harder than any other male group.

An analysis of marriage statistics by the Office for National Statistics (ONS) in 2007 concludes that marriage is good for the health of couples and that married people live longer than single or **divorced** people, although Murphy (2007) suggests that it could be bad relationships rather than divorce that makes people unhappy and hence ill.

However, fears about what marriage statistics reveal are probably exaggerated for four reasons:

1 People are delaying marriage rather than rejecting it. Most people will marry at some point in their lives. However, people are now marrying later in life, probably after a period of cohabitation. The average age for first-time brides in 2003 was 29 years and for all grooms 31 years, compared with 22 for women and 24 for men in 1971. Women may delay marriage because they want to develop their careers and enjoy a period of independence.

2 British Social Attitude Surveys indicate that most people, whether single, divorced or cohabiting, still see marriage as a desirable life-goal. People also generally believe that having children is best done in the context of marriage. Few people believe that the freedom associated with living alone is better than being married to someone.

3 Two fifths of all marriages are remarriages (in which one or both partners have been divorced). These people are obviously committed to the institution of marriage despite their previous negative experience of it. (An interesting new trend is the number of young men – aged under 25 – who are marrying women significantly older than them, i.e. 'toy-boy' marriages. One in three of first-time grooms in 2004 was younger than his bride, more than double the number in 1963.)

4 Despite the decrease in the overall number of people marrying, married couples are still the main type of partnership for men and women in the UK. In 2005, seven in ten families were headed by a married couple.

Wilkinson (1994) notes that female attitudes towards marriage and family life have undergone a radical change or 'genderquake'. She argues that young females no longer prioritize marriage and children, as their mothers and grandmothers did. Educational opportunities and the feminization of the economy have resulted in young women weighing up the costs of marriage and having children against the benefits of a career and economic independence. The result of this is that many females, particularly middle-class graduates, are postponing marriage and family life until their careers are established. This is supported by the statistics which show that births to women aged between 35 and 39 have dramatically increased in the last 20 years.

Other feminist sociologists are sceptical about the value of marriage. Smith (2001) argues that marriage creates unrealistic expectations about **monogamy** and faithfulness in a world characterized by sexual freedom. She argues that at different points in people's life cycles, people need different things that often can only be gained from a new partner. Campbell (2000) suggests that marriage benefits men more than it does women.

Cohabitation

A constant source of concern to the New Right has been the significant rise in the number of couples cohabiting during the last decade. The proportion of non-married people cohabiting has risen sharply in the last 20 years from 11 per cent of men and 13 per cent of women in 1986 to 24 per cent and 25 per cent respectively. In 2007, the ONS suggested that cohabiting couples are the fastest growing family type in the UK. Around 2.2 million families are cohabiting couples with or without children. This family type has grown by 65 per cent since 1997. In fact, the numbers are likely to be higher than this because the ONS data did not include same-sex couples living together. The ONS predict that by 2014, as a consequence of this growth, married couples could account for less than half of British families. The ONS data also suggests that a third of teenagers in 2007 are destined to cohabit rather than marry, compared with one in ten of their grandparents.

New Right commentators claim that cohabitation is less stable than marriage. A report by the Institute for the Study of Civil Society (Morgan 2000) claimed that cohabiting couples were less happy and less fulfilled than married couples, and

Focus on research

Smart and Stevens (2000)
Cohabitation: testing the water?

Smart and Stevens (2000) carried out interviews with 20 mothers and 20 fathers who were separated from cohabiting partners with whom they had had a child. They found that most of the sample were either indifferent to marriage or had been unsure about marrying the person with whom they had lived. Many of the female respondents had wanted their partners to become more 'marriage-worthy', especially in terms of expressing emotional commitment and helping more with the children. Cohabitation, then, was generally a test of their own and their partner's commitment. Many felt that their level of commitment to each other was the same as married couples but they believed it was easier to leave a cohabiting relationship than it was to leave a marriage.

Smart, C. and Stevens, P. (2000) *Cohabitation Breakdown*, London: The Family Policy Studies Centre

1   **What does this research tell us about the meaning of cohabitation?**

2   **What effect might the choice of sample have had on the findings?**

more likely to be abusive, unfaithful, stressed and depressed. In 2007, ONS data analysed by Murphy suggested that children whose parents live together but are not married get worse results at school, leave education earlier and have a higher risk of developing a serious illness.

However, surveys indicate that few people see cohabitation as an alternative to marriage. The fact that cohabiting couples are much younger than married couples suggests cohabitation is seen by many participants as a test of compatibility and a prelude to marriage. Kiernan (2007) notes that it is difficult to generalize about cohabiting couples. These may include people who are about to marry, those who oppose marriage and those who are just testing the strength of their relationship in a

situation that has become more socially acceptable in the last ten years. Kiernan also points out that the educational and health disadvantages that the ONS study purports to identify might come about because people in cohabiting relationships are more likely to be socially disadvantaged and poor in the first place.

Other research suggests that cohabitation is a temporary phase lasting on average about five years. Approximately 60 per cent of cohabiting couples eventually marry – usually some time after the first child is born. Although cohabitation marks a dramatic change in adult living arrangements – as recently as the 1960s, it was regarded as immoral – cohabiting couples with and without children only accounted for 10 per cent of households in 2006. There is also some evidence that a significant number of people live together simply because they are waiting for a divorce. For example, in 2005, 23 per cent of cohabiting men were separated from a previous partner whilst 36 per cent were divorced. Finally, as we saw earlier, marriage rather than cohabitation is still the main cultural goal for most people in the UK.

Marital breakdown

Types of marital breakdown

Marital breakdown can take three different forms: divorce, separation and **empty-shell marriages**:

- *Divorce* refers to the legal ending of a marriage. Since the Divorce Reform Act of 1969, divorce has been granted on the basis of '**irretrievable** breakdown' and, since 1984, couples have been able to petition for divorce after the first anniversary of their marriage. 'Quickie' divorces are also available, in which one partner has to prove the 'fault' or 'guilt' of the other, for matrimonial 'crimes' such as adultery, although these tend to be costly.
- *Separation* is where couples agree to live apart after the breakdown of a marriage. In the past, when divorce was difficult to obtain or too expensive, separation was often the only solution.
- *Empty-shell marriages* are those in which husband and wife stay together in name only. There may no longer be any love or intimacy between them. Today, such marriages are likely to end in separation or divorce, although this type of relationship may persist for the sake of children or for religious reasons.

The divorce rate

Britain's divorce rate is high compared with other European societies. In 1938, 6000 divorces were granted in the UK. This figure had increased tenfold by 1970, and in 1993, numbers peaked at 180 000. By 2000, this figure had fallen to 154 600 although the years 2001–04 have seen a gradual rise to 167 100. People who had been divorced before constitute about 20 per cent of this total. There are now nearly half as many divorces as marriages and, if present trends continue, about 40 per cent of current marriages will end in divorce.

New Right sociologists argue that such divorce statistics are one of the symptoms of a serious crisis in the family. They suggest that divorce is too easily available, with the result that people are not as committed to marriage and the family as they were in the past. Many New Right sociologists see a direct relationship between divorce, one-parent families and antisocial behaviour among the young, and argue for a return to traditional family values as well as a toughening up of the divorce laws.

New Right sociologists argue that children who experience the divorce of their parents suffer a range of problems as they get older, such as being more prone to crime and unemployment. It is claimed that such children are themselves likely to experience divorce when they marry. Research by Rodgers and Pryor (1998) found that children from separated families are more likely than children from two-parent families to suffer behavioural problems, to underachieve at school, to become sexually active and, if female, become pregnant at an early age, and to smoke, drink and use drugs during adolescence. When they become adults, they are more likely to experience poverty.

Flouri and Buchanan's (2002) study of 17 000 children from families that had experienced separation and divorce found that in families where fathers were still involved with their children, the children were more successful in gaining educational qualifications and continued to seek out educational opportunities in adult life. They are less likely to get into trouble with the police and less likely to become homeless. Such children also grow up to enjoy more stable and satisfying relationships with their adult partners. However, Buchanan found that if conflict continued after divorce between parents, children could become vulnerable to mental health problems.

Why is the divorce rate increasing?

Changes in divorce law have generally made it easier and cheaper to end marriages, but this is not necessarily the cause of the rising divorce rate. Legal changes reflect other changes in society, especially changes in attitudes. In particular, sociologists argue that social expectations about marriage have changed. Functionalist sociologists even argue that high divorce rates are evidence that marriage is increasingly valued and that people are demanding higher standards from their partners. Couples are no longer prepared to put up with unhappy, 'empty-shell' marriages. People want emotional and sexual compatibility and equality, as well as companionship. Some are willing to go through a number of partners to achieve these goals.

Feminists note that women's expectations of marriage have radically changed, compared with previous generations. In the 1990s, most **divorce petitions** were initiated by women. This may support Thornes and Collard's (1979) view that women expect far more from marriage than men and, in particular, that they value friendship and emotional gratification more than men do. If husbands fail to live up to these expectations, women may feel the need to look elsewhere.

Women's expectations have probably changed as a result of the improved educational and career opportunities they have experienced since the 1980s. Women no longer have to be unhappily married because they are financially dependent upon their husbands. Moreover, Hart (1976) notes that divorce may be a reaction to the frustration that many working wives may feel if they are responsible for the bulk of housework and childcare. Similarly, it may also be the outcome of tensions produced by women taking over the traditional male role of breadwinner in some households, especially if the male is unemployed.

Figure 3.6 Reasons for increasing divorce rate

Changes in divorce law have generally made it easier and cheaper to end marriages but legal changes reflect other changes in society, especially changes in attitudes.

Functionalist sociologists argue that high divorce rates are evidence that marriage is increasingly valued and that people are demanding higher standards from their partners.

Thornes and Collard: women value friendship and emotional gratification more than men do. If husbands fail to live up to these expectations, women may feel the need to look elsewhere.

Divorce may be the outcome of tensions produced by women taking over the traditional male role of breadwinner in some households.

Divorce is no longer associated with stigma and shame. The view that divorce can lead to greater happiness for the individual is more acceptable.

Beck and Beck-Gernsheim (1995): rising divorce rates are the product of a rapidly changing world in which the traditional rules, rituals and traditions of love, romance and relationships no longer apply.

Women's improved educational and career opportunities mean that they no longer have to be unhappily married because they are financially dependent upon their husbands.

Hart: divorce may be a reaction to the frustration that many working wives may feel if they are responsible for the bulk of housework and childcare.

Divorce is no longer associated with stigma and shame. This may be partly due to a general decline in religious practices. The social controls, such as extended families and **close-knit communities**, that exerted pressure on couples to stay together and that labelled divorce as 'wicked' and 'shameful', are also in decline. Consequently, in a society dominated by **privatized nuclear families**, the view that divorce can lead to greater happiness for the individual is more acceptable. It is even more so if divorce involves escaping from an abusive relationship or if an unhappy marriage is causing emotional damage to children. However, it is important to recognize that such attitudes are not necessarily a sign of a casual attitude towards divorce. Most people experience divorce as an emotional and traumatic experience, equivalent to bereavement. They are usually also aware of the severe impact it may have on children.

Postmodern approaches to divorce

Beck and Beck-Gernsheim (1995) argue that rising divorce rates are the product of a rapidly changing world in which the traditional rules, rituals and traditions of love, romance and relationships no longer apply. In particular, they point out that the modern world is characterized by individualization, choice and conflict.

- *Individualization* – We are under less pressure to conform to traditional collective goals set by our extended family, religion or culture. We now have the freedom to pursue individual goals.
- *Choice* – Cultural and economic changes mean that we have a greater range of choices available to us in terms of lifestyle and living arrangements.
- *Conflict* – There is now more potential for antagonism between men and women because there is a natural clash of interest between the selfishness encouraged by individualization and the selflessness required by relationships, marriage and family life.

Beck and Beck-Gernsheim argue that these characteristics of the modern world have led to personal relationships between men and women becoming a battleground (they call it the 'chaos of love') as evidenced by rising divorce rates. However, Beck and Beck-Gernsheim are positive about the future because they note that people still generally want to find love with another in order to help them cope with a risky, rapidly changing world. In particular, love helps compensate for the stress and, particularly, the impersonal and uncertain nature of the modern world. Love is the one thing people feel is real and that they can be sure of. Divorce and remarriage may simply be signs that people still have faith that they will one day find the true love they need to help them cope with the complexity of modern life.

Divorce trends suggest that monogamy (one partner for life) will eventually be replaced by **serial monogamy** (a series of long-term relationships resulting in cohabitation and/or marriage). However, the New Right panic about divorce is probably exaggerated. It is important to remember that although four out of ten marriages may end in divorce, six out of ten succeed; over 75 per cent of children are living with both natural parents who are legally married. These figures suggest that society still places a high value on marriage and the family.

One-parent families

The number of one-parent families with dependent children tripled from 2 per cent of UK households in 1961 to 7 per cent in 2005. There are now approximately 1.75 million lone-parent families in Britain, making up about 23 per cent of all families. About 26 per cent of people under the age of 19 live in a one-parent family. Ninety per cent of single-parent families are headed by women. Most of these are ex-married (divorced, separated or widowed) or ex-cohabitees. The fastest growing group of single parents is made up of those who have never married or cohabited. Haskey estimated this group to be 26 per cent of all single mothers in 2002. Contrary to popular opinion, most single mothers are not teenagers – teenage mothers make up just 3 per cent of lone parents. The average age of a lone parent is actually 34.

Focus on research

Burghes and Brown (1995)
Teenage single mothers

A qualitative study using unstructured interviews with 31 mothers who were teenagers at conception and who have never been married was carried out by Burghes and Brown in 1995. They found that most of the pregnancies were unintended. However, nearly all the respondents expressed strong anti-abortion views and adoption was rarely considered. Most of the mothers reported that their experience of lone motherhood was a mixture of hard work and enormous joy. For the most part, the mothers interviewed preferred to be at home caring for their children. All the mothers intended to resume training or employment once their children were in school. Marriage was also a long-term goal.

Burghes, L. and Brown, M. (1995) *Single Lone Mothers: Problems, prospects and policies*, York: Family Policy Studies Centre

How does this research challenge stereotypes about teenage mothers?

Ford and Millar (1998) note that lone parenthood is seen by some as an inherently second-rate and imperfect family type, reflecting the selfish choices of adults against the interests of children. For example, New Right thinkers see a connection between one-parent families, educational underachievement and delinquency. They believe that children from one-parent families lack self-discipline and can be emotionally disturbed because of the lack of a firm father figure in their lives. In addition, New Right thinkers are concerned about the cost of one-parent families to the state. Public expenditure on such families increased fourfold in the 1990s. It is suggested that the state offers 'perverse incentives', such as council housing and benefits, to young females to get pregnant.

Ford and Millar note that the 'perverse incentives' argument is flawed when the quality of life of lone parents is examined. Many experience poverty, debt and material hardship, and try to protect their children from poverty by spending less on themselves. Ford and Millar also suggest that poverty may be partly responsible for lone parenthood. Single women from poor socio-economic backgrounds living on council estates with higher than average rates of unemployment are more likely than others to become solo mothers. Motherhood is regarded as a desired and valued goal by these women and may be a rational response to their poor economic prospects. Surveys of such women suggest that children are a great source of love and pride, and most lone parents put family life at the top of things they see as important.

Feminist sociologists maintain that familial ideology causes problems for the one-parent family because it emphasizes the nuclear family ideal. This ideal leads to the **negative labelling** of one-parent families by teachers, social workers, housing departments, police and the courts. Single parents may be **scapegoated** for inner-city crime and educational underachievement, when these problems are actually the result of factors such as unemployment and poverty. The New Right also rarely consider that single parenthood may be preferable to the domestic violence that is inflicted by some husbands on their wives and children – or that the majority of one-parent families bring up their children successfully.

Reconstituted families

The **reconstituted** or stepfamily is made up of divorced or widowed people who have remarried, and their children from the previous marriage (or cohabitation). Such families are on the increase because of the rise in divorce. In 2003, it was estimated that 726 000 children were living in this type of family.

Reconstituted families are unique because children are also likely to have close ties with their other natural parent. An increasing number of children experience co-parenting, where they spend half their week with their mother and stepfather and spend the other half with their father. Some family experts see co-parenting as a characteristic of binuclear families – two separate post-divorce or separation households are really one family system as far as children are concerned.

De'Ath and Slater's (1992) study of step-parenting identified a number of challenges facing reconstituted families. Children may find themselves pulled in two directions, especially if the relationship between their natural parents continues to be strained. They may have tense relationships with their step-parents, and conflict may arise around the extent to which the step-parent and stepchild accept each other, especially with regard to whether the child accepts the newcomer as a 'mother' or 'father'. Strained relations between step-parents and children may test the loyalty of the natural parent and strain the new marriage. These families may be further complicated if the new couple decide to have children of their own, which may create the potential for envy and conflict among existing children.

Singlehood

One of the most dramatic post-war changes in Britain has been the increase in single-person households. More than 6.5m people now live on their own – three times as many as 40 years ago – and 29 per cent of all households comprised just one person in 2005. We saw in Topic 4 that some of this is due to an increase in elderly households because of longer life expectancy. However, we have also seen a corresponding

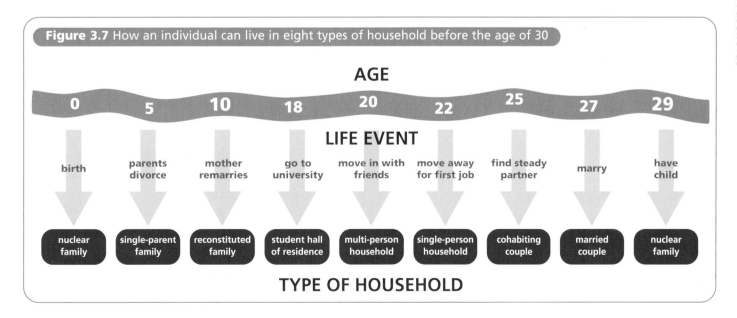

Figure 3.7 How an individual can live in eight types of household before the age of 30

AGE

| 0 | 5 | 10 | 18 | 20 | 22 | 25 | 27 | 29 |

LIFE EVENT

| birth | parents divorce | mother remarries | go to university | move in with friends | move away for first job | find steady partner | marry | have child |

TYPE OF HOUSEHOLD

| nuclear family | single-parent family | reconstituted family | student hall of residence | multi-person household | single-person household | cohabiting couple | married couple | nuclear family |

increase in young, single-person households. For example, in 1971, only 6 per cent of households were made up of single people under state pension age. This had increased to 15 per cent by 2005. There are a number of explanations for this increase:

- *The increase in female employment/career opportunities* – More women are gaining financial independence and choosing singlehood as a creative option for themselves before they elect eventually to settle down, although some are opting for voluntary childlessness.
- *The expansion of higher education* – More people are now going to university. This obviously delays the start of their careers and thus is likely to delay 'settling down' tendencies.

- *Changes in attitude/priorities* – Trends in marriage suggest that people are marrying later and have other priorities, such as education and careers. For example, Sharpe (1994) found girls in the 1970s were concerned with love, marriage, husbands, children, jobs and careers, in that order. In the 1990s, when she repeated the research, she found that girls' priorities had changed and that they were more focused on jobs and careers. The pressure to 'settle down and have children' is not as great as it used to be.
- *The increase in divorce* – Divorce creates both single-parent families and single-person households.

However, it is also important to note that for some young people, singlehood might only be a temporary phase before they establish a couple relationship and a nuclear family.

Key terms

Close-knit community a community in which there are close relationships between people (everyone knows everyone else).

Divorce the legal ending of a marriage.

Divorce petition a legal request for a divorce.

Empty-shell marriage a marriage in which the partners no longer love each other but stay together, usually for the sake of the children.

Irretrievable unable to be recovered. Broken down for ever.

Monogamy the practice of having only one partner.

Negative labelling treating something as being 'bad' or 'undesirable'.

Privatized nuclear family a home-centred family that has little contact with extended kin or neighbours.

Reconstituted families stepfamilies.

Scapegoated unfairly blamed.

Serial monogamy a series of long-term relationships.

Activities

Research ideas

1 Carry out a mini-survey across three different age groups (e.g. 15 to 20, 25 to 30, and 35 to 40), investigating attitudes towards marriage, cohabitation, one-parent families, step-families, co-parenting, teenage pregnancy, etc.

2 Interview two males and two females to find out what characteristics they are looking for in a future partner. Do your findings support the view that females set higher standards in relationships?

Web.tasks

1 Use the archives of either the *Guardian* or the *Daily Telegraph* websites to research the debate about divorce. The latter is excellent for links to relevant sites such as www.divorce-online.co.uk, the family law consortium and the Lord Chancellor's Department.

2 Visit the websites of the following organizations and work out whether they support familial ideology:

- www.themothersunion.org
- www.civitas.org.uk – this site has a collection of interesting fact sheets on the family, plus excellent links to traditionalist family sites
- www.oneplusone.org.uk

3 Use the web to research one-parent families. The following websites contain a range of useful data and information:

- www.gingerbread.org.uk
- www.opfs.org.uk
- www.oneparentfamilies.org.uk
- www.spsw.ox.ac.uk/

Check your understanding

1 Why have marriage rates declined in recent years?

2 Why is cohabitation not a threat to marriage?

3 Why are women more likely to initiate divorce proceedings than men?

4 What social problems are caused by divorce according to New Right sociologists?

5 What reasons, apart from legislation making divorce easier, might be responsible for the rise in divorce since the 1970s?

6 How might reconstituted family life differ from that experienced in nuclear families?

7 Why do feminist sociologists think that one-parent families are seen as a 'problem'?

Marriage, divorce and family diversity

Item A

The family seems to be dwindling as a social institution. The stark figures would suggest that British society has turned its back on those things normally associated with the idea of 'the family'. Within one generation, we have seen the following changes: only half as many people are getting married, lone-parent families have increased threefold, children born outside marriage have quadrupled in number, and the number of divorces has trebled. However, there is strong evidence that these things indicate a change in the nature of the family, rather than its death. The family remains a cornerstone of British society in terms of people's lives and their sense of identity. Families are still a crucial source of care and support for the elderly and the disabled. Nearly two in three working mothers turn to relatives for help with childcare. Most people are in regular contact with relatives and see them at least once a month. At Christmas, more than four in five people join in some form of family gathering.

Adapted from Denscombe, M. (1998) *Sociology Update*, Leicester: Olympus Books, p. 20

Item B

Marriage is a normal and expected part of women's lives in Western society. However, although the vast majority of women will expect to marry at some time and at least once, in recent years there has been some decline in the popularity of marriage. In 1971, only 4 per cent of women remained unmarried by the age of 50, but by 1987, the proportion had grown to 17 per cent. Women today are marrying older and marrying less. The Family Policy Studies Centre estimates that one in five young women will remain childless. Typically, those who defer motherhood are educated women. A recent study showed that women who have qualifications are twice as likely as those with no qualifications to say they expect to have no children.

Adapted from Chandler, J. (1993) 'Women outside marriage', *Sociology Review*, 2(4), and Jorgensen, N. *et al.* (1997) *Sociology: An Interactive Approach*, London: Collins Educational, pp. 100–1

Item C

Despite all the arguments about the decline of marriage, the increase in illegitimacy and so on, it continues to be the case that most people in Britain grow up, get married and form a nuclear family for part of their adult life. Nine out of ten people get married at some time in their lives; 90 per cent of women are married by the age of 30 and over 90 per cent of men before the age of 40. Most couples who get married (or have stable cohabitation relationships) have children. Thus nine out of ten married women have children, and four out of five children live with their two natural parents. Seventy-nine per cent of families with children are headed by a married couple.

Adapted from Abbott, P. and Wallace, C. (1997) *An Introduction to Sociology: Feminist Perspectives* (2nd edn), Routledge

(a) Explain what sociologists mean by 'serial monogamy'. (2 marks)

(b) Suggest two reasons for the growth of one-parent families (Item A). (4 marks)

(c) Suggest three reasons for increase in the divorce rate (Item A). (6 marks)

(d) Using information from the Items and elsewhere, examine the reasons for changing patterns of marriage, cohabitation and childbearing in the last 40 years. (24 marks)

Grade booster Getting top marks in the 24-mark question

Use the Items to identify some of the patterns of marriage, cohabitation and childbearing. For marriage, make sure you include remarriages as well as first marriages, and changes in the age at which people first marry. For cohabitation, describe the extent of the increase and look at different reasons why couples cohabit. For childbearing, include information on lone-parent families. You need to consider reasons for changes in all three aspects, such as the changing role of women, high divorce rates, the financial costs and benefits of cohabitation, and changes in attitudes to sexual relationships outside marriage.

TOPIC 6

Power and control in the family

Getting you thinking

(a) Making sure that you had sandwiches for lunch or the money to pay for a school dinner.

(b) Making sure that your favourite food was in the fridge.

(c) Arranging with other parents for you to go to a party or around to somebody's house for tea.

(d) Making sure that you had a clean swimming costume and towel on the days of school swims.

(e) Changing the sheets on your bed.

(f) Supervising your bathtime.

(g) Picking you up from school.

(h) Buying a present for you to take to another child's birthday party.

(i) Reassuring you if you had a bad dream in the night.

(j) Anticipating that you needed a new pair of shoes because you were about to grow out of your old pair.

1 Consider the list of tasks above. Which adult in your home was mainly responsible for each task when you were aged 5 to 7?

2 What other aspects of power and control in the home are neglected if we only focus on household tasks?

3 Who exercises power in your home and what forms does this take?

In 1973, Young and Willmott claimed that the traditional **segregated division of labour in the home** – men as breadwinners and women as housewives/mothers – was breaking down. The relationship between husband and wife (the **conjugal relationship**) was becoming – at least in middle-class families – more joint or **symmetrical**. This trend towards **egalitarian** marriage, they argued, was caused by the decline in the extended family, and its replacement in the late 20th century by the privatized nuclear family, as well as by the increasing opportunities in paid employment for women. Some media commentators were so convinced by these arguments that in the 1980s, it was claimed that a 'new man' had appeared, i.e. males

who were in touch with their feminine side and who were happy to meet women's emotional and domestic needs.

However, the exercise above should have shown you that much of women's labour in the home is neglected by studies that focus only on obvious and highly visible tasks. A good deal of what women do in the home is mental and emotional as well as physical, involving anticipating and fulfilling the needs of family members. These more subtle responsibilities tend to be missed by researchers, some of whom have concluded that men and women are becoming more equal in the home on the basis of their sharing some of the more glamorous domestic tasks, such as cooking. These sorts of surveys can also miss other influences that ensure that power and control in the home remain firmly in male hands – violence, the lack of status associated with the full-time mother/housewife role, the belief that working mothers damage children, the fact that being a mother limits job opportunities, and so on.

Studies of housework and childcare

The idea that equality is a central characteristic of marriage is strongly opposed by feminist sociologists. Studies of professional couples indicate that only a minority genuinely share housework and childcare. For example, Dryden's (1999) qualitative study of 17 married couples found that women still had major responsibility for housework and childcare.

Surveys investigating the distribution of housework and childcare tasks suggest that men today are more involved in domestic tasks than their fathers and grandfathers. However, the Time Use Survey of 2005 carried out by Lader *et al.* (2006) found that women in paid work spent 21 hours a week on average on housework, compared with only 12 hours spent by men on the same. Overall, this survey found that 92 per cent of women do some housework per day, compared with only 77 per cent of men. Surprisingly, there was little sign that the traditional sexual division of labour in the home was changing. In 2005, women still spent more time than men cooking, washing up, cleaning, tidying, washing clothes and shopping. DIY and gardening tasks were still male dominated.

Furthermore, data from the British Household Panel Survey (2001) suggests that whatever the work–domestic set-up, women do more in the home than men. For example, when both spouses work full time, and even when the man is unemployed and his wife works, women put more hours into domestic labour than men. Some sociologists have suggested that unemployed men actually resist increased involvement in housework because they interpret it as unmasculine and as further threatening their role as breadwinner. McKee and Bell (1986) found that unemployed men in their study found it degrading to do housework and to be 'kept' by their employed wives.

The quantifiable evidence, therefore, indicates that women are still likely to experience a **dual burden or double shift** – in that they are expected to be mainly responsible for the bulk of domestic tasks, despite holding down full-time jobs. Sclater (2000) points out that household technologies, such as washing machines and vacuum cleaners, advertised as making life easier for women have actually increased this burden because they have raised household standards of cleanliness and increased time spent on housework.

Sociological studies have also noted that the distinction between work and leisure or free time is less clear cut for married women. For example, Green (1996) found that wives usually interpret leisure time as time free from both paid work and family commitments, whereas husbands saw all time outside paid work as their leisure time.

It has been suggested by Kilkey (2005) that working parents are now experiencing a 'time famine' with regard to childcare, which is resulting in the delegation of some childcare to external carers, especially kin such as grandparents. Brannen's observations about beanpole families outlined in Topic 4 seem to support this. However, Dryden found that gender inequality in the distribution of childcare and housework tasks was still a major source of dissatisfaction in marriage for women. Indeed, studies, such as the one by Bittman and Pixley (1997), suggest this inequality is a major cause of divorce today

Women are also responsible for the emotional wellbeing of their partners and children. Studies such as that carried out by Duncombe and Marsden (1995) have found that women felt that their male partners were lacking in terms of 'emotional participation', i.e. men found it difficult to express their feelings, to tell their partners how they felt about them and to relate emotionally to their children. Duncombe and Marsden argue that this increases the burden on women because they feel they should attempt to compensate and please all parties in the home. Consequently, women spend a great deal of time soothing the emotions of partners and children. This leads to the neglect of their own psychological wellbeing, and can have negative consequences for their mental and physical health. For example, Bernard's study of marriage (1982) confirms this – she found that the men in her study were more satisfied with their marriage than their wives, many of whom expressed emotional loneliness. Moreover, these men had no inkling that their wives were unhappy.

Decision-making

Surveys of young married couples with children conclude that the decision to have children, although jointly reached, dramatically changes the life of the mother rather than the father. As Bernardes (1997) notes, in the UK, most female careers are interrupted by childbirth, but only a small minority of mothers return to their pre-baby jobs and most experience downward mobility into precarious, low-paid, part-time jobs with few rights.

Some sociologists have focused on the distribution of power within marriages. Hardill *et al.* (1997) discovered that middle-class wives generally deferred to their husbands in major decisions involving where to live, the size of the mortgage, buying cars etc. They concluded that the men in their sample were able to demand that the interests of their wives and families should be subordinated to the man's career because he was the major breadwinner. However, Gillian Leighton (1992) discovered that the power to influence and make family decisions changed when males became unemployed. In her study of professional couples, working wives often took over responsibility for bills and initiated cutbacks in spending.

Fatherhood

An important part of the New Right critique of one-parent families is the view that most of them lack fathers. Dennis and Erdos (2000), for example, suggest that fatherless children are less likely to be successfully socialized into the culture of discipline and compromise found in nuclear families, and so are less likely to be successful parents themselves. It is suggested that such children lack an authority figure to turn to in times of crisis and, as a result, the peer group and mass media have an increased influence. It is argued that such influence is likely to lead to an increase in social problems, such as delinquency, sexual promiscuity, teenage pregnancy and drug use.

There is no doubt that de-partnering, whether from marriage or cohabitation, leads to some degree of de-parenting, i.e. one or other parent, usually the father in the UK, becomes less involved in the parenting of a child. Furthermore, the law in the UK tends to uphold traditional ideas about gender roles, and custody of children is mainly awarded to the mother. Bernardes notes that the Children Act clearly states that the mother should have parental responsibility for a child if the parents are not married. It is estimated that 40 per cent of fathers lose touch completely with their children after two years; others will experience irregular contact or conflict with their ex-partners about access arrangements.

Other commentators have suggested that we should focus on the quality of fathering. In the early 1990s, many sociologists concluded that the role of fathers was changing. For example, men in the 1990s were more likely to attend the birth of their babies than men in the 1960s, and they were more likely to play a greater role in childcare than their own fathers. Burghes (1997) found that fathers were taking an increasingly active role in the emotional development of their children. Beck (1992) notes that, in the postmodern age, fathers can no longer rely on jobs to provide a sense of identity and fulfilment. Increasingly, they look to their children to give them a sense of identity and purpose.

However, Warin *et al.* (1999), in their study of 95 families in Rochdale, found that fathers, mothers and teenage children overwhelmingly subscribed to the view that the male should be the breadwinner, despite changes in employment and family life, and that mothers were the experts in parenting. The researchers do note that children increasingly expected their fathers to support them emotionally as well as provide for their material comforts. Research by Gray (2006) supports this view. Her research showed that fathers emphasized the need to spend quality time with their children. They wanted more time to get to know their children, to take them out, to help them with homework and to talk to them. Fathers viewed time spent with children in outings, sport, play and conversation as an expression of fatherhood rather than as a form of domestic work.

However, it is important not to exaggerate men's role in childcare. Looking after children is still overwhelmingly the responsibility of mothers, rather than jointly shared with fathers. Recent research has focused on the pressures of work in the 21st century. A survey by Dex in 2003 found that 30 per cent of fathers (and 6 per cent of mothers) worked more than 48 hours a week on a regular basis. Gray found that many fathers would like to spend more time with their children but are prevented by long work hours from bonding effectively with their children.

The social capital approach

Lately, researchers have taken a 'social capital' approach to childcare. This has resulted in parenting being re-defined as investing time in children which will benefit them educationally, economically and emotionally. Social capital research therefore focuses on how parents interpret time spent with children. Gray's research found that both male and female parents in her study saw spending time with children as an important aspect of family relationships. Fathers, in particular, saw spending time alone with a child as quality time because they were more likely than women to be doing it out of choice rather than obligation.

Patriarchal ideology

Feminists have highlighted the influence of patriarchal ideology (see Chapter 1, p. 18) on the perceptions of both husbands and wives. Surveys indicate that many women accept primary responsibility for housework and childcare without question, and believe that their career should be secondary to that of their husband. Such ideas are also reflected in state policy, which encourages female economic dependence upon men. Moreover, patriarchal ideology expects women to take on jobs that are compatible with family commitments. Surveys suggest that a large number of mothers feel guilty about working. Some actually give up work altogether because they believe that their absence somehow damages their children.

The mother/housewife role and work

Some feminist sociologists have concluded that women's participation in the labour market is clearly limited by their domestic responsibilities. Because of these responsibilities, very few women have continuous full-time careers. Mothers, then, tend to have 'jobs', while their husbands have 'careers'. As a result, women don't have the same access to promotion and training opportunities as men. Some employers may believe that women are unreliable because of family commitments and, consequently, discriminate against them.

Modern marriages, therefore, do not appear as equal as functionalists suggest. On all the criteria examined so far – the distribution of housework and childcare tasks, decision-making, and the impact of being a mother/housewife on employment – we see women at a disadvantage compared with men.

Violence in families

Another important aspect of power within marriage is domestic violence – the power of men to control women by physical force. This type of violence is estimated to be the most common type of violence in the UK although, because it takes place behind closed doors, often without witnesses, it is notoriously difficult to measure and document. It is also difficult to define – as Sclater (2000) notes, some behaviour, such as kicking and punching, is easily recognizable as violent, but behaviours such as threats, verbal abuse, psychological manipulation and sexual intimidation are less easy to categorize and may not be recognized by some men and women as domestic violence.

The official statistics tell us that violence by men against their female partners accounts for a third of all reported violence. Stanko's (2000) survey found that one incident of domestic violence is reported by women to the police every minute in the UK. Mirrlees-Black (1999), using data from the British Crime Survey, found that women were more likely to suffer domestic violence than men – 70 per cent of reported domestic violence is violence by men against their female partners. These figures are thought to be an underestimate because many women are reluctant to come forward for various reasons:

- They love their partners and think they can change them.
- They blame themselves in some way for the violence.
- They feel they may not be taken seriously.
- They are afraid of the repercussions.

Some sociologists have reported increases in female violence on men, but it is estimated that this constitutes, at most, only 5 per cent of all domestic violence. Moreover, as Nazroo's (1999) research indicates, wives often live in fear of men's potential domestic violence or threats, while husbands rarely feel frightened or intimidated by their wives' potential for violence.

Feminists suggest that domestic violence is a problem of patriarchy. In particular, research indicates that men's view that women have failed to be 'good' partners or mothers is often used to justify attacks or threats. These gendered expectations may be particularly reinforced if a woman goes out to work and earns more than her partner. Many boys and men are still brought up in traditional ways to believe that they should have economic and social power as breadwinners and heads of household. However, the feminization of the economy and male unemployment has led to some sociologists suggesting that men are undergoing a 'crisis of masculinity'. Violence may be an aspect of the anxiety men are feeling about their economic and domestic role, an attempt to re-exert and maintain power and control in a rapidly changing world. Feminists also point out that society has, until fairly recently, condoned male violence in the home. Both the state and the criminal justice system have failed to take the problem seriously, although there are positive signs that the Labour government and police forces are now willing to condemn and punish such violence. Whatever the explanation, some feminists would argue that as long as men have the capacity to commit such violence, there can never be equality within marriage.

Focus on research

British Crime Survey
Computer-assisted interviewing

Questions on domestic violence are now part of British Crime Surveys, which aim to gain an insight into the true amount of crime in society by talking to victims. The designers of this survey realized that face-to-face interviewing was an unreliable method because victims are often too embarrassed to talk about their experiences of violence. The 1996 survey was the first to use the alternative method of computer-assisted interviewing, in which a laptop is passed over to the respondent, who reads the questions on screen and enters their answers directly onto the computer without the interviewer being involved. It is thought that the confidentiality factor associated with this type of interviewing on such a sensitive issue has improved both the reliability of the method (and produced on average a 97 per cent response rate) and the validity of the data collected, i.e. people are more willing to open up.

1 What is computer-assisted interviewing?

2 Identify the advantages and disadvantages of computer-assisted interviewing.

3 To what extent is computer-assisted interviewing likely to achieve valid and reliable data about domestic violence?

Theoretical explanations of inequalities in power and control in families

There are four major theoretical perspectives on the distribution of power and control in the family:

1 *Functionalists* see the sexual division of labour in the home as biologically inevitable. Women are seen as naturally suited to the caring and emotional role, which Parsons terms the 'expressive role'.

2 *Liberal feminists* believe that women have made real progress in terms of equality within the family and particularly in education and the economy. They generally

believe that men are adapting to change and, although they culturally lag behind women in terms of attitudes and behaviour, the future is likely to bring further movement towards domestic and economic equality.

3 *Marxist–feminists* argue that the housewife role serves the needs of capitalism in that it maintains the present workforce and reproduces future labour-power (see Topic 2, p. 83).

4 *Radical feminists* such as Delphy (1984) believe that 'the first oppression is the oppression of women by men – women are an exploited class'. The housewife role is, therefore, a role created by patriarchy and geared to the service of men and their interests (see Topic 2, p. 83).

Criticisms of these theories

- These theories fail to explain why women's roles vary across different cultures. For example, the mother/housewife role does not exist in all societies.

- Feminism may be guilty of devaluing the mother/housewife role as a 'second-class' role. For many women, housework and childcare, like paid work, have real and positive meaning. Such work may be invested with meaning for women because it is 'work done for love' and it demonstrates their commitment to their families. Thus, boring, routine work may be transformed into satisfying, caring work.

- Feminists may underestimate the degree of power that women actually enjoy. Women are concerned about the amount of housework men do, but they are probably more concerned about whether men show enough gratitude or whether men listen to them, etc. The fact that many women divorce their husbands indicates that they have the power to leave a relationship if they are unhappy with it. Catherine Hakim (1996) suggests that feminists underestimate women's ability to make rational choices. It is not patriarchy or men that are responsible for the position of women in families. She argues that women choose to give more commitment to family and children, and so have less commitment to work than men have.

Key terms

Conjugal relationship the relationship between married or cohabiting partners.

Double shift or dual burden refers to wives taking responsibility for the bulk of domestic tasks as well as holding down full-time jobs.

Egalitarian based on equality.

Segregated division of labour in the home a traditional sexual division of labour in which women take responsibility for housework and mothering, and men take responsibility for being the breadwinner and head of the household.

Symmetrical similar or corresponding.

Check your understanding

1 What did Young and Willmott claim about conjugal roles in the 1970s?

2 What have recent surveys concluded about the distribution of domestic tasks between husbands and wives?

3 In what circumstances might wives acquire more power over decision-making in the home?

4 What do sociological studies tell us about fatherhood?

5 What effect does the mother/housewife role have on women's job opportunities?

Activities

Research ideas

1 Conduct a survey of parents using the lists of tasks in the 'Getting you thinking' exercise on p. 108. An interesting variation is to ask parents separately whether they think they and their partner are doing enough around the home. Ask a set of parents to keep a time-use diary documenting time spent on housework and childcare.

2 Interview a selection of mothers in different social situations – e.g. full-time mothers, those who have full-time or part-time jobs, those who have children who have left home. Try to construct an interview schedule that measures how they feel about the mother/housewife role.

Web.task

Use the web to research domestic violence. The following websites contain a range of useful data and information:

- www.homeoffice.gov.uk/crime-victims/reducing-crime/domestic-violence/
- www.womensaid.org.uk
- www.met.police.uk/dv/
- www.womenandequalityunit.gov.uk/domestic_violence

Item A

<<Working mothers spend more hours a week on housework than on their full-time job, a survey revealed yesterday. The survey of 543 parents of children under 18 was carried out for Legal & General. It found that full-time working mothers spend 56 hours a week on housework, part-time working mothers do 68 hours and housewives put in 76 hours, while fathers do only 31. Mothers spend around 14 hours a week cooking, compared with fathers' four hours, and 21 hours washing and ironing, compared with eight-and-a-half hours for men. Mothers clean for 13 hours a week, compared with their husbands' four hours, and women spend about an hour sewing compared with 10 minutes for men. Fathers do four hours a week of gardening, an hour more than mothers.>>

Source: *The Guardian*, 10 March 2000

Item B

Why does such a pronounced division of domestic labour persist? Women who continue to see housework and childcare as an essential part of being a 'good wife and mother' are more likely to be satisfied with an unequal domestic division of labour than women who reject such roles. Baxter and Western (1998) argue that women may deal with situations over which they have little control by defining them as 'satisfactory'. Men may have inflexible and demanding work schedules that make it difficult for them to meet family obligations. However, in criticism of this, men do tend to have greater control and freedom over how they spend their time outside of work. Women are often unable to 'clock on and off' from their caring responsibilities. The most plausible explanation for the persistence of an unequal domestic division of labour is that it suits men and so they resist change.

Adapted from Leonard, M. (2000) 'Back to the future: the domestic division of labour', *Sociology Review*, 10(2)

Item C

According to radical feminists, the family is the main source of men's oppression of women and the root of gender inequality in society. This is expressed in the fact that women are expected to do most of the unpaid labour of housework and childcare, as well as servicing men's sexual and emotional needs. Radical feminists argue that men use domestic violence or the threat of it to keep women subordinated to their will and that other institutions such as the police and courts turn a blind eye to this violence or treat it as trivial.

(a) Explain what is meant by the phrase 'domestic division of labour' (Item B). (2 marks)

(b) Identify two reasons for the trend towards egalitarian marriage. (4 marks)

(c) Suggest three ways in which men's role as parents may have changed in recent years. (6 marks)

(d) Using material from the Items and elsewhere, assess sociological explanations for inequalities between husbands and wives. (24 marks)

Grade booster — Getting top marks in the 24-mark question

For this question, note that 'inequalities' is plural and that these include not just housework and childcare, but also emotion work (the 'triple shift'), earning an income for the family, domestic violence and decision-making. You need to review the evidence for these, some of which should come from the Items, but you should also use studies such as Dryden's. You should evaluate competing explanations and perspectives on the division of labour, power and control, including functionalism and different varieties of feminism, using ideas such as patriarchy, dual burden, earning power, segregated and joint conjugal relationships, biological factors and expressive role.

TOPIC 7

The nature of childhood

Getting you thinking

Gun-toting children in Sierra Leone

Friendship in childhood

Funeral of a Palestinian child killed in an Israeli attack

Abused children can't speak up.

Image used in an NSPCC campaign against child abuse

1   **What does the cartoon on the right tell us about family life in the Middle Ages?**

2   **How does the experience of medieval childhood differ from that of today?**

3   **What do the images above tell us about the experience of childhood today?**

What is a child? Innocent, cute, funny? That's certainly the popular image suggested by birthday cards, magazines and so on. However, the cartoon on the right and some of the images above give a different impression. We can see that ideas about childhood appear to vary between different societies and different historical periods. This means that childhood is a **social construction** – something created by society, rather than simply a biological stage.

Childhood in pre-industrial society

The social historian Philippe Aries (1962) suggested that what we experience today as childhood is a recent social invention. He claimed that in pre-industrial society, childhood as we know it today did not exist. Children were 'little adults' who took part in the same work and play activities as adults. Toys and games specifically for children did not exist. Moreover, Aries argued

that children were regarded as an **economic asset** rather than as a symbol of people's love for one another. Investing emotionally in children was difficult when their death rate was so high.

Aries's evidence for this view of childhood has been questioned, but other historians agree that the pre-industrial family was a unit of production, working the land or engaged in crafts. Children were expected to help their parents from a very young age. Those who did not help with domestic production usually left home to become servants or apprentices.

Childhood and industrialization

After industrialization these attitudes continued, especially among the working classes, whose children were frequently found working in factories, mines and mills. Aries argued that middle-class attitudes towards children started to change during

Figure 3.8 Childhood in the Middle Ages

Children dressed like their parents

In the Middle Ages, young and old played together in games and festivals, as in this scene based on Brueghel's painting, the 'Battle between Carnival and Lent', where the children are depicted as small adults.

Everyone worked together

At 8 years, I was put out as an apprentice

So he could learn his trade from me.

Everyone was held responsible

Tudor law says a 7 year old can be hanged for stealing

In many cases, houses were not split up into special rooms for eating, sleeping, working or cooking, so children could not escape from the adult world.

this period. There was a growth in marital and parental love in middle-class families as the **infant mortality rate** started to fall.

Social attitudes towards children really started to change in the middle of the 19th century. Many 19th-century campaigners were concerned about juvenile delinquency, beggars and child prostitution, and consequently wanted to get children off the streets. Children were excluded from the mines and factories where thousands of them had been killed or injured. Some working-class parents, however, resisted these moves, because they depended on their children's wages.

Cunningham (2006) notes that the 19th century saw the social construction of childhood by adults. This 'childhood' had three major characteristics:

● It was the opposite of adulthood – children were seen to be in need of protection, to have the right not to work, and to be dependent on adults.
● The world of the adult and the world of the child were to be kept separate – the home and the school were regarded as the ideal places for children and they were often banned from adult spaces, such as the pub.
● Children were seen to have the right to 'happiness'.

However, there is considerable evidence that children continued to be badly treated in this period, and child prostitution and abuse were common features of most cities. It was not until the turn of the 20th century that the age of sexual consent was raised to 16.

Childhood in the 20th century

The 20th century saw the emergence of a **child-centred** society. This was probably the result of improved standards of living and nutrition in the late 19th century, which led to a major decline in the infant mortality rate. The higher standard of living also meant that having children became more expensive. The increased availability and efficiency of contraception allowed people to choose to have fewer children. Consequently, parents were able to invest more in them in terms of love, socialization and protection.

Childhood and adolescence were consequently seen as separate categories from adulthood. Children were seen as being in need of special attention and protection.

Children and the state

Concern over the rights of children can be seen in greater state involvement in protecting them. The state supervises the socialization of children through compulsory education, which lasts 11 years. The role of social services and social workers is to police those families in which children are thought to be at risk. The government also takes some economic responsibility by paying child benefit and children's tax credits to parents. The 2004 Children Act has produced the influential policy 'Every Child Matters' which focuses on the wellbeing of children and young people from birth to age 19. This stresses 'better outcomes' for children, such as 'being healthy, staying safe', and 'achieving economic wellbeing' at the centre of all government policies. In 2007, the government set up the Department for Children, Schools and Families to ensure that all children and young people:

- stay healthy and safe
- secure an excellent education and the highest possible standards of achievement
- enjoy their childhood
- make a positive contribution to society and the economy
- have lives full of opportunity, free from the effects of poverty.

Increasingly, children have come to be seen as individuals with rights. The Child Support Act (1991) deals with the care, bringing up and protection of children. It protects children's welfare in the event of parental separation and divorce, emphasizing that the prime concern of the state should be the child, and what children themselves say about their experiences and needs. Some children have recently used the act to 'divorce' their parents, while others have used it to 'force' their separated/divorced parents to see them more regularly.

Theoretical approaches to childhood

The conventional approach

Many functionalists and New Right thinkers tend to subscribe to what has been termed a 'conventional' approach to childhood. This sees children as a vulnerable group – both under threat from and in need of protection from adult society. This approach suggests that successful childrearing requires two parents of the opposite sex, and that there is a 'right' way to bring up a child. Such views often 'blame' working mothers or single mothers, and/or inadequate parents, for social problems such as delinquency. They also see children as in need of protection from 'threats' such as homosexuality and media violence. Postman (1982), for example, sees childhood as under threat because television exposes them too soon to the adult world (see Focus on research below).

Melanie Phillips' book *All Must Have Prizes* (1997) is typical of this conventional approach to childhood. She argues that the culture of parenting in the UK has broken down and the 'innocence' of childhood has been undermined by two trends:

1 The concept of parenting has been distorted by liberal ideas, which have given too many rights and powers to children. Phillips argues that children should be socialized into a healthy respect for parental authority. However, she argues that children's rights have undermined this process, and parents are increasingly criticized and penalized for resorting to sanctions such as smacking.

2 Phillips believes that the media and the peer group have become more influential than parents. She sees the media in the form of magazines aimed at young girls, pop music videos and television as a particular problem, because they encourage young girls to envisage themselves as sexual beings at a much younger age.

These trends mean that the period of childhood has been shortened – it is no longer a sacred and innocent period lasting up to 13 or 14 years. Phillips complains that adulthood

---

Focus on research

Neil Postman (1982)
Is childhood disappearing?

Postman argues that childhood is disappearing. His view is based on two related ideas.

1 The growth of television means that there are no more secrets from children. Television gives them unlimited access to the adult world. They are exposed to the 'real world' of sex, disaster, death and suffering.

2 'Social blurring' has occurred so there is little distinction between adults and children. Children's games are disappearing and children seem less childlike today. They speak, dress and behave in more adult ways, while adults have enjoyed looking more like their kids and youth generally. Over time, nearly all the traditional features that mark the transition to adulthood – getting a job, religious confirmation, leaving home, getting married – no longer apply in any clear way.

Postman's analysis has been heavily criticized. His arguments do not appear to be based on solid evidence, while recent studies indicate that adults are actually taking more and more control of their children's lives. For example, David Brooks (2001) diagnoses parents today as obsessed with safety, and ever more concerned with defining boundaries for their kids and widening their control and safety net around them.

Perhaps it is children that are disappearing rather than childhood. Children are a smaller percentage of our overall population today and are diminishing in relative proportion to other age groups.

Adapted from Allen, D. (2001) 'Is childhood disappearing?', *Studies in Social and Political Thought*, 6(1), 2001

1 What methods could be used to collect data about the impact of television on children?

2 To what extent do you believe that childhood is disappearing? What evidence can you use to support your view?

encroaches upon the experiences of children a great deal earlier than in the past. She argues that many children do not have the emotional maturity to cope with the rights and choices that they have today. The result, she believes, is an increase in social problems such as suicide, eating disorders, self-harm, depression and drug/alcohol abuse.

In *Toxic Childhood* (2007), Sue Palmer argues that adults are benefiting enormously from living in a wealthier society in which electronic technologies have enriched their lives. However, the same technologies are harming children because all too often parents are using them as an alternative to traditional parenting practices. Instead of spending quality time with their children and reading them stories, Palmer claims parents are too happy to use television, electronic games and junk food to keep them quiet. Children are therefore deprived of traditional childhood and family life, and she claims that 'every year children become more distractible, impulsive and self-obsessed – less able to learn, to enjoy life, to thrive socially' because of these trends.

Another trend that has alarmed some sociologists is the rise of children as consumers. It is estimated that children aged between 7 and 11 are worth about £20 million a year as consumers. Advertisers have therefore targeted children in order to encourage 'pester power' – the power of children to train or manipulate their parents to spend money on consumer goods that will shape and increase the status of their children in the eyes of their peers. Three related sociological concerns have arisen out of this trend:

- Commentators often hark back to a so-called 'golden age' of childhood; they see their own lives as children as being much less pressurized and complex, and suggest that the shift into a more consumer-orientated society has resulted in children cynically manipulating their parents with regard to consumer goods. Pugh (2002), for example, suggests that parental spending on children is 'consumption as compensation' – parents who are 'cash-rich but time poor' alleviate their guilt about not spending time with their children by buying them whatever consumer goods they desire.
- Evans and Chandler (2006) found that peer pressure was an important aspect of children's rationale for consumption. The children in their study were very aware of what clothing and labels were approved by their peers and which were not. Moreover, they were very aware of the possibility of the teasing, name-calling and bullying that might result if they did not conform or fit in because they lacked a particular item. Evans and Chandler found that the parents and children from poorer families felt this pressure the most.
- Some commentators claim that the marketing of children's products is often 'anti-adult' – for example, advertising aimed at children often suggests that rebellion is 'cool'. It is argued that this undermines parental authority and contributes to a perceived increase in antisocial behaviour among children and teenagers.

An alternative view

This conventional approach has been criticized by sociologists who have focused on researching how children see and

Focus on research

Julie Evans & Joan Chandler (2006) Family dynamics and children's consumption

Evans and Chandler focused on a sample of 45 children aged 7 to 11 years: 24 girls and 21 boys. The children were asked to complete diaries. They also took part in small-group discussions about how they might negotiate with adults to obtain toys, games and clothing. Nineteen parents were also interviewed.

Many parents justified their consumption of children's products on the basis that the world had become a much riskier place for children and that children spent more time in the home than previous generations. Parents justified their spending on items such as DVDs and computer games as 'safer leisure options'.

Most parents and children saw buying consumer goods for their children as indicative of 'good parenting'. There were signs too that both parents and children interpreted the giving of material possessions as a means of communicating and measuring love respectively.

Evans, J. and Chandler, J. (2006) 'To buy or not to buy: family dynamics and children's consumption', *Sociological Research Online*, 11(2)

1 **How might the research methods used by this study contribute to the validity of the findings?**

2 **How might the conventional approach to children view these findings?**

interpret the world around them. They suggest that functionalist and New Right arguments assume that children are simply empty vessels. Family life is presented as a one-way process in which parenting and socialization aim to transform children into good citizens. However, this view ignores the fact that children have their own unique interpretation of family life, which they actively employ in interaction with their parents. In other words, the relationship between parents and children is a two-way process in which the latter can and do influence the nature and quality of family life. For example, research by Morrow (1998) found that children can be constructive and reflective contributors to family life. Most of the children in Morrow's study had a pragmatic view of their family role – they did not want to make decisions for themselves but they did want a say in what happened to them.

Conventional approaches are also criticized because they tend to generalize about children and childhood. This is dangerous because, as we saw earlier, childhood is not a fixed, universal experience. Historical period, locality, culture, social class, gender and ethnicity all have an influence on the character and quality of childhood. This can be illustrated in a number of ways:

- In many less developed nations, the experience of childhood is extremely different from that in the industrialized world. Children in such countries are constantly at risk of early death because of poverty and lack of basic health care. They are unlikely to have access to education, and may find themselves occupying adult roles as workers or soldiers. In many countries, children are not regarded as special or as in need of protection. For example, in Mexico, it is estimated that 1.9 million children live rough on the streets – 240 000 of these have been abandoned by their parents. In Brazil, 1000 homeless children are shot dead every year by people who regard them as vermin.
- Even in a country such as Britain, experience of childhood may differ across ethnic and religious groups. For example, there is evidence that Muslim, Hindu and Sikh children generally feel a stronger sense of obligation and duty to their parents than White children. Generational conflict is therefore less likely or is more likely to be hidden.
- Experiences of childhood in Britain may vary according to social class. Upper-class children may find that they spend most of their formative years in boarding schools. Middle-class children may be encouraged from an early age to aim for university and a professional career, and they are likely to receive considerable economic and cultural support from their parents. Working-class childhood may be made more difficult by the experience of poverty. For example, research by Jefferis *et al.* (2002) found that children who experienced poverty had significantly fallen behind children from middle-class backgrounds in terms of maths, reading and other ability tests by the age of 7.
- Experiences of childhood may differ according to gender. Boys and girls may be socialized into a set of behaviours based on expectations about masculinity and femininity. For example, there is some evidence that girls are subjected to stricter social controls from parents, compared with boys, when they reach adolescence.

We also need to acknowledge that some children's experiences of childhood may be damaging. Different types of child abuse have been rediscovered in recent years, such as neglect and physical, sexual and emotional abuse. The NSPCC points out that each week at least one child will die as a result of an adult's cruelty, usually a parent or step-parent, while 30 000

children are on child protection registers because they are at risk of abuse from family members. The negative effects of divorce have been documented in several surveys of teenagers. In conclusion, not all children experience the family or their parents as positive – for many children and teenagers, the family is exploitative and dangerous.

Check your understanding

1. What do sociologists mean when they describe childhood as a 'social construction'?

2. How does Aries believe children were treated in pre-industrial society?

3. What were the main causes of society becoming more child-centred at the end of the 19th century?

4. How does the conventional approach to childhood view children?

5. What problems are associated with this approach?

Activities

Research ideas

1. In order to document the changing experience of and attitudes towards childhood, design a survey asking three generations about their experience of being a child.

2. Using textbooks, CD-Roms and government websites, such as those of the Home Office and Lord Chancellor's department (accessible via www.open.gov.uk), compile a detailed time-line outlining state intervention in children's lives and the rights children now have.

Web.tasks

1. Visit the websites www.child-abuse.com/childhouse and www.unicef-irc.org/research/

   These contain links to a number of excellent sites that look at childhood and children's rights across the world.

2. Visit the NSPCC website www.nspcc.co.uk to get an idea of the degree of child abuse in UK society.

3. Visit the government websites www.dfes.gov.uk and www.everychildmatters.gov.uk to see how social policy is now shaped by official concerns for the welfare of children.

Key terms

Child-centred treating the needs of children as a priority.

Economic asset something that brings money in.

Infant mortality rate the number of babies who die in their first year of life, as a proportion of all live births.

Social construction something that is created by society.

The nature of childhood

Item A

<< Most of us tend to think of childhood as a clear and distinct stage of life. 'Children', we suppose, are distinct from 'babies' or 'toddlers'. Childhood intervenes between infancy and the onset of adolescence. Yet the concept of childhood, like so many other aspects of our social life today, has only come into being over the past two or three centuries. In traditional and pre-industrial cultures, the young move directly from a lengthy infancy into working roles within the community. Right up to the start of the 20th century, in the UK and most other Western countries, children as young as 7 or 8 years old were put to work at what now seems a very early age. There are many countries in the world today, in fact, in which young children are engaged in full-time work, often in physically demanding circumstances (coal-mines, for example). The idea that children have distinctive rights, and the notion that the use of child labour is morally wrong, are quite recent developments. >>

Source: Giddens, A. (1997) *Sociology* (3rd edn),
Cambridge: Polity Press

Item B

The changing nature of legislation concerning children has reflected the changing views towards children over time. In the 19th century, the idea gradually developed that children were not simply little adults, but were vulnerable members of society who needed care and protection. This concept of the child as vulnerable dominates 20th-century thinking. For example, the Children Act of 1908 resulted in the criminal justice system treating and punishing criminal adults and children in different ways for the first time. In 1952, local authorities were given the duty to investigate cases of neglect or cruelty with regard to children, while the 1989 Children Act made it clear that the child's best interests must be central to any decision made about the welfare of the child. The child's views are therefore sought and taken into account. Such legislation reflects the fact that we are now a child-centred society.

Adapted from Moore, S. (1998) *Social Welfare Alive*
(2nd edn), Cheltenham: Stanley Thornes, pp. 366–7

Item C

Childhood is tremendously varied, from the sheltered pre-schooler of Western nations to the maimed street beggar or gun-carrying 'freedom fighter' of less industrialized nations. Even in the UK, children may grow up in a wide variety of different and potentially damaging situations. There are occasional alarming reports of child prostitution linked to runaway children and drug use. We know from recent studies that many children of less than 10 years old may be the main carer in family situations where their parent is chronically ill or disabled. For many children, childhood may involve the direct experience of oppression, abuse, exploitation, not to mention parental divorce, poor health and poverty. Childhood experience, then, is extremely diverse by way of region, social class, housing quality, income, culture and ethnicity, prejudice, diet, disease and abuse.

Adapted from Bernardes, J. (1997) *Family Studies: An Introduction*, London: Routledge, p. 115

(a) Explain what sociologists mean by a 'child-centred society' (Item B). (2 marks)

(b) Suggest two differences between childhood in pre-industrial societies and contemporary industrial societies. (4 marks)

(c) Identify three ways in which the state protects the rights of children today. (6 marks)

(d) Using information from the Items and elsewhere, assess the view that childhood is not a fixed universal experience. (24 marks)

Grade booster — Getting top marks in the 24-mark question

It would be a good idea to start with the concept of social construction and then go on to explain how childhood can be seen as socially constructed. You should make use of examples from the Items to illustrate your answer. These can include cross-cultural comparisons between developed and less developed societies and differences within societies, as well as historical comparisons, e.g. between pre-industrial and industrial societies. You should evaluate the importance of different factors producing differences in the experience of childhood, such as compulsory schooling, government policy, the media and poverty.

Exam practice

1 Read **Item A** below and answer and answer parts (a) to (d) that follow.

> ### Item A
>
> Functionalist sociologists have argued that with the transition from pre-industrial society to industrial society, the family has undergone a change in its structure. For example, Talcott Parsons has argued that while in pre-industrial society the family is extended in structure and performs a wide variety of functions, in industrial society the nuclear family becomes the dominant family structure.
>
> Some sociologists also argue that the modern family is much more equal than in the past. For example, Young and Willmott claim that in today's 'symmetrical' nuclear family, husbands' and wives' conjugal roles have become much more equal than in the patriarchal family of the Victorian era. However, feminists have criticized this view of the modern family.

(a) Explain what is meant by the 'patriarchal family' (**Item A**). *(2 marks)*

0/2 *A family found in a society which is patriarchal.*

(b) Suggest **two** criticisms which feminist sociologists might make of the view that 'husbands' and wives' conjugal roles have become much more equal' (**Item A**). *(4 marks)*

2/4 *Firstly, there is still domestic violence by men towards women.*

Secondly, men and women have different functions.

(c) Suggest **three** functions that the extended family might perform. *(6 marks)*

6/6 *1. It can provide a babysitting service, where grandparents look after young children while the parents go out to work.*

2. It can arrange marriages between families.

3. It can provide support, e.g. when migrating to a new area in search of work, having extended family contacts there can help a person find somewhere to live.

(d) Examine the reasons for changes in the position of children in the last 200 years. *(24 marks)*

Childhood has changed a great deal in the last 200 years. As Item A shows, we have gone from an extended to a nuclear family structure, where people no longer work together as a family unit but each adult goes out to work in factories, offices, etc. This means that we are no longer a unit of production and this has its effects on the family and children.

One important change has been education. In the past, children rarely got much education if any, whereas it was made compulsory to go to school in the late 19th century and since then the school leaving age has gone up to sixteen. This means that today children are better educated and so are prepared to achieve their social status and have career opportunities.

Another change is the improvement in children's health and welfare. With the introduction of the NHS, children now have a better chance of surviving and the infant mortality rate is now very low compared to the last two centuries. This means parents don't have to have as many children in order to get enough to look after them in old age. Also, there is less need to have many children because of the welfare state, which can provide for the elderly instead of their children having to do so.

An examiner comments

This just repeats the question. You must define patriarchal using different words, e.g. a male-dominated family.

A good first point, but the second scores no marks because the meaning is unclear and it's not linked particularly to feminism. A better point would be to say that although married women are more likely to go out to work nowadays, they are still expected to do most of the housework and childcare.

Three good points, so full marks.

This shows knowledge, but it's not been made very relevant and needs to focus on childhood more.

A good point about compulsory schooling, but needs to say more about its impact on children, not just on their future as adults.

Some good points here about infant mortality rate and family size – but what impact did these have on children's position?

Another big change is child labour laws, banning children from working in mines, factories, etc., until they are old enough. This means fewer children die in workplace accidents, but it also makes children dependent on their parents financially. Because they cannot go out to work from their early years, children are no longer an economic asset to their parents, who have to pay to support them through school.

Therefore, as we can see, there have been major changes in childhood in the last two centuries, including education, banning children from working and smaller families. All these have had a great impact on their position in modern society.

> A good point about child labour laws here. It would be a good idea to link the point about children as economic assets back to the one about declining family size.

> A summary to conclude, but this only repeats points already made. Better to use the time to look at another reason.

13/24

An examiner comments

Answer (d) gets off to a badly focused start, describing the extended to nuclear family transition and industrialization when it really needs to be concentrating on childhood – perhaps because the question itself has a historical angle. However, it begins to improve in the main body of the answer, and looks at several reasons for changes in children's position: education, the welfare state, infant mortality, family size and labour laws.

However, the answer could explain the impact of these factors more fully and it could also look at other issues, e.g. the effect of the media, children as consumers, children's rights, and gender, ethnic or other differences in childhood. It also needs to use concepts such as child-centred society and social construction of childhood. It should also offer some analysis or evaluation, for example by considering whether children's position today is better than in the past, or whether childhood as we understand it today is disappearing.

One for you to try

(e) Using information from **Item B** and elsewhere, assess sociological explanations of changes in the rate of divorce. *(24 marks)*

Item B

The last three decades of the twentieth century showed a very striking trend towards much higher divorce rates than had been the case previously. For example, in the British case, compared with the figures for the early 1970s, the statistics for the late 1990s showed about twice as many divorces.

Although Great Britain had the highest divorce rate in Europe, the same trends were evident elsewhere, especially in the more economically developed and less religious countries of northern Europe, but the same trend is also evident even in the more conservative, religious and less developed regions of southern Europe.

There are also social class differences in the rate of divorce. Broadly speaking, the lower the social class, the higher the rate of divorce has tended to be. Similarly, those who marry young are at greater risk of divorce.

An examiner comments

You need to outline the changes in the divorce rate. Concentrate on the period since about 1970. Use the Item to help you (e.g. mention international trends as well as British ones). Look at a range of explanations, such as modernization, industrialization, the decline in religion, individualism, changes in the law and in the position of women (e.g. education and career opportunities), and changing expectations of marriage. You should contrast different perspectives on divorce, e.g. New Right and feminist approaches.

Answers to the 'One for you to try' are available **free** on **www.collinseducation.com/sociologyweb**

Chapter 3 Summary

Functionalism
- Nuclear family norm
- Industrialization
- Structural differentiation

Historical perspectives
- Gradual evolution
- Symmetrical family

Marxism
- Ideological capitalist apparatus
- Promotes ruling-class ideology

Feminism
- Marxist-feminist: family benefits capitalism & men
- Radical feminist: family benefits men – patriarchal

G.P. Murdock
- Family as universal institution
- Performs repro-ductive, sexual, educational and economic functions

Marxism
- Family functions to distract working class from inequality

Parsons
- Primary socialization of children
- Stabilization of adult personalities

Feminism
- Family is patriarchal and promotes male dominance

Family functions

Family, social structure & change

Demographic trends & family life

Birth rates & fertility rates
- Effect on family size
- Effect of birth control, educational opportunity and genderquake

Death rate
- Life expectancy
- Ageing population
- Beanpole families

Migration
- Cultural diversity in family life

Family, morality & state policy

Familial ideology
- Nuclear family as ideal
- Nuclear family under moral attack

State policy
- Supportive of or undermining familial ideology?

Families and households

Marriage, divorce & family diversity

Marriage
- In decline or merely postponed?
- Effect of genderquake
- Threat of cohabitation

Marital breakdown
- Divorce rate
- Effects of divorce on children
- Influence of postmodern world

One-parent families
- Stereotypes vs facts
- Reconstituted families

Childhood

Social construction of childhood
- Children as economic assets
- Child-centred societies
- Relativity of childhood experiences

Theoretical approaches
- Conventional
- Interpretivist

Power & control in families

Housework and childcare
- Equality vs dual burden
- Decision-making
- Fatherhood

Violence
- Definitions
- Role of patriarchy

Wealth, poverty and welfare

THE HENLEY COLLEGE LIBRARY

AQA Specification	Topics	Pages
Candidates should examine:		
Different definitions and ways of measuring poverty, wealth and income.	Definitions of income and wealth are covered in Topic 1, poverty in Topic 2.	124–35
The distribution of poverty, wealth and income between different social groups.	Explanations of the distribution of income and wealth are covered in Topic 1. Topic 2 discusses the distribution of poverty.	124–35
The existence and persistence of poverty in contemporary society.	Topic 3 investigates the groups most at risk of poverty. Topic 4 covers sociological explanations of poverty.	136–41 142–47
Different responses to poverty, with particular reference to the role of social policy since the 1940s.	Topic 5 looks at possible solutions to poverty.	148–53
The nature and role of public, private, voluntary and informal welfare provision in contemporary society.	Topic 6 focuses on welfare provision.	154–59

Getting you thinking

Times Rich List: The top 11

Name	Worth	Industry
Results (Last year's results in brackets)		
1 (1) Lakshmi Mittal & family	£19 250m	Steel
2 (2) Roman Abramovich	£10 800m	Oil & industry
3 (3) The Duke of Westminster	£7000m	Property
4 (7) Sri & Gopi Hinduja	£6200m	Industry & finance
5 (99) David Khalili	£5800m	Art & property
6 (4) Hans Rausing & family	£5400m	Packaging
7 (5) Sir Philip & Lady Green	£4900m	Retailing
8 (10) John Fredriksen	£3500m	Shipping
9 (8) David & Simon Reuben	£3490m	Metals & property
10 (45) Jim Ratcliffe	£3300m	Chemicals
11 (9) Sir Richard Branson	£3100m	Transport & mobile phones

Source: http://business.timesonline.co.uk/
tol/business/specials/rich_list/rich_list_search/

<< The Conservatives sought last night to re-establish some of their tax cutting credentials by unveiling plans to abolish inheritance tax.

The proposals, to be published today but yet to be endorsed by David Cameron, the Tory leader, would mean a tax reduction that would cost the Treasury £2.6 billion and would free roughly 40,000 families a year from the unpopular levy ... The plan is part of John Redwood's policy review on competitiveness. >>

Source: Carlin, B. *Daily Telegraph*, 31 August 2007

1 Do you think that people should have a right to pass wealth on to their children, or does it give some people an unfair advantage in life?

2 Do you think that we ought to have much higher rates of tax for the better off, to ensure that there is less inequality in society?

3 In your opinion, should we have inequalities in income, or do you think that everyone should have the same wage? Give the reasons for your answer.

Wealth

Problems of definition

Wealth is defined as the ownership of property, shares, savings and other assets. However, within that overall definition, there is some debate about exactly what we should include as property and 'assets'. For example, does a person's house constitute wealth? Yes, of course, if they sold it, then they would receive a very large amount of money – but where would they live? But even that is too simple. Some people live in houses which are enormous and far exceed what they need – so does the excess beyond their needs count as wealth?

A similar debate surrounds **pensions** – some argue that pensions must be defined as wealth, because they are savings, while others argue that pensions are essential and so they do not actually constitute wealth.

So how we define wealth is not as easy as first appears. The answer to the problem of definition faced by sociologists is that we normally talk about **marketable wealth**. By this, we mean the range of assets that a person is reasonably able to dispose of, if they should so wish. Marketable wealth, therefore, is generally taken to exclude house and pension.

Problems of measurement

A further problem with wealth is actually measuring it. Unlike income, which we discuss later, the **Inland Revenue** does not conduct a yearly assessment of wealth. So, researchers obtain their information in one of the following two ways:

1 looking at the assessment of wealth made for tax purposes when someone dies

2 asking a sample of rich people the extent of their wealth.

Problems arise with both methods.

Inland Revenue statistics based on inheritance tax

Using information obtained from wills usually only provides us with out-of-date figures. What is more, wealthy people will attempt to limit the amount of wealth that they declare for tax purposes. Charitable trusts, early distribution of wealth to younger family members before death and financial holdings abroad are all common ways to avoid tax. All of this means that the wealth of the rich may be underestimated. On the other hand, poorer people who do not pay **inheritance tax** are excluded from Inland Revenue statistics, so their wealth may be underestimated too.

Surveys

Because of these problems, sociologists turn to surveys, but rich people are extremely reluctant to divulge their true wealth. Either way, the figures will probably be inaccurate.

Changes in wealth distribution over time

We have just seen some of the difficulties of trying to define wealth. However, even bearing in mind the differences that occur if we include such things as house values and occupational pensions, we can still make the simple, clear statement that wealth is distributed very unequally in British society.

In the 1920s, one per cent of the population owned over 60 per cent of all marketable wealth. A further 9 per cent owned 29 per cent, leaving 90 per cent of the population with about 11 per cent of marketable wealth. By the 1970s, however, the share of the top one per cent had halved to about 30 per cent, while the wealthiest 10 per cent (including the top one per cent) owned about 50 per cent of wealth. However, after 20 years in which this pattern of inequality stabilized, inequality began growing again during the 1990s.

Patterns of wealth today

If we include houses and pensions in the definition of wealth, then **personal wealth** more than doubled in the period between 1980 and the early part of the 21st century. This reflects the growth in home ownership. As house prices have increased faster than inflation, those who own homes (over 70 per cent of householders) have become 'richer'. However, for those who do not own their homes or have no pension, their personal wealth declined. In fact, during the period 1980 to 2000, the number of people without any assets (and therefore no wealth) increased from 5 per cent to 10 per cent of the population.

However, if we look only at personal marketable wealth – which consists largely of property, shares and other savings/investments – the situation is very different. Shares in companies are now held by a relatively high proportion of the

Table 4.1 Distribution of marketable wealth

	1991	1996	2001	2002	2003
Percentage of marketable wealth owned by:					
Most wealthy 1%	17	20	22	24	21
Most wealthy 25%	71	74	72	75	72
Most wealthy 50%	92	93	94	94	93
Total marketable wealth (£ billion)	1711	2092	3477	3588	3783

Source: HM Revenue and Customs/*Social Trends 37*

population, as a result of the 1980s government sell-off of public utilities such as water, electricity and gas – and more recently as a result of some building societies 'giving' shares to their account holders, when they became banks.

Despite this increase in share ownership, a very large proportion of shares and assets is owned by very few people. The wealthiest 1 per cent of the population own about 21 per cent of total marketable wealth, and the wealthiest 25 per cent own 72 per cent of all marketable wealth – mainly in the form of company shares (see Table 4.1). If we compare the total wealth of the richest one thousand families with the total wealth of the least wealthy half of the population – about 28 million people – then the richest one thousand has 15 000 times more total wealth!

Income

Defining income

Like wealth, income is difficult to measure. Once again, those with large amounts of income (who are of course often 'the wealthy') will seek to minimize their income levels on their income tax returns, and will employ accountants and tax experts to do just that.

But there are also methodological problems that sociologists face in trying to measure income levels. They have to decide whether to calculate income by household or by individual (poverty statistics, for example, are increasingly based on households). They must decide which is more important, income before tax, or income after tax? And what about people who work for 'cash in hand'? Finally, many people receive state benefits, but also receive some services free (bus passes, for example) which others have to pay for – is this income?

Income distribution

Overall, income is more evenly distributed than wealth, but that does not mean there is any great amount of equality. The income of the highest-earning 20 per cent of households is four times higher than the lowest-earning 20 per cent – even after tax and including benefits for the lowest income earners. Furthermore, it appears that income inequalities are actually

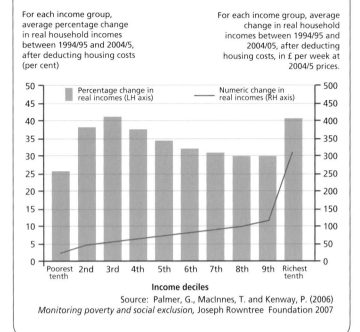

Figure 4.1 Changes in income, poorest to richest, 1994/5 to 2004/5

For each income group, average percentage change in real household incomes between 1994/95 and 2004/5, after deducting housing costs (per cent)

For each income group, average change in real household incomes between 1994/95 and 2004/05, after deducting housing costs, in £ per week at 2004/5 prices.

Percentage change in real incomes (LH axis)

Numeric change in real incomes (RH axis)

Income deciles

Source: Palmer, G., MacInnes, T. and Kenway, P. (2006) *Monitoring poverty and social exclusion,* Joseph Rowntree Foundation 2007

increasing. As Figure 4.1 above shows, the richest tenth of the population have seen their income increase the most, while the poorest tenth have seen their income increase the least. While the richest and poorest have moved further apart, other 'better off' groups have not done as well.

Changes over time

Income inequality is actually increasing, and has been doing so since the early 1980s. On average, income has risen by 44 per cent since 1979, with the wealthiest 10 per cent of the population experiencing an increase of 70 per cent in real terms. On the other hand, the poorest 10 per cent have had an income decrease of 9 per cent.

Income and the life cycle

Income inequality needs to be seen as a dynamic, changing concept. It is not that the same people are necessarily in the lowest (or highest) wage earners for their entire lives. The research suggests that income is closely related to the **life cycle** – people's earnings gradually rise over their lifetime and when their children leave home, but when they reach pensionable age, income declines sharply again.

Redistribution and the impact of taxation

We have seen that income and wealth are unequally distributed in the UK. However, as people pay higher rates of tax the more

they earn, and as the lowest income groups receive a range of state benefits, the outcome should be that the levels of inequality are much lower. The evidence suggests that this is partly true, in that tax and benefits do redistribute, but not as much as might be expected.

Redistribution in the UK is based upon a mixture of taxes and benefits. These include the following:

- *Direct taxes* – These are taken straight out of a person's wage. These tend to be 'progressive', in that the more a person earns, the more they must pay in tax. Over the last 20 years, direct taxes have been reduced.
- *Indirect taxes* – These include taxes (such as **VAT**) which are added to purchases. Indirect taxes tend to be 'regressive' in that they hit poorer people harder, as they spend a higher proportion of their incomes on necessities. People with higher incomes can choose to save money if they wish. Indirect taxes have increased over the last 20 years.
- *Cash benefits* – These include payments by the government to lower earners and unemployed people. Depending upon how high these benefits are, they can significantly redistribute income or not. Since 1997, there has been a real increase in cash benefits, so that it has had a redistributive effect. The bottom 30 per cent of households have received about £20 a week more because of an increase and restructuring in benefits.
- *Benefits in kind* – These are services provided by the state which are freely available, such as education and health services. Currently, the lowest earning 20 per cent of households receive on average about £5200 worth of benefits per year.

What effects do these taxes and benefits have on the redistribution of income?

If we start by looking at incomes before tax, then the richest 20 per cent earn about 18 times more than the poorest 20 per cent. After income tax and the addition of various benefits, the ratio drops to 4 to 1. However, there are still some adjustments to be made. Most goods have VAT (value-added tax) charged on them, and this has a greater proportional impact on poorer families (because more of their income is spent, and less is saved). As a result, the actual ratio of incomes between the richest and poorest is about 6 to 1.

The tax and social security systems, therefore, do have an impact – they reduce inequalities by about two-thirds – but this still leaves considerable inequality.

Explanations for inequalities of wealth and income

Explanations for the continuing existence of – and indeed growth in – inequalities in income and wealth can be divided into two main categories: specific explanations and theoretical explanations.

Focus on research

Kawachi, Kennedy & Wilkinson
Crime and inequality

In 1996, Wilkinson published a famous study which linked income inequalities with high mortality and morbidity among poorer people. In a later study, Kawachi, Kennedy and Wilkinson wanted to see if inequality levels could also explain higher crime rates. They compared statistics on crime levels in different areas in the USA with various levels of income inequality. This, then, was a comparative study using official statistics on crime and income inequality. They found that *in general*, crime rates were highest when levels of inequality were at their highest and, conversely, where inequality was lowest, so too were crime rates – but this was not always the case.

The key factor which influenced the outcome of the relationship was the degree of *social capital*. This term describes the sense individuals have of belonging to a network of people living in a particular neighbourhood. Crime rates were a direct outcome of the two linked factors of inequality and social capital. The higher the level of inequality and the lower the degree of social capital, the higher the crime rate. They concluded that focusing solely on levels of inequality in income and wealth in understanding social problems ignored the key factor of social capital.

Kawachi, I., Kennedy, B.P. and Wilkinson, R.G. (1999) 'Crime, social disorganisation and relative deprivation', *Social Science and Medicine*, 48, pp. 719–31

1 In what way was the study 'comparative'?

2 What is meant by the term 'social capital'?

3 What did the study find about the relationship between inequality, social capital and crime?

Specific explanations for increases in income inequality

Government policy

Changes in taxation and state benefits have actually lowered taxes on the rich in real terms, while state benefits have declined relative to the increase in average earnings for those employed.

Two-earner households

Pahl (1988) has pointed out that there is an increasing division between households. On the one side, there are households in which there is no adult worker at all; on the other side, the number of two-earner households is rising. The divide is increasing because there is a decline in single-earner households, while the other two household types are growing – and as they do so, the differences in earnings are also growing.

Growth of lone-parent families

This links to the point above. The fastest growing type of family is the one-parent family. Because of childcare responsibilities, the parent (usually a woman) is more likely to work part-time or to have no employment.

Job insecurity

Employment patterns are changing, and the prospect of a job for life is gradually being replaced by job insecurity. People are now expected to perform a range of jobs in their working careers. For example, a Joseph Rowntree Foundation survey in 2006 (*Monitoring Poverty and Social Exclusion*) found that half of men and a third of women applying for Jobseekers Allowance (an indication of unemployment) had last been on the same benefit less than six months before – showing that unemployment is now a normal expectation for some employees, as employers demand more 'flexible' labour. The impact on income is that those with more reliable work can expect a regular income, while the increasing numbers in 'flexible' employment often experience peaks and troughs of income.

Specific explanations for the retention of wealth

Globalization

Most economies in the world are now linked in a **global economy**. If a democratically elected government were to seek to take wealth away from the very richest, the rich would move their money out of the country. This would have a huge impact on the British economy. Governments are therefore very cautious about upsetting the very rich.

The nature of the taxation system

The tax system in the UK allows a substantial proportion of wealth to be passed from one generation to another. This maintains wealth within the same small group.

Political decisions

If governments wanted to reform the tax system, increase benefits for lower-income families or raise the minimum wage, they could do so. Therefore, a key factor in maintaining inequalities of wealth and income is the choices made by politicians.

Entrepreneurial talent

It is possible for very clever (and possibly fortunate) people, from relatively humble backgrounds, to become rich – although, in practice, very few do so.

Theoretical explanations for income and wealth inequalities

There are three broad types of explanation for inequalities in wealth and income: functionalist (see pp. 12–15), Marxist (see pp. 17–19) and Weberian (see p. 18).

Functionalist-based theoretical explanations

These argue that society needs inequality in order to reward the more able, who undertake the most important social and economic positions. Critics have pointed out that this is more of a justification than an explanation. For example, it could be argued that nurses or social workers contribute more to society than advertising executives, yet they earn far less.

Marxist–based theories

Marxist theories claim that capitalism is based upon inequality, with the rich actively seeking to exploit the rest of society. Inequality is, therefore, inevitable in capitalism.

Weberian-based explanations

These suggest that society is best seen as various interest groups competing among themselves to ensure that they benefit the most. Weber argues that this results in more powerful groups finding ways to obtain the highest incomes and maintain their wealth.

Check your understanding

1 Explain why it is difficult to define 'wealth'.

2 Why might the statistics we have on wealth be inaccurate?

3 What changes in wealth distribution have taken place since the 1970s?

4 Which is less unevenly distributed across the nation, income or wealth?

5 In your own words, describe any one specific and one theoretical reason for the continuing inequalities in income and wealth.

6 How does the 'global economy' have an impact on wealth distribution within the UK?

Key terms

Global economy refers to the way in which investment and trading now span the entire world. This hinders individual governments' control of the economy, because companies can simply move to other countries.

Inheritance tax tax on wealth when a person dies.

Inland Revenue the government department responsible for taxes on earnings and wealth.

Life cycle refers to the changes in a person's economic and social situation over their lifetime.

Marketable wealth all a person possesses (does not include their pension or house).

Pension a regular payment made to someone when they retire from paid employment.

Personal wealth wealth owned by individuals. This can be compared with institutional wealth, which is wealth owned by companies.

Redistribution the transfer of wealth from the rich to the poor. In theory, the taxes the rich pay are used to fund services for the poor.

VAT (value-added tax) a tax charged on most goods and services. It is an indirect tax because it is not taken directly from people's wages.

Wealth the ownership of property, shares, savings and other assets.

Activities

Research idea

Organize a small focus group (perhaps from another student group not studying sociology). Show them the figures on the differences in wealth and income. Ask them to discuss the reasons for such differences. Compare their views with the theoretical explanations in this topic. Which theory comes closest to their views?

Web.tasks

1 Go to http://ucatlas.ucsc.edu/income.php, the site of the UC Atlas of Inequality. This explores inequality across the world. How does the information contained here put the inequality within UK society into perspective?

2 The House of Commons Library produced a detailed research report on income and wealth in 2004. It can be found at www.parliament.uk/commons/lib/research/rp2004/rp04-070.pdf Look at page 39. Find out which countries in Europe had the highest and lowest levels of income inequality.

Wealth and income

Item A

Distribution of real household disposable income (UK)

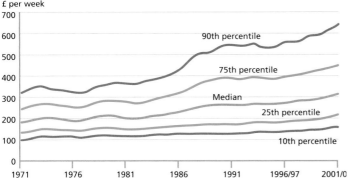

£ per week

- Median refers to the level of income of the middle range of people in the UK.
- The 90th percentile refers to the richest 10 per cent and the 10th percentile refers to the poorest 10 per cent.

Source: *Social Trends* 34, London: Office for National Statistics, 2004

Item B

<< Several explanations have been put forward to account for both shifts in individual earnings and the overall growth in inequality of earnings since the mid-1980s. The growth of unemployment, changing forms of work, the decline of the male 'breadwinner' and the increase in women's labour-force participation, the decline of trade-union influence and national collective bargaining structures, and changes in the taxation and benefit systems are among the factors that have influenced the rapid growth of income inequality in the UK. >>

Source: Abercrombie, N. and Warde, A. (2000)
Contemporary British Society (3rd edn),
Cambridge: Polity Press, p. 119

Item C

<< Among the factors found to affect wealth accumulation, the most important was ability to accumulate wealth – those with higher incomes and lower outgoings were most likely to put money into financial savings, mortgages and occupational or personal pension schemes. Attitudes towards saving and knowledge about different schemes also had an effect on wealth accumulation. Finally, the availability of suitable savings and investment schemes was also a key factor. >>

Source: Joseph Rowntree Foundation, *Findings*, July 1999

(a) Explain the difference between wealth and income. (4 marks)

(b) Identify two trends in the graph shown in Item A. (4 marks)

(c) Suggest two problems of defining and/or measuring wealth. (4 marks)

(d) Using information from Items B and C and elsewhere, assess sociological explanations of the distribution of wealth and income. (24 marks)

Grade booster Getting top marks in the 24-mark question

You need to deal with both wealth and income. Describe the patterns of wealth and income distribution and discuss a range of different explanations, e.g. the impact of government tax and benefits policies, changes in family structure, globalization. Relate these to sociological theories, e.g. functionalism and Marxism. Make sure you use information from the Items – for example, how might the changes listed in Item B affect income inequality?

Defining and measuring poverty

Getting you thinking

A national survey was carried out in order to find out how 'ordinary people' defined poverty. The respondents were offered the three definitions shown in the table below and asked which one(s) they agreed with (they could agree with more than one). The (cumulative) percentage agreeing with each definition is shown in the right-hand column.

Public definitions of poverty

Someone in the UK was in poverty if …	% agreeing
…they had enough to buy things they really needed, but not enough to buy the things that most people take for granted	28%
…they had enough to eat and live, but not enough to buy other things they needed	60%
…they had not got enough to eat and live without getting into debt	90%

Source: Jowell, R., Witherspoon, S. and Brook, L. (eds) (1995) *British Social Attitudes Survey*, Aldershot: Gower

1 If someone could not afford to buy the items pictured, which of the definitions of poverty in the table (if any) would you consider applied to them? Look at each item separately.

2 Which definition of poverty do you agree with? Explain your answer.

3 Look at the items in Figure 4.2 opposite (used in research on defining and measuring poverty). Do you think they accurately represent a measure of 'poverty'?

4 Break into small groups. How would you measure poverty if you were doing sociological research on its existence in Britain?

5 Do you think it is possible to talk about poverty in the UK when we can see such extreme deprivation in other parts of the world?

Figure 4.2 Affordability of household items

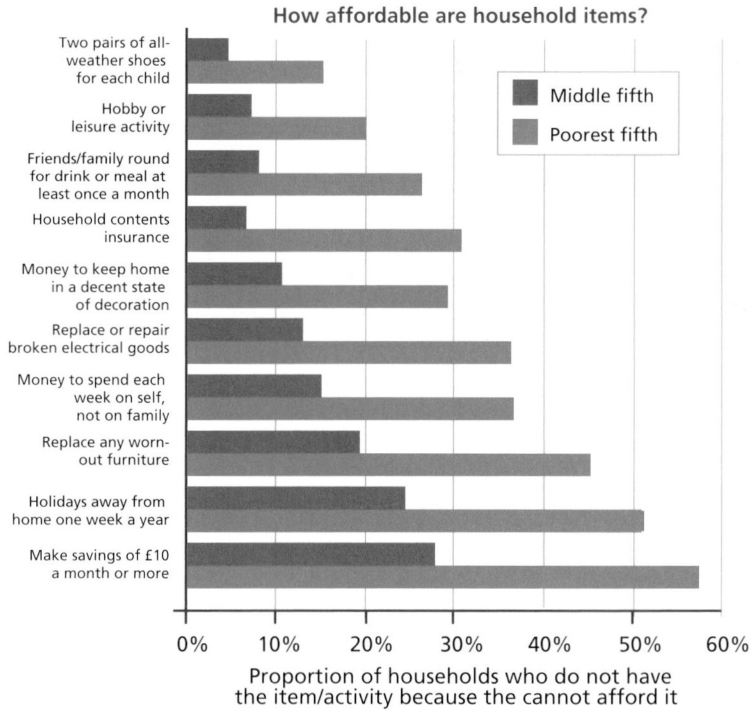
How affordable are household items?
Two pairs of all-weather shoes for each child
Hobby or leisure activity
Friends/family round for drink or meal at least once a month
Household contents insurance
Money to keep home in a decent state of decoration
Replace or repair broken electrical goods
Money to spend each week on self, not on family
Replace any worn-out furniture
Holidays away from home one week a year
Make savings of £10 a month or more
Middle fifth
Poorest fifth
0%
10%
20%
30%
40%
50%
60%
Proportion of households who do not have the item/activity because the cannot afford it

Source: Palmer, G., MacInnes, T. and Kenway, P. (2006) *Monitoring poverty and social exclusion*, Joseph Rowntree Foundation 2007

Each time there is an election, the political party in government will announce all that they have achieved in combating poverty. They will manage to produce convincing statistics to show that poverty has decreased under their government. The opposition parties will angrily denounce these statistics as biased, and produce a completely different set, which show, quite clearly, that poverty has *increased* during the governing party's time in office. How do we make sense of this? The answer lies, quite simply, in the different definitions and measurements that can be used.

Sociologists have defined poverty in two different ways:

1 **absolute poverty**
2 **relative poverty**.

Absolute poverty

This definition is usually traced back to the 19th-century antipoverty campaigner Seebohm Rowntree. Rowntree was concerned that politicians refused to recognize the sheer extent of poverty in the UK. Therefore, in the 1890s, he conducted a 'scientific' survey to discover the real extent of poverty (Rowntree 1901). Part of this survey involved constructing a clear definition that distinguished the poor from the non-poor. The definition was based on deciding what resources were needed for a person to be able to live healthily and work efficiently.

To find the amount of income a person needed, Rowntree added together:

- the costs of a very basic diet
- the costs of purchasing a minimum amount of clothes of minimum quality
- the rent for a basic level of housing.

The 'poverty line' was then drawn at the income needed to cover these three costs.

Advantages of an absolute definition of poverty

An absolute definition provides us with a clear measure of who is in poverty at any one time. It also provides us with a tool to compare the extent of poverty in different societies, and in the same society at different periods of time.

Disadvantages of an absolute definition

An absolute definition fails to take into account the fact that what is regarded as poverty changes over time. What is a luxury today may be a necessity tomorrow, as fashion, acceptable standards of housing and general standards of living change. This makes it very hard to decide exactly what constitutes a 'minimum' standard of clothes or an 'acceptable' diet. The absolute definition of poverty is, in fact, a measure of destitution – that is, the failure to obtain the absolute necessities to keep life going. But poverty is not actually **destitution** – someone can be poor, but still be able to struggle on.

The 'budget standard measure'

A contemporary version of the absolute definition is the 'budget standard measure', which is a rather more sophisticated version of Rowntree's original work. One version of this was developed by the Family Budget Unit, led by Bradshaw (1990). Bradshaw used detailed research information on the spending patterns of the poorest to construct an income that would provide a 'modest but adequate budget'. According to this measure, any family living below this income would be regarded as poor by any reasonable person.

Relative poverty

An alternative way of looking at poverty is to see it in terms of the normal expectations of any society. As societies change and become more (or less) affluent, so the idea of what is poverty will change too. Central heating and colour televisions were at one time luxuries – yet today the majority of homes have them. More recently, mobile phones and home computers have become part of a 'normal' standard of living for a very large section of the British population.

Relative poverty places poverty in relationship to the 'normal' expectations of society. If a person, or family, is unable to achieve a moderate standard of living, then they are poor.

Advantages of the relative definition of poverty

The relative definition links poverty to the expectations of society – reflecting the fact that people do measure their own quality of life against that of other people. It also broadens the idea of what poverty is – from lacking basic necessities to lacking a range of other 'needs', such as adequate leisure.

Disadvantages of the relative definition

The relative definition does have a number of disadvantages, however:

- It can only be used within any one society; it does not help with cross-cultural comparisons. (You are measuring poverty by asking people what is acceptable within their society – not across the world.)
- There is the difficulty of deciding what is or is not a 'normal' standard of living.
- It also has the rather absurd implication that, no matter how rich people become, there will always be poverty, as long as not everybody is equally rich. This is because relative poverty is as much a measure of inequality as poverty. As long as there is inequality, it could be argued, there is poverty.

Measuring relative poverty

There are two ways of **operationalizing** (measuring) the concept of poverty within the relative approach:

1 the **relative income measure**
2 the **consensual measure**.

The relative income measure (HBAI)

This approach measures income as a proportion of typical household income – the idea being that, if a family has a lower-than-average income, they cannot afford an acceptable standard of living. The most commonly used measure is that a household is in poverty if it receives less than 60 per cent of the **median** British income. This approach is now used by the British government and the European Union as the threshold measure of poverty. It is called **Households Below Average Income** or **HBAI** approach.

A consensual measure of poverty

A second approach is to measure the extent of poverty in terms of what possessions and services the majority of people think are necessary in a society. The measure is constructed by asking people to rank in order a list of possessions and services which they consider to be necessities. The resulting list is used as the basis to work out what most people regard as an unacceptable

level of deprivation. This approach was used originally by Mack and Lansley in *Breadline Britain* (1993), and developed later by David Gordon and colleagues in *Poverty and Social Exclusion in Britain* (2000). Gordon and colleagues' consensual definition of poverty was derived using the following methods. (Please note that Table 4.2 below is a much shortened version of the full table used in the research and referred to in the following extract.)

<< *The table ranks the percentage of respondents identifying different adult items as 'necessary, which all adults should be able to afford and which they should not have to do without'. People of all ages and walks of life do not restrict their interpretation of 'necessities' to the basic material needs of a subsistence diet, shelter, clothing and fuel. There are social customs, obligations and activities that substantial majorities of the population also identify as among the top necessities of life.* >>

Source: Gordon, D. et al. (2000) *Poverty and Social Exclusion in Britain*, York: Joseph Rowntree Foundation

Table 4.2 Essential requirements (1999)

	Necessary	Not necessary
Bed and bedding for everyone	95	4
Heating to warm living areas of the home	94	5
Damp-free home	93	6
Visiting friends or family in hospital	92	7
Two meals a day	91	9
Medicines prescribed by doctor	90	9
Refrigerator	89	11
Fresh fruit and vegetables daily	86	13
Warm waterproof coat	85	14
Replacement or repair of broken electrical goods	85	14
Visits to friends or family	84	15
Celebrations on special days such as Christmas	83	16

Poverty and social exclusion

The concept of poverty is closely linked to that of **social exclusion**, and there is some debate over whether the term social exclusion should replace 'poverty'.

Poverty is usually seen as lack of income to purchase the goods and services that allow people to participate fully in society. In many ways, it is a 'static' concept, based on inability to purchase a socially accepted standard of living. Social exclusion, on the other hand, widens the horizon of analysis and looks at a range of interconnecting disadvantages from which certain groups in society suffer. These groups have the

Focus on research

New Policy Institute
Monitoring poverty and social exclusion

The New Policy Institute has been undertaking a series of annual reports monitoring the latest changes in poverty levels. This is the ninth in the series, which began in 1997, the year that New Labour were elected. The researchers reanalysed a wide range of official statistics from government departments in order to see exactly what was happening. The Institute concluded that overall poverty was decreasing, influenced by the growing numbers of people in employment. This was strengthened by the introduction of a system of *tax credits,* which provided

additional income for low-earning households. However, in terms of wider social exclusion, educational inequalities remained static, health inequalities were still high and certain parts of the country, particularly the North East, had a noticeably higher range of social problems than elsewhere.

Palmer, G., MacInnes, T. and Kenway, P. (2007) *Monitoring Poverty and Social Exclusion 2006*, York: Joseph Rowntree Foundation

1   What reasons did the report identify for the decrease in poverty?

2   What did the report find out about the level of social exclusion?

worst housing, health, education and job prospects in society, while suffering from the highest levels of stress, crime victimization and unemployment.

The idea of social exclusion comes from two sources. In the UK, it was originally developed by Townsend (1979), the very person who first introduced the notion of relative poverty. Townsend amended his definition of poverty to argue that poverty turned into social exclusion when it denied people full membership of society. This also coincided with the European Commission rejecting the idea that poverty in any meaningful financial sense (such as exists in developing countries or was

experienced in Europe in the 1920s and 1930s) continued to exist. Instead, the Commission saw a wide range of extreme inequalities in European societies which could not be remedied solely by increasing the income of the poor.

This is the crucial distinction between the ideas of poverty and of social exclusion. For poverty campaigners, if low incomes can be eradicated, then the problem of poverty will disappear. For campaigners who wish to eradicate social exclusion, extreme inequalities in health, housing, environment, crime victimization and education would all have to be tackled. Finally, social exclusion is seen as a problem that continues

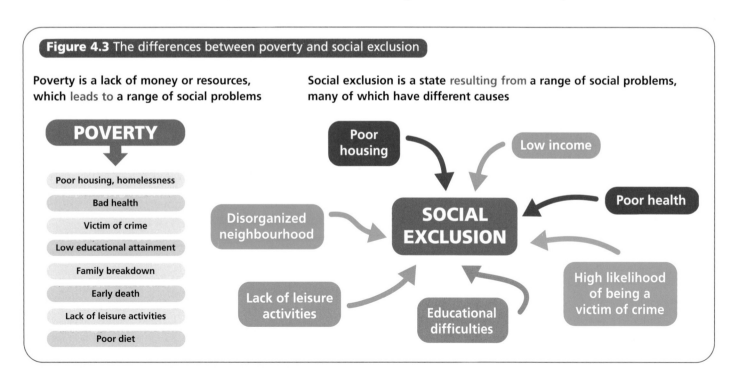

Figure 4.3 The differences between poverty and social exclusion

Poverty is a lack of money or resources, which leads to a range of social problems

Social exclusion is a state resulting from a range of social problems, many of which have different causes

POVERTY

- Poor housing, homelessness
- Bad health
- Victim of crime
- Low educational attainment
- Family breakdown
- Early death
- Lack of leisure activities
- Poor diet

Poor housing → SOCIAL EXCLUSION
Low income
Poor health
Disorganized neighbourhood
Lack of leisure activities
Educational difficulties
High likelihood of being a victim of crime

across generations, so that patterns of poor health, low educational attainment and high levels of victimization continue within the same families and neighbourhoods. Social exclusion is, therefore, a much wider and more complex issue.

Measuring social exclusion

According to the government's Social Exclusion Unit:

>> *Social exclusion is a shorthand term for what can happen when people or areas suffer from a combination of linked problems such as unemployment, poor skills, low incomes, poor housing, high crime environments, bad health and family breakdown.* >>

Because social exclusion is something which is manifested in virtually every aspect of life, actually measuring it is difficult. As a result, various 'indices' or measures have been developed which try to capture a snapshot of a wide range of disadvantages that the socially excluded face in life. The New Policy Institute, for example has developed 50 indicators which measure levels of:

- income
- employment
- educational attainment
- mental and physical health
- housing and homelessness
- living in a disadvantaged neighbourhood.

Key terms

Absolute definition of poverty a person is in poverty if they are unable to afford the most basic necessities of life. Poverty is seen as destitution.

Consensual measure (of poverty) a form of the relative definition of poverty, based on a lack of the goods and services deemed necessary by most people in society.

Destitution failure to obtain the absolute necessities to keep life going.

Households Below Average Income (**HBAI**) the measure used by the British government which puts the poverty threshold at 60 per cent of median income.

Median income the middle band of income.

Operationalize how sociologists go about finding a way to measure a concept (e.g. poverty).

Relative definition of poverty a person is in poverty if they are unable to afford the standard of living considered acceptable by the majority of people.

Relative income measure (of poverty) a form of the relative definition of poverty, based on having only a certain proportion of the average income in a society.

Social exclusion when people suffer a series of linked problems, such as unemployment, poor skills, low incomes, poor housing and high crime, which prevent them from enjoying full membership of society.

Check your understanding

1 Explain the difference between an absolute and a relative measure of poverty.

2 What criticisms have been made of absolute definitions of poverty?

3 Relative definitions of poverty have been criticized by campaigners against poverty in developing countries – why might this be?

4 Give two examples of how researchers have actually 'operationalized' the relative poverty concept.

5 Why has there been criticism of the concept of poverty and a move towards the use of the term 'social exclusion'?

Activities

Research ideas

1 Draw up your own list of ten essential items for an AS-level student today. Ask a representative sample of students which items they agree are necessary: 'which all [AS-level students] should be able to afford, and which they should not have to do without' (see quote from Gordon *et al.* (2000) on p. 132).

2 At the time of writing, the government guarantees all people over retirement age a minimum income of £119.05 per week. Check for the latest update at **www.thepensionservice.gov.uk/pensioncredit/** Now work out (a) your weekly income (b) how much you spend per week *including* (if you are living with parents) an estimate of the cost of your food, travel, heating and lighting and council tax. What are your views on the incomes of retired people on minimum income?

Web.tasks

1 Find out what the British government is doing about social exclusion – this is on the Social Exclusion Unit website at **www.communities.gov.uk/communities/ neighbourhoodrenewal/socialexclusion/**

2 Find detailed information on poverty and further research at the poverty site of the New Policy Institute at **www.poverty.org.uk/**

An eye on the exam Defining and measuring poverty

Item A

<< So, for example, a widely accepted indicator of third world poverty is the numbers of people living on less than $1 per day, on the grounds that people on such incomes are literally in danger of starving to death. This threshold is often termed 'absolute income poverty'. But the use of such a threshold in the UK would obviously be completely inappropriate. >>

Source: New Policy Institute/Joseph Rowntree Foundation *Measuring Poverty and Social Exclusion*
www.poverty.org.uk/income/income_choices.htm

Item B

<< The main causes and consequences of social exclusion are: poverty and low income; unemployment; poor educational attainment; poor mental or physical health; family breakdown and poor parenting; poor housing and homelessness; discrimination; crime; and living in a disadvantaged area. The risk factors for social exclusion tend to cluster in certain neighbourhoods, but not everybody at risk lives in a deprived area. Poverty and social exclusion can also pass from one generation to the next. >>

Source: Social Exclusion Unit (2004) *Breaking the Cycle* London: HMSO

(a) Explain what sociologists mean by 'absolute income poverty' (Item A). (2 marks)

(b) Suggest two criticisms of the notion of relative poverty. (4 marks)

(c) Suggest three ways in which poverty may lead to social exclusion (Item B). (6 marks)

(d) Using information from Item A and elsewhere, examine the problems of defining and measuring poverty. (24 marks)

Grade booster Getting top marks in the 24-mark question

You need to examine both the problems of defining poverty and the problems of measuring it. You need to consider absolute and relative definitions. Consider problems such as how to establish what is a minimum standard of clothing, diet and so on (absolute definitions), or what counts as a 'normal' standard of living and who decides this (relative definitions). When it comes to measurement, consider problems of operationalizing the definitions. You should discuss measures using budget standards, HBAI and consensual measures. Item A can be used to discuss the usefulness of absolute measures.

TOPIC 3

The extent of poverty

Getting you thinking

<< We tend to think that poverty hits family members equally, yet research indicates that this is not the case. There can be affluence for some and poverty for others, within the same household. A household with a high income could, in fact, contain a number of poor people, because the main income earner might not want to share 'his' (it is usually the male) wages.

Studies have shown that income is not shared equally within families, with men having greater 'personal spending money' than women and more control over financial decisions. Bringing money into the household seems to bring a sense of entitlement as to how it is spent, with the man generally as the higher earner being the one with greater control over family expenditure. >>

Source: Flaherty, J., Veit-Wilson, J. and Dornan, P. (2004) *Poverty: the facts* (5th edn) London: CPAG

1 In your opinion, does the person who earns the highest income in the family have the greatest right to say how it is spent if there is a dispute?

2 Should both earners in a marriage/partnership keep their own money and only pool their earnings to pay for 'family' expenses?

3 What rights should the children have to decide how the money is spent?

4 If the parents have low incomes, should the children take on a part-time job?

5 If they do, should the children keep the money they earn?

6 How might the results of the studies mentioned above help us to appreciate the complexity of understanding who is in poverty?

As we saw in Topic 2, the numbers of people living in poverty will vary according to which definition and measurement are used. But if we take the measure most commonly used by the government – that is, the number of households with incomes below 60 per cent of median income after housing costs – then the figures indicate that about 22 per cent of the population are in poverty. In total, there are about 12.8 million people living in poverty.

Poverty, then, is very widespread in Britain and not just restricted to a few 'unfortunates'.

Who are the poor?

The answer to this is a lot more complicated and confusing than simply identifying a particular group of the population. It depends first upon:

● how you wish to *classify* people, and then once you have done this:
● whether you wish to know the *composition* of the poor by percentages
● whether you wish to know the *risk* of being in poverty according to membership of a group.

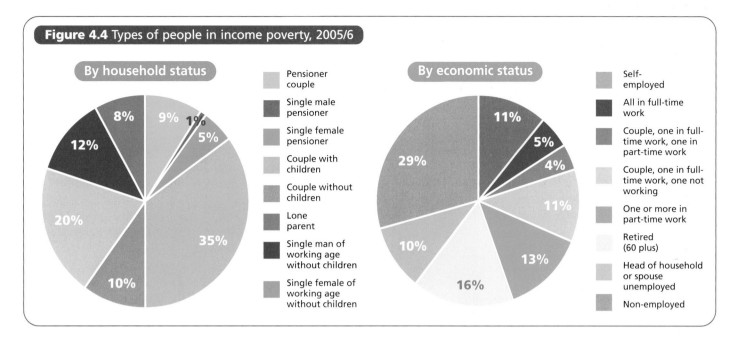

Figure 4.4 Types of people in income poverty, 2005/6

By household status

- Pensioner couple
- Single male pensioner
- Single female pensioner
- Couple with children
- Couple without children
- Lone parent
- Single man of working age without children
- Single female of working age without children

9%, 1%, 5%, 35%, 10%, 20%, 12%, 8%

By economic status

- Self-employed
- All in full-time work
- Couple, one in full-time work, one in part-time work
- Couple, one in full-time work, one not working
- One or more in part-time work
- Retired (60 plus)
- Head of household or spouse unemployed
- Non-employed

11%, 5%, 4%, 11%, 13%, 16%, 10%, 29%

Classifying by family type or economic status

Sociologists have chosen two ways of classifying people when they wish to measure the extent of poverty. These involve viewing the poor through the lens of **family** or **household status** on the one hand (for example 'lone parent family') or by **economic status** on the other (for example 'unemployed'). These are complementary methods which simply involve sociologists shifting their gaze at poverty from one angle to another. So we are looking at the same 'panorama', but seeing it from different directions.

The composition of the poor

The first piece of information sociologists want is the **composition of the poor**, that is what percentage of all poor people are formed by particular categories of households or economic status groups. The pie charts in Figure 4.4 illustrate the composition of the poor.

When we classify the poor by family (household) status, the single largest category in poverty is composed of couples with children, followed by single people and third, lone parents. When, instead, we break down the groups of people living in poverty by using the classification 'economic status', then the largest group consists of the long-term **sick**, **disabled people** and lone parents unable to work (classified as 'non-employed' in Figure 4.4). The next largest group is composed of retired people.

If you look at the pie charts in Figure 4.4, you will see that 35 per cent of all poor people are couples with children, when classified by household, and 29 per cent of all poor people are non-employed, when classified by economic status.

These two different ways of classifying and counting the composition of the poor are very useful, but it should be remembered that these are largely the same people, just looked at from a different perspective.

Measuring poverty by risk groups

An alternative method of measuring poverty is by **risk groups**. By this, we mean looking at the poor once again in terms of both household composition and economic status, but this time instead of dividing them according to what percentage of all poor people these groups provide, we look at what proportion of each group are in poverty. Figure 4.5 illustrates this. It shows that 48 per cent of all lone parents live in poverty, and 'only' 11 per cent of couples without children do.

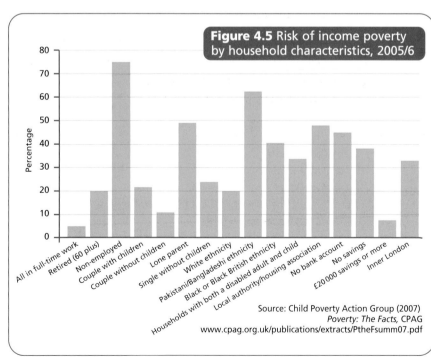

Figure 4.5 Risk of income poverty by household characteristics, 2005/6

Source: Child Poverty Action Group (2007)
Poverty: The Facts, CPAG
www.cpag.org.uk/publications/extracts/PtheFsumm07.pdf

The single highest risk group is the non-employed, with 75 per cent of them living in poverty, while the lowest risk group is composed of those in full-time employment, with only 4 per cent in poverty.

'Composition of the poor' or 'risk of poverty' – which is the better measure?

The answer is that neither is better (or worse), just different. We can see the composition of the poor in terms of absolute numbers or we can see how different groups run higher or lower risks of being in poverty. Both of these approaches help understand poverty and allow policymakers to develop ways of combating poverty.

Extending the range of risk groups

In recent years, the concept of risk groups has been extended beyond economic or household groups to include such things as gender, disability, age and ethnicity. Increasingly, sociological research has sought to find out what specific risks of being in poverty are associated with these categories.

What complicates matters, however, is that all of these groups overlap. For example, disabled people are more likely to be unemployed than the population average, while older people are more likely to be disabled.

Because of the history of immigration to the UK and birth patterns, ethnic minority families are heavily overrepresented among couples with children, but are also more likely to be unemployed. However, it is important to remember that although there are numerous overlaps, each way of classifying is simply looking at that same 22 per cent of the population but from different angles. Also, none of this alters the fact that whichever classification you use, there are about 12.8 million people in the UK who are living in households with incomes below 60 per cent of the median.

High risk groups and poverty

Below, we look at a 'snapshot' of groups who have a high risk of living in poverty – drawing examples from all of the classifications above.

Lone-parent families

Forty-nine per cent of people in lone-parent households are income poor, compared with 24 per cent of single people without children and 22 per cent of people in couple households with children. Lone-parent families are more likely to be poor for two, possibly overlapping, reasons:

1   Women from poorer backgrounds have a higher risk of becoming lone parents in the first place. So they are already more likely to be at risk of poverty before having children.
2   Any lone parent is likely to be poorer because they have to combine childcare with employment. This means that they are more likely to work part time, so their incomes on average will be lower.

It is important to remember, however, that not all lone mothers are poor – it is just that they are more at risk of poverty.

Children

Some 30 per cent of children are living in low-income families. In 2005/6, there were 3.8 million children living in poverty. This is a decline of almost three-quarters of a million since 1998, but an increase of 1.9 million compared to 1979.

Approximately 75 per cent of all children living in households where the parent or parents are unemployed live in poverty. However, because there are high levels of employment, it is still true to say that over half of all children in poverty are living in households with at least one parent working, and just under half are living in households with no employed parent.

The unemployed

About 1.8 million children come from households with no parent in employment. But it is not just children who are hit by unemployment. About 75 per cent of unemployed people now live in poverty.

Those who are unemployed for a long time face much greater problems than those who are out of work for a short period. These problems include a lower level of income, the gradual exhaustion of savings, and deterioration in the condition of clothing, furniture and general possessions. After three months of unemployment, the average **disposable income** of a family drops by as much as 59 per cent. It is not just financial losses that occur as a result of long-term unemployment – there are psychological effects too, such as lack of confidence, stress and depression. These further undermine people's ability to obtain work.

The low paid

Thirty-one per cent of all poor people are in full- or part-time employment, but simply do not earn enough to live on. People who are low paid tend to be those with fewer skills, and they often live in areas where there are relatively few jobs, so competition keeps wages low. As we have seen, there is a link between **low pay** and lone parenthood, in that lone parents usually have to take part-time jobs because of childcare responsibilities – and approximately 70 per cent of part-time work is low paid according to the Low Pay Commission (2003).

Sick and disabled people

According to government statistics, there are approximately 6.2 million adults (14 per cent of all adults) and 36,000 children (3 per cent of all children) who suffer from one or more disabilities. Of these, 34 per cent are living in poverty. The average income for a disabled adult, under pensionable age, is 72 per cent of that for non-disabled people. The impact of disability also goes beyond the individual person concerned, with 52 per cent of working-age adults with a disabled child themselves living in poverty.

There are several reasons for the poverty of long-term sick and disabled people, and their carers. They may be unable to work, or the work they can do may be limited to particular kinds of low-paid employment. At the same time, people with disabilities often have higher outgoings, such as having to pay for a special diet or having to pay for heating to be on all day.

Older people

About 18 per cent of the population – over 11 million people – are over retirement age, and over 65 per cent of **older people** are women. With the gradual rise in life expectancy, the number of older people in the population is likely to continue to increase.

Because of government policies since 2000, the number of older people in poverty has declined, from about 33 per cent of older people in 2000 to 20 per cent in 2005/6. In 2006, 1.8 million retired people lived in poverty.

Being old does not necessarily make people poor – it is just that the risk increases. Those people who are poor in old age are most likely to be those who have earned least in their working lives.

Ethnic minorities

People from ethnic minority backgrounds run a substantially higher risk than the majority population of living in poverty – 69 per cent of people of Pakistani and Bangladeshi origin, 46 per cent of people of African origin and 32 per cent of people of African-Caribbean origin are poor.

Ethnic minority groups have substantially higher rates of unemployment than the majority of the population. This holds true even if the person has the same educational qualifications as the majority population. Those of African-Caribbean origin and a majority of those of Asian origin have a greater chance of earning lower wages than the majority population, and they are more likely to work in the types of employment where wages are generally low.

Women

The majority of the poor in the UK are women – most of the groups we have discussed above are likely to have a majority of women members. Lone parents are overwhelmingly women who are more likely to be in part-time work, to be in low-paid work, or to be unemployed, leading to the situation where 51 per cent of lone families are poor. Single female pensioners are also slightly more likely to be poor (21 per cent) than single male pensioners (17 per cent). This is because they are less likely to have savings, as a result of low earnings throughout their lives.

Risk of poverty and region

The chances of living in poverty vary considerably across the country and within cities. Indeed, in relative terms, the UK lies only second to Mexico in the industrialized world for the extent of regional inequalities in living standards.

People living in Wales, the North East, Inner London and Yorkshire are most likely to be poor, and those living in Outer London and the South East are least likely to be poor. These largely reflect differences in rates of pay and in levels of unemployment.

Poverty: a risk not a state

When we talk about poor people, it is rather misleading, because it gives the impression that there is a group of people

Focus on research

Blanden et al. (2002)
Poverty and social mobility

Blanden and colleagues were interested in finding out whether poverty persisted over generations and to what extent the increased levels of social mobility experienced in the UK had helped eliminate poverty. In order to do this, they reanalysed two well-known longitudinal studies – the 1958 National Child Cohort Study and the 1970 British Cohort Study (both of which had been used for a range of purposes including medical and educational studies). The researchers concluded that the chance of being better off than one's parents had reduced for those who grew up in the 1970s and 1980s, compared to the earlier cohort. More of the 1970s cohort were in poor families at the age of 16 than the older cohort. In the majority of cases, children remained in the same quarter of the income distribution as their parents. In the 1958 cohort, almost 20 per cent of males and females rose from the lowest earning quarter of families to the top. But in the 1970s cohort, the figures had fallen to 15 per cent. The increase in educational opportunities in the last 30 years has been more likely to benefit the children of the more affluent, rather than the poor.

Blanden, J., Goodman, A., Gregg, P. and Machin, S. (2002)
Changes in Intergenerational Mobility in Britain,
Royal Economic Society

1 What is meant by the term 'social mobility'?

2 What did the researchers conclude about the relationship between increased social mobility and poverty?

who live in poverty all their lives. This is true for some people, but the majority of the poor are people who live on the margins of poverty, moving into poverty and out again, depending upon a range of economic factors, government decisions, family responsibilities and their earning possibilities. Nearly a fifth of the population – around 10 million people – continues to experience low income at least two years in three (see Fig. 4.6).

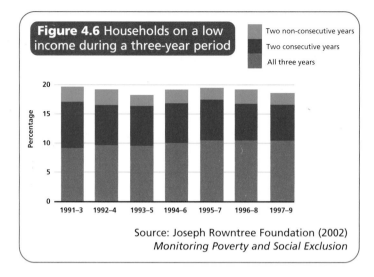

Figure 4.6 Households on a low income during a three-year period

- Two non-consecutive years
- Two consecutive years
- All three years

Source: Joseph Rowntree Foundation (2002)
Monitoring Poverty and Social Exclusion

Key terms

Composition (of the poor) refers to a way of analysing poverty figures by illustrating which groups provide the largest proportions of people living in poverty.

Disposable income how much people actually have left to spend after paying fixed bills (such as council tax or housing costs).

Economic status refers to a way of classifying poor people by how they obtain their income.

Family status refers to a way of classifying poor people by the sorts of family types they belong to. Used interchangeably with 'household status'.

Household status used interchangeably with 'family status'.

Low pay defined as earning less than half the average male wage (women's average wages are lower than men's).

Older people refers to people of pensionable age, currently 60 for women and 65 for men.

Risk groups refers to a way of analysing poverty figures by classifying groups by their chance of being in poverty.

Sick and disabled people 'sick' refers to chronic illness, where people are unwell on a long-term basis. 'Disabled' refers to people officially classified by the government (on the basis of a medical report) as suffering from some form of disability.

Check your understanding

1 According to the text, how many people in the UK are living in poverty?

2 What percentage of the population is this?

3 Identify the different ways of classifying and measuring those who are in poverty.

4 What are the implications of the fact that these classifications overlap?

5 Why is long-term unemployment so much worse a problem than shorter-term unemployment?

6 Are all old people poor? What does poverty in old age reflect?

7 Poverty is 'a risk not a state'. Explain what this means in your own words.

Activities

Research ideas

1 Go through job adverts in your local paper and a couple of national papers, ideally *The Daily Telegraph* and *The Guardian*. Compare the salaries on offer and identify the lowest- and highest-paid jobs? What weekly wages before tax do they offer? What is the median pay rate in your area?

2 Ask a sample of people to estimate the proportions of the various groups shown in Figure 4.5 who are actually living in poverty. Then show them the actual percentages. How closely do their estimates match the figures? Are they surprised at the figures?

Web.tasks

1 Find out the latest figures on 'households below average income', and the latest figures for the 'poverty line'. Search the website of the Child Poverty Action Group at www.cpag.org.uk to find this and much more information.

2 To explore world poverty go to www.poverty.com/

To what extent and in what ways are women poorer across the world? www.womankind.org.uk/statistics.html

Explore the links between disability and poverty on a global basis at www.healthlink.org.uk/PDFs/kar_learn.pdf

3 The BBC News website gives a simple summary of some of the facts on the extent of poverty:

http://news.bbc.co.uk/1/shared/spl/hi/pop_ups/03/uk_poverty_and_social_exclusion/html/1.stm

Item A

Lone-parent families are more than twice as likely to be on low incomes as couples without children, and three times as likely as adults without children.

Source: Department for Work and Pensions (2002) Households below Average Income series 1994/5 to 2000/1, Corporate Document Services, reproduced in Joseph Rowntree Foundation (2002) Monitoring Poverty and Social Exclusion

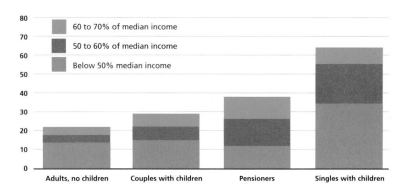

Proportion of individuals in each family type on low income after housing costs (per cent)

Legend:
- 60 to 70% of median income
- 50 to 60% of median income
- Below 50% median income

Categories: Adults, no children · Couples with children · Pensioners · Singles with children

Item B

Poverty in the UK is the result of three main factors. First, access to the labour market: poverty is caused by not having access to well-paid work. Second, extra costs: poverty is caused by having to meet the extra costs of, for example, having a child or a disability. Poverty is likely to be particularly acute when these two factors combine. Third, there is the failure of policies to deal with these two causes. The benefits system often fails to meet the needs created by disability, ill health, low pay, unemployment or having children. In other words, poverty is also caused by government policies – it is not simply the result of random misfortune. And the risk of poverty is not equal for all groups – it depends on class, age, gender and ethnicity.

Adapted from Oppenheim and Harker, quoted in Beresford, P., Green, D., Lister, R. and Woodward, K. (1999)
Poverty First Hand London: CPAG

(a) Explain what sociologists mean by the 'composition' of the poor. (2 marks)

(b) Suggest two reasons why pensioners may be at risk of poverty (Item B). (4 marks)

(c) Identify three groups, in addition to those referred to in Item A, who are likely to experience poverty. (6 marks)

(d) Using information from the Items and elsewhere, examine the reasons why women and ethnic minorities are more likely to experience poverty. (24 marks)

Grade booster · Getting top marks in the 24-mark question

Make sure you deal with both women and ethnic minorities, and that you draw upon information from the Items – for example, apply the three causes identified in Item B to women and ethnic minorities. Consider how far each group is likely to face risk factors such as low pay, unemployment and old age. Why might they be at greater risk of these? How far and why might women's childbearing and childrearing role put them at risk of poverty?

TOPIC 4

Explaining the existence and persistence of poverty

Getting you thinking

<< What thoughtful rich people call the problem of poverty, thinking poor people call, with equal justice, the problem of riches. >> R.H. Tawney

1   Write down the first four words that come into your head when you look at the photos above.

2   If a homeless person were to ask you for money, what would you reply?

3   Compare your responses to questions 1 and 2 with those of with people sitting around you. Discuss with them the reasons for your replies.

4   Why do you think people like those shown in the photo live the way they do? Is it their own fault? Bad luck? The fault of an unjust society?

5   How would you resolve their problems?

Arguments about the causes of poverty can be traced back as far as we have written records. Intriguingly, it seems that, although the terminology has changed, the actual explanations for the existence of poverty have not changed over the centuries. On the one side, there are those who claim that affluence is a combination of natural ability and hard work; on the other side, there are those who argue that the poor are unfortunate, or that the 'system' is against them. So one argument lays the blame at the feet of the poor themselves, while the other blames the society that condemns some people to poverty:

● **Dependency**-based explanations argue that poverty is the result of individual or cultural deficiency. Such explanations include the belief that there is a specific section

of the working class that does not want to work, called the **underclass**.

● **Exclusion**-based explanations focus on the way in which some people are 'made to be poor' by the economic and political system.

Dependency-based explanations

These sorts of explanations argue that the poor are, in some way, the cause of their own poverty. At their most extreme, they suggest that the welfare system in the UK actually makes people dependent on it by providing an attractive alternative to work. Three different approaches exist, outlined on the next page.

1 Individual deficiency

Individual deficiency explanations centre on the concept of dependency; they stress that people who are poor are in that state because of some personal or cultural deficiency. Essentially, it is their fault if they are poor.

The individual as scapegoat

This is the approach that many 19th-century writers took, and it remains, to some extent, in the idea of the '**scrounger**'. There is little evidence that this could explain any more than a tiny proportion of poverty. However, the myth of the scrounger was used powerfully in the 1980s as a justification for cutbacks in welfare.

The dependent individual

This idea was developed by Marsland (1996) who argued that the individual's will to work was undermined by excessively generous state welfare benefits, and that the need to look after other family members was weakened by the extensive provision of state services. The result was a high level of dependence on the state.

2 The culture of poverty

This idea of a **culture of poverty** was originally suggested by Oscar Lewis (1966) in his study of poor people in Mexico. Lewis argued that poor people in a 'class-stratified and highly individualistic society' were likely to develop a set of cultural values that trapped them in their poverty. It is important to stress the ideas of class and **individualism**, for Lewis is not arguing that these people are necessarily deficient. He believes that they are caught in a society that really does put barriers in their path – but that the poor themselves help ensure that they

are trapped by developing a set of values that prevent them from breaking out of poverty. These cultural values include:

- a sense of **fatalism** and acceptance of their poverty
- an inability to think for the long term
- a desire for immediate enjoyment.

Critics of this approach argue that there is no such thing as a culture of poverty – rather, such cultural values are a perfectly rational reaction to conditions of hopelessness. In the USA, the poorest groups really are excluded, and they are unlikely to be allowed to break out of their poverty. In such a situation, the poor may feel that there is no point in long-term planning.

3 The underclass

The underclass approach is a development of the cultural explanations for poverty, but it extends the analysis much further and introduces a very radical critique of the American and British welfare systems. In the culture of poverty thesis (see above), the 'cause' of poverty lies in a cultural adaptation to a highly class-stratified society; in the underclass approach, on the other hand, poverty is a response to cultural, economic and welfare changes.

The argument, first developed by an American writer, Charles Murray, is that an underclass (see Chapter 1, p. 8) exists, consisting of people who are lazy and make no effort to work or look after themselves (see Figure 4.7). These people prefer to live off the state rather than work. By underclass, Murray means a significant and self-reproducing group who form a distinctive bottom element of the class structure in British and American societies.

Murray accepts that there are poor people who are poor through no fault of their own. Nevertheless, he believes that

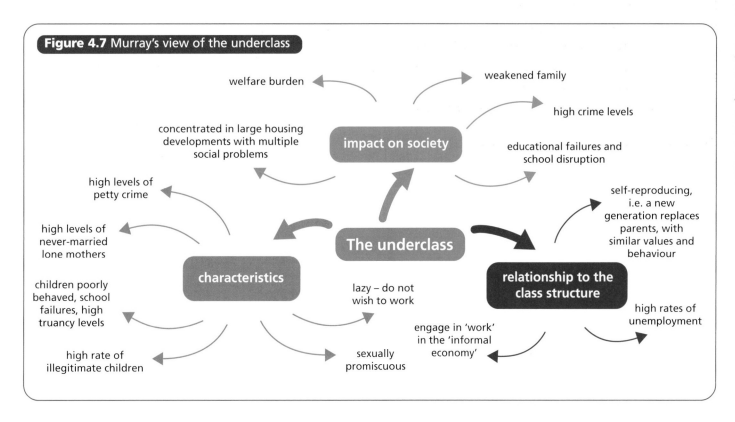

Figure 4.7 Murray's view of the underclass

welfare burden

weakened family

high crime levels

concentrated in large housing developments with multiple social problems

impact on society

educational failures and school disruption

high levels of petty crime

self-reproducing, i.e. a new generation replaces parents, with similar values and behaviour

high levels of never-married lone mothers

The underclass

characteristics

relationship to the class structure

children poorly behaved, school failures, high truancy levels

lazy – do not wish to work

high rates of unemployment

high rate of illegitimate children

sexually promiscuous

engage in 'work' in the 'informal economy'

the bulk of poverty is caused by those who do not make the effort to earn a living, and/or waste what they do have. Murray's analysis (1994) is slightly different for the USA and the UK. His analysis of the USA focuses heavily on 'American Blacks' as the source of the underclass; in the UK, his analysis is not race based.

Murray argues that a clear segment of the working class distinguishes itself through the following factors:

● *Crime* – Murray points out that a very high proportion of violent and property crime is carried out by a small proportion of the population.
● *Illegitimacy* – There are very high levels of children born outside marriage (and in particular to never-married women). These children are the outcome of casual sex, and the fathers have no interest in supporting the child or mother.
● *Economic inactivity* – Here, Murray is referring to the high levels of long-term unemployment that characterize the same relatively small group of people. Murray argues that it is not that they are unemployed in any traditional sense, but that they prefer to collect state benefit and to work in the **'hidden' economy**. Poverty is a way of life and is chosen by members of the underclass.

Murray's work has been fiercely attacked by a wide range of writers. The consensus among critics is that Murray is, quite simply, factually wrong. There is no evidence from social surveys that a group exists that rejects the work ethic. Research shows that the majority of lone parents would like a stable relationship. There is also no evidence of an automatic overlap between lone-parent families and crime.

Exclusion-based explanations

Exclusion-based explanations argue that the poor are poor because they are prevented from achieving a reasonable standard of living by the actions of the more powerful in society. This approach stresses differences in power between the various groups in society. Those who have least power – the disabled, older people, women, ethnic minorities and, of course, children – have significantly higher chances of living in poverty. Within this approach we can distinguish three strands.

1 Poverty, powerlessness and the labour market

In all societies, the least powerful groups are the most likely to lose out economically and socially, and they will form the bulk of the poor. Indeed, poverty and powerlessness go hand in hand. The powerless include women, lone parents (usually women), the very young and the very old, as well as those with disabilities. When these powerless groups do get employment, it is likely to be in short-term, low-paid, temporary and possibly 'unofficial' work. For many supporters of the welfare state, it is these groups who deserve help, because they are blameless 'victims' of the economic system. A good example of this is the situation of disabled people who are twice as likely to be poor than non-disabled adults (see Figure 4.9). This is mainly because they are unable to obtain work.

2 Citizenship and exclusion

Field (1989) has developed this argument, and linked it to the idea of 'citizenship'. Field argues that three groups in society

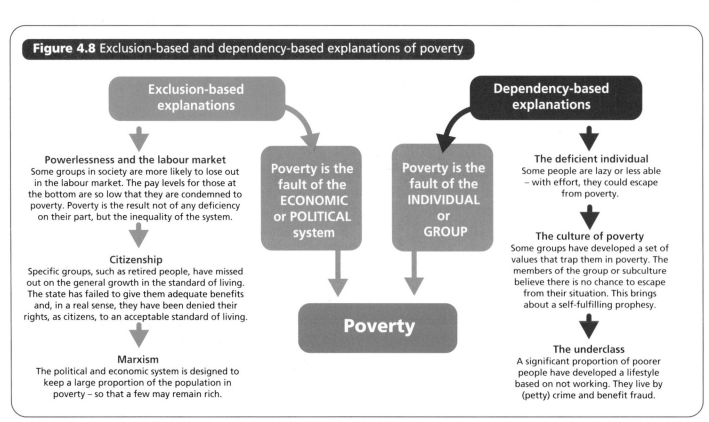

Figure 4.8 Exclusion-based and dependency-based explanations of poverty

Exclusion-based explanations

Powerlessness and the labour market
Some groups in society are more likely to lose out in the labour market. The pay levels for those at the bottom are so low that they are condemned to poverty. Poverty is the result not of any deficiency on their part, but the inequality of the system.

Citizenship
Specific groups, such as retired people, have missed out on the general growth in the standard of living. The state has failed to give them adequate benefits and, in a real sense, they have been denied their rights, as citizens, to an acceptable standard of living.

Marxism
The political and economic system is designed to keep a large proportion of the population in poverty – so that a few may remain rich.

Poverty is the fault of the **ECONOMIC** or **POLITICAL** system

Poverty is the fault of the **INDIVIDUAL** or **GROUP**

Dependency-based explanations

The deficient individual
Some people are lazy or less able – with effort, they could escape from poverty.

The culture of poverty
Some groups have developed a set of values that trap them in poverty. The members of the group or subculture believe there is no chance to escape from their situation. This brings about a self-fulfilling prophesy.

The underclass
A significant proportion of poorer people have developed a lifestyle based on not working. They live by (petty) crime and benefit fraud.

Poverty

have, over the last 20 years, been excluded from the rights that citizens should enjoy, including the right to a decent standard of living. These are:

- the long-term unemployed
- lone-parent families
- those on state retirement pensions.

Together these groups comprise what he calls (rather confusingly) the 'underclass'. Field argues that these groups have been particularly hit by several factors:

- government policies, which have increased the gap between rich and poor
- increases in the core number of long-term unemployed

- an increasing tendency to **stigmatize** and blame the poor for their poverty, rather than look at wider economic and social factors.

Once again, the answer to the problem of poverty lies in a better-organized and comprehensive welfare state.

3 Poverty and capitalism: the economic-system approach

The final, and most radical, explanation for poverty is provided by those in the Marxist tradition (see Chapter 1, p. 17). They see poverty as an inevitable outcome of the capitalist system. According to Marxist theory, the economy is owned and run

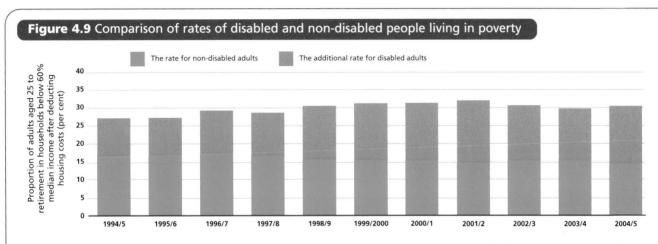

Figure 4.9 Comparison of rates of disabled and non-disabled people living in poverty

Source: Palmer, G., MacInnes, T. and Kenway, P. (2006)
Monitoring poverty and social exclusion, Joseph Rowntree Foundation 2007

Focus on research

Beresford et al. (1999)
Poverty first hand

Beresford and his colleagues pointed out that most research undertaken on poverty had been by 'experts' and pressure groups. Typically, they collected statistics on poverty and then worked out the numbers of people in that situation. Even the definition of poverty was provided by these experts. Beresford and colleagues wanted to find out the views and attitudes of poor people themselves. In order to do so, they approached a wide variety of local groups across the country, mainly composed of people on low income, and then interviewed representatives from each. In all, 137 people were interviewed.

The results showed that living in poverty was a

difficult and demoralizing situation, in which they felt stigmatized by the attitudes of others. The majority of the people believed that the causes of poverty were in the way society was organized, rather than in individual failings. They vehemently rejected the notion of the underclass. They would like to find work if they could or, if they were already in employment, in better-paid work.

Beresford, P., Green, D., Lister, R. and Woodard, K. (1999) *Poverty First Hand*, London: CPAG

1 Typically, who does most research on poverty?

2 How representative of the poor do you think the sample was likely to be?

3 What were the views of the sample on the causes of poverty?

by a small ruling class, who exploit the majority of the population who work for them. Poverty emerges from three main causes:

1 The wealth of the ruling class is created from paying the lowest possible wages to people – because it is the profits that produce the wealth.
2 The poor act as a warning – having a group in poverty provides a direct warning to the rest of the workforce of what could happen to them if they didn't work hard.
3 Poor people provide a 'starting point' against which other workers can measure their own income (rather than against the income of members of the ruling class).

For Marxists, the welfare state is a means of hiding exploitation, and it is used by the rich and powerful to provide just enough in the way of healthcare and income support benefits to prevent a serious challenge to their authority.

Check your understanding

1 Explain how, according to some writers, the welfare state can actually be the cause of poverty?

2 What is the 'culture of poverty'? Give two examples of the values of the 'culture'.

3 According to Charles Murray, what is the 'underclass'?

4 What do sociologists mean by 'exclusion-based approaches'?

5 What three groups have been excluded from the rights of citizenship, according to Field?

6 From a Marxist perspective, how does capitalism cause poverty?

Activities

Research ideas

1 Carry out a 'content analysis' of newspapers to see what approach they take in their stories to the issue of poverty (or people in poverty, the homeless, etc). Do they blame the victims or other factors?

You should do this by finding newspaper sites on the web and then searching them for the stories.

2 Look over this chapter and make notes on the causes of poverty. Form into small groups. Using this information, construct a simple questionnaire with a maximum of six or seven 'closed' questions. Then each member of the group should ask a maximum of 10 people what they regard as the main reason why people are poor in the UK and how we should eliminate poverty. Pool your answers.

Web.tasks

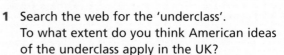

1 Search the web for the 'underclass'. To what extent do you think American ideas of the underclass apply in the UK?

2 Go to the following site at *The Guardian* newspaper http://society.guardian.co.uk/socialexclusion/story/0,,631442,00.html

This explains more about social exclusion. What policies have been followed to tackle social exclusion? What is the relationship to lack of income?

There are further links which can be explored from this page.

Key terms

Citizenship refers (in this particular case) to the belief that people living in British society have certain 'rights', including the right to have a decent standard of living.

Culture of poverty a set of values that some poorer people in society share, which they pass on to their children. The result is that they get trapped in poverty.

Dependency the state of being dependent. It is used to refer to the idea that some people live off the hard work of others.

Exclusion the idea that some people are prevented from being able to get on in life and enjoy the benefits of an affluent society.

Fatalism acceptance that what happens is the result of luck or 'fate'.

'Hidden' economy all the 'cash-in-hand' and casual work that is never reported to

authorities such as the Inland Revenue.

Individual deficiency refers to a person's specific faults or weaknesses which make them unable to get on in society and be successful.

Individualism the belief that individuals are far more important than social groups.

Labour market refers to the sorts of jobs and employment conditions that people have.

'Scrounger' someone who claims welfare benefits they are not entitled to, and/or who manipulates the benefits system to their own advantage.

Stigmatize to mark something out as bad.

Underclass a term first used by Charles Murray to describe those people whom he claims have developed a lifestyle which depends upon state support and who have no desire to seek employment.

An eye on the exam The existence and persistence of poverty

Item A

<< So, let us get it straight from the outset: the underclass does not refer to a degree of poverty, but to a type of poverty.

It is not a new concept. I grew up knowing what the underclass was; we just didn't call it that in those days. One class of poor people was never even called poor – they simply lived with low incomes. Then there was another set of poor people … these poor people didn't lack just money. They were defined by their behaviour. Their homes were littered and unkempt. The men in the family were unable to hold a job for more than a few weeks at a time. Drunkenness was common. The children grew up ill-schooled and ill-behaved and contributed a disproportionate share of the local juvenile delinquents.>>

Source: Murray, C. (1990) *The Emerging British Underclass*, London: IEA (Health and Welfare Series), p. 1

Item B

The British labour market has many of the worst features of the USA – ranging from high turnover of staff to inequality of income – but without the compensating virtues of mobility and managerial dynamism. In the UK, there is a search for maximum and immediate profit to meet the demands of shareholders. This means that firms are less willing to offer lifetime employment and less willing to undertake training, as both of these are costly. The result is that employees are paid the lowest possible wages, while the social benefits of pensions, healthcare, holidays and a general sense of caring for workers, both as employees and citizens, are largely absent. The underlying belief is that, in this kind of market economy, everybody looks after themselves.

Adapted from Hutton, W. (1995) *The State We're In*, London: Vintage, pp. 281–4

Item C

The problems of social exclusion are often linked and mutually reinforcing. The risk of social exclusion is highest for those with multiple disadvantages. The figure on the right illustrates this, showing that the likelihood of being out of work increases with the number of disadvantages experienced by an individual. For example, more than 50 per cent of those with three or more labour-market disadvantages are nonemployed, compared with 3 per cent without any of these characteristics.

Likelihood of non-employment amongst multiple disadvantaged groups

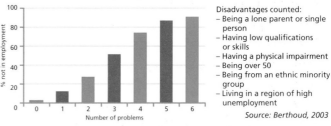

Disadvantages counted:
– Being a lone parent or single person
– Having low qualifications or skills
– Having a physical impairment
– Being over 50
– Being from an ethnic minority group
– Living in a region of high unemployment

Source: Berthoud, 2003

Non-employment is defined as being either not working at least 16 hours a week or not in full-time education, and not having a working partner.

(a) **Explain what sociologists mean by the 'underclass' (Item A).** (2 marks)

(b) **Explain the difference between the 'underclass' and 'culture of poverty' approaches.** (4 marks)

(c) **Suggest three ways in which the disadvantages referred to in Item C may put individuals at risk of unemployment.** (6 marks)

(d) **Using information from the Items and elsewhere, assess the view that poverty is the result of the way in which the labour market operates.** (24 marks)

Grade booster Getting top marks in the 24-mark question

Make sure you use information from the Items. For example, explain how each of the features of the British labour market identified in Item B may lead to poverty. Consider issues such as low pay and unemployment. Link the view in the question to issues of how powerlessness in the labour market can cause poverty (e.g. the position of the disabled) and also to Marxist views about how capitalism produces poverty. You can evaluate the view by considering alternative explanations such as the underclass (using Item A) and culture of poverty approaches.

Competing approaches to poverty and the welfare state

Getting you thinking

Look at each of the photographs.

1 **What is causing the people above to be in poverty?**

2 **Suggest different ways in which the people in each situation might be taken out of poverty.**

3 **What are the advantages and disadvantages of these approaches? Which do you favour, if any? Explain your answer.**

We have seen in earlier topics that there is considerable debate over the definitions, causes and even the extent of poverty in the UK. Clearly, if there is no agreement on any of these, then finding one programme to eradicate poverty that is acceptable to all is, to say the least, difficult. This topic explores the various solutions to poverty that have been put forward, and gives some examples of actual policies that have been tried. It looks at the four main approaches to solving the problem of poverty:

● the New Right approach
● the social democratic approach
● the late-modern approach or 'Third Way'
● the Marxist approach.

The New Right approach

The New Right have developed a series of arguments which attack the welfare state and see it, both directly and indirectly, as one of the main causes of poverty. New Right theorists, such as Marsland (1996) argue that, in a democratic, capitalist society, wealth is created by those people who successfully run companies, and by others who innovate, have entrepreneurial ideas and start new companies. Everyone else relies upon these people for jobs, and therefore incomes. These **entrepreneurs** are motivated by money, and it is therefore up to government

to encourage entrepreneurs and owners of successful companies to flourish. This is best done where there is a 'free market' – that is, an economic system where there are a number of competing firms seeking to offer their services, and where the government does not interfere.

Welfare as an indirect cause of poverty

In order to ensure that entrepreneurs are well rewarded, taxation must be kept as low as possible. This is done by minimizing the size of the government and by keeping expenditure as low as possible. The **welfare state** – including provision of **state benefits** for those without employment – is the largest area of government spending, employing a massive array of people to deliver benefits and services. Without the costs of employing the staff and the expenditure on welfare payments, taxes could be much lower. The welfare state is, therefore, an indirect cause of poverty, because:

● it discourages the efforts of entrepreneurs to start new companies which would create new jobs
● it hinders successful, established companies by burdening them with taxes.

Welfare as a direct cause of poverty

Welfare also has a direct role in causing poverty. This is because the welfare state actually undermines the will to work. It does

'Outsider' approaches to poverty and welfare

Running parallel to the major approaches to welfare of the right, the social democrats, the Third Way and Marxism, is a radical critique by those who feel they are 'outsiders' in the proposals put forward in these models of welfare. These outsiders are women, the ethnic minorities and the disabled. Each category has a similar story to tell of being pushed to the edge of welfare concern.

Gender, welfare and poverty

Women have always been more heavily affected by poverty than men, as a result of earning lower wages and, increasingly, by being heads of lone-parent households. Feminist writers, such as Glendinning and Millar (1992), have argued that the welfare state, far from challenging the poverty of women, has often ignored their plight. The welfare state, in its initial form in the late 1940s, was actually based on the idea that women would stay at home looking after the children, with benefits such as pensions and tax incentives being channelled through the husband. The ambivalence about the role of women has only recently started to be addressed with the new tax credits offered by New Labour since 2002. However, feminists point out that the different patterns of work of males and females mean that women are less likely to have decent pensions than men and that, despite the support of tax credits from the government, lone parenthood tends to leave women in much greater risk of poverty.

Ethnicity, welfare and poverty

A second group who feel they have been marginalized by welfare and are consistently at higher risk of poverty are ethnic minority groups. Writers such as Modood (1997) have argued that the welfare state has been ineffective in combating the poverty of ethnic minorities and, indeed, might well contribute to it. Very high numbers of the ethnic minorities work in the welfare system, particularly in hospitals and care homes. Yet they are consistently among the lowest paid. So, the very welfare system which sets out to solve social problems is one of the sources of poverty for ethnic minority people. Furthermore, the welfare system has failed to respond to the particular cultural and family differences of some ethnic minorities. We have just commented on the difficulties faced by lone-parent families headed by women; women of African-Caribbean origins have high rates of lone parenthood. Those of Bangladeshi and Pakistani origins have much lower rates of employment, and therefore the new tax credit system which rewards women for going out to work does not help them. The issue for writers such as Modood is not so much direct racism, as a lack of flexibility and response to different cultural circumstances by the welfare state.

Disability, welfare and poverty

Disabled people might well claim to be the most marginalized of all groups when it comes to welfare and poverty. Disabled people are heavily overrepresented among the poor. It is difficult to find employment and even more difficult to find

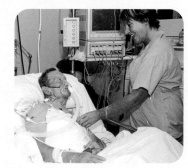

Focus on research

Taylor-Gooby and Hastie (2003)
Higher taxes, better welfare

The different approaches to solving the problem of social exclusion suggest different ways of paying for it. Social Democratic and Marxist approaches argue for higher taxes, while the New Right suggest that lower taxes are the way forward. Taylor-Gooby and Hastie wanted to find out if people were really prepared to pay higher taxes for better welfare services. They found mixed responses.

The methodology they used was very interesting, as they paid for an additional set of questions (a 'module') to be added to an existing national survey which takes place each year. The British Social Attitudes Survey asks a cross-section of the British public for its opinions on a range of issues. Between 2000 and 3000 respondents (for technical reasons, the numbers varied across different areas of the questionnaire) were interviewed using closed questions. The researchers found strong support for 'hypothecated taxes' – that is tax earmarked for one specific public service – as long as the identified service was the NHS. There was also support for higher taxes in general for other welfare services, but the level of support was much lower. This suggests that if people had a choice, they would fund the health service much more highly than other welfare services.

Taylor-Gooby, P. and Hastie, C. (2003) 'Paying for world class services: A British dilemma', *Journal of Social Policy*, 32(2)

1 **What were the advantages and disadvantages of using closed questions in this survey?**

2 **In what ways did the researchers find 'mixed' responses?**

adequately paid employment. According to Oliver (1996), this is because society stigmatizes disabled people by seeing them as less able, which makes it difficult for them to obtain decent employment. Oliver also argues that assumptions about what is 'normal' means that workplaces, leisure facilities and public transport are organized on the basis of able-bodied people. In the last 10 years, legislation has been introduced to bring about a degree of equality and there is now a Disability Rights Commission to enforce the law.

Table 4.3 Solutions to poverty – summary of different approaches

Approach	View of welfare state	View of poor people	Strategy to eliminate poverty	Role of government
New Right	BAD – wasteful and inefficient; undermines the will to work	Lazy or less able than successful people	To let entrepreneurs create wealth for themselves and, therefore, jobs for others	To create the conditions for successful commerce, e.g. low taxes, few regulations
Social democratic	GOOD – role is to ensure a fair society	Unfortunate people	An all-encompassing welfare state paid for through tax	To organize, provide and fund a 'free' welfare state
Late modern or Third way	Essentially good, but too expensive and inefficient	Most poor people could work but they either can't (the majority) or don't want to (the minority)	Make a society in which all people can get employment with adequate income to live on	To overcome the barriers that prevent people working
Marxist	Hides the true exploitation of the majority of the population by the few rich	Exploited by the ruling class	REVOLUTION! – Take over control of the economy and the state	Governments in capitalist societies are just there to represent the interests of the ruling class
Outsider critique	Ineffective, out of touch with cultural realities for groups such as women, ethnic minorities & disabled	Excluded and stigmatized	Citizenship and equal rights	To ensure that all groups have access to employment and services

Check your understanding

1 According to the New Right:
   (a) How do entrepreneurs help to solve the problem of poverty?
   (b) How can the welfare state undermine the 'will to work'?

2 Which approach is associated with the introduction of the welfare state?

3 What is the role of the welfare state, according to social democrats?

4 What is the role of the welfare state, according to Marxists?

5 Explain in your own words what the term 'disciplinary tendency' means, and give one example.

Key terms

Child tax credits give wage earners (up to a certain level of salary) additional payments for each child they have.

Disciplinary tendency where people are forced into certain patterns of behaviour, e.g. the unemployed are forced to undertake skills training or lose their rights to state benefits.

Entrepreneur person who takes risks in order to make a profit.

Minimum wage the lowest legal wage an employer can pay.

Poverty trap where a person who gets a job experiences a drop in income, because their wages are lower than the welfare benefits they were receiving when unemployed.

Tax credits (see also **Child tax credits**) a way of helping people in low-wage jobs or part-time employment. People in work have their tax adjusted so that the government will add money to their salary, rather than take it away.

Tax incentives encouraging a particular course of action by rewarding people with tax relief or extra tax benefits.

Welfare benefits/state benefits the financial support that the government gives people as part of the welfare state, e.g. disability benefits and pensions.

Welfare state a system of welfare benefits and services provided by central or local government.

Activities

Research idea

In couples, organize a small discussion group (maximum 8 people). Present them with a series of very short statements that summarize the approach of each political party (which you have found out from your web task) towards the elimination of poverty. Tell them that in 20 minutes they need to come to a majority agreement on selecting one of these approaches. Which do they select? Why?

Web.task

Use the websites of the main political parties to compare their approaches to welfare and poverty (and remember that each party is going to be biased in the information it gives you).

Conservative Party	www.conservatives.com
Labour Party	www.labour.org.uk
Liberal Democrats	www.libdems.org.uk
The Green Party	http://policy.greenparty.org.uk/

Item A

From 1997, the Labour government effectively placed work at the centre of its social policies, with initiatives aimed not merely at increasing employment or reducing unemployment, but also at using work to tackle social exclusion.

The government wanted to devise a system that was more 'active', offering claimants a 'hand up, not a hand-out'. In practice, this meant making benefit payments more conditional on undertaking activities geared to labour market (re-)entry. The government has introduced a minimum wage and a series of tax credits to help those in low pay with families ... all this based on the belief in making work pay, because benefit claimants would only take work if there was sufficient financial incentive to do so. Supporting people in work costs a lot less than paying social security benefits.

Adapted from Bochel, H., Bochel, C., Page, R. and Sykes, R. (2004) *Social Policy: Issues and Developments,* Harlow: Pearson (pp. 67 & 76)

Item B

According to David Marsland (1996), the welfare state and its services can be criticised on several grounds. First, he claims that the 'monopolistic position of the welfare services' means that they face no competition from which they could learn and so improve. Second, these services are very bureaucratic and this stops them from responding flexibly to changing circumstances. This is unlike the private sector of the economy, where we as consumers take it for granted that businesses will be focused on our needs. Third, Marsland argues that the 'colossal scale' of the welfare state (for example, the NHS is the biggest employer in western Europe) prevents new ideas and practices from emerging and encourages a depersonalized approach to clients. Similarly, the managers of state welfare services favour centralized planning and this blocks 'local and individual initiative and enterprise'.

Adapted from Marsland, D. (1996) *Welfare or Welfare State?* Basingstoke: Macmillan

Item C

Thus, in contrast to the social democratic view, it is insisted that, under capitalism, the functioning and management of state welfare remain part of a capitalist state. The benefits of the welfare state to the working class are not generally denied, but they are seen to be largely the by-product of securing the interests of [the ruling class]. The role of the welfare state is not to eliminate poverty, but to maintain a basic standard of living to ensure the continuation of capitalism. Furthermore, by paying benefits to the poor, capitalism gives the appearance of being 'caring'.

Adapted from Pierson, C. (1991) *Beyond the Welfare State?* Cambridge: Polity Press, p. 53

(a) Explain what is meant by 'tax credits' (Item A). (2 marks)

(b) Identify the two approaches to the welfare state represented by Item B and Item C. (4 marks)

(c) Suggest three criticisms of the social democratic approach to welfare. (6 marks)

(d) Examine the New Right view that the welfare state is in fact the principal cause of poverty today. (24 marks)

> **Grade booster** Getting top marks in the 24-mark question
>
> You need to describe the New Right view in detail, including the welfare state's direct and indirect role in causing poverty. You can link this to ideas about the underclass. You should also make some points of evaluation, for example by contrasting the New Right view of the welfare state with the social democratic, 'Third Way' and/or Marxist approaches. Use specific aspects of welfare provision to illustrate your answer, such as the minimum wage, tax credits, the poverty trap, and so on.

Welfare provision

Getting you thinking

Does an elderly man in a home have a right to pay for sex?

The tale is told by James Barrett, consultant psychiatrist at the Charing Cross Hospital, London, who was called to see 'Mr Cooper' (not his real name) after staff at the old people's home where he lived complained that he had been pestering them for sex. Mr Cooper, who was in his 80s, had been paying an elderly woman to visit him to provide sexual services. When she stopped visiting, he asked staff to arrange another prostitute, difficult for him as his eyesight and hearing were failing.

The staff demurred and Mr Cooper made advances to female carers. Dr Barrett suggested the simplest way of resolving the matter would be to comply with Mr Cooper's wishes but staff thought it illegal and didn't want 'someone like that' at the home. 'They seemed disappointed I was not going to prescribe a drug to lower Mr Cooper's libido,' Dr Barrett writes in the British Medical Journal.

The matter was referred to the head of social services for the elderly in the borough, who took legal advice. This suggested 'the crime of procurement would not have been committed' were staff to call prostitutes. Managers now found a new worry – that once his modest savings ran out,

they might have to pay for the visits, if the encounters proved to control his advances towards staff.

Matters got worse and the old people's home had to hire a male member of staff to follow Mr Cooper's 'every tottering step'. Eventually it relented and arranged for Mr Cooper to meet a prostitute at a neutral venue.

The cab was called and Mr Cooper was 'tremulous with anticipation', when it was called off. Managers had decided the arrangement could only be justified if it could be shown to have 'a beneficial effect on his behaviour in an NHS setting'.

The case was passed to the local NHS hospital, which reluctantly accepted there was no other solution. A room was allocated and staff told a special 'therapist' would call the day after Mr Cooper was transferred to the hospital. But before he could be admitted to enjoy the liaison he had long sought, he developed pneumonia and died.

The British Medical Association said: 'It is not an appropriate use of NHS facilities. Seeing a prostitute is not about improving people's health.'

Source: *The Independent*, 23 October 2004, p. 27

1 Read the article above. Do you think that the gentleman should have had sex paid for by the state?

2 Do you think his 'needs' should be regarded as legitimate?

3 What are the limits to a welfare state?

The development of welfare

The situation before the welfare state

Before the introduction of the welfare state, there had been a variety of forms of welfare provision, most of them based on charity, though the state did intervene over some issues.

Combating poverty

Measures to combat poverty date back as far as 1601, when the government introduced what we might now call a 'minimum wage'. In 1834, the Poor Law (Amendment) Act introduced the workhouse system: the poor and the old had to go and live in workhouses if they were destitute. In order to ensure that people did not 'abuse' the system, the conditions

inside the workhouses were deliberately made worse than the conditions outside – on the principle of 'less eligibility', which assumes that people will always take from the state unless they find conditions would be worse than those they already had.

The conditions in which the poor lived in the 19th century were appalling, so it is difficult for us to imagine just how bad workhouse standards were. Indeed, for a very large number of people, entry to the workhouse was a death sentence.

Workhouses remained in various forms until 1928, although in 1908 and 1912 the Liberal governments introduced sickness benefits (for males only) and old age pensions, which meant that the workhouses were no longer needed.

Healthcare was largely based on charity or payment until the Second World War (1939), with poorer people having no access to doctors at all, apart from the charitable clinics. In the 1920s and 1930s, working-class people took out insurance with local doctors, paying a small amount each week to have the right to call out a doctor.

Housing

Housing conditions were appalling in 19th-century Britain and a number of **philanthropists** raised funds and built housing projects (many still existing in the old ex-industrial cities) for the poor. However, only the 'respectable' poor were allowed to rent these properties. By the 1920s, the demand for housing was so great that local authorities were given power to build social-housing projects, although it was still necessary to prove respectability to get a property.

The welfare state

The coming of the welfare state dramatically changed all this. A 'system' of welfare based on charity was seen as demeaning and was replaced with one based on the right to welfare, where the only criterion for help was that of being in need.

The welfare state followed the **Beveridge Report** of 1942, which analysed the flaws of the previous system based on a mixture of charity, local authority intervention and private provision by the more affluent.

Beveridge identified what he called the five 'evils' which he felt the government needed to wipe out (see Table 4.4). These were: want (poverty), ignorance, disease, squalor and idleness. The resulting policies introduced between 1944 and 1948, brought about the NHS, the extension of schooling, the social security system, an increase in social housing and a commitment to full employment. This system became known as the 'welfare state'.

Explanations for the introduction of the welfare state

The question that many academics have asked is: why was the welfare state introduced in the 1940s and not before, as the 'evils' identified by Beveridge were not new?

Pluralist explanations

The most common explanation is that a general consensus was reached during the Second World War that it would be impossible to ask the people who were suffering so greatly to return to a society of high unemployment and poverty – a situation which had characterized the 20th century up to that time. The major political parties agreed that an organized system of welfare needed to be introduced which provided a safety net for ordinary people, but did not disturb the unequal nature of British society. This is a **pluralist** explanation, which sees the various power groups in society vying with each other and arriving at an agreement.

Marxist explanation

A more radical view of the situation has been suggested by Marxist-influenced writers such as Ginsberg (1998). They argue that the welfare state can best be understood in a more complex, 'two-sided' way. On the one hand, the welfare state

Table 4.4 Tackling social evils: the welfare state

Social evil	Welfare state
Want (poverty)	Poverty was to be tackled by payment of unemployment and sickness benefits, and a 'safety net' benefit that would cover everyone not covered by these other benefits. Today, this safety-net benefit is known as 'income support'.
Ignorance	Free schooling was to be extended (to age 15), and new schools were to be built.
Disease	A National Health Service (NHS) was to be set up, whereby everyone would have a right to free healthcare. Before this, people either paid for their healthcare, or applied to charitable hospitals.
Squalor (poor housing)	A massive programme of house-building was to be undertaken to get rid of poor-quality housing ('slums').
Idleness (unemployment)	The government was to commit itself to ensuring that never again would there be a return to mass unemployment.

was a true advance for the working class, emerging from the class conflict as a concession wrestled from capitalism. However, it was also a way for the ruling class to control the mass of the population by giving them a safety net which would prevent them falling into extreme poverty. It would provide them with housing and give healthcare (and so maintain a healthy working population). At the same time, education would provide a better disciplined workforce and full employment was not a problem in the years following the Second World War. However, the most important thing was that the welfare state maintained the capitalist system with its inequalities of income and wealth intact.

The welfare state in context

During the early to mid 20th century, other countries also began to introduce welfare systems. However, their answers to the problems of poverty, education, housing and so on were quite different. In fact, a wide variety of different systems of welfare have developed across the world. In a famous study, Esping-Andersen (1990) has suggested that all capitalist **welfare regimes** can be divided into three main types:

1 Liberal welfare states

These provide only a minimum level of services and cash benefits. In these societies, the poor, sick and disabled are helped by their families, by charitable organizations and religious groups. Those people in employment usually pay into insurance schemes to ensure that they receive health, pensions and unemployment benefits. The state provides services for those most in need but these are 'means tested' – that is, people have to prove that they are in real need before they can receive help, and their situation (their 'means') is thoroughly examined to decide whether or not they should receive help.

Examples of this type of welfare regime include the USA, Portugal and Spain.

2 Corporatist welfare states

These systems have high-quality health, education and welfare services organized by the state, but are funded by a mixture of state support and insurance schemes. Other non-government organizations, such as churches, trades unions and employers' organizations, are heavily involved in providing services. Corporatist welfare states are usually conservative in their views on society. They tend to fund people in conventional families and provide less support for lone parents and women (who are expected to obtain help through their husbands and/or family). These services are means tested, as in the liberal welfare regimes. Examples of this sort of regime include France, Belgium and Germany.

3 Social democratic welfare states

Social democratic welfare states place considerable emphasis on equality. There is a high level of taxation and a very high-quality, extensive set of welfare services. Because the state-provided services are so high, there is very little private provision of welfare. There is great emphasis on full employment, so that the costs of the system can be supported, because relatively few people are out of work and because most of those in work are also paying taxes. People have a right to state services and these are 'universal', in the sense that anyone has access to them. Examples of this regime can mainly be found in Scandinavia, with Sweden most commonly being given as the prime example.

Welfare regime debates

We have just seen how the welfare state emerged in the UK. In other countries, different forms of welfare regime were adopted. The different regimes reflect different decisions as to how to resolve the problems of:

- who should receive services and cash benefits
- what agencies should provide the services – the state, or a mixture of private companies and charities.

Who should receive benefits?

Philosophical arguments

One debate that has dogged the provision of welfare has been the question of who should receive state benefits. Those who support the idea of universal benefits (**universalism**) argue that state benefits – such as free healthcare, pensions and child allowances – should be given to all those who need them, irrespective of their income. The thinking behind this is that it helps to draw society together and promotes social harmony.

Those who support the targeting of benefits (**selectivism**) argue that universalism simply wastes resources on those who have no need of them. It also undermines people's desire to look after themselves, their family and other members of the community. Universalism thus weakens rather than strengthens social harmony and any sense of community.

Practical arguments

The debate between those who support the universal provision of welfare and those who support selective provision also involves arguments about practicality.

It is true that universalism does provide help to those who have no need of it. However, because everyone gets the same benefits, and there is no complex bureaucratic mechanism to assess who is eligible, the costs of providing the benefits are actually quite low. Furthermore, universal provision ensures that everyone who needs help gets it (because everyone does), and it also eliminates the stigma attached to claiming state benefits.

Selectivists point out that universal benefits are wasteful. By targeting the more needy, the levels of benefit could be higher and the quality of services could be better. It is true that, for some benefits, the administrative costs of targeting are expensive, but, despite this, overall, money would be saved on most benefits.

The state or the mixed economy of welfare?

The **'mixed economy' of welfare** refers to the move away from a state monopoly of health and care provision, to having a number of different providers, including:

- **for-profit/private organizations**
- **voluntary (charitable) organizations**
- **informal care** provided by family and friends.

Before the introduction of the welfare state, many services we now associate with it, such as healthcare, were provided either by profit-making organizations or by charities. In the last 20 years, there has been a resurgence of both private companies and charitable (or non-profit-making) organizations. The main reason for this has been the influence of the New Right on Conservative governments during the 1980s and 1990s, and the subsequent acceptance of many of their arguments by succeeding Labour governments, which have incorporated these ideas into their late-modern, 'Third Way' ideology (see Topic 5).

The New Right has argued that the state provision of welfare is both inefficient and of a poor standard, because there is no incentive for the providers of welfare either to attract 'customers' or to save money. The employees of the NHS, for example, continue to receive their salaries no matter how inefficient the system or how rude they are to the people who use their services. This is because the NHS has been, until recently, a **monopoly** – that is, the only provider of health services. Supporters of the New Right argue that, if the NHS had to make a profit, its employees would certainly have to act differently. The term used to describe this is the 'discipline of the market'.

Since the 1980s, governments have partially accepted these arguments, and a number of reforms have been introduced that attempt to bring the discipline of the market into the provision of health and welfare. These changes include:

- handing over some areas of welfare and healthcare provision (e.g. housing and the care of older people) to private or charitable organizations

Focus on research

Karen Rowlingson
Pension planning

The mixed economy of welfare is based on the idea that people make rational choices about spending their money and, if they had less tax, they would spend their money on the most sensible services they need. Perhaps the most important welfare service that most people need after health is pension planning – yet relatively few people save for a pension from an early age. Rowlingson decided to interview a small cross section of people of different ages, sexes and incomes, to find out why so few people who do not have compulsory occupational pension schemes actually save for their pensions. Rowlingson was interested in attitudes and so undertook a series of in-depth, qualitative interviews. In all, she questioned 41 people. After the interview, each person was given a £10 voucher as a token of appreciation. Interviews took place in the respondents' homes and lasted between 45 minutes and three hours. She found that people did not save for a number of reasons, which included the following:

- It is difficult to imagine growing old (when you are young) and having need of a pension.
- Financial constraints mean that people have to spend the money even if they wish to save.
- It 'tempts fate' to plan ahead (if you save a lot, you tempt fate that you will die early).

Rowlingson therefore concluded that it is mistaken to rely on voluntary pension plans if society is not to face major problems in the future.

Rowlingson, K. (2002) 'Private pension planning: the rhetoric of responsibility, the reality of insecurity', *Journal of Social Policy*, 32(4)

1 Suggest reasons why Rowlingson used in-depth interviews for this research.

2 To what extent do you think the sample used was representative of the British population?

3 Why does the researcher conclude that it is wrong for society to rely on voluntary pension plans?

- encouraging the NHS to subcontract certain activities to private organizations (e.g. private hospitals may undertake routine operations such as removal of cataracts and hip replacements)
- the building of new NHS hospitals that are shared with private healthcare organizations.
- grants to voluntary organizations to help support their activities
- requiring local healthcare trusts to operate to stringent financial and customer-care standards.

Another area of this 'mixed economy' of welfare is the growing emphasis on informal care by family members. The government strongly supports this form of care, primarily because it is cheap. For example, grants are available to enable family carers to stay at home to look after family members with disabilities.

Criticisms of the mixed economy of welfare

Critics of the mixed economy of welfare argue that the state is abandoning its responsibilities, and that it is a step back to the time before the welfare state. The main criticisms are these:

- The growth of private healthcare and its funding by government means that a two-tier system has developed, in which the more affluent are able to buy better healthcare, while the majority of the population have to make do with second-class services.
- Charitable organizations, which are often staffed by volunteers, may have less expertise than professionals.
- Feminist sociologists, in particular, have pointed out that the burden of informal care usually falls upon the women in families.

Who has benefited from the welfare state?

The main aim of the welfare state has been to ensure a certain minimum quality of life for all citizens of the UK. For many commentators, this suggests that the welfare state is a mechanism for redistributing wealth from the better off to the less well off. It does this by taxing the affluent at a higher rate and then using the surplus taxes to pay for welfare services, which are more likely to be used by the poorer groups in society. But does it actually do this?

To answer this question we need to look at the different services provided by the state. In the 1990s, Hills (1998) undertook a massive overview of the state of the welfare services and, although there have been changes since then, the overall conclusions he reached are still accepted as largely accurate today.

Education

Hills concluded that this favoured the middle-income groups overall. The most affluent pay both taxes and fees for private schools, so do not benefit, while the poorer groups tend to have the worse-quality schools and the lowest educational outcomes. In terms of value, therefore, the middle class benefit.

Health

According to Le Grand (1982), cited in Hills (1998), the middle class benefited more from the health service. According to Le Grand, this was because they ask for more services, are more knowledgeable about the system and have greater awareness of possible health risks. Le Grand called this the 'inverse care law'. However Hills' research found no evidence to support this 'law' and points out that, in fact, the health service is highly beneficial to poorer groups in society and widely used by them.

Social security and tax credit payments

Hills suggests that households earning below the median income do actually benefit more from the social-security and tax-credit system, while those in the top half pay more in tax and receive less in benefits.

It appears therefore that the welfare state does redistribute income and wealth. However, the next question is: by how much does it redistribute? According to the Office for National Statistics – the government's own statistical department – the overall degree of redistribution is fairly small. Before tax and redistribution via the welfare state, the highest-earning 20 per cent of households receive over 50 per cent of all income, while the lowest-earning households receive 2 per cent of income. After tax and taking into account the redistribution which occurs, the highest-earning 20 per cent receive 44 per cent of income and the lowest-earning 20 per cent receive 7 per cent of all income (ONS statistics cited in Palmer *et al.* 2004).

Hills also points out the importance of seeing the redistributive effects of the welfare state over a person's lifetime. He argues that, although over a full lifetime the poorest are likely to benefit from the welfare state, the majority of the population actually finance themselves over their lifetime. This is because people pay higher taxes during their adulthood when their demands upon the welfare state are relatively low. In old age, they then return to take from the welfare state through demands upon health services and pensions. However, as lower-paid people are more likely to die younger, although they will have paid less into the system, proportionately they will take less out.

Check your understanding

1 What three types of welfare regimes are there?

2 What are the advantages of:
   (a) the universal provision of benefits?
   (b) the selective provision of benefits?

3 Why has there been a resurgence in the provision of welfare services by private companies and voluntary organizations?

4 How has the New Right attacked the welfare state?

5 Which members of the family are most likely to provide 'informal care'?

Activities

Research idea

In small groups construct a simple questionnaire. Use this to question people about their attitude to particular 'welfare groups'. In particular, ask them to rate from 1 to 5 how sympathetic they feel towards these groups receiving state support, where 1 = not sympathetic at all, 2 = not particularly sympathetic, 3 = neutral, 4 = quite sympathetic, 5 = very sympathetic. Ask a maximum of 10 people.

- retired people
- young lone parents
- unemployed people
- people dependent on drugs or alcohol.
- disabled people
- homeless people
- ex-prisoners

Web.task

Go to the NCVO website at **www.ncvo-vol.org.uk**

What is the NCVO? What does it do? Go to the 'press briefing' section and see what information you can find about the importance of voluntary organizations. Should we need so much voluntary provision when the welfare state exists?

Key terms

Beveridge Report introduced the welfare state in the UK.

For-profit/private organizations organizations that provide services in order to make a profit.

Informal care care provided by family or friends.

'Mixed economy' of welfare refers to the fact that welfare is provided not just by the state, but also by private and voluntary organizations.

Monopoly a situation in which there is only one provider of goods or services and, therefore, no competition.

Philanthropy another term for charity, usually used when rich people give large amounts to charity.

Pluralism a theoretical position in sociology which sees society consisting of competing groups seeking to get the best for themselves. Society is the result of this managed competition.

Selectivism/targeting the belief that only those with limited financial resources should receive welfare services and benefits.

Universalism the belief that everyone should be entitled to free welfare services and benefits.

Voluntary (charitable) organizations independent organizations that provide health or welfare services, but do not seek to make any profit.

Welfare regime 'ideal type' term used to categorize similar sorts of welfare provision in different countries.

An eye on the exam Welfare provision

Item A

<<Britain's history of welfare development has shown that, along with Sweden, the UK led Europe in introducing a comprehensive and universal welfare system. In that sense, the early emphasis on equality and citizenship, rights to a wide range of benefits, and 'free' healthcare, all point to the UK being a prototype of the social democratic model. However, over time, the UK developed a welfare system that was founded on liberal rather than social democratic principles and a rather basic or minimal idea of how much help people should receive in times of need.

Britain's welfare system today represents an interesting mix of principles and influences from the past. There is still a relatively strong commitment to welfare state principles and a high proportion of the nation's wealth is spent on welfare. However, the recent revival of the concept of the mixed economy of welfare emphasizes the role of private and voluntary organizations. For all these reasons, therefore, the British model combines elements of the liberal type of welfare system and remnants of a social democratic approach.>>

Source: Blakemore, K. (2003) *Social Policy: An Introduction,* Buckingham: Open University Press, p. 57

Item B

<< The welfare state functions in various ways to bolster and renew capitalism. First, its existence makes capitalism seem more humane and acceptable, disguising its underlying brutality. Second, the welfare state ensures that a sufficiently educated, healthy and securely housed working population is available in the labour market. Third, the welfare state contributes directly to capital accumulation through its investment in infrastructure, such as hospitals, schools, etc. (thereby making profit for capitalists).>>

Source: Ginsberg, N. (1998) 'The socialist perspective', in P. Alcock, A. Erskine and M. May *The Student's Companion to Social Policy,* Oxford: Blackwell

Item C

Universal welfare benefits and services are those that are made available to everybody, both rich and poor, as a right. For example, every child has the right to free state education up to the age of 16; everyone has the right to free hospital treatment, while all parents are automatically entitled to receive child benefit. However, those on the New Right argue strongly against universalism in welfare provision. Instead, they favour the principle of selectivism. In welfare systems based on this principle, there is no automatic entitlement to welfare benefits and services. Those who seek help from the state must first prove that they are genuinely in need before they are given assistance. They do this by passing a 'means test'. However, even those who pass the means test are unlikely to receive particularly generous benefits.

(a) Explain what sociologists mean by a 'mixed economy of welfare' (Item A). (2 marks)

(b) Explain the difference between private and voluntary organizations in the provision of welfare (Item A). (4 marks)

(c) Suggest three reasons why some writers may be in favour of selectivism as a principle of welfare (Item C). (6 marks)

(d) Examine the role of different types of providers of welfare services. (24 marks)

Grade booster Getting top marks in the 24-mark question

You need to examine the full range of different welfare providers: state (or public), private, voluntary (e.g. charities) and informal (e.g. family, friends and neighbours). You should consider the effectiveness of each type, e.g. that private providers are motivated by profit or may create a two-tier system (one for the rich, one for the poor), or that informal care is likely to be more personalized but lacks expertise, or that the burden of informal care falls mainly on women. You should use concepts such as the mixed economy of welfare, universalism versus selectivity, and so on.

1 Read **Item A** below and answer and answer parts (a) to (d) that follow.

Item A

Mack and Lansley used a democratic or consensual definition of poverty. In a survey in 1983, they presented their respondents with a list of 35 items and asked them to choose those items that they thought necessities. Over 90 per cent of respondents said that heating, an indoor toilet and a bath, a damp-free home, and beds for everyone were necessities. Over two-thirds also included three meals a day for children, a warm waterproof coat, a refrigerator, children's toys, carpets and a washing machine.

Altogether, there were 22 items which over half the respondents deemed to be necessities. Mack and Lansley defined as poor anyone who lacked three or more of these items because they could not afford them.

Mack and Lansley carried out a follow-up study in 1990. They found that the public's perceptions of necessities had changed. For example, more people now thought a fridge essential (92 per cent, as against 77 per cent in 1983).

(a) Explain what is meant by a 'democratic or consensual definition of poverty' (**Item A**). *(2 marks)*

2/2 Consensus means agreement, so a consensual definition is one agreed by most people (which is also what democratic means – majority agreement or rule). A definition of poverty shared by most of society.

> **An examiner comments**
>
> A good answer. Mack and Lansley's approach was to ask the public what they thought were necessities and so arrive at the public's shared definition of poverty.

(b) Suggest **two** criticisms of the idea of absolute poverty. *(4 marks)*

2/4 One criticism is that absolute definitions of poverty assume that everyone has the same basic needs, which is not true. A building worker needs more calories than an office worker, because he does a heavy manual job, so he uses up much more energy fulfilling his role. Also it is likely that office workers will have different non-basic needs as well, e.g. they will probably have different leisure needs.

> The first criticism is correct: absolute definitions assume there is a single fixed minimum standard of living needed for health and efficiency, yet people with different jobs will have different food needs. But the second one is wrong, because the idea of absolute poverty is based solely on basic needs. A second valid criticism would be that absolute definitions are really about destitution, rather than poverty.

(c) Identify **three** criticisms that could be made of the research described in **Item A**. *(6 marks)*

One criticism is that their definition of poverty isn't really a democratic one because the public didn't really choose the necessities. They only chose from a list that the researchers had drawn up for them. What if the public had wanted to include other things that they thought were necessities? This wouldn't have been possible – they could only pick from what was there.

Another problem is that when you repeat the research, as Mack and Lansley did, if you add extra items to the list of necessities, you won't be able to make a true comparison over time, since poverty at one time will be a lack of one set of things and at another it will be a lack of different things.

6/6 Third, if you asked people in a different country, e.g. Ethiopia, they would probably give a different answer about what items were necessities, so it would be impossible to compare levels of poverty between societies.

> Three very good criticisms, but no need for lengthy explanations.

(d) Examine the reasons why the welfare state has not necessarily met the needs of the poor. *(24 marks)*

The welfare state was set up in the 1940s after the Second World War by the Labour government. Its aim was to eradicate poverty, bad housing, bad health, etc. However, many sociologists think that it has failed to help those who need it, i.e. the poor.

New Right thinkers argue that poverty is the fault of the poor themselves, but that the welfare state makes this worse, for example by giving council flats to teenage single mothers. Charles Murray (a US sociologist) calls this 'perverse incentives', i.e. the state is rewarding bad behaviour and thus so encouraging the problem to grow. If young girls know that they will get a flat if they get pregnant – some will do so, for example to escape their parents' authority. This then means they won't be able to work and so they will live off benefits instead.

> Good idea to contrast why the welfare state was set up with what it has actually done for the poor. But some sociologists claim its aim was to manage poverty, not eradicate it – so better to say 'Some say its aim was…'

> Good – the New Right blame the welfare state for creating poverty, not reducing it. Good example too.

The New Right solution is to cut the welfare state back. It seems that they think that the less the state does for the poor, the more it will in fact be helping them. This is because they will learn to get out of their culture of dependency and stand on their own feet.

> Builds on previous paragraph, and but could explain 'culture of dependency' and could mention underclass too.

Some sociologists don't really look at the welfare state in their explanation of why poverty exists. For example, Oscar Lewis puts forward the culture of poverty thesis. He argues that the poor create a subculture of 'live for today' to help them cope with poverty, unskilled labour, etc. The trouble is that when opportunities do arise to get out of poverty, the poor are too 'adapted' to it to change their ways.

> The first sentence gives the game away – this paragraph isn't really relevant. It's drifted into a general 'explanations of poverty' answer, unlinked to the question.

Marxists think that the welfare state is part of capitalism and works to benefit the ruling class, e.g. the National Health Service patches up workers so they can keep working to make profits for the bourgeoisie.

> Potentially a very useful paragraph, but needs further explanation. Also, the example is about health, not poverty.

Feminists think that the welfare state benefits men, not women (though some of them, e.g. Marxist feminists, think it serves the ruling class rather than working-class men). This is why women are more likely to be in poverty – the welfare state keeps them trapped there.

> Again, relevant to the question, but needs more. An example or two would be good.

So although some sociologists think the welfare state has failed to help the poor, others explain poverty as a culture of poverty.

> A conclusion of sorts, but to a slightly different question. Could end with a contrast as to why the New Right, Marxism, etc think it has failed the poor.

 16/24

An examiner comments

Overall, this answer shows a good deal of knowledge, but it isn't always applied well to the question. For example, the paragraph on the culture of poverty is not well linked to the issue of the welfare state (though it could have been tied in perhaps by saying that the education system – part of the welfare state – provides opportunities). Some points need developing further – e.g. the paragraph on the Marxist view of the welfare state could be developed by spelling out the Marxist idea that it maintains the poor as a reserve army of labour on low benefit levels to hold down the wages of those in work. Likewise, concepts such as patriarchy should be brought into the paragraph on feminism. The answer also needs a sharper conclusion: the present one seems to be summing up a different question – 'What causes poverty: is it the state or not?' You could conclude by contrasting Marxist and new Right views, for example. Both criticize the welfare state for failing to meet the needs of the poor, but for very different reasons.

One for you to try

(e) Using information from **Item B** and elsewhere, assess sociological explanations of why some groups are at greater risk of poverty than others.

(24 marks)

Item B

61 per cent of people of Pakistani and Bangladeshi origin are in the bottom fifth of incomes, as compared with 34 per cent of Black Caribbeans and only 18 per cent of Whites At the other extreme, 21 per cent of Whites had incomes in the top fifth as compared to only 3 per cent of Pakistanis and Bangladeshis.

A woman's chances of being in poverty are 14 per cent higher than for a man. There are more than twice as many women in the bottom fifth of incomes, and almost three times as many men in the top fifth.

53 per cent of lone parents are poor, but only 20 per cent of couples with children and only 11 per cent of couples without children.

22 per cent of pensioners are poor. 61 per cent of sick or disabled people not in paid work live in poverty.

An examiner comments

You need to make sure you use material from the Item. You need to look at a range of different groups, and the Item gives you a good start, with examples of ethnicity, gender, age, household structure and disability.

You need to consider and evaluate competing explanations, e.g. structural versus cultural or individualistic theories of why some are poor. Look at the role of the benefits system, the labour market, discrimination (racism, sexism and ageism), capitalism, low pay, unemployment, the underclass approach, etc., in putting some groups at greater risk.

Answers to the 'One for you to try' are available free on **www.collinseducation.com/sociologyweb**

Chapter 4 Summary

Competing approaches

Social democracy
- Traditional approach
- Underpins 'cradle to grave' welfare state

Third way
- Mix of private and state provision
- Approach of late modernity & New Labour

New Right
- Welfare state causes problems
- Abandon welfare state

Marxism
- Welfare state is victory for workers
- Welfare state also controls workers

Wealth and income

Wealth — Unequal distribution — **Income**

= What you own

= Flow of cash into household

Change over time
- Slight decline in % owned by richest
- Slight growth in inequality

Reasons for change
- Globalization
- Capitalism
- Entrepreneurial talents
- Government policy
- Lone-parent families
- Job insecurity

Welfare provision

Welfare state
Types of regime:
- Liberal
- Corporatist
- Social democratic

Who should receive benefits?
- Universal vs selective

Who should provide benefits?
- State vs mixed economy

Who benefits?
- Tax + welfare services redistribute from rich to poor BUT
- Mainly across individual's lifetime

Wealth, poverty and welfare

Defining and measuring poverty

Social exclusion
- Sees poverty in broadest sense
- Exclusion from leisure, health, education, etc.

Absolute poverty
- Based on minimum living standards
- 'Budget standard measure'

Relative poverty
- Consensual – based on research
- Based on accepted standard of living
- Relative income measure

Existence and persistence of poverty

Dependency explanations
- Individual – personal faults
- Culture – culture of poverty
- Underclass – behaviour of distinct social class

Exclusion explanations
- Labour market – poorly paid work
- Marxist – outcome of capitalism
- Citizenship – groups are stigmatized and excluded

Extent and causes of poverty

Extent
- Total poverty in UK
- How to measure who is in poverty:
  - Household or Economic status
  - % of total poor or Risk of being poor

High-risk groups
- Low paid
- Older people
- Unemployed
- Women
- Children
- Lone-parent families
- Ethnic minorities
- Sick or disabled

Sociological methods

AQA Specification	Topics	Pages
Candidates should examine:		
Quantitative and qualitative methods of research; their strengths and limitations; research design.	Quantitative research: Topic 3. Qualitative research: Topic 4. Research design in Topics 1 and 2.	175–80 181–86 164–74
Sources of data, including questionnaires, interviews, participant and non-participant observation, experiments, documents, and official statistics; the strengths and limitations of these sources.	Questionnaires and interviews in Topic 5. Participant and non-participant observation in Topic 4. Experiments in Topic 3. Documents, official statistics in Topic 5. Sources of secondary data in Topic 6. Strengths and limitations of these sources in the relevant topics.	187–92 181–86 175–80 187–92 193–97
The distinction between primary and secondary data, and between quantitative and qualitative data.	Introduced in Topic 1, and then followed up with detailed discussions in Topics 3 to 6.	164–68 175–97
The relationship between positivism, interpretivism and sociological methods; the nature of 'social facts'.	Covered in Topic 2 and related discussions in Topic 1.	164–74
The theoretical, practical and ethical considerations influencing choice of topic, choice of method(s) and the conduct of research.	Covered in Topic 2.	169–74

Researching social life

Getting you thinking

A scene from inside the Big Brother house 2007, as the housemates perform one of the tasks set by Big Brother

Big Brother is a television series in which a group of people are required to live together in a house for a period of several months. During that time all their activities and conversations are monitored. Edited versions are shown to a television audience, which then votes contestants out each week, until the last remaining 'survivor' is declared the winner.

1 **Do you think that people who live in the Big Brother household are representative of the country as a whole?**

2 **Do you think the people in the household act naturally? If not, why do they behave the way they do?**

3 **Does Big Brother therefore give a 'true' picture of what life would be like if a group of young people lived together? Explain your answer.**

4 **Do you think that a lot of what goes on is 'edited out' by the producers? What kinds of things are left out? Why?**

Sociologists generally try to take a 'sideways' look at social life – seeking to provide insights into the social world that the ordinary person would not normally have. In some ways, this interest in society is shared by journalists and other 'interested observers' of the world, but whereas these people tend to rely heavily on their *common sense* or *personal experience* in exploring society, sociologists reject these as adequate ways of explaining society. Common sense and personal experience, they argue, are usually based on our own limited and **biased** opinions already held, which override our objectivity. In research, bias occurs where the researchers' views affect the research. Instead, sociologists claim that the best way to study society is to conduct research which uncovers patterns that would normally remain hidden. This research is ideally founded on facts rather than opinions. However, the activities of sociologists do not stop at undertaking research – once they have uncovered these patterns, they then seek explanations for the relationships between them. This process of constructing explanations for the social patterns is known as 'theorizing'.

So, research leads – eventually – to theories.

Even that is not the end of it. For once theories exist, other sociologists are influenced by them and will use them as the starting point for their research.

So, research leads to theories, which lead to more research and – yes, you've guessed it – more theories!

What does sociological research set out to do?

Sociological research does three main things: gathers data, makes correlations and suggests or confirms theories.

Gathering data

The first task of research is simply to gather information about the social world. This very basic function is the starting point for any kind of sociological understanding. Knowledge can take the form of statistical information, such as the numbers of marriages and divorces, and sociological 'facts', such as the attitudes of people in society towards marriage as an institution. (This sort of research is conducted by the Office for National Statistics – a government organization which collects data about the UK.) It can also include observations of people in social situations – such as Philippe Bourgois' study of crime and drugs in a New York 'ghetto' (2003) – or people talking about their own lives – Ken Plummer has used this form of biographical research with gay men (1995).

However, we need to be wary about accepting these data at face value. As we shall see later, what is a 'fact' for someone may not be for others, as they may use different theories and methods to interpret the facts. A famous example of this is research on suicide by Durkheim (1897/1952). He collected a large number of

Figure 5.1 Research and common sense: why common sense is faulty

Common sense		Research
What is common sense for one person is not common sense for another.	✘ ✔	Research is based on evidence.
Common sense derives from personal experience and people have limited experience.	✘ ✔	Research can be conducted in areas where most people have little experience.
Common sense is not objective.	✘ ✔	Research is objective.
Common sense can be based on false beliefs and information.	✘ ✔	Research can be tested.
Common sense is often based upon memories which may be faulty.	✘ ✔	Research can compare memories with other evidence to check their accuracy.

statistics and then based his theory of the causes of suicide on these statistics. However, much later, other sociologists looked at exactly the same statistics and produced very different interpretations of these same 'facts'. They argued that the statistics on which Durkheim had based his research were fundamentally flawed. These sociologists said that in only a few cases can we know for certain whether the death was suicide or not, as there are rarely suicide notes. The real research, they argued, was in studying how coroners go about making their decision as to whether or not to classify a death as suicide.

Much effort is made in sociological research to make sure that the data gathered is as clear and accurate as possible, but sociologists always approach any data – whether in the form of statistics, observation or narrative – in a very cautious way.

Establishing correlations

Research can go further than just gathering information. It can help us explore relationships between different elements of society. At its most basic it can be in the form of simple **correlations**. Sociologists describe a correlation as the situation where when one social event occurs, another one tends to do so as well. This is clearer if we use an illustration. Bennett and Holloway (2005) conducted a national research project over a number of years which involved testing the urine of people immediately after they were arrested by the police and being held in police cells. The results of the urine tests demonstrated that the offenders had a very high chance indeed of showing evidence of illegal drug use (as well as alcohol). The statistical results therefore show that there is a correlation between drug use and crime, as when one social event (committing crime) occurs, then another (taking drugs) tends to do so as well.

Cause and effect

The immediate conclusion that most people would draw from this correlation is that drug use causes crime. But this may

not be true. It could be argued that people who commit crime are more likely to take drugs – and indeed there is considerable evidence to support this argument (Pudney 2002)**.** We could also argue that people who like to do drugs also like to commit crime. Therefore a completely different social event causes people both to commit crime and do drugs. There is considerable evidence for this explanation too (Hough and Roberts 2004).

Just because statistics demonstrate that two social events tend to occur together – *a correlation* – it does not mean there is actually a **causal relationship**. Identifying and agreeing a causal relationship between social events is often complicated and linked with developing a sociological theory.

Developing theories

The final role of research is to support or disprove a **sociological theory**. (A theory is simply a general explanation of social events.) Researchers gather information and statistics which help sociologists explain why certain social events occur. This often involves providing an explanation for correlations. So, if a correlation exists between drug use and crime, various theories can be developed. One theoretical explanation for heroin users having high rates of burglary is that they need money to pay for their drug habit. An alternative is that burglars have a high income and so are more likely to have a pleasurable lifestyle that involves using drugs. A third theoretical explanation could be that people with unhappy home backgrounds turn to crime and drugs. It was just this sort of problem that Pudney (2002) tackled in a research project on whether young offenders started taking drugs before they committed crimes or after.

Sources and types of data

Data can come from either primary or secondary sources:

- **Primary data** are those collected directly by the researchers themselves. The most common methods of providing primary data are surveys, observational studies, questionnaires, interviews and experiments.
- **Secondary data** are those which are used by sociologists but have been collected by other people. These include official and commercial statistics; radio, internet and TV; historical and official documents; personal letters and diaries.

There are two types of data (see Table 5.1 on next page):

- **Quantitative data** is the term used for statistical charts and tables.
- **Qualitative data** is the term used to describe data in the form of observation or other published or broadcast sources.

Evaluating data

When conducting research or reading sociological research reports written by others, sociologists are always very critical of the methods employed and the data used. They know that if the **methodology** is weak, then the research may well be inaccurate. All sociologists are committed to making sure that

Table 5.1 Types of data

Types of data	Sources of data	
	Primary data	*Secondary data*
Qualitative data	Interviews, observations	Historical documents, TV programmes
Quantitative data	Statistical surveys	Official statistics

their research is of the highest quality and achieves what it sets out to do. When sociologists evaluate research, they need to look at its reliability, validity, representativeness, generalizability and objectivity. We will look at each of these in more detail.

Reliability

The very nature of sociology means that it has to use a variety of very different methods, in a range of circumstances, to study people. In these circumstances, it can often be quite difficult to compare one piece of research with another and sociologists accept this. However, what is always expected is that if the same piece of research were repeated by different sociologists, then it should produce the same results. If this is not the case, then we could not rely upon the evidence produced.

Sociologists, therefore, always ask questions about whether or not the research, if repeated, would be likely to produce the same results – the issue of **reliability**. Some methods of research are much more likely to produce results which can be repeated than others. Well-designed questionnaires are probably the method most likely to produce similar research results each time and are therefore regarded as highly reliable. At the other extreme, when a lone sociologist engages in participant observation (that is, joins a group of people and observes their behaviour), the research is likely to be far less reliable, as the research is affected by the specific circumstances surrounding the group and the relationship of the observer to the group. Overall, quantitative methods tend to be more reliable, qualititative methods less reliable.

Validity

The second crucial factor in evaluating research is the extent to which it is **valid**, i.e. how far it gives a true picture of the subject being studied. In evaluating a piece of research, sociologists will ask whether the methods used were those most likely to get to the truth of the matter. Interestingly, validity and reliability do not always go hand in hand. We saw before that questionnaires are likely to be highly reliable, but this does not necessarily mean that they are valid. For example, when asked about embarrassing subjects, such as sex or criminal activity, people often lie. Therefore, if the study were repeated, the results would be exactly the same, yet they would never be true! Observational studies are usually difficult to repeat and so are fairly unreliable. However, if the observation has been done well, then it may actually be very valid.

Representativeness

The third crucial element in any evaluation is that of **representativeness**. Does the sample of people chosen for the research reflect a typical cross section of the group or society the researcher is interested in gaining information about? If the respondents in the study are not representative, then it is simply not possible to generalize to the whole group or society (see the following point). For example, if sociologists wish to talk about the population as a whole, then the chosen group must be representative of society as a whole. Similarly, if they wish to comment on people who are terminally ill, then the study must be of a representative group from this section of society.

Generalizability

The aim of most (though not all) sociological research is to produce knowledge which can aid us in understanding the behaviour of people in general – not just the specific group being studied. If the knowledge gained from studying the group cannot be **generalized** to all society, then it has limited use. This is why many sociologists are concerned that the people they study are typical or representative of a cross section of the society which they wish to generalize about. Overall, the

Key terms

Bias where the views of the researchers affect the research.

Causal relationship where there is a relationship between two social events with one causing the other.

Correlation a statistical relationship between two things. It does not necessarily mean that one causes the other. For example, over 70 per cent of burglars drink coffee, but this does not mean that drinking coffee causes someone to commit burglary.

Data the information uncovered by research.

Generalizability if the group sociologists choose to study are representative of the population as a whole, then they will be able to make generalizations about the whole society. If the group is not representative, they will only be able to speak about the particular group studied.

Methodology the process of undertaking research using the appropriate sociological methods

Objectivity quality achieved when a researcher's values do not affect their work.

Primary data information obtained directly by the sociologist.

Qualitative data information from a range of sources which are not statistical, such as observation.

Quantitative data statistical information.

Reliability quality of repeatability: if the same piece of research were repeated by different sociologists, then it should produce the same results.

Representativeness situation where the people sociologists study are a cross section of the

group they wish to generalize about.

Secondary data information obtained from sources originally collected by someone other than the sociologist conducting the research.

Sociological theory (or **theorizing**) an explanation of how different parts of society or different events relate to one another.

Validity the extent to which data give a true picture of the subject being studied.

larger the numbers of people in the study and the more sophisticated the methods used to select these people, the greater the chance of the study being representative.

Objectivity

The final key element in ensuring that research is of high standard is the extent to which the researchers have ensured that their own values and beliefs have not had any influence on the design or the carrying out of the research. This is known as **objectivity**. If sociologists allow their own values to intrude into the research process, then this will seriously weaken the

research and certainly impact upon the validity of the research. However, we cannot say that all values should be kept out of research, as this is simply impossible, just that there should never be intentional bias.

Research methods

Reay et al. (2001)
Choice in higher education

Diane Reay and her colleagues wished to study the choices and views of people entering higher education made by people who were not school leavers from traditional middle-class backgrounds.

The researchers studied people from six different educational institutions. They gave out 502 questionnaires and followed this up with 53 interviews with students and 'a small number of interviews with parents' and others. The study drew upon the 'qualitative' interviews with the 53 students who Reay says were 'not representative of the sample as a whole'. The students were asked to define their ethnicity themselves and the result was that only 23 of the 53 people in the sample defined themselves as being 'White'. One of the interviewees defined himself as 'Irish', rather than any other category such as 'White'.

The students were also classified by the researchers into social-class groupings. The researchers used the registrar-general's five-point scale, but in order to simplify things, did not use one of the categories (III Non-manual).

Reay, D., Davies, J., David, M. and Ball, S.J. (2001) 'Choices of degree or degrees of choice? Class, 'race' and the higher education process', *Sociology*, 35(4)

1 The researchers quantify various elements of the research, but not the 'small number' of interviews. Why not?

2 If the students are not 'representative', how easy is it to generalize?

3 What problems can you identify regarding 'self-definition' of ethnicity?

4 The researchers adopted the reliable Registrar-General categorisation, but chose to leave one grouping out. What implications could this have for their research?

Check your understanding

1 Explain the three main aims of sociological research in your own words.

2 Give two reasons why sociological research is more trustworthy than 'common sense'.

3 Explain the difference between a 'correlation' and a 'causal relationship'.

4 What term is used by sociologists for statistical data?

5 Give two examples of:
  (a) primary data
  (b) secondary data.

6 Why is it important for a sociological study to be 'valid'?

Activities

Research idea

Divide into small groups. Each group should write a short questionnaire consisting of three questions. The questions should aim to collect opinions on:

(a) whether cannabis should be legalized

(b) whether the use of drugs causes crime.

Decide on the wording of your questions and then put them to a sample of six people.

Compare the answers of the different groups. Are they all similar? If they are different, can you think of reasons why? What might this tell us about validity, bias and representativeness?

Web.task

Find some of the statistics on drugs and crime. These are available through the Home Office website at
www.homeoffice.gov.uk

You will need to select or search for the section on 'Drugs' or 'Drugs and crime'. Give examples of the sort of figures and information provided. Comment on their validity, reliability and representativeness.

Item A

Dissatisfaction with the NHS by age, income and experience of the NHS

	% Dissatisfied		
	1987	*1999*	*2001*
Age			
18–36	42	36	44
54+	30	28	35
Household Income			
High	46	41	48
Low	35	28	34
Health Service Experience			
NHS inpatient in previous 12 months	40	40	33
Has private medical insurance	42	41	45

Adapted from Park, A. *et al.* (2002) *British Social Attitudes*, London: Sage (Table 4.6, p. 81)

Item B

You have been asked to assess a research design in terms of its reliability, validity, representativeness and generalizability. The research is about the relationship between drugs and crime. The research design consists of the following steps:

● selecting a large sample of convicted offenders in prison
● giving each of them a list of reasons why they felt they had committed their crime and asking them to rate these in order of importance
● collecting all the results and making one list using all their replies.

(a) Explain what is meant by 'generalizability' (Item B).   (2 marks)

(b) Suggest two weaknesses of the research design proposed in item B.   (4 marks)

(c) Using information from Item A, give two examples of a correlation.   (4 marks)

(d) Examine one qualitative and one quantitative method or source of data that could be used to investigate patient dissatisfaction with the NHS (Item A).   (20 marks)

Grade booster   Getting top marks in the 20-mark question

You need to be clear about what quantitative and qualitative data mean, and what methods and sources produce each type (e.g. surveys and official statistics versus interviews and historical documents). Explain what the advantages and disadvantages are of each type of data. This could be done in terms of issues of reliability, validity, representativeness, generalizability and objectivity, so you need to explain these concepts. You must link these ideas to the issue of patient dissatisfaction, e.g. official statistics might provide reliable data on which patients were most dissatisfied, but interviews might give a valid picture of their attitudes to healthcare.

TOPIC 2

Choices in research: methods, theories and ethics

Getting you thinking

Karen Sharpe studied the lives of prostitutes by acting as a 'secretary' for them. Read the passage (right) about the aims of her research and then answer the questions that follow.

« The central objective of my research was to understand why and how women entered the world of prostitution: to discover the motivating factors, the dynamics of the introductory process, and how they learnt the skills, values and codes of conduct of the business. I wanted to explore the importance and impact of prostitution on their lifestyles and to put the 'deviance' of prostitution into context with other aspects of their criminality. I also wanted to discover how the women themselves and their families and friends, subjectively defined, perceived and rationalized their activities. »

1   Suggest two possible ways of undertaking this. List the advantages of your choices and the disadvantages.

2   This research was conducted by a woman. Do you think it would be possible for a male researcher to have done this? Explain the reasons for your answer.

3   Do you think that there is any point in doing this research? Explain your answer.

4   If during your research you found that one of the women was very unhappy and you knew you could help her, but if you did so it would ruin the research – what would you do?

In the previous topic, we found that objective research and the creation of theories comprise the key elements that distinguish sociology as a distinct academic subject. However, the reality of actually undertaking research and creating theories is complex and full of pitfalls. Several important issues arise:

1   Why do some topics of research occur again and again (e.g. young people and offending), while other issues are rarely explored (e.g. the breaking of ecological rules by multinational companies)? Could it be that the more commonly researched issues are easier or perhaps cheaper or more interesting for sociologists to do? Perhaps more worryingly, is funding less likely to be obtained for research into subject areas that threaten the interests of more powerful groups?

2   If the aim of research is to generate or to confirm theoretical approaches, why do different, conflicting theories continue to exist in sociology? Surely, by now research would have provided enough evidence for one theoretical approach to be seen as correct and deny the claim of others?

3   Sociology seeks to provide objective information about society – but is that possible? After all, sociologists are people like anyone else, with values, beliefs and prejudices. Can they really put these values to one side? Even if they can, don't they have to take into account when starting their research that their results may well have significant consequences for people's lives? For example, sociological research is largely responsible for the move away from grammar/secondary modern schools to the comprehensive system.

4   The final big issue is the choice of methods. Sociologists have a wide range of methodological approaches to use. These range from questionnaires handed out to thousands of people which are then subjected to statistical analysis, to a sociologist hanging around with young, homeless people simply being part of their lives. Which method is more useful in which circumstances? Are there any implications for the research project in using one method rather than another?

In this topic, we seek some answers to these questions and provide a few signposts to help guide us through the complex issues of ethical and theoretical debates and their relationship to research methods.

The relationship between research and ethics

Research can have a powerful impact on people's lives. It can do so in both harmful and beneficial ways. Therefore, researchers must always think very carefully about the impact of the research and how they ought to behave, so that no harm comes to the subjects of the research or to society in general. These sorts of concerns are generally discussed under the umbrella term **ethical issues**.

Most sociological researchers would agree that there are five areas of ethical concern.

1 Choice of topic

The first ethical issue relates to the decision about what to study. Merely by choosing an area, the researcher might be confirming some people's prejudices about a particular issue. For example, many sociologists are concerned about the extent of research into the 'negative' side of African-Caribbean life, with studies on school failure, lower levels of job success and even the claimed higher rate of criminality. Critics argue that merely by studying this, a continued association is made between race and criminality or race and failure.

2 Choice of group to be studied

One of the trickiest problems that sociologists face is gaining access to study particular groups. The more powerful the group, the less likely it is that the sociologist will manage to obtain agreement to study its members. The result, as you will see, is that the groups most commonly studied by sociologists are the least powerful – so students, petty criminals and less-skilled workers are the staple diet of sociological research. The really powerful evade study. Does sociology have a duty to explore the lives of the powerful?

3 Effects on the people being studied

Research can often have an effect on the people being studied. So, before setting out to do research, sociologists must think carefully about what these effects will be, although it is not always possible to anticipate them.

One of the reasons why sociologists rarely use experiments, for example, is that these may lead to the subjects being harmed by the experiment. In participant observational studies, where the researcher actually joins in with the group being studied (see Topic 4), the researcher can often become an important member of the group and may influence other members to behave in ways they would not normally.

4 Effects on the wider society

It is not only the people being studied who are potentially affected by the research. The families of those being researched may have information given about them that they wish to keep secret. Also, victims of crime may be upset by the information that researchers obtain about the perpetrators, as they may prefer to forget the incident.

5 Issues of legality and immorality

Finally, sociologists may be drawn into situations where they may commit crimes or possibly help in or witness deviant acts. While undertaking research on a prisoner in the USA, Kenneth Tunnell (1998) discovered that the prisoner had actually taken on the identity of someone else (who was dead), in order to avoid a much longer prison sentence. The prison authorities became suspicious and investigated the prisoner's background. Though Tunnell knew the truth, he felt that he owed the prisoner confidentiality and deliberately lied, stating that he knew nothing about the identity 'theft'. As a result, the prisoner was released many years early.

The relationship between theories and methods

Earlier, we saw that research findings could be used either to generate new sociological theories, or to confirm or challenge existing theories. However, the relationship between research and theory is even more complicated than this. If a sociologist has a particular interest in a theoretical approach, then this may well influence their research methodology. There are three areas in which theory has a strong influence on research.

1 Theory and choice of an area of research

One of the great joys of studying sociology is that the variety of different views and theories generates so many different opinions about society. However, when reading sociological research, you must always be aware that sociologists who hold strong theoretical beliefs about society are bound to study the topics that, in their eyes, are the most important, and to be less interested in other areas.

- **Feminist sociologists** see it as their role to examine the position of women in society, and to uncover the ways in which **patriarchy**, or the power of men, has been used to control and oppress women. Consequently, their choice of research projects will be influenced by this.
- **Marxist or critical sociologists** argue that the most important area of study is the question of how a relatively small group of people exploits the vast majority of the population. They will study issues such as the concentration of power and wealth, and the importance of social class divisions.
- **Functionalist-oriented sociologists** think that society is based on a general consensus of values. They are interested in looking at the ways in which society maintains agreement on values and solves social problems. Therefore, they will look at the role of religion or schools in passing on values.

2 Theory and techniques of study

Various theories may point to different areas of interest, but theories also nudge sociologists into different ways of studying society. Theories in sociology usually fall into two camps – **top-down** and **bottom-up** theories.

Top-down approaches

Top-down approaches, such as functionalism and Marxism, say that the best way to understand society is to view it as a real 'thing' which exists above and beyond us all as individuals. It shapes our lives and provides us with the social world in which we live. Our role is generally to conform. These sorts of theoretical approaches emphasize that any research ought to bear this in mind and that the researcher should be looking for general patterns of behaviour – which individuals may not even be aware of.

The favoured research methods used by these sociologists tend to be those that generate sets of statistics (such as questionnaires), known as **quantitative methods** (see Topic 3). Sociologists sympathetic to the use of these more 'scientific' methods are sometimes known as **positivists**.

Bottom-up approaches

Bottom-up approaches, such as interactionism (see Chapter 1, p. 20), stress that the only way to understand society is to look at the world through the eyes of individuals, as it is the activities and beliefs of individuals that make up the social world. Research must start at 'the bottom' and work upwards. The sorts of research methods favoured by those who advocate this approach (known as **interpretive sociologists**) tend to be those that allow the researcher to see the world from the same perspective as those being studied (known as **qualitative methods**). An example is participant observation (see p. 182).

Triangulation and mixed methods research

Although one group of sociologists is largely in favour of using quantitative methods and others prefer qualitative methods, in practice both groups will dip into the 'other side's' methods if they think it will be useful. This mixing of methods has become known as **triangulation**.

Triangulation can improve the validity, reliability and generalizability of a particular piece of research. The results gathered using one method can be checked against those derived from another and the advantages and disadvantages of quantitative and qualitative approaches can be 'balanced out'.

So, quantitative researchers may well back up their work by including some observation or some in-depth, unstructured interviewing, whilst qualitative researchers may well engage in some structured interviewing or draw upon secondary sources.

3 The interpretation of research findings

The final impact of theory on research comes when interpreting the research findings. The research is completed and the results are all there in the computer. How does the researcher make sense of the results? This will depend, of course, on what they are looking for, and that, in turn, depends upon what theoretical approach the researcher sympathizes with. This is very different from bias or personal values – rather, it is a matter of choosing which results are most important, and this will always depend upon what best fits the theoretical framework of the researcher. A feminist researcher will be keen to understand the position of women; the Marxist will be looking for signs of class struggle; the functionalist will be looking at the key indicators to prove that a set of common beliefs exists.

The relationship between practical issues and research

So far we have looked at the ethical and theoretical issues which have an important influence on the research process. As you can see, these are quite difficult 'abstract' issues, which sometimes seem far removed from the reality of everyday life. However, just as important are a range of very down-to-earth influences on the research process.

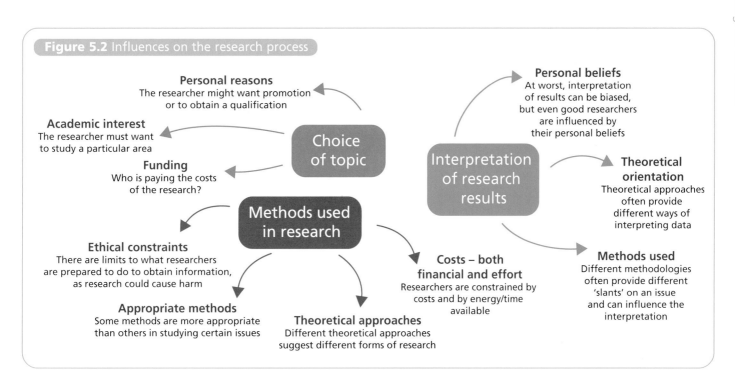

Figure 5.2 Influences on the research process

Personal reasons
The researcher might want promotion or to obtain a qualification

Academic interest
The researcher must want to study a particular area

Funding
Who is paying the costs of the research?

Choice of topic

Methods used in research

Ethical constraints
There are limits to what researchers are prepared to do to obtain information, as research could cause harm

Appropriate methods
Some methods are more appropriate than others in studying certain issues

Theoretical approaches
Different theoretical approaches suggest different forms of research

Personal beliefs
At worst, interpretation of results can be biased, but even good researchers are influenced by their personal beliefs

Interpretation of research results

Theoretical orientation
Theoretical approaches often provide different ways of interpreting data

Costs – both financial and effort
Researchers are constrained by costs and by energy/time available

Methods used
Different methodologies often provide different 'slants' on an issue and can influence the interpretation

Research methods

Mac an Ghaill (1998)
Ethnographic studies in educational research

In *Young, Gifted and Black*, Mairtin Mac an Ghaill carried out two ethnographic studies in inner-city educational institutions in which he worked. The first study looks at the relations between White teachers and two groups of antischool male students – the Asian Warriors and the African-Caribbean Rasta Heads – and the second study looks at a group of black female students, of African-Caribbean and Asian parentage, called the Black Sisters.

Why study this subject?

Originally, Mac an Ghaill wanted to study Irish school students for his PhD, but no university supervisor was available to do so. He was advised to study students of African-Caribbean origin instead and agreed to do so. He then began his study of (male) Asian Warriors and the African-Caribbean Rasta Heads.

Similarly, his later study of ethnic-minority females was also not planned. As Mac an Ghaill puts it: 'I had not intended to carry out a study of black female students. In fact it would be more accurate to say that they chose me.' Mac an Ghaill was teaching sociology at the time in a sixth-form college and, because he was seen to be on the side of the students, the Black Sisters were happy to talk to him about their views of racism.

The relationship between theory and method

Mac an Ghaill started his research by accepting the then current sociological explanation for the underachievement in school of young people of African-Caribbean origin, namely that there were cultural differences with the dominant White culture. Initially, therefore, he wanted to research the problem of young African-Caribbean students as trapped between two cultures.

Because Mac an Ghaill wanted to understand the nature of the cultural differences, he decided to use participant observational methods, which would give him a close insight into the values and beliefs of the students. As Mac an Ghaill says: 'Intensive participant observation of the antischool Rasta Heads led me to shift my theoretical perspective, identifying racism rather than the students themselves as the main problem in their schooling.

Adopting a Black perspective – that is, the view that the Black community experiences the social world in a systematically different way from Whites – was vital here. It enabled me to reinterpret the students' subcultural responses, not as primarily causal of their academic underachievement but as symptoms of their coping with a racially structured institution.'

Although he used participant observational methods, he also collected a range of quantitative information, including data on school absences, lateness, suspensions, the ethnic composition of students in academic/non-academic teaching groups and examination results. As the study developed, he used this material, linking it with what the students told him, to provide a deeper understanding of the students' perspectives.

Objectivity

During the research, Mac an Ghaill became friendly with the students, as he puts it: 'Over the research periods the Rasta Heads, the Warriors and the Black Sisters visited my home regularly. The experience of talking, eating, dancing and listening to music together helped to break down the potential social barriers of the teacher–researcher role that may have been assigned to me and my seeing them as students with the accompanying status perception.'

Mac an Ghaill does not claim to be value free in his research, and states that he was committed to helping the students to overcome the racially based barriers they faced in life.

Practical issues and research

Mac an Ghaill was able to gain entry into the research because he was a teacher in both educational institutions over the period of research. Beyond that, his sympathy and support for the students convinced them that he was a trustworthy person who was 'on their side'. Mac an Ghaill also lived in the area and was recognized as a local. However, there was always tension between his role as a teacher and that of a friend and researcher of the young people. He found that in the staff room he became the defender of the ethnic-minority students and a critic of the institutional racism he believed existed in the school and wider society. This position sometimes caused conflict with other members of staff.

Mac an Ghaill, M. (1998) *Young, Gifted and Black: Student-teacher relations in the schooling of black youth*, Milton Keynes: Open University Press

1 What factors influenced the choice of subject Mac an Ghaill studied?

2 What was the relationship between theoretical perspective and methods?

3 What methodology did Mac an Ghaill use?

4 Do you think that Mac an Ghaill found it difficult to remain objective in his research? Give reasons for your answer.

5 How did 'practical issues' impact upon his research activities and his relationship with staff and students?

Funding

All research has to be paid for by someone and those who pay for research have a reason for doing so. These funding organizations may vary from those who wish to extend knowledge about society and to improve the quality of life (such as the Joseph Rowntree Foundation), to private companies wanting to sell more products or services (such as market research organizations). Despite the differences between the funding organizations, each has an aim that constrains the research choices and activities of sociologists.

Probably the largest funder of sociological research in Britain is the government, which pays for a wide range of research into areas such as transport, health, crime and housing. However, anyone conducting research for the government signs a contract that restricts what they can say and publish about their findings.

Academic specialism

Sociologists at university specialize in particular areas within sociology – for example, some will only study the family and others only health issues. Clearly, the research they will wish to undertake will be within their specialism.

Personal reasons

Sociologists, like everyone else, want to have successful careers, be promoted and become respected. Research choices are often influenced by these desires. If there are various areas of research to choose from, the ambitious sociologist chooses that one that may lead to promotion.

Appropriate methods

The research method is often dictated by the situation and the sociologist has no choice, even if they have misgivings. Generally, if a large number of people need to be studied, then the sociologist will use questionnaires or possibly interviews. If a few people need to be studied in depth, then some form of observation will be generally employed.

Key terms

Bottom-up theories (generally called 'micro' or 'interpretive' approaches) sociological theories that analyse society by studying the ways in which individuals interpret the world.

Ethical issues moral concerns about the benefits and potential harm of research to the people being researched, to researchers themselves and to society.

Feminist sociology an approach within sociology that concerns itself with studying the way in which women are oppressed by men.

Functionalism an approach within sociology that stresses that society is based on a general agreement of values.

Interpretive sociology an approach favouring the use of qualitative methods, such as participant observation, that allow the researcher to see the world from the same perspective as those being studied.

Marxist or critical sociology an approach within sociology that stresses the exploitation of

the majority of the population by a small and powerful 'ruling class'.

Patriarchy the oppression of women by men.

Positivism the view that sociology should try to use more 'scientific' approaches and methods, such as questionnaires and official statistics.

Qualitative methods methods, such as participant observation, that produce primarily written data and allow the researcher to see things from the same perspective as those being studied.

Quantitative methods methods, such as questionnaires, that produce primarily statistical data.

Top-down theories (often called 'macro' or 'structural' approaches) sociological theories that believe it is important to look at society as a whole when studying it.

Triangulation term often used to describe the use of multiple methods (qualitative and quantitative) in research.

Check your understanding

1 Name the three main aims that sociological researchers set out to achieve.

2 Explain in your own words what is meant by the term 'ethical issues'.

3 Illustrate how ethical issues may emerge in:
   (a) the choice of topic to be studied
   (b) the effects on the people being studied.

4 How can a theoretical approach influence:
   (a) the area of study?
   (b) the methodological techniques chosen?

5 Give two examples that show the influence of practical issues on the nature of research.

Activities

Research idea

Look in your school or college library for resources about drugs and alcohol. Who published the material? Can you suggest reasons why they published the material? Could this affect the content of the material in any way?

Web.task

Go to the website of the British Sociological Association and find the section on 'The Statement of Ethical Practice'. Make a brief list of the key elements.
Do you think they are all necessary?
How could 'informed consent' cause problems for studying young people or deviant groups?

Item A

≪ The topic of Catrin's [research] very much evolved out of two fundamental concerns: women's health and women's imprisonment. Emma's interest, similarly, developed when she began to read a number of highly critical accounts of women's imprisonment ...

Both pieces of research were primarily influenced by what could loosely be termed a 'feminist' criminological perspective. In the 1970s and afterwards, feminist concern was directed at the misrepresentation and/or absence of women in conventional criminological research ... 'We were aware of the incomplete nature of this knowledge and were keen to address some of the gaps.' ≫

Source: Smith, C. and Wincup, E. (2000) 'Breaking in: researching criminal justice institutions for women' in R.D. King and E. Wincup (eds), *Doing Research on Crime and Justice*, Oxford: OUP, pp. 332–3

Item B

Carolyn Hoyle conducted research into domestic violence against women. She told victims what the research was about, how it was funded and how she would use the data. Hoyle describes how the violent husband and his victim were interviewed in separate rooms of their homes. The husbands were told that they were being asked the same questions as their wives. This was not true – they were misled as to the true nature of the questions asked of the wives.

Hoyle argues that this deception allowed the victims to speak freely and be assured that the husband/perpetrator would not know what they were really asked. She believes that ethical principles are important but have to be weighed against other factors such as the need to obtain reliable evidence about a controversial topic, evidence which could help bring about an improvement in the lives of the research subjects – in this case, the wives. The greater the social problem, the more it may be justified to attach less weight to ethical principles.

Adapted from Hoyle, C. (2000) 'Being "a nosy bloody cow": ethical and methodological issues in researching domestic violence', in R.D. King and E. Wincup (eds), *Doing Research on Crime and Justice*, Oxford: OUP, pp. 401–2

(a) Explain what is meant by 'quantitative methods'. (2 marks)

(b) Suggest two situations, other than that described in Item B, where it might be justified to mislead respondents or withhold information from them. (4 marks)

(c) Using information from Item A or elsewhere, suggest two ways in which theory might influence a sociologist's research. (4 marks)

(d) Examine the ways in which ethical issues are relevant to sociological research. (20 marks)

Grade booster · Getting top marks in the 20-mark question

For this question, you need to be clear about the meaning of the term 'ethical issues'. Look at a range of ways in which these are relevant to sociologists' work. These can include choice of research topic as well as decisions about which social groups ought to be studied (e.g. should we just focus on the powerless because they are less able to stop us from studying them?). Look also at ways in which research might harm those being studied, or even society at large, and at whether sociologists should become involved in illegality or dishonesty in their research.

TOPIC 3

Quantitative methods of primary research

Getting you thinking

Young men most likely to binge drink

In Great Britain, men aged 16–24 are the most likely to binge drink (consume twice the recommended daily amount of 3 to 4 units of alcohol for men). In 2005, 30 per cent had done so on at least one day in the previous week, a slightly higher proportion than among the 25–44 age group at 25 per cent. Among women aged 16–24, 22 per cent had consumed twice the recommended daily amount on at least one day during the preceding week, twice the proportion of those in the 25–44 age group, (who were the next most likely age group to have consumed at least twice the recommended daily level).

Source: *Health Statistics Quarterly*

Every year a survey called the Health Related Behaviour Questionnaire takes place. Young people are asked about their experiences of a range of health issues. According to the latest, conducted in 2002:

- Up to 21 per cent of 10- to 11-year-olds had consumed an alcoholic drink during the previous week.
- 19 per cent of 15 year old males drank more than 11 units of alcohol in the previous week.
- Up to 65 per cent of young people will have smoked by Year 10.
- About one in four pupils in Year 10 have tried at least one illegal drug.
- Up to 8 per cent of 12 to 13 year olds have taken cannabis.

Adapted from: Schools Health Education Unit (2003), *Young people in 2002*, Exeter: SHEU

1 **How can anyone make the above claims? For example, did they ask every school student in Britain? If they didn't, how is it possible to arrive at these figures?**
2 **Do you believe these figures. Why?**
3 **How honestly do you think pupils will answer these questions?**
4 **On what sort of questions do you think people would lie? Why?**
5 **Do you think that males and females might lie over different sorts of questions? Give examples.**

Sociologists choose different methods of research depending upon what method seems most appropriate in the circumstances, and the resources available to them. The approach covered in this topic is quantitative research. This stresses the importance of gathering statistical information that can be checked and tested. Quantitative research usually involves one or more of the following:

- **surveys**
- **experiments**
- **comparative research**
- **case studies**.

Quantitative research methods are most often chosen by sociologists who believe that sociology should attempt to be similar to the natural sciences in the way it researches. Sociologists who prefer the natural sciences model of research argue that the closest they can get to scientific research is if they use highly advanced statistical methods, which can, they argue, factually prove the relationship between different social events. Therefore, statistical analyses have demonstrated beyond doubt that social class, ethnicity and gender are all directly related to educational success. This approach to sociological research is known as **positivism**.

Positivists reject qualitative research, which is based on the principle that people construct the social world through their perceptions of what is real or true. Positivists argue that only through obtaining verifiable and objective information about the social world can knowledge be generated.

Surveys

A social survey involves obtaining information in a standardized manner from a large group of people. Surveys usually obtain this information through questionnaires or, less often, through interviews. The information is then analysed using statistical techniques. There are three possible aims of social surveys. They can be used to:

- find out 'facts' about the population – e.g. how many people have access to the internet
- uncover differences in beliefs, values and behaviour – e.g. whether young people have a more positive view of the internet than older people
- test 'a hypothesis' – e.g. that women are less confident in using the internet than men.

A good example of a survey is the British Crime Survey, which takes place every two years and asks people about their experience of crime. This survey has helped sociologists gain a fuller understanding of patterns of crime. We now know a lot more about issues such as people's fear of crime, the factors affecting the reporting of crime and the likelihood of different social groups becoming victims of crime.

Before a full social survey is carried out, it is usual for a researcher to carry out a **pilot survey**. This is a small-scale version of the full survey, which is intended to:

- help evaluate the usefulness of the larger survey
- test the quality and the accuracy of the questions
- test the accuracy of the sample
- find out if there are any unforeseen problems.

Longitudinal surveys

Social surveys are sometimes criticized for providing only a 'snapshot' of social life at any one time. Sociologists often want to understand how people change over time and in these circumstances the typical **cross-sectional survey** (as these 'snapshot surveys' or 'social surveys' are sometimes called) is not appropriate. **Longitudinal surveys**, however, get around this problem by studying the same people over a long period of time (as the name suggests) – sometimes over as long as 20 years. Such surveys provide us with a clear, moving image of changes in attitudes and actions over time. The Longitudinal Study of Young People in England is a new(ish) longitudinal survey which began in 2004 and will continue to track the sample throughout their education and onwards. In 2004, students in Year 9 (born 1989/1990) were interviewed and completed a questionnaire regarding their views on education. In all, over 15000 young people were interviewed. Since then, the interviews have been carried out yearly and are still

ongoing. The information obtained is used to plan educational provision, amongst other things.

Longitudinal surveys suffer from a number of problems, but the main one is that respondents drop out of the survey because they get bored with answering the questions, or they move and the researchers lose track of them. If too many people drop out, this may make the survey unreliable, as the views of those who remain may well be significantly different from the views of those who drop out.

Some of the problems faced by interviewers...

Sampling

It is usually impossible for sociologists to study the entire population, on the grounds of cost and practicality. Instead, they have to find a way of studying a smaller proportion of the population whose views will exactly mirror the views of the whole population. There are two main ways of ensuring that the smaller group studied (the sample) is typical – or **representative** – of the entire population:

1 some form of **random sampling**
2 **quota sampling**.

There are also other forms of sampling which are not representative but are sometimes used. These include:

3 **snowball sampling**
4 **theoretical sampling**.

Random sampling

This is based on the idea that, by choosing randomly, each person has an equal chance of being selected and so those chosen are likely to be a cross section of the population. A simple random sample involves selecting names randomly from a list, known as a **sampling frame**. If the sampling frame is inaccurate, this can lead to great errors in the final findings. Therefore, it needs to be a true reflection of the sort of people whom the researcher wishes to study. Examples of commonly used sampling frames are electoral registers (lists of people entitled to vote, which are publicly available) or the Postcode Address File (see Research methods on the next page).

Research methods

The Health Survey for England

The Health Survey for England (HSE) is part of a programme of surveys commissioned by the Information Centre for health and social care, and has been carried out regularly since 1994; they have become increasingly broader over time. The study provides information on changing health trends and risk factors linked to certain health conditions.

Sampling

The most recent survey, the HSE 2005, included a general population sample of adults and children, representative of the whole population at both national and regional level. In total, 7200 addresses were randomly selected in 720 postcode sectors.

At each address, everyone in them was eligible for inclusion in the survey. However, where there were three or more children aged 0–15 in a household, two of the children were selected at random.

As the 2005 survey was focusing on older people, a booster sample of people aged 65 and over was selected which consisted of 11 520 addresses in the same 720 postcode sectors as the main sample.

Interviews were held with 7630 adults aged 16 and over, and 1852 children from the general population. The boost sample resulted in an additional 2673 adults aged 65 and over, and 1142 children aged 2 to 15 being interviewed.

Response rate: 89 per cent of adults in the general households agreed to be interviewed, and 97 per cent of older people chosen agreed.

Interview and questionnaire

The survey used a mixture of interviews and self-completed questionnaires. The interview included questions on core topics such as general health, alcohol consumption, smoking, and fruit and vegetable consumption. Older informants were also asked about use of health, dental and social care services, cardiovascular disease (CVD), chronic diseases and quality of care, disabilities and falls.

Craig, R. and Mindell, J. (eds) (2007) *Health Survey for England 2005. The health of older people: Summary of key findings*, Joint Health Surveys Unit
www.ic.nhs.uk/webfiles/publications/hseolder/HSESummary.pdf

1 What sampling frame was used in this research?

2 How many households were chosen in (a) the main sample and (b) the booster sample? How can this number of households represent the views of the British population?

3 Why did they use a 'booster sample'?

4 Why do you think they obtained such a high response rate (a typical response rate is lower than 60 per cent)?

5 What problems do you think might occur when interviewing older people?

However, a simple random sample does not guarantee a representative sample – you may, for instance, select too many young people, too many males or too many from some other group. For this reason, many sociologists break down their list of names into separate categories (for example, males and females) and then select from those lists.

Types of random sampling

There are a number of commonly used types of random sampling which aim to guarantee a representative sample. These include the following:

- **Systematic sampling** – where every *n*th name (for example, every tenth name) on a list is chosen. It is not truly random, but it is close enough.
- **Stratified sampling** – where the population under study is divided according to known criteria (for example, it could be divided into 52 per cent women and 48 per cent men, to reflect the sex composition of the UK). Within these broad strata, people are then chosen at random. The strata can become quite detailed – for example, with further divisions into age, social class, geographical location.

- **Cluster sampling** – where the researcher selects a series of different places and then chooses a sample at random within the cluster of people within these areas. This method is sometimes used where the population under study is spread over a wide area and it is impossible for the researcher to cover the whole area.

Quota sampling

This form of sampling is often used by market research companies and is used purely as the basis for interviews. Since the main social characteristics of the UK population (age, income, occupation, location, ethnicity, etc.) are known, researchers can give interviewers a particular quota of individuals whom they must find and question – for example, a certain proportion of women of different ages and occupations, and a certain proportion of men of different ages and occupations. The results, when pieced together, should be an accurate reflection of the population as a whole. This form of sampling can only be used where accurate information about the major characteristics of the population is available.

The major advantage of quota sampling over random sampling is the very small number of people needed to build up an accurate picture of the whole. For example, the typical surveys of voting preferences in journals and newspapers use a quota sample of approximately 1200 to represent the entire British electorate.

Non-representative sampling

Sometimes researchers either do not want a cross section of the population, or are unable to obtain one.

Snowball sampling

This method is used when it is difficult to gain access to a particular group of people who are the subjects of study, or where there is simply no sampling frame available. It involves making contact with one member of the population to be studied and then asking them to name one or more possible contacts. An example of this is McNamara's study of male prostitutes in New York (1994) where he simply asked prostitutes to identify others, gradually building up enough contacts for the research.

Theoretical sampling

Glaser and Strauss (1967) argue that sometimes it is more helpful to study non-typical people, because they may help generate theoretical insights. Feminist sociologists have deliberately studied very untypical societies, where women occupy non-traditional roles, in order to show that gender roles are socially constructed – if they were based on biology, we would expect to see the same roles in every society.

Experiments

Experiments are very commonly used in the natural sciences (e.g. physics and chemistry). An experiment is basically research in which all the variables are closely controlled, so that the

effect of changing one or more of the variables can be understood. Experiments are widely used in psychology, but much less so in sociology. There are several reasons for this:

- It is impossible to recreate normal life in the artificial environment of an experiment.
- There are many ethical problems in performing experiments on people.
- There is the possibility of the experimenter effect, where the awareness of being in an experiment affects the behaviour of the participants.

Occasionally, sociologists use **field experiments**, where a form of experiment is undertaken in the community. Rosenhan (1982) sent 'normal' people to psychiatric institutions in the USA in the late 1960s to see how they were treated by the staff. (Rather worryingly, the staff treated ordinary behaviour in institutions as evidence of insanity!)

Comparative research

The sociological version of an experiment is the **comparative method**. When a sociologist is interested in explaining a particular issue, one way of doing so is by comparing differences across groups or societies, or across one society over time. By comparing the different social variables in the different societies and their effects upon the issue being studied, it is sometimes possible to identify a particular social practice or value which is the key factor in determining that issue. Emile Durkheim (1897/1952) used the comparative method in his classic study of the different levels of suicide in societies, concluding that specific cultural differences motivated people to commit suicide. In order to arrive at this conclusion, Durkheim collected official statistics from a number of different countries and then compared the different levels of suicide, linking them to cultural differences, including religion and family relationships, which varied across the different countries.

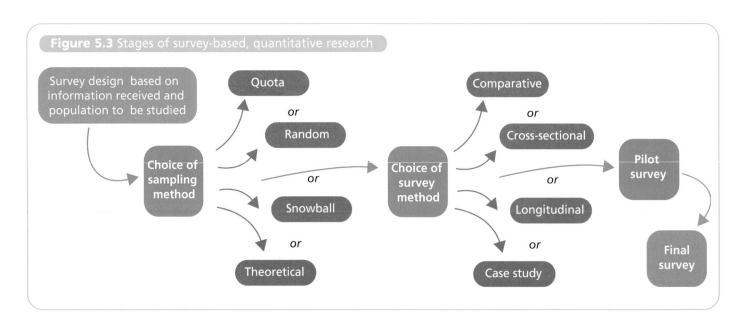

Figure 5.3 Stages of survey-based, quantitative research

Case studies

A case study is a detailed study of one particular group or organization. Instead of searching out a wide range of people via sampling, the researcher focuses on one group. The resulting studies are usually extremely detailed and provide a depth of information not normally available. However, there is always the problem that this intense scrutiny may miss wider issues by its very concentration. An example of a case study is Grieshaber's work (1997), where she conducted case studies of how families ate their meals, and the rules that the parents and their children negotiated.

Check your understanding

1 What do we mean by 'quantitative research'?

2 Explain in your own words the importance of sampling.

3 Why are random samples not always representative?

4 What is 'quota' sampling? What is the main drawback of this method?

5 Identify and explain, in your own words, three types of random sampling.

6 In what situations might a sociologist use:
    (a) snowball sampling?
    (b) theoretical sampling?

7 Why do sociologists rarely use experiments?

8 What is a case study?

9 Give one example of a research project that has used the comparative method.

Activities

Research ideas

1 Work out the proportions needed in your sample if you were to do a quota sample of your school or college.

2 Conduct a small survey to discover the patterns of alcohol use in your college. Ask males and females how much they drink per week on average and when they drink. Construct charts to demonstrate the patterns that emerge. What explanations could you suggest? You will need to work out your statistics based on alcohol units, and to do this, you should go to: www.at-bristol.org.uk/Alcoholandyou /Facts/units.html

Web.tasks

1 Go to the website 'School Surveys' at www.schoolsurveys.co.uk, where you can organize your own online survey. You will need to get your teacher to register first.

2 Go to www.nextstepsstudy.org.uk/who-is-the-study-for.asp

    Find out all you can about 'Next Steps'.

Key terms

Case study a highly detailed study of one or two social situations or groups.

Cluster sampling the researcher selects a series of different places and then chooses a sample at random within the cluster of people within these areas.

Comparative method a comparison across countries or cultures; sociology's version of an experiment.

Cross-sectional survey (also known as **social survey** or **snapshot survey**) a survey conducted at one time with no attempt to follow up the people surveyed over a longer time.

Experiment a highly controlled situation where the researchers try to isolate the influence of each variable. Rarely used in sociology.

Field experiment an experiment undertaken in the community rather than in a controlled environment.

Longitudinal survey a survey carried out over a considerable number of years on the same group of people.

Pilot survey a small-scale survey carried out before the main one, to iron out any problems.

Positivism the belief that the methods of the natural sciences are best suited to the study of society. Positivists prefer, wherever possible, to use statistics.

Quota sampling where a representative sample of the population is chosen using known characteristics of the population.

Random sampling where a representative sample of the population is chosen by entirely random methods.

Representative a sample is representative if it is an accurate cross section of the whole population being studied.

Sampling frame a list used as the source for a random sample.

Snowball sampling where a sample is obtained using a series of personal contacts. Usually used for the study of deviant behaviour.

Stratified sampling where the population under study is divided according to known criteria, such as sex and age, in order to make the sample more representative.

Survey a large-scale piece of quantitative research aiming to make general statements about a particular population.

Systematic sampling where every *n*th name (for example, every tenth name) on a list is chosen.

Theoretical sampling where an untypical sample of the population is chosen to illustrate a particular theory.

Item A

The North-West Longitudinal Study involved following several hundred young people for five years between the ages of 14 and 18. The overall aim of this study was to assess how 'ordinary' young people, growing up in England in the 1990s, developed attitudes and behaviour in relation to the availability of illegal drugs, alongside other options such as alcohol and tobacco.

The main technique was a self-report questionnaire initially administered personally by the researchers (and then by post) to several hundred young people within eight state secondary schools in two non-inner-city boroughs of metropolitan north-west England.

At the start of the research the sample was representative of those areas in terms of gender, class and ethnicity. However, attrition (losing participants) partly reduced this over time with the disproportionate loss of some 'working-class' participants and some from Asian and Muslim backgrounds.

A longitudinal study is able to address issues of validity and reliability far more extensively than one-off snapshot surveys, but in turn must also explain inconsistent reporting that occurs over the years.

In general, the research provides a detailed account of how young people develop attitudes and behaviours through time.

Adapted from Parker, H., Aldrige, J. and Measham, F. (1998) *Illegal Leisure*, London: Routledge, pp. 48–9

Item B

Brewer and his colleagues studied the way in which local communities managed to control and limit crime, given that the police were often not welcome in certain areas of Belfast.

They worked through local community-based organizations in order to gain access to general members of the public. Initial contact with the organizations was made possible by the network of contacts possessed by the authors and by the snowball technique. The authors believe that the organizations selected were an accurate political and social representation of the locality.

Adapted from Brewer, J.D., Lockhart, B. and Rodgers, P. (1998) 'Informal social control and crime management in Belfast', *British Journal of Sociology*, 49, December

(a) Explain what is meant by the 'snowball technique' of sampling (Item B).   (2 marks)

(b) Identify two types of quantitative research method.   (4 marks)

(c) Identify one advantage and one disadvantage of selecting a non-representative sample.   (4 marks)

(d) Using information from Item A and elsewhere, examine the advantages and disadvantages of longitudinal studies.   (20 marks)

Grade booster   Getting top marks in the 20-mark question

You should begin by defining 'longitudinal studies' and be able to give some examples of them, such as the North-West study described in Item A or the Health Survey for England. You should also make use of Item A to identify some of the possible advantages and disadvantages of this method. One approach is to contrast longitudinal studies with 'one-off' social surveys. Advantages include greater validity and reliability (e.g. in giving a picture of how behaviour develops over time). For disadvantages, consider issues of sample attrition, loss of representativeness and cost.

Qualitative methods of research

Getting you thinking

The extract on the right is from a research project which studies the lives and attitudes of door staff ('bouncers') working in night clubs. The researcher narrating the story is a student who has got a job as a bouncer as part of the research project.

1 What is your immediate reaction to the story?

2 Why do you think the girl was attacked by her friend?

3 Have you ever seen a fight outside a club at night? What happened? What did the doorstaff do?

4 Why do you think the researcher chose to get a job as a bouncer in order to study their lives? Could you think of a better way?

<<It's Friday evening outside a club in a city centre … one young woman has shouted an insult at another, the recipient of which has turned on her heel and begun to walk away. The first young woman continues to throw insults until the retreating young woman seemingly has a change of heart, turns, picks up an empty lager bottle from the street and hits the first young woman in the face with it.

A hush descends on the busy street. It isn't funny any more. Nobody is laughing; in fact there was a palpable 'Oh!' sound emitted from the spectators, mixed with the sound of thick glass crashing into tender flesh and bone. The injured young woman has her hand pressed to her mouth – she isn't screaming or crying, but instantly it is possible to tell that she is badly injured.

I snap out of my shocked state when I see Paul (bouncer and colleague) putting his arm around her back to support her unsteady steps … After some gentle coaxing, the woman releases her grip on the wound … blood spurts all over Paul's shirt. Her upper lip is split entirely, right up to her right nostril. It's a wide gash and through the resulting hole it becomes apparent that the woman has also lost at least three teeth. Blood is everywhere. Paul's shirt now appears tie-dyed red with blood.

Later when a policeman calls to take a statement, he informs me that I may be called as a witness in any resulting court case. When I ask how the young woman is, he informs me that 'She lost four teeth, 28 stitches to the upper lip, the usual bruising and swelling … Shame really. Pretty girl.' Turns out she's only 15.>>

Source: Winlow, S., Hobbs, D., Lister, S. and Hadfield, P. (2001) 'Get ready to duck: bouncers and the realities of ethnographic research on violent groups', *British Journal of Criminology*, 41, pp. 536–48

Have you ever watched a sporting event on television and heard the commentator saying what a fantastic atmosphere there is? Yet, at home, you remain outside it. You know there is a fantastic atmosphere, you hear the roar of the crowd, yet you are not part of it. For the people actually in the stadium, the experience of the occasion is quite different. The heat, the closeness of thousands of others, the noise and the emotional highs and lows of the actual event, all combine to give a totally different sense of what is happening.

Some sociologists 'stay at home' to do their research. They may use questionnaires, interviews and surveys to obtain a clear, overall view. On the other hand, there are sociologists who are more interested in experiencing the emotions and sense of actually being there. These sociologists set out to immerse themselves in the lifestyle of the group they wish to study.

Because this form of research is less interested in statistics to prove its point (that is, quantitative research), and more interested in the qualities of social life, it is sometimes known as **qualitative research**. Qualitative approaches are based on the belief that it is not appropriate or possible to measure and categorize the social world accurately – all that is possible is to observe and describe what is happening and offer possible explanations.

There are three common forms of qualitative research:

- observational studies
- informal interviews
- focus groups.

In this topic we will concentrate on observational studies, as many of the issues surrounding asking questions and discussion are covered in the following topic. However, we should remember that, strictly speaking, qualitative research can include a wide variety of other approaches, such as video and audio recording of activities, interviews, analysis of the internet, or even non-statistical analysis of books, magazines and journals.

Although there is still some debate, the general consensus is that qualitative research is a naturalistic, interpretative approach concerned with understanding the meanings which people attach to actions, decisions, beliefs, values, etc., within their social world; it is also about understanding the mental mapping process that respondents use to make sense of and interpret the world around them (Ritchie and Lewis 2003).

The most common form of qualitative research consists of observational studies in which a particular group of people is closely observed and their activities noted. The belief is that, by exploring the lives of people in detail, insights may be gained that can be applied to the understanding of society in general. Observational studies derive from **ethnography**, which is the term used to describe the work of anthropologists who study simple, small-scale societies by living with the (usually tribal) people and observing their daily lives.

Observational research

Observational research is a general term that covers a range of different research techniques. Observational studies vary in two main ways (see Fig. 5.4 opposite):

1 the extent to which the researcher joins in the activities of the group – the researcher may decide to be a participant or not. The choice is between **participant observation** and **non-participant observation**

2 whether the researcher is honest and tells the group about the research, or prefers to pretend to be one of the group. The choice is between **overt** and **covert** research.

Participant observation

The most common form of observational study is participant observation, where the researcher joins the group being studied.

The advantages of participant observation

- *Experience* – Participant observation allows the researcher to join the group fully and see things through the eyes (and actions) of the people in the group. The researcher is placed in exactly the same situation as the group under study, fully experiencing what is happening. This results in the researcher seeing social life from the same perspective as the group.
- *Generating new ideas* – Often this can lead to completely new insights and generate new theoretical ideas, unlike

traditional research, which undertakes the study in order to explore an existing theory or hypothesis.

- *Getting the truth* – One of the problems with questionnaires, and to a lesser extent with interviews, is that the respondent can lie. Participant observation prevents this because the researcher can see the person in action – it may also help them understand why the person would lie in a questionnaire or interview.
- *Digging deep* – Participant observation can create a close bond between the researcher and the group under study, and individuals in the group may be prepared to confide in the researcher on issues and views that would normally remain hidden.
- *Dynamic* – Questionnaires and interviews are 'static': they are only able to gain an understanding of a person's behaviour or attitudes at the precise moment of the interview. Participant observation takes place over a period of time and allows an understanding of how changes in attitudes and behaviour take place.
- *Reaching into difficult areas* – Participant observation is normally used to obtain research information on hard-to-reach groups, such as religious sects and young offenders.

The disadvantages of participant observation

- *Bias* – The main problem lies with bias, as the observer can be drawn into the group and start to see things through their eyes. This may blind the observer to the insights that would otherwise be available.
- *Influence of the researcher* – The presence of the researcher may make the group act less naturally as they are aware of being studied. Of course, this is less likely to happen if the researcher is operating covertly.
- *Ethics* – If the researcher is studying a group engaged in deviant behaviour, then there is a moral issue of how far the researcher should be drawn into the activities of the group – particularly if these activities are immoral or illegal.
- *Proof* – Critics have pointed out that there is no way of knowing objectively whether the findings of participant observation are actually true or not, since there is no possibility of replicating the research. In other words, the results may lack reliability.
- *Too specific* – Participant observation is usually used to study small groups of people who are not typical of the wider population. It is therefore difficult to claim that the findings can be generalized across the population as a whole.
- *Studying the powerless* – Finally, almost all participant observational studies are concerned with the least powerful groups in society – typically groups of young males or females who engage in deviant activities. Some critics argue that the information obtained does not help us to understand the more important issues in society.

Non-participant observation

Some researchers prefer to withdraw from participation and merely observe.

Figure 5.4 Types of observational research

COVERT

Laud Humphries (1975) studied homosexual activity in public toilets. He pretended to be a gay voyeur.

Amy Flowers (1998) got a job as a telephone sex line worker and studied the way that the women learned to mask their feelings and emotions when talking to clients. Neither employees nor managers knew about her research.

NON-PARTICIPANT

Heidi Safia Mirza and Diane Reay (2000) studied two African-Caribbean 'supplementary' schools, run by the African-Caribbean-origin community for their children. The researchers attended and observed the classes (as well as using in-depth interviews).

PARTICIPANT

Stephen Lyng (1990) studied 'high risk' groups (sky divers and motorcyclists) to find out why they did it. Lyng never hid the fact he was an academic but joined in all the dangerous activities.

OVERT

Advantages of non-participant observation

- *Bias* – As the researcher is less likely to be drawn into the group, the researchers' views are also less likely to be biased.
- *Influencing the group* – As the researcher is not making any decisions or joining in activities, the group may be less influenced than in participant observation.

Disadvantages of non-participant observation

- *Superficial* – The whole point of participant observation is to be a member of the group and experience life as the group experiences it. Merely observing leaves the researcher on the outside and may limit understanding.
- *Altering behaviour* – People may well act differently if they know they are being watched.

Covert and overt methods

Observational research is usually carried out amongst deviant groups or other groups who are unusual in some way, such as religious cults. Usually, these groups will not be very welcoming to a researcher. Before researchers begin their work, therefore, they must decide whether they wish to conduct the research in a covert or overt way.

The advantages of covert research

- *Forbidden fruit* – Researchers can enter forbidden areas, be fully accepted and trusted, and immerse themselves totally in the group being studied. This can generate a real sense of understanding of the views of the group.
- *Normal behaviour* – The group will continue to act naturally, unaware that they are being studied.

The disadvantages of covert research

- *Danger* – If the researcher's true role is uncovered, it may place the researcher in danger.
- *Ethical dilemmas* – First, there is the issue that it is wrong to study a group without telling them. Second, if the group engages in illegal or immoral activities, the researchers may have to engage in these activities as well. They may then find themselves in possession of knowledge that it may be immoral to withhold from the authorities.

The advantages of overt observation

- *The confidante* – As someone who has no role within the group, the researcher may be in the position of the trusted outsider and receive confidences from group members.
- *Honest* – The researcher is also able to play an open, clear and honest role, which will help minimize ethical dilemmas.
- *Other methods* – Researchers can supplement their observation with other methods, such as interviews and questionnaires.

The disadvantage of overt observation

- *Outsider* – There will be many situations where only a trusted insider will be let into the secrets. Anyone else, even a sympathetic observer, will be excluded.

Doing ethnographic research

The process of doing ethnographic research involves solving some key problems.

Joining the group

Observational studies usually involve groups of people on the margins of society, and the first problem is actually to contact and join the group. The sociologist has to find a place where the group goes and a situation in which they would accept the researcher. Shane Blackman (1997) (see the Eye on the exam on p. 186) studied a group of young homeless people, whom he met at an advice centre for young people. Sometimes sociologists make use of **gatekeepers** – members of the group who help the sociologist become accepted and introduce them to new people and situations. Andy Bennett (2004) describes how his route 'into' the local hip hop scene in Newcastle was facilitated by a local breakdancer who also worked as an instructor at a community dance project. Through this contact, he gained access to, or learned of, key figures in the scene. He would accompany the gatekeeper and a number of his dance students and other friends to around a dozen weekly hip hop nights held in a bar.

Acceptance by the group

There are often barriers of age, ethnicity and gender to overcome if the group are to accept the researcher. Moore (2004) researched young people 'hanging around'. He was initially unable to gain full acceptance because of his age. He overcame this by using young, female researchers.

Recording information

When researchers are actually hanging around with a group, it is difficult to make notes – particularly if engaged in covert research. Even if the group members are aware of the research, someone constantly making notes would disrupt normal activity and, of course, the researcher would also be unable to pay full attention to what was going on. In participant observational studies, therefore, researchers generally use a **field diary**. This is simply a detailed record of what happened, which the researcher writes up as often as possible. However, the research diary can also be a real weakness of the research.

Research diaries

Ethnographic researchers do not keep regular hours. Their observation may well go on into the night. It can be difficult to write up a diary each evening. Therefore, there is plenty of time to forget things and to distort them. Most observational studies include quotes, yet as it is impossible to remember the exact words, the quotes reflect what the researcher thinks the people said. This may be inaccurate.

Maintaining objectivity

In observational research, it is hard to remain objective. Close contact with the group under study means that feelings almost always emerge. In the introduction to Bourgois' (2003) study of crack cocaine dealers, he comments on how these dealers are his friends and how much he owes to the 'comments, corrections and discussions' provided by one particular dealer.

Influencing the situation

The more involved the researcher is with the people being studied, the greater the chance of influencing what happens. Stephen Lyng (1990) joined a group of males who engaged in 'edgework' – that is, putting their lives at risk through skydiving and (illegal) road motorcycle racing. Lyng became so entangled in this style of life that he actually helped encourage others into life-risking behaviour.

Research methods

Dympna Devine (2003) Observational research with primary-school children

Devine studied primary school pupils in three schools in Ireland: one was in a working-class area, another in a slightly more mixed area and the third in an affluent area. She mainly used 'extended observation' of the classroom and the playground, although she also used a range of other qualitative methods, including interviews and children's drawings and diaries. The interviews were friendly and informal and developed out of her observations.

The observational work was done by her joining classes and sitting in the room with them. In order to demonstrate that she was not a teacher or an adult in charge, she sat on a low chair at a desk, the same as the children. Furthermore, she was careful never to take the role of teacher by trying to impose any discipline or reporting any misbehaving. According to Devine, she was thus able to gain their trust. During school breaks, Devine usually went into the playground with the children and not to the staffroom. When she did go into the staffroom, it was not as another adult, but as an outsider and she tended to listen to the conversations of the

teachers about the pupils. All this allowed her to build up a picture, from the children's perspective, of life in a primary school.

According to Devine, her conclusions are that what children want most from schooling is 'to be taught clearly, to be treated fairly and to be taken seriously by adults in school'. Devine suggests that the power in primary schools is too much in the hands of adults and teachers, and that children are unable to put their views across in such a way as to change things.

Devine, D. (2003) *Children, Power and Schooling*, Stoke on Trent: Trentham Books

1 Why can this research be best described as qualitative?

2 Of the four types of observational techniques we discuss in this topic, which do you think are used here?

3 How did Devine obtain the children's trust?

4 Devine claims to provide the perspective of the children. Do you think this is possible? Explain your answer.

5 Could this work claim to be generalizable? Explain your answer.

6 What other way of finding out about the views of young children could you use?

Informal interviews

We discuss interviewing techniques in some detail in Topic 5, but it is worth stressing that informal interviewing is a very important part of qualitative research. The aim of informal interviews is to try to focus on a particular issue with one person and to guide them into explaining how they perceive that issue. It is better to view such an interview as a sort of 'controlled conversation'. Qualitative interviews tend to use '**open questions**', which allow the respondent to talk in some depth, choosing their own words.

Usually, the conversations are recorded (with the respondent's permission) and the sociologist later listens again to the interview and makes notes. If a large number of interviews are conducted, sociologists tend to use special software which analyses conversations and collects words or themes which recur.

The advantage of qualitative interviews is that they allow a person to talk in depth about their views and it is often possible to get a real sense of a person's understanding of a situation. Often, new ideas are generated which the researcher had not previously thought of.

The disadvantage is that qualitative interviews do not lend themselves to statistical analysis and so it is difficult to generalize from them.

Focus groups

Focus groups are one of the more common types of research now used in sociology. These groups consist of a group of people who are gathered together by the researcher and asked to discuss a particular issue. In many ways, focus groups can be seen as a group informal interview. The researcher leads with an introduction and then allows the group to discuss the particular issue. The role of the researcher is simply to ensure that the discussion does not drift too far away from the desired research topic.

Focus groups can be very useful in providing insights into complex problems, although the researcher must be very careful not to 'lead' the group into any particular direction.

Check your understanding

1 What forms of observational studies are there?

2 What advantages does observational research have over quantitative methods?

3 Identify three problems associated with participant observation.

4 Suggest two examples of research where it would be possible to justify covert observation.

5 Suggest two examples of research situations where observational methods would be appropriate.

6 Suggest two examples of research situations where it might be more appropriate to undertake a survey.

Key terms

Covert observation where the sociologist does not admit to being a researcher.

Ethnography describes the work of anthropologists who study simple, small-scale societies by living with the people and observing their daily lives. The term has been used by sociologists to describe modern-day observational studies.

Field diary a detailed record of events, conversations and thoughts kept by participant observers, written up as often as possible.

Gatekeeper person who can allow a researcher access to an individual, group or event.

Non-participant observation where the sociologist simply observes the group but does not seek to join in their activities.

Open questions allow respondents to express themselves fully.

Participant observation where the sociologist joins a group of people and studies their behaviour.

Qualitative research a general term for approaches to research that are less interested in collecting statistical data, and more interested in observing and interpreting the ways in which people behave.

Overt observation where the sociologist is open about the research role.

Activities

Research ideas

1 Carry out these two pieces of observation:

- Go to your local library. Spend one hour watching how people behave. Write down as accurate a description as you can.
- Then spend an evening at home 'observing' your family. Write down as accurate a description of home behaviour that evening as you can.

2 Which study is likely to be more biased? Why? Does this make it any less accurate? Are you able to get greater depth studying your family? Why? Do you think it would make a difference if you operated in a covert rather than an overt way with your family?

Web.task

Is it possible to do observational studies on the internet? Try observing a chat room or MSN Messenger. What behaviour occurs? Why?

Item A

In 1992, Shane Blackman spent several months with a group of young homeless people in Brighton.

≪ As the study proceeded my research role expanded to also include that of action researcher, drinking partner, friend, colleague and football player. In terms of techniques, I found that the conventional social research interview was an impossibility with the individuals in the study, due to their suspicion of such forms of enquiry. The main research instrument was the field diary.

Where social research focuses on individuals and groups who are on the margins of society, the method through which data is collected is often of a highly intimate nature. The researcher is drawn into the lives of the researched and the fieldworker feels emotions while listening to respondents' accounts of their own lives ...

Ethnographic descriptions are able to convey experience from the perspective of the subject of the research and to develop theories based on feeling. ≫

Source: Blackman, S. (1997) 'An ethnographic study of youth underclass' in R. McDonald (ed.), *Youth, the Underclass and Social Exclusion*, London: Routledge

Item B

In the late 1990s, Fleisher spent a year with a violent gang in Kansas City.

≪ Genuine ethnography, spending six months to a year with informants in natural settings, creates a sort of 'marriage' between researcher and the researched. When I commit myself to a neighbourhood and its people, that commitment obtains the right to see things other researchers never see, ask questions others never ask, get answers others never get. But that privilege has a dark side. That dark side is the personal damage that seeing kids in pain who inflict pain on others has caused me. I see child abuse and teenage prostitution, drug addiction and drug dealing and have even heard murder contracts and street-to-prison drug smuggling being arranged over the phone. For this privilege I pay a heavy price.

My research and my bad dreams are worth it, only if my writing results in a better life for these people. But that's not up to me. ≫

Source: Fleisher, M.S. (1998) 'Ethnographers, Pimps and the Company Store' in J. Ferrell and M.S. Hamm *Ethnography at the Edge*, Boston: Northeastern University Press

(a) Explain what is meant by a 'field diary' (Item A). (2 marks)

(b) Suggest one reason why interviews may not be an effective way to study groups such as those in Item A. (2 marks)

(c) Identify three problems of keeping a field diary while carrying out participant observation. (6 marks)

(d) Using information from the Items and elsewhere, assess the advantages and disadvantages of participant observation as a research method. (20 marks)

Grade booster — Getting top marks in the 20-mark question

It's a good idea to describe the different types of participant observation, especially covert and overt, since the advantages and disadvantages of each vary considerably. Make sure you use information from both the Items. For example, Item A suggests that participant observation enables the researcher to feel the same emotions as the subjects, while Item B claims that it allows the researcher to 'get answers others never get'. Link these to issues such as lack of objectivity and insight. You should also consider issues such as danger, ethics, problems of recording information and bias.

TOPIC 5

Asking questions: questionnaires and interviews

Getting you thinking

Are you a top scorer in the friendship game, or someone your mates could do without? Take our quiz to find out.

Are You a Good Mate?

Start here!

Do you have a new best bud almost every week?

No →

Is fessing up your friend's secret the very worst friendship crime?

No →

Are you always doing things for your pals?

Yes ↓

You always stick by your mates, no matter what.

Yes →

Do you often end up doing your pal's homework for her?

Yes →

It's your big party and your mate cancels. D'ya give her grief?

No ↓

Do you put yourself before your pals?

No →

Are you always totally honest with your best mate?

No ←

Do you spend most of your time listening to your pal's probs?

Fake Friend

Oh dear! With mates like you, who needs enemies? Try sticking by your pals a bit more and you'll see how fun it is being a premier league pal. Go on, give it a go!

Fab Friend

Whoah! Prepare your acceptance speech, Missy, cos you just won the tournament of friendship. You're kind and fun to be around. We bet that everyone loves having you as a friend.

Good Friend

Hello Little Miss Nice Girl! You'd do almost anything when it comes to your mates, but be careful not to be walked all over, you need to stand up for yourself too.

1 Complete this questionnaire from *Go Girl* magazine to find whether or not you are a 'good mate'.

2 Do you think the conclusion about your strengths and weaknesses as a friend is justified? Explain your answer.

3 Do you think people will answer all the questions honestly? Explain your answer.

4 How good a questionnaire do you think this is? Why?

The most obvious way of finding out something is to ask questions. It is not surprising, then, to find that one of the most common methods of research used by sociologists is just to ask people questions about their attitudes and actions.

Sociologists ask questions in two main ways:

1 asking the questions face to face – the interview
2 writing the questions down and handing them to someone to complete – the questionnaire.

Which of the two methods is chosen depends upon which way of asking questions seems to fit the circumstances best – and has the best chance of gaining the information required.

Questionnaires

Questionnaires are used for reaching:

- a large number of people, since the forms can just be handed out
- a widely dispersed group of people, as they can simply be posted out.

Self-completion questionnaires are also less time-consuming for researchers than interviewing, as they do not require the researcher to go and talk to people face to face.

Anonymous questionnaires are also very useful if the researcher wishes to ask embarrassing questions about such things as sexual activities or illegal acts. People are more likely to tell the truth if they can do so anonymously than if they have to face an interviewer.

Questionnaires – particularly **closed** questionnaires – are a favourite method used by positivist sociologists (see Topic 2, p. 171), as they can be used in large numbers and the answers can be codified and subjected to statistical tests.

Types of questionnaires

There are many different types of questionnaire. They vary in the way in which they expect the person to answer the questions set. At one extreme are closed questionnaires, which have a series of questions with a choice of answers – all the respondent has to do is tick the box next to the most appropriate answer. At the other extreme are **open** questionnaires that seek the respondent's opinion by leaving space for their response. Some questionnaires contain a mixture of both open and closed questions.

The essence of a good questionnaire

When constructing a questionnaire, the sociologist has to ensure that:

- it asks the right questions to unearth exactly the information wanted
- the questions are asked in a clear and simple manner that can be understood by the people completing the questionnaire
- it is as short as possible, since people usually cannot be bothered to spend a long time completing questionnaires.

Issues in undertaking questionnaires

- Unfortunately, many people cannot be bothered to reply to questionnaires – that is, unless there is some benefit to them, such as the chance to win a prize. This is a serious drawback of questionnaires in research.
- A low **response rate** (the proportion of people who reply) makes a survey useless, as you do not know if the small number of replies is representative of all who were sent the questionnaire. Those who reply might have strong opinions on an issue, for example, whereas the majority may have much less firm convictions. Without an adequate number of replies, you will never know.
- It is difficult to go into depth in a questionnaire, because the questions need to be as clear and simple as possible.

- You can never be sure that the correct person answers. If you mail a questionnaire to one member of a household, how do you know that that person answers it?
- You can never be sure that the person who replies to the questionnaire interprets the questions in the way that the researcher intended, so their replies might actually mean something different from what the researcher believes they mean.
- Lying is also a danger. People may simply not tell the truth when answering questionnaires. There is little that the researcher can do, apart from putting in 'check questions' – questions that ask for the same information, but are phrased differently.

Interviews

An interview can either be a series of questions asked directly by the researcher to the respondent or it can be conducted as a discussion. Sociologists generally use interviews:

- if the subject of enquiry is complex, and a questionnaire would not allow the researcher to probe deeply
- when they want to compare their observations with the replies given by the respondents, to see if they appear true or not.

Advantages of interviews

- The interviewer can help explain questions to the respondent if necessary.
- Researchers are also sure that they are getting information from the right person.
- They can be organized virtually on the spot and so can be done immediately – as opposed to preparing a questionnaire, finding a sampling frame and posting the questionnaires out.
- There is a much higher response rate with interviews than with questionnaires, as the process is more personal and it is difficult to refuse a researcher when approached politely.

Types of interviews

Interviews fall between two extremes: **structured** and **unstructured**. At their most structured, they can be very tightly organized, with the interviewer simply reading out questions from a prepared questionnaire. At the other extreme they can be unstructured, where the interviewer simply has a basic area for discussion and asks any questions that seem relevant. Interviews that fall between the two extremes are known as 'semi-structured' interviews.

There are also individual and group interviews. Most people assume that an interview is between just two people, but in sociological research a group of people may get together to discuss an issue, rather than simply giving an answer to a question. Group interviews are commonly used where the researcher wants to explore the dynamics of the group, believing that a 'truer' picture emerges when the group are all together, creating a 'group dynamic'. An example of this is Mairtin Mac an Ghaill's *The Making of Men: Masculinities,*

Sexualities and Schooling (1994), in which a group of gay students discuss their experiences of school.

Issues in undertaking interviews

Influencing the replies

Interviews are a form of conversation between people and, as in any conversation, likes and dislikes emerge. The problem is to ensure that the interviewer does not influence the replies provided by the respondent in any way – known as **interviewer bias**. For example, respondents may want to please the interviewer and so give the replies they think the interviewer wants. Influences that can affect the outcome of the interview include manner of speech, ethnic origin, sex or personal habits.

Lying

There is no reason why people should tell the truth to researchers, and this is particularly true when a sensitive issue is being researched. When questioned about sexual activities or numbers of friends, for example, people may exaggerate in order to impress the interviewer.

Interview reliability

The aim of the research process is to conduct enough interviews for the researcher to be able to make an accurate generalization. However, if interviews are actually different from each other as a result of the interaction, then it is wrong to make generalizations.

Recording the information

Unstructured interviews are generally recorded and usually require **transcribing** (writing up), which is time-consuming. Tizard and Hughes (1991) recorded interviews with students to find out how they went about learning – every hour of interview took 17 hours to transcribe and check! However, writing down the replies at the time is slow and can disrupt the flow of an interview.

Operationalizing concepts

Ideas that are discussed in sociology, such as 'sexual deviance', 'educational failure', or 'ill health', are all pretty vague when you spend a few moments thinking about them. Take educational failure – does this mean not having A levels? Perhaps it means having 'low' grades at GCSE (whatever the concept 'low grades' means)? Or only having one or two GCSEs? You can see that a concept as apparently simple as 'educational failure' is actually capable of having different meanings to different people.

However, concepts such as educational failure or ill health are used all the time in sociological research, so sociologists have had to find a way around this problem when they ask people questions about the concepts. For example, if you were

to ask somebody if they 'suffered from ill health', the reply would depend upon the individual definition of ill health and different people might (in fact we know they *do*) use very different definitions of ill health.

In research, we need to use concepts such as sexual deviance, educational failure and ill health, but in a way which is valid and reliable (see p. 166). By this, we mean that the concepts are accurately measured (valid), and that each time we use them, we are sure that every respondent understands the concept in the same way (reliable).

When concepts are used in research, sociologists say that they are **operationalizing** them. So, if there is a piece of research to find out the levels of ill health amongst retired people, the concept 'ill health' will need to be operationalized. The problem when operationalizing a concept is how to ensure that it is accurately and reliably measured.

Indicators

The answer is that sociologists use **indicators**. An indicator is something 'concrete' that stands in for the abstract concept, but which people can understand and sociologists can actually measure. Let us return to the example of 'ill health'. It is possible to ask people the following:

- whether they suffer from any specific diseases or any long-term disability
- whether they are receiving any specific medication
- how frequently they have attended a GP surgery or clinic in the last year.

Problems with indicators

An indicator then, is a short cut sociologists use to measure an abstract concept. Unfortunately, short cuts in any academic area of study bring problems. We need to remember that what is actually being measured are the *indicators, not the actual concept*. This may not be a problem if the indicators are a perfect reflection of the original concept, but this is rarely the case. Let's go back to ill health. One question used is how often people have visited the GP surgery in the last year. However, this does not necessarily tell us about *levels* of health, it may just tell us that some people tend to visit the GP (whether they need to or not) more than others. Someone might be very ill but refuse to visit a GP. For example, there is considerable evidence that older people visit GPs less often than their medical conditions warrant.

Furthermore, it is not the actual number of visits that could be considered important, but the reasons why they went. A younger person may be seeing a GP for contraceptive advice, while an older person may be concerned about a heart condition.

Coding

Using clear indicators in research allows answers to be **coded** – that is broken down into simple, distinct answers that can be counted. The researchers can simply add up the numbers of people replying to each category of indicator and then make statements such as '82 per cent of people have seen a doctor on their own behalf in 2002' (Department of Health 2003).

Questions and values

Both questionnaires and interviews share the problem of the values of the researcher creeping into the questions asked. Two problems are particularly important – using leading questions and using loaded words:

- *Leading questions*: Researchers write or ask questions that suggest what the appropriate answer is, e.g. 'Wouldn't you agree that …?'
- *Loaded words and phrases*: Researchers use particular forms of language that either indicate a viewpoint or will generate a particular positive or negative response – for example, 'termination of pregnancy' (a positive view) or 'abortion' (a negative view); 'gay' or 'homosexual'.

Research methods

Stephen Frosh *et al.* (2002) Asking boys questions

Stephen Frosh wanted to find out how boys in the early years of secondary school came to an idea of what masculinity means to them and how this impacts upon their behaviour and their learning. Frosh undertook two main types of qualitative research: group interviews/focus groups and informal interviews. In total, 78 boys were interviewed.

Each interviewer was given a list of topics and possible questions which guided them through the interview. This is a perfect example of qualitative, semi-structured interviewing methods. All the answers were recorded and then transcribed, and the researchers looked for the key themes that emerged.

General self-description

- Could you tell me three things you think are important about yourself?

Ethnicity

- What ethnic group do you think you belong to?
- Do you see some boys as belonging to a different ethnic group to you? How would you describe their background? Do you go around with boys from this/these backgrounds? Why/why not? Do you do the same things with them as boys from your 'own' ethnic background?
- Can you imagine having a girlfriend from a different ethnic group?
- Do you think boys are treated differently because of where their parents come from? Is your ethnic background important to you? What difference does it make being a boy from this background? Are you pleased you are from this background?
- Have you ever thought you'd not like to be?
- Are there things you dislike about boys from other ethnic and cultural backgrounds?
- Are there things you admire about boys from other ethnic and cultural backgrounds?

Sources: Frosh, S., Phoenix, A. and Pattman, R. (2002) *Young Masculinities: Understanding Boys in Contemporary Society,* Basingstoke: Palgrave Macmillan; Youth Lifetime Leisure Survey, Home Office, www.data-archive.ac.uk/doc/4345/mrdoc/pdf/a4345uab.pdf

Youth Lifetime Leisure Survey

The following questions were taken from a quantitative study into bullying by young people. It was part of a Home Office national survey and was completed by 4800 people between the ages of 12 and 30.

2.2 BULLYING

Would you say that students are bullied by other students …

a   a lot   b   a little   c   or not at all?

In the last 12 MONTHS, have you been bullied by other students?

a   Yes   b   No

If yes … how often has this happened in the last 12 months?

a   Every day   e   Once a month
b   A few times a week   f   Less often than this
c   Once or twice a week   g   It varies
d   Once every two weeks

In the last 12 months, have other students made you give them money or your personal possessions?

a   Yes   b   No

1   Compare the questions in the two extracts

2   What are the advantages and disadvantages of each type of questioning?

3   Which type of questioning do you think is more time consuming? Why?

4   Which type of questioning do you think is likely to lead to greater reliability? Explain your answer.

5   Which type of questioning do you think is likely to lead to greater validity? Explain your answer.

6   Considering only the second set of questions on ethnicity, do you think that there might be different answers if the questions were asked by:

   (a) females rather than males?
   (b) African-Caribbean-origin researchers rather than White researchers?

   Explain your answer.

7   Explain how bias might possibly creep into this form of research interview?

Interviews and scientific methods

Interviews are used by all kinds of sociologists. The more structured the interviews, the more likely they are to be used in a quantitative way to produce statistics. The more unstructured the interviews (including group interviews), the more likely they are to be of use to interpretive sociologists.

Issues of validity and reliability

Validity

Questions asked should actually produce the information required. This is a crucial issue in sociological research and is known as the issue of **validity** (i.e. getting at the truth). The type of questions asked in the questionnaire or interview must allow the respondent to give a true and accurate reply.

Reliability

The researcher must ensure not only that the design of the question gets to the truth of the matter, but also that it does so consistently. If the question means different things to different people, or can be interpreted differently, then the research is not reliable. **Reliability**, then, refers to the fact that all completed questionnaires and interviews can be accurately compared.

Check your understanding

1 What are the three elements of a good questionnaire?

2 Why are response rates so important?

3 In what situations is it better to use self-completion questionnaires rather than interviews?

4 When would it be more appropriate to use open questions? Give an example of an open question.

5 Explain the difference between structured, semi-structured, unstructured and group interviews

6 What do we mean by 'transcribing'?

7 What do we mean when we talk about 'loaded questions' and 'leading questions'? Illustrate your answer with an example of each and show how the problem could be overcome by writing a 'correct' example of the same questions.

Activities

Research idea

Working with a partner of the opposite sex, draft guide questions for an unstructured interview with young men about their attitudes to sex. Each partner should then conduct three of these interviews.

Discuss the different ways interviewees responded. Are the young men more honest and open with a male or female interviewer or is there no difference? Do you think that one of the interviewers obtained more valid results? If so, what reasons can you suggest for this?

Web.tasks

1 Go to the website of the opinion polling organization Market and Opinion Research International at www.mori.com

Find out how MORI go about asking questions.

2 Search the world wide web for other examples of questionnaires. Assess the strengths and weaknesses of the question design.

Key terms

Closed questions require a very specific reply, such as 'yes' or 'no'.

Coding questionnaire replies are given a number or code, making it easier for the researcher to construct statistics from them.

Indicator something easily measurable that can stand for a particular concept.

Interviewer bias the influence of the interviewer (e.g. their age, 'race', sex) on the way the respondent replies.

Open questions allow respondents to express themselves fully.

Operationalizing concepts the process of defining concepts in a way which makes them measurable.

Reliability quality achieved when all questionnaires and interviews have been completed consistently. This means that the data gathered from each can be accurately compared.

Response rate the proportion of the questionnaires returned (could also refer to the number of people who agree to be interviewed).

Structured interview where the questions are delivered in a particular order and no explanation or elaboration of the questions is allowed by the interviewer.

Transcribing the process of writing up interviews that have been recorded.

Unstructured interview where the interviewer is allowed to explain and elaborate on questions.

Validity quality achieved when questions provide an accurate measurement of the concept being investigated.

Item A

≪ From my own experience in researching white British and Caribbean people with diabetes, I would argue that there is evidence suggesting that my own Caribbean background was a distinct advantage … Rapport [a good relationship] with the Caribbeans developed fairly spontaneously … We traded stories about how we ended up in England, what part of Jamaica or the Caribbean we are from and generally how we coped with the cold weather and lack of sunshine.

… The interviews with the white British sub-sample differed significantly. Initial conversations were polite and were confined to matters relating to the interview … Generally, there was no sharing of personal details and the interviewees did not elaborate on the issues of the research in the way that the Caribbean sample had. ≫

Source: Scott, P. (1999) 'Black people's health: ethnic status and research issues' in S. Hod, B. Mayall and S. Oliver, *Critical Issues in Social Research*, Buckingham: Open University Press

Item B

≪ The first time we had this questionnaire, I thought it was a bit of a laugh. That's my memory of it. I can't remember if I answered it truthfully or not … It had a list of drugs and some of them I'd never heard of, and just the names just cracked me up. ≫

Source: Youth quoted in Parker, H., Aldrige, J. and Measham, F. (1998) *Illegal Leisure*, London: Routledge, pp. 46–7

(a) Explain what is meant by 'interviewer bias'. (2 marks)

(b) Explain the difference between structured and unstructured interviews. (4 marks)

(c) Suggest one advantage and one disadvantage of researchers establishing rapport with their interviewees (Item A). (4 marks)

(d) Using information from Item B and elsewhere, examine the usefulness of questionnaires in sociological research. (20 marks)

Grade booster Getting top marks in the 20-mark question

You could start by briefly describing the main features of questionnaires as a way of gathering data, and the main steps in conducting questionnaire research (e.g. closed questions, coding, operationalizing concepts, etc.). You need to consider a range of advantages and disadvantages. These include the problems of a low response rate, the lack of depth, not knowing if the right person has completed it, misinterpretation of questions, lying, etc. Advantages include gaining large quantities of data from widely dispersed groups, the fact that they are quick and cheap and they can be used to gather sensitive data anonymously. Remember to make use of information from Item B – for example, you could discuss the problems of respondents not understanding the questions or not taking them seriously.

TOPIC 6

Secondary sources of data

Getting you thinking

You are a sociologist in the future – 100 years from now. You have access to Facebook profiles in 2008 and want to use them to find out about people's lives in the early years of the 21st century.

1   What insights into life in 2008 could be gained from looking at Facebook profiles?

2   Suggest some ways in which these profiles could be analysed. Think of both qualitative and quantitative approaches.

3   Evaluate the validity and representativeness of Facebook profiles as sources of secondary data.

4   Discuss the usefulness of the worldwide web as a source of secondary data. Use examples to support your points.

Not all research uses primary sources – that is, observing people in real life, sending out questionnaires or carrying out interviews. Many sociologists prefer to use material collected and published by other people. This material is known as **secondary data**.

Secondary data consist of a very wide range of material collected by organizations and individuals for their own purposes, and include sources as complex as official government statistics at one extreme and as personal as diaries at the other. These data include written material, sound and visual images. Such material can be from the present day or historical data. Finally, and most commonly, secondary sources include the work of sociologists, which is read, analysed and commented on by other sociologists.

Secondary sources are invaluable to sociologists, both on their own and in combination with primary sources. It is unheard of for a researcher not to refer to some secondary sources.

Why sociologists use secondary sources

Some of the main reasons for using secondary sources include the following:

- The information required already exists as secondary data.
- Historical information is needed, but the main participants are dead or too old to be interviewed.
- The researcher is unable for financial or other reasons to visit places to collect data at first hand.
- The subject of the research concerns illegal activities and it is unsafe for the researcher to collect primary data.
- Data need to be collected about groups who are unwilling to provide accounts of their activities – for instance, extreme religious sects who do not want their activities to be open to study.

Errors and biases

Whenever sociologists use a secondary source, they must be aware that the person who first created the source did so for a specific reason, and this could well create **bias**. A diary, for example, gives a very one-sided view of what happened and one that is most likely to be sympathetic. Official statistics may have been constructed to shed a good light on the activities of the government – for example, so that they can claim they are 'winning the war against crime'. Even the work of previous sociologists may contain errors and biases.

Types of secondary data

Sociologists commonly use all these types of secondary data:

- previous sociological research
- official publications, including statistics and reports
- diaries and letters
- novels and other works of fiction
- oral history and family histories
- the media.

Previous sociological research

Previous studies as a starting point

Whenever sociologists undertake a study, the first thing they do is to carry out a **literature search** – that is, go to the library or the internet and look up every available piece of sociological research on the topic of interest. The sociologist can then see the ways in which the topic has been researched before, the conclusions reached and the theoretical issues thrown up. Armed with this information, the researcher can then construct the new research study to explore a different 'angle' on the problem or simply avoid the mistakes made earlier.

However, there are sometimes methodological errors in published research, as well as possible bias in the research findings. There have been many examples of research that has formed the basis for succeeding work and that only many years later has been found to be faulty. A famous piece of

Research methods

George Davey Smith *et al.* (2003) The health of ethnic minorities: a meta-study

George Davey Smith and his colleagues were concerned that there was relatively little information on the health of ethnic minorities in Great Britain. They therefore conducted a **meta-study** to try to provide an overall picture of health care. They looked at data from a range of surveys including official publications, small-scale surveys and earlier sociological studies. Putting all of this together, they provided a picture of standards of health for different ethnic groups in Britain, taking into account the impact of social class. In order to do this, they also had to review a wide range of theoretical and methodological books and articles. The study therefore includes secondary research based upon both theoretical and statistical studies, from government as well as academic sources.

They found that, overall, the health standards of ethnic minorities in Britain were worse than those of the general population, and that these differences were most apparent in childhood and old age. They found that most previous studies tended to explain any differences in health between ethnic minorities and the majority population in terms of cultural, dietary or genetic differences. However, they concluded that ethnicity by itself does not explain these differences. They suggest instead that differences in health are closely linked to social class and income.

Davey Smith, G., Chaturverdi, N., Harding, S., Nazroo, J. and Williams, R. (2003) *Health Inequalities: Lifecourse approaches*, Bristol: Policy Press

1 **Why did the researchers use a meta-study?**

2 **How did the use of secondary sources allow them to reach different conclusions from earlier research?**

anthropological research that was used for 40 years before it was found to be centrally flawed was Mead's *Coming of Age in Samoa* (1928). Mead made a number of mistakes in her interpretation of the behaviour of the people she was studying, but as no one knew this, many later studies used her (incorrect) findings in their work.

Reinterpreting previous studies

Often sociologists do not want to carry out a new research project, but prefer instead to examine previous research in great detail in order to find a new interpretation of the original research results. Secondary data then provides all the information that is needed.

Official publications

Statistics

Statistics compiled by governments and reputable research organizations are particularly heavily used by sociologists. These statistics often provide far greater scale and detail than a sociologist could manage. It is also much cheaper to work on statistics already collected than repeating the work.

The government will usually produce these statistics over a number of years (for example, the government statistical publication *Social Trends* has been published for 30 years), so comparisons can be made over a long period of time.

However, while these official statistics have many advantages, there are also some pitfalls that researchers have to be aware of. The statistics are collected for administrative reasons and the classifications used may omit crucial information for sociologists. For example, sociologists may be interested in exploring issues of 'race' or gender, but this information might be missing from the official statistics.

Official statistics may be affected by political considerations, such as when they are used to assist the image of the government of the day. They may also reflect a complex process of interaction and negotiation – as is the case with crime statistics – and may well need to be the focus of investigation themselves!

Reports and government inquiries

The civil service and other linked organizations will often produce official reports which investigate important problems or social issues. However, although they draw together much information on these issues, they are constrained by their 'remit', which states the limits of their investigations. The government and other powerful bodies are therefore able to exclude discussion of issues that they do not want to become the centre of public attention. Government discussions on issues related to drugs, for example, are usually carefully controlled so that legalization of drugs is simply not discussed.

Diaries and letters

It is difficult to understand a historical period or important social events if the researcher has no way of interviewing the people involved. Usually, only the official information or media accounts are available. Using such things as letters and diaries helps to provide an insight into how participants in the events felt at the time.

However, problems can occur, as the writers may have distorted views of what happened, or they may well be justifying or glorifying themselves in their accounts. Almost any politician's memoirs prove this.

Research methods

Gina Oliver (2004)
Alone in the mainstream

Gina Oliver's book combines a detailed autobiography of the experience of being deaf throughout the education system in the USA, from primary school to university, and the obstacles which are placed on deaf schoolchildren who seek to be integrated into mainstream schooling.

In order to go beyond her personal experience, Gina Oliver posted a notice on a US website for people who have hearing problems, asking them to contact her with their experiences in the education system. Oliver also wrote to a range of educational institutions and to her own university, asking them to provide publicity for her research. Oliver then asked the respondents to write an essay about their experiences:

≪ *Please write a short (or long, if you like) essay describing the reasons why you would like to be included in this research project. Feel free to share anything you would like about your experience as the only deaf or hard of hearing child in your mainstream school. Feel free to include your suggestions for children who are currently mainstreamed.* ≫

More than 100 respondents chose to respond to this essay question; many wrote quite profusely. Their essays illustrated their eagerness to share their stories and pervasive concern for today's young deaf people.

Having analysed these essays, Oliver then asked a number of people to write about four key themes which she identified, and 60 deaf adults then wrote about their experiences.

Source: Oliver, G. (2004) *Alone in the Mainstream: A Deaf Woman Remembers Public School*, Washington, DC: Gallaudet University Press

1 **Why would reading Oliver's work provide us with an unusual insight into the educational experience of deaf children?**

2 **Why might this be better than asking her and other deaf people about their experiences directly?**

3 **What weaknesses can you see in Oliver asking other deaf people to write 'essays' about their childhood experiences?**

4 **Is this work 'value free'? Justify your answer. What issues are raised by your answer?**

5 **What other ways could this research be done:**

   (a) from a quantitative approach?
   (b) from a qualitative approach?

Novels

Novels can give an insight into the attitudes and behaviour of particular groups, especially if the author is drawn from one of those groups. However, they are fiction and will exaggerate actions and values for the sake of the story. Also, writing books is typically a middle- or upper-class activity, which may limit the insight that can be gained about the particular group featured.

Oral history and family histories

The events to be studied may have taken place some considerable time ago, but there may be older people alive who can recall the events or who themselves were told about them. There may be recordings available of people (now dead) talking of their lives. People often have old cine-film or family photos of events of interest. All of these can be collected and used by the researcher to help understand past events. Of course, the best of all these methods is the interview, with the older person recalling events of long ago (although quite where the line can be drawn between this as secondary research and as a simple interview is rather unclear).

These approaches do all share the usual problems, for instance that events may be reinterpreted by older people or by families to throw a positive light on their actions and, of course, to hide any harm they did to others. Also, memories may be faulty or influenced by intervening knowledge.

The media and content analysis

A huge amount of material is available from newspapers, the internet, magazines and television. In fact, so much material is available that one of the major problems of using the mass media as secondary data lies with the selection of material: on exactly what grounds are items included or excluded? Researchers have to be very careful to include all relevant material and not to be biased in their selection in order to 'prove' their point. Two of the best-known studies using **content analysis** have been strongly criticized for just this. The Glasgow University Media Group's publications have explored a range of topics including television news,

representations of mental illness in the media and the portrayal of the 1991 Iraq war; critics claim that they were selective in their choice of material and that they applied their own interpretations to the selections.

However, trying to understand accurately the printed and broadcast media is not just a matter of watching out for bias; there is also the issue of how we interpret the material. When looking at pictures or reading a story in a magazine, different people find different meanings in the material. There are many factors influencing this, but one crucial factor is our own beliefs and attitudes towards the subject that we are reading about. The importance of this for research using secondary data is that we must not assume that what we read or see is the same as it was for the original readers or viewers.

Check your understanding

1 **What are secondary data?**

2 **Why do sociologists use secondary sources?**

3 **What are the disadvantages of using secondary sources?**

4 **What are the advantages and disadvantages of using official statistics and other government documents?**

5 **What are the advantages and disadvantages of using qualitative secondary data such as diaries?**

Activities

Research idea

Collect the prospectuses of various universities, colleges or schools. Look at the photographs in each. How do they portray their students? From your own experience of education, do you think this is an accurate portrayal? What motives might there be for the particular images presented? Are there any negative photographs or comments in the text about the educational institution?

Web.task

Find the website 'Corporate Watch' at www.corporatewatch.org.uk

Look up information about any two huge corporations (for example, Microsoft or Disney). Then go to the website belonging to that corporation. What are the differences between the information given? Which do you think is more accurate? Why?

Key terms

Bias where the material reflects a particular viewpoint to the exclusion of others. This may give a false impression of what happened. This is a particularly important problem for secondary sources.

Content analysis exploring the contents of the various media in order to find out how a particular issue is presented.

Literature search the process whereby a researcher finds as

much published material as possible on the subject of interest. Usually done through library catalogues or the internet.

Meta-study a secondary analysis using all or most of the published information on a particular topic.

Secondary data data already collected by someone else for their own purposes.

An eye on the exam — Secondary sources of data

Item A

Forest is a pressure group that supports the right of people to smoke cigarettes. It is largely supported by funding from the tobacco industry. In May 2004, it produced the results of a report, a random sample of 10,000 adults aged 18+ in eight cities. Below are the answers to one question asked and the summary by the report.

≪*Which one of the following statements is closest to your view about the way smoking should be dealt with in pubs, clubs and bars?* ≫

- Smoking should be allowed throughout all pubs, clubs and bars — 6%
- All pubs, bars and clubs should be mainly smoking with separate non-smoking areas — 19%
- All pubs, bars and clubs should be mainly non-smoking with separate areas for smoking — 49%
- Smoking should be banned completely in all pubs, bars and clubs — 24%

The replies were summarized in the report as follows:

≪Presented with four options of how smoking should be handled in pubs, clubs and bars – 74 per cent prefer to retain some smoking facility rather than banning it altogether, with 24 per cent agreeing with a complete ban on smoking. Just over two-thirds of non-smokers (67 per cent) agreed with one of the options that would retain some smoking facility, compared with 90 per cent of smokers. The proportion of non-smokers opting for a complete ban was 32 per cent compared with only 24 per cent of smokers. Of those visiting pubs frequently or often, only 19 per cent would prefer to see a ban. ≫

Source: Forest (2004) *Smoking in Public Places*

Item B

Stephen Bourne grew up in London in the 1960s and his family was regularly visited by his Aunt Esther, a black woman. Stephen Bourne thought nothing about this until he saw a television programme about black people in Britain and he also found some old family photos showing his aunt and his mother's family when they were young:

≪The point of departure for me came in 1974 when I watched … *The Black Man in Britain 1550–1950*. This documented the history of black people in Britain over 400 years …
By this time I had discovered a shoe box in Mum's wardrobe which was full of old family photographs. Several featured Aunt Esther …
Hungry for information, I was disappointed to find that, apart from the slave trade, there was no mention of black people in our school history books … However, through inter-library loans, I accessed two books then available on the subject: James Walvin's *Black and White: The Negro and English Society 1555–1945* (1973) and Folarin Shyllon's *Black People in Britain 1555–1833* (1977) …
I realized that my quest for knowledge would have to come from first-hand accounts, so I began to ask Aunt Esther questions …
[She] gave me first-hand accounts of what life was like for a working-class black Londoner throughout the century… ≫

Source: Bourne, S. (2000) 'My Aunt Esther', *History Today*, Feb, pp. 62–3

(a) Explain what is meant by 'content analysis'. (2 marks)

(b) Identify two advantages of official statistics to sociologists. (4 marks)

(c) Suggest two problems that the author of Item B might have had in interviewing Aunt Esther. (4 marks)

(d) Using information from Items A and B and elsewhere, assess the usefulness of documents in sociological research. (20 marks)

Grade booster — Getting top marks in the 20-mark question

You should look at a range of different documents. Remember to use information from both the Items. For example, from Item B, you could consider the usefulness of family photos, television programmes and history books. From Item A, you can discuss the advantages and disadvantages of using other sources' interpretations of statistical data. You can also look at the use of other sociologists' work, diaries, letters, novels, government reports (e.g. the Black Report), etc. To evaluate the usefulness of documents, you can consider issues such as their authenticity, validity and representativeness.

1 This question permits you to draw examples from **any areas** of sociology with which you are familiar.

(a) Explain what is meant by 'validity'. *(2 marks)*

Giving a true picture of something. For example, participant observation is said to give the researcher a true picture of the group being studied.

> A correct explanation of the term, so full marks.

(b) Suggest **two** advantages of laboratory experiments as a method of research. *(4 marks)*

First, they allow the researcher to control key variables and discover cause and effect relationships.

Second, supporters of the experimental method in sociology say that they give a valid picture of the things they study.

> The first advantage suggested is correct, so it scores two marks. However, the second one is incorrect and fails to score. This advantage might be true of field experiments, but not laboratory experiments. You could give 'replicability' as a second advantage of experiments.

(c) Suggest **two** problems of using questionnaires in sociological research. *(4 marks)*

1. One problem of using questionnaires in sociological research is that if they are posted out to respondents (as is usually the case), there is no way of knowing if the person who filled it in is the person who it was intended for.

2. A second problem with questionnaires is that because the researcher is not normally present when it is being filled in, they cannot be sure that the respondent has understood the questions correctly, so this may make the results invalid.

> Two good points made here. Both are very clearly explained, so full marks.

(d) Examine the usefulness of official statistics in sociological research. *(20 marks)*

Official statistics have many advantages. They are readily available because the government publishes them and they cost the sociologist nothing to use. Because the government collects them, this also saves the sociologist time as well. Also, very often, official statistics may be the only source of data available to the researcher in a particular area, for example births and deaths.

> Good start – the answer quickly identifies several relevant advantages of official statistics.

Because official statistics are usually collected on a regular basis, they also allow the sociologist to study trends over time, for example to see if birth rates are rising, or death rates declining. (Likewise, the Census is carried out every ten years.) If the statistics are changing, then the researcher can perhaps develop a hypothesis to explain the trend, and then use other statistics to test it out. For example, Durkheim did this with suicide statistics and rates.

> Good use of example of population statistics to illustrate the point about trends over time. The 'Durkheim' point is potentially a good one, but it needs developing.

Also, as official statistics are large scale (for instance total UK employment figures), so they are representative of the whole society and we can use them to make generalizations about society. Sometimes they might be the only source of information on a particular subject.

> Useful point about generalization. However, the point about statistics being the only source of data is needless repetition.

Official statistics can also be useful as background information on a given topic as a starting point before going on to research it in other ways. For example, the statistics might show that a particular ethnic group has a higher rate of truancy from school than other groups. The sociologist could then go on to do a small-scale study on a sample of that group to explore why this pattern was happening, for instance by using in-depth interviews. (This is known as triangulation, where two methods are used together with one another.)

> Good idea to show how official statistics can complement other methods, and effective use of truancy as an example.

As official statistics are collected by professional people, they are also likely to be reliable. Reliability means being able to get the same results when the method is repeated, for example by a different researcher. The high degree of reliability of official statistics is one important reason why they are often favoured by positivist sociologists.

> An interesting point, but too brief. Why is reliability important to positivists? It needs linking up with the earlier points about Durkheim/suicide, hypotheses and generalization.

However, on the other hand, interpretivist sociologists (such as interactionists) do not trust official statistics. For example, they have often been collected for a different purpose than the one that the sociologists want to use them for, and this will influence how they were collected, when and for who. For example, the government might choose to collect unemployment statistics in a particular way so as to make themselves look good, for instance by keeping the figures low.

Also, if the police decide not to record a crime that someone has reported to them, then it won't enter into the official crime statistics, even though it actually occurred. Also, if the police can get a criminal to confess to a lot of crimes that he didn't actually commit, then this will improve their clear-up rate and will make them look more efficient.

Therefore, although official statistics have their uses, they suffer from many drawbacks and disadvantages. In the end, it all depends on the perspective of the sociologist. Positivists see them as reliable, whereas interpretivists see them as biased.

This doesn't link the points about interpretivists and about the government very well. It needs a clear explanation of why interpretivists don't like official statistics. It would be better to link the point about unemployment to Marxism instead of interpretivism.

Suitable examples, but they need explaining sociologically, e.g. by linking to interpretivism or the concept of validity.

Tries to tie it up – but does it really 'all' depend on perspective? If so, the point should have been made near the beginning of the answer.

An examiner comments

This answer needs more careful planning – the point in the last paragraph should have been introduced much earlier if it's as important as is claimed. It could have then linked up to the paragraphs on positivism and interpretivism. It would also be a good idea to spell out what these perspectives are and then explain why they take their particular views of official statistics. This should also include the idea that they are criticized for lack of validity. You can also bring in the Marxist view of official statistics as ideology. You should also avoid sweeping conclusions that are not supported by what you have already written. In this case, the conclusion claims that it 'all' depends on perspective – yet much of the answer claims it is also to do with practical advantages and disadvantages.

One for you to try

This question permits you to draw examples from **any areas** of sociology with which you are familiar.

(e) Examine the usefulness of different types of interview to sociologists.   *(20 marks)*

An examiner comments

You need to consider both structured and unstructured interviews in your answer. Link these to the different types of question (e.g. open and closed). You need to look at a range of advantages and disadvantages, e.g. practical factors (such as time, cost, how many can be studied, training of interviewers, etc.) as well as issues such as validity, reliability, representativeness and generalization. You should illustrate your answer by using examples from studies that have used these methods.

Answers to the 'One for you to try' are available **free** on **www.collinseducation.com/sociologyweb**

Types of quantitative method

- Case studies
- Comparative research
- Experiments
- Surveys
  - Cross-sectional
  - Longitudinal

Why use?

- Allows use of statistical test
- Less bias
- Good overview of society

Problems of quantitative methods

- Fails to get 'lived experience'
- Validity
- Reliability

Ways of asking questions

- Interviews
- Questionnaires

Types of observational method

- Participant
- Non-participant — *Covert or overt?*

Why use?

- Useful for illegal or deviant activities
- Gives real insight

Problems of qualitative methods

- Bias
- Generalizability
- Reliability
- Influence on group being studied

Quantitative methods

Qualitative methods

What does sociological research do?

Sociological research methods

Mixed methods or triangulation

Sociologists often use two or more approaches

Gathers data

- Primary
- Secondary

Makes correlations

Suggests/confirms correlations

Secondary data

Theoretical and ethical issues

Why use?

- Allows historical research
- Good where 'primary methods' (surveys, participant observation, etc.) not possible

Problems of secondary data

- Inaccuracy or bias in original source
- Censorship

Types of secondary data

- Previous research
- Official publications
- Diaries and letters
- Novels and fiction
- Oral and family history
- The media

How theoretical issues influence research

- Suggest one research topic rather than another
- Influence research method chosen
- Influence interpretation of research findings

How ethical issues influence research

- Influence choice of research topic
- Ask researcher to consider the effects of the research
- Influence who is chosen to be researched
- Raise issue of whether researcher may act immorally or illegally during research

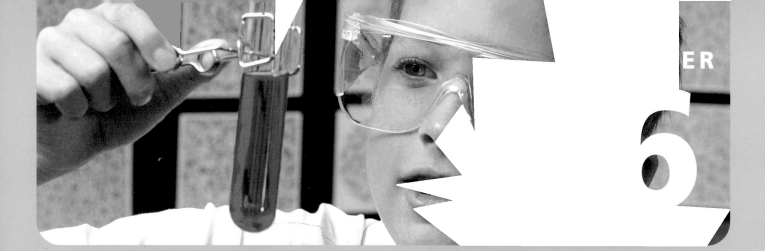

Education

AQA Specification	Topics	Pages
Candidates should examine:		
The role and purpose of education, including vocational education and training, in contemporary society.	Topic 1 covers the key theoretical perspectives on the role of education. Topic 6 discusses vocational education in detail.	202–7 235–41
Differential educational achievement of social groups by social class, gender and ethnicity in contemporary society.	These are covered at length in Topics 2, 3 and 4.	208–27
Relationships and processes within schools, with particular reference to teacher/pupil relationships, pupil subcultures, the hidden curriculum, and the organization of teaching and learning.	Topic 5	228–34
The significance of educational policies, including selection, comprehensivization and marketization, for an understanding of the structure, role, impact and experience of education.	Topic 6	235–41
The application of sociological research methods to the study of education.	All topics	202–41

Getting you thinking

1   Look at the photographs above. Using these and any other ideas you may have, make a list of the purposes of school for:

    (a) individuals   (b) society as a whole.

2   Is there anything that occurs in schools that you feel has no purpose? If so, what?

3   What have you really learned at school/college this week? Who will gain from your acquiring this knowledge, set of attitudes or skills?

4   Could you learn effectively without school?

5   Would society suffer if schools did not exist? Explain your answer.

The education system is one of the most influential institutions in society. It takes individuals from the age of 4 or 5, for six or so hours per day, over a period of at least 11 years. It bombards them with a vast amount of knowledge, attitudes and skills. These are acquired either formally through set lessons or informally through what is known as the **hidden curriculum** – the processes involved in being 'schooled' and the various interactions that take place while in school. By the time they finish compulsory education, most pupils will have spent over 15 000 hours in lessons.

Compulsory education for all

This has not always been the situation for all children. While those of the upper and middle classes have always had the option of private schooling, and relatively few members of the working class did receive mainly religious instruction in church schools, **state education** for all has only been available in Britain since 1880, when it was made compulsory for children up to the age of 10.

Forster's 1870 Education Act declared that school boards could be set up in districts where school places were inadequate. Between 1870 and 1880, about 4000 schools were started or taken over by boards. The school boards were replaced with around 300 Local Education Authorities in 1902, by which time about 20 000 board and voluntary schools served 5.6 million pupils. The Fisher Education Act of 1918 made the state responsible for **secondary education**, and attendance was made compulsory up to the age of 14. The school-leaving age was raised to 15 in 1947, and to 16 in 1972. Currently, over 10 million 5 to 16 year olds attend school in the UK.

A number of factors have been cited which together are said to account for this educational revolution. The driving force behind much educational reform since 1870 has been a perceived need for Britain to remain competitive in the world by being at the forefront of manufacture and improvement. In 1870, this dominance was being challenged by other industrialized nations such as Germany. (In 1870, only 1 in 10 British children was attending school compared with 1 in 6 German children.) The earlier introduction of state education there and elsewhere was seen as partly responsible for the weakening position of Britain as a world power.

There was initial hostility from some towards the idea of mass education, because it was feared it would make labouring classes 'think', perhaps seeing their lives as dissatisfying, possibly encouraging them to revolt. This was challenged by others who felt it could have a civilizing role and would better serve the interests of the powerful in society as an agency of **ideological control**. There were also powerful **liberal** lobbyists in favour of education for all, who campaigned for the poor, seeing education as a way out of poverty and a basic human right. These sometimes contradictory positions have continued to resurface throughout the history of state education.

Since the 1960s, post-compulsory education to age 18 in school sixth forms and further education colleges has expanded dramatically, as has higher education (see Topic 6). By 2002/3, UK government expenditure on education was £53 billion, 13.5 per cent of total government spending (*Annual Abstract of Statistics* 2005).

So why do modern societies invest so much in **schooling** the next generation? Sociologists are divided in their views about this. Most agree that education is important, both in teaching skills and in encouraging certain attitudes and values, but they disagree about why this occurs and who benefits from it.

Functionalist approach

Functionalists argue that education has three broad functions:

1 *Socialization* – Education helps to maintain society by socializing young people into key cultural values, such as achievement, competition, **equality of opportunity**, social solidarity, democracy and religious morality. Durkheim was particularly concerned that education should emphasize the moral responsibilities that members of society had towards each other and the wider society. In his view, the increasing tendency towards **individualism** in modern society could lead to too little social solidarity and possibly anomie (a state of normlessness or lack of shared norms). This emphasis can be seen today through the introduction of Citizenship and the maintenance of religious education as compulsory subjects, as well as incorporating the *Every Child Matters* agenda into tutorial work (see below). Parsons also recognized the social significance of education. He suggested that it forms a bridge between the family and the wider society by socializing children to adapt to a **meritocratic** view of achievement. In the family, **particularistic standards** apply – a child's social status is accorded by its parents and other family members. However, in wider society, **universalistic standards** apply – the individual is judged by criteria that apply to all of society's members. Education helps ease this transition and instil the major value of achievement through merit.
2 *Skills provision* – Education teaches the skills required by a modern industrial society. These may be general skills that everyone needs, such as literacy and numeracy, or the specific skills needed for particular occupations. As the division of labour increases in complexity and occupational roles become more specialized, increasingly longer periods in education become necessary.

> ### Every Child Matters
>
> In November 2004, the DfES released *Every Child Matters: Change for Children*, setting out the national framework for local change programmes led by local authorities and their partners. Schools were required to work with other agencies to ensure that children would have the support that they need to:
>
> - be healthy
> - stay safe
> - enjoy and achieve
> - make a positive contribution
> - achieve economic wellbeing.

3 *Role allocation* – Education allocates people to the most appropriate job for their talents, using examinations and qualifications. This ensures that the most talented are allocated to the occupations that are the most functionally important for society. This is seen to be fair because there is equality of opportunity – everyone has the chance to achieve success in society on the basis of their ability. Critics consider the ideas of equality of opportunity and meritocracy to be a **myth** and question the correspondence between occupational status and talent.

Functionalists are criticized for failing to recognize the diversity of values in modern society and the extent to which the main beliefs of some groups, notably the powerful, are promoted through the education system.

Marxist approach

For Marx, education is seen as an important part of the superstructure of society. Along with other institutions (e.g. the mass media, family, religion and the legal system), it serves the needs of the economic base, which contains everything to do with production in society (bosses, workers, factories, land and raw materials). This base shapes the superstructure, while the superstructure maintains and justifies the base (see Fig. 6.1).

For Marx then, education performs two main functions in capitalist society:

1 It reproduces the inequalities and social relations of production of capitalist society.
2 It serves to legitimate (justify) these inequalities through the myth of meritocracy.

The neo-Marxist Althusser (1971) also disagrees that the main function of education is the transmission of common values. He argues that education is, rather, an ideological state apparatus (ISA). Its main function is to maintain, legitimate and reproduce, generation by generation, class inequalities in wealth and power, by transmitting ruling-class or capitalist values disguised as common values. Along with other ISAs, such as the media and the legal system, education reproduces the conditions needed for capitalism to flourish without having to use force, which would expose it as oppressive. Instead, **ideology** gets the same results exerting its influence subconsciously. Althusser argues that this is done through the hidden curriculum: the way that schools are organized and the way that knowledge is taught means that working-class people are encouraged to conform to the capitalist system, and accept failure and inequality uncritically.

Bourdieu (1977) has called the means by which the working classes are effectively duped into accepting their failure and limited social mobility as justified, 'symbolic violence'. Their cultural attributes are rejected because the system is defined by, and for, the middle classes who, in turn, succeed by default rather than greater ability. Their cultural assets are seen as worthy of investment and reward and hence have greater value as **cultural capital**. This is discussed more fully in the next topic.

Correspondence theory

Bowles and Gintis (1976) argue that education serves to reproduce directly the **capitalist relations of production** – the hierarchy of workers from the boss down – with the appropriate skills and attitudes. Education ensures that workers will unquestioningly adapt to the needs of the system. Bowles and Gintis's '**correspondence theory**' suggests that what goes on in school corresponds directly to the world of work. Teachers are like the bosses, and pupils are like the workers, who work for rewards (wages or exam success). The higher up the system the individual progresses, however, the more personal freedom they have to control their own educational or working experiences, and the more responsibility they have for the outcomes.

Bowles and Gintis point out, however, that success is not entirely related to intellectual ability. Those pupils who fit in and conform, rise above those who express attitudes or display behaviour which challenge the system. Bowles and Gintis go as far as to say that this is irrespective of ability, some of the most creative and talented being among the latter group. Schools, therefore, reproduce sets of workers with the appropriate ways of being for the position that they come to occupy. This explains why White middle-class pupils tend to do better whatever their ability. The education system disguises this injustice through the myth of meritocracy, whereby those denied success blame themselves rather than the system. The hidden curriculum of the school not only reproduces the relations of production, it makes inequality in society appear legitimate and fair.

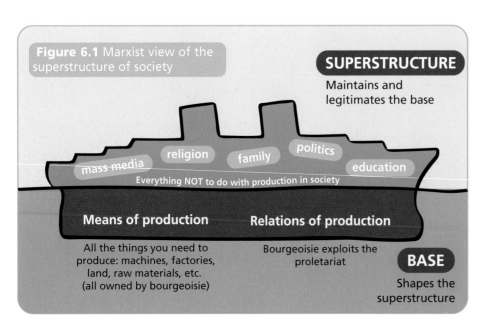

Figure 6.1 Marxist view of the superstructure of society

SUPERSTRUCTURE
Maintains and legitimates the base

mass media   religion   family   politics   education

Everything NOT to do with production in society

Means of production
All the things you need to produce: machines, factories, land, raw materials, etc. (all owned by bourgeoisie)

Relations of production
Bourgeoisie exploits the proletariat

BASE
Shapes the superstructure

Criticisms of Bowles and Gintis

Many writers have criticized Bowles and Gintis for their failure to recognize a lack of correspondence between schools and the needs of the economy, in particular in terms of the content of the formal curriculum. Reynolds (1984) claims that the curriculum does not seem designed to teach either the skills needed by employers or uncritical passive behaviour that makes workers easy to exploit. He points out that the survival of liberal humanities-based subjects and limited emphasis on science and applied knowledge suggest a lack of correspondence. How, for example, can Sociology itself be such a popular A-level subject if schools and colleges are all about developing unthinking workers?

Employers are highly critical of the low level of employability skills possessed not only by school leavers, but even graduates. Brown (1997) points out that modern businesses require shared creativity and teamwork. However, the exam system in which people are judged and compete with one another as individuals discourages the development of these skills.

Furthermore, numerous studies show that many pupils have little regard for the rules of the school, and little respect for the authority of the teacher. Paul Willis's research *Learning to Labour* (1977) showed that working-class 'lads' learned to behave at school in ways quite at odds with capitalism's supposed need for a docile workforce. Willis, however, supported the principle that schools reproduce the relations of production by demonstrating that the boys in the antischool subculture he observed, shared a similar outlook to the workers in the factories they were likely to end up in. They accepted the inevitability of educational failure and so developed strategies ('having a laff') to deal with the boredom of school which would also serve them well in the boring jobs they were destined for.

While the work of Bowles and Gintis has been criticized for failing to live up to its claims of direct correspondence on a number of levels, recent developments are causing some writers to revisit their work. For example, local authorities have lost some of their power over education because they no longer run colleges. At the same time, the freedom of teachers has been restricted by the introduction of a national curriculum, and education has become more explicitly designed to meet the needs of employers – not only in curriculum terms, with the introduction of more vocational education such as GNVQ, BTECs and the new Diplomas (formerly Specialist diplomas), but also through the influence of the work-oriented ethos characteristic of many **specialist schools** and City academies. Employers also have more direct say in the organization and curriculum of such schools. This is more fully discussed in Topic 6.

Research methods

The British Cohort Study – evidence on education and social mobility

The British Cohort Study is a longitudinal piece of research which takes as its subjects all those living in England, Scotland and Wales who were born in one particular week in April 1970. Data were collected about the births and families of just under 17 200 babies; since then, there have been five more attempts to gather information from this group. With each successive 'sweep', the scope of enquiry has broadened and it now covers physical, educational, social and economic development.

Data have been collected in a variety of ways. In the 1986 research, 16 separate methods were used, including parental questionnaires, school-class and head-teacher questionnaires and medical examinations. The sample completed questionnaires, kept two diaries and undertook some educational assessments. In both 1975 and 1980, immigrants to Britain who were born in the target week in 1970 were added to the sample. Over the period of the research, the sample has reduced to 15 500.

Jo Blanden, Paul Gregg and Steve Machin have used data from The British Cohort Study to compare the life chances of British children with those in other advanced countries, and the results are disturbing. In a comparison of eight European and North American countries, Britain and the United States have the lowest social mobility (movement between classes). Social mobility in Britain has declined, whereas in the USA it is stable. Part of the reason for Britain's decline has been that the better off have benefited disproportionately from increased educational opportunity

Comparing surveys of children born in the 1950s and the 1970s, the researchers went on to examine the reason for Britain's low, and declining, mobility. They found that it is partly due to the strong and increasing relationship between family income and educational attainment.

For these children, additional opportunities to stay in education at age 16 and age 18 disproportionately benefited those from better-off backgrounds. For a more recent group born in the early 1980s, the gap between those staying on in education at age 16 narrowed, but inequality of access to higher education has widened further: while the proportion of people from the poorest fifth of families obtaining a degree has increased from 6 per cent to 9 per cent, the graduation rates for the richest fifth have risen from 20 to 47 per cent.

Sources: Blanden, *et al.* (2005);
The Centre for Longitudinal Studies (www.cls.ioe.ac.uk)

1 Explain how the British Cohort Study is a longitudinal piece of research.

2 Suggest reasons why the sample size was increased in 1975 and 1980.

3 What reasons might there be for the reduction in sample size over the period of the study?

4 What does this research by Blanden *et al.* tell us about the functionalist view that education allocates roles efficiently in modern societies?

Key terms

Capitalist relations of production how members of the workforce are organized in relation to each other under capitalism. (In capitalist industrial societies, this is usually hierarchical, with a few at the top making all the decisions and giving out orders, while the majority do what they are told.)

Correspondence theory Bowles and Gintis's theory that various aspects of economic production (work) have corresponding features in the education system.

Cultural capital cultural skills, such as knowing how to behave, speak and learn, passed on by middle-class parents to their children.

Equality of opportunity every person having the same chances.

Hidden curriculum the informal learning of particular values and attitudes in schools.

Ideology a set of interconnected ideas that serve the interests of a particular group.

Ideological control getting people to behave in a desired way by convincing them that it is in their interests to behave in that way.

Individualism the belief that individuals are far more important than social groups.

Liberals open-minded people who believe in personal freedom, democracy (the involvement of everyone in decision-making) and the rights of others.

Meritocracy system where people are rewarded on the basis of ability and talent.

Myth of meritocracy the view that it is not true that the education system rewards pupils on the basis of merit, i.e. intelligence and ability, usually via examinations and qualifications.

Particularistic standards judgements based on the exclusive views of a particular group.

Schooling the process of compulsory education.

Secondary education education between the ages of 11 and 16.

Specialist schools schools that have a particular focus within their curriculum and links to specialist areas of work, e.g. arts and media, business, languages, healthcare and medicine. They can select 10 per cent of their intake on the basis of ability.

State education education provided by local and central governments.

Universalistic standards judgements based upon universally agreed principles.

Check your understanding

1. Which act recommended the introduction of compulsory state education?

2. Why do you think it took ten years before it became law?

3. Give three of the main reasons why education was made compulsory in 1880.

4. According to functionalists, what are the main functions of schools?

5. What does Althusser consider to be the main purpose of education, and how is it achieved?

6. Why do you think the theory of Bowles and Gintis is sometimes called 'correspondence' theory? Give examples.

7. Why, according to Bowles and Gintis, do White, middle-class pupils do better?

8. How does Willis's work appear to support the views of Bowles and Gintis?

9. Give three reasons why what goes on in schools would appear to contradict the correspondence with the world of work that Bowles and Gintis claim.

10. In what ways might it be said that Bowles and Gintis's theory now has more relevance?

Activities

Research ideas

1. Interview a range of your teachers. Ask them to explain the values which they consider are encouraged by the following aspects of school organization and routine: assemblies, speech days, sports days, school uniform, registration, house competitions, school rules, prefects, detention.

   Evaluate the extent to which their responses subscribe to functionalist, Marxist or liberal views of education.

2. Organize a small research project to discover what people consider to be the primary purpose of education. Compare class, gender and age patterns in terms of the extent to which the wider social purposes are recognized. Which groups see school as most individually beneficial – for example, as helping someone to get a better job?

Web.task

Search for government educational policy documents and statements at www.dfes.gov.uk. What are the government's stated aims? How do these aims relate to the sociological views you have been introduced to in this chapter?

Item A

If Britain is ever to achieve economic prosperity again, schools should encourage competition, discipline, decency, self-reliance and eventually prosperity through a return to hard work, selection, higher standards and biblical morality. The classroom should be a place where results are expected; a place where the teacher gets it across that our second best is not good enough; a place where the shortcomings of even the worst homes are to some extent rectified and not used as a constant excuse for inaction. Schools should get a hard grip on the surly and uncooperative. They must support the hardworking, the inventive and the original. This means selection. We must toughen up the educational process so that everything else – learning, creativity, technical skills, wealth-creating potential – can flourish properly. Children must learn biblical stories such as the Good Samaritan because the stories will speak for themselves.

Adapted from a speech made in 1984 by Tom Howarth, Senior Tutor, Cambridge University, quoted in R. Burgess (ed.) (1986) *Education, Schools and Schooling*, Walton-on-Thames: Thomas Nelson

Item B

Extract 1

<< The space won from the school and its rules by the 'lads' is used for the shaping and development of particular cultural skills devoted to 'having a laff'. The 'laff' is of particular importance to the 'lads'. It is used in many contexts – to defeat boredom and fear, to overcome hardship and problems – as a way out of almost anything. Specific themes of authority are explored and used in their humour. When a teacher comes into the classroom he is told 'It's alright, Sir, the deputy's taking us, you can go. He said you can have the period off.' The 'lads' stop younger pupils around the school and say 'Mr Argyle wants to see you.' Argyle's room is soon choked with worried kids.>>

Extract 2

<< **Joey:** On a Monday afternoon, we'd have nothing right? Nothing hardly relating to schoolwork, Tuesday afternoon we have swimming and they stick you in a classroom for the rest of the afternoon, Wednesday afternoon you have games and there's only Thursday and Friday afternoon that you work, if you call that work. The last lesson Friday afternoon we used to go and doss…

Spanksy: Skive this lesson, just go up on the bank, have a smoke, and the next lesson go to a teacher who you know will call the register…

Eddie: I ain't supposed to be in school this afternoon, I'm supposed to be at college on a link course.

Fuzz: Last time [I did any writing] was in careers, 'cos I writ 'yes' on a piece of paper, that broke me heart 'cos I was going to try and go through the term without writing anything.>>

Source: Willis, P. (1977) *Learning to Labour*, Aldershot: Ashgate

(a) Explain what is meant by the statement that education is an 'ideological state apparatus'. (2 marks)

(b) Suggest three ways in which the lads' attitudes to school might prepare them for unskilled rather than skilled work (Item B). (6 marks)

(c) Using information from Item A and elsewhere, outline some of the ways in which the education system performs functions for both individuals and society. (12 marks)

(d) Using information from Items A and B and elsewhere, assess the view that the education system serves to maintain capitalist society. (20 marks)

Grade booster Getting top marks in the 20-mark question

You need to identify the view in the question as a Marxist one and consider a range of ways in which education may maintain capitalism. You should examine how it both legitimates and reproduces capitalist relations of production and ensures that working-class pupils end up in working-class jobs. Give an account of different Marxist approaches such as Althusser, Bowles and Gintis, and Paul Willis. You need to make use of material from the Items, e.g. how 'having a laff' (Item B) prepares the lads to cope with manual work. You can evaluate the view from a functionalist perspective, e.g. via the idea that all pupils have equal opportunity to achieve.

Class and educational achievement

Getting you thinking

- Smaller percentages of children in Sure Start (more deprived) areas achieved a 'good' level of development by the end of the 'foundation' stage in school (3 to 5 year olds) than in non-Sure Start (less deprived) areas (DfES 2006).

- Analysis of 2006 Key Stage 2 results – for 11 year olds achieving Level 4 – reveal an attainment gap of 22 percentage points in children receiving free school meals compared to those not doing so.

- 38.5 per cent of children from the quarter of UK districts with the lowest incomes achieve five or more GCSE passes at Grade C or above; 72.5 per cent of children from the quarter of UK districts with the highest incomes achieve five or more GCSE passes at Grade C or above.

- More than half of young people who were NEET (not in education employment or training) or in jobs without training were from routine or manual backgrounds compared with only around 18 per cent who were from higher professional backgrounds (DfES 2006).

In addition, children from working-class backgrounds:

- are less likely to be found in nursery schools or pre-school playgroups
- are more likely to start school unable to read
- are more likely to fall behind in reading, writing and number skills
- are more likely to suffer from ill health, which can affect their attendance and performance at school
- are more likely to be placed in lower sets or streams
- are more likely to leave school at the age of 16
- are less likely to go on to sixth form and university.

1 **Make a list of possible explanations for the points in the list on the right. Use the photographs above to help you.**

2 **Compare your list with those of others. Rank the explanations you have identified in order, with the most important first.**

3 **Explain why you have ranked some explanations higher than others.**

It seems obvious: our educational success or failure is simply the result of our ability and motivation. When sociologists look at educational achievement, however, they find that there are distinct patterns. It seems that ability and motivation are closely linked to membership of certain social groups.

Class: patterns of achievement

Differential educational attainment refers to the tendency for some groups to do better or worse than others in terms of educational success. The issue was initially considered by sociologists solely in terms of class, as they attempted to explain the huge class differences that existed between schools within the **tripartite system** (see Topic 6, p. 236). Differences between boys and girls and between different ethnic groups are a more recent focus, which will be explored in later topics.

Much of the government's focus over the last decade has been about raising the standards of teaching and learning in schools, and many reports suggest that school quality does have an impact on achievement across all social classes. Such research, however, needs to be put into context. According to DfES research (2004):

- The effectiveness of teaching only contributes to an 8 per cent difference in achievement.
- However, the proportion of pupils receiving free school meals has a 19 per cent impact, whereas the most significant impact is made by the SATs scores on entry to secondary school, at 73 per cent impact.

A recent large-scale study of over a million secondary-school pupils by Butler and Hamnetta (2007) has shown that a school's performance directly corresponds to the number of middle-class pupils that attend it, as evidenced by their postcode.

Explanations of class differences in educational attainment

Differential educational attainment has been explained in a number of ways:

- **material deprivation**
- **cultural disadvantages**
- cultural capital.

Material deprivation

Certain groups have less money than others and so are not able to make the most of their educational opportunities. For example, in a study of the effects of poverty on schooling, Smith and Noble (1995) list the 'barriers to learning' which can result from low income. These include the following:

- If families are unable to afford school uniforms, school trips, transport to and from school, classroom materials and, in some cases, school textbooks, this can lead to children being isolated, bullied and stigmatized. As a result, they may fall behind in their school work.
- Low income reduces the likelihood of a computer with internet access, a desk, educational toys, books, space to do homework and a comfortable well-heated home.
- The marketization of schools means that there will be better-resourced, oversubscribed schools in more affluent areas, while socially disadvantaged children are concentrated in a limited number of increasingly unpopular schools.

Furthermore, older working-class children are more likely to have to work part time to support their studies, or to have to care for younger siblings if informal childcare networks break down, affecting their attendance at school, whereas middle-class parents can more easily afford to pay for childcare.

Material deprivation has been shown to impact upon the selection of a higher-education institution, whereby choice can be severely limited by low income. According to Reay *et al.* (2005), many working-class students intended to apply for the nearest university, not for reasons of educational quality, but because they felt they could not afford the costs of travel and/or accommodation away from home. Only 32 per cent of the working-class students in the study were considering moving out of the family home to attend university, compared to over 70 per cent of the middle-class students.

Once at university, students from poorer backgrounds suffer material disadvantages that affect their capacity to study. A survey was conducted to examine the effect of term-time working on academic attainment (Universities UK 2005). The survey found that students from the poorest homes were most likely to be working and to be working the longest hours. As a result, they often missed lectures, handed in work late and produced poor-quality assignments.

Governments have attempted to reduce the material disadvantages faced by working-class pupils through **positive discrimination**. This takes the form of programmes of **compensatory education** that plough more resources into poorer areas. The Conservative government in the 1990s allocated up to 25 per cent more money to local authorities in poor areas, and the introduction of Educational Action Zones by the Labour government in the late 1990s was also an attempt to raise standards by compensating for deprivation. Schools in deprived areas were given extra funding and allowed more independence than other state schools. One of the most recent initiatives, Excellence in Cities, aims to improve the education of children in the inner cities by providing a number of measures, including:

- better resourcing schools to enable them to specialize in particular vocational areas
- providing learning mentors to reduce the number of pupils excluded
- special provision for those in danger of being excluded
- other resources to encourage gifted and talented pupils to stay in education post-16 and aspire to higher education, especially those from families who had not themselves been to university.

The expansion of **Educational Maintenance Allowances** (EMA) for post-16 students is another compensatory scheme that has two main aims:

1 to offset the need for older students to work part time, often for long hours, to support their studies
2 to support parents by removing the need for them to pay for their child's travel, equipment and food costs while they remain in schooling.

Many proponents of New Right thinking are highly sceptical about the value of compensatory education, seeing it as an initiative of the 'nanny state'. Underclass theorists such as Marsland (1996) and Murray (1994) have long argued that the unstable family life, inferior socialization and lack of discipline experienced by the poor, result in increased levels of crime, educational underachievement, and higher levels of single parenthood. The journalist Melanie Phillips, in her critique of the comprehensive system, *All Must Have Prizes* (1997), further argues that working-class educational underachievement arises as a result of teachers being too willing to blame poverty for underachievement, when the real reason is poor teaching and parenting. Phillips and Murray (2001) further argue that the increase in children's rights introduced by liberal social policy makers, has led to parents taking less responsibility for the parenting process and pupils taking less responsibility for themselves, further undermining educational achievement.

Cultural disadvantages

The education system is mostly controlled by middle-class people, many of whom are White. Those who share these characteristics may well be viewed more positively and be more likely to succeed in the tests and exams created to assess their abilities. The 11+ test (see Topic 6) was criticized for middle-class bias. Being able to unscramble an anagram (a jumbled-up word) such as 'ZOMRAT' to form the name of a famous composer (MOZART) is much easier for a child familiar with anagrams (because their parents do crosswords) and classical composers (because they have seen their names on CD covers in their parents' music collection).

Much (now dated) research into language has identified class differences in spoken and written language which disadvantage working-class children. The middle classes succeed not because of greater intelligence but merely because they use the preferred way of communicating.

Cultural capital

The idea of cultural capital (see Topic 1, p. 204) is used by Marxists to explain cultural influences on educational success. Bourdieu and Passeron (1977) suggested that middle-class culture (cultural capital) is as valuable in educational terms as material wealth (economic capital). Schools are middle-class institutions run by the middle class. The forms of knowledge, values, ways of interacting and communicating ideas that middle-class children possess are developed further and rewarded by the education system. Working-class and ethnic-minority children may lack these qualities and so do not have the same chances to succeed. Bourdieu's theory of cultural

Research methods

Alice Sullivan (2001)
A test of Bourdieu's theory of cultural capital

Although many sociologists have used Bourdieu's concept of cultural capital to understand and explain inequality of educational achievement, there have been few attempts to test Bourdieu's theory directly. One such attempt is provided in a study by Alice Sullivan (2001). In 1998, Sullivan carried out survey research on children approaching school-leaving age in four schools in England and received questionnaire data from a total of 465 pupils. The occupation of the parent in the highest-status job was used to determine the class of the children, and parents' educational qualifications were used to measure their cultural capital. A number of measures of pupils' cultural capital were used. Pupils were asked about the books they read, the television programmes they watched, the music they listened to, whether they played a musical instrument, and attendance at art galleries, theatres and concerts; they were also tested on their knowledge of cultural figures and on their vocabulary.

The research then examined which of these factors affected educational performance in GCSEs. Sullivan found that pupils were more likely to be successful if they read more complex fiction and watched TV programmes such as arts, science and current affairs documentaries and

more sophisticated drama. Watching programmes such as soap operas and game shows did not improve GCSE performance. Attendance at cultural events and involvement in music had no significant effect, suggesting that these should not be considered important aspects of cultural capital. Pupils who read widely and watched sophisticated television developed wider vocabularies and greater knowledge of cultural figures, and this was reflected in exam performance. Sullivan found that pupils' cultural capital was strongly correlated with parental cultural capital (i.e. their educational qualifications), which in turn was closely linked to their social class. Graduate parents in higher professions had children with the most cultural capital and who were most successful in exams.

Adapted from Haralambos, M. and Holborn, M. (2008) *Sociology: Themes and Perspectives* (7th edn), London: Collins Educational

1 **How was the concept of social class operationalized in Sullivan's research?**

2 **What indicators were used to measure cultural capital?**

3 **Which cultural factors correlated with educational performance? Suggest reasons why this might be the case.**

capital was tested in research by Alice Sullivan. Her research is discussed on p. 210 (see Research methods).

Ball *et al*. (1994) showed how middle-class parents are able to use their cultural capital to play the system so as to ensure that their children are accepted into the schools of their choice. The strategies they use include attempting to make an impression with the headteacher on open day, and knowing how to mount an appeal if their child is unsuccessful in their application to a particular school. West and Hind (2003) found that interviews were also often used to exclude certain types of families, particularly working-class and poor families, whereas middle-class parents often had the cultural capital to negotiate such interviews successfully. The government banned such interviews in 2005.

In *Education and the Middle Class* (2003), Power *et al*. note that, once middle-class parents had secured a place in the school of their choice, 'travelling time, homework and the schools' perceived exclusiveness made it difficult for children to maintain an "external" social life, thus focusing peer-group activity within the school territories and in the company of academically able and often ambitious students like themselves'. They conclude that an important aspect of cultural capital is the pursuit of 'conspicuous academic achievement' by both middle-class parents and children.

The influence of the school: interactionist explanations

Interactionist explanations of differential educational achievement – based on 'labelling theory' (see Chapter 1, p. 22) – look at what goes on in schools themselves, and, in particular, teacher–pupil relationships. Labelling theories suggest that teachers judge pupils not by their ability or intelligence, but by characteristics that relate to class, gender and ethnicity, such as attitude, appearance and behaviour. Becker (1971) showed how teachers perceive the 'ideal pupil' to be one who conforms to middle-class standards of behaviour. Middle-class teachers

are more likely to perceive middle-class behaviour as evidence of commitment to study, and working-class cultural demeanour as evidence of indiscipline, lower ability or motivation. They may hold different expectations of eventual achievement, which in turn can affect pupils' progress according to the ways in which they are labelled and sorted into ability groups. In other words, a **self-fulfilling prophecy** can be seen to occur, whereby teachers' expectations are translated into actual outcomes. Labelling and the self-fulfilling prophecy concentrate on effects on the individual. Ball (1981) in his study of 'Beachside Comprehensive' argued that the same effects can be observed in whole groups. Pupils at this school were put into three 'bands' on the basis of information about their ability given by primary schools: band 1 mostly contained pupils from non-manual backgrounds; those in band 2 were socially mixed; while those in band 3 were mostly from manual backgrounds.

Ball argues that all students entered the school eager to learn but due to the effects of teacher attitudes and expectations, band 1 'warmed to education' and did well in school, whereas bands 2 and 3 'cooled down' and underachieved.

The impact of banding or streaming (being placed in a particular ability group for all lessons) and setting (being placed by ability for some lessons), is more fully discussed in Topic 5.

The interactionist perspective has the advantage of focusing directly on small-scale interaction situations in schools and colleges. In doing so, it provides detailed evidence of what actually happens within educational institutions. However, critics contend that this focus can lead researchers to ignore the wider society, which clearly plays a major role in relation to class differences in attainment. Although they are no longer fashionable and seen as rather dated, these theories had a major impact on the development of both the comprehensive system and the idea of 'progressive' education (see Topic 6).

The curriculum

Some sociologists have argued that what is taught in schools – the curriculum – actually disadvantages the working class. The knowledge that they encounter at school does not connect with their own cultural experience. Working-class experience is almost invisible in the school curriculum. History, for example, tends to deal with the ruling classes – such as kings, queens and politicians – rather than with the vast majority of ordinary people. The study of Shakespeare is still a compulsory component of English GCSE specifications.

We have seen how the cultural bias of the hidden curriculum favours the middle classes. Other sociologists have expressed concern about the impact of the hidden curriculum in relation to school attendance, suggesting its often disapproving and oppressive emphasis contributes to working-class underachievement by causing increased levels of truancy. The neo-Marxist Ramsay (1983) claimed that knowledge is being used as a form of social control, and that behind the façade of Maths and English, there is a 'hidden curriculum' to keep working-class and ethnic-minority children in their place. Truancy is, he argues in part, a protest against this pressure.

As is further discussed in Topic 6, recent government policies have emphasized the importance of differentiating between pupils to provide a more personalized educational experience. On the one hand, this promotes the idea that pupils need to be taught in different ways depending upon factors such as their ability and their learning styles. On the other hand, differentiation between pupils also now takes place through the creation of different types of school – some of these emphasize an academic curriculum, some specialize in particular subject areas that have currency in the local job market and some emphasize work-related learning and vocational studies. The encouragement of differing curriculum models in schools means that, increasingly, a less comprehensive intake will be attracted. Academically focused schools, high in the league tables, are more populated by middle-class, able pupils. Specialist and foundation schools are allowed to continue to select 10 per cent of their pupils on the basis of aptitude. The remaining comprehensive schools will have an ability range skewed towards the lower end and populated by a higher proportion of working-class pupils. Research by the Education Network in 2002 found that specialist and foundation schools have an advantaged intake compared with their comprehensive school neighbours, and less than half the number of deprived children, as measured by the number of free school meals.

Class is still considered by far the most significant factor influencing educational attainment – thought to have twice the effect on educational achievement of ethnicity and five times the effect of gender (Gillborn and Mirza 2000). However, these other dimensions are still important and will be explored in the following two topics.

Sociology AS for AQA

Check your understanding

1 Outline in your own words the meaning of the phrase 'differential educational attainment'.

2 How do material factors influence working-class students' experience of school?

3 How do material factors influence working-class students' experience of higher education?

4 How has recent government policy attempted to address material deprivation?

5 Give three examples of ways in which differences in class culture might affect achievement in education.

6 How does Ball argue that cultural capital helps middle-class children to gain a place in the school of their choice?

7 Using examples, explain how labelling can affect educational success.

8 Why might the formal curriculum appear less relevant to working-class children? Give examples.

9 In what ways might the hidden curriculum appear oppressive to working-class pupils? Give examples.

10 How does the recent development of differentiation within and between schools impact on class and educational achievement?

Key terms

Compensatory education making more resources available to schools in poorer areas in order to compensate (make up) for deprivation.

Cultural disadvantage 'cultural deprivation' theory suggests that some pupils' backgrounds are in some way deficient or inferior; 'cultural difference' explanations suggest that pupils' backgrounds are simply different, and that the mismatch with the culture of the school places them at a disadvantage.

Differential educational attainment the extent to which educational achievement differs between social groups.

Educational Maintenance Allowance (EMA) a means-tested sum of up to £30 per week given to post-16 students to support them in meeting the daily costs of coming to school.

Material deprivation lack of money leading to disadvantages such as an unhealthy diet and unsatisfactory housing.

Positive discrimination treating certain groups more favourably than others, usually to help overcome disadvantages.

Self-fulfilling prophecy a prediction that causes the outcome it predicts.

Tripartite system system that offered three types of school (grammar, secondary technical and secondary modern), with students allocated according to abilities and the results of the 11+ test.

Activities

Research ideas

1 Interview other people in your class to find out their experiences of setting and banding. Compare their experiences with Ball's views on p. 211.

2 Conduct a survey to establish the most popular secondary schools in your area. Use the internet and the local press to investigate relative house prices for similar styles of property.

Web.task

Use the UCAS website at www.ucas.ac.uk to investigate class differences in higher-education applications. What patterns can you find and how do they appear to be changing? Has the reduction in government financial support for students in the last few years had any effect on applications?

Item A

<<Children from working-class homes are no more likely to get educational qualifications than they were 20 years ago, writes Geraldine Hackett. Research from the Institute of Education's centre for longitudinal studies suggests that social class remains a major factor in determining life chances. According to the early study, 'Obstacles and Opportunities on the Route to Adulthood', for those born into poverty, there remains persistent underachievement. The report says that education provides an avenue for children from disadvantaged backgrounds, but their peers from advantaged families gain even more from school.

The report says: 'Class of origin and childhood poverty make educational attainment more difficult for children of similar test scores.' For children from disadvantaged backgrounds, the die is cast by the time they reach the third year of secondary schools, when they may have already started to truant.>>

Source: *Times Educational Supplement*, 23 December 2000

Item B

Despite efforts from many sides, social class still dictates educational prospects.

Student applicants from the upper social classes are more likely to be admitted to the London School of Economics than any other university, the latest official statistics reveal. The LSE leads a batch of elite London academic institutions, including King's College and University College London, where a much larger proportion of students from posh backgrounds have successful applications than students from poorer backgrounds.

The figures have emerged as two Oxford academics reiterate their calls to abolish the interview system at the Oxbridge universities, after research showed that half of all independent school students attaining three A grades at A-level ended up at Oxbridge universities, compared to just under a third of those with the same grades from state schools.

Adapted from *Times Educational Supplement*, 16 November 1999

(a) Explain what is meant by the 'ideal pupil'. (2 marks)

(b) Suggest three reasons why students from the upper social classes and those who have attended independent schools are more likely to gain places at elite universities such as LSE and Oxbridge, even when they have the same A-level grades as students from state schools. (6 marks)

(c) Outline some of the reasons why childhood poverty makes educational attainment more difficult (Item A). (12 marks)

(d) Using information from Items A and B and elsewhere, assess the view that factors within schools are the greatest influence on social-class differences in educational achievement. (20 marks)

Grade booster Getting top marks in the 20-mark question

You need to consider a range of different factors within school, such as labelling, the self-fulfilling prophecy, the ideal pupil, streaming, the hidden curriculum and so on. Use interactionist studies to illustrate these ideas and how they affect achievement. Remember that this is a question about social class and educational achievement – so don't start discussing gender or ethnic differences in achievement. Make use of the Items, for example by using them to evaluate the role of factors outside school, such as poverty and material deprivation, cultural disadvantage or cultural capital.

Ethnicity and educational achievement

Getting you thinking

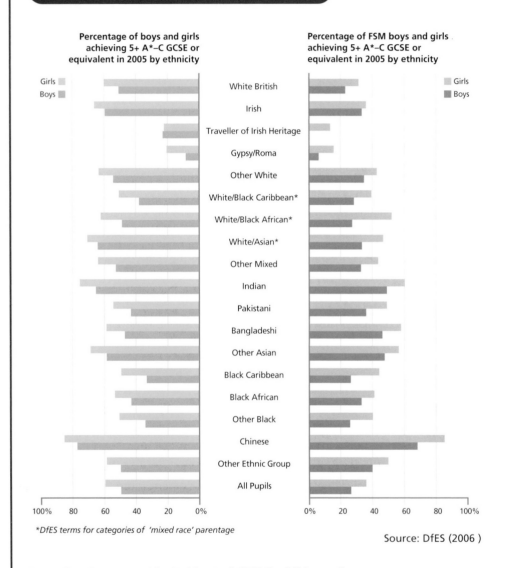

Percentage of boys and girls achieving 5+ A*–C GCSE or equivalent in 2005 by ethnicity

Girls
Boys

White British
Irish
Traveller of Irish Heritage
Gypsy/Roma
Other White
White/Black Caribbean*
White/Black African*
White/Asian*
Other Mixed
Indian
Pakistani
Bangladeshi
Other Asian
Black Caribbean
Black African
Other Black
Chinese
Other Ethnic Group
All Pupils

100% 80 60 40 20 0%

*DfES terms for categories of 'mixed race' parentage

Percentage of FSM boys and girls achieving 5+ A*–C GCSE or equivalent in 2005 by ethnicity

Girls
Boys

0% 20 40 60 80 100%

Source: DfES (2006)

The bar charts on the left show achievement by ethnicity for all pupils (on the left), and achievement by ethnicity for just those on free school meals (FSM) (on the right).

1 Roughly what difference does relative deprivation as indicated by FSM eligibility make for all pupils?

2 For which ethnic group does relative deprivation appear to make little or no difference?

3 For which ethnic group does relative deprivation appear to make the most difference?

4 How would you summarize the impact of ethnicity on educational attainment?

According to a report by Babb *et al.* (2004), children who are most likely to be low educational achievers in England are:

- male
- from a low socio-economic background
- with parents who have low or no qualifications
- living in a single-parent household
- having many siblings
- attending a state school rather than an independent school
- attending a school with a high rate of free-school meal eligibility.

5 How many of the factors listed on the left do you think apply to ethnic minorities?

6 Why do you think they have such a significant impact on educational achievement?

Material and cultural factors affecting underachievement

Material and cultural explanations of educational disadvantage referred to in the previous topic also apply to the experience of ethnic minorities, because a higher proportion than White British pupils tend to be working-class.

It is clearly not possible to argue that the worst case systematically happens to every minority ethnic child. The interplay between class, gender and ethnicity is highly complex and is affected by a multitude of factors both inside and outside school. However, as we saw from the 'Getting you thinking' exercise, relative deprivation is a key factor and higher proportions of people from ethnic minorities, than White British, are from lower-income households (see Table 6.1).

There are clearly noteworthy differences from the norm for certain ethnic categories. African-Caribbean males are near the bottom of each class group in terms of attainment. However, working-class African-Caribbean females, although they suffer from initial disadvantages in school, tend to do significantly better than working-class White pupils by the time they take their GCSEs. Fuller (1984) suggests that they may appear 'cool' in order to present a positive self-image to boys and teachers, but that they recognize the importance of getting good qualifications.

Children of Indian, Chinese and African-Asian origin also do very well within the education system. There is a strong emphasis on self-improvement through education in these cultures, and many of the children come from professional backgrounds, providing support, appropriate role models and material advantages. Their culture is perceived more positively by teachers than that of, for example, African-Caribbean males. In addition to all of the points listed in the previous topic (for children from working-class backgrounds), many pupils from particular ethnic-minority groups are relatively disadvantaged within the education system.

According to a recent report commissioned for the DfES (Wanless Report 2007), Black pupils:

- are significantly more likely to be permanently excluded and routinely punished more harshly
- are praised less and told off more often
- are 1.5 times as likely as White British pupils to be identified with behaviour-related special needs
- outperformed White pupils in school entry tests (but when these were changed to teacher observations, the pattern was reversed)
- are disproportionately put in bottom sets – due to behaviour rather than ability
- are much less likely than the average to be identified as gifted and talented.

While some Pakistani and Bangladeshi children still do relatively badly in school, recent research has shown these groups to be catching up. Bangladeshi pupils have made the greatest gains since 2000 with a gain of 28 percentage points, which brings them to the national average, followed by Pakistani pupils with a gain of 22 percentage points.

Table 6.1 Percentage of pupils entitled to a Free School Meal (FSM) by ethnicity

Ethnic group	per cent entitled to FSM
White British	12.8
Mixed heritage	25.2
Indian	13.7
Pakistani	38.2
Bangladeshi	58.5
African-Caribbean	26.2
Black African	41.4
Any other group	29.6

Source: Strand, S. (2007)

However, the length of time Asian immigrant groups have lived in Britain varies. A study by Haque and Bell (2001), showed that recent arrival into the UK had a significant negative effect on performance (by the equivalent of more than one level in each core subject). Like social class and recent arrival, as we saw in Topic 2, parental education is a significant influence on their children's achievement, in particular the level of the mother's education. However, while 83 per cent of Bangladeshi parents have no qualifications, compared with 16 per cent of White British parents, the children of those who have been here longer achieve more highly in the education system. This is because older siblings, educated here, are able to help their younger brothers and sisters. Also, as we have seen, reflecting changes within the White community, females generally tend to perform better than males within each ethnic group (see Topic 4).

However, a significant **anomaly** is that compared to Whites, minority ethnic groups have a larger proportion of members with working-class backgrounds in higher education. This is particularly true for Pakistanis and Bangladeshis – nearly two-thirds of the entrants to higher education from these groups came from households headed by manual workers or the unemployed (Modood 2004).

Some African-Caribbean pupils have very high attainment and make excellent progress. On the other hand, some White British pupils have extremely low attainment, particularly those from economically disadvantaged groups, and make poor progress. For example, national statistics highlight the fact that only 24 per cent of White British boys entitled to FSM achieved 5 or more GCSE grades at A* to C compared to 27 per cent of African-Caribbean boys entitled to FSM (DfES 2007). Also, White British working-class pupils in inner-city areas have recently emerged as the group making the least progress over the secondary phase.

Highlighting a relatively long-term trend, Strand (2007) focuses on two ethnic groups of particular interest, as both vary considerably in terms of progress throughout the first four years of secondary school, relative to their White British peers. Indian pupils widen the gap by achieving significantly better than their White peers, whereas African-Caribbean pupils do so by achieving considerably less progress. According to Strand, Indian pupils' relative progress can in part be explained by positive factors such as:

- high parental and pupil educational aspirations
- undertaking high levels of homework
- low levels of truanting, exclusion, or social services/ Educational Welfare Service involvement
- high resource provision at home (computers and private tuition)
- high parental monitoring of their children's whereabouts.

However, his research can not fully account for the poor progress of the African-Caribbean group. Relative to White British pupils generally, African-Caribbean pupils on average experience greater poverty (entitlement to FSM), are more likely to live in rented accommodation and to attend schools that are more deprived, as well as live in more deprived neighbourhoods, as is the case for Indian pupils. In terms of social class and mother's educational qualifications, however, African-Caribbean pupils do not differ markedly from White British pupils. In addition, African-Caribbean pupils (and their parents) have higher educational aspirations, have a more positive attitude to school, a higher academic self-concept and are more likely to be actively planning for the future. Despite this, African-Caribbean pupils, especially boys, are (in addition to their lower level of achievement) much more likely to have identified special educational needs and to be temporarily excluded from school, and are less likely to do homework. Given the similar socio-economic background and, if anything, more favourable balance of advantage/disadvantage relative to Indian pupils, Strand concludes that it is difficult to explain the poor progress of the African-Caribbean group.

It is, therefore, necessary to look at wider explanations of ethnic group differences, beyond those described above.

African-Caribbean underachievement has been blamed on the high numbers of one-parent families in African-Caribbean communities (57 per cent compared with 23 per cent for White British families). Some politicians have suggested that, because many of these families are female-headed, African-Caribbean boys, in particular, lack the discipline of a father-figure, which they suggest may account for the high percentage of African-Caribbeans in special schools. For girls, on the other hand, the role model provided by a strong, independent single mother is a motivating influence, and this helps to explain their relative success in education. Living in a single-parent household is not necessarily a cause of low attainment where it occurs, but according to Strand, it is a significant risk factor. Single-parent households have, on average, lower income, greater levels of parental stress and less time for educational input to the child, all of which may impact negatively on educational attainment. However, although a higher number of African-Caribbeans do live in one-parent families, it should be noted that most children of African-Caribbean origin live in nuclear families.

Many working-class and ethnic-minority pupils may feel undervalued and demotivated by an educational system that does not recognize their qualities, which are based on their class and ethnic culture.

Language has also been seen as a problem for children of African-Caribbean origin, who may speak different dialects of English, and for children from other ethnic groups who come from homes where a language other than English is spoken.

This language difference may cause problems in doing schoolwork and communicating with teachers, leading to disadvantage at school.

Ball (2002) shows how ethnic-minority parents are at a disadvantage when trying to get their children into the better schools. The parents, especially if born abroad, may not have much experience of the British education system and may not be able to negotiate the system. This may be compounded by a lack of confidence in their English-language skills.

Issues such as uniform (which markets a school well and fosters an impression of discipline) may disrupt teacher–pupil relationships, particularly between teachers and ethnic-minority pupils whose cultural influences may exert more pressure on them to subvert the formal dress codes of the school, e.g. by refusing to remove baseball caps. This may provoke more antischool behaviour, truancy and the constructive exclusion of 'problem children'. Gewirtz (2002) identifies further socially exclusive practices, such as the creation of complex application forms requiring high levels of literacy and often available only in English.

In-school factors
Labelling, racism and pupil responses

Ethnic-minority boys

Boys of African-Caribbean origin often have the label 'unruly', 'disrespectful' and 'difficult to control' applied to them. Gillborn (1990) found that African-Caribbean pupils were more likely to be given detentions than other pupils. This was because the teachers interpreted (or misinterpreted) the dress and manner of speech of African-Caribbean pupils as representing a challenge to their authority. In perceiving their treatment to be unfair, the pupils responded, understandably, in accordance with their labels. Tony Sewell (1996) claimed that many teachers were fearful of Black boys in school, the result of socialization into stereotypical assumptions. Jasper (2002) goes further to suggest that the expectations that White female teachers have of Black boys' behaviour dictate the form and style of the teaching that they offer them, a style less conducive to learning than they offer to other groups. O'Donnell (1991) showed how the various ethnic subcultures have distinctive reactions to racism, prejudice and discrimination, which may have different effects on educational performance. African-Caribbean males often react angrily to and reject the White-dominated education system, gaining status and recognition through other means. Indians show their anger, but do not tend to reject the education system. Instead, they succeed because they use the education system to their advantage.

According to Sewell (1996) and O'Donnell and Sharpe (2000), in responding to teacher's labels, racism and poor economic prospects, Black males construct a form of masculinity that earns respect from peers and females. This macho response may have little relevance for males in general with the decline in manual work and increasing opportunities within the **service sector**. However, for young Black men, with more limited

employment prospects, opposition to schooling still has some relevance in highlighting their masculinity and alternative attributes of success. Despite the fact of their relatively high academic self-concept (Strand 2007), educational success is seen as a feminine thing. The way for them to get respect is through the credibility of the street. In Sewell's words, the young man wants to be a 'street hood'. Success in the school room marks the Black boy out from his peers or classmates and is likely to make him the target of ridicule or bullying. According to Sewell, educational failure becomes a badge to wear with pride. Aspects of this view have been reflected in concerns about the development of 'gangsta' culture and the absence of positive Black male role-models at home as well as in schools. The current moral panic over gun and knife crime is in part supported by such assertions.

A similar response has been identified among some Asian youths – in particular, Bangladeshi boys, whose economic prospects are generally bleaker than those of other Asian groups. O'Donnell and Sharpe (2000) recognized that this macho 'warrior' perception by peers existed alongside perceptions of other Asian youths as 'weaklings' conforming to demands of the school or 'patriarchs', whose loyalty lay with the prescriptions of the male-dominated Asian family.

Connolly (1998) also examined the treatment in school of boys of South Asian origin. He found that teachers tended to see some South Asian boys as immature rather than as seriously deviant. Much of their bad behaviour went unnoticed by teachers and was not punished to the same extent as that of Black boys. The South Asian boys, therefore, had difficulty in gaining status as males, which made it more difficult for them to enjoy school and feel confident. However, teachers did have high expectations of their academic potential and they were often praised and encouraged.

Ethnic-minority girls

Connolly (1998) found in his recent investigation of three classes of 5 to 6 year olds in a multi-ethnic, inner-city primary school that some negative stereotypes are not just confined to boys. Like Black boys, girls were perceived by teachers as potentially disruptive but likely to be good at sports. The teachers in one school tended to 'underplay the Black girls' educational achievements and focus on their social behaviour'. Like their male counterparts, they were quite likely to be disciplined and punished, even though their behaviour did not always seem to justify it.

While few would argue that teachers display overt racism, Wright (1992) found considerable discrimination in the classroom. She observed Asian and African-Caribbean children in primary schools and found that teachers paid Asian pupils, especially girls, less attention. They involved them less in discussion and used simplistic language, assuming that they had a poor command of English. Teachers also lacked sensitivity towards aspects of their culture and displayed open disapproval of their customs and traditions. Teachers also made little effort to ensure that they pronounced names correctly, causing embarrassment and unnecessary ridicule. This had the effect of making the girls feel less positive towards the school. It also

Research methods

Tikly et al. (2006)
Aiming high

In 2003, the government set up a programme called 'Aiming High' to help raise the achievement of African-Caribbean pupils. It provided extra resources to 30 schools where African and Caribbean pupils were performing below the average for all pupils between the ages of 11 and 16. In 2006, a team of sociologists led by Leon Tikly evaluated the success of the project.

Tikly's team used postal questionnaires to produce quantitative information about setting, examination tiers and rates of exclusion. The questionnaires were returned by only 18 schools at the start of the project and 11 at the end. One third of the sample (10 schools) were subsequently involved in semi-structured interviews with, for example, governors, headteachers, pupils, parents and teachers. These produced qualitative data about the extent to which schools recognized and valued ethnic diversity and the ways they treated ethnic-minority pupils in relation to behaviour and discipline. Those that did most appeared to have fewer behavioural problems and lower exclusion rates.

Tikly, L. et al. (2006) Evaluation of Aiming High: African Caribbean Achievement Project, Bristol: University of Bristol

1 Identify the quantitative and qualitative methods used in this research.

2 What are the advantages and disadvantages of using postal questionnaires?

3 To what extent do you think the results of this research can be generalized to other schools?

4 What was the benefit for the schools who valued ethnic diversity?

attracted hostility from other pupils, who picked up on the teachers' comments and attitude towards the Asian pupils. Despite this, teachers did have high expectations of Asian pupils with regard to academic success. According to Connolly (1998), South Asian girls, though generally successful in the education system, may be overlooked because of their perceived passivity, or they may feel marginalized and left out of **discourses** relating to intimacy, love and marriage because of stereotypical assumptions about Asian family life. Connolly also challenged the stereotypical assumptions many teachers made, noting that the behaviour of South Asian girls pointed towards a similar mix of work and avoidance of work and obedience and disruption, making their behaviour largely indistinguishable from that of their female peers. It would appear, therefore, that high expectations may to some extent be responsible for creating a self-fulfilling prophecy in terms of Asian girls' relative success.

Some evidence indicates that Black girls are antischool, but pro-education. They resent low teacher expectations and labelling, but are more determined to succeed than many other groups, especially Black boys. Both Fuller (1984) and Mirza (1992) have noted how Black girls respond to the failure of the school to address their needs by rejecting the help of teachers, which they regard as patronizing and, though sometimes well-meaning, misguided. For example, the girls were entered for fewer subjects 'to take the pressure off' or given ill-informed, often stereotypical careers advice. The girls respond outwardly by appearing to reject the values of the school through their dress, attitudes and behaviour. In terms of academic achievement, however, Fuller is more optimistic than Mirza about the outcomes and suggests that the strategies that they adopt in working with and helping each other enable them to succeed academically and prove their teachers wrong. In Mirza's study, on the other hand, rejection of teachers' help and limited involvement in lessons were seen to place them at a disadvantage academically, even though they preserved high self-esteem. They were not victims of overt racism or labelling, they were simply held back by the well-meaning but misguided behaviour of most of their teachers.

While teachers may have certain expectations of ethnic-minority groups, some of which may have been detrimental to their success, pupils of both Asian and African-Caribbean origin are, according to Connolly (1998), often victims of racism from White pupils. The impact of this on educational commitment and performance is inevitably negative.

Other authors argue that racism, at least in the overt sense, cannot be a complete explanation for ethnic-group differences in attainment. Modood (2003) argues: 'If racism leads to the victim being turned off school and dropping out, why do Asian men and women have such high staying-on rates and make academic progress?' This does not discount the possibility of social stereotyping or **institutional racism** against some ethnic groups, but does highlight the importance of being sceptical with regard to generalized explanations.

The curriculum

Some sociologists have argued that the curriculum – what is taught in schools – actually disadvantages ethnic minorities.

The knowledge that they encounter at school may not connect with their own cultural experience, while **ethnocentrism**, resulting from the use of out-of-date material, could be potentially offensive by reflecting old colonial values and racial stereotypes. Coard (1971) showed how the content of education also ignored Black people. The people who are acclaimed tend to be White, while Black culture, music and art are largely ignored. Coard argued that this led to low self-esteem among Black pupils. However, this assertion was refuted by both the Swann Report (1985) and Stone (1981), who noted that, despite feeling discriminated against by some teachers, African-Caribbean children had been able to maintain an extremely positive self-image.

Since the 1970s, some effort has been made to address the neglect of other cultures in the curriculum. **Multicultural education**, which acknowledges the contribution of all of the world's cultures, has become more common, although it has been criticized for focusing only on external factors ('saris and samosas') and failing to address the real problem of racism. Ethnic-minority languages still do not have the same status as European languages, and schools are still required to hold Christian assemblies. The National Curriculum itself has also been criticized for being ethnocentric – especially in its focus on British history and literature. Geography also emphasizes Britain's positive contribution to the rest of the world, rather that the negative consequences of unfair trade and employment practices. Tikly *et al.* (2006), in their study of 30 comprehensive schools (see also Research methods, p. 217), found that a significant number of African-Caribbean pupils noted their invisibility in the curriculum and were exasperated by the White European focus. Moreover, when Black history was acknowledged within the curriculum, many pupils reported their frustration with the tendency to focus on slavery. However, while the curriculum may be ethnocentric, it is unlikely that this, in isolation, is a major factor in the underachievement of ethnic minorities, as it is not the case that all pupils from ethnic-minority backgrounds underachieve to similar degrees. Indian and Chinese pupils' achievement, for example, is above the national average.

Institutional racism?

Gillborn (2002) argues that schools are institutionally racist as teachers interpret policy in a way that disadvantages Black pupils. For example, setting, schemes for gifted and talented pupils, and vocational schemes for the less academic all underrate the abilities of Black children, relegating them to low-ability groups, a restricted curriculum and entry for lower-level exams. The increased marketization of schools (see Topic 6), has led to what some writers have called an 'A to C economy'. According to Gillborn and Youdell (1999) this creates a rationing of education, whereby teachers are forced to focus on those in danger of not realizing their potential for an above C grade. They thus neglect the no-hopers and high achievers, leaving them to their own devices. Many ethnic-minority pupils are judged, often subjectively, to belong to the former group. Hatcher (1996) examined the role of school governing bodies and found that they gave low priority to race issues, failing to deal adequately with pupil racism. Furthermore, formal links with ethnic-minority parents tended not to exist, which meant that little was done to address their concerns. Ethnic-minority pupils' needs therefore tended to be low priority or disregarded. Ranson (2005) highlights the unrepresentativeness of school governing bodies which are 'disproportionately White, middle-aged, middle-class, middle-income, public/community service workers'.

Problems of categorization

Classifying according to ethnic origin is by no means simple. The term 'ethnic minorities', for example, includes many different groups and does not take account of class and gender differences within those groups. Gillborn and Gipps (1996) argue that terms such as 'White', 'Black', 'Asian' and 'other' actually prevent any real understanding of differences in achievement. Postmodernists go further; they argue that the increasingly diverse nature of contemporary societies makes it impossible to explain educational achievement (or anything else) in terms of broad categories such as class or ethnicity, and that

the generalizations that are made actually do more harm than good. They suggest that a conscious attempt needs to be made to understand the complexities of cultural difference and identity in modern society.

Key terms

Anomaly an odd, peculiar, or strange condition, situation, quality, etc.

Discourse a set of ideas that tell us how to make sense of the world, what kind of questions to ask, what counts as a problem and how to solve problems.

Ethnocentric emphasizing White middle-class culture at the expense of other cultures.

Institutional racism racism that is built into the normal day-to-day practices of an organization.

Multicultural education education that recognizes cultural diversity.

Service sector a group of economic activities loosely organized around finance, retail and personal care.

Activities

Research ideas

1 Analyse the content of a sample of text books at your school or college. Focus on visual images, examples and case studies. To what extent do they recognize the variety and contribution of ethnic groups in contemporary Britain?

2 Look at the distribution of students in your school or college in terms of lower-level ability groups or courses. Interview a range of students to ascertain how they feel about this. Is there any evidence of uneven distribution on the basis of ethnicity?

Web.tasks

1 Search for statistics about ethnic groups and education at the websites of the Department for Children, Schools and Families and the Department for Innovation, University and Skills at www.dfes.gov.uk/ and www.dius.gov.uk/

What statistics and reports are available? Do they tell us anything about the government's priorities?

2 Use the UCAS website at www.ucas.ac.uk to investigate class and ethnic differences in higher education applications. Select 'Statistics' and then choose from the menu.

What patterns can you find and how do they appear to be changing? Has the reduction in government financial support for students in the last few years had any effect on applications?

Check your understanding

1 Briefly describe some of the material disadvantages that might be faced by ethnic minorities from working-class backgrounds (see also previous topic).

2 What are the possible reasons for differences in educational achievement between Asian groups?

3 What has recently become a concern in relation to White British working-class pupils?

4 Why do you think a higher proportion of members of ethnic minorities than White students attend university?

5 Explain how Indian pupils and African-Caribbean pupils demonstrate a widening of the achievement gap in relation to White pupils.

6 Give three examples of ways in which cultural differences may affect ethnic achievement in education. Include some reference to Tony Sewell's research.

7 How do pupil subcultures illustrate aspects of ethnic-minority experience of school?

8 How may the labelling of Black boys have a negative impact upon their achievement?

9 How, despite generally high expectations, does the behaviour of teachers towards Asian children impede their success?

10 How might the curriculum itself disadvantage ethnic-minority pupils?

Ethnicity and educational achievement

Item A

The evidence that many teachers continue to have low expectations of pupils from some ethnic and linguistic minorities can be found in the impact of largely hidden, day-to-day decisions about such issues as placement in streamed classes. Evidence from school inspectors suggests that in schools that emphasize tight setting, some groups learning English as an additional language are likely to be placed disproportionately in low sets, especially in English (Ofsted 1999).

The introduction of tiered GCSE examinations has added new risks of discriminatory decision-making at that stage. Gillborn and Youdell (1999) have shown that Black children are markedly less likely to be entered for higher-tier examinations, depriving them of the opportunity to win higher grades.

Adapted from Cline, T. and Shamsi, T. (2000) Language Needs or Special Needs? The assessment of learning difficulties in literacy among children learning English as an additional language: a literature review, London: DfEE

Item B

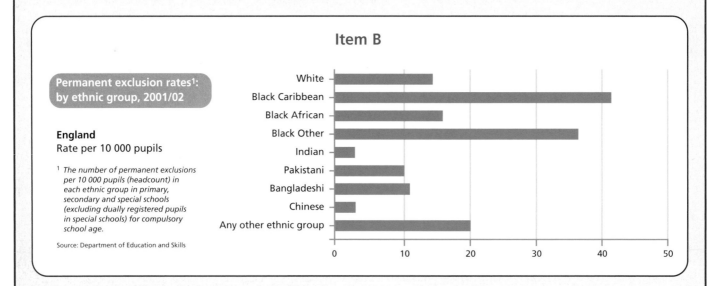

Permanent exclusion rates[1]: by ethnic group, 2001/02

England
Rate per 10 000 pupils

[1] *The number of permanent exclusions per 10 000 pupils (headcount) in each ethnic group in primary, secondary and special schools (excluding dually registered pupils in special schools) for compulsory school age.*

Source: Department of Education and Skills

(a) Explain what is meant by 'ethnocentrism'. (2 marks)

(b) Suggest three reasons why Black girls tend to do better than Black boys in education. (6 marks)

(c) Outline some of the material and cultural factors affecting educational achievement. (12 marks)

(d) Using information from Items A and B and elsewhere, assess the view that processes in schools themselves are mainly responsible for ethnic differences in attainment. (20 marks)

Grade booster Getting top marks in the 20-mark question

You need to look at a range of different processes inside schools, such as labelling, streaming or the self-fulfilling prophecy. Remember to relate these processes to ethnic differences (rather than say social-class or gender differences) in achievement. Make sure you use information from both the Items. This could include ethnic differences in rates of exclusion (Item B) and information about teachers' expectations, streaming and entry for tiered GCSE examinations. You need to assess the view, and you could do this by considering the role of factors outside schools, such as home background.

Gender and educational achievement

Getting you thinking

The table below highlights the extent to which girls outperform boys at GCSE and at A-level in a range of subjects, with girls outperforming boys in every subject.

Girls' achievement of A*–C grades in GCSE subjects relative to boys' in 2006

	No. sat ('000s)		% diff A* to C		No sat ('000s)		% diff A* to C
	M	F			M	F	
Art	86	126	+19	Information technology	50	40	+8
Design & technology	203	168	+16	Geography	104	83	+7
English	306	305	+15	History	106	102	+6
Drama	35	59	+14	Science single award	36	35	+5
English literature	255	271	+13	Business studies	46	33	+4
French	93	116	+13	PE	91	61	+3
Religious studies	63	81	+12	Science double award	220	223	+3
All GCSE subjects	3180	3110	+9	Mathematics	310	305	+2

Girls' achievement of A–E grades in A-level subjects relative to boys' in 2006

	No. sat ('000s)		% diff A to E		No sat ('000s)		% diff A to E
	M	F			M	F	
Law	5.4	8.1	+2.7	Sociology	5.7	18.6	+1
Psychology	12.4	35.2	+2.7	Mathematics	30.6	19.1	+0.9
Music	5	4	+2.2	Drama	4.5	10.5	+0.8
Physics	18.7	5	+2	Media Studies	10	13	+0.8
ICT/Computing	12.5	4.7	+1.9	History	20.5	20.1	+0.8
Design & technology	9.7	7	+1.9	Geography	15.5	12.7	+0.7
PE	12.5	9	+1.6	Economics	9.5	4	+0.5
English	24	54	+1.3	Religious Studies	4.7	10.2	+0.4
Art	11	26	+1.1	Spanish	1.7	3.5	+0.2
Chemistry	17.7	16.8	+1.1	German	2	3.5	+0.1
Biology	19.3	27.3	+1	Politics	5.7	3.8	0
All A-level subjects	328	387	+1.2	French	3.9	8.3	0

1 What is the general pattern of female achievement at GCSE and A-level?

2 Why do you think more girls than boys enter for A-levels even though they take fewer GCSEs?

3 Significant differences in entry numbers at A-level are highlighted above. How would you personally account for the variation in entry numbers between males and females in each subject? Share your explanations with your peers.

Until the late 1980s, there was considerable concern about the underachievement of girls. They did not do quite as well as boys in exams, and were also less likely to take A-levels and enter higher education. However, since the early 1990s, girls have begun to outperform boys at most levels of the education system. For example, they do better at every stage of the National Curriculum SAT results in English, Maths and Science, and in all subjects at GCSE and A-level. In 2006, 48 per cent of females progressed to higher education, compared with 38 per cent of males. With regard to the number achieving first-class

and second-class degrees, the gender gap has remained consistent, with women outperforming men by about 7 per cent (Higher Education Statistics Agency 2007).

However, there are still concerns about the subject choices made by girls. Boys dominate in maths, science and technology at A-level and far more men than women study these subjects in higher education. This has significant implications for men's and women's career choices and future earnings: 60 per cent of working women are clustered in only 10 per cent of occupations.

Why has girls' achievement improved?

The job market

There are increasing job opportunities for women in the service sector of the economy, while the availability of traditional male manual work has reduced considerably. About half of all women of working age were in employment in 1960. By 2006, the proportion had risen to three-quarters, with many more in higher-status, relatively well-paid positions. Many girls have mothers in paid employment providing positive role models and contributing, often equally, to the household economy. As a result, girls recognize that the future offers them more choices – they are provided with the incentive to seek economic independence, and careers are now a real possibility.

Female expectations

Many women are now looking well beyond the mother/housewife role. In a 1976 survey, Sue Sharpe discovered that girls' priorities were 'love, marriage, husbands, children, jobs and careers, more or less in that order'. When the research was repeated in 1994, she found that the priorities had changed to 'job, career and being able to support themselves' above all other priorities. Studies of girls in primary and secondary schools illustrate this change in emphasis. According to Francis and Skelton (2005), 'The majority (of primary and secondary school female pupils) appear to see their chosen career as reflecting their identity and as a vehicle for future fulfilment, rather than as simply a stopgap before marriage'. The growth in employment opportunities, along with the rise in young women's occupational ambitions, have increased their incentives to gain educational qualifications. Studies of both primary and secondary school pupils show that many girls are now looking forward towards jobs that require degree-level qualifications (Francis and Skelton 2005).

Feminism

The work of feminist sociologists in the 1970s and 1980s led to a greater emphasis on equal opportunities in schools. Teaching approaches and resources were monitored for sex bias to ensure more 'girl-friendly schooling', especially in the sciences. Consequently, teachers are now more sensitive about avoiding gender stereotyping in the classroom. Various antisexist initiatives have raised both teachers' and girls' consciousness. Single-sex classes in some subjects, the exploration of sexism through **PSE**, and citizenship classes have all made a difference. Boys, especially in mixed schools, are more aware of equal opportunities and of the unacceptability of sexist behaviour. Weiner (1995) has argued that teachers have more forcefully challenged stereotypes since the 1980s and many sexist images have been removed from learning materials. However, research by Best (1993) and Abraham (1996) found that women continue to be presented as passive or in a narrow range of often domestic jobs (shopping or buying domestic appliances) whilst men are shown as active, running a business or investing.

Behaviour

There is mounting evidence that girls work harder and are more motivated than boys. On average, girls put more effort into their work and spend more time on homework. They take more care with presentation of their work, are better organized and, consequently, meet deadlines more successfully than boys. Many boys believe school work should be done at school and, unlike girls, are not prepared to draft and redraft assignments (Burns and Bracey 2001).

Research shows that, from the age of 6, girls read more books than boys, and this trend continues through their lives. Girls are three times more likely than boys to borrow books from a public library (Book Marketing Limited 2000).

Changes in the organization of education

Before the introduction of the GCSE examination, the gender gap at age 16 was either slightly in favour of girls or non-existent. From 1988, when GCSEs replaced O-levels, the gender gap steadily widened. Pirie (2001) has argued that the old O-level was a boy's exam with its 'high-risk, swot it all up for the final throw' approach to assessment. By contrast, the coursework involved in GCSE and some A-levels requires organizational skills and sustained motivation – skills that girls seem to be better at than boys. However, Debra Myhill (1999) has pointed out that shifts in assessment to increase the proportion of unseen examinations in English have actually been paralleled by an increase in the extent to which girls outperform boys in that subject. Recent changes in the assessment of GCSE and A-level, reducing the level of coursework may not, therefore, make any significant difference to the gender gap.

Better socialization for schooling

Research by Hannan (2000) shows that girls spend their leisure time differently from boys. Whereas boys relate to their peers by doing (i.e. being active in a range of ways), girls relate to one another by talking. This puts girls at an advantage, because school is essentially a language experience – most subjects require good levels of comprehension and writing skills. Among boys, peer-group pressure is often very strong. It is noticeable from research that boys who do well at school are often helped at home, away from the view of the peer group. Boys often consider it weak to request help from a teacher and it is also especially difficult for a boy to accept help from another boy. Girls, on the other hand, are happy to help each other. It is an acceptable part of being female. (Look at the photos on p. 224 and think about the questions beneath.)

Kirby (2000) has suggested that communicative play through organized social games has been replaced with TV, DVD and computer games. In addition, there has been a decline in family discussion time, through occasions such as mealtimes. Both changes have reduced opportunities for boys to catch up with girls in terms of language development. He points out that, while modern computer games (more popular with boys than girls) may exercise already advanced spatial and visual abilities, they do little to address language deficiency.

Research methods

Becky Francis
Gender and learning

Becky Francis studied the ways in which gender affects students learning in school and ambitions once they finish compulsory education. The project involved research in three different London secondary schools. Observation was used to record classroom interaction and student behaviour during GCSE lessons as well as individual interviews. The schools were all mixed-sex comprehensives with a large majority of working-class pupils. Approximately one third of the sample were from African-Caribbean origin, one third were White and one third from other ethnic groups.

The observation was conducted in English lessons (a traditionally feminine subject) and Maths lessons (a traditionally masculine subject) – both important for acceptance to certain levels of post-compulsory education and for future employment. A top set and a lower set lesson were observed, so four lessons were observed at each school (12 classes in all). Each class had three lessons observed. A limitation of the classroom observation was an inability to faithfully record all the interaction, due to the sheer noise levels in some of the classes.

In terms of power, boys gained status by taking up 'laddish' or 'class clown' roles. Many used these roles to dominate the classroom interaction, marginalizing girls and other boys. In eight of the twelve lessons observed, boys dominated the classroom interaction by being louder than girls, making greater use of the classroom space, shouting out questions and answers, being disruptive, and/or taking up more of the teachers' attention.

However, the research also showed how the view of femininity as 'sensible' fits more easily with the qualities required for educational success such as concentration and hard work.

Girls' choices of future occupations were as diverse and ambitious as those of boys. They did, however, believe that gender discrimination at work still exists. Their ambition for a 'good job' and the need to compete with men may be motivating them to perform well at school.

Francis, B. (2005) *The Impact of Gender Constructions on Pupils' Learning and Educational Choices: Final project report*, London: ESRC

1 To what extent is Francis' sample representative of secondary pupils across the UK?

2 Why did Francis choose to observe GCSE lessons in English and Maths?

3 How might the presence of an observer in the classroom have affected the validity of the data collected?

4 What problem did Francis encounter when observing in classrooms?

5 What does the research suggest might be the cause of some girls' educational success?

6 What does the research suggest might be the cause of some boys' educational underachievement?

What are the concerns about boys' achievement?

The increased success of girls relative to boys has caused considerable alarm and, some would argue, overreaction, with some politicians going as far as to warn of the prospect of 'a wasted generation of boys' (Gordon Brown in 2006). Evidence, however, shows that the achievement of both boys and girls has increased over the last 20 years; it is just that girls have improved at a faster rate, resulting in a significant widening of the gender gap. This applies to boys and girls from *all* social classes. Whether this should be seen as 'boys' underachievement' is a matter of opinion. One might well ask why girls are not being enthusiastically applauded for their accomplishments. Some of the concerns over boys are these:

- Boys are behind girls at reading and writing by the age of 6.

- At age 11, the average boy is nine months behind the average girl in development of speaking skills, 12 months behind in literacy and six months behind in numeracy.

- Traditionally, boys have matured later than girls, who have always been ahead in language at primary level, but boys no longer appear able to catch up, remaining, for example, 15 per cent behind at GCSE in English with half the number choosing the subject at A-level.

- White working-class boys are for the first time the lowest achieving group.

- There is a view that less-able boys are virtually unemployable because they lack interest, drive, enthusiasm and social skills (Burns and Bracey 2001), and this increases government anxiety over future generations' dependency on the state.

- Young men are much more likely than young women to be excluded from school (DfES 2006) and, it is feared, increasingly likely to be exposed to deviant and antisocial behaviour.

Why are boys making slower progress?

Changes in the job market/status frustration

Some commentators, notably Mac an Ghaill (1994), suggest that working-class boys are experiencing a 'crisis of masculinity' (see Chapter 2, p. 51). They are socialized into seeing their future male identity and role in terms of having a job and being a 'breadwinner'. However, the decline of **manufacturing industry** and the rise in long-term unemployment make it increasingly unlikely that males will occupy these roles. Moreover, new jobs in the service sector are often part-time, desk-based, and suited to the skills and lifestyles of women. In some families, females may be the primary breadwinners. Consequently, traditional masculine roles are under threat. Working-class boys' perception of this may influence their motivation and ambition. They may feel that qualifications are a waste of time because there are only limited opportunities in the job market. They may see their future as bleak and without purpose. Consequently, they don't see any point in working hard at school and seek other ways of defining their masculinity.

'Laddish' behaviour and peer-group status

Early research into **peer-group status** highlighted the development of antischool subcultures that tended to be developed by some working-class boys, particularly those placed in lower streams, bands and sets. Studies by Hargreaves (1967) and Willis (1977), for example, showed how such boys were either fatalistic in accepting school failure as inevitable and so developed anti-educational **coping strategies,** or sought to compensate for status frustration by gaining credibility in the eyes of their peers. However, studies now indicate that 'laddish' behaviours have spread to most boys – both working-class and middle-class – and to some extent to girls.

Social control differences

According to Mitsos and Browne (1998), teachers are not as critical with boys as with girls. They may have lower expectations of boys, expecting work to be late, rushed and untidy, and expecting boys to be disruptive. Some research suggests that boys are less positively influenced than girls, or even turned off, by primary-school environments, which are female dominated and may have an emphasis on neatness and tidiness.

Unrealistic attitudes

There are signs that boys' overconfidence may blind them to what is actually required for educational success. Research indicates that they are surprised when they fail exams and tend to put their failure down to bad luck rather than lack of effort. On the other hand, girls are more realistic, even self-doubting, and try that much harder in order to ensure success. However,

1   *What features of schooling might seem more in line with girls' experiences outside school?*
2   *What features of schooling might seem to conflict with boys' experiences outside school?*

according to Francis (2000), boys are no longer likely to consider themselves more able than girls, as was the case in the 1970s and 1980s. Also, Francis notes that boys are more likely to have career aspirations that are not only unrealistic, but less likely to require academic success, e.g. professional footballer, whereas girls' career ambitions more often require academic success, e.g. doctor, and hence a commitment to schoolwork.

What about the future?

According to a number of writers, the solutions to boys' underachievement are couched within a number of discourses, some of which are sympathetic to boys' predicament while others are more critical:

- Epstein (1998) refers to the 'poor boys' discourse that blames schools for failing to cater for boys. Teachers, the exam system, and female concerns and interests ignore boys' learning needs and fail to appreciate and understand their masculinity, especially during primary school. To resolve this, proponents argue that schools should be made more 'masculine', and attention and resources should be directed from girls to boys. However, recent research by Carrington *et al.* (2007) suggests that the gender of the teacher has little or no impact on boys' or girls' learning.
- Second, the 'boys will be boys' discourse suggests that, while boys may be naturally clever, they also tend to be lazy and difficult to motivate, slap-dash, noisy, competitive and demanding. The solution lies with setting clear targets for boys and strong discipline while respecting their masculinity.

- Francis and Skelton (2005) identify two further discourses. The first sees boys themselves as the barrier. The so-called 'problem boys discourse' suggests that boys are to blame for their own underachievement. They get involved in behaviour that is troublesome to themselves and society. The solution lies with strong discipline and more social control.
- They finally recognize a more sympathetic view – the 'boys at risk' discourse – which sees boys as vulnerable, confused, insecure, and with low self-esteem. They suggest that while the underachieving boy may appear tough on the outside, seeking to impress and boost his self-image, on the inside he is insecure and has low self-esteem. Schools need to be sensitive to and appreciate this and provide opportunities for such boys to rebuild their sense of worth.

Some feminist researchers are concerned that girls are still underachieving because of disruptive boys. Teachers may be so tied up with controlling boys that girls don't get the attention they deserve. Recent research shows that girls' educational achievement has improved despite continuing male dominance of the classroom, curriculum content (for example History's focus on the lives of men) and greater demands on teacher time (Francis 1998). By implication, without boys holding them back, it could have improved even more.

Feminists are also still concerned about the narrow subject choices that females are making at further and higher education level. Females are still more likely to take arts subjects, and males are more likely to take scientific and technological subjects. Such gender stereotyping may be the result of gender socialization in early childhood (e.g. different toys and activities around the home), teacher advice on subject choice, and a continuing perception that the sciences are masculine subjects.

Many feminists believe that the current concern about boys and achievement is simply a 'moral panic'. Weiner *et al.* (1997) argue that the media see the underachievement of Black and working-class boys as a problem because it may lead to the creation of a potentially dangerous underclass, and failure to celebrate girls achievement is merely part of a backlash against female success.

Some critics have argued that the whole question of equality of educational opportunity has now been reduced to gender and the focus on boys. A number of costly government

Research methods

Carolyn Jackson (2006)
Lads and ladettes in school

Carolyn Jackson's research investigates a growing culture of 'laddishness' among girls at school. She calls these girls 'ladettes'.

Jackson used a variety of methods, including self-completion questionnaires and interviews. Year 9 pupils completed three questionnaires. The first two concerned their educational goals and behaviour; the third, their views about 'laddishness' and popularity. Pupils were required to respond to statements on a five-point scale according to levels of agreement, and there were slightly different questionnaires for girls and for boys.

Semi-structured interviews were also used. Jackson herself interviewed 153 pupils: 75 girls and 78 boys. The audio tapes were transcribed and then analysed with the help of computer packages which identified key themes: academic pressure, academic self-presentation, SATs, 'lads', 'ladettes'. Some of the key themes were further subdivided into ability, aggression, loudness, language, drinking and dress.

According to Jackson, laddish behaviour can have important advantages from the perspectives of many boys and girls. First, it makes them appear 'cool' if they have a laugh and mess about in class. This aspect of laddishness was accepted by the vast majority of boys and girls, whatever their social-class background. Second, there is so

much academic pressure due to teachers' concerns about their school's league table that there is a fear of failure and of being regarded as stupid. Being laddish allows pupils to appear workshy and unconcerned with failure. If they do succeed, they are seen to be 'a genius' because they have apparently done so without doing any work.

Jackson claims that there are no quick fixes for laddish behaviour, but she suggests that it could probably be reduced if the culture of competition in schools was replaced with a more supportive atmosphere where developing ideas was more important than passing tests.

Sources: Jackson, C. (2006) *Lads and Ladettes in School: Gender and a Fear of Failure*, Buckingham: Open University Press ; and Blundell, J. and Griffiths, J. (2008) *Sociology since 2000*, Lewes: Connect Publications

1 What are the advantages and disadvantages of using self-completion questionnaires to find out about 'laddishness'?

2 What are the advantages and disadvantages of using interviews to find out about 'laddishness'?

3 How does Jackson operationalize the concept of 'laddishness' when analysing interview data?

4 What does Jackson identify as the advantages of 'laddishness' for both boys and girls?

measures aimed at raising boys' educational attainment have been initiated. However, as noted earlier, class has over five times the effect on educational attainment as gender, and ethnicity has twice the effect (Gillborn and Mirza 2000). According to some researchers, the focus on boys has diverted attention from not only underachieving girls but from pupils disadvantaged by their class and/or ethnic background. Osler (2006) picks up on this. She highlights one key area which the Report identifies as a priority for action, namely 'reducing school exclusions among boys and certain ethnic minorities'.

She points out that the current focus on boys' exclusion (and underachievement) is masking a serious problem of exclusion and underachievement among girls, which is increasing at a faster rate than that of boys. African-Caribbean girls are often hailed as one of education's success stories. Yet girls classified as African-Caribbean are more vulnerable to disciplinary exclusion than their White female peers. Despite this, mentoring schemes and other support systems are targeting Black boys. Furthermore, girls who are excluded from school are less likely than their male counterparts to access appropriate

support or secure places in pupil referral units or other alternative schemes. Not only do they fail to access the appropriate resources but their right to education is also denied. The research also revealed that official disciplinary exclusion rates mask a wider problem of exclusion from school among girls, which is expressed in a number of hidden ways, including self-exclusion, withdrawal from learning, and truancy. The report advocates a move away from the 'gender see-saw' (in both exclusions and achievement), where we focus on girls for a while and then on boys, to a more integrated approach.

Key terms

Coping strategies ways of 'getting by' in an unpleasant situation.

Manufacturing industry industries that actually make goods. Most of the work in such industries is manual and based in factories.

Peer-group status being seen as 'big' or important in the eyes of friends and other people around you.

PSE Personal and Social Education. Sometimes known as PSHE (including Health Education) or PSME (including Moral Education).

Check your understanding

1 What have been the overall trends in male and female achievement in the last 20 years?

2 How might changes in the economy affect both female and male attitudes towards education?

3 How have changes in girls' aspirations given them more ambition to succeed academically?

4 What effects might gender stereotyping have on female subject choice at school and university?

5 How may aspects of boys' socialization explain why they underachieve at school?

6 How do boys' aspirations sometimes fail to match up with commitment to study?

7 What solutions have been proposed to address boys' underachievement?

8 (a) Why do male and female students adopt 'laddish' behaviour?
(b) What form does it take?
(c) How is increased academic pressure contributing to laddish behaviour?
(d) What is the solution proposed?

9 Explain how class and ethnicity may be just as important as gender in explaining the current achievement patterns of boys?

10 What does Audrey Osler see as the main problem being caused by the exclusive focus on boys' so-called underachievement?

Activities

Research ideas

1 Conduct a content analysis of two science and technology textbooks used at your school or college. One should be significantly older than the other, if possible. Count the number of times that males and females appear in diagrams, photographs, etc., and record how they are shown. Find examples that are gender specific. What roles do they suggest as typical for each gender? Is there a change over time?

2 Interview a sample of boys and girls. Try to find out if they have different expectations about future success. Are there differences in the amount of time they spend on homework?

Web.task

The government's concern about gender and achievement is demonstrated by their creation of a website devoted to the issue. Visit it at www.standards.dfee.gov.uk/genderandachievement for statistical data and summaries of research. In particular, look at the case studies and latest research detailing how certain schools are tackling boys' underachievement.

An eye on the exam   Gender and educational achievement

Item A

Debates about boys and schooling take three main forms. There are stories about 'poor boys', who are victims of feminism or teachers, about schools which fail them and about their laddishness. 'Poor boys' stories call for alterations to the curriculum and teaching to favour boys. 'Failing schools' stories lead to punitive inspection processes, hit squads and action zones. Like 'poor boys' the 'boys will be boys' stories call for alterations to teaching to favour boys and, in addition, seek to use girls to police, teach, control and civilize boys. But these responses are based on oversimplified explanations of what is happening in schools. Not all boys are doing worse than girls. The picture is far from simple. Rather than spending our time in handwringing, we must try to understand the complexity of the situation. If we ask 'Which boys, in which areas, are doing badly?', we find that the impact of class and ethnicity on achievement is greater than that of gender.

Adapted from Epstein, D. *et al.* (eds) (1999) *Gender and Achievement*, Milton Keynes: Open University Press

Item B

'Reports of girls' GCSE success obscure the true picture,' says Gillian Plummer. Yet another simplistic, statistical interpretation of gender differences in examination results makes the national news: 'Boys are outperformed by girls in GCSEs.' As a result, the government wants all education authorities to take action in raising the academic performance of boys.

But beware: simplistic statistical analyses are dangerously misleading. We do not have a hierarchy in which girls are positioned in the top 50 per cent and boys in the bottom 50 per cent at GCSE. It is social class, not gender or race differences, which continues to have the single most important influence on educational attainment in Britain.

The majority of boys and girls from socially advantaged families do much better in all subjects at GCSE than the majority of girls from socially disadvantaged families.

While, overall, girls do outperform boys at GCSE, working-class girls do only marginally better than working-class boys in public examinations.

It is dangerous and inaccurate to imply that all boys underperform and that all girls do well.

The real question is: what action is being taken to raise the academic performance of working-class girls (as well as other underachievers)?

Adapted from *Times Educational Supplement*, 23 January 1998

(a) Explain what is meant by 'peer-group status'.   (2 marks)

(b) Suggest three ways in which teaching might be altered to favour boys.   (6 marks)

(c) Outline some of the factors outside the education system that have affected gender
     differences in school.   (12 marks)

(d) Using information from Items A and B and elsewhere, assess sociological explanations
     of why girls achieve better results than boys.   (20 marks)

Grade booster   Getting top marks in the 20-mark question

You need to outline the patterns of achievement of boys and girls (e.g. which subjects do they choose and which do they do best in?). You should examine the different reasons that have been put forward for the gender gap in achievement, such as changes in the job market, girls' expectations, the effect of differences in the ways boys and girls socialize, laddish behaviour, the impact of school organization, the curriculum, and so on. Make sure you use information from both the Items in your answer – for example, remember to point out the importance of class as an influence on achievement.

Getting you thinking

1 Look at the first three photographs above. What do you think pupils learn from:

  ● wearing school uniform?
  ● team sport?
  ● classes where teachers stand at the front talking, with students sitting in rows listening or taking notes?

2 The fourth photograph shows an American classroom. Every day students pledge their allegiance to the American flag. Why do you think they have to do this?

3 Think of three other routines that go on in a typical school. What do pupils learn from these?

4 What does the *Beano* cartoon of the Bash Street Kids tell us about the way some pupils respond to attempts by schools to control their behaviour?

Topic 1 showed us that a 'hidden curriculum' exists in which children are socialized into various norms and values. This topic explores in more detail how the hidden curriculum is transmitted, the messages it conveys and how different groups of pupils respond to it. Some may accept it unquestioningly, for example, while others, like the Bash Street Kids, may reject it and gain pleasure from disrupting the school's attempts to socialize them.

The hidden curriculum

The hidden curriculum involves messages and ideas that schools do not directly teach but which are part and parcel of the normal routines and procedures of the organization. It involves norms, values, beliefs and practices that are taken for granted. They appear as common sense, in total, as an **ethos** reinforced by all of the school's managers, teachers and processes.

We saw in Topic 1 that functionalists value not only the *formal* curriculum that develops the skills and knowledge needed by modern industrial society, but also the *hidden* curriculum, as it helps foster cooperation, healthy competition (but not at the expense of solidarity) and the spirit of meritocracy. Marxists and feminists are critical of all aspects of the school curriculum for the way it legitimates male and ruling-class dominance, and helps maintain and reproduce it.

How is the hidden curriculum transmitted?

This occurs through the standard, everyday aspects of school life, such as:

- the hierarchy of management that places White, generally male headteachers at the top, female classroom practitioners in the middle and Black, working-class service workers, e.g. kitchen staff and cleaners, near the bottom (and pupils at the very bottom!)
- an insistence on punctuality at key points within the rigid pattern of the day
- wearing a uniform, which imposes the identity of the school over that of the individual
- the various sets and levels defined by age and ability
- elements of the curriculum and the school's pastoral system
- the organization of the classroom, e.g. with the teacher at the front for pupils to look up to and be looked down upon
- the expectations teachers bring with them about particular categories of pupils.

Taken together, these elements shape pupils' experiences, producing particular outcomes which are positive for some, while being negative for, and often challenged by, others.

Pupil subcultures

Some groups accept the rules and the authority of teachers without question, while others may devote all their attention to rule-breaking and avoiding work. You have probably encountered examples of both during your compulsory education. Sociologists are interested in these subcultures. Why do they form, and what effect do they have on their members, other pupils, teachers and schools?

In the 1970s, a great deal of media concern was directed at inner-city comprehensives and the alleged misbehaviour of their pupils. This prompted sociologists such as Paul Willis (see p. 205) to examine the possible reasons for the development of these mainly male, working-class groups of 'undisciplined' school pupils, or antischool subcultures. As we saw in Topic 1, Willis identified a group of 'lads' – whose main aim at school was to have a 'laff' by rejecting the values of the school – and a more conformist group, referred to by the 'lads' as 'earoles'.

On a general level, all subcultures have things in common: their members gain status, mutual support and a sense of belonging from the subculture. According to Hargreaves (1967), antischool working-class subcultures are predominantly found in the bottom streams of secondary schools. In fact, he argued, they are caused by the labelling of some pupils as 'low-stream failures'. Unable to achieve status in terms of the mainstream values of the school, these pupils substitute their own set of delinquent values by which they can achieve success in the eyes of their peers. They do this by, for example, not respecting teachers, messing about, arriving late, having fights, building up a reputation with the opposite sex, and so on.

Writers such as Hargreaves and Willis refer to the pro- and antischool cultures as **homogeneous**, coherent groups that share their own uniform sets of values. Peter Woods (1983), however, argues that this is too simplistic. He argues that pupils use a variety of **adaptations**, depending upon the ways in which the values of the school are accepted or rejected. Some pupils may partially accept aspects of the school's values but reject others. It is now recognized that responses will also differ within and between the different categories of pupils, and in different school situations. The study of school subcultures is, therefore, a lot more complex than it used to be.

Male subcultures

The antischool male subcultures of the early 1970s made a degree of sense in that their members nearly all got jobs, despite their lack of qualifications. Their coping strategies – what the 'lads' in Willis's study called 'having a laff' – also equipped them for the monotony of the work they were destined for.

The economy has changed, however, and very few working-class jobs remain in manufacturing. Has this changed the antischool subculture of the 'lads'? There is concern that some working-class boys are stuck in a time warp. That is, they imagine that work will be available whatever happens to them in school, and so they make little effort. In a sense the 'laff' is on them when they find that this is not the case and they are forced to join training schemes. Riseborough (1993) describes how boys on **YTS schemes** show some awareness and resentment of their predicament. They quickly realize that there is little likelihood of a job at the end of the scheme, and that they are being exploited.

Mac an Ghaill (1994) illustrates the complexity of subcultural responses by examining the relationship between schooling, work, masculinity and sexuality. He identifies a range of school subcultures, as follows.

The 'macho lads'

This group was hostile to school authority and learning, not unlike the lads in Willis's study. Willis had argued that work – especially physical work – was essential to the development of a sense of identity. By the mid-1980s, much of this kind of work was gone. Instead, a spell in youth training, followed very often by unemployment, became the norm for many working-class boys.

The academic achievers

This group, who were from mostly skilled manual working-class backgrounds, adopted a more traditional upwardly mobile route via academic success. However, they had to develop ways of coping with the stereotyping and accusations of effeminacy from the 'macho lads'. They would do this either by confusing those who bullied them, by deliberately behaving in an effeminate way, or simply by having the confidence to cope with the jibes.

The 'new enterprisers'

This group was identified as a new successful proschool subculture, who embraced the 'new vocationalism' of the 1980s and 1990s (see Topic 6). They rejected the traditional academic curriculum, which they saw as a waste of time, but accepted the new vocational ethos, with the help and support of the new breed of teachers and their industrial contacts. In studying subjects such as business studies and computing, they were able to achieve upward mobility and employment by exploiting school–industry links to their advantage.

'Real Englishmen'

These were a small group of middle-class pupils, usually from a **liberal professional** background (their parents were typically university lecturers, or writers, or had jobs in the media). They rejected what teachers had to offer, seeing their own culture and knowledge as superior. They also saw the motivations of the 'achievers' and 'enterprisers' as shallow. While their own values did not fit with doing well at school, they did, however, aspire to university and a professional career. They resolved this dilemma by achieving academic success in a way that appeared effortless (whether it was or not).

Gay students

Finally, Mac an Ghaill looked at the experience of a group neglected entirely by most writers – gay students. These students commented on the **heterosexist** and **homophobic** nature of schools, which took for granted the naturalness of heterosexual relationships and the two-parent nuclear family.

Female subcultures

Mac an Ghaill refers to the **remasculinization of the vocational curriculum**. By this he means the higher-status subjects such as business studies, technology and computing, which have come to be dominated by males. Girls are more often on lower-level courses – doing stereotypical work experience in retail or community placements, for example. In Mac an Ghaill's study, although girls disliked the masculinity of the 'macho males', most sought boyfriends. Lower-class girls, in particular, even saw work as a potential marriage market. More upwardly mobile girls saw careers more in terms of independence and achievement.

Griffin (1985) studied young White working-class women during their first two years in employment. Rather than forming a large anti-authority grouping, they created small friendship groups. Their deviance was defined by their sexual behaviour rather than 'trouble-making'. Most importantly, there was not the same continuity between the school's culture and that of their future workplace as there had been for the lads in Willis's study. Instead, there were three possible routes for the girls, which they could follow all at the same time:

- the labour market – securing a job
- the marriage market – acquiring a permanent male partner
- the sexual market – having sexual relationships, while at the same time maintaining their reputation so as to not damage marriage prospects.

Ethnic subcultures

Ethnic-minority subcultures were discussed in Topic 3. However, it is worth reiterating here some of the key issues. For both males and females, their subcultural responses to school reflect a rejection of differential treatment on the basis of their ethnicity and gender. Such responses enable them to cope with and counter the negative experiences they suffer, and to redeem themselves, sometimes to their educational cost. Many Black boys reject school and education in favour of a culture of **conspicuous consumption** and street credibility, while Black girls strive to achieve in alternative ways, as they reject their teachers' low expectations of them. Other ethnic groups, such as Bangladeshi males, have adopted aspects of Black subcultural responses, while many Asian girls, though perceived as passive and relatively invisible, achieve while disguising their rebellion. However, all groups have substantial numbers of conformists who attract little attention.

It is clearly the case that the actual or perceived membership of subcultures in school has an impact on pupils' experience of schooling and their achievement, in a variety of ways. But the situation can be highly complex and it is difficult to generalize. There is considerable evidence, however, that teachers do respond to groups of students differently, whether they project a particular identity or not. Teachers bring with them certain expectations about particular groups and they may ascribe characteristics erroneously, which in turn can have particular consequences.

Labelling and the self-fulfilling prophecy

As we saw earlier in Topic 2, teachers' expectations can have the effect of creating a self-fulfilling prophecy, whereby whatever they anticipate comes to be translated into actual outcomes. This happens in one of two ways:

- Pupils accept the label teachers give them as being true and internalize it as part of their self-concept, seeing themselves as, for example, having low ability.
- They react against the labelling process and thus conform to negative assumptions, by exhibiting poor behaviour and/or underachievement.

The self-fulfilling prophecy was a very influential concept throughout the 1970s and 80s, and led to considerable educational reform. Educationalists began to acknowledge that placing pupils in different classes or schools on the basis of ability could damage the prospects of the less able considerably. Since the 1990s, these concerns have been abandoned as the quest for higher grades and **league table** positions has become more important (see Topic 6).

Teacher–pupil relationships

As the section on pupil subcultures showed, teachers' perceptions and subsequent interactions with students have a significant impact on pupils' educational experiences.

Teachers prefer to teach pupils whom they perceive to be well behaved, well motivated, well mannered, reserved and compliant. They tend to reward such pupils with praise and with good marks and subsequent placement in higher sets. Such pupils tend to be middle-class and White, not because of overt prejudice but because teachers tend to judge them by their own cultural standards, being generally members of the White middle classes themselves.

We saw in Topic 2 how interactionist sociologists identified teacher's perceptions of the 'ideal pupil' to be one who conforms to middle-class standards of behaviour. However, this earlier research (by Becker 1971) noted that teachers did not consciously ascribe low ability to working-class pupils. Rather, as is also confirmed by more recent research, teachers have a 'commonsense understanding of ability' which they think to be fair and without particular bias. Gillborn and Youdell (1999) suggest that teachers systematically discriminate against

working-class pupils by failing to recognize their intelligence because they do not exhibit it in the right way. Instead, they use their blinkered judgement to allocate working-class pupils to lower sets and foundation-tier examinations. Such pupils may respond with resentment, perceiving their treatment to be unfair. This may cause hostility, discipline problems and reduced motivation, impacting negatively on achievement and their relationship with their teachers.

We also saw in Topic 3 how differential treatment by teachers of particular ethnic-minority pupils can have negative consequences for the teacher–pupil relationship and for learning. Many, in particular, feel angry at the way they tend to be singled out for punishment when White pupils are often just as guilty. This too may lead to antischool sentiments and negative subcultural responses that make interaction with teachers even more confrontational. Many Black pupils, particularly boys, get drawn into this downward spiral of disengagement from schooling (Connolly 1998).

The organization of teaching and learning

The way pupils are allocated to teaching groups on the basis of the sometimes unfair judgements teachers make, shapes what pupils are taught and their ultimate success, both in terms of the qualifications that they achieve and their subsequent progression opportunities. These groupings can in themselves involve labelling and the self-fulfilling prophecy. The main methods of grouping are as follows:

- *Mixed ability* – where pupils of all abilities are taught together. Teaching tends to be differentiated to allow weaker pupils to engage, while stretching and challenging the more able. Proponents feel that there are both social and educational benefits. This approach allows for a broader social mix, reducing conflict in society and ensures that labelling on the basis of behaviour does not affect attainment. It also recognizes the fact that ability is not fixed, as children develop in spurts rather than all at the same rate.
- **Streaming** – where pupils are grouped by ability for most or all of their lessons. The top stream is the most academic group; the bottom streams the low achievers. Supporters believe that this ensures that the most able are not held back and the least able can be given the extra support they need.
- *Setting* – where pupils are placed in ability groups for particular subjects and so may be in the top set for one subject and a lower set in another. This is the most common form of ability grouping in England and Wales, especially as pupils approach GCSE, as it helps teachers to prepare pupils for a particular examination tier.
- *Within-class grouping*, where the teacher makes ability groups within the class, is the most common type of grouping. However, research into primary schools has shown that pupils are aware of which ability group or table they have been put with, and this does impact on motivation and self-esteem.

Numerous writers have suggested that the influence of league tables has increased the tendency for schools to separate pupils on the basis of ability. Ireson *et al.* (2002) notes that such

Research methods

Tony Sewell
Black masculinities and schooling

Tony Sewell (1996) conducted research in comprehensive schools in London. The bulk of the study took place in what Sewell refers to as 'Township School'. This school was a boys' comprehensive for children aged 11 to 16. There were 61 students of Asian origin, 63 of African origin, 140 of African-Caribbean origin, 31 mixed race students, 127 White boys and 23 'others'.

Sewell gathered his material through an ethnographic approach using semi-structured interviews and observation. At the time, he was in his early 30s and describes himself as Black. He is careful to point out that he was able to make very good relationships with the boys and was able to mix with them socially. He describes this process as being able to 'chill'.

Sewell found that some Black pupils were disciplined excessively by teachers who were socialized into racist attitudes and who felt threatened by these students' masculinity, sexuality and physical skills. Furthermore, the boys felt that their culture received little or no positive recognition.

Adapted from Blundell, J. and Griffiths J. (2002) *Sociology since 1995,* Lewes: Connect Publications

1 Why do sociologists such as Sewell often change the names of the schools in which they conduct research?

2 Why was it important for Sewell to make good relationships and 'chill' with the boys?

3 To what extent did Sewell's own social identity help his relationships with the boys?

4 Do you think the boys would have been completely honest with Sewell? Explain your answer.

5 What are the dangers for a researcher in identifying too strongly with the group being studied?

grouping is not always based on attainment within specific subjects – it has also been based on behaviour and used as a means of socially controlling particular groups of pupils. Ireson's research survey indicates that setting tends to be beneficial for the more able pupils in the top groups, while those in bottom sets generally receive little challenge or stimulation, and so can easily become demoralized, disruptive and disaffected.

Recent evidence from the Evaluation of the DfES African Caribbean Achievement Project (Aiming High) (Tikly *et al.* 2006 – see Research methods, p. 217) does appear to indicate that African-Caribbean pupils are underrepresented in higher-ability sets, higher test and examination tiers, and in gifted and talented cohorts.

Although there has been a lot of research on the academic, social and personal outcomes of grouping pupils by ability, there has been little from the pupils' perspective. Research by Hallam *et al.* (2004) illustrates the impact of ability grouping as pupils perceive it. Six pupils, of high, moderate or low ability, mixed in gender, in each Key Stage 2 class were interviewed in each of six primary schools adopting different combinations of grouping practices, including streaming, setting, within-class ability and mixed-ability grouping.

At primary level, the authors found the following:

- In reading, most pupils wished to be in the top group because it gave them status and a feeling of superiority. However, most pupils (excluding the top groups) preferred whole-class or individual work because they didn't like to feel left out.

- Social adjustment, social attitudes and attitudes to peers of different ability were 'healthier' among children in non-streamed classes.

- The more streams there were, the more negative were the attitudes of those in the lower streams.

- Pupils of below-average ability who were taught by teachers who believed in streaming could become friendless or neglected by others.

According to the authors, what research there is on ability grouping in secondary schools suggests the following:

- *Streaming* may play a major role in polarizing pro- and antischool attitudes among pupils (with higher-level students being pro and lower ones anti).

- *Setting* may produce more negative than positive consequences among mathematics students, with a high proportion of students wanting to move sets or change to mixed-ability teaching.

- *Ability grouping* – when it involves setting – is the preferred form of grouping among secondary pupils, but the greater the level of mixed-ability teaching in the school, the more it is the preferred option among students.

The research on ability grouping is inconclusive, generally demonstrating that, overall, it has little or no impact on school achievement levels, but that those in the top sets do better than they otherwise might, while those in the bottom sets do worse. The winners tend to be the White middle classes; the losers, working-class and ethnic-minority pupils. Streaming and setting had been in decline throughout the 1970s and 1980s. As the final topic shows, however, since results were published from secondary schools in 1992 and from primary schools in 1997, league tables (where schools are ranked on the basis of their highest results) have forced many schools to return to various systems of ability grouping. This is because schools now operate in a marketplace where they compete for pupils and resources.

Check your understanding

1 How do the views of functionalists and Marxists differ with regard to the role of the hidden curriculum?

2 For three of the bullet points illustrating the means by which the hidden curriculum is transmitted (see p. 229), suggest the impact they may have on pupils.

3 How, according to Hargreaves, did 'low-stream failures' respond to their label?

4 Explain in your own words why the work of early writers on pupil cultures has been criticized.

5 How has the economic situation for working-class males changed since the 1970s?

6 Which of Mac an Ghaill's male subcultures were proschool, and which antischool? What were the reasons for this?

7 Give two examples of the ways in which the experience of female subcultures is said to be different from that of male subcultures.

8 How might pupils react to negative labels and low expectations from teachers?

9 Why do working-class and ethnic-minority pupils get assigned to lower-ability groups?

10 Describe three ways in which teachers group pupils by perceived ability. How might each arrangement affect pupils of high and low ability?

Key terms

Adaptations refers here to different ways of responding to compulsory schooling (e.g. by being a teacher's pet, by going through the motions but not trying to achieve anything, or by doing your own thing).

Conspicuous consumption public enjoyment of possessions that are known to be expensive so that the ability to pay for such things is 'shown off'.

Ethos the arrangement, character, or fundamental values peculiar to a specific person, people, culture or organization.

Heterosexist biased against homosexuals.

Homogeneous the same throughout, undifferentiated.

Homophobic fearing that homosexuals pose a threat of some kind.

League tables rank ordering of schools according to their test and examination results.

Liberal professional university-educated (usually in the arts/humanities) people who tend to be open-minded and encourage personal freedom and self-expression, and who tend to work in areas that enable this outlook to thrive.

Remasculinization of the vocational curriculum term used by Mac an Ghaill to describe the process whereby higher-status subjects such as business studies and technology come to be dominated by boys, while girls are more often on lower-level or stereotypically female courses.

Streaming where pupils are taught in groups according to their perceived ability.

YTS Youth Training Scheme (see Topic 6).

Activities

Research ideas

1 Conduct a participant observational survey of your school or college to identify pro- and antischool subcultures. (Use Mac an Ghaill's categories as well as some of your own.)

2 Design a questionnaire to examine the relationships between class, ethnicity and gender and subcultural membership.

Web.task

Go to www.chavscum.co.uk – this is a humorous site that claims to have identified a subculture called 'chavs'. Look around the site. To what extent do you think that this group actually exists? And, if they do exist, what attitudes towards education are they likely to have?

Relationships and processes in schools

Item A

Despite being fresh out of Torquay Boys' Grammar, Adrian Bougourd, 18, Will Rushmer, 19, and Ryan Hayward, 18, beat the other five teams on the Channel 4 fantasy share game show, *Show Me The Money*, at the end of the ten-week series. The youngest contestants [on the show] have made a profit of over £55,000 on an imaginary £100,000 lump sum in only eight weeks.

The teenagers started taking an interest in the stock market last year when their school entered the ProShare national investment programme. Both Will, who is studying economics at Warwick, and Ryan are hoping for a career in the City in either fund management or investment banking once they have finished their degrees. Adrian, who is studying finance, accounting and management at Nottingham University, is toying with the idea of financial journalism. The Three Freshers, as they called themselves for the show, are just one of thousands of investment clubs in the UK.

Adapted from *The Times*, 11 November 2000

Item B

Gang culture in the north east of England means teenagers deliberately fail exams to stay cool, a study says. A poll of 4000 Tyneside teenagers says peer pressure stops many pupils from studying or taking part in lessons.

Researchers say an antischool subculture known as 'charvers' reject school as uncool and refuse to do GCSE course work, meaning they fail their exams. The charvers typically wear fake designer and sports gear and are usually from poor backgrounds.

Researchers questioned teenagers aged between 15 and 17. They found the charvers' attitude was that school was uncool but college was OK, and that most expected to resit their GCSEs at FE colleges. The research was by Lynne Howe, director of the South Tyneside Excellence in Cities programme. She said: 'For some youngsters – those known as charvers – being cool and well thought of among their peers is the most important thing.

'These youngsters were largely from a deprived population but they didn't lack confidence or self-esteem. They deliberately fail their GCSEs because their social standing outside school is more important than any qualification. They were scared of being called names, physical threats and damage to the family home and property if they were seen doing homework or answering questions in class.'

The former teacher said the teenagers identified five different groups in school, including charvers, radgys (more aggressive than charvers), divvies (impressionable hangers-on to the charvers), goths (wear dark clothes but often work hard) and freaks, who work hard and are considered 'normal' by teachers.

Nearly a third of the 15 year olds said they had been picked on for doing well at school, while the same proportion admitted teasing others who participated in lessons. Some said they would rather fail their GCSEs and take resits at college, hoping to get into higher education later, than risk being targeted by bullies at school.

Adapted from BBC Online News, September 2004

(a) Explain what is meant by 'antischool subcultures' (Item B). (2 marks)

(b) Describe three different subcultures that sociologists have identified among male pupils. (6 marks)

(c) Outline some of the reasons why pupils form subcultures. (12 marks)

(d) Using information from the Items and elsewhere, assess the extent to which pupil subcultures are the cause of failure in school. (20 marks)

Grade booster Getting top marks in the 20-mark question

Remember to make use of both the Items. Item A could be used to illustrate a proschool subculture, while B provides examples of both pro- and antischool subcultures. You need to link these to sociological explanations and studies of pupil subcultures (such as Willis, Hargreaves, Mac an Ghaill, Griffin or others). Explain why some pupils join these subcultures and what effect this has on their achievement. Remember to deal with proschool as well as antischool subcultures. For this question you need to evaluate the sociological explanations, for example by considering other factors (such as home background) that may cause pupils to fail.

Social policy and education

Getting you thinking

SECONDARY SCHOOL PERFORMANCE

BOLTON	PUPILS AGED 14	(% achieving level 5 or above in test)			PUPILS AGED 15	5 or more Grades A*-C	5 or more Grades A*-G	% in age group who passed
		ENGLISH	MATHS	SCIENCE				
Al Jamiah Al Islamiyyah	22	55%	59%	36%	23	0%	22%	26%
Bolton Muslim Girls' School	65	95%	71%	54%	61	54%	97%	0%
Bolton School Boys' Division	-	-	-	-	139	96%	96%	4%
Bolton School Girls' Division	-	-	-	-	120	99%	99%	1%
Canon Slade CofE School	270	90%	90%	88%	246	81%	98%	0%
The Deane School	154	46%	53%	47%	175	27%	80%	15%
George Tomlinson School	123	41%	42%	42%	85	22%	91%	6%
Harper Green School	288	68%	59%	59%	258	36%	92%	2%
Hayward School	260	63%	58%	56%	232	31%	91%	3%
Little Lever School Specialist Language College	210	64%	70%	63%	231	47%	97%	2%
Lord's College	-	-	-	-	9	44%	89%	0%
Mount St Joseph RC High School, Bolton	183	63%	67%	69%	205	42%	92%	5%
Rivington and Blackrod High School	310	70%	71%	69%	303	52%	94%	2%
St James's Church of England Secondary School	200	80%	83%	84%	178	56%	98%	1%
St Joseph's RC High School and Sports College	174	73%	85%	78%	154	69%	98%	0%
Sharples School	214	48%	56%	66%	203	42%	90%	

1 Why do so many schools produce glossy brochures? Where does the money to produce these come from? What else could it be spent on?

2 Why have recent governments been keen to produce education 'league tables'?

3 Apart from improving quality, what can schools do to improve their position in league tables?

4 Why do you think the developments discussed here are sometimes referred to as the 'marketization' of education?

5 What arguments can be put forward:

(a) in favour of marketization?   (b) against marketization?

The questions above should have encouraged you to think about the effects of what sociologists have called the '**marketization**' of schools. The idea behind marketization is that schools compete for pupils; the best schools attract the most pupils and the weaker schools have to improve. As you may have noticed from your own experiences, the idea of marketization is still very much alive. This topic traces the origins of this and other key themes in social policy on education.

1870 to 1944

Since its introduction in 1880, compulsory education had been a haphazard affair, controlled by local administrators who oversaw the provision of basic skills, along with religious and moral instruction. Boys and girls were often taught separately, with boys trained in technical skills, and girls in domestic competence. Socialization into obedience and deference (respect for superiors) was the norm. A small proportion of bright working-class children won scholarships to continue their education free at fee-paying schools.

Social democracy and educational reform

Ideas began to change between the wars – in particular, away from the idea that society had a natural order based on ascribed status. In 1918, all men over the age of 21 were given the right to vote, while women gained equal voting rights in 1928. The social democratic idea took hold that all citizens should have a say in the way society operates.

From a **social democratic perspective**, society should be based on justice and fairness; everyone should have an equal chance to succeed. In other words, society should be meritocratic – based on equality of opportunity. Education had an important part to play in this meritocracy, as it could be the mechanism through which individuals had equal chances to develop their talents.

1944 to 1965

Up until the end of the Second World War, it was clear that those with the most access to education and the opportunities it provided were the sons and daughters of the middle and upper classes. Social democratic thinkers believed that social inequalities could be reduced by providing greater educational opportunities. This approach to educational policy dominated thinking between 1945 and 1979, and has reappeared – at least partially – since New Labour came to power in 1997.

The tripartite system

As part of their aim to create a 'land fit for heroes' after the Second World War, Butler's Education Act of 1944 introduced **secondary education** for all pupils. The act may have had no effect on the **public schools**, but it did aim to abolish class-based inequalities within state education. A tripartite system was to be introduced, providing three types of secondary school, each suited to one of three types of ability:

- grammar schools for academically able pupils
- technical schools
- secondary modern schools for everyone else.

Underpinning this system was the idea of equality of opportunity. All children would take an **IQ test** at the age of 11 in order to discover which kind of school most suited their abilities. The government accepted the view that intelligence was innate (in-born) and could be scientifically measured. While only those who passed the **11+ test** went to grammar or technical schools, each of the three types of school was supposed to have similar standards of provision and be considered as equals ('**parity of esteem**'), as each school would provide the most suitable education for the development of each type of learner, irrespective of their background.

Problems of the tripartite system

1   For most pupils only two types of school were available – grammar and secondary moderns. Few technical schools were built because of the cost of equipping them.
2   Grammar schools, attended by around 20 per cent of pupils, were seen as the most prestigious type of state secondary school. They specialized in academic subjects that led to university and a well-paid job. The 75 per cent of pupils who attended secondary moderns were seen as 'failures'. Many were not allowed to take exams, so were denied opportunities to progress. There was no 'parity of esteem', instead a huge wastage of talent.
3   Some pupils ended up in secondary modern schools irrespective of their ability. Girls generally achieved better marks than boys in the 11+, yet the pass mark for girls was set higher as there were fewer girls' grammar school places available (many grammar schools being single-sex).
4   The social class divide remained intact. Two thirds of grammar school places were taken by middle-class pupils. The mainly working-class pupils in secondary moderns were effectively labelled 'failures' and so lacked the means and motivation to succeed.

The system still had its supporters. It served many middle-class families very well, such that even today it survives in a few areas of the country. It must also be remembered that it did provide almost guaranteed social mobility for those working-class pupils who made it to grammar schools. Some recent research has gone so far as to suggest the system gave working-class pupils more chances than they have today – see Research methods, p. 205.

1965 to 1979

Comprehensive schools

The tripartite system had not succeeded in creating equality of opportunity. What might bring that ideal closer was to abolish selection at 11 and educate all children in the same school, regardless of their class, ethnicity, gender or ability. In 1965, the Labour government instructed all local authorities to submit plans for comprehensive reorganization. Facilities were upgraded so that the new comprehensive schools could provide a broad curriculum and more sporting and recreational activities.

Problems of comprehensive schools

1   In practice, comprehensive schools did not live up to their ideal. Admissions were based on geographical catchment areas, often inhabited mainly by one social class, so social mixing at school was limited. Also, the tripartite system continued in some areas and independent education remained an option for the most wealthy.
2   Most comprehensive schools organized their classes by ability, for example by streaming. Because of the links between social class and achievement, this meant that higher streams were dominated by middle-class pupils and lower streams by working-class. Sociological studies by writers such as Hargreaves (1967) and Ball (1981) showed that the class divide that existed between grammar and secondary modern schools was reappearing within comprehensives (see p. 231 for more detail on the effects of streaming and banding).

During the 1970s, comprehensive schools came under increasing attack. From the social democratic perspective, class differences were not budging, so equality of opportunity still remained some distance away.

But the loudest criticisms came from what has become known as the New Right. The focus was lack of discipline, poor results, large classes and failure to prepare pupils for the world of work. It did not matter that there seemed little evidence to support these criticisms (for example, exam results were improving during this period) – momentum grew for change. In 1997, the Conservative Party won the general election, and Margaret Thatcher became prime minister.

1979 to 1997

Education and the New Right

New Right policies became increasingly influential during the Conservative governments of 1979 to 1997. New Right policies favour the use of market forces as a method of distributing resources. In a free market, consumers have choice and choose between a range of products. Producers compete to produce the best product at the best price. In this way, schools compete to attract pupils and educational standards improve.

Their first actions, though, involved trying to tackle the growing problem of youth unemployment.

Vocational education and training

The Conservatives felt that youth unemployment was the result of schools' failure to teach appropriate work skills. This 'skills crisis' was to blame for Britain's economic decline. A number of schemes were developed that aimed to reduce youth unemployment, increase young people's skill levels and make them more aware of the world of work. These became known as the '**New vocationalism**' (see Table 6.2).

Criticisms of the New vocationalism

Vocational education and training have had many critics, particularly from neo-Marxist writers. Finn (1987) argues that there is a hidden political agenda to vocational training:

- It provides cheap labour for employers and keeps the pay rates of young workers low.
- It undermines the bargaining power of the unions (because only permanent workers can be members).
- It reduces politically embarrassing unemployment statistics.
- It may also be intended to reduce crime by removing young people from the streets.

Critics such as Phil Cohen (1984) argued that the real purpose of vocational training is to create 'good' attitudes and work discipline rather than actual job skills. In this way, young people come to accept a likely future of low-paid and unskilled work. Those young unemployed who view training schemes as cheap labour, and refuse to join them, are defined as irresponsible and idle, and are 'punished' by the withdrawal of benefits.

It is not proven that young people lack job skills. Many have already gained a lot of work experience from part-time jobs. Youth unemployment is the result not of a shortage of skills, but of a shortage of jobs. Critics also point out that the sorts of skills taught to YTS trainees are only appropriate for jobs in the secondary labour market. This consists of jobs that are unskilled, insecure, and pay low wages – such jobs offer little chance of promotion, employer investment is very low, and labour turnover is consequently very high.

In practice, it is lower-ability students who tend to be channelled into vocational courses. The new vocationalism thus introduced another form of selection, with working-class and ethnic-minority students being disproportionately represented on these courses.

Training schemes were also criticized for failing to break down traditional patterns of sex stereotyping found in employment and education; nor are they encouraging girls to move into nontraditional areas. In fact, according to Buswell (1987), they are structured so as to reproduce gender inequality. She pointed out that the types of schemes into which girls are channelled, such as retail work, lead to occupations where they are low paid when young, and work part time when older,

Table 6.2 Conservative work-based education and training initiatives	
National Vocational Qualifications (NVQs)	In 1986, the National Council for Vocational Qualifications was set up to introduce standardized vocational qualifications for particular occupations. These were job-specific qualifications which demonstrate 'on-the-job' competencies, such as 'production machine sewing', and are often studied part time in college in the evening, or on day release, alongside full-time work. They now cover about 88 per cent of all occupations.
General National Vocational Qualifications (GNVQs)	GNVQs are studied in school as an alternative to academic courses and cover wider areas – for example, leisure and tourism and health and social care; GNVQs were available from 1995.
Modern Apprenticeships (renamed as **Apprenticeships** in 2005)	From 1995, these programmes combined training at work with part-time attendance at college with the aim of achieving an NVQ qualification at Level 3 (equivalent to an A-level) as well as other accreditation and skills.
Training schemes	A Youth Training Scheme (YTS) was a one-year training scheme combining work experience with education for school leavers. In 1986, YTS was extended to a two-year scheme. YTS was replaced in 1990 with Youth Training. The only requirement in this scheme was for employers to ensure that trainees followed some sort of training programme which led towards a Level 2 NVQ.

reflecting women's position in the labour market. This problem has remained up to the present day. For example, according to figures from the DfES, in 2006, 6 per cent of Apprenticeships in hairdressing were taken up by males compared with 94 per cent by females. Retail fares slightly better with a 38/62 split, whereas in construction crafts, the male-to-female ratio is 99 to 1.

The 1988 Education Reform Act

The influence of the New Right is clearly seen in this Act, the most influential in education since 1944. It introduced a new emphasis on competition and choice in education. Its key elements consisted of the following.

Marketization

Competition between schools was to be encouraged. The greater the competition, the greater the incentive for schools to improve. Successful schools could expand; unsuccessful schools would have to improve or face the possibility of funding cuts and, ultimately, closure. Parents would be given a real choice between schools.

Testing

Parents would need a way of judging the quality of schools. It was decided that all pupils would sit national tests at the ages of 7, 11 and 14. These, along with GCSE and A-level results, would be used to draw up league tables so that parents could make an informed choice of school.

The National Curriculum

In order to develop meaningful standards for comparison and to ensure that all pupils received teaching in appropriate knowledge and skills, a **National Curriculum** was introduced. This prescribed knowledge in a range of subjects that every school would have to teach. In addition, the influence of local authorities on education was reduced. Schools could decide how to manage their own budgets and even opt out of local authority control altogether, enabling them to make their own decisions about which pupils to admit, even introducing selection if they wished.

Criticisms of the Education Reform Act

1 Concerns were expressed over the damaging, stressful effects of testing children so often – also, that testing could distort what was taught so that schools would 'teach to the test'.
2 League tables were felt to be counterproductive. They meant that some schools might not admit low achievers and difficult pupils or enter them for exams. Competition might also force schools to spend large amounts of money on marketing rather than on the education of pupils (see 'Getting you thinking' on p. 235).
3 Very few extra places were available in popular schools, so many parents had very little or no choice of school.
4 Some critics felt that the Act was more motivated by the Conservative government's desire to reduce the power of Labour-controlled local authorities than improving education.
5 Class differences were reinforced by the Act. Middle-class parents were able to use their cultural capital (see Topic 2) to make sure that their children got into the best schools. Research by Ball *et al.* (1994) showed that middle-class parents were better able to impress at interview, write convincing letters and manipulate the system, for example by making multiple applications to schools. They could also use their economic capital (money) to pay transport costs if better schools were further away and even move nearer their favoured school if necessary.

1997 onwards

New Labour: New Right influences

New Right thinking has continued to influence the New Labour government elected in 1997. Many of the policies begun by the Conservatives have been continued and developed. One example is the expansion of **specialist schools**.

Specialist schools

Schools have been encouraged to specialize in particular subjects. The aim has been to increase choice, encourage competition, raise standards and allow schools to excel at their specialisms. No longer do school pupils have to attend what the Education secretary of the day David Blunkett referred to as the 'bog standard' local comprehensive school.

State secondary schools can apply to become a specialist school in one of ten specialisms – art, business and enterprise, engineering, humanities, languages, mathematics and computing, music, science, sports and technology. They must raise £50 000 from sponsors, which will be matched by government funding. Once a specialist school, they can select up to 10 per cent of their pupils who show an aptitude for their specialism.

In 1997, New Labour inherited 196 specialist schools from the Conservatives. Ten years later, there were 2500 – about 80 per cent of all secondary schools in England.

Work-related learning

Another strand of policy inherited from the Conservatives is a focus on work-related learning and training. A number of initiatives illustrate New Labour's continued commitment to the aim of improving the skills of the workforce in order for Britain to remain competitive in the global marketplace. In particular, the raising of the minimum age of leaving full-time education to 18 has brought with it various initiatives to allow schools and colleges more options in providing vocational education and training (see Table 6.3).

New Labour: social democratic influences

By no means all New Labour's educational policies have reflected New Right thinking, however. The influence of social democratic viewpoints has also been apparent. Here are some examples of policies which aim to reduce **social exclusion** and promote equality of opportunity.

- *Academies* – In 2001, it was proposed that Academies should be established in partnership with employers and other sponsors to replace failing schools and provide high-quality education for all in deprived areas. The best teachers would be encouraged to work in these schools and there would be a high level of resourcing. Sponsors can have a say in how the school is run and what curriculum is on offer. In the sense that Academies represent private companies becoming involved in state education, there is also a New Right influence visible in this policy.
- *Sure Start* – This term describes a wide range of programmes targeted at giving young children a better start in life. Free nursery education is now available, and Sure Start children's centres bring together a range of educational and other support services in disadvantaged communities.
- *Educational Maintenance Allowances* – Students between the ages of 16 and 19 who are in full-time education and training can now apply for Educational Maintenance Allowances of up to £30 a week. These are available to families on lower incomes and aim to encourage young people to stay in education.

Evaluation of New Labour policies

The influence of New Right ideas on government thinking has meant that competition and choice have continued to be seen as the key way to improve educational standards. However, as Sally Tomlinson has pointed out, in practice, the middle classes have gained most from these policies (Tomlinson 2005). In addition, the focus on exams and league tables has meant that

Table 6.3 Labour's work-based education and training initiatives

New Deal for Young People (NDYP)	In 1998, Labour introduced the DNYP, with the aim of reducing youth unemployment. The programme was designed for 18 to 24 year olds who had been unemployed and claiming Jobseeker's Allowance for six months. They were provided with Personal Advisors to guide them through the various options: (1) full-time education or training for up to 12 months; (2) work for six months in either the Environmental Task Force or the voluntary sector; (3) a subsidized job with at least one day a week of training; (4) loss of benefits if they refused to take part in the programme. From April 1998 to the end of May 2005, 567 900 (46 per cent) of those leaving the programme entered employment (*Social Trends* 2006). Most jobs were relatively short term.
Apprentice-ships	Labour also expanded the Apprenticeship scheme (finally dropping the term 'Modern' in 2005). More NVQs at Level 2 or 3 were offered, as well as a technical certificate and Key Skills to complete a full framework. Young apprenticeships at Level 1 for 14 to 16 year olds in schools and colleges have also been introduced.
Vocational GCSEs/AVCEs	These replaced GNVQs in an attempt to create parity of esteem with academic courses.
Increased Flexibility programme	Pupils at Key stage 4 (14 to 16) were allowed to attend college for one or two days per week to follow vocational qualifications not available at school. Most schools used the IFP to re-engage disaffected young people.
Diplomas (formerly Specialist diplomas)	A combination of vocational and academic learning studied alongside other complementary qualifications and embedded skills. The aim is to engage all 14 to 19 year olds in education and further study, delivered in partnerships between schools, colleges and employers.

much education has become, as she puts it, 'examination techniques, rote learning and revision'.

Social democratic influences on educational policy have resulted in the directing of resources towards deprived groups and areas. This may have resulted in some improvements although these are not yet clear (McKnight *et al.* 2005).

New Labour policy on higher education presents an interesting case study of the way in which New Labour has tried to increase opportunities.

Higher education

A stated aim of the government has been to increase the numbers of students in higher education. The target is that 50 per cent of young people will be entering higher education by 2010. To meet this target, university facilities have been expanded, funded by the replacement of student grants with loans, to be repaid once the graduate's salary has reached a certain level. Also, students now have to meet some of the cost of their tuition fees. Financial support for less affluent applicants is available.

So, is the government's plan to encourage a wider range of young people to apply to university working? In one sense it is:

the percentage of young people from manual working-class backgrounds going to university increased from 11 per cent to 19 per cent between 1991/2 and 2001/2 (*Social Trends 34*). However, over the same period, the percentage from middle-class backgrounds increased from 35 to 50 per cent. Recent statistics from the Higher Education Statistics Agency show that only 28.7 per cent of young entrants to university in 2004/5 came from lower socio-economic groups. If anything, class inequalities in higher education have increased (McKnight *et al.* 2005).

What is more, a range of research evidence shows that university students from a working-class background are more likely to:

- study at local institutions with limited course options
- live at home while studying
- study part time
- have family or work commitments
- incur high levels of student debt
- drop out from their initial choice of course.

See also the Research methods on 'Fear of debt' on p. 240.

Conclusion

The changes in higher education under New Labour reflect the overall pattern of their policies on education: opportunities have increased for everybody, but class inequalities remain stubbornly present. Back in 1971, Basil Bernstein wrote that 'education cannot compensate for society' – in other words, education will tend to reflect social inequalities rather than eliminate them. That seems to be the story of education under New Labour.

Key terms

11+ IQ test taken at the age of 11 to determine what sort of school you would attend under the tripartite system.

IQ tests supposedly objective tests that establish a person's 'intelligence quotient' (how clever they are).

Marketization the move towards educational provision being determined by market forces.

National Curriculum what every pupil in every state school must learn, decided by the government.

New vocationalism a series of measures in the 1980s that re-emphasized the importance of work-related education.

Parity of esteem equal status, equally valued.

Public schools the top private fee-paying schools, e.g. Eton, Harrow, Roedeen.

Secondary education education between ages 11 and 16.

Social democratic perspective supports the view that a democratically elected government can work to reduce the perceived injustices of the capitalist market system.

Social exclusion the situation where people are unable to achieve a quality of life that would be regarded as acceptable by most people.

Specialist schools schools which have a particular focus within their curriculum and links to specialist areas of work, e.g. arts and media, business, languages, healthcare and medicine. They can select 10 per cent of their intake on the basis of ability.

Vocational work-related.

Research methods

Callendar and Jackson (2004)
Fear of debt

One policy of the Labour Government elected in 1997 was to increase numbers going to university. At the same time, the cost to students of a university education has been going up. Student grants have been replaced as the main source of funding by loans that have to be repaid once they graduate and are earning a reasonable income.

Callendar and Jackson's study investigates whether students from poorer families were more likely than those from better-off backgrounds to be deterred from applying to university by concerns about cost and debts, especially the student loan debt.

The research involved a survey of prospective higher-education students producing quantitative data. 101 school sixth forms and further education colleges agreed to take part, and 3582 questionnaires were sent out. A national stratified random sample of schools and colleges was used. Responses were received from 1954 students in 82 schools and colleges; a 55 per cent response rate was achieved.

Self-completion questionnaires were handed out to students in classes by teachers. Three questions were asked to gather information on general level of debt aversion; students were asked to what extent they agreed or disagreed with these statements:

- 'Owing money is basically wrong.'
- 'There is no excuse for borrowing money.'
- 'You should always save up first before buying something.'

Students were then asked their attitudes towards statements about the costs and benefits of going to university, e.g. 'Borrowing money to pay for a university education is a good investment.'

Callendar and Jackson's conclusion is that, 'Debt aversion is a class issue'. Those from lower income groups were more debt averse (more likely to see debt as negative, to be avoided) than the other classes. This was true even holding constant the type of institution they attended (college or state or independent school), gender, ethnicity and age. The lower income group was also more likely to see more costs than benefits in going to university.

Adapted from Blundell, J. and Griffiths, J. (2008)
Sociology since 2000, Lewes: Connect Publications

1 Explain how the researchers attempted to make their sample representative of prospective university applicants.

2 What is meant by a 'response rate'?

3 What are the advantages and disadvantages of using a quantitative approach to investigate fear of debt and its influence on university application?

4 What problems may have been caused by the method used to distribute the questionnaires?

Check your understanding

1 How was the education system organized prior to 1944?

2 Why was Butler's Education Act introduced?

3 Give three reasons why the tripartite system was gradually phased out.

4 Why did comprehensivization create less social mixing than was anticipated?

5 What key principles lie behind the New Right approach to education?

6 Describe three criticisms of the 'New vocationalism'.

7 How did the Education Reform Act 1988 attempt to create a more unified and accountable education system?

8 How can it be argued that the Act failed to achieve this?

9 Give one example of a New Labour educational policy influenced by New Right thinking. Explain your answer.

10 Give one example of a New Labour educational policy influenced by social democratic thinking. Explain your answer.

11 Explain the phrase 'Education cannot compensate for society' using New Labour's higher education policy as an example.

Activities

Research idea

Interview an experienced member of your school or college staff. Ask them to describe the impact that the following changes had upon their educational career and experiences: the introduction of the National Curriculum, school/college inspections, league tables, competition between schools/colleges, parental choice and Educational Maintenance Allowances.

Web.task

Visit the Standards site www.standards.dfes.gov.uk and find information on different types of schools and key educational initiatives.

Social policy and education

Item A

Ex-private (fee-paying) school students hold upwards of 75 per cent of the top jobs in British institutions, including the government, the civil service, the church, the legal system, the armed forces and the financial system in the City. Yet they make up only about 7 per cent of the school population. Furthermore, those who control these institutions come overwhelmingly from a few exclusive private schools – for example, Eton, Harrow, Winchester and Westminster – and have attended Oxford or Cambridge universities (the so-called 'Oxbridge connection'). Those who occupy the top jobs perpetuate these inequalities in two ways:

● by sending their own sons and daughters to these same schools
● by appointing new recruits to top jobs from these schools.

This restrictive elite self-recruitment is known as the 'old-boy' (or 'school-tie') network. (Private schools don't have to follow the National Curriculum, nor are their teachers inspected by central government officers.)

Adapted from Denscombe, M. (1993) *Sociology Update*, Leicester: Olympus Books

Item B

There is often a gap between the image promoted of youth training and its reality. The literature of YT often suggested that it could open up exciting and creative opportunities for young people regardless of social background. However, youth trainees have long complained that they are being trained for 'Noddy jobs'. Certainly, there is evidence that the majority of YT places are provided by the big retailers – e.g. supermarkets and department stores, such as BHS and Marks and Spencer. Consequently, YT trainees have generally found themselves trained in a narrow range of skills, such as working on the till, shelf-filling and stocktaking, which are common to most retail jobs. One study found that 80 per cent of the jobs that YTS trainees went into required no entry qualification. There is also evidence that some employers are using YT as a screening device. If the trainee is uncomplaining, docile and flexible about the mundane tasks they are allocated, there is a good chance that they will be offered a post. Finally, while YT schemes emphasize equal opportunities for females and ethnic minorities, there is evidence that female training places reinforce traditional gender roles, while in some areas youth training places with major employers have been monopolized by White youth.

Adapted from Maguire, S. (September 1993) 'Training for a living? The 1990s youth labour market', *Sociology Review*, 3(1)

(a) **Explain the difference between vocational education and vocational training.** (4 marks)

(b) **Suggest two policies that could be introduced to reduce the inequalities perpetuated by public schools (Item A).** (4 marks)

(c) **Outline some of the policies that have attempted to overcome the academic/vocational divide in education.** (12 marks)

(d) **Using information from Item B and elsewhere, assess the view that vocational education and training schemes have done nothing to reduce social inequality.** (20 marks)

Grade booster Getting top marks in the 20-mark question

You need to identify a range of different schemes (e.g. YTS, Apprenticeships, NVQs, GNVQs). You should consider different views of vocational education and training (e.g. Cohen, Finn) and the functions they see it as performing, and contrast these with the idea that it opens up opportunities. Remember that you should use information from Item B – for example, to evaluate the view in the question. This could include the idea that youth training schemes in reality offer few skills, that they are used to select compliant employees, that they reinforce gender roles or discriminate against ethnic minorities.

Exam Practice

1 Read **Item A** below and answer parts (a) to (d) that follow.

Item A

From as early as 22 months, children of parents in the higher social classes I and II with higher educational levels are already 14 percentage points further up the scale of educational development than children of classes IV and V parents with low educational attainment.

Poverty also affects the likelihood of progressing through school to attain formal educational qualifications. For example, truants are more likely to have parents from poorer backgrounds, in low-skilled rather than managerial jobs, living in council housing. Similarly, children excluded from school are more likely to be from poorer families, have disrupted family circumstances or be from schools with a high level of disadvantage.

At GCSE, West found that low income could account for 66 per cent of the difference in attainment within a local authority area. Similarly, McCallum and Redhead found that GCSE success was associated with higher levels of home ownership and lower levels of unemployment.

An examiner comments

(a) Explain what is meant by 'anti-school subculture'. *(2 marks)*

2/2 It means a group of pupils who adopt norms, values etc that oppose those of the school.

> Clear and correct.

(b) Suggest **three** cultural factors that may affect educational achievement. *(6 marks)*

First, there is the attitude to education adopted by parents and children. For example, working-class children may be taught that education is a waste of time.

Second, some ethnic-minority groups may not see the point of education and so their children fail to take school seriously and so they under-achieve.

2/6 Third, not being able to afford books and similar items means children will be held back educationally.

> The first point is valid, but the second one is really just a repetition of the first, even though it refers to ethnicity rather than class.

> The third point – not being able to afford something – is a material not a cultural factor.

(c) Outline some of the functions of the education system. *(12 marks)*

The education system performs many different functions. Functionalists such as Durkheim and Parsons, and Marxists such as Bowles and Gintis, have different views on this question. Functionalists believe that the education system is beneficial for society as a whole, whereas Marxists see it as serving only the interests of the ruling class.

Durkheim believes that the main functions of education include socializing young people into society by integrating children and encouraging them to make friends. Durkheim also sees education as teaching norms and values to the next generation. Another main function is to prepare people for their roles in their future careers.

8/12 Parsons agrees with Durkheim. He believes in meritocracy, and that the talented will be able to rise to the top. However, Marxists disagree, arguing that functionalists ignore the negative side of the education system. They believe that education's main function is to produce a hardworking labour force to be exploited by the ruling class.. Bowles and Gintis claim that teaching people skills only allows them to make more profit for the capitalists. New vocationalist courses such as NVQ help to prepare people for particular jobs, but as Marxists would say, they just produce cheap labour for employers.

> Good start – shows awareness of different sociological perspectives on the question.

> Quite good but a bit brief – e.g. could say why integrating children or teaching them norms and values is important.

> Quite good, but needs to bring out the contrast between the views – e.g. by using the 'myth of meritocracy' and the correspondence principle.

> Overall, quite a good answer to part (c), identifying a range of functions from two different perspectives. However, it would benefit from a fuller explanation of some of these – e.g. how does the education system ensure that pupils will allow themselves to become willing workers for capitalism to exploit? The answer needs more concepts, such as those identified above, to help with these explanations.

(d) Using information from Item A and elsewhere, assess the view that poverty is the main cause of social-class differences in achievement. *(20 marks)*

Education is supposed to be available to all children, no matter what their class background. Unfortunately, however, poverty does affect educational achievement. Working-class children who are in poverty do badly academically. This is mainly because of their lack of facilities, e.g. they cannot afford school equipment, computer, books etc. They lack a quiet place to work at home because of overcrowding. Their parents can't afford educational visits to museums etc. They're likely to have a poor diet, which can affect the ability to concentrate or to stay healthy, so they miss school through illness.

Sociologists such as Douglas have shown that most of the children who achieve high grades are middle-class children. This is because the education system is designed for them. Children from poor families have less parental support, e.g. because their parents are working long hours to make a living. Douglas found that many working-class parents did not attend parents' evenings and this could be why.

According to Item A, 'truants are more likely to have parents from poorer backgrounds'. This may be because their parents don't offer encouragement to do well, so the children don't see any point in being in school and so they are more likely to truant. Middle-class children are likely to be given maximum encouragement and support and the importance of staying on and gaining qualifications will be stressed to them from an early age.

In my view, poverty plays an important part in differences in achievement. This is because the system is designed to benefit the middle classes. As a result, working-class children don't fit in, so they have no way of bettering themselves and no support from their parents. Other children look down on them for being poor and teachers ignore them in favour of brighter children. But as well as poverty, ethnicity and gender also play a part in achievement. **13/20**

An examiner comments

This answer makes some use of Item A, but it could also use the references to council housing, unemployment, disrupted family circumstances, etc, by linking them to both poverty and low achievement. Other material factors could be mentioned, such as the hidden costs of schooling. Concepts such as material deprivation and cultural deprivation could be used. You could also bring in the idea of cultural capital to show how cultural and material factors are connected.

There is some analysis and evaluation here (e.g. in terms of why parents may not attend parents' evenings), but more is needed. You can begin to do this by bringing in a range of different concepts and explanations, and explaining how they differ and criticize each other. For example, not all poor children do badly, so there must be other factors at work, such as cultural differences (some poor parents offer more encouragement than others). You should also consider factors inside school, such as labelling by teachers and bullying by other pupils. It might be these things, rather than poverty as such, that cause many poor children to fail.

Beware of bringing in ethnicity and gender in inappropriate ways. The question is about class, and you can't easily explain class differences in achievement by talking about non-class factors such as these. In any case, ethnic differences in achievement may themselves be caused by poverty.

243

One for you to try

This question requires you to **apply** your knowledge and understanding of sociological research methods to the study of this **particular** issue in education.

2   Read **Item B** and answer the question that follows.

Item B

There is considerable evidence to show that pupils from some ethnic-minority backgrounds fall behind in school, particularly during the secondary phase. These include Black, Pakistani and Bangladeshi pupils. By contrast, Indian and Chinese pupils do better than the average. There are also class and gender differences in achievement within all these groups, just as there are among White pupils.

One explanation for these patterns of achievement lies in the school itself and the processes at work there. For example, Black pupils are more likely to be excluded from school than members of other ethnic groups. Other factors within school include peer groups and subcultures. For example, Sewell found that a minority of Black boys joined 'rebel' subcultures. However, he also found that some teachers labelled all Black boys as rebels, regardless of the facts.

An examiner comments

Remember that you need to know what the main features are of the method that you choose to write about, and you need to be able both to outline and to evaluate the method's advantages and disadvantages. These include practical, theoretical and ethical factors, such as time, cost, reliability, and validity. You need to apply these to the study of educational achievement among ethnic-minority pupils. For example, official statistics might be useful in obtaining an overall picture of rates of exclusion of different groups, but without giving any insight into reasons. By contrast, unstructured interviews might be useful in understanding the meanings behind the labelling process, but would be very time-consuming.

Using information from **Item B** and elsewhere, assess the strengths and limitations of **one** of the following methods for the study of educational achievement among ethnic-minority pupils:

(a) unstructured interviews

(b) official statistics. *(20 marks)*

Answers to the 'One for you to try' are available **free** on **www.collinseducation.com/sociologyweb**

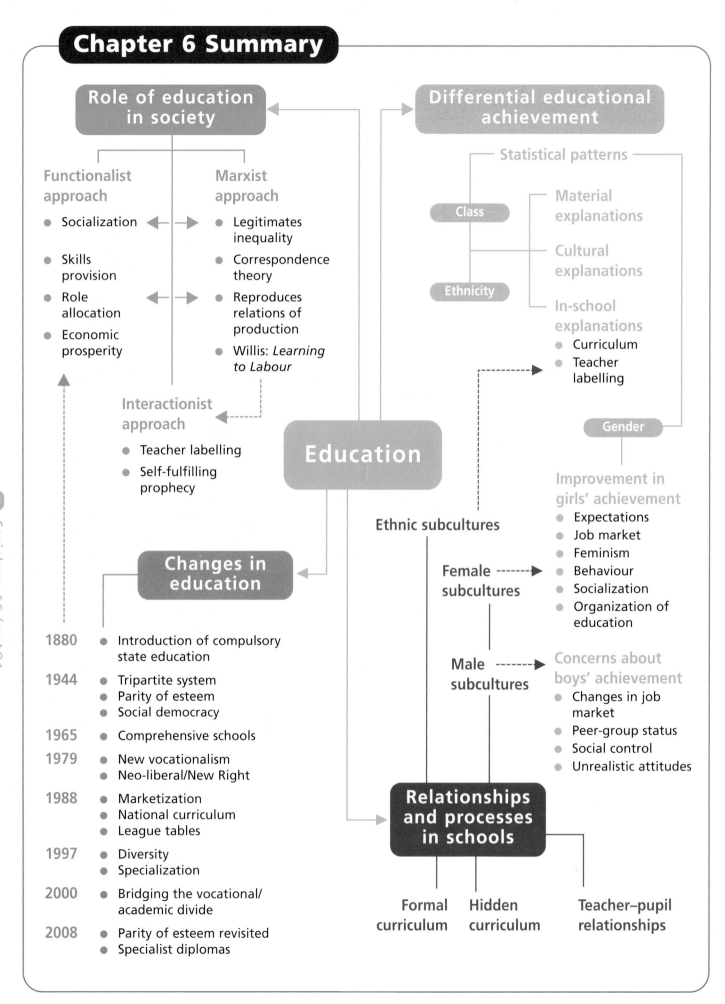

Role of education in society

Functionalist approach
- Socialization
- Skills provision
- Role allocation
- Economic prosperity

Marxist approach
- Legitimates inequality
- Correspondence theory
- Reproduces relations of production
- Willis: *Learning to Labour*

Interactionist approach
- Teacher labelling
- Self-fulfilling prophecy

Education

Changes in education

1880 ● Introduction of compulsory state education
1944 ● Tripartite system
 ● Parity of esteem
 ● Social democracy
1965 ● Comprehensive schools
1979 ● New vocationalism
 ● Neo-liberal/New Right
1988 ● Marketization
 ● National curriculum
 ● League tables
1997 ● Diversity
 ● Specialization
2000 ● Bridging the vocational/academic divide
2008 ● Parity of esteem revisited
 ● Specialist diplomas

Differential educational achievement

Statistical patterns

Class
Ethnicity

Material explanations

Cultural explanations

In-school explanations
- Curriculum
- Teacher labelling

Gender

Improvement in girls' achievement
- Expectations
- Job market
- Feminism
- Behaviour
- Socialization
- Organization of education

Ethnic subcultures

Female subcultures - - - - ▶

Male subcultures - - - - ▶

Concerns about boys' achievement
- Changes in job market
- Peer-group status
- Social control
- Unrealistic attitudes

Relationships and processes in schools

Formal curriculum Hidden curriculum Teacher–pupil relationships

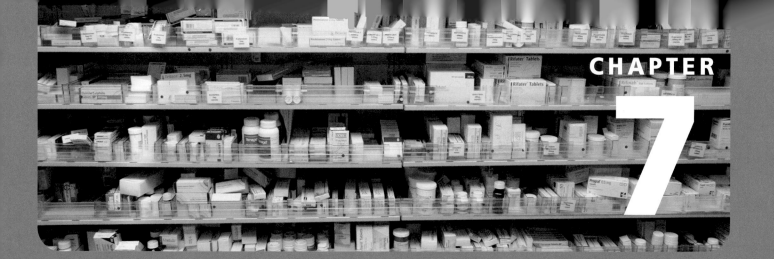

Health

AQA Specification	Topics	Pages
Candidates should examine:		
Health, illness, disability and the body as social and as biological constructs.	Covered in Topic 1	246–53
The unequal social distribution of health and illness in the United Kingdom by social class, age, gender, ethnicity and region, and internationally.	Covered in Topic 2	254–59
Inequalities in the provision of, and access to, health care in contemporary society.	Covered in Topic 3	260–65
The sociological study of the nature and social distribution of mental illness.	Covered in Topic 4	266–71
The role of medicine and the health professions.	Covered in Topic 5	272–77
The application of sociological research methods to the study of health.	Covered in every topic and the Exam Practice	278–79

TOPIC 1

Defining health, illness and disability

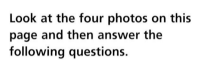

Look at the four photos on this page and then answer the following questions.

1 Which of these people are, in your opinion, 'abnormal' and which are 'normal'?

2 What suggestions can you make for helping 'abnormal' people make themselves 'normal'?

3 Next, indicate which of these people, if any, are 'ill'.

4 In small groups, compare your answers and explain how you made your decisions.

5 Do you think that health and illness and normal bodies have anything to do with society, or are they just natural, biological states?

This topic investigates the ways in which **health**, **illness** and **disability** are defined in our society and the implications for people who are defined as ill or disabled. The majority of the population pass most their lives taking for granted the normal, routine state of their bodies, until this 'normality' is disrupted in some way. At this point, people often say they are 'ill'. However, it is very unclear just what illness is. Surely, such an important concept does not vary simply according to how each individual feels? Anyway, how does anyone know what is 'normal'?

A second, linked area is the notion of 'abnormality'. If there is such a thing as 'normality', then there must be something which is 'abnormal'. This category might include those suffering from chronic (long-term) illness, such as multiple sclerosis, those with a 'mental illness' or those with a physical 'disability'.

Sociologists also want to understand how terms such as 'abnormality' and 'disability' are constructed and what implications there are for the people so labelled.

We begin by looking at how health and illness are defined and the implications of these definitions for society. We then extend our analysis to issues of disability and mental illness, and their implications for people labelled with these terms.

Definitions of health and illness

At some time, most of us will have woken up in the morning not really feeling very well. Despite telling our parents this, it may have been difficult to persuade them that we really were too ill to go to school or college (particularly if there was an exam that day or a particular lesson they knew we loathed). Only when we produced some real evidence, such as vomiting or a rash, were we believed. Our parents may also be rather less than supportive when it turns out that we have been drinking pretty heavily the night before. Ill or just hung over? And anyway, why is being hung over not being ill – after all, we feel awful? The answer from disapproving parents might well be that being hung over is the price we pay for a night's drinking and that it therefore does not count as a 'real' illness.

This situation illustrates a number of issues. First, it is not clear exactly what we mean by being 'healthy' and being 'unwell'. It seems that these concepts may well have different meanings depending upon who is defining them. In this case, us and our parents. Furthermore, there is a 'moral' element involved. If feeling ill is a result of having drunk too much, then this may be classified as just a 'hangover' and hence our own fault.

Definitions of illness and their consequences (get the day off college or have to endure a miserable day attending) form the starting point for the sociology of medicine.

To unravel this complex issue, we will look first at how ordinary, or **lay**, people construct their definitions of health and illness. We will then move on to look at the competing models amongst health practitioners themselves.

Lay definitions of health and illness

If definitions of health and illness vary, then we need to know just what factors appear to influence the way in which individuals define their sense of being healthy or ill. Sociologists have suggested that culture, age, gender and social class are particularly important.

Cultural differences

Different social groups have differing ideas of what constitutes illness. For example, Krause (1989) studied Hindu and Sikh Punjabis living in Bedford, and in particular focused on their illness called 'sinking heart' (*dil ghirda hai*) which is characterized by physical chest pain. According to Krause, this illness is caused by a variety of emotional experiences – most importantly, public shame of some sort. No such illness exists in other mainstream cultures in Britain.

Age differences

Older people tend to accept as 'normal' a range of pains and physical limitations which younger people would define as symptoms of some illness or disability. As we age, we gradually redefine health and accept greater levels of physical discomfort. In Blaxter's (1990) national survey of health definitions, she found that young people tend to define health in terms of physical fitness, but gradually, as people age, health comes to be defined more in terms of being able to cope with everyday tasks. She found examples of older people with really serious arthritis, who nevertheless defined themselves as healthy, as they were still able to carry out a limited range of routine activities.

Gender differences

According to Hilary Graham (2002), men have fewer consultations with doctors than women and appear to have lower levels of illness. This is partly due to the greater number of complications associated with childbirth and menopause that

Talcott Parsons
The sick role: sickness as deviance

According to Talcott Parsons (1975), being sick is a deviant act which can prevent a person undertaking their normal social functions. Society therefore controls this deviance through a device known as 'the sick role'. This is illustrated in Figure 7.1 below.

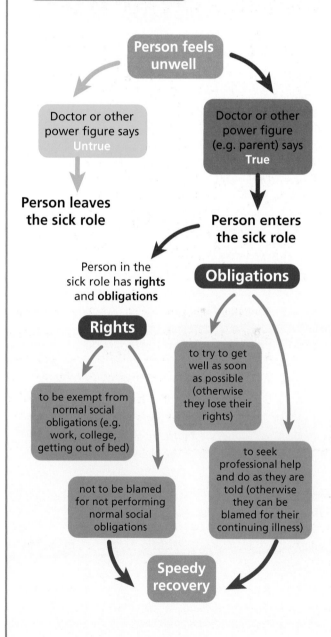

Figure 7.1 The sick role

1 **Think of examples of people you know who have 'unfairly' claimed the sick role. What do you think about them and their behaviour?**

2 **Are there some illnesses which, in your opinion, do not deserve the 'rights' of the sick role?**

women face, but it is also partly due to the fact that men are less likely to define themselves as ill or as needing medical attention. The idea of 'masculinity' includes the belief that a man should be tough and put off going to the doctor.

Despite the greater readiness of men to define themselves as healthy and to visit **GPs** less often, men have considerably higher mortality (death) rates than women.

Social class differences

Blaxter's research also showed that working-class people were far more likely to accept higher levels of 'illness' than middle-class people. Blaxter describes working-class people as 'fatalistic' – that is, they accepted poor health as 'one of those things'. As a result, people from lower social classes are less likely to consult a GP than middle-class people. This may be because they will accept a higher level of pain and discomfort before considering themselves ill enough to visit a doctor.

Medical definitions of health and illness

There is a distinction in most people's minds between those who think they are ill and those who really are ill. In contemporary society, the role of deciding whether the person is truly ill lies with doctors. If they decide that a person is ill, then a series of benefits flow, both formal (in the provision of medical help, or time off work or college) and informal (such as sympathy, release from household tasks and so on).

However, if they decide that you are not really ill, then you receive no benefits and may, in fact, be open to accusations of **malingering**.

Doctors use a particular 'scientific' measure of health and illness in order to decide whether someone really is ill or not. This model is known as the **biomedical model**, and it is the basis of all Western medicine. The elements of this model include the following:

● Illness is always caused by an identifiable (physical or mental) reason and cannot be the result of magic, religion or witchcraft.
● Illnesses and their causes can be identified, classified and measured using scientific methods.
● If there is a cure, then it will almost always be through the use of drugs or surgery, rather than in changing social relationships or people's spiritual lives.
● This is because the cause almost always lies in the actual physical body of the individual patient.

At its simplest, this model presents the human body as a type of machine and, just as with a machine, parts can go wrong and need repairing. Over time, the body 'wears out' just as a machine does and will eventually stop working completely. This is why the contemporary medical model is sometimes referred to as the 'bio-*mechanical*' model.

Illness and disease

What emerges from the discussion of health and illness is that individuals, using lay concepts of health, may define themselves as 'ill' or not, depending upon a range of social factors. On the other hand, doctors claim that they can scientifically determine, via medical tests, whether or not a person is ill. Eisenberg (1977) has therefore suggested that we should make a distinction between illness and disease. Illness is an individual's subjective experience of symptoms of ill health, whereas diseases are clinical conditions defined by medical professionals. It is therefore perfectly possible, as Blaxter has pointed out, to have an illness without a disease and a disease without an illness!

Traditional and non-Western definitions of health and illness

The biomedical model contrasts markedly with concepts of illness in traditional and non-Western societies, where illness is seen as the result of a wider range of factors than just the body itself.

In traditional societies, for example, these factors could include witchcraft – where the blame for the illness lies in the bad wishes of others, or possibly the 'will of God'. A more complex model of health exists in non-Western societies, where the body and the mind are seen as completely linked. Any understanding of the body must be linked with the person's mental state, and the two need to be treated together.

However, over the last two hundred years, the biomedical model of health has come to dominate healthcare and has excluded other approaches. This supremacy is linked to the wider development of science and scientific methods as the predominant form of knowledge in modern societies.

Complementary medicine

In recent years, there has been a major growth in alternative or **complementary** forms of health provision. These include therapies such as homeopathy, herbal medicines and acupuncture. Following the ideas of Giddens (1991) about the development of new ways of thinking and acting in contemporary society, which he characterizes as **late modernity** (see p. 276), Hardey (1998) has argued that in late modernity, there has been a decline in the uncritical acceptance of the authority of professionals, such as doctors. A second relevant feature of late modernity has been the growth in self-expression and individual choice. The idea that some people should give themselves completely into the power of doctors, and subject themselves to treatments which they may not even understand has therefore become increasingly questioned.

The result of this has been a partial rejection of the traditional biomedical model in favour of seeking alternative therapies from the wide range available.

Research methods

Timotijevic and Barnett (2006)
Researching perceptions of the risks of mobile phone masts

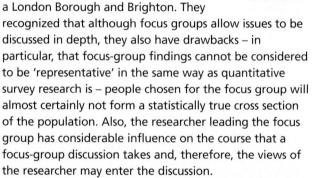

Lada Timotijevic and Julie Barnett wanted to find out the sense of risk to their health that people felt when living near a mobile phone mast. They decided that they needed in-depth information and that the best method to use was that of focus groups. Timotijevic and Barnett organized nine focus groups in two areas: a London Borough and Brighton. They recognized that although focus groups allow issues to be discussed in depth, they also have drawbacks – in particular, that focus-group findings cannot be considered to be 'representative' in the same way as quantitative survey research is – people chosen for the focus group will almost certainly not form a statistically true cross section of the population. Also, the researcher leading the focus group has considerable influence on the course that a focus-group discussion takes and, therefore, the views of the researcher may enter the discussion.

People were recruited through schools (to obtain the views of parents of young children) and through recruitment agencies in London. Participants were paid between £30 and £35 for attending the one-hour focus group. All the focus groups were recorded and then transcribed. Once this was done, they were analyzed using computer software to divide the discussion into various themes.

The authors concluded that people's perceptions of the risks of mobile phone masts were far more complex than generally thought, with most people having awareness of the possible dangers, although this did not influence their behaviour over much.

Timotijevic, L. and Barnett, J. (2006) 'Managing the possible health risks of mobile telecommunications', *Health, Risk and Society,* June 8(2), pp. 143–64

1 **What is a focus group?**

2 **Name one advantage of a focus group.**

3 **Why is it considered a drawback that focus groups are not 'representative'?**

4 **When leading a focus group, why must researchers be careful?**

5 **What problem(s) can you think of which might result from paying people to join focus groups?**

Criticisms of the biomedical and complementary models of health

According to Coward (1989), both the biomedical and the complementary models of health tend to stress that health problems are individual, both in terms of the causes and the cures. Coward argues that this ignores the wider social factors that cause ill health, such as poverty, poor housing, job-related stress and pollution, amongst others.

The body

So far in this chapter, we have questioned common-sense ideas held about what is sickness and health and have raised some challenging questions about these ideas. However, we can go further and question a closely related concept upon which notions of illness are ultimately based: the concept of 'the body'.

All of us exist in 'bodies' that, *objectively,* are different shapes, heights, colours and physical abilities; they are also *subjectively valued* as attractive or ugly, young or old, short or tall, weak or strong.

Let us look first at the objective differences. The two most common explanations for objective differences between bodies are, first, that people's bodies vary according to genetic differences (height, weight, etc.) and, second, that bodies change as people age. However, sociologists point out that the shapes of people's bodies are often actually linked to diets, type of employment and general quality of life. A huge range of research indicates that poorer people are more likely to:

- eat 'unhealthy' foods and to smoke cigarettes
- be employed in repetitive, physically demanding work or the other extreme of boring, sedentary employment
- have worse housing conditions
- live in more deprived neighbourhoods.

All of these factors impact upon the condition of a person's body and health. We can see then that the physical shapes of bodies are strongly influenced by social factors.

If we look next at the differences in how bodies are subjectively valued, we can see that the culture – and media – of different societies promote very different valuations of body shapes. What is considered as attractive or ugly, normal or abnormal has varied over time and society. Currently, for example, in affluent societies the idea of slimness is highly valued, yet historically in most societies the ideal body shape for a woman was a 'full figure' with a noticeable belly, while in middle-aged men, a large stomach indicated that they were financially successful in life – poor people looked thin and ill nourished.

Body shapes and appearance have never been neutral; they have always sent out social messages which others evaluate. However, in late modernity, the body has become an especially important 'site' for making statements about oneself. Giddens (1991) argues that in contemporary society our individual identity has come to be something which people 'work at', with everyone consciously constructing the image (personality, clothing, style of speech, ethnic affiliation) which they want to present to others as their real 'selves'. Giddens calls this **reflexive mobilization**. One very important part of this is how we wish our body to be viewed by others and what message we wish it to give. Chris Shilling (2003), for example, has pointed out that bodies are coming to be seen more and more as **unfinished products**, by which he means that bodies are no longer seen as something which people just 'have', to be accepted as they are. Increasingly, he argues, people wish to alter their bodies in order to express their individuality or to achieve some desired state. Shilling points to the growth of cosmetic surgery, tattooing, dieting and body building, all of which are undertaken by individuals to achieve a desired image of themselves.

Sociologists, then, are suggesting that we should not just view the body in biological terms, but also in social terms. The physical body and what we seek to do with it change over time and society. This has significant implications for medicine and ideas of health. Thus, the idea of people being 'obese' is *physically* related to excessive amounts of processed food, coupled with lack of exercise. However, *socially* it has become a medical problem as a result of people coming to define this particular body shape as 'wrong' and unhealthy. In many traditional African and Pacific island cultures, however, a large or (as we now call it) **obese** body shape was a sign of success and a shape to be aimed at.

Defining disability

One particularly interesting area where ideas of health and body shapes overlap is the topic of disability. According to Friedson (1965), the common perception of disability is that disabled people have some impediment that prevents them from operating 'normally'. This perception starts from the assumption that there is a clear definition of the 'normal' body, and a 'normal' range of activities associated with it.

However, it has been pointed out by critics such as Michael Oliver (1996) that the impediments imposed by society are at least as great as those imposed by the physical impairment. In other words, disability is a social construction, rather than just a physical one.

Not everyone is able to do everything as well as others – for example, run, catch or throw a ball – yet we do not describe those who are less able as being 'disabled'. We just accept these differences as part of the normal range of human abilities. This range of normality could be extended to include those defined as 'disabled'. This could occur, it is argued, if physical facilities and social attitudes were adjusted to include those with disabilities – for example, by altering the way we construct buildings, and by regarding sport played by disabled people as equal to 'traditional' types of sport.

It is with this in mind that the World Health Organization has distinguished between impairment, disability and handicap:

- *Impairment* refers to the abnormality of, or loss of function of, a part of the body.
- *Handicap* refers to the physical limits imposed by the loss of function.

- *Disability* refers to the socially imposed restriction on people's abilities to perform tasks as a result of the behaviour of people in society.

According to this approach, disability has to be understood as much in social terms as physical ones; so, a person can have an impairment without being disabled.

The origins of disability

If disability is a socially constructed concept, how did it come about? According to Finkelstein (1980), the modern idea of the dependent disabled person is largely the result of industrialization and the introduction of machinery. People with impairments were excluded from this type of work and came to be viewed as a burden. The rise of the medical profession in the early 19th century led them to become labelled as sick and in need of care.

Oliver (1990) takes Finkelstein's analysis further, by suggesting that the medical profession not only imposed the label of sickness and abnormality on people with impairments, but also helped to construct a way of looking at disability which saw it as a **personal tragedy**.

This concept of personal tragedy stresses that the individual disabled person has to be 'helped' to come to terms with the physical and psychological problems that they face. According to Oliver, this draws attention away from the fact that impairment is turned into disability by the wider economic, physical and social environment that discriminates against disabled people.

Stigma, illness and disability

Stigma is an important term in helping us to understand how people with disabilities are excluded from social activities. The idea of 'stigma' does not just apply to disabled people, but also to those with certain illnesses, such as Aids. The concept was first used in sociology by Erving Goffman (1963), who suggested that certain groups of people are defined as 'discredited' because of characteristics that are seen as 'negative'.

Types of stigma

Goffman suggested that there are two types of stigma.

1 *Discrediting* – These are obvious types of stigma, such as being in a wheelchair. People find it awkward to have normal social relations with those who are 'discredited'. They may be embarrassed, avoid eye contact or ignore the 'obvious' disability.
2 *Discreditable* – Here, the stigma is one of potential, dependent on whether other people find out about the discreditable illness or disability. Examples of this might include HIV status or epilepsy. In this situation, the person with the illness may find it difficult to act 'normally' in case they are 'found out'.

The concept of 'master status'

When the discrediting or discreditable status becomes the main way in which people are seen by others, then Goffman calls this a 'master status'. The stigma then completely dominates the way the person is treated, and any other attributes are seen as less important. The person who is unable to walk unaided is seen simply as 'wheelchair-bound' (not as an intelligent, articulate woman, for example), and the happy family man is seen as an 'Aids victim'. Finally, Goffman points out that the individuals themselves may accept this master status and come to see themselves solely in terms of their stigmatized status.

However, Goffman's argument that the individuals with stigma may well accept this as a master status has been criticized by other sociologists. According to Scambler and Hopkins (1986), for example, people with stigma may react in a number of different ways, using different tactics to manage their stigma:

- *Selective concealment* – If the stigmatizing condition is not obvious, the person may only tell a few trusted friends and family.
- *Covering up* – The person may tell no one.
- *Medicalizing the behaviour* – If the person cannot hide (or does not choose to hide) the condition, they could emphasize the medical aspect of it, as opposed to the social or moral aspect, and thus make a bid for sympathy (a link to the sick role here – see p. 247).
- *Condemning the condemners* – This is where people with a stigmatized condition take on those who impose the stigma and engage in forms of political action to have the

Research methods

Green and Platt (2004) Studying stigma and illness by 'mixed methods'

Gill Green and Stephen Platt wished to explore the experience of stigma by people who are HIV positive. Obtaining a sample of people with this condition was difficult and there were also a number of ethical issues involved.

As it was extremely difficult to obtain a random sample from the general population, Green and Platt used a theoretical or purposive sample – that is, they set out to recruit respondents in settings where they knew they could be sure of finding HIV+ people and then selected as broad a range of respondents as possible within these settings. The recruitment took place in outpatient clinics, prisons, drug rehabilitation centres, voluntary organizations and GP practices. How the respondents were approached depended upon what was permitted by these organizations. Usually, a member of the organization arranged an interview after gaining permission from the HIV+ person. Initially, 61 people were interviewed; then, one year later in the follow-up interview, 40 of these people were interviewed. The drop in the number of interviewees was caused by deaths and by the refusal of some people to give a second interview. The researchers accept that this is a large 'rate of attrition', but they believed that the normal procedure of contacting respondents a number of times to urge them to be interviewed again was inappropriate in the situation of these people who were in considerable stress over their condition. Green and Platt were not willing to add to their stress.

The first interview used semi-structured questions and respondents were encouraged to elaborate their answers. They were also asked to rate their satisfaction of the services they had received from the NHS using a five-point scale (from 'very dissatisfied' to 'very satisfied'). The second interview asked a series of more factual questions (e.g. had any GP refused treatment?) and then the respondents were encouraged to talk openly about their experiences. The information obtained was therefore both quantitative and qualitative. The combined and integrated use of both these forms of methods is sometimes known as 'mixed-method research'.

All interviews were recorded and later transcribed. They were then analysed using special software which helped to identify themes that emerged from the interview.

Green, G. and Platt, S. (2004) 'Fear and Loathing in healthcare settings reported by people with HIV', in E. Annandale, M.A. Elston and L. Prior (eds) *Medical Work, Medical Knowledge and healthcare*, Oxford: Blackwell

1 Why would it have been extremely difficult to obtain a sample from the general population?

2 What is meant by a 'theoretical' or 'purposive' sample? Why was this method most appropriate?

3 Explain why there was such a large drop-out between the first and second interviews.

4 How could the research claim to be both quantitative and qualitative?

5 When studies explicitly set out to use both quantitative and qualitative methods together, what term is sometimes used?

stigma reviewed. Examples of this include the activities of HIV/Aids pressure groups and of pressure groups set up by disabled people.

The origins of stigma

Goffman never explained the origins of stigma, that is, why some people are stigmatized and others not. His main interest was in the effect of stigma on people and their interactions with others. However, other writers have suggested reasons why certain categories of people come to be stigmatized.

Clarke (1992) conducted a content analysis survey of magazines over a 20-year period and concluded that certain illnesses are linked to leading the 'wrong' sorts of lifestyles. HIV/Aids is viewed as discreditable, as are lung cancer and obesity. However, heart disease had no negative image.

Oliver (1990), as discussed earlier, sees the role of the medical profession as being crucial in defining how certain conditions are viewed.

Key terms

Biomedical model of health the conventional Western model. It sees the body as very much like a biological machine, with each part of the body performing a function. The doctor's job is to restore the functions by solving the problem of what is wrong. Ideas about the environment or the spiritual health of the person are not relevant.

Complementary medicine alternative forms of health intervention, such as homeopathy.

Disability the socially imposed restriction on people's abilities to perform tasks as a result of the behaviour of people in society.

General practitioner (GP) a local doctor who deals with general health issues.

Health a person's perception of the state of their body's wellbeing.

Illness perception of feeling unacceptably worse than normal body state.

Late modernity a term used to describe contemporary

society, where choice and individuality have become more important than conformity and group membership.

Lay definitions of health 'lay' refers to the majority of the public who are not medical practitioners and who therefore use common-sense ideas about health and illness.

Malingering pretending to be ill in order to avoid work or other responsibilities.

Obesity a medical term for being overweight.

Personal tragedy a term used by Oliver to describe the way disability is seen as a personal as opposed to a social problem.

Reflexive mobilization within late modernity the process of seeing oneself as others see you and using this to construct an individual identity.

Unfinished product (the body as) in late modernity, the human body is not regarded as a biological fact that one must accept, but as something that can be amended according to one's wishes.

Check your understanding

1 How does the public define health?

2 Identify and explain any three factors that affect the definition of health and illness.

3 Who 'sanctions' illness (officially approves it), and what are the benefits of being 'sanctioned' as ill?

4 Construct a table summarizing the three types of medical models: biomedical, traditional and complementary.

5 What do we mean when we say that in late modernity, the body is something which is an 'unfinished product'?

6 What is the difference between 'impairment' and 'disability'?

7 Explain the difference between 'stigma' and 'disability'.

8 Why might certain types of people become stigmatized?

Activities

Research idea

Select a small sample of people, ideally from different generations, and ask them to rate their degree of sympathy on a scale of 1 to 5 for people with the following 'illnesses': hangover, headache (not caused by a hangover!), impotence, cirrhosis of the liver (caused by drinking too much alcohol), anorexia, heart disease, breast cancer, lung cancer caused by smoking, sexually transmitted disease.

Do your results show any different attitudes to illness and disease amongst people? What explanations can you suggest for your findings?

Web.task

Search online for information and advice on health – for example, *Men's Health Magazine* at www.menshealth.co.uk

Does the advice make an assumption about what is normal and abnormal in terms of body shape and styles of life?

An eye on the exam Defining health, illness and disability

Item A

The Ndembu explain all persistent or severe health problems by reference to social causes, such as the secret malevolence of sorcerers or witches, or punishment by the spirits of ancestors. These spirits cause sickness in an individual if his or her family and kin are 'not living well together', and are involved in grudges or quarrelling.

The Ndembu traditional healer, the *chimbuki*, conducts a séance attended by the victim, their kin and neighbours. By questioning these people and by shrewd observation, he builds up a picture of the patient's social situation and its various tensions. The diviner calls all the relatives of the patient before a sacred shrine to the ancestors, and induces them 'to confess any grudges and hard feelings they may nourish against the patient'. By this process all the hidden social tensions of the group are publicly aired and gradually resolved.

Treatment involves rituals of exorcism to withdraw evil influences from the patient's body. It also includes the use of certain herbal and other medicines, manipulation and cupping, and the application of certain substances to the skin.

Adapted from Helman, C. (2000) *Culture, Health and Illness*, Oxford: Butterworth/Heinemann, pp. 197–8

Item B

In the biomedical model, information is gathered by means of indicators like X-rays, blood sugar levels, electroencephalograph readings or biopsies, which are thought to measure these biological processes directly.

This framework is closely associated with developments in Western science. Physicians can readily reach agreement on the functioning of the body by reference to well-defined criteria which are known to all members of the medical profession and which become progressively more precise with advances in scientific knowledge. The doctor will be able to use signs derived from these tests as objective indicators of biological malfunction or irregularity – regardless of whether the supposed patient actually feels ill.

Adapted from Dingwall, R. (1976) *Aspects of Illness*, Basingstoke: Palgrave

(a) Explain what is meant by 'disability'. (2 marks)

(b) Identify three characteristics of the traditional model of health, illness and medicine (Item A). (6 marks)

(c) Outline the main features of the biomedical model of health, illness and medicine (Item B). (12 marks)

(d) Using information from Items A and B and elsewhere, assess the view that health and illness are socially constructed. (20 marks)

Grade booster Getting top marks in the 20-mark question

Don't confuse the idea of *social construction* with *social causes* such as poverty, bad housing, poor diet, etc. Use examples from different cultures of the ways in which health and illness have been defined differently, or contrast lay and medical definitions. Use information from the Items to do this. Make sure you refer to health as well as illness. It's also legitimate to discuss how disability is socially constructed.

TOPIC 2

Health inequalities

Getting you thinking

Look at the graph on the right.

1 Who is likely to live longer on average, men or women?

2 Approximately, what is the highest age that women could expect to live to in 2001 (the latest figures currently available) and what is the highest age for men?

3 What impact does social class have on age expectancy?

4 What explanations can you offer for these differences?

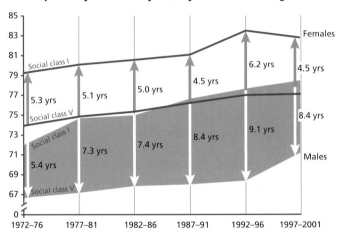

Life expectancy at birth in years, by social class and gender

Source: Department of Health (2005) *Tackling Health Inequalities*, London: DoH

Sociology AS for AQA

Life expectancy, healthy life expectancy and disability-free life expectancy at birth: by gender (Great Britain)

	Years			
	Males		*Females*	
	1981	2002	1981	2002
Life expectancy	70.9	76.0	76.8	80.5
Healthy life expectancy	64.4	67.2	66.7	69.9
Years spent in poor health	6.4	8.8	10.1	10.6
Disability-free life expectancy	58.1	60.9	60.8	63.0
Years spent with disability	12.8	15.0	16.0	17.5

Source: *Social Trends 37*, 2007

Look at the table on the left.

5 Although people live longer nowadays, what does the table tell us about the health of older people? What implications might this have for women in particular?

6 In your opinion, is it a curse or a blessing to live longer (on the basis of these statistics)?

If ever anyone sought proof that social factors have a significant impact upon people's lives, then they only have to look at the relationship between a person's life experiences and their chances of illness and early death. The chances of an early death, of a serious long-term illness and of a disability are closely related to social class, income, gender, area of residence and ethnic group.

But why should this be? Health, illness and disability are generally thought of as linked to the luck of our genes – that is, they are biologically caused. Yet sociologists argue that the evidence from research indicates that it is the interaction of our social experiences with our biological make-up that determines our health. If pressed, they might well argue that the more important of the two sets of factors is actually the social rather than the biological. In this chapter, we will explore the major

social determinants of our health: geography, social class, gender and ethnicity. We will look at each area in turn.

Geographical differences

The simplest way of finding out the impact of place of residence on health is to compare the health differences between **parliamentary constituencies** in Britain. Mary Shaw and a group of researchers (1999) used the available statistics to compare the health of one million people living in the constituencies that had the very worst health records with the one million people living in the constituencies that had the very best health records. The gap between these groups surprised even the researchers themselves.

The comparison showed that, in the worst health areas:

- children under the age of 1 are twice as likely to die
- there are ten times more women under the age of 65 who are permanently sick (including those who are disabled)
- adults are almost three times as likely to state that they have a serious 'chronic' (long-term) illness or disability
- adults have a 70 per cent greater chance of dying before the age of 65.

These geographical differences generally reflect differences in income and levels of deprivation. However, they are not simply a reflection of these, because poorer people living in the richer areas tend to have higher standards of health. It seems that quality of life in poorer areas is generally lower and, as a result, health standards are worse.

Social class

Mortality

Over the last 25 years, **life expectancy** has risen for both men and women, in all social classes. But overall they have risen more for those in the higher social classes, so that the difference between those in the higher and those in the lower social classes has actually grown. For example, in the 1970s, the **death rate** among men of working age was almost twice as high for those in class V (unskilled) as for those in class I (professional). By 2003, it was almost two and a half times as high. Men in social class I can expect to live for almost eight and a half years longer than men from social class V, while women in social class I can expect to live four and a half years longer than their social class V counterparts.

Deaths from heart disease and lung cancer (the two most common causes of death for people aged 35 to 64) are twice as high in people from manual backgrounds as non-manual backgrounds.

Morbidity

Although death rates have fallen and life expectancy has increased, there is little evidence that the population is experiencing better health than 20 years ago. In fact, there has actually been a small increase in **self-reported** long-standing illness, and differences between the social classes are still quite clear. However, as we saw in Topic 1, what is defined as 'health' changes over time. So it may be that people are actually in better health but don't believe it. Bearing this in mind, among the 45 to 64 age group, 18 per cent of people from 'managerial or professional backgrounds' reported a limiting long-standing illness, compared to over 32 per cent of people from 'routine or manual backgrounds' (ONS 2007).

In adulthood, being overweight is a measure of possible ill health, with obesity a risk factor for many chronic diseases. There is a noticeable social-class gradient in obesity, which is greater for women than men. According to the Department of Health (2007), about 32 per cent of women in the poorest fifth of the population are obese, compared to 16 per cent of women in the richest fifth of the population.

Explanations for differences in health between social classes

Different ways of explaining class differences in **mortality** and **morbidity** have been suggested.

The artefact approach

An **artefact** is something observed in a scientific investigation that is not naturally present, but occurs as a result of the investigative procedure. Perhaps the link between class and health is not real but a statistical illusion. Illsley (1986) argues that the statistical connection between social class and illness exaggerates the situation. For example, he points out that the number of people in social class V has declined so much over the last 30 years that the membership is just too small to be used as the basis for comparisons with other social classes.

However, the 'Independent Inquiry into Inequalities in Health' (Acheson 1998) showed that, even when the classes were regrouped to include classes IV and V together, significant differences remained. For example, in the late 1970s, death rates were 53 per cent higher among men in classes IV and V, compared with those in classes I and II.

Social selection

This approach claims that social class does not cause ill health, but that ill health may be a significant cause of social class. For example, if a person is chronically ill (i.e. has a long-term illness) or disabled in some way, it is usually difficult for them to obtain a secure, well-paid job. The fit and healthy are more likely to be successful in life and upwardly mobile in terms of social class.

The problem with this approach is that studies of health differences indicate that poor health is a result of poverty rather than a cause of it.

Cultural explanations

The **cultural explanations** approach stresses that differences in health are best understood as the result of cultural choices made by individuals or groups in the population.

- *Diet* – Manual workers consume twice as much white bread as professionals, and have higher sugar consumption and eat less fresh fruit.
- *Cigarette smoking* – Over 40 per cent of males and 35 per cent of females in social classes IV and V regularly smoke, whereas only about 12 per cent of males and females in social class I smoke.
- *Leisure and lifestyle* – Middle-class people are more likely to take exercise and have a wider range of social activities than the working classes. These reduce levels of stress and help maintain a higher standard of health.
- *Alcohol* – Alcohol consumption is directly related to social class, with much higher consumption amongst the 'lower' social classes.

The cultural approach, however, fails to ask why these groups have poor diets and high alcohol and cigarette consumption. Critics point out that there may be reasons why people are 'forced' into an unhealthy lifestyle. These critics have put forward an alternative **material explanation**.

Material explanations

Some analysts see a direct relationship between differences in health and the unequal nature of British society. Supporters of this approach accept the behavioural differences pointed to earlier, but claim that this behaviour has to be seen within a broader context of inequality. So, poor health is the result of 'hazards to which some people have no choice but to be exposed given the present distribution of income and opportunity' (Shaw *et al.* 1999).

● *Poverty* – This key factor links a range of health risks. Poorer people have worse diets and worse housing conditions. They are more likely to be unemployed and generally to have a more highly stressed, lower quality of life. According to the British Regional Heart Survey (cited in Shaw *et al.* 1999) – a study of 8000 middle-aged men – over half of those who did not own a car or a home were reported to be in poor health, compared to a tenth of those who owned both.

● *Position at work* – Workers with little power or control over their work are likely to experience worse health than those given more responsibility. Research on civil servants (Davey Smith *et al.* 1990) has shown that routine clerical workers are much more likely to die young than workers in higher grades. If the lowest and highest grades are compared, those in the lowest grades are actually three times more likely to die before reaching the age of 65.

● *Unemployment* – According to Moser's long-term study of the relationship between income and wealth (Moser *et al.* 1990), unemployed men and their wives are likely to die younger than those in employment.

● *Types of industry* – industries vary in how dangerous they are to their employees. For example, respiratory diseases are common amongst those working in road and building construction, as a result of the dust inhaled, while various forms of cancer are associated with chemical industries.

The material approach has the advantage of explaining why there are cultural differences in behaviour between various groups in society. The argument advanced by those who support this approach is that people may make choices about their behaviour, but that the circumstances within which they make their choices are strongly affected by the extent of inequality existing in Britain.

Gender and health

Women live longer than men, but are more likely to visit their GPs for treatment. They also have higher levels of mental illness. This apparently contradictory pattern – higher morbidity combined with a longer life span – has led some observers to argue that it is not that women are more likely to be ill than men, but that they are more willing to visit the doctor. Yet MacIntyre (1993) shows that women are, in fact, no more likely than men to report symptoms. The answer lies perhaps in a combination of biological factors and social roles.

Explanations for the link between gender and health

Biology

There is some evidence to suggest that women are biologically stronger than men (for instance, female foetuses are less likely to die than male foetuses) and they have a greater biological possibility of living longer. However, this does not mean that they are less immune to illness. In addition, they can suffer from a range of health problems associated with reproduction and the menopause.

Social role

Women may also live longer because their social role tends to prevent them from taking risks. Their social role discourages them from violence, fast driving and excess alcohol consumption. Women are also less likely to smoke than men. However, the social role that limits their activities also places considerable stress upon women, by restricting opportunities in employment and in life in general. Furthermore, women are more likely than men to be living in poverty. They are also more likely to be lone parents. Both place considerable burdens upon their health.

Work

According to Ellen Annandale (1998), women who go out to work have better levels of health than those who do not. Annandale argues that this is not just because of the financial benefits, but also because work gives women a sense of

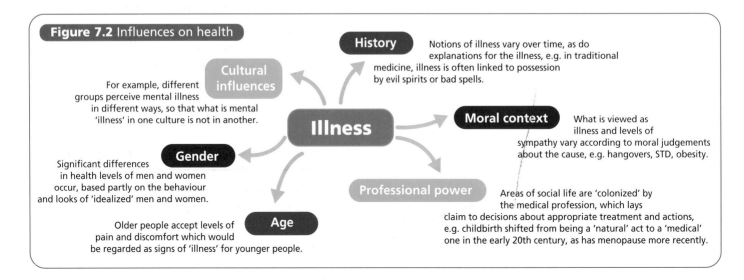

Figure 7.2 Influences on health

History – Notions of illness vary over time, as do explanations for the illness, e.g. in traditional medicine, illness is often linked to possession by evil spirits or bad spells.

Cultural influences – For example, different groups perceive mental illness in different ways, so that what is mental 'illness' in one culture is not in another.

Illness

Moral context – What is viewed as illness and levels of sympathy vary according to moral judgements about the cause, e.g. hangovers, STD, obesity.

Gender – Significant differences in health levels of men and women occur, based partly on the behaviour and looks of 'idealized' men and women.

Professional power – Areas of social life are 'colonized' by the medical profession, which lays claim to decisions about appropriate treatment and actions, e.g. childbirth shifted from being a 'natural' act to a 'medical' one in the early 20th century, as has menopause more recently.

Age – Older people accept levels of pain and discomfort which would be regarded as signs of 'illness' for younger people.

independence and a wider social network. Both of these have the effect of lowering stress levels – and stress is closely related to standards of health.

Ethnicity and health

Surprisingly, there is only limited information available on ethnicity and illness. This is partly because of the complex make-up of ethnic groups in the UK and the difficulty of making generalizations across these groupings. However, some specific health problems can be linked with particular groups – for example, those of Afro-Caribbean origin are much more likely to suffer from sickle cell disease.

The research that has been done – mainly by the Health Education Authority (Sproston and Mindell 2006) shows that members of minority ethnic groups are more likely to define themselves as having poor health than the majority population. For example, just under 50 per cent of ethnic-minority members described themselves as having fair or poor health. This compared with just under 30 per cent of the majority population.

As for mortality, all ethnic-minority groups have a shorter life expectancy than the majority population. Patterns in the causes of death do seem to vary, with groups from the **Indian subcontinent** having the highest levels of coronary heart disease of the whole population, while those from the **Caribbean commonwealth** have the lowest levels of death from this cause. Although, overall, health levels are worse and life expectancy is lower, one striking difference is that all of the ethnic-minority groups have lower rates of deaths from cancers than the majority population.

Explanations for the link between ethnicity and health

'Race' and inequality

We saw earlier the profound effects of inequality in helping to explain different levels of health. Minority ethnic groups have some of the lowest incomes, worst housing and highest unemployment rates in Britain. Even without any specific explanations related to 'race', the higher levels of morbidity and higher early mortality rates could largely be explained by their relative social deprivation.

'Race' as a specific factor

Some analysts have gone further than this, however, and have argued that 'race' is important by itself. First, much of the poverty and exclusion is actually caused by racism. Second, the experience of living in a racist society can place great stress upon people and this may impact upon health levels.

Research methods

English Longitudinal Study of Ageing

In order to ensure that government policies are working effectively and to find out the needs of the British population, the government is constantly carrying out surveys of various kinds. One of these, known as the English Longitudinal Study of Ageing (ELSA), obtains information on the health of approximately 8500 people over the age of 50. The research takes place every two years and follows one nationally representative sample of people aged 50 or more. It is drawn from households and is intended to be a longitudinal survey. The first phase of the survey took place in 2002/3 and the second in 2004/5. The statistics are so complex that it takes two years before the reports can be published.

The sampling was conducted by a random sample of postcode selected from the Postcode Address File. These were then 'stratified' to ensure that a range of health authorities and a true cross section of social class groups were represented. Addresses were then selected 'systematically' from each sector.

Each selected household was sent a letter explaining the research and asking if they would agree to be interviewed and to complete a questionnaire. They achieved a response rate of 84%, which is extremely high. This may have been because it was an official piece of research or because people are likely to be interested in their health and prepared to answer questions about it.

First, there was an interview which covered a wide range of subjects including the demographics of the household, the health of the people living there, their income and their activities. Each chosen person was left a questionnaire to complete, covering such things as life satisfaction, views of ageing, social networks and alcohol consumption.

Finally, the respondents were examined by a nurse to collect data on their physical health. The result is extremely detailed information on a wide range of factors that impact on a person's health and longevity.

Source: Banks, J., Breeze, E., Lessof, C. and Nazroo, J. (2007) *Retirement, Health and Relationships of the Older Population in England: The 2004 English Longitudinal Study of Ageing (Wave 2)*

1 What do we mean by a 'longitudinal survey'?

2 How can it be argued that 8500 people represent an accurate image of health and ageing in Britain?

3 How was the sample obtained?

4 What is meant by the 'postcode address file'?

5 The results of surveys often take years to be published. Why might this be?

6 This survey has a very high response rate – what factors might influence these response rates?

7 Why do you think that some information was obtained by interview and some by questionnaire?

Culture and ethnicity

The final approach argues that cultural differences, in terms of diet and lifestyle, may influence health. For example, diets using large amounts of 'ghee' (clarified butter) can help cause heart disease amongst those of South Asian origin. Asian diets also tend to lack vitamin D. Long work hours and relatively little physical leisure activity may also lower the health levels of some minority ethnic groups.

Health inequalities in an international perspective

Although inequalities in health are quite marked within the UK, the differences between the richer and poorer countries of the world make quite stark reading. The probability of premature adult death (before the age of 65) varies widely between (and within) different regions of the world. For example, the probability of premature adult death in some parts of sub-Saharan Africa is nearly four times higher than that observed in low-mortality countries of the Western Pacific region (such as Japan). Yet men in some eastern European countries are also three to four times more likely to die prematurely than men in Western Europe. Perhaps most shocking is that, while expectation of life is increasing overall in the world, in Africa the reverse is true with adults today more likely to die at a younger age than 1990.

The obvious reasons for the differences in life expectation and levels of illness lie in the extremes of poverty that exist in the less developed nations as well as in their lack of health systems. However, perhaps more surprising were the findings of Richard Wilkinson (1996), who compared the health and economic data for 23 different countries. He found very strong evidence to link the overall health of the population with the degree of economic inequality. Once a certain basic level of overall economic wealth had been attained by a country, then the greater the economic inequality which existed, the wider the health differentials.

Interestingly, no matter how high the general standard of living became, as long as there were economic inequalities, there was no increase in the general standards of health. This meant that a country with a high standard of living, but considerable economic inequality, actually had lower standards of health for the majority of the population than a poorer country with greater social equality. Cuba, for example, has better standards of health and expectation of life overall than the USA, despite being much poorer. Wilkinson's conclusions were that societies with low levels of inequality had high levels of 'social capital' – that is a sense of belonging and place in a society. This sense of belonging had the effect of increasing the sense of wellbeing, which in turn improved standards of health.

Check your understanding

1 Identify four factors that are closely linked to health.

2 Why might some areas of Britain have worse health than others?

3 Give one example of health differences between the social classes.

4 What explanations have been suggested for health differences between the social classes?

5 Explain, in your own words, the meaning of the 'artefact approach'.

6 Do biological factors alone explain the differences in health between men and women?

7 What three explanations have been given for the differences in health between the various ethnic minorities and the majority of the population?

Key terms

Artefact approach an approach that believes that the statistics about class and health exaggerate the real situation.

Caribbean commonwealth parts of the West Indies that are in the Commonwealth, such as Barbados.

Cultural explanations explanations that emphasize lifestyle and behaviour.

Death rate the number dying per 1000 of a population per year.

Indian subcontinent the section of south Asia consisting of India, Pakistan and Bangladesh.

Life expectancy the number of years that a person can expect to live on average in a given population.

Material explanations explanations that focus on the make-up of society: for example, on inequalities of income and wealth.

Morbidity refers to statistics about illness.

Mortality refers to statistics of death.

Parliamentary constituency an area that elects one MP. The UK is divided into over 600 constituencies.

Self-reported the result of asking people themselves.

Activities

Research idea

Ask a sample of 20 people how much fresh fruit they eat each day. You might wish to divide the sample by gender or by age or even by parental occupation. Do any differences emerge?

Web.task

Go to the Department of Health's Community Health Profiles website at:

www.communityhealthprofiles.info/index.php

Here you can look up your own area and obtain a full health profile.

An eye on the exam — Health inequalities

Item A

Percentage of people in England and Wales reporting long-term illness or disability that restricts daily activities: data from Census 2001

Great Britain	Males (%)	Females (%)
White British	15.9	15.3
White Irish	17.7	15.7
Mixed	18.3	17.8
Indian	16.5	19.8
Pakistani	22.1	25.4
Bangladeshi	23.6	24.9
Other Asian	16.7	18.6
Black Caribbean	17.9	19.3
Black African	14.1	16.7
Other Black	18.8	19.9
Chinese	11.4	12.1
All ethnic groups	16.0	15.4

Adapted from ONS
www.statistics.gov.uk/cci/nugget.asp?id=464
www.empho.org.uk/products/ethnicity/inequalities.htm

Item B

<< Alongside these material and behavioural determinants, research is uncovering the psychosocial [social and psychological] costs of living in an unequal society. For example, perceiving oneself to be worse off relative to others may carry a health penalty, in terms of increased stress and risk-taking behaviour. Attention has also focused on the health effects of the work environment and particularly on the control that individuals exercise over the pace and content of work.

Material, behavioural and psychosocial factors cluster together: those in lower socio-economic groups are likely to be exposed to risks in all three domains. Health-damaging factors also accumulate together: children born into poorer circumstances clock up more by way of material, behavioural and psychosocial risks as they grow up and grow older. For example, girls and boys born into social classes IV and V are more likely than those in higher social classes to grow up in overcrowded homes, to develop health-damaging habits like smoking and to be exposed to stressful life-events and work environments.>>

Source: Graham, H. (ed.) (2000) *Understanding Health Inequalities*, Buckingham: Open University Press

---

(a) Explain what sociologists mean by 'behavioural factors' (Item B). (2 marks)

(b) Using Item A, identify the ethnic group with:
   (i)   the highest level of female long-term illness
   (ii) the lowest level of female long-term illness
   (iii) the biggest gap between male and female levels of long-term illness. (6 marks)

(c) Outline some of the causes of gender inequalities in health. (12 marks)

(d) Using information from the Items and elsewhere, assess the view that inequalities in health are the result of material factors. (20 marks)

Grade booster — Getting top marks in the 20-mark question

Be clear what 'material factors' means and what kinds of health inequalities they might cause. Discuss how different material factors, such as low income, unemployment, poor housing, etc., affect health. Make sure you use information from the Items. Use other explanations, such as cultural/behavioural, artefact and social selection, to assess the materialist view. How far can material and behavioural factors be linked? Most of your answer can be about class inequalities, but mention other types too, e.g. gender, ethnic, age or regional.

Inequalities in the health service

Getting you thinking

GP Health promotion claims, by Jarman (UPA) score of health authority, London Boroughs, October 1995

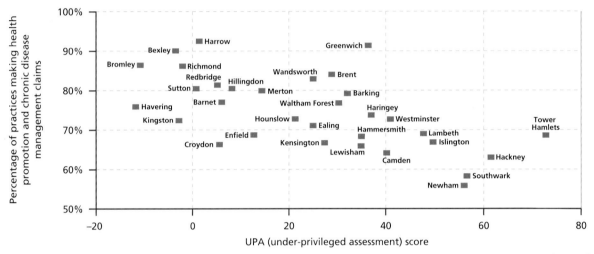

Source: www.archive.official-documents.co.uk/document/doh/ih/fig17.gif

The graph above shows the amount of preventive health work done by GPs in London boroughs in relation to the extent of deprivation in those boroughs. The higher the borough on the vertical axis, the more preventive work it is doing. The more deprived the borough is, the further to the right it is along the horizontal axis.

<<Is the day of rationing the US healthcare services on the basis of age close at hand?

The fastest-growing age group is the population aged 80 and over – the very segment of the population that tends to require expensive and intensive medical care. The projected demands from a growing elderly population on the healthcare system have led to troubling questions about society's ability to meet future healthcare demands.

Daniel Callahan has proposed that the US government refuse to pay for life-extending medical care for individuals beyond the age of 70 or 80, and only pay for routine care aimed at relieving their pain. While the health of the young can be ensured by relatively cheap preventive measures such as exercise programs and health education, the medical conditions of the elderly are often complicated, requiring the use of expensive technologies and treatments. In short, the costs that are incurred to prolong the life of one elderly person might be more productively directed toward the treatment of a far greater number of younger persons.>>

Source: Andre, C. and Velasquez, M. (1990) 'Aged-based healthcare rationing: challenges for an aging society', *Issues in Ethics*, 3(3)

1 Look at the chart above. Identify the two boroughs in the graph where the lowest levels of health prevention are carried out. What other social characteristic do they share?

2 'If more money is spent on health in poorer areas then more affluent areas are deprived.' Do you agree with this statement? Give your reasons.

3 In small groups discuss the position put forward by Callahan regarding older people – do you agree with his argument?

4 Do you think there are some (other) groups in society whose access to healthcare should be restricted?

Despite the National Health Service (NHS) being free to users, and despite taxpayers spending over £115 million *each day* on paying for the NHS, it is a fact that some groups in the population are more likely to receive medical help than others. This contradicts the fundamental notion of 'equity' – the principle that provision of services is based solely upon need. According to this principle, the health services serving disadvantaged populations should not be of poorer quality or less accessible than those serving the more affluent groups in society. Furthermore, it implies that more resources should be allocated to the poorer groups in society, as they have worse levels of health. However, sociologists argue that there is not actually equity in the NHS, for two reasons:

1   The NHS fails to provide equal services for all in relation to their relative needs.
2   Certain groups are less likely to demand services than others.

Issues of provision

The NHS is the main provider of healthcare for the population and it needs to plan how best to provide this care. Provision is influenced by several factors, discussed below.

Geographical and social inequalities

Each area is allocated a certain amount of money by the government to provide healthcare for its residents. The amount of money given to each **health authority** is based on the principle of giving more money to poorer areas and less to richer areas. Unfortunately, this has never worked out as planned, and the poorer areas have never received adequate funding. Reasons for this include:

● *Foundation trust hospitals* – These are usually located in the richer areas of the country and have traditionally been given considerably higher levels of funding than other hospitals.
● *Political pressures* – Certain areas, such as London, have historically received more money than other regions. Over time, the reasons for this extra funding have disappeared – with shifts in population, for example. Each time plans have been put forward to reallocate money to other areas, the politicians have blocked them for fear of losing votes.

An example of this is provided by the Healthcare Commission, an official government body set up to oversee equity in healthcare. Easington in County Durham, a very deprived area, should be receiving an additional £26.5 million a year in funding, while Kensington and Chelsea, one of the richest places in Britain, is receiving £30.3 million a year, more than the official government funding formula requires.

The Healthcare Commission also found variations between England and Wales, with patients more likely to wait longer for hospital appointments in Wales than in England. In March 2004, 50 people were waiting more than nine months for an operation in England, yet in Wales, 8457 patients had been waiting longer than 12 months, of whom over 1000 had been waiting longer than 18 months.

The medical professions

The medical professions are extremely influential in determining how the different areas or specialisms of healthcare are funded. There are some specialisms that are seen as much more important and prestigious, while others are viewed as less important or less attractive. In general, chronic illness (that is, long-term illnesses for which there is no cure), mental health and geriatric (elderly people's) healthcare are seen as much less attractive areas than surgery, pharmaceuticals and high-technology medicine.

Hospital and primary care trust quality

Different hospitals and **primary care trusts** appear to be organized in very different ways, which results in great differences in the chances of survival from serious operations, and in the chances of catching some form of infection in hospital (known as **iatrogenesis**). In a study of all English hospitals in 2000, the researchers found that 17 people were likely to die in the worst hospitals for every 10 in the best. For instance, the death rate from cancer is 60 per cent higher in Liverpool than in east Dorset.

Private healthcare

Although there is much evidence of inequalities within the NHS, greater inequalities in access to healthcare exist between those who rely upon the NHS and those who use the private sector.

Private healthcare is used by those who pay directly for medical services or who have private health insurance. The total spending on private healthcare in Britain is about £2.5 billion each year, and those doctors who provide private healthcare earn about £550 million each year.

Private healthcare increases inequalities in healthcare by:

● allowing those who can pay to have treatment without waiting, whereas NHS patients have to join a waiting list
● giving private patients access to a range of medical services that may not be available on the NHS
● limiting the number of hours worked by some consultants (senior specialists) in the NHS, who prefer to earn more money in the private sector
● employing nurses and other specialists who have been trained by the NHS – thus contributing to the shortage of trained staff.

Issues of demand
Social class variations

Although the health of the population as a whole has improved, there is no evidence to show that inequalities between the social classes have decreased. As we saw in Topic 2, despite the fact that members of the working class are more likely to be ill and to have accidents, they are actually less likely to attend doctors' surgeries. They are also less likely to take part in any form of **screening programme** that can discover disease (such as certain forms of cancer) at an early stage. They are, however, more likely to use accident and emergency services – often because conditions that have not been attended to have become acute.

The reasons for this are not that they care less about illness, but that there are more barriers to them accessing healthcare. They are less likely to be able to:

● afford to take time off work
● travel a considerable distance to a GP's surgery – this is a particular problem because there are far fewer GPs in poorer areas, in proportion to the population, than in more affluent areas
● notice signs of health problems.

Gender

Women live approximately seven years longer than men, but they do not necessarily do so in good health. In fact, on average, they have only two extra years of healthy life without significant chronic illness. During their lifetimes, too, women appear to have higher levels of illness and higher rates of attendance at doctors' surgeries. However, this needs to be set against women's needs. Women give birth, and also take on the main childcare role, both of which put great strain upon their bodies.

Feminist sociologists argue that women actually under-use the health services, if their use is compared to their actual needs. They argue that, instead, the health services spend much of their resources on controlling women, by turning many 'normal' physical activities, such as giving birth, into medical ones. This takes power away from women and hands it to men, who form the majority of doctors.

As a result of these concerns, a national screening programme for breast cancer was introduced in 1988, and for cervical cancer in 1995. However, within these programmes, considerable differences in attendance have occurred, related to social class and ethnicity. Overall, the take-up rates have been approximately 75 per cent, but the poorer the social group, the less likely women are to attend. Similarly, the attendance rates for those of Bangladeshi and Pakistani origin are particularly low.

Ethnicity

There is a lower use of medical services by certain ethnic-minority groups. Several reasons have been suggested for this:

● *Language barriers* – Until recently, there was little attempt to provide translation facilities or to publicize the NHS in minority languages.
● *Cultural differences* – The traditional acceptance of male doctors has been challenged by many women from ethnic minorities, whose ideas of modesty have meant that many are unwilling to be seen by male doctors.
● *Poverty* – Ethnic minorities contain some of the lowest-income families in Britain, and so the factors that limit working-class use of health services (time off work and public transport difficulties) apply equally to them.

Age

Older people's approach to healthcare provision is different from that of middle-aged and younger people. Although they are the age group who are most in need of health services and who use them most, they tend to under-use them relative to their needs. Older people see themselves as 'wasting the doctor's time' if they consider that they may be consulting the doctor unnecessarily. What is more, geriatric medicine (the care of older people) is seen by doctors and nurses as an area of low prestige, and staffing and funding levels are extremely low. Therefore, both in terms of demand and provision, older people do particularly badly. However, stratification by class and geography also cuts across age lines – for example, the proportion of older people in the population receiving flu vaccinations varies from 49 per cent to 78 per cent across England.

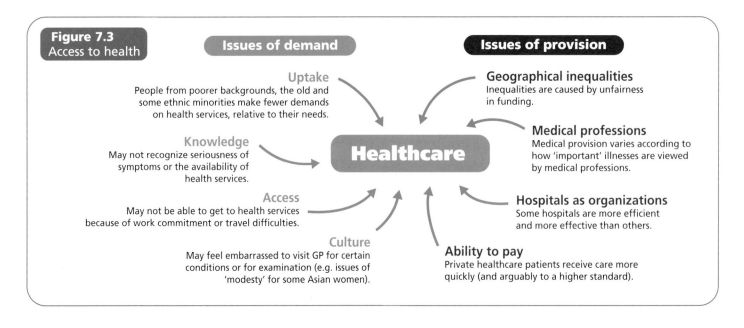

Figure 7.3 Access to health

Issues of demand

Uptake
People from poorer backgrounds, the old and some ethnic minorities make fewer demands on health services, relative to their needs.

Knowledge
May not recognize seriousness of symptoms or the availability of health services.

Access
May not be able to get to health services because of work commitment or travel difficulties.

Culture
May feel embarrassed to visit GP for certain conditions or for examination (e.g. issues of 'modesty' for some Asian women).

Healthcare

Issues of provision

Geographical inequalities
Inequalities are caused by unfairness in funding.

Medical professions
Medical provision varies according to how 'important' illnesses are viewed by medical professions.

Hospitals as organizations
Some hospitals are more efficient and more effective than others.

Ability to pay
Private healthcare patients receive care more quickly (and arguably to a higher standard).

Research methods

Meershoek et al. (2007)
Doctors' power of judgement

The Netherlands and the UK operate a similar system whereby people applying for long-term state benefits on the grounds of disability will be assessed by a specialist doctor. Because of the difficulty in deciding precisely what 'disabled' means, a great deal of discretion is given to the doctors. Meershoek and colleagues set out to uncover the grounds on which the doctors made their judgements about whether a person was truly disabled or not and hence about their entitlement to state benefits.

Meershoek and colleagues undertook an ethnographic study of the specialist doctors employed to do this work in The Netherlands. This involved observing over 500 consultations between clients and 20 different doctors, in different phases of the sick leave, including final judgments for long-term disability pension. They made field notes of the consultations and of the doctors' comments beforehand and afterwards. They also interviewed the 20 physicians about their decision-making processes. In order to have a background understanding, they also followed the doctors in their contacts and meetings with other experts and employers, but did not make any detailed notes.

They made notes of all the consultations and then agreed between them on certain themes and patterns which emerged on the basis of 'grounded theory' (that is, not making any assumptions before gathering data and then building up a theory as the information becomes available). They then re-analysed their notes to look at the specific responses of doctors to the replies of people claiming disability benefit whom the doctors considered 'problematic'.

Meershoek, A., Krumeich, A. and Vos, R. (2007) 'Judging without criteria? Sickness certification in Dutch disability schemes', *Sociology of Health and Illness* 29(4), pp.497–514

1 What is meant by an ethnographic approach?

2 The researchers made notes of the meetings, but did not make any (electronic) recordings. Do you think this might present some problems?

3 The researchers did not make detailed notes of their interviews with the experts and employers. Do you think making detailed notes would have been useful?

4 Grounded theory is commonly used in ethnographic research – how does this compare with more positivistic approaches?

Theoretical approaches

So far, we have seen how patterns of inequalities in the usage of the NHS can best be grasped in terms of provision of services on the one hand and demand for healthcare on the other. However, some writers have suggested that these explanations can also be included within wider theoretical perspectives. In particular, Ham (1999) has suggested that Marxism, pluralism and structuralism are the best ways of understanding the inequalities in health provision.

Marxist approaches to inequalities in health provision

Marxist writers on health, such as Doyal (1979) and O'Connor (1973), argue that the health service exists for two reasons. First, it has a 'legitimation' role, in that it persuades the bulk of the population that capitalism 'cares' for them. In this role, it acts to limit class conflict and social unrest by creating a sense of harmony. The health service therefore legitimates capitalism and is a subtle form of social control. However, the second role of health services helps the capitalist economy more directly. The health service maintains a healthy and hardworking – and therefore productive – workforce. Workers who are ill or injured are returned to work and therefore continue to make profits for the owners of capital.

Using this approach, inequalities in health provision are directly related to how productive people are. This explains why there are low levels of expenditure on people with mental illness, people with learning difficulties and the oldest and frailest members of society. The low levels of expenditure on the working class is explained by the presence of social-class divisions throughout society, whereby working-class people consistently receive worse treatment across the range of services in housing, education and health.

There are a number of problems with the Marxist analysis. It could equally be argued that, rather than being a form of social control, the National Health Service provides a very powerful alternative message to that of capitalism. The NHS is based on the socialist principle of giving to people in need, irrespective of income. Capitalism is based on people choosing to buy services, which depends upon their levels of income.

Also, some of the largest areas of NHS expenditure are actually with groups who are not 'productive'. For example, the largest group of users of the NHS are older, retired people.

Pluralist approaches

This approach suggests that the best way to understand any society (or large organization) is to examine the way that power is distributed within it. More powerful groups will be more likely to gain benefits compared to less powerful groups. This differs from the Marxist model in a number of ways, but, most importantly, pluralism argues that no one group has all the power – instead, there are numerous ('plural') competing groups who need to accommodate each other. The resulting social inequalities will be much more complex and fragmented than in the ruling-class/working-class division in Marxist theory.

Applying pluralist theory to inequalities in health service provision, we can understand these inequalities (both of provision and demand) in terms of the differences in power between the various groups. In terms of the provision of services, there is the interplay between the various professional groups (surgeons, dentists, nurses, pediatricians, geriatricians) and between managers and, finally, political interests. Demand for services consists of competing demands from the various 'illness categories' (mentally ill, children, older people, cancer patients, etc.) and from groups stratified according to ethnicity, age, gender and class.

The outcome in terms of provision and use will constantly vary according to shifts in power between these groups.

Structuralist approaches

Alford (1975) has suggested that both the Marxist and the pluralist approaches are useful, but that combining elements of both produces a better theory.

According to Alford there are three groups of interested parties in the health service: dominant, challenging and repressed. These groups operate on different levels and there is conflict both *between* them and *within* them. The dominant group consists of the established medical professions who vie with each other for dominance. Whatever the outcome of their struggles, the winners will have greater power over decision-making than the next 'challenging' group – which consists of senior health managers and health-service policy planners. The third group, the 'repressed', consists of patients and other consumer groups. Different categories of patients compete for their health needs to be addressed, but they do so within the framework set out by the dominant and challenging groups.

This may seem rather complex, but Alford is essentially arguing that the competing interest groups in the health service can be grouped together in terms of the power they hold. In doing so, Alford presents a modified version of pluralism. The elements of Marxism incorporated into his theory include the point that the dominant and challenging groups draw their power from established social hierarchies and so the divisions in health-service provision reflect the divisions in the wider capitalist society.

Check your understanding

1. What do we mean by 'issues of provision and demand' when discussing inequalities in access to healthcare?

2. What impact can doctors and hospitals have on inequalities of provision?

3. What three factors help to restrict the use of health services by ethnic minorities?

4. How does the medical profession view geriatric medicine?

5. Explain what impact private medicine may have on health inequalities?

6. Explain the structuralist explanation of inequalities in healthcare provision, using examples from the main text where appropriate.

Activities

Research idea

Interview a sample of older people (over the age of 60) and ask them:

- whether they get their 'flu jab' each autumn and why they do or don't
- whether they think older people are treated any differently by the NHS than younger people.

Compare your answers in class.

Web.task

Go to the site of the Healthcare Commission at **www.healthcarecommission.org.uk/homepage.cfm**

Find out what the Commission does and look up how well your local healthcare trust is performing.

- How does your area compare with others?
- Do links appear to exist between the richer areas and 'better performance'?
- How useful do you think these tables are?

Key terms

Health authorities the National Health Service is actually a system of local health services. Health authorities are the bodies responsible for ensuring that local people get adequate health services by overseeing the local healthcare trusts which actually provide the health services.

Iatrogenesis illness caused by the medical professions (e.g. as a result of poor care or inaccurate diagnosis).

Primary care trusts the NHS organizations responsible for local health- and social-care services (including GPs).

Private healthcare healthcare that is not provided by the NHS, but which people pay for themselves.

Screening programmes programmes where particular sections of the population are tested to see if they have signs of a particular disease.

An eye on the exam   Inequalities in the health service

Item A

Julian Tudor-Hart has argued that there exists an 'inverse care law' in healthcare, in which those groups and neighbourhoods most in need of good healthcare in fact have least access to it. For example, in working-class neighbourhoods, there are fewer GPs, dentists and so on than in more affluent middle-class areas. It has been suggested that one reason for this may be because the medical professionals are middle-class themselves.

More recently, Gordon *et al.* (1999) have argued that there now exists a large body of evidence to support what they describe as the 'inverse prevention law' in front-line healthcare. By this, they mean that those social groups who are in greatest need of preventive care – that is, the ones whose risk of ill health is greatest, such as manual workers, the unemployed and many ethnic minorities – are least likely to have access to preventive services such as health promotion, dental check-ups, immunization, cancer screening and so on.

By contrast, the middle classes are more aware of such services and make greater use of them.

Item B

<< The way that [health] services are organized and offered is based on indigenous British culture and is often inflexible so that members of ethnic-minority groups may find vital provision irrelevant, offensive, unhelpful or threatening.

Aspects of racism that are implicated here include the failure to provide health information in appropriate languages, the failure to make knowledge of religious, dietary and cultural imperatives basic to health professional training, and the failure to provide amenities to support cultural beliefs in the importance of running water for washing, death rites, prayer in hospital, visiting times, food in hospital, etc., as an automatic inclusion in health service budgets.>>

Source: Culley, L. and Dyson, D. (1993) '"Race", inequality and health', *Sociology Review*, 3(1)

(a) Explain what sociologists mean by 'iatrogenesis'.   (2 marks)

(b) Identify three reasons for gender differences in use of health services.   (6 marks)

(c) Outline some of the causes of ethnic differences in access to healthcare.   (12 marks)

(d) Using information from Item A and elsewhere, assess the reasons for class differences
     in use of health services.   (20 marks)

Grade booster   Getting top marks in the 20-mark question

You need to focus on differences in healthcare rather than in health chances, but make sure you stick to social class differences (not ethnicity, gender, etc.). Make use of the information in Item A. You should discuss a range of class differences, e.g. in uptake of different types of services, the inverse care law and the inverse prevention law (both in Item A), and a range of reasons, e.g. cultural factors and knowledge of services, material factors (e.g. being able to afford private care), labelling by professionals, and so on.

Mental health and mental illness

Getting you thinking

'Normal children given drugs'

By **David Derbyshire** and **Roger Highfield** at the British Association science festival The Daily Telegraph (filed: 09 September 2004)

THE RISE OF attention deficit hyperactivity disorder has led to concerns that doctors and drugs companies are turning unpleasant, but essentially normal, human behaviour into medical conditions. Its most serious form, known as hyperkinetic disorder, affects 1.4 per cent of children. Sufferers are unable to concentrate, forgetful, disorganized and easily distracted. At school they are disruptive, find it almost impossible to learn ...

While the most serious cases are generally recognized as psychiatric disorders, diagnosis of milder forms of ADHD, is more controversial. One person's ADHD victim is another's naughty child. Some researchers are concerned that drugs such as Ritalin, the 'chemical cosh', are used to suppress essentially normal but disruptive behaviour. In the UK, only 0.3 per cent of all children receive medication for ADHD, compared with six per cent in America.

Prevalence of mental disorders among children: by gender and gross weekly household income, Great Britain, 2004

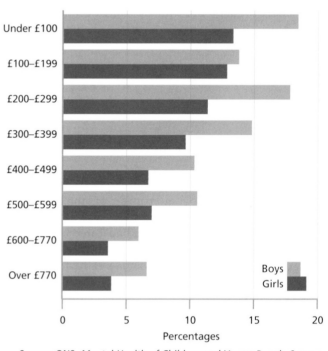

Source: ONS, *Mental Health of Children and Young People Survey*

1 Provide a short summary of what the chart above tells you about the relationship between mental illness and (a) gender (b) family income.

2 Can you suggest any explanations for these links?

3 There is considerable debate concerning the very existence of ADHD. Some people argue that it is simply a way of labelling bad behaviour as mental illness and therefore taking the blame away from parents and the children. What is your view?

4 Do you think that it is right to use drugs to alter the behaviour of children?

5 Look at the photo of the anorexic/very thin young women. Is anorexia a mental illness in your opinion?

6 What conclusions can you draw about how we define mental illness and who decides whether it exists or not?

Mental illness has been the forgotten twin to physical illness, in terms of the attention paid to it and the funding provided by the NHS. The issue only comes to the fore when a particularly spectacular event hits the headlines. However, mental health is a major problem in society, with about one in seven of the population claiming to have mental health problems at some point in their lives. But mental health is dogged with debates over definitions and over the differences in the extent of mental health problems across different groups in society.

According to the government publication *Social Trends 2007* (Self and Zealey 2007), about one in six British people aged 16 to 74 reported experiencing a neurotic disorder (self-diagnosed), such as depression, anxiety or a phobia, in the seven days before a national survey on mental health. A higher proportion of women (19 per cent) than men (14 per cent) experienced such a disorder.

Defining mental illness

Sociology is split between two different approaches regarding how to define mental illness. The two approaches are **social realism** and **social constructionism**.

Social realism

Social realism is a general term used to describe the approaches of sociologists who, broadly speaking, accept that there are distinctive sets of abnormal behaviour that cause distress to individuals and to those around them. These forms of abnormal behaviour are classified as mental illness. Social realists such as Pilgrim and Rogers (1999) accept that, at different times and in different cultures, there are variations in what is considered as mental illness. Nevertheless, they argue that, although mental illness may have different names and may or may not be recognized in different cultures, it does actually exist as a real condition.

Social constructionism

Social constructionist perspectives have been very influential in sociological approaches to mental illness and start from the argument that what is considered normal varies over time and from society to society. For example, over the last two hundred years in Britain, alcohol consumption has been seen variously as normal, as morally wrong or even illegal, as a sign of being mentally ill and as a central part of a religious ritual. In fact, most of these different attitudes to alcohol can still be found in Britain today!

Even greater extremes of behaviour have been seen as normal in some societies and as evidence of madness in others. For example, saying that you are possessed by the spirit of your ancestor would suggest madness in contemporary Britain, but for native Americans, or in some West African religions, it would be a perfectly reasonable statement which most people would believe was true.

Mental illness: real or culturally created?

All sociologists agree that there are forms of behaviour that cause considerable stress to the individual involved, and that prevent them from engaging in any meaningful participation in society. They also recognize that how it comes to be defined depends upon cultural differences. Where the difference between realist and constructionist perspectives emerges is more in the stress they place on how far the cultural context determines the levels and types of mental illness.

The best way to understand the sociology of mental health is to see it as a continuum, with those who argue for the overwhelming importance of culture at one extreme and those who argue for the existence of common illnesses (which might go under different names, but are essentially the same) at the other extreme.

Mental illness: the labelling perspective

The degree of flexibility about what constitutes normal and abnormal behaviour has been taken furthest by so-called 'labelling theorists'. Labelling theory (as we saw in Chapter 1, p. 22) examines how labelling occurs in the first place and what effects it has on those who are labelled. Thomas Szasz (1973), for example, argues that the label 'mental illness' is simply a convenient way to deal with behaviour that people find disruptive. Labelling theory rests firmly upon a social constructionist definition of mental illness.

The effects of labelling

According to Scheff (1966), whether someone becomes labelled or not is determined by the benefits that others might gain by labelling the person 'mentally ill'. So, those people who become a nuisance, or who prevent others from doing something they want to do, are far more likely to be defined as being mentally ill than those who pose no threat or inconvenience, and may be ignored.

Once labelled, there are a number of negative consequences for the person, because it is then assumed that all their behaviour is evidence of their mental state. A famous study by Rosenhan (1973) illustrates this. In the early 1970s in the USA, Rosenhan asked eight perfectly 'normal' researchers to enter a number of psychiatric institutions after phoning up and complaining that they were 'hearing voices'. Once the researchers had been admitted into the institutions, doctors and staff regarded them as truly mentally ill and reinterpreted all their behaviour as proof of this. However, the researchers were under strict instructions to behave completely normally at all times.

In a later study, new staff in a psychiatric hospital were told that this experiment was to be repeated in their institution, and they were asked to uncover these researchers who were just pretending to be ill. In this study, staff routinely judged people who were 'genuinely ill' as merely pretending. It would seem, therefore, that there is some confusion as to how even experts can decide who is actually mentally ill.

Erving Goffman (1961) followed the **careers** of people who were genuinely defined as being mentally ill. He suggested that, once in an institution, people are stripped of their **presenting culture** – by which he means the image that we all choose to present to the world as 'us'. This may include a style of haircut, make-up, or the requirement that people address us as 'Mr' or 'Mrs' rather than 'Michael' or 'Sarah'. The 'patient' may also lose their right to make decisions about their life and may be required to take medication, which can disorientate them.

Quickly, the self-image that a patient has – perhaps of being a respectable, witty, middle-aged person – is stripped away, leaving them bewildered, vulnerable and ready to accept a new role. In this powerless situation, any attempts to reject the label of mental illness can actually be interpreted as further signs of illness, and perhaps as indicating a need for increased medication or counselling. In fact, accepting the role of being mentally ill is seen as the first sign of recovery.

Criticisms of the labelling perspective

The labelling perspective on mental illness has not gone unchallenged. Gove (1982) suggests that the vast majority of people who receive treatment for mental illness actually have serious problems before they are treated and so the argument that the label causes the problem is wrong. Furthermore, he argues that labelling theory provides no adequate explanation for why some people start to show symptoms in the first place.

According to Gove, labelling may help explain some of the responses of others to the mentally ill, but it cannot explain the causes of the illness.

Foucault's perspective on mental illness

A second, very distinctive version of social constructionist theory emerges in the work of the French sociologist, Foucault (1965). He explains the growth in the concept of mental illness by placing it in the context of the changing ways of thinking and acting which developed in the early 18th century. According to Foucault, during the **Enlightenment**, more traditional ways of thinking, based on religious beliefs and on emotions, were gradually replaced by more rational, intellectually disciplined ways of thinking and acting. These eventually led to the significant scientific and engineering developments that formed the basis of the 'industrial revolution'. Foucault argues that as rationality developed into the normal way of thinking, irrationality began to be perceived as deviant.

This shift away from the irrational and towards the rational was illustrated, according to Foucault, by the growth in asylums for those considered mad. Foucault suggests that having mad people in asylums, both symbolically and literally, isolated mad people away from the majority of the population. The asylums

symbolized the fact that madness or irrationality was marked out as behaviour that was no longer acceptable.

Although Foucault's writing is very dense and complicated, the essential message is that madness, as we understand it, is a relatively modern invention which emerged from the development of modern 'rational' ways of thinking and acting.

Structuralist perspectives on mental health

Structuralist perspectives on mental health are closely tied to the social realist definition of mental illness. These approaches accept the reality of mental illness and set out to discover what factors in society might cause the illness. As a result of research by sociologists working within this tradition, evidence of clear mental health differences between social groups has emerged. Some of these are discussed next.

Mental illness and ethnicity

Members of ethnic minorities have significantly different chances of mental illness compared to the majority White population. According to Nazroo (2001) people of 'South Asian origin' have very low rates of mental illness, while those of African-Caribbean origins have particularly high levels of **schizophrenia**, with levels between three and five times higher than the population as a whole. Writers within the structuralist perspective, such as Virdee (1997), explain this by arguing that the sorts of pressures and stresses that can cause people to develop mental illness are more likely to be experienced by members of ethnic minorities because they encounter racism and disadvantage throughout their lives.

However, labelling theorists have argued that some of the behaviour of Afro-Caribbean adults, in particular, has been seen as inappropriate in British society, and has therefore been labelled as a symptom of mental illness. Nazroo points out that people of Bangladeshi origin, who are amongst the most deprived groups in the British population and are also recipients of racism, actually have lower levels of mental illness than the general population. They therefore argue that it cannot just be racism and deprivation.

Mental illness and gender

Women are more likely than men to exhibit behaviour defined as mental illness. Overall, women have rates about one third higher than men, but in some specific forms of mental illness the figures are much higher. For example, women are at least three times more likely to suffer from depression. Structuralists, such as Brown et al. (1995), argue that women are more likely to lead stressful lives – combining careers and the responsibility for childcare, for example, and being more likely to experience poverty and poor housing conditions.

However, labelling theorists and feminist sociologists, such as Chesler (1972), go further and argue that the behaviour of women is more likely to be defined as evidence of mental illness because the defining is done by a male-dominated profession. Rather than looking for the real reasons – which are most likely to be stress and poverty – psychiatrists are more interested in defining the problem in terms of an individual's mental state.

Busfield (1988) has suggested that the structuralist position and the labelling approach are not irreconcilable and that women are under pressure in their lives, which leads to higher levels of mental illness, but are also more likely to have their problems defined as mental illness by psychiatrists.

Inequality, social class and mental illness

Overall, when looking at which group is most likely to suffer from high rates of mental illness, the poorest and most excluded are massively overrepresented.

Link and Phelan (1995) reviewed all the evidence over a period of 40 years of connections between social class and mental illness, concluding that all the research clearly pointed

to the close relationship between deprivation and low levels of mental health. A government study (Office for National Statistics Study 2004) found that children from the poorest backgrounds were three times more likely to have conduct disorders than those whose parents were in professional occupations. Structuralist writers, such as Myers (1975), have

---

Research methods

Emma Rich (2006)
Research into how women manage anorexia

Emma Rich set out to explore the ways in which young women 'manage' the difficulties associated with having an anorexic identity, the stigma attached to it, and the relationships they develop with fellow sufferers.

The style of the research was complex and used a number of methods. First, the researcher undertook semi-structured interviews with young women who were experiencing anorexia or bulimia. These interviews were with young women (all under the age of 16) who were attending a special school for the treatment of eating disorders. The aim of the interviews was to collect 'narratives' of the young women's experiences in previous schools as well as their current views and feelings.

As well as this, an academic researcher in her early twenties engaged in an ethnographic study of the young girls at the school. Rich developed her ideas by using the field notes of this researcher, but she restricted her research to the interviews only. This researcher was, according to Rich, of 'slim build' and she stayed at the centre interviewing and interacting with the girls during their daily routines. This allowed her to share some of the experiences and interact in greater depth with the young women. However, she was still always an outsider. Rich describes the researcher's relationship to the young women as follows: the researcher reports being 'invited into' this subculture, with a number of intimate

experiences and practices shared, against which the ethnographer reports having to renegotiate relationships and taken-for-granted assumptions about anorexia.

Conversely, there are other occasions where these young people remain protective of certain social spaces.

A third element of Rich's research was her use of the internet to enter support networks and chatrooms – even websites which support anorexia.

Finally, she conducted a full literature review of academic sources.

Rich states that her research was conducted from a clear feminist standpoint and that her interpretation of the research results was conducted through this perspective.

Rich, E. (2006) 'Anorexic dis(connection): managing anorexia as an illness and an identity', *Sociology of Health and Illness*, 28(3), pp. 284–305

1 How many methods did Emma Rich use?

2 Which part of the work was undertaken by another researcher? Can you see any difficulties this might create for (a) Rich's research process and (b) the analysis of the results?

3 What are the strengths and weaknesses which she identified of the ethnographic element of her research?

4 What perspective guided her research? What views do you have of an explicit 'political' perspective being applied to the research process and analysis?

suggested a '**life-course**' model, which explains the higher levels of mental illness as a result of poorer people consistently encountering higher levels of social problems over their lifetimes, but having limited educational, social and economic resources to continue overcoming the problems. They argue that, eventually, the stress of coping emerges and is expressed through mental illness.

A second form of structuralist explanation is that of **social capital**. The concept of social capital derives from the writings of Putnam (2000) who argues that people who have social networks of friends and relatives are more likely to be happy, to have lower levels of stress and to feel they 'belong' to their local community. The result of this is that they are less likely to suffer from mental illness.

Pilgrim and Rogers (1999), however, point to the arguments of labelling and feminist theorists, who note that within the most deprived groups, there are also higher levels of women suffering from mental illness compared to men and they would suggest that women are more likely to have their problems defined in terms of mental illness.

Mental illness: conclusion

Mental illness is a highly contested issue in sociology. There are arguments over the very definition of the term and how to explain the differences in mental illness rates in the population. However, the approaches are not entirely irreconcilable and Busfield's approach is one that has received much support. She argues that it is probably true that some groups are much more likely to find their behaviour defined as mental illness,

compared to the behaviour of other groups. However, it is also true that these very same groups – ethnic minorities, women and the socially excluded – all suffer high levels of stress and so one would expect them to have higher levels of illness. Both processes reinforce each other.

Key terms

Career refers, in this context, to the gradual changes in people as a response to a label (for example, 'mental patient').

Enlightenment a period of intellectual change in the late 17th to the late 18th centuries.

Life-course model suggests that the accumulation of social events experienced over a whole lifetime, not just individual important events, influence people and their mental state.

Presenting culture a term used by Goffman to refer to how people like to portray themselves to others.

Schizophrenia a form of mental illness where people are unable to distinguish their own feelings and perceptions from reality.

Social capital refers to a network of social contacts.

Social constructionism the approach which suggests that mental illness (and all other social phenomena) exists because people believe it does.

Social realism a sociological approach which suggests that mental illness does really exist.

Activities

Research idea

Conduct a small-scale survey. Ask 20 people:

1 what the first words are that pop into their minds when you say the words 'mental illness'
2 to suggest the two main reasons for people being mentally ill.

Collate your answers – what do they suggest about people's views of mental illness. Do the sociological ideas contained in this topic ring true?

Web.tasks

1 Find the website of the mental health charity MIND at **www.mind.org.uk**. Use the 'links' section to explore the work of some of the organizations connected with mental health issues. Make a list of all the mental health issues covered. How important an issue is mental health in the UK today?

2 Key the words 'mentally ill people' into Google and then list the themes that emerge.

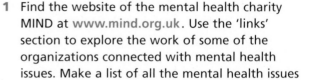

Check your understanding

1 Identify the two sociological approaches to defining mental illness.

2 Explain the key differences between the two approaches you have identified.

3 How does the idea of 'labelling' help us to understand mental illness?

4 What is meant by a structural explanation for mental illness?

5 How does Busfield suggest that the structuralist and labelling approaches can be combined?

6 Why are people from certain ethnic minorities more likely to be defined as suffering from mental illness?

7 What argument do feminist writers use to explain why women are more likely to be defined as suffering from mental illness?

An eye on the exam Mental health and mental illness

Item A

<<It affects your mind. If you feel depressed that you are not treated as other people are, or they look down on you, you will feel mentally ill, won't you? It will depress you that you are not treated well racially, it will affect your health in some way. It will cause you depression, and that depression will cause the illness.>>

Source: Quoted in Annandale, E. (1998) *The Sociology of Health and Medicine*, Cambridge: Polity Press, p. 187

Item B

People of African-Caribbean origin are far more likely to reach the mental health system via the police, the courts and prisons, and to experience the more harsh and invasive forms of treatment (such as electro-convulsive therapy), than other groups.

Recorded rates of schizophrenia are considerably higher for people of African-Caribbean origin than for other groups. However, it is not clear how far this is due to a greater willingness of psychiatrists to diagnose the condition in this group. Littlemore and Lipsedge argue that schizophrenia among Black patients is simply misdiagnosed paranoia resulting from the racism they have encountered in British society.

With regard to mental illness, for all diagnoses combined, women's rate of admission to hospitals in England and Wales was 29 per cent above the rate for men.

Adapted from Annandale, E. (1998) *The Sociology of Health and Medicine*, Cambridge: Polity Press, pp. 143 & 186

Item C

Katz examined the process of psychiatric diagnosis among both British and American psychiatrists. Groups of British and American psychiatrists were shown films of interviews with patients and asked to note down all the pathological symptoms and make a diagnosis. Marked disagreements in diagnosis between the two groups were found. The British saw less evidence of mental illness generally. For example, one patient was diagnosed as 'schizophrenic' by one-third of the Americans, but by none of the British.

Adapted from Helman, C. (2000) *Culture, Health and Illness*, Oxford: Butterworth/Heinemann, p. 80

(a) **Suggest two reasons why the British and American psychiatrists in Item C may have diagnosed the same individual differently.** (4 marks)

(b) **Using material from Items A and B, suggest two reasons for ethnic differences in mental health.** (4 marks)

(c) **Outline the reasons for gender differences in the patterns of mental illness.** (12 marks)

(d) **Using information from the Items and elsewhere, assess the usefulness of labelling theory in understanding mental illness.** (20 marks)

Grade booster Getting top marks in the 20-mark question

Outline the labelling theory, linking it to the idea that mental illness is socially constructed (a product of social definition). Use 'realist' approaches (i.e. that mental illness is a real illness, not merely a label) to criticize it. These can include structuralist views that see mental illness as resulting from society's unequal structure. Make sure you use relevant information both from the Items and from studies of mental illness, e.g. of class, ethnic or gender differences in rates of mental illness.

Getting you thinking

Trust me, doctors are paid too much

By Nick Britten

A JUNIOR DOCTOR yesterday called for doctors' pay to be reduced into line with that of nurses and other public sector workers, saying that his senior colleagues enjoyed an 'opulent' way of life while other hospital staff had to get by on a 'piffling' amount.

Mark Jopling, a first-year pre-registration house officer, said doctors allowed themselves to be placed on a 'golden pedestal' and were happy to be regarded as 'awesome life savers', earning large amounts of money, driving luxury cars and living in grand houses.

The British Medical Association said Dr Jopling's views were 'not widely held' among doctors, but he won support from the Royal College of Nursing for 'helping expose nurses' poor pay'.

Dr Jopling, 24, yesterday accepted that his comments might well upset his senior colleagues. He said: 'If I became a consultant, the taxpayer would be sending me home with about £90,000. Were I to prefer a nine-to-five job as a GP, I would be raking in a fat £100,000 – even more, if I played the system well.'

Doctors, Dr Jopling said, were 'quick to justify' their salaries 'with a series of compelling arguments: we work hard, we have big responsibilities, we are also well qualified and have to endure a protracted training'. But he added: 'Teachers, social workers and other professionals in the public sector work long hours too, however, some of these at home and unrecognised.

It is unfair that our salaries dwarf theirs. In medicine there has been a long-standing acknowledgment that nurses work hard and are underpaid. A nurse starts on a relatively modest £16,000 and regularly works nights and weekends. It is usually nurses who give patients most support during their stay in hospital.'

A spokesman for the BMA said: 'This is one doctor's point of view. Unsurprisingly, it isn't widely held in the medical profession. The facts support the case for paying doctors more, not less. The new GP contract pays doctors for raising the quality of patient care they provide.'

Source: nbritten@telegraph.co.uk

Nurses fear for futures as morale plummets

By Nicole Martin

MORALE AMONG NURSES has reached an all-time low, according to a survey that paints a picture of a profession in crisis.

A poll of 9,000 nurses found that despite the Government pouring billions of pounds into the health service, many still feel overworked, under-valued and fear for their futures.

More than half – 55 per cent – said they were too busy to deliver the level of care they would like, and 30 per cent said they would quit the profession if they could.

Source: www.telegraph.co.uk/news/
main.jhtml?xml=/news/2007/07/16/nnurse116.xml

1 Why are doctors paid higher salaries than nurses or teachers?

2 Do you think that only outstanding people can become doctors?

3 Break into small groups and decide whether, as a group, you agree with Dr Jopling's arguments or those of the BMA.

4 Which occupational group, if any, do you trust more than doctors?

Members of the medical profession are among the most prestigious and well-paid groups in society. But how did they get this superior status? Was it really through their greater abilities, as they would have us believe? Sociologists are always suspicious of the claims groups make about themselves and, as you might expect, their views are not always totally supportive of the caring, dedicated image the medical professions like to present. In this topic, we are going to explore the reasons that sociologists suggest provide the basis for the power, prestige and affluence of the medical professions. This exploration of the medical professions is useful in its own right, helping us to understand the nature of medical provision in Britain, but it is also a helpful model for understanding how other occupational groups have arrived in their particular position. Some of these, such as the legal profession, have been successful in obtaining prestige and financial rewards, while others, such as the teaching profession, have been much less successful.

There are five main sociological approaches to understanding the position and role of the medical professions. These are:

● *the functionalist argument* – that the medical profession benefits society

● *the Weberian approach* – that the medical profession is just an occupational strategy to get higher income and status

- *the Marxist view* – that the medical profession acts to control the majority of the population and is rewarded for this by the ruling class
- *Foucault's suggestion* – that the power of the medical profession has emerged as a result of their ability to define what is prestigious knowledge
- *the feminist approach* – that the medical profession can best be understood by seeing how it has controlled and marginalized women.

The functionalist approach: professions as a benefit to society

The first approach to understanding the role of the professions developed from the functionalist school of sociology (see Chapter 1, p. 12), associated with the writing of Talcott Parsons, which seeks to show what functions the various parts of society play in helping society to exist.

Barber (1963) argued that professions, especially the medical professions, are very important for society because they deal with people when they are in particularly vulnerable positions. It is, therefore, in the interests of society to have the very best people, who maintain the highest standards, to provide medical care. These people must not only be competent but they must also be totally trustworthy. According to functionalists, true professions can be recognized by the fact that they share a number of 'traits'. These are as follows:

- They have a *theoretical basis* to their knowledge – Doctors have a full understanding of medical theories about the body. This allows them to make independent decisions about the cause of illness and the best cure.
- They are *fully trained* to the highest possible standards – Only the most intelligent can enter and succeed.
- Competence is *tested by examination* – There is no favouritism and doctors are in their position as a result of their ability alone.
- The profession has a *strict code of* **ethics** – Doctors deal with people at their most vulnerable and the code of ethics ensures that no patient is exploited.
- They are *regulated and controlled* through an organization (in the case of doctors it is the General Medical Council) which decides who can enter the profession and has the power to punish and exclude for any misconduct.

Critics of the functionalist approach, such as Waitzkin (1979), while agreeing that high standards and trust are all

needed, argue that these 'traits', rather than simply justifying the high status of doctors, are used by the medical profession as barriers to prevent others from entering. This criticism was for a long time supported by the fact that entry to medicine remained largely the preserve of males from higher social-class backgrounds. Only in the last 20 years has there been a significant inflow of women and ethnic minorities into the medical profession. This inflow has largely coincided with an acceptance of the criticisms of the functionalist approach.

The Weberian approach: professionalization as a strategy

The second approach to understanding the power of the medical professions is that, rather than being constructed for the good of the community, they are, in fact, constructed for the good of the medical professions themselves. This argument has developed from the original writings of Max Weber, an early 20th-century sociologist who argued that all occupational groups are constantly vying with one another to improve their prestige and financial bargaining power. There are a number of different techniques used, but the two main ones are the creation of trades unions (which has traditionally been used by the working class) and the construction of professions (which has been used by the middle class).

Overall, **professionalization** of an occupational group has actually been a more effective method to gain status and financial rewards. It is for this reason that many other groups, such as teachers and social workers, have tried to gain professional status. The process of professionalization has four important dimensions:

1. *The production of a body of* **esoteric** *knowledge* – This means creating an apparently complex body of knowledge which must be placed in the hands of experts.
2. *Educational barriers* – Professionals construct a series of specialist educational courses and qualifications in order to limit the numbers of entrants.

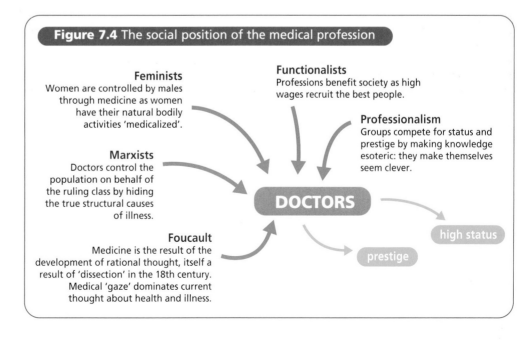

Figure 7.4 The social position of the medical profession

Feminists
Women are controlled by males through medicine as women have their natural bodily activities 'medicalized'.

Functionalists
Professions benefit society as high wages recruit the best people.

Professionalism
Groups compete for status and prestige by making knowledge esoteric: they make themselves seem clever.

Marxists
Doctors control the population on behalf of the ruling class by hiding the true structural causes of illness.

Foucault
Medicine is the result of the development of rational thought, itself a result of 'dissection' in the 18th century. Medical 'gaze' dominates current thought about health and illness.

DOCTORS

high status

prestige

3 *Exclusion of competition* – The profession must wipe out any possible competitors, such as faith healers, homeopaths and herbalists. They do this by claiming that only scientific medicine and surgery are effective.

4 *Maintenance of privilege* – The professional group will fight all attempts to have others impose any control over them. So, doctors will demand **clinical freedom** – the right to do what they think best – and they will fight any attempts to hand over part of their work to others, such as allowing nurses to prescribe medicines.

These four methods of professionalizing are very similar to the traits suggested by functionalist writers. From a Weberian perspective, therefore, the medical profession is looking after its own interests as well as those of the patients.

A good example of the Weberian approach is provided by Cant and Sharma (2002), who studied the relationship between the medical profession and the practitioners of chiropractic. (Chiropractic is the manipulation of the spine, joints and muscles in order to realign them.) For over 60 years, chiropractors campaigned to gain legal recognition, which was finally granted

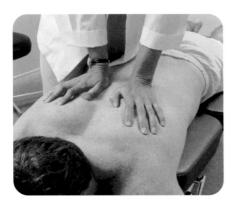

in an act of parliament in 1994. But Cant and Sharma point out that in order to get this recognition, chiropractors effectively had to subordinate themselves to doctors.

Marxist approaches

Marxists, such as Navarro (1977), argue that in capitalist societies such as Britain, a small ruling class exploits society for its own benefit. In order to hide this exploitation from people and to maintain its power, the ruling class employs a number of mechanisms which involve distorting 'reality', so that people come to accept exploitation as 'natural'.

The medical profession plays an important role in this by misleading the population as to the real cause of their illnesses. The medical profession explains health and illness in terms of individuals' actions and genetics – they point the finger away from the poor working conditions, poverty, poor housing and inequalities in society, which are the true, underlying causes of ill health, according to Marxist writers (see Chapter 1, pp. 17–18, for more details on Marx). But what doctors do succeed in doing for the health of the population is to keep them fit enough to work.

Marxists also point out that health and illness in a capitalist society are carefully linked to being able or not able to work. Doctors play a key role in deciding who is fit to work and who is sick enough to be eligible for state disability and sickness benefits.

Critics have pointed out that this perspective ignores the genuinely beneficial work that doctors do, and that to characterize their work as only misleading and controlling the population is inaccurate. Doctors do work very much within the framework of looking at individual problems, but stress in the workplace and the role of poverty are well known and recognized by doctors.

Foucault's approach

There is an old saying, 'knowledge is power', and in Foucault's analysis of society this is literally true. According to Foucault (1976), in every society, groups are 'battling' to look after their own interests. The best way of doing this is to get control of what is regarded as 'truth' or 'knowledge'. If other people believe that what you say is 'true' and what others say is 'false', then you have a high chance of getting them to do what you want. So you seek to create an overall framework of thought and ideas, within which all the more specific debates (what Foucault calls '**discourses**') are conducted. This argument is similar in some ways to the Marxist argument we saw earlier.

Foucault argues that, over time, doctors have led the way in helping to construct an idea of 'science', through their activities in dissecting bodies and demonstrating to people the ways in which bodies are constructed in the form of a 'biological machine'. This has resulted in a society where rational scientific thought is prized above all else, where other forms of thought are regarded as inferior, and where doctors have significant prestige and power.

So, medicine has played a major part in constructing the way we think and act in contemporary society. In the process, the medical professions have gained considerable benefits in terms of prestige and financial rewards.

Feminist approaches

Feminist sociologists, such as Oakley (1986) and Witz (1992), suggest that the activities of doctors contribute to the social control of women, both as patients and as medical practitioners. They point out that medicine has traditionally been a male occupation, with women excluded or marginalized into junior roles. This simply reinforces the subordinate position of women in society. (However, in the last 15 years, roughly equal numbers of men and women have been training to be doctors.)

Historically, women had always held a key role in healing and traditional healthcare. For example, the women whom we now refer to as 'witches' were very often herbal healers who were eagerly sought out in rural areas. There had always been a degree of competition between male and female healthcare practitioners, and it was not until 1885 that a law was passed that legally recognized a closed medical profession. Although women were not legally prevented from entering the medical profession, the values of Victorian Britain and the nature of the educational system, which generally excluded women from higher education, meant that the outcome of the act was effectively to prevent women from becoming doctors.

Techniques to exclude women from the medical profession

According to Witz, the male-dominated medical profession was successful in excluding females for over half a century by using two techniques – exclusion and demarcation:

- *Exclusion* involves creating barriers so that it is virtually impossible for other groups (in this case females) to enter the profession.
- *Demarcation* involves creating a restricted area of competence and then allowing people to enter this area. At the same time, this area of competence is still controlled by the medical profession. Examples of this include nursing and radiography.

Witz further argues that to combat these techniques, women have used two strategies – inclusion and dual closure:

- *Inclusion* involves using any possible method of gaining entry through, for example, political and legal action.
- The aim of *dual closure* is to accept, in part, a restricted area of competence, but then to close this off to others and to seek to turn it into a profession. It is exactly this process that is happening to nursing.

The 'medicalization' process

Feminist sociologists, such as Lupton (1994), also claim that the male-dominated profession of medicine has successfully 'medicalized' a number of female activities or problems. By this, they mean that normal or natural activities of women (such as childbirth and menopause), or problems faced more often by women (such as depression), have been taken over by the medical profession and turned into medical issues. So, for example, women are expected to give birth in the manner and in the place determined by 'the experts'. For Lupton, this means that male doctors can use this as a means of controlling how women ought to act. According to Lupton, through this process 'women are placed in a position of compliance with expert advice throughout their pregnancy and delivery, and their personal needs and wishes tend to be ignored' (Lupton 1994, p. 148).

Research methods

Lorelei Jones and Judith Green (2006) The attitudes of younger GPs

Lorelei Jones and Judith Green wanted to find out whether newly qualified GPs had different views from older GPs about the nature of professionalism. Traditionally, GPs have perceived their jobs as a vocation, in which they had a duty to their patients and society. Their motivation was as much moral as financial. Jones and Green wished to know if, in late modernity, this vocational attitude to being a GP was still dominant. They discovered that the traditional vocational approach had been replaced by one in which younger GPs seek nice work, by which they meant good pay, pleasant surroundings, interesting and varied work and decent patients.

A purposive sampling strategy was used to select interviewees who were working in general practice from across England, Wales and Scotland in a range of rural and urban locations. In total, 20 GPs, aged 32–37 (14 women, 6 men) were included in the study, reflecting the gender composition of new GPs.

Interviews, lasting about an hour, were audio-taped and transcribed. In all interviews, participants were prompted for reasons for choosing general practice, career histories, descriptions of their work, satisfactions and dissatisfactions with the job and plans for the future. Participants were encouraged to elaborate when they raised other topics. The results were transcribed and formed the basis of a second interview.

Follow-up interviews took place some months later and participants were asked to reflect on questions arising from analysis of the earlier replies. These second replies were also transcribed.

The research was based on 'grounded theory', in which the theoretical ideas emerge during the research in the process of discussion and analysis. The researchers used computer software which can be used to generate 'themes'. The analysis of the transcripts showed the key theme of 'nice work'.

Before the research, the interviewees were assured that they would remain anonymous and all the interviewees were given pseudonyms in the published academic article.

Jones, L. and Green, J. (2006) 'Shifting discourses of professionalism: a case study of general practitioners in the United Kingdom', *Sociology of Health and Illness*, 28(7), pp. 927–50

1 What sort of sampling technique was used?

2 The researchers interviewed a total of 20 GPs. Do you think that it is possible to make generalizations for all younger GPs based upon this number?

3 What do we mean by 'grounded theory'? How does this differ from traditional positivistic research methods?

4 Why was it important to the accuracy of the research that the GPs remained anonymous?

When it comes to an 'illness' such as depression – which feminists argue is partly a result of the restricted role of women in society – the medical profession turns it into a medical problem that can be solved by prescribing medicines. This shifts the issue away from the position of women in general, to the particular medical condition of a single woman. One example of the creation of female illness and resulting medical treatment, according to Wertz and Wertz (1981), was the treatment of upper-class women in Victorian Britain. Links were made between the female reproductive and sexual organs and a whole range of illnesses including headaches, sore throats, indigestion and 'inappropriate libido'. This resulted in 'routine' hysterectomies, removals of ovaries and clitorectomies.

The rise of complementary medicine

The traditional male-dominated medical profession's monopoly of healthcare has been strongly challenged over the last 20 years. Within the profession, there has been an influx of ethnic minorities and women, and from outside the profession the claim to sole expertise on health matters has been challenged by a wide range of groups. Perhaps the biggest external challenge has come from complementary or alternative medicines, which include homeopathy, herbal remedies, acupuncture and a range of other techniques.

Giddens (1991) has argued that this is the result of the development of late-modern society. Two particularly relevant characteristics of late modernity are:

1 a decline in conformity, with a greater stress on individual desire and choice
2 disillusionment with the claims of professionals and experts in general to have a monopoly of knowledge. The particular result for healthcare and medicine has been a decline in the acceptance that 'doctor knows best' and an increased demand for choice in what 'cures' and interventions the ill person should undergo.

A third, less significant element of late modernity, which is particularly relevant to mental illness, is that a much wider range of behaviour is tolerated. This makes the distinction between deviant or marginally tolerated behaviour and mental illness far less clear.

Key terms

Clinical freedom the right of doctors to do what they think is best without other people having a say.

Discourse a way of thinking about issues.

Esoteric obscure and accessible only to a few.

Ethics a code of behaviour.

Professionalization tactic used by occupational groups to gain prestige and financial rewards.

Check your understanding

1 Give two examples of the 'traits' of a profession, according to functionalists.

2 According to the 'professionalization' approach, how do professions exclude other competing occupational groups?

3 How do the actions of doctors, in explaining why we are ill and then prescribing medicines, help capitalism?

4 Give one example of how doctors have 'medicalized' a normal activity of women?

5 According to Foucault, what is the relationship between knowledge and power over people?

Activities

Research ideas

1 Ask a small sample of people to identify five characteristics they associate with doctors. Do your results support the points made in the topic?

2 Identify a small sample of people who have actually used some form of 'alternative' healing. Conduct unstructured interviews to uncover their motives in seeking the treatment and the meaning they gave to their experiences.

Web.tasks

1 Visit the Royal College of Nursing website at **www.rcn.org.uk**

What aspects of the discussion in this topic are illustrated here? You will find useful to look at the section on the RCN's 'mission'.

2 Visit the General Medical Council website at **www.gmc-uk.org**

What points in this topic does this website illustrate (and also perhaps challenge!)?

3 Visit the Institute for Complementary Medicine website at **www.icmedicine.co.uk**

What ideas about 'the body' and healing lie behind these therapies and treatments? To what extent are they similar to, or different from, the conventional Western 'biomedical model'?

The medical professions in society

Item A

<< It is commonly held that nursing, since becoming a profession (the first register was set up in 1919), has progressed to become a higher-status, centrally recognized healthcare profession. Yet the crucial distinction between nursing and medicine remains: that of curing versus caring. Nursing's professional bodies are caught in a double-bind: in order to be of high status, the profession must lay claim to clinical and curative skills, but in order to remain as 'nursing', the practice must be centred on caring for, not curing, patients.

This dilemma has been addressed in part by the conscious formation of a body of theoretical knowledge, the nursing process, which is particular to nursing and distinct from medicine. To some extent, this has also been the rationale behind the most recent developments in nurse education, for example, the creation of the new Project 2000 and the possibility of a degree in nursing, which superseded the old apprentice-style ward-based training of 'pupil' nurses.>>

Source: Marsh, I. (2000) *Sociology: Making Sense of Society*, Harlow: Prentice Hall

Item B

Professional bodies (such as the General Medical Council) are charged with supervising the profession. But, being members of that profession, they usually whitewash or ignore cases of incompetence, etc. Final sanctions, like striking a doctor off the medical register, are used only rarely and then more often for sexual misconduct than for gross incompetence.

The medical profession also do a bad job. Their drug prescriptions often cause bad side effects and sometimes dependency. Their diagnostic tests sometimes do more harm than good. Women in particular suffer at their hands. Many iatrogenic (doctor-caused) diseases affect women only, for example those stemming from using contraceptive pills and devices, and from hysterectomies. Doctors medicalize pregnancy and birth, taking control away from women and treating them merely as 'cases'.

Adapted from: Trowler, P. (1996) *Investigating Health, Welfare and Poverty*, London: Collins Educational

Item C

<< For functionalist sociologists the higher professions such as medicine are virtually beyond reproach. Professionals are seen as selfless individuals working for the good of the community, often making great personal sacrifices. They need to be of the highest intelligence and skill, have to undergo years of training and in their early careers earn very little. High levels of reward later, then, are necessary to attract, retain and motivate the best people into the professions.>>

Source: Trowler, P. (1996) *Investigating Health, Welfare and Poverty*, London: Collins Education

---

(a) Explain what is meant by a 'professional body'. (2 marks)

(b) Identify three features that functionalists see as typical of professions. (6 marks)

(c) Using information from Item A and elsewhere, outline some of the ways in which doctors and nurses have tried to raise their power and status. (12 marks)

(d) Using information from Items B and C and elsewhere, assess the view that the medical profession enjoys high status and rewards because of its contribution to society. (20 marks)

Grade booster Getting top marks in the 20-mark question

You could begin with Barber's functionalist view, linking it to Item C. You need to evaluate this view in the light of other theories, such as Marxist, Weberian and feminist approaches to the medical profession's status and rewards. Consider who the medical profession serves – is it their patients, themselves, capitalism, or patriarchy? – and link this to the different theories. Use Cant and Sharma or Items A and B when examining the Weberian approach that professionalization is a strategy.

Exam Practice

1 Read **Item A** below and answer and answer parts (a) to (d) that follow.

Item A

Of the population of England and Wales, those people born in the Indian subcontinent have higher than average rates of tuberculosis, heart disease and diabetes, but lower rates of certain cancers. Those born in Africa or the Caribbean have higher rates of strokes, diabetes and high blood pressure. About a third of all male deaths in the UK are from circulatory diseases (such as heart attacks and strokes), but this rises to about a half among men under 50 from the Indian subcontinent, while Indian men in their 20s have over three times the national death rate from heart disease. Those born in Africa, the Caribbean and the Indian subcontinent are also more likely to suffer death from accidents.

There are also important differences in the birth weight of babies born to different ethnic groups. The average birth weight of babies born to mothers from India, Bangladesh and East Africa is about 300 grams lower than for babies of women who were born in the UK. These differences in some ways mirror social-class differences; for example, babies born to working-class mothers have a lower average birth weight than those born to middle-class mothers.

(a) Explain what is meant by 'morbidity'. *(2 marks)*

0/2 The term 'morbidity' means death. The morbidity rate is the death rate.

An examiner comments

Wrong – morbidity means sickness. Death is 'mortality', not morbidity.

(b) Suggest **three** reasons why women on average live longer than men in modern society. *(6 marks)*

First, women live longer than men because they don't smoke as much as men, so they don't get lung cancer, etc., as much.

Second, they go to the doctor's more often than men, e.g. to take the children when they are sick, so they can get early medical attention themselves at the same time and this can sometimes save their lives.

4/6 Third, women are biologically different from men and this accounts for their longer life expectancy.

The first two reasons are fine, but the third one isn't. It needs to say at least which biological differences are important or how they may prolong women's lives. A better approach is to suggest other aspects of women's lifestyle or social role, e.g. they drink less, drive less, work in less dangerous jobs, and so on.

(c) Outline some of the reasons for class differences in healthcare. *(12 marks)*

Health statistics show that the working class have a shorter life expectancy than the middle class and that they are more likely to be ill. Sociologists have found many reasons for this.

One explanation is the cultural and behavioural explanation. This states that the class differences are due to different behaviour, for example manual workers smoke and drink more, eat less healthy foods and don't go to the doctor's for check-ups and screening.

However, other sociologists argue that class differences in healthcare are due to material factors, e.g. not being able to afford healthy foods. Also, working class people are less likely to get paid time off work to go to the doctor's compared to, say, a businessman who can take time off whenever he likes.

Another reason for the differences is the fact that in working-class neighbourhoods there are not as many doctors' surgeries, so it is harder to get treatment than in middle-class neighbourhoods. This may be because doctors are middle-class and prefer to work in these areas. Working-class people may also have to rely on public transport to get to the surgery because they can't afford private transport.

This is related to poverty, because the working-class earn less and this can cause further health problems. Lack of money makes life stressful and causes mental health problems. Doctors are more likely to treat working-class patients with drugs rather than psychotherapy, perhaps because they are not so good at communicating with middle-class doctors.

6/12

Needs to focus on healthcare rather than health *chances*.

Still too much on health chances. Begins to touch on care via check-ups and screening – but needs to explain reasons.

Again, it's the last part that scores by giving a reason for differences in take-up of healthcare.

Good focus on care here, but should mention the inverse care law.

Overall, this is a reasonable answer, but it needs to be clearer about the difference between chances and care, and to focus on the latter. It could mention differences in consultation times, referrals and preventive treatment. It's also rather descriptive and should say more about reasons, such as speech codes, cultural capital or the inverse care law.

Drifts into health chances at first but comes back to focus on mental healthcare. Good point about communication – could mention speech codes here.

278

Sociology AS for AQA

(d) Using information from **Item A** and elsewhere, assess sociological explanations of differences in the health chances of different ethnic groups. *(20 marks)*

As Item A shows, different ethnic groups have different health chances, and ethnic minorities tend to have worse health than the White majority in Britain. There are various reasons for this difference, which sociologists have tried to identify.

Genetic causes can play a part. For example, Black people are more likely to get inherited diseases like sickle cell anaemia, which is very rare in White people.

Cultural factors can also be important. For example, if a group has a particular norm which requires women to marry very young and not to go out to work, but to stay at home, and the religion of the group forbids them to use contraception, then it is likely that there will be a high birth rate and the risk of worse health for both mother and children. Some groups also practise female circumcision (also known as genital mutilation), which can harm women's health.

Another example of how a group's culture can affect the health of ethnic minorities is in the fact that Asian children have higher rates of rickets (a bone deformity) as a result of their diet, which lacks vitamin D. Another source of vitamin D is sunlight and some sociologists have argued that rickets is also due to wearing clothes which cover up so much of the skin and prevent sunlight reaching it.

Language is an important aspect of culture. If a person's first language is not English, they may not be able to communicate with doctors, nurses, etc., so they may fail to get the treatment they need. They may also be unable to understand health education campaigns, so this will worsen their health chances. However, many minorities speak English, e.g. people of Caribbean origin, plus most second-generation immigrants, so language is not always a factor.

Housing can also be a cause of ill health. Ethnic-minority groups are more likely to live in substandard housing. Marxists would argue that this is the result of discrimination against ethnic minorities, so that they get pushed into the worst housing, with overcrowding, damp, etc., and this in turn leads to health problems for the family members.

Although ethnic minorities generally have worse health than the majority of the population, it can be difficult to explain, partly because we don't have proper figures, e.g. in Item A it only tells us about people who were born in India, Africa and the Caribbean, but a lot of the ethnic minorities were born in the UK so they wouldn't appear in the figures.

12/20

An examiner comments

A good way to approach this question would be to identify different types of explanation. These could be, for instance, cultural, structural, biological and labelling.

You could then organize the answer into sections on each, with an account of the explanation plus some evidence for and against it. This answer has a good account of some cultural factors but much less on other approaches – a little on genetic factors and a mention of Marxism.

There's a brief reference to Item A, but it should be used much more, e.g. by linking low birth weight to poverty among minorities (who are more likely to be working-class). You could also ask why minorities are at greater risk of accidental death (e.g. link to poorer working conditions, housing). Does racism and discrimination cause stress and affect high blood pressure and strokes?

Look at mental as well as physical health. Some studies indicate that Black people are more likely to be labelled schizophrenic, given harsher treatment and 'sectioned' against their will. Is this because of institutional racism, more stressful lives, or both?

The answer needs more theory and debate between views – e.g. a better account of Marxism, plus a functionalist view. You could link the latter to cultural differences, e.g. the idea that some minorities may not share the mainstream 'modern' culture and so may engage in practices harmful to health – and you can criticize this view as ethnocentric and as neglecting material factors, as well as the effects of racism.

One for you to try

This question requires you to **apply** your knowledge and understanding of sociological research methods to the study of this **particular** issue in health.

2 Read **Item B** and answer the question that follows.

Item B

One way of studying mental illness is to see it as a type of labelling. This is strikingly illustrated by Rosenhan's (1973) pseudo-patient study, entitled 'On being sane in insane places'. A team of researchers presented themselves at a number of different hospitals in California claiming, falsely, to have been hearing voices. Once admitted, they behaved normally. Yet, having been diagnosed as schizophrenic, all their subsequent behaviour was interpreted by staff in terms of this label. Interestingly, though, some of the other patients suspected that the pseudo-patients were not genuinely ill.

Using information from **Item B** and elsewhere, assess the strengths and limitations of **one** of the following methods for the study of mental illness:

(a) participant observation
(b) questionnaires. *(20 marks)*

An examiner comments

Remember that you need to know what the main features are of the method that you choose to write about, and you need to be able both to outline and to evaluate the method's advantages and disadvantages. These include practical, theoretical and ethical factors, such as time, cost, reliability, validity, etc. You need to apply these to the study of mental illness. For example, Rosenhan's participant observation study might be seen as valid yet unethical, because it involved covert observation. By contrast, questionnaires might be both a cheap and reliable method, but how would you gain access to a mental hospital to give them out?

Answers to the 'One for you to try' are available free on **www.collinseducation.com/sociologyweb**

What is meant by 'normal' bodies and 'normal' functionality?

- Disability as abnormal – stigma model
- Disability as different – impairment model
- Normal bodies as social constructions as well as physical entities

Illness and health socially constructed

Traditional models

- Based on mind/body explanations
- Linked to complementary medicine

Lay definitions

- Based on common sense
- Vary by culture, age, gender, etc.

Patterns of health

Vary according to social group:

- Ethnicity
- Social class
- Gender
- Geographical location

Explanations for variations

- Artefact/statistical
- Cultural
- Structural

Health inequalities

Physical illness

Mental illness

Health, illness and medicine

Social realism

Causes of mental illness located in living experiences of oppressed groups:

- Ethnic minorities
- Women
- Poor

Social constructionism

- Foucault – shift to rational thinking
- Labelling theory

Services delivered unequally to different groups

- Social class
- Age
- Gender
- Ethnicity

Health service inequalities

The medical professions

Reasons for inequalities

Supply reasons

- Differences in funding
- Priority given to prestige services
- Inefficiency of local NHS
- Ability to pay for private healthcare

Demand reasons

- Lack of knowledge of the system
- Cultural barriers
- Ignorance of warning signs of ill health

To whose benefit do they operate?

- Men – the feminist approach
- Themselves – Weberian approach
- The ruling class – Marxist approach
- For the increasing dispersal of power – Foucault
- Society as a whole – the functionalist approach

Preparing for the AS exam

TOPIC 1

Preparing for the AQA AS-level exam

What will I study?

For the AQA AS Sociology examination, you have to sit two exam papers. Each paper examines a unit of study. Each unit contains three sociological topics, which are shown in Table 8.1.

For Unit 1, you must study a minimum of one topic from the three options shown and answer a question on it in the exam paper. Thus, for example, you could study and answer a question on Culture and Identity. For Unit 2, as a minimum, you must study either Education or Health, plus Sociological Methods.

As well as leading to a qualification in its own right, the two units at AS-level Sociology together make up the first half of a full A-level qualification in Sociology. However, the two units are not equally weighted. Table 8.2 shows the balance of marks for the units both as a proportion of the total AS-level and the total A-level marks.

Table 8.2 Weighting given to AS units at AS- & A-level		
Unit of Assessment	AS-level weighting	A-level weighting
Unit 1	40% of the total AS-level marks	20% of the total A-level marks
Unit 2	60% of the total AS-level marks	30% of the total A-level marks

How will I be assessed?

Knowledge and skills

The knowledge, understanding and skills that you develop in studying the AS-level Sociology course are assessed in terms of two assessment objectives. Each of these is worth approximately half the total marks in the examination.

Assessment Objective 1 (AO1): knowledge and understanding

To meet this objective successfully, you have to show your knowledge and understanding of the chosen topic on which you are answering an exam question (e.g. Families and Households, or Health). This knowledge and understanding coves the full range of relevant sociological material, including concepts, theories, perspectives, the findings of sociological

studies, relevant facts (e.g. from official sources) and sociological methods.

AO1 also includes assessment of the quality of your written communication. In other words, you need to be able to express yourself clearly in writing. Obviously, if don't do so, the examiner will have difficulty in deciding whether you actually know and understand the material that you are using in your answers.

Assessment Objective 2 (AO2): application, interpretation, evaluation and analysis

While it is probably obvious that you need to know some sociological material, you also need to be able to use and discuss it in ways that actually answer the question. For example, you need to be able to *interpret* what the question is about, select relevant material (e.g. theories, studies) from what you know, and *apply* it to the question appropriately. Similarly, you need to be able to *analyse* arguments logically, showing in detail how their ideas fit together. You also need to be able to *evaluate* sociological material and issues. This involves being able to weigh up strengths and weaknesses, advantages and disadvantages, evidence and arguments, to reach an appropriate conclusion.

Table 8.1 Unit content and forms of assessment			
Unit	Subjects covered	Form of assessment
1	● Culture and Identity ● Families and Households ● Wealth, Poverty and Welfare	Written examination paper of one hour. Answer one data-response question on one topic area.
2	● Education ● Health ● Sociological Methods	Written examination paper of two hours Answer one data-response question on either Education or Health, plus one data-response question on either Education with Research Methods or Health with Research Methods, plus one question on Sociological Methods.

Know the meaning of the key command words

● *'Explain what is meant by…'* – In a short question, this means define the term or concept given, using different words from those in the question. An example on its own, while it will throw some light on the point, will not be enough to answer such a question fully. Watch out also for terms that might have a slightly different meaning from their everyday meaning when used by sociologists, e.g. 'socialize'.

● *'Identify…'* – Here you must show that you can recognize an argument, example, idea, fact, viewpoint, etc. (depending on what the question is about) and briefly explain/describe it. You need to develop further the point you have identified to show your understanding of it.

● *'Explain…'* – In an essay, this means that you must show a detailed knowledge and understanding of something, and apply it in a way that is relevant to the question. 'Explain' often implies that you need to know 'why' as well, so be prepared to give reasons or causes for the things you are writing about.

● *'Examine…'* – This term means that you must consider in detail the relevant information – for example, sociological arguments, factors, reasons, evidence, concepts, views, methods and sources, facts and findings, and so on.

● *'Using information from Item B…'* – This means that you *must* select relevant information from the Item and use it to help answer the question. Remember – there may be more than one point you could use from the Item. Bear in mind, too, that this is an instruction, not an option – so you will miss out on marks if you fail to make appropriate use of information from the Item.

● *'Assess…'* – This term signals that you must show the skill of evaluation, weighing up the arguments and/or the evidence for and against, the advantages and disadvantages of something (e.g. a theory, explanation or method), considering different viewpoints, and drawing an appropriate conclusion. Sometimes you may be asked to assess the strengths and limitations of something. This means you need to look at both sides (or all sides, if there are more than two) and draw a conclusion as to whether one side outweighs the other(s), based on your arguments and evidence for each. It's important in the essays to write a brief conclusion to your answer summing up your main arguments and evidence.

How can I do well in the written exams?

Question style and structure

AS-level questions are data-response questions. Each question has either one or two Items of information. These Items have a dual purpose:

1 They provide the basis for some of the shorter questions. For example, you may be asked to explain the meaning of a concept or phrase that occurs in the Item, or to give examples of something referred to in the Item, or to interpret some statistical data from a graph or table.

2 The Items also provide helpful information to assist you in answering some of the longer, higher-mark essay-style questions.

In both Unit 1 and Unit 2, you will be required to answer both short questions and essays. The short questions are marked out of 2, 4, 6 and 12. The longer, essay-style questions are marked out of 24 (on Unit 1) or 20 (on Unit 2).

Short-answer questions (a), (b) and (c)

The 2-mark question will usually ask you to explain the meaning of a concept or phrase taken from one of the Items. You should do this in your own words. If the phrase has several elements, such as 'infant mortality rate', make sure that your answer explains all the parts: what is an infant, what is mortality, and what is a rate? Here, the answer should be 'the number of deaths, per year, of young children (under the age of 1), per thousand born'. If you only explain part of the term you will not score full marks for this question.

The 4-mark and 6-mark questions will ask you to do two or three things, each of which will carry 2 marks. Typical questions would be:

● 'Give two reasons why …'
● 'Give three examples of …'
● 'Suggest two explanations of …'
● 'Identify three criticisms which could be made of …'

If you are asked for two things, make sure that the two things you give are clearly distinct from one another. If asked for three, make sure you give three. Giving fewer means you cannot score all the marks available, giving more means that you are wasting time that could be better spent on your next answer.

Some 4-mark questions may carry the instruction to 'Identify and briefly explain' something. The 'something' could refer to criticisms, reasons why, disadvantages of, etc., in just the same way as the other examples of 4- and 6-mark questions above. As you have been asked to do two things (first, identify, and second, briefly explain), you will gain 2 marks for the identification and two marks for the explanation (assuming that you answer correctly!).

In Unit 2, you will find 12-mark questions. These ask you to 'outline'. For example, this could be some of the reasons for or causes of something. Note that this is plural and so you would be expected to deal with at least two reasons, causes, etc. For example, you might be asked to outline some of the reasons for the underachievement of boys in the education system, such as changes in the curriculum or the negative influence of peer pressure or boys' antischool subcultures on their attitudes to education.

Longer-answer questions (d) and (e)

In Unit 1, the (d) question carries 24 marks, and will typically ask you to 'discuss' or 'examine' something. Note that this question carries 14 of the 24 available marks for knowledge and understanding (AO1) and the remaining 10 marks for the AO2 skills. This question will usually not be based on one of the Items, but will focus on a different aspect of the topic area than that covered in the Items, allowing you to demonstrate the breadth of your knowledge.

In Unit 1, the (e) question also carries 24 marks, and will typically ask you to 'assess' something. It is important to realize that this question carries 14 of the 24 available marks for the AO2 skills, particularly analysis and evaluation, and the remaining 10 marks for knowledge and understanding. Since you are being asked to assess something, it is reasonable to spend a short time describing briefly what it is you are assessing, but the bulk of your answer must focus on the evaluation. This usually involves either empirical evidence for and against an explanation or a point of view, or a consideration of other theories. Attempt to be balanced. Give both sides equal weight and equal time, if possible. At the end, try to come to a conclusion that is based on the information you have given in your answer. Sitting on the fence and saying both sides might be right, does not always follow from what the rest of your essay suggests.

The two longer-answer questions do not allocate specific marks for each of the two assessment objectives. In other words, you do not get a mark out of 14 and a mark out of 10. Examiners allocate marks using a mark scheme with three broad bands, and are they awarded on the basis of descriptions of typical answers. The greater focus of the (d) mark scheme is on rewarding you for displaying the relevant knowledge and understanding (AO1), while in the (e) mark scheme the emphasis is on the skills of application, interpretation, evaluation and analysis (the AO2 skills) that you have shown in your answer.

In Unit 2, you will find that the longer questions are similar in style to those in Unit 1. However, there are some minor differences between the two units:

- In Unit 2, the longer questions are marked out of 20 and not 24.
- The 'examine' questions in Unit 2 split the 20 marks equally between knowledge and understanding (10 marks) and the AO2 skills (10 marks), rather than 14/10 as in Unit 1.
- As in Unit 1, the 'assess' questions in Unit 2 focus on the AO2 skills, but they award 12 marks for showing these (not 14), with the remaining 8 marks for knowledge and understanding.

Now that you know what the exam papers contain and how you will be assessed, why not try taking a mock exam? The next few pages contain mock papers for both Unit 1 and Unit 2 for you to try. But remember to keep an eye on the clock and try to do them under exam conditions.

Exam tips

- Read the whole question very carefully before you begin your first answer. Reading the whole question will give you an understanding of which aspects of the topic have been covered.

- Read the Item(s). They are there to help you and often contain essential information. Make sure you use them – if you don't do so when the question tells you to, you will be throwing away marks. To make the most of the Items, read them through several times, picking out or underlining key points and letting your mind digest them. Think how they link up with your own knowledge.

- When you have read the question and Items, make a brief plan for your answers to the longer part questions before you begin any writing. As you write your other answers, you may well remember things that you will wish to slot into these answers. Stick to your plan and refer back to it throughout when you are writing your answer.

- Keep an eye on the time. Use the marks available as a rough guide to how much to write for each question. Make sure you allow yourself enough time to answer the longer questions fully, since these carry most of the marks.

- In short questions where you are asked to give two reasons, suggest three examples, etc., it is quite acceptable to answer using bullet points if you wish. For these questions there is no need to write a lengthy paragraph for every point you make.

- Start each point on a separate line. You can add extra points if you want – you won't be penalized for giving wrong ones, but you will be rewarded for correct ones, up to the maximum marks available for that question.

- If you find you are using the same information in different answers, check carefully that you are answering the question set. The examiner attempts to cover as much of the specification as possible and so is unlikely to be asking the same question twice.

- Particularly in the longer, higher-mark questions, you should refer to appropriate theories, perspectives, studies and evidence to support and inform your answer. Where possible, bring in examples of recent or current events, policies, etc., to illustrate the points you are making. Make quite sure that in the 'assess' questions, you have given sufficient demonstration of the AO2 skills, especially analysis and evaluation.

- Finally, make sure that you answer the question that the examiner has set, rather than the one that you wished had been set! This is a serious point – many candidates fail to achieve good marks because they have not kept to the focus of the question. No question is likely to ask you simply to write everything you know about a certain topic and yet this is what some students do.

Choose **either** Section A **or** Section B and answer **all** the questions from that Section.

Section A: CULTURE & IDENTITY

Total for this section: 60 marks

1   Read **Items 1A and 1B** below and answer parts (a) to (e) that follow.

Item 1A

In distinguishing between sex and gender, sociologists argue that we acquire our gender identity and gender roles initially through the process of primary socialization, during which the family encourages the child to develop their gender identity as a boy or a girl.

Subsequently, secondary socialization via institutions and groups such as education, the mass media, the workplace and peer groups, plays an important part in the ongoing development and reinforcement of gender identity.

However, while boys and girls are certainly socialized differently, there are also important differences *within* each gender, for example between different social classes: middle-class children may be socialized into very different values and behaviour patterns from working-class children.

Item 1B

Complex modern industrial societies such as the United Kingdom frequently contain a wide range of different ethnic groups and identities. For example, well over 100 different languages are spoken by schoolchildren in UK schools.

There are many reasons for this diversity of ethnic identities. In the UK case, one reason is the fact that Britain was for several centuries a major imperial power, creating an empire throughout Asia, Africa and the Americas. Subsequent immigration from the former colonies into Britain from the late 1940s onwards has helped to make today's Britain much more ethnically diverse. However, this is not the only source of diversity in ethnic identity.

(a)   Explain the difference between sex and gender (**Item 1A**).   *(4 marks)*

(b)   Suggest **two** ways in which the family may encourage children to develop their gender identity (**Item 1A**).   *(4 marks)*

(c)   Identify **two** differences in the socialization patterns of children of different social classes (**Item 1A**).   *(4 marks)*

(d)   Examine the process of secondary socialization.   *(24 marks)*

(e)   Using information from **Item 1B** and elsewhere, assess the reasons for ethnic differences in identity.   *(24 marks)*

Total for this section: 60 marks

2   Read **Items 2A and 2B** below and answer parts (a) to (e) that follow.

Item 2A

The family does not exist in isolation from the rest of society. It is both influenced by what goes on around it, and it acts as an influence on other areas of social life. Wider society, in the form of the mass media, government economic or social policies and the economy, for example, all influence the structure of the family and the roles and relationships of its members. As a result, therefore, sociologists are interested in exploring the interrelationships between the family and the wider social structure.

Marxists, for instance, try to identify the different ways in which family life is shaped by the needs of capitalism.

Item 2B

Ann Oakley has described the image of the typical or 'conventional' family as 'nuclear families composed of legally married couples, voluntarily choosing the parenthood of one or more (but not too many) children'. Leach has called this the 'cereal packet image of the family'. The image of the happily married couple with two children is prominent in advertising and the 'family sized' packets of cereals and other products are aimed at just this type of grouping.

However, the view that this image equals reality has been attacked. Robert and Rhona Rapoport draw attention to the fact that in 1978, for example, just 20 per cent of families consisted of couples with children in which there was a single breadwinner. There has been a steady decline in the proportion of households consisting of married couples with dependent children, from 38 per cent of all households in 1961 to 23 per cent in 2002.

The Rapoports argue that this change is part of the growing diversity of family forms in Britain today. They identify five types of diversity: organizational; cultural; class; life cycle and generational.

Source: adapted from M. Haralambos and M. Holborn (2004) *Sociology: Themes and Perspectives* (6th edn), London: Collins Educational

---

(a)   Explain what is meant by a 'household' (**Item 2B**, line 9). *(2 marks)*

(b)   Identify **two** ways in which the family might be 'shaped by the needs of capitalism' (**Item 2A**). *(4 marks)*

(c)   Suggest **three** government economic or social policies which might influence the structure of the family or the roles and relationships of its members (**Item 2A**). *(6 marks)*

(d)   Examine the factors affecting the division of labour between couples. *(24 marks)*

(e)   Using material from **Item 2B** and elsewhere, assess sociological contributions to an understanding of the diversity of family forms found in society today. *(24 marks)*

Section C: WEALTH, POVERTY & WELFARE

Total for this section: 60 marks

3 Read **Items 3A and 3B** below and answer parts (a) to (e) that follow.

Item 3A

Sociologists argue that there has been a feminization of poverty. There are also significant differences in the risk of poverty depending on age. Older people are more likely to be living in poverty than other age groups, and in all societies, older women are especially vulnerable to poverty. In Great Britain in 2001/2, for example, women in pensioner couples had the lowest average individual income of all, at around £70 per week. By contrast, men in such couples had a weekly income of around £180. Older women are more likely than older men to live in poor households. Some of these are single-pensioner households.

Item 3B

Explanations offered as to the causes of poverty are often divided into two main types. The first type, 'individualistic' theories, identifies the main causes of poverty as being within the individuals themselves, or in the characteristics of the subculture to which they belong. This approach tends, therefore, to place the blame for poverty on the poor themselves. The idea of the poor as 'undeserving' was popular in Victorian times, and echoes of that view can be found in the writings of some commentators from the New Right today.

Sociologists supporting the second type of explanation see poverty as a product of the structure of society itself, or of the inability of the welfare state either to prevent or to eradicate poverty. These 'structural' theories are predominantly advocated by Marxists, but also by writers such as Gans, who believes that poverty exists because it benefits the non-poor and therefore performs functions for society in general.

(a) Explain what is meant by the 'feminization of poverty' (**Item 3A**).   *(2 marks)*

(b) Suggest how each of the following is a provider of welfare:

    (i) voluntary organizations
    (ii) the private sector.   *(4 marks)*

(c) Suggest **three** reasons why older women are more likely to be in poverty than older men (**Item 3A**).   *(6 marks)*

(d) Examine some of the different ways that researchers have attempted to measure poverty.
                                                                              (24 marks)

(e) Using information from **Item 3B** and elsewhere, assess the usefulness of 'individualistic' theories of the causes of poverty.   *(24 marks)*

Choose **either** Section A **or** Section B and answer **all** the questions from that Section.

Section A: EDUCATION WITH RESEARCH METHODS

You are advised to spend approximately 50 minutes on Question 1.
You are advised to spend approximately 25 minutes on Question 2.
You are advised to spend approximately 40 minutes on Question 3.

Total for this section: 90 marks

1 Read **Item A** below and answer parts (a) to (d) that follow.

Item A

The Marxist view of education starts from the idea that in capitalist society, all social institutions, such as the family, religion, the mass media and so on, exist to serve the interests of the ruling class and to maintain the system of exploitation on which capitalism is based. In the view of most Marxists, this is also the basic role or purpose of the education system.

A major example of this approach comes from the American Marxist writers, Bowles and Gintis. In their view, the education system performs two essential functions for capitalism. Firstly, it performs a legitimation function, legitimating the inequalities of the capitalist system. Secondly, it performs a reproduction function, reproducing the existing class inequalities of capitalist society, for example through the 'correspondence principle'.

(a) Explain what is meant by the 'hidden curriculum'. *(2 marks)*

(b) Suggest **three** reasons for ethnic differences in educational achievement. *(6 marks)*

(c) Outline some of the reasons for gender differences in educational achievement. *(12 marks)*

(d) Using information from **Item A** and elsewhere, assess sociological explanations of the role of the education system. *(20 marks)*

2 This question requires you to **apply** your knowledge and understanding of sociological research methods to the study of this **particular** issue in education.

Read **Item B** below and answer the question that follows.

Item B

There is considerable evidence to show that pupils from some ethnic-minority backgrounds fall behind in school, particularly during the secondary phase. These include Black, Pakistani and Bangladeshi pupils. By contrast, Indian and Chinese pupils do better than the average. There are also class and gender differences in achievement within all these groups, just as there are among White pupils.

One explanation for these patterns of achievement lies in the school itself and the processes at work there. For example, Black pupils are more likely to be excluded from school than members of other ethnic groups. Other factors within school include peer groups and subcultures. For example, Sewell found that a minority of Black boys joined 'rebel' subcultures. However, he also found that some teachers labelled all Black boys as rebels, regardless of the facts.

Using information from **Item B** and elsewhere, assess the strengths and limitations of **one** of the following methods for the study of educational achievement among ethnic-minority pupils:

  (i) unstructured interviews

  (ii) official statistics. *(20 marks)*

3 This question permits you to draw examples from **any areas** of sociology with which you are familiar.

  (a) Explain what is meant by 'operationalizing' concepts. *(2 marks)*

  (b) Identify **two** sources of secondary data. *(4 marks)*

  (c) Suggest **two** advantages of questionnaires. *(4 marks)*

  (d) Examine the advantages and disadvantages of observational methods in sociological research. *(20 marks)*

Section B: HEALTH WITH RESEARCH METHODS

You are advised to spend approximately 50 minutes on Question 4.

You are advised to spend approximately 25 minutes on Question 5.

You are advised to spend approximately 40 minutes on Question 6.

Total for this section: 90 marks

4 Read **Item C** below and answer parts (a) to (d) that follow.

Item C

Cultural or behavioural explanations of the distribution of health in modern industrial society give an independent causal role to ideas and behaviour in the onset of disease and the event of death. Such explanations often focus on the individual, emphasizing unthinking, reckless or irresponsible behaviour or incautious life-style as the determinant of poor health status. What is implied is that people harm themselves or their children by the excessive consumption of refined foods, lack of exercise and so on.

There are class differences in these patterns of behaviour. For example, the bottom income group eats more white bread and sugar, but less brown or wholemeal bread and fresh fruit, than other income groups.

Some sociologists see such differences in behaviour as the cause of class inequalities in health and illness. They also argue that these behavioural differences between members of different social classes are the result of subcultural differences.

Source: adapted from M. Whitehead, P. Townsend and N. Davidson (eds) (1992) *Inequalities in Health*, London: Penguin

---

(a) Explain what is meant by the 'inverse care law'. *(2 marks)*

(b) Identify **three** characteristics of the biomedical model of health, illness and medicine. *(6 marks)*

(c) Outline some of the reasons why doctors enjoy high status and rewards. *(12 marks)*

(d) Using information from **Item C** and elsewhere, assess the view that class inequalities in health and illness are the result of cultural and behavioural differences. *(20 marks)*

5 This question requires you to **apply** your knowledge and understanding of sociological research methods to the study of this **particular** issue in health.

Read **Item D** below and answer the question that follows.

Item D

On being sane in insane places

One way of studying mental illness is to see it as a type of labelling. This is strikingly illustrated by Rosenhan's (1973) pseudo-patient study, entitled 'On being sane in insane places'. A team of researchers presented themselves at a number of different hospitals in California claiming, falsely, to have been hearing voices. Once admitted, they behaved normally. Yet, having been diagnosed as schizophrenic, all their subsequent behaviour was interpreted by staff in terms of this label. Interestingly, though, some of the other patients suspected that the pseudo-patients were not genuinely ill.

Using information from **Item D** and elsewhere, assess the strengths and limitations of **one** of the following methods for the study of mental illness:

(i)   participant observation

(ii) questionnaires.   *(20 marks)*

6 This question permits you to draw examples from **any areas** of sociology with which you are familiar.

(a)   Explain what is meant by operationalizing concepts.   *(2 marks)*

(b)   Identify **two** sources of secondary data.   *(4 marks)*

(c)   Suggest **two** advantages of questionnaires.   *(4 marks)*

(d)   Examine the advantages and disadvantages of secondary data in sociological research.
                                                                                       (20 marks)

REFERENCES

Abbott, D. (1998) *Culture and Identity*, London: Hodder & Stoughton

Abraham, J. (1996) *Are Girls Necessary? Lesbian writing and modern histories*, London: Routledge

Acheson, Sir Donald (1998) *Independent Inquiry into Inequalities in Health: Report*, London: The Stationery Office

Alford, R.R. (1975) *Health Care Politics: Ideological and interest group barriers to reform*, Chicago: The University of Chicago Press

Ali, S. (2002) 'Interethnic families', *Sociology Review*, 12(1)

Allan, G. (1985) *Family Life: Domestic roles and social organization*, London: Blackwell

Althusser, L. (1971) 'Ideology and ideological state apparatuses', in *Lenin and Philosophy and Other Essays*, London: New Left Books

Anderson, M. (1971) 'Family, Household and the Industrial Revolution', in M. Anderson (ed.) *The Sociology of the Family*, Harmondsworth: Penguin

Anderson, P. and Kitchin, R.M. (2000) 'Disability, space and sexuality: Access to family planning services', *Social Science and Medicine*, 51

Annandale, E. (1998) *The Sociology of Health and Illness*, Cambridge: Polity Press

Antle, B.J. (2000) 'Seeking strengths in young people with physical disabilities', *Dissertation Abstracts International, Humanities and Social Sciences*, 60

Anwar, M. (1981) *Between Two Cultures: A Study of Relationships Between Generations in the Asian Community*, London: CRE

Arber, S. and Ginn, J. (1993) 'Class, caring and the life course' in S. Arber and M.E. Vandrow (eds) *Ageing, Independence and the Life Course*, London: Jessica Kingsley

Aries, P. (1962) *Centuries of Childhood*, London: Random House

Babb, P., Haezewindt, P. and Martin, J. (eds) (2004) *Focus on Social Inequalities*, London: Office for National Statistics

Ball, S. (1981) *Beachside Comprehensive*, Cambridge University Press

Ball, S. (2002) *Class Strategies and the Education Market: The Middle Classes and Social Advantage*, London: RoutledgeFalmer

Ball, S.J., Bowe, R. and Gerwitz, S. (1994) 'Market forces and parental choice', in S. Tomlinson (ed.) *Education Reform and Its Consequences*, London: IPPR/Rivers Oram Press

Barber, B. (1963) 'Some problems in the sociology of professions', *Daedalus*, 92(4)

Barnett, S. and Curry, A. (1994) *The Battle for the BBC: a British Broadcasting Conspiracy?*, London: Aurum

Barrett, M. and McIntosh, M. (1982) *The Anti-social Family*, London: Verso

Bauman, Z. (1990) *Thinking Sociologically*, Oxford: Blackwell

Baumeister, R. (1986) *Identity: Cultural Change and the Struggle for Self*, Oxford University Press

Beck, U. (1992) *Risk Society: Towards a New Modernity*, London: Sage

Beck, U. and Beck-Gernsheim, E. (1995) *The Normal Chaos of Love*, Cambridge: Polity Press

Becker, H. (1963) *Outsiders: Studies in the Sociology of Deviance*, London: Macmillan

Becker, H. (1971) 'Social class variations in the teacher–pupil relationship', in B. Cosin (ed.) *School and Society*, London: Routledge & Kegan Paul

Bennett, A. (2004) 'Rap and Hip Hop: community and identity', in S. Whiteley, A. Bennett and S. Hawkins (eds) *Music, Space and Place*, Aldershot: Ashgate

Bennett, T. and Holloway, K. (2005) *Understanding Drugs Alcohol and Crime*, Milton Keynes: Open University Press

Benston, M. (1972) 'The political economy of women's liberation', in N. Glazer-Malbin and H.Y. Waehrer (eds) *Women in a Man-Made World*, Chicago: Rand McNally

Bernard, J. (1982, originally 1972) *The Future of Marriage*, Yale: Yale University Press

Bernardes, J. (1997) *Family Studies: An Introduction*, London: Routledge

Bernstein, B. (1971) *Class, Codes and Control* (Vol. 1), London: Routledge & Kegan Paul

Berthoud, R. (2000) 'Family formation in multi-cultural Britain: three patterns of diversity', *Working Paper of the Institute for Social and Economic Research*, Colchester: University of Essex

Berthoud, R. (2003) Lecture at ATSS Conference 2004, based on research conducted in 2003

Best, L. (1993) '"Dragons, dinner ladies and ferrets": Sex roles in children's books', *Sociology Review*, 2(3), Oxford: Philip Allan

Best, S. (2005) *Understanding Social Divisions*, London: Sage

Billington, R., Hockey, J. and Strawbridge, S. (1998) *Exploring Self and Society*, Basingstoke: Macmillan

Bittman, M. and Pixley, J. (1997) *The Double Life of the Family*, St Leonards, NSW: Allen & Unwin

Blackman, S. (1997) 'An ethnographic study of youth underclass' in R. McDonald (ed.) *Youth, the Underclass and Social Exclusion*, London: Routledge

Blanden, J., Gregg, P. and Machin, S. (2005) *Intergenerational Mobility in Europe and North America*, London: The Sutton Trust

Blaxter, M. (1990) *Health and Lifestyles*, London: Tavistock

Blundell, J. and Griffiths, J. (2002) *Sociology since 1995*, Lewes: Connect Publications

Blundell, J. and Griffiths, J. (2008) *Sociology since 2000*, Lewes: Connect Publications

Book Marketing Limited (2000) *Reading the Situation: Book Reading, Buying and Borrowing Habits in Britain*, Library and Information Commission Research Report 34, Book Marketing Limited

Bourdieu, P. (1977) 'Cultural reproduction and social reproduction', in J. Karabel and A.H. Halsey (eds) *Power and Ideology in Education*, New York: Oxford University Press, pp.487–511

Bourdieu, P. and Passeron, J. (1977) *Reproduction in Education, Society and Culture*, London: Sage

Bourgois, P. (2003) *In Search of Respect* (2nd edn), Cambridge University Press

Bowles, S. and Gintis, H. (1976) *Schooling in Capitalist America: Educational Reform and the Contradictions of Economic Life*, New York: Basic Books

Bradley, H. (1996) *Fractured Identities: Changing Patterns of Inequality*, Cambridge: Polity Press

Bradshaw, J. and Ernst, J. (1990) *Establishing a Modest but Adequate Budget for a British Family*, Family Budget Unit

Brah, A. (1993) 'Race and culture in the gendering of labour markets: South Asian young women and the labour market', *New Community*, 19(3)

Brannen, J. (2003) 'The age of beanpole families', *Sociology Review*, September

Brookes-Gunn, J. and Kirsch, B. (1984) 'Life events and the boundaries of midlife for women', in G. Baruch and J. Brookes-Gunn (eds) *Women in Midlife*, New York: Plenum Press

Brown, C. (1979) *Understanding Society*, Harlow: Longman

Brown, D. (1994) 'An ordinary sexual life? A review of the normalization principle as it applies to the sexual options of people with learning disabilities', *Disability and Society*, 9(2)

Brown, G.W., Harris, T.O. and Hepworth, C. (1995) 'Loss, humiliation and entrapment among women developing depression', *Psychological Medicine*, 25, pp.7–21

Brown, Gordon (2006) Donald Dewar memorial lecture, Glasgow, 12 October 2006

Brown, S. (1997) 'High and low quality performance in manufacturing firms', *TQM Journal*, 9(4), pp.292–9

Burghes, L. (1997) *Fathers and Fatherhood in Britain*, London: Policy Studies Institute

Burghes, L. and Brown, M. (1995) *Single Lone Mothers: Problems, prospects and policies*, York: Family Policy Studies Centre with the support of the Joseph Rowntree Foundation

Burns, J. and Bracey, P. (2001) 'Boys' underachievement: Issues, challenges and possible ways forward', *Westminster Studies in Education*, 24, pp.155–66

Busfield, J. (1988) 'Mental illness as a social product or social construct: a contradiction in feminists' arguments?', *Sociology of Health and Illness*, 10, pp.521–42

Buswell, C. (1987) *Training for Low Pay*, Basingstoke: Macmillan

Butler, T. and Hamnetta, C. (2007) 'The Geography of Education: Introduction', *Urban Studies*, 44(7), June 2007, pp.1161–74

Callendar, C. and Jackson, J. (2004) *Fear of Debt and Higher Education Participation*, London: South Bank University

Campbell, B. (2000) *The Independent*, 20 November 2000

Cant, S. and Sharma, U. (2002) 'The state and complementary medicine: a changing relationship?', in S. Nettleton and U. Gustafsson (eds) *The Sociology of Health and Illness, A Reader*, Cambridge: Polity

Carrington, B., Francis, B., Skelton, C., Hutchings, M., Read, B. and Hall, I. (2007 in press) 'A Perfect Match? Pupils' and teachers' views of the impact of matching educators and learners by gender', Research Papers in Education.

Chamberlain, M. and Goulborne, H. (1999) *Caribbean Families in Britain and the Trans-Atlantic World*, Basingstoke: Macmillan

Chapman, T. (2004) *Gender and Domestic Life: Changing Practices in Families and Households*, Basingstoke: Palgrave Macmillan

Charlesworth, S. (2000) *A Phenomenology of Working Class Experience*, Cambridge University Press

Cheal, D. (2002) *Sociology of Family Life*, Basingstoke: Palgrave

Chesler, P. (1972) *Women and Madness*, New York: Doubleday

Clark, J. and Hein, J. (2000) 'The Political Economy of Welfare Reform in the United States' in J. Clark *et al. (eds) Welfare, Work and Poverty*, London: Institute for the Study of Civil Society

Clarke, J.N. (1992) 'Cancer, heart disease and AIDS: What do the media tell us about these diseases?', *Health Communication*, 4(2)

Coard, B. (1971) *How the West-Indian Child is Made Educationally Sub-normal in the British School System*, London: New Beacon Books

Cohen, P. (1984) 'Against the new vocationalism', in L. Bates, J. Clarke, R. Moore and P. Willis *Schooling for the Dole*, Basingstoke: Macmillan

Cohen, S. (1980) *Folk Devils and Moral Panics* (2nd edn), Oxford: Martin Robinson

Collier, R. (2002) 'Masculinities', *Sociology*, 36(3), pp.737–42

Connell, R.W. (2002) *Gender*, Cambridge: Blackwell

Connolly, P. (1998) *Racism, Gender Identities and Young Children*, London: Routledge & Kegan Paul

Cote, J. (2000) *Arrested Adulthood: The Changing Nature of Maturity and Identity*, New York University Press

Coward, R. (1989) *The Whole Truth; The Myth of Alternative Health*, London: Faber

292

Sociology AS for AQA

Crosland, C.A.R. (1956) *The Future of Socialism*, London: Jonathan Cape

Cumberbatch, G. and Negrine, R. (1992) *Images of Disability on Television*, London: Routledge

Cunningham, H. (2006) *The Invention of Childhood*, London: BBC Books

Curtice, J. and Heath, A. (2000) 'Is the English Lion about to roar? National identity after the devolution', in R. Jowell *et al.* (eds) *British Social Attitudes, 17th Report: Focusing on Diversity*, London: Sage

Davey Smith, G., Shipley, M.J. and Rose, G. (1990) 'The magnitude and causes of socio-economic differentials in mortality: further evidence from the Whitehall study', *Journal of Epidemiology and Community Health*, 44, pp.265–70

De'Ath, E. and Slater, D. (eds) (1992) *Parenting Threads: Caring for children when couples part*, Stepfamily Publications

Delphy, C. (1984) *Close to Home*, London: Hutchinson

Dennis, N. and Erdos, G. (2000) *Families Without Fatherhood* (3rd edn), London: Civitas

Department for Education and Skills (DfES) (2004) *Every Child Matters. Change for Children in Schools*, London: DfES/HMSO

Department for Education and Skills (DfES) (2006) *Social Mobility: Narrowing Social Class Educational Attainment Gaps*, London: Office for National Statistics

Department for Education and Skills (DfES) (2007) *Green Paper: Raising Expectations: Staying in education and training post-16*, London: DfES

Department of Health (2003) *NHS Patient Survey Programme: GP Survey 2003*, London: DoH

Department of Health (2007) *Health Survey for England*, London: DoH

Dex, S. (2003) *Families and Work in the Twenty-first Century*, York: Joseph Rowntree Foundation

Doyal, L. (1979) *The Political Economy of Health*, London: Pluto

Drew, D. (1995) *Race, Education and Work: The Statistics of Inequality*, Aldershot: Avebury

Dryden, C. (1999) *Being Married Doing Gender*, London: Routledge

Duncombe, J. and Marsden, D. (1995) 'Women's "triple shift": paid employment, domestic labour and "emotion work"', *Sociology Review* 4(4)

Dunne, G A. (ed.) (1997) *Lesbian Lifestyles: Women's Work and the Politics of Sexuality*, Basingstoke: Macmillan

Durkheim, E. (1897, reprinted 1952) *Suicide: a Study in Sociology*, London: Routledge

Durkheim, E. (1912, reprinted 1961) *The Elementary Forms of Religious Life*, London: Allen & Unwin

Durkheim, E. (1893, reprinted 1960) *The Division of Labour in Society*, Glencoe: Free Press

Durkin, K. (1995) *Developmental Social Psychology, from Infancy to Old Age*, Oxford: Blackwell

Eisenberg, L. (1977) 'Disease and illness: distinction between professional and popular ideas of sickness', *Culture, Medicine and Psychiatry*, 1, pp.9–23

Elias, N. (1978) *The Civilising Process*, Oxford: Blackwell

Epstein, D. (1998) 'Real boys don't work: "underachievement", masculinity and the harassment of "sissies"', in D. Epstein, J. Ellwood, V. Hey and J. Maw (eds) *Failing Boys? Issues in Gender and Achievement*, Buckingham: Open University Press

Esping-Andersen, G. (1990) *The Three Worlds of Welfare Capitalism*, Cambridge: Polity Press

Evans, J. and Chandler, J. (2006) 'To buy or not to buy: family dynamics and children's consumption', *Sociological Research Online*, 11(2)

Field, F. (1989) *Losing Out: The Emergence of Britain's Underclass*, Oxford: Blackwell

Finkelstein, V. (1980) *Attitudes and Disabled People: Issues for Discussion*, New York: World Rehabilitation Fund

Finkelstein, V. (1980) *Attitudes and Disabled People: Issues for Discussion*, New York: World Rehabilitation Fund

Finn, D. (1987) *Training without Jobs*, Basingstoke: MacMillan

Fletcher, R. (1988) *The Shaking of the Foundations: Family and Society*, London: Routledge

Flouri, E. and Buchanan, A. (2002) 'Father involvement in childhood and trouble with the police in adolescence: Findings from the 1958 British birth cohort', *Journal of Interpersonal Violence*, 17, pp.689-701

Flowers, A. (1998) *The Fantasy Factory: An insider's view of the phone sex industry*, Philadelphia: University of Pennsylvania Press

Ford, R. and Millar, J. (eds) (1998) *Private Lives and Public Costs: Lone parents and the state*, London: Policy Studies Institute

Foster, J. (1990) *Villains: Crime and Community in the Inner City*, London: Routledge

Foucault, M. (1965) *Madness and Civilization*, New York: Random House

Foucault, M. (1976) *The Birth of the Clinic*, London: Tavistock

Fox Harding, L. (1996) *Family, State and Social Policy*, Basingstoke: Macmillan

Francis, B. (1998) *Power Plays: Primary School Children's Constructions of Gender, Power and Adult Work*, Stoke-on-Trent: Trentham Books

Francis, B. (2000) *Boys, Girls and Achievement. Addressing the Classroom Issues*, London: Routledge Falmer

Francis, B. (2005) *The Impact of Gender Constructions on Pupils' Learning and Educational Choices: Final project report*, London: ESRC

Francis, B. and Skelton, C. (2005) *Reassessing Gender and Achievement*, London: Routledge/Falmer

Friedson, E. (1965) 'Disability as social deviance', in M.B. Sussman (ed.) *Sociology of Disability and Rehabilitation*, Washington, DC: American Sociological Association

Fuller, M. (1984) 'Black girls in a London comprehensive', in R. Deem (ed.) *Schooling for Women's Work*, London: Routledge

Gershuny, J. (2000) ISER, University of Essex with the Future Foundation for Abbey National

Gewirtz, S. (2002) *The Managerial School: Post-welfarism and social justice in education*, London, Routledge

Giddens, A. (1991) *Modernity and Self-Identity: Self in Society in the Late Modern Age*, Cambridge: Polity

Giddens, A. (1997) *Sociology* (3rd edn), Cambridge: Polity Press

Giddens, A. (1999) *The Third Way: The Renewal of Social Democracy*, Cambridge: Polity Press

Gillborn, D. (1990) *'Race', Ethnicity and Education: Teaching and Learning in Multi-ethnic Schools*, London: Unwin Hyman

Gillborn, D. (2002) *Education and Institutional Racism*, London: Institute of Education

Gillborn, D. and Gipps, B. (1996) *Recent Research in the Achievement of Ethnic Minority Pupils*, London: HMSO

Gillborn, D. and Mirza, H.S. (2000) *Educational Inequality: Mapping Race and Class*, London: OFSTED

Gillborn, D. and Youdell, D. (1999) *Rationing Education: Policy, Practice, Reform and Equity*, Milton Keynes: Open University Press

Ginsberg, N. (1998) 'The socialist perspective', in P. Alcock, A. Erskine and M. May (eds) *The Student's Companion to Social Policy*, Oxford: Blackwell

Glaser, B. and Strauss, A. (1967) *The Discovery of Grounded Theory*, Chicago: Aldine

Glendinning, C. and Millar, J. (1992) *Women and Poverty in Britain: The 1990s* (2nd edn), Hemel Hempstead: Harvester Wheatsheaf

Goffman, E. (1961) *Asylums*, Harmondsworth: Penguin

Goffman, E. (1963) *Stigma: Notes on the Management of Spoiled Identity*, New York: Prentice Hall

Goffman, E. (2004, originally 1959) *The Presentation of Self in Everyday Life*, Harmondsworth: Penguin

Gordon, D., Adelman, L., Ashworth, K., Bradshaw, J., Levitas, R., Middleton, S., Pantazis, C., Patsios, D., Payne, S., Townsend, P. and Williams, J. (2000) *Poverty and Social Exclusion in Britain*, York: Joseph Rowntree Foundation

Gottman, J.S. (1990) 'Children of gay and lesbian parents', in F.W. Bozett and M.B. Sussman (eds) *Homosexuality and Family Relations*, New York: Harrington Press

Gove, W.R. (1982) 'The current status of the labeling theory of mental illness', in W.R. Gove (ed.) *Deviance and Mental Illness* (pp.273–300), Beverly Hills, CA: Sage Publications

Graham, H. (2002) 'Inequality in Men and Women's Health', in S. Nettleton and U. Gustafsson (eds) *The Sociology of Health and Illness, A Reader*, Cambridge: Polity

Gray, A (2006) 'The time economy of parenting', *Sociological Research Online*, 11(3)

Grieshaber, S. (1977) 'Mealtime rituals: power and resistance in the construction of mealtime rules', *British Journal of Sociology*, 48(4)

Griffin, C. (1985) *Typical Girls: Young Women from School to the Job Market*, London: Routledge & Kegan Paul

Guibernau, M. and Goldblatt, D. (2000) 'Identity and nation', in K.Woodward (ed.) *Questioning Identity: Gender, Class, Nation*, London: Routledge/Open University Press

Hakim, C. (1996) *Key Issues in Women's Work*, London: Athlone

Hall, S. and Jefferson, S. (eds) (1993) *Resistance through Rituals: Youth Subcultures in Post-war Britain*, London: Routledge

Hallam, S., Ireson, J. and Davies, J. (2004) 'Primary pupils' experiences of different types of grouping in school', *British Journal of Educational Research*, 30, pp.515–33

Ham, C. (1999) *Health Policy in Britain*, Basingstoke: Palgrave

Hannan, J. (2000) Improving Boys' Performance, Dunstable: Folens

Haque, Z. and Bell, J.F. (2001) 'Evaluating the performances of minority ethnic pupils in secondary schools', *Oxford Review of Education*, 27(3), pp.359–68

Haralambos, M. and Holborn, M. (2008) *Sociology: Themes and Perspectives* (7th edn), London: Collins Educational

Hardey, M. (1998) *The Social Context of Health*, Buckingham: Open University Press

Hardill, I., Green, A., Dudlestone, A. and Owen, D.W. (1997) 'Who decides what? Decision making in dual career households', *Work, Employment and Society*, 11(2)

Hargreaves, D.H. (1967) *Social Relations in a Secondary School*, London: Routledge & Kegan Paul

Hart, N. (1976) *When Marriage Ends*, London: Tavistock

Hatcher, R. (1996) 'The Limitations of the New Social-Democratic Agendas: Class, equality and agency', in R. Hatcher and K. Jones (eds) *Education after the Conservatives*, Stoke-on-Trent: Trentham Books

Heath, S. (2004) 'Transforming friendship', *Sociology Review*, 14(1), September 2004

Hennink, M. *et al.* (1999) 'Young Asian women and relationships: traditional or transitional', *Ethnic and Racial Studies*, 22(5)

Higher Education Statistics Agency (2007) *Higher Education Students Early Statistics Survey 2007–08*, HESES07, London. Higher Education Funding Council for England

Hills, J. (1998) *Income and Wealth: The latest evidence*, York: Joseph Rowntree Foundation

Hockey, J. and James, A. (1993) *Growing Up and Growing Old*, London: Sage

Hooks, B. (2003) *Rock My Soul: Black People and Self-Esteem*, New York: Pocket Books

Hough, J.M. and Roberts, J.V (2004) *Juvenile Delinquency in England*, Oxford: Polity Press

Humphreys, L. (1975) *Tearoom Trade: Impersonal sex in public places*, New York: Aldine De Gruyter

Hunt, S. (2001) 'Dying to be thin', *Sociology Review*

293

References

Illsley, R. (1986) 'Occupational class, selection and the production of inequalities in health', *Quarterly Journal of Social Affairs*, 2(2), pp.151–64

Ireson, J., Hallam, S. and Hurley, C. (2002) *Ability grouping in the Secondary School: Effects on GCSE attainment in English, mathematics and science,* Paper presented at the British Educational Research Association Annual Conference, Exeter University, Exeter, 10–14 September, 2002.

Jackson, C. (2006) *Lads and Ladettes in School: Gender and the fear of failure,* Milton Keynes: Open University Press

Jasper, L. (2002) 'School system failing black children', *Guardian*, 16 March

Jefferis, B., Power, C. and Hertzman, C. (2002) 'Birth weight, childhood socioeconomic environment, and cognitive development in the 1958 British birth cohort study', *British Medical Journal*, 325, p.305

Johal, S. (1998) 'Brimful of Brasia', *Sociology Review*, 8(1)

Johnson, J. and Bytheway, B. (1993) 'Ageism: concept and definition', in J.Johnson and R.Slater (eds) *Ageing and Later Life*, London: Sage

Jones G. and Wallace, C. (1992) *Youth, Family and Citizenship*, Milton Keynes: Open University Press

Jordan, B. (1992) *Trapped in Poverty: Labour Market Decisions in Low Income Households*, London: Routledge

Joseph Rowntree Foundation Survey (1999, 2002) *Monitoring Poverty and Social Exclusion*, York: Joseph Rowntree Foundation

Jowell, R., Curtice, J., Park, A., Brook, L. and Ahrendt, A. (eds) (1995) *British Social Attitudes: the 12th Report,* Aldershot: Dartmouth

Kallianes, V. and Rubenfeld, P. (1997) 'Disabled women and reproductive rights', *Disability and Society,* 12(2)

Kidd, W. (2002) *Culture and Identity*, Palgrave: Basingstoke

Kiernan, K. (2007) quoted in '"Marriage still the best way to play happy, healthy families", says study', Polly Curtis, *The Guardian*, 5 October 2007

Kilkey, M. (2005) 'New Labour and reconciling work and family life; making it fathers' business', *Social Policy and Society*, 5(2), pp.167–75

Kirby, R. (2000) *Underachievement in Boys*, Winchester: www.practicalparent.org.uk

Krause, I.B. (1989) 'Sinking heart: a Punjabi communication of distress', *Social Science and Medicine*, 29, pp.563–75

Lader, D., Short, S. and Gershuny, J. (2006) *The Time Use Survey, 2005*, London: Office for National Statistics

Laslett, P. (1972) 'Mean household size in England since the sixteenth century', in P. Laslett (ed.) *Household and Family in Past Time*, Cambridge University Press

Le Grand, J. (1982) *The Strategy of Equality: Redistribution and the Social Services*, London: Allen & Unwin

Lees, S. (1986) *Losing Out: Sexuality and Adolescent Girls*, London: Hutchinson

Leighton, G. (1992) 'Wives' paid and unpaid work and husbands' unemployment', *Sociology Review*, 1(3)

Lewis, J. (2007) *Families and Labour's Family Policies*, posted on www.lse.ac.uk/collections/pressAndInformationOffice/newsAndEvents/archives/2007/BlairsLegacyJune07.htm

Lewis, O. (1966) *La Vida*, New York: Random House

Link, B. and Phelan, J. (1995) 'Social conditions as fundamental cause of disease', *Journal of Health and Social Behaviour*, pp.80–94

Lobban, G. (1974) 'Data report on British reading schemes', *Times Educational Supplement*, 1 March 1974

Longmore, F. (1987) 'Screening stereotypes: images of disabled people in TV and motion pictures', in A. Gartner and T. Foe (eds) *Images of the Disabled, Disabling Images*, New York: Praeger

Lupton, D. (1994) *Medicine as Culture: Illness, Disease and the Body in Western Societies*, London: Sage

Lyng, S. (1990) 'Edgework: a social psychological analysis of voluntary risk-taking', *American Journal of Sociology*, 95(4), pp.851–6

McAllister, F. with Clarke, L. (1998) *Choosing Childlessness*, York: Family Policy Studies Centre and Joseph Rowntree Foundation

Mac an Ghaill, M. (1991) 'Young, gifted and Black: methodological reflections of a teacher/researcher', in G.Walford (1991) *Doing Educational Research*, London: Taylor & Francis

Mac an Ghaill, M. (1994) *The Making of Men: Masculinities, Sexualities and Schooling*, Milton Keynes: Open University Press

Mac an Ghaill, M. (ed.) (1996) *Understanding Masculinities: Social Relations and Cultural Arenas*, Buckingham: Open University Press

MacIntyre, S. (1993) 'Gender differences in the perceptions of common cold symptoms', *Social Science and Medicine*, 36(1), pp.15–20

Mack, J. and Lansley, S. (1993) *Breadline Britain*, London: Unwin Hyman

McKnight, A., Glennerster, H. and Lupton, R. (2005) '"Education, education, education": An assessment of Labour's success in tackling education inequalities', in J. Hills and K. Stewart (eds) *A More Equal Society: New Labour, Poverty, Inequality and Exclusion*, Bristol: Policy Press

McNamara, R.P. (1994) *The Times Square Hustler: Male prostitution in New York City*, Westport: Praeger

Marcuse, H. (1964) *One Dimensional Man*, London: Routledge & Kegan Paul

Marsh, I. and Keating, M. (2006) *Sociology: Making Sense of Society* (3rd edn), Harlow: Pearson Education

Marshall, G. (1998) *Oxford Dictionary of Sociology*, Oxford University Press

Marshall, G., Newby, H., Rose, D. and Vogler, C. (1988) *Social Class in Modern Britain*, London: Hutchinson

Marsland, D. (1996) *Welfare or Welfare State?*, Basingstoke: Macmillan

Marx, K. and Engels, F. (1974) *The German Ideology* (2nd edn), London: Lawrence & Wishart

Mead, M. (1928) *Coming of Age in Samoa*, New York: Morrow

Mirrlees-Black, C. (1999) 'Domestic violence: findings from a new British Crime Survey self-completion questionnaire', *Home Office Research Study 191*

Mirza, H. (1992) *Young, Female and Black*, London: Routledge

Mirza, H. and Reay, D. (2000) 'Spaces and places of Black educational desire: rethinking Black supplementary schools as a new social movement', *Sociology*, 34, pp.521–44

Mitsos E. and Browne, K. (1998) 'Gender differences in education: the underachievement of boys', *Sociology Review*, 8(1)

Modood, T. (1997) *Ethnic Minorities in Britain: Diversity and Disadvantage*, London: Policy Studies Institute

Modood, T. (2003) 'Ethnic differentials in educational performance', in D. Mason (ed.) *Explaining Ethnic Differences: Changing Patterns of Disadvantage in Britain*, Bristol: The Policy Press.

Modood, T. (2004) 'Capitals, ethnic identity and education qualifications', *Cultural Trends*, 13(2), pp.87–105.

Modood, T. (2005) *Multicultural Politics Racism, Ethnicity and Muslims in Britain*, Minneapolis: University of Minnesota Press

Moore. S. (2004) 'Hanging around: the politics of the busstop', *Youth and Policy*, 82, pp.47–59

Morgan, D.H.J. (1996) *Family Connections: An Introduction to Family Studies*, Brighton: Polity

Morgan, P. (2000) *Marriage-Lite: the Rise of Cohabitation and its Consequences*, London: Civitas

Morris, D. (1968) *The Naked Ape*, London: Corgi

Morrow, V. (1998) *Understanding Families: Children's Perspectives*, York: National Children's Bureau in association with the Joseph Rowntree Foundation

Mort, F. (1996) *Cultures of Consumption: Masculinities and Social Space in Late Twentieth-Century Britain*, London: Routledge

Moser, K., Goldblatt, P., Fox, J. and Jones, D. (1990) 'Unemployment and mortality', in P. Goldblatt (ed.) *Longitudinal Study: Mortality and Social Organisation*, London: HMSO

Mount, F. (2004) *Mind the Gap: The New Class Divide in Britain*, London: Short Books

Murdock, G.P. (1949) *Social Structure*, New York: Macmillan

Murphy, M. (2006) *Household and Family: Past, Present and Future,* taken from presentation made to ESRC/BSPS/ONS Public Policy Seminar 'Changing Household and Family Structure Including Complex Living Arrangements', 18 May 2006

Murphy, M. (2007) quoted in '"Marriage still the best way to play happy, healthy families", says study', Polly Curtis, *The Guardian*, 5 October 2007

Murray, C. (1990) *The Emerging British Underclass*, London: IEA

Murray, C. (1994) *Underclass: The Crisis Deepens*, London: IEA

Myers, J. (1975) 'Life events, social integration and psychiatric symptomatology', *Journal of Health and Social Behaviour*, 16, pp.121–7

Myhill, D. (1999) 'Bad boys and good girls: patterns of interaction and response in whole class teaching', Exeter University School of Education paper

Navarro, V. (1977) *Medicine under Capitalism*, London: Martin Robertson

Nazroo, J. (1999) 'Uncovering gender differences in the use of marital violence: the effect of methodology' in G. Allan (ed.) *The Sociology of the Family: A Reader*, Oxford: Blackwell

Nazroo, J.Y. (2001) *Ethnicity, Class and Social Health*, London: PSI

Oakley, A. (1982) *Subject Women*, London: Fontana

Oakley, A. (1986) 'Feminism, motherhood and medicine – Who cares?', in J. Mitchell and A. Oakley (eds) *What is Feminism?*, Oxford: Blackwell

O'Brien, M. and Jones, D. (1996) 'Revisiting family and kinship', *Sociology Review*, February 1996

O'Connor, J. (1973) *The Fiscal Crisis of the State*, Basingstoke: Macmillan

O'Donnell, M. (1991) *Race and Ethnicity*, Harlow: Longman

O'Donnell, M. and Sharpe, S. (2000) *Uncertain Masculinities: Youth, Ethnicity and Class in Contemporary Britain*, London: Routledge

Office for National Statistics (2004) *Mental health of children and young people in Great Britain*, Basingstoke: Palgrave Macmillan

Office for National Statistics (2007) cited in www.poverty.org.uk/36/index.shtml#g4

Oliver, M. (1990) *The Politics of Disablement*, Basingstoke: Macmillan

Oliver, M. (1996) *Understanding Disability*, London: Macmillan

Olney, M.F. and Kim, A. (2001) 'Beyond adjustment: integration of cognitive disability into identity', *Disability and Society*, 16

Osler, A. (2006) *Response to the Equalities Review Interim Report of the Cabinet Office (2006)* sponsored by the Joseph Rowntree Foundation, Centre for Citizenship and Human Rights Education, University of Leeds

Pahl, R.E. (1988) 'Some remarks on informal work, social polarisation and the class structure', *International Journal of Urban and Regional Research*, 12(2), pp.247–67

Palmer, G., Carr, J. and Kenway, P. (2004) *Monitoring Poverty and Social Exclusion 2004*, York: Joseph Rowntree Foundation

Palmer, S. (2007) *Toxic Childhood: How the modern world is damaging our children and what we can do about it*, London: Orion

Parsons, C., Godfrey, R., Annan, G., Cornwall, J., Dussart, M., Hepburn, S., Howlett, K. and Wennerstrom, V. (2005) *Minority Ethnic Exclusions and the RR (A)A 2000*, Report 616/2004, London: DfESResearch

Parsons, T. (1955) 'The social structure of the family', in T. Parsons and R.F. Bales (eds) *Family, Socialization and Interaction Process*, New York: The Free Press

Parsons, T. (1965) 'The normal American family', in S.M. Farber (ed.) *Man and*

Civilization: the Family's Search for Survival, New York: McGraw Hill

Parsons, T. (1975) 'The sick role and the role of the physician reconsidered', *Millbank Memorial Fund Quarterly: Health and Society*, 53, pp 257–78

Phillips, M. (1997) *All Must Have Prizes*, London: Little Brown

Phillips, M. and Murray. C. (2001) *Charles Murray and the Underclass (Civil Society) Ten Years On*, London: Civitas

Phillipson, C. and Downs, M. (1999) *The Futures of Old Age*, London: Sage

Pilcher, J. (1996) *Age and Generation in Modern Britain*, Oxford University Press

Pilgrim, D. and Rogers, A. (1999) *A Sociology of Mental Health and Illness* (2nd edn), Buckingham: Open University Press

Pirie, M. (2001) 'How exams are fixed in favour of girls', *The Spectator*, 20 January

Plummer, K. (2000) *Documents of Life*, Thousand Oaks, CA: Sage

Postman, N. (1982) *The Disappearance of Childhood*, New York: Delacorte Press

Power, S., Edwards, T., Whitty, G. and Wigfall, V. (2003) *Education and the Middle Class*, Milton Keynes: Open University Press

Pryke, R. (2000) 'Poverty-wallahs, the underclass and incentives', in J. Clark, N. Dennis, J. Hein, R. Pryke and D. Smith (eds) *Welfare, Work and Poverty*, London: Institute for the Study of Civil Society

Pudney, S. (2002) *The Road to Ruin? Sequences of initiation into drug use and offending by young people in Britain,* Home Office Research Study 253, www.homeoffice.gov.uk/rds/pdfs2/hors253.pdf

Pugh, A. (2002) *From 'Compensation' to 'Childhood Wonder': Why Parents Buy*, Working Paper No 39. University of California Berkeley: Centre for Working Families

Putnam, R. (2000) *Bowling Alone*, New York: Simon and Schuster

Ramsay, P. (1983) 'Fresh perspectives on the school transformation-reproduction debate: a response to anyon from the antipodes', *Curriculum Enquiry*, 13

Ranson, S. (2005) 'The participation of volunteer citizens in school governance', *Education Review*, 57

Rapoport, R.N., Fogarty, M.P. and Rapoport, R. (eds) (1982) *Families in Britain*, London: Routledge

Reay, D., David, M. et al. (2005) *Degrees of Choice: Social class, race and gender in higher education*, New York: Oxford University Press

Reynolds, D. (1984) Constructive Living, *Hawaii: Kolowalu Books,* University of Hawaii Press

Reynolds, T., Callender, C. and Edwards, R. (2003) *Caring and Counting: The impact of mothers' employment on family relationships*, Bristol: The Policy Press

Rich, A. (1984) 'Compulsory heterosexuality and lesbian existence', in A. Snitow et al. (eds) *Desire: The Politics of Sexuality*, London: Virago

Riseborough, G. (1993) 'The gobbo barmy army: one day in the life of YTS boys', in I. Bates (ed.) *Youth and Inequality*, Milton Keynes: Open University Press

Ritchie, J. and Lewis, J. (eds) (2003) *Qualitative Research Practice A Guide for Social Science Students and Researchers*, London: Sage Publications

Roberts, K. (2001) *Class in Modern Britain*, Basingstoke: Palgrave Macmillan

Rodgers, B. and Pryor, J. (1998), *Divorce and separation: The outcomes for children*, York: Joseph Rowntree Foundation

Rosenhan, D.L. (1973/1982) 'On being sane in insane places', *Science*, 179, pp.250–8; also in M. Bulmer (ed.) (1982) *Social Research Ethics*, London: Holmes and Meier

Ross, N., Hill, M., Sweeting, H. and Cunningham-Burley, S. (2006) *Grandparents and Teen Grandchildren: Exploring Intergenerational Relationships*, Edinburgh: Centre for Research on Families and Relationships

Rowntree, S. (1901) *Poverty: A Study of Town Life*, London: Macmillan

Savage, J. (2007) *Teenage: The Creation of Youth Culture*, London: Chatto & Windus

Savage, M. (1995) 'The middle classes in modern Britain', *Sociology Review*, 5(2), Oxford: Philip Allan

Scambler, G. and Hopkins, A. (1986) 'Being epileptic; coming to terms with stigma', *Sociology of Health and Illness*, 8, pp.26–43

Scheff, T. (1966) *Being Mentally Ill: A Sociological Theory*, Chicago: Aldine

Schudsen, R. (1994) 'Culture and integration of national societies', in D. Crane (ed.) *The Sociology of Culture*, Oxford, Blackwell

Sclater, S.D. (2000) *Access to Sociology: Families*, London: Hodder Arnold

Scott, J. (1991) *Who Rules Britain?*, Cambridge: Polity Press

Scott, R.A. (1969) *The Making of Blind Men*, New Brunswick, Transaction Publishers

Scott, S. (2003) 'Symbolic interactionism and shyness', *Sociology Review,* 12(4)

Self, A. and Zealey, L. (eds) (2007) *Social Trends 37*, Basingstoke: Office for National Statistics/Palgrave Macmillan

Sewell, T. (1996) *Black Masculinities and Schooling*, Stoke on Trent: Trentham Books

Shakespeare, T. and Watson, N. (1997) 'Defending the social model', in L. Barton and M. Oliver (eds) *Disability Studies: Past, Present and Future*, Leeds: The Disability Press

Sharpe, S. (1976, 1994 2nd edn) *Just Like a Girl*, Harmondsworth: Penguin

Shaw, M., Dorling, D., Gordon, D. and Davey Smith, G. (1999) *The Widening Gap*, Bristol: Policy Press

Shilling, C. (2003) *The Body and Social Theory* (2nd edn), London: Sage

Singh Ghumann, P.A. (1999) *Asian Adolescents in the West*, Leicester: BPS Books

Skelton, C. (2001) *Schooling the Boys: Masculinities and Primary Education*, Buckingham: Open University Press

Smith, J. (2001) *Moralities, Sex, Money and Power in the 21st Century*, Allen Lane

Smith, T. and Noble, M. (1995) *Poverty and Schooling in the 1990s*, London: Child Poverty Action Group

Sontag, S. (1978) 'The double standard of ageing', in V. Carver and P. Liddiard (eds) *An Ageing Population*, London: Hodder & Stoughton

Sproston, K. and Mindell, J. (2006) *Health Survey for England 2004: the health of ethnic minorities*, Leeds: The Information Centre

Stanko, E. (2000) 'The day to count: a snapshot of the impact of domestic violence in the UK', *Criminal Justice*, 1(2)

Statham, J. (1986) *Daughters and Sons: Experiences of Non-Sexist Childraising*, Oxford: Blackwell

Steel, E. and Kidd, W. (2001) *The Family*, Basingstoke: Palgrave

Stone, M. (1981) *The Education of the Black Child in Britain*, Glasgow: Fontana

Strand, S. (2007) *Minority Ethnic Pupils in the Longitudinal Study of Young People in England (LSYPE)*, Centre for Educational Development Appraisal and Research, University of Warwick/Department for Children, Schools and Families

Sullivan, A. (2001) 'Cultural capital and educational attainment', *Sociology*, 35(4), pp.893–912

Swann Report (1985) *Education for All*, London: HMSO

Swingewood, A. (2000) *A Short History of Sociological Thought*, Basingstoke: Macmillan

Szasz, T. (1973 first published 1962) *The Myth of Mental Illness*, London: Paladin

Taylor, P. (1997) *Investigating Culture and Identity*, London: Collins Educational

Taylor, S. (1999) 'Postmodernism: a challenge to sociology', *'S' Magazine*, 4

Thornes, B. and Collard, J. (1979) *Who divorces?*, London: Routledge & Kegan Paul

Thornton, S. (1995) *Club Cultures: Music, media and subcultural capital*, Cambridge: Polity Press

Tikly, L., Haynes, J., Caballero, C., Hill, J. and Gillborn, D. (2006) *Evaluation of Aiming High Report*, University of London Research Report RR801, London: DFES/HMSO

Tizard, B. and Hughes, M. (1991) 'Reflections on young people learning', in G. Walford (ed.) *Doing Educational Research*, London: Routledge

Tizard, B. and Phoenix, A. (1993) *Black, White or Mixed Race: Race and Racism in the Lives of Young People of Mixed Parentage*, London: Routledge

Tomlinson, S. (2005) *Education in a Post-welfare Society* (2nd edn), Maidenhead: Open University Press

Townsend, P. (1979) *Poverty in the United Kingdom*, Harmondsworth: Penguin

Tunnell, K.D. (1998) 'Honesty, secrecy, and deception in the sociology of crime: confessions and reflections from the backstage', in J. Ferrell and M.S. Hamm (eds), *Ethnography at the Edge*, Boston: Northeastern University Press

Universities UK (2005) *Survey of Higher Education Students' Attitudes to Debt and Term-time Working and their Impact on Attainment*, London South Bank University, London

Virdee, S. (1997) 'Racial harassment', in T. Modood, R. Berthoud, J. Lakey, J. Nazroo, P. Smith, S. Virdee and S.

Beishon (eds) *Ethnic Minorities in Britain: Diversity and Disadvantage*, London: PSI

Vulliamy, G. (1978) 'Culture clash and school music: a sociological analysis', in L. Barton and R. Meighan (eds) *Sociological Interpretations of Schooling and Classrooms: a Re-appraisal*, Driffield: Nafferton Books

Waitzkin, H. (1979) 'Medicine, superstructure and micropolitics', *Social Science and Medicine*, 13a, pp.601–9

Walter, N. (1999) *The New Feminism*, London: Virago

Wanless Report (2007) *Getting It, Getting It Right*, London: Department for Education and Skills (HMSO)

Warin, J., Solomon, Y., Lewis, C. and Langford, W. (1999) *Fathers, Work and Family Life*, York: Joseph Rowntree Foundation

Waters, M. (1995) *The Death of Class*, London: Sage

Watson, N. (1998) 'Enabling identity: disability, self and citizenship', in Shakespeare, T. (ed.) *The Disability Reader: Social Science Perspectives*, London, Cassell

Weeks, J. (2003) *Sexuality* (2nd edn), London: Routledge

Weiner, G. (1995) 'Feminisms and education', in *Feminism and Education*, Buckingham: OUP

Weiner, G., Arnot, M. and David, M. (1997) 'Is the future female? Female success, male disadvantage, and changing gender patterns in education', in A.H. Halsey et al. (2002) *Education: Culture, Economy, Society*, Oxford: OUP

Wertz, R.W. and Wertz, D.C. (1981) 'Notes on the decline of midwives and the rise of medical obstetricians', in P. Conrad and R. Kerns (eds) *The Sociology of Health and Illness: Critical Perspectives*, New York: St Martin's Press

West, A. and Hind, A. (2003) *Secondary School Admissions in England: Exploring the extent of overt and covert selection*, Centre for Educational Research, Department of Social Policy, London School of Economics and Political Science.

Wilkinson, H. (1994) *No Turning Back: Generations and the Genderquake*, London: Demos

Wilkinson, R.G. (1996) *Unhealthy Societies: The Afflictions of Inequality*, London: Routledge

Willis, P. (1977) *Learning to Labour*, Aldershot: Ashgate

Witz, A. (1992) *Professions and Patriarchy*, London: Routledge

Woods, P. (1983) *Sociology and the School: An Interactionist Viewpoint*, London: Routledge & Kegan Paul

Wright, C. (1992) 'Early education: multi-racial primary classrooms', in D. Gill, B. Mayor and M. Blair (eds) *Racism and Education: Structures and Strategies*, London: Sage

Young, M. and Willmott, P. (1957) *Family and Kinship in East London*, Harmondsworth: Penguin

Young, M. and Willmott, P. (1973) *The Symmetrical Family*, Harmondsworth: Penguin

Zaretsky, E. (1976) *Capitalism, the Family and Personal Life*, London: Pluto Press

INDEX

Note: page numbers **in bold** refer to definitions/explanations of key terms.